FIGH'

To

Aubrey Silkoff with
best wishes

Martin Sugarman

2015

The publication of this book would not have been possible without the generous support of The Pears Foundation

Fighting Back

British Jewry's Military Contribution
in the Second World War

MARTIN SUGARMAN

VALLENTINE MITCHELL
LONDON • PORTLAND, OR

First published in 2010 by Vallentine Mitchell

Middlesex House,
29/45 High Street, Edgware,
Middlesex HA8 7UU, UK

920 NE 58th Avenue, Suite 300
Portland, Oregon,
97213-3786, USA

www.vmbooks.com

British Library Cataloguing in Publication Data
Sugarman, Martin.
    Fighting back : British Jewry's miltary contribution in the
Second World War.
    1. World War, 1939-1945—Participation, Jewish. 2. World
War, 1939-1945—Jews—Great Britain.
    I. Title
    940.5'404-dc22

ISBN 978 0 85303 900 6 (cloth)
ISBN 978 0 85303 910 5 (paper)

Library of Congress Cataloging in Publication Data

Printed by T J International, Padstow, Cornwall

I dedicate this book to

Acting Sergeant Israel 'Ted' Sugarman, RASC
Warrant Officer Leon Joseph Sugarman, 1/7 Middlesex Regt,
wounded in action
Rifleman Isaac 'Jack' Kruyer, Rifle Brigade, att. SAS, MiD
Private Chaim 'Harry' Kruyer, 11th 'Red' Devons,
Glider Paras, wounded in action
Able Seaman Dennis Andrews, RN, MiD,
wounded in action
Able Seaman Sidney (Ames) Hyams, RN
Pte John Kruyer, 1st Berkshires, killed in action at
Kohima, April 1944.

And to the parents and women who waited and overcame
throughout the London Blitz – Kruyers – Marie, Phillip,
Mary, Alf, Millie, Jenny, Leah, Julie, Sarah, Eva, Anne, Tony,
Rachel, Winnie and Sarah Hyams;
and the Sugarmans – Woolf, Esther and Helena

Bless them all

Contents

Foreword

This book makes a most important contribution to our knowledge of a remarkable aspect of British-Jewish history: the Jewish military contribution. Its author, Martin Sugarman, deserves the profound thanks of all British Jews, and of all Britons who wish to know the full scale of Jewish participation in the Second World War.

There was no aspect of Britain's five-and-a-half-year struggle on land, at sea and in the air in which Jews did not participate, and indeed play an important part. This deeply researched and in many ways passionate book is their story, and their memorial. The statistics alone are remarkable. More than 60,000 Jews out of a total Jewish community of no more than 350,000 served in the British armed forces. Of these, more than 3,000 were killed, as well as almost 700 of the 30,000 Jewish volunteers from British Mandate Palestine. Among the awards for bravery in action given to Jews were three Victoria Crosses, 168 Military Crosses and 188 Distinguished Flying Crosses. More than a thousand Jews were Mentioned in Despatches for their actions on the battlefields of Europe, the Middle East, Africa and the Pacific.

Martin Sugarman has given flesh and blood to these statistics. He gives the names and tells the stories of many of those who fought, and explores in absorbing detail the individual contributions of Jews in every sphere of the war. This includes the Jewish pilots who flew in the Battle of Britain, the Jews who served on many dangerous raids carried out by the commandos, the Jews who risked – and often lost – their lives after being parachuted behind enemy lines in France and Burma as members of the Special Operations Executive (SOE), and the Jews who were among the top-secret code breakers at Bletchley Park, enabling the Allied Commanders-in-Chief to take full advantage of the orders and commands of their German, Italian and Japanese opposite numbers.

Thanks to this remarkably comprehensive study, Martin Sugarman has ensured that every future book, television programme and feature film about Britain at war will be able to include the extraordinary role of British and Palestinian Jews, wearing British uniforms, first in ensuring that Britain was not defeated, and then in fighting on with courage and tenacity until victory was secured.

Sir Martin Gilbert

Acknowledgements

The research in this book has been carried out by the author over more than a decade, and at the end of each chapter I have thanked those people and organizations who have been of specific assistance in each study. However, the following have been a constant source of help and I wish to thank them particularly. The staff of:

The AJEX Jewish Military Museum
The British Library
Colindale Newspaper Library
The Commonwealth War Graves Commission
The Imperial War Museum Reading Room, and Sound and Film Archives Dept.
The National Archives in Kew
The Tower Hamlets Local History Library

Introduction

The studies in this book were written over a period of years as a response to the myths often perpetrated and perpetuated by anti-Semites and sceptics about British Jewry's alleged lack of fighting spirit and participation in the Second World War. Similar myths circulated during and after the First World War. Some of these papers have been published by the Jewish Historical Society of England and the Military Historical Society, but this reaches only a small readership in terms of national exposure. The issuing of this book, with the enthusiastic and inspired support of the publisher and The Pears Foundation, is thus a powerful and robust attempt to redress the balance and our determination to see that it reaches a far wider audience in the English-speaking world, and so stand as a tribute for posterity to what the Jewish People achieved.

The topics focussed on are random and reflect my own interest; neither do I claim that the subjects or the content are exhaustive; indeed the book is a snapshot only of the British Jewish contribution to the victory of democracy and freedom, over Nazism, Japanese imperialism, fascism and anti-Semitism those seven decades ago. We intuitively know, especially the veterans of that war, that Jews, for example, were prominent among the Paratroopers at the Battle of Arnhem; but what were their names and who were they? My research sets out to *detail the details* for historians and general readers everywhere and has met with great approval by the veterans who have read them, in particular and gratifyingly from the non-Jewish men and women who assisted me so much and know the truth of the huge Jewish participation, because they served alongside the Jewish veterans and *know that truth*.

I am especially proud to include in this book also some tribute to the much neglected and almost forgotten Auxiliary Services of Civil Defence, who did so much and sacrificed so greatly in the Second World War, in this case the Fire Service of the National and Auxiliary Firemen and Women (NFS and AFS). This has been written in collaboration with Stephanie Maltman of 'Firemen Remembered'; she has been zealous in her determination to remember the Jewish personnel and her support has been invaluable. We have produced a groundbreaking study on this but here only the introduction and the Roll of Honour is included. As it is work in progress, we hope to produce a full list of a Record of Honour of all Jewish Firemen and Women who served, which at time of writing already runs into several thousands.

British Jewry has never been more than about one half of 1 per cent of the general population, yet the figures show (and in some articles I have made the calculations) that our fighting contribution always has been way out of proportion to our numbers, both in frontline units and in the receiving of awards for courage; the table of awards here, shown in the first pages, reveals this, and those interested in statistics can do the sums themselves.[1] But as an illustration, at Arnhem for example, Jewish Paras were 2 per cent of the strength (four times our numbers), and as aircrew in the Battle of Britain, 1.2 per cent (over twice). If British Jewry numbered at the time, as a guestimate, 300,000–350,000, and we know that we had 60,000–70,000 in the Forces, then Jewish participation can be modestly assessed at least at 20 per cent of our Jewish population, a truly astonishing figure. Our British Jewish dead, together with Jews from Israel, numbered more than 3,000, 1 per cent of our tiny population, which represents in real terms a huge sacrifice from a small community.

In addition I have been able in some of my work to expose the huge part played by Palestinian Jewish volunteers from Israel in the 'good fight'. As part of the British Empire and Commonwealth Forces, 130,000 of them registered to serve and 60,000 of them volunteered – virtually every able-bodied Jewish man and woman from the relatively small Jewish population – and 30,000 were finally accepted; almost 700 were killed and hundreds were decorated for valour; they served in every branch and theatre of war, many in Special Forces. Four were even POW of the Japanese in the Far East. The true picture of the huge contribution of the Palestinian Jews from Israel may also be studied in the companion volume to this book, *We Will Remember Them* by Henry Morris and Martin Sugarman, and many other works on this subject.

Sadly, the part played by Palestinian Jewry from Eretz Yisroel, the Yishuv of Israel, nation-in-waiting, has been deliberately erased from the memory of those who are keepers of the British war remembrance communities, by those who should know better. They never appear in British tributes to the Commonwealth/Empire Forces who served, be it at historical exhibitions or commemorations, or on any memorial in Britain, whilst those of many other ethnic groups are well represented. Most disgracefully, Israel is never invited to attend at the Cenotaph in Whitehall each Remembrance Sunday, to lay a wreath for their war dead who, although they lie under Commonwealth War Graves Commission headstones around the world, are clearly not considered worthy. The Palestinian Jewish/Israeli proportionately huge contribution has been made totally invisible.

Meanwhile, and in stark contrast, it is well recorded how the Arab world at best remained indifferent to the struggle against the Nazis and at worst openly collaborated. Few Palestinian Arabs volunteered and a diplomatic attempt to keep the numbers of Palestinian Jews and Arabs at even recruitment in the British Forces, for example with the forming of the Palestine Regiment in 1942, was embarrassingly abandoned early on by the British authorities as the Jews came forward in droves to fight, in stark comparison to the Arab population. It is well documented that the Palestinian Arab leader, the Mufti of Jerusalem, Haj Amin El Husseini, was wanted by the British for treachery and fled to Berlin in 1939 where he planned with Hitler to construct gas chambers outside Nablus on the present West Bank, to exterminate the Jews of the Middle East; that hundreds of Arabs and Moslems served in the SS battalions in the Balkans and took part in atrocities there, and hundreds belonged to the notorious 'Freies Arabien' (Arab volunteers serving in SS units of the German Army[2]). As Rommel approached Cairo in the dark days of 1942, the Egyptians prepared to welcome him and the young army officer Anwar Sadat was arrested with a group of traitors, on the way to receive Rommel in the desert in October 1942, and guide him into Cairo. Rashid Ali led a pro-Nazi Fascist revolt against the British in Iraq in 1941, which was put down by British and Commonwealth troops spearheaded by Jewish Palestinian scouts and commandos. The record of such Arab treachery is huge.[3]

British Jewry, with Jews from Israel, may thus be deeply and justly proud of this history of fighting back, fighting for democracy and peace, dispelling the myths that we were just civilians or victims or bystanders in the struggle. So let this book, and the companion volume by Henry Morris and myself, stand as permanent testimony to the truth.

The many pictures that are included in this volume are credited wherever the copyright holder is known. However, while every effort has been made to obtain permission to reproduce the pictures, I will rectify any omissions if I receive further information as to the copyright holder.

I wish finally to thank AJEX and its staff; Stewart Cass and his late, great father Frank, and Heather Marchant, Joanna Lawson, Jenni Tinson and others of Vallentine Mitchell, for their enthusiasm and support for this project; and of course Trevor Pears. Sir Martin Gilbert, our greatest historian, has given me unflagging support and friendship. And of course my wife Jane, who persistently put up with my many absences when I was delving into archives and interviewing veterans in far-flung locations. The book itself I devote to her, to our amazing Jewish veterans, to our Jewish Military Museum and to my three flowers, Gideon, Joel and Leah, together with the next generation, Lauryn and Lylah Sugarman, and Polly and Mia Pyman.

Authors note: the abreviations PRO and TNA refer, of course to the same archives at Kew. They are used interchangeably in the book. The views expressed in this book are, along with any errors and omissions, those of the author only.

Martin Sugarman
Hackney, 2009

Notes

1. In some chapters it has not been possible to separate British Jewish personnel from Allied Jewish personnel serving in British units; in others, for the sake of completeness, some Allied Jewish personnel have been deliberately included.
2. Antonio J. Munoz, 'Lions of the Desert: Arab volunteers in the German Army', undated, private publication available at the University of London, SOAS Library; copy at AJEX Museum. Also in Axis Europa Books, 2001, USA, pp.203–38. Other Arab battalions serving willingly in Axis Enemy Forces were the Phalange Africaine (largely but not totally North African Arabs), Brigade North Africaine (mostly Algerian), The Free Arabia Battalion and the Deutsche-Arabische Legion. These all served around the Mediterranean and North African Theatre including southern France and Yugoslavia – totalling as many as 13,000 troops. See Robert Satloff, *Among the Righteous: The Lost Stories from the Holocaust's Long Reach into Arab Lands* (New York: Public Affairs, 2006) and Jonathan Trigg, *Hitler's Jihadists* (London: History Press, 2008), passim. However, it should be noted that Arab troops served in some Free French units and a few were involved in saving Jews in North Africa and France as 'Righteous Moslems', as were some Moslems in the Balkans.
3. Readers are urged to Google some of these topics, especially on the Mufti as well as 'Arabs in the German Army', to see numerous studies on this non-PC subject.

Jewish Awards and Casualties
1939–45 and Post War

Casualties
(Most Commonwealth Forces and Auxiliary Services are excluded here)

British Jews killed:	3,024:
Army:	1,896
Royal Navy/Marines and Merchant Navy:	221
RAF:	907
Palestinian Jews killed:	694

Honours

VC:	3	MM and bar	3
GC:	3	DFM	64
CB:	6	DFM and bar	5
CBE:	28	AFC	19
OBE:	97	GM	20
MBE:	164	BEM	96
DSO:	44	Mention in Despatches	1,103
DSC:	25	US LoM	6
DSC and bar:	3	US DSO/DFC	8
MC:	168	US Bronze Star	12
MC and bar	3	Legion d'Honneur	9
DFC	188	Croix de Guerre	40
DFC and bar	43	Cert. of Gallantry	40
DCM	30	Foreign Awards	33
DSM	35	Colonial Police Medal	14
DSM and bar	1	AFM	5
CGM	3	Air Efficiency Award	3
MM	152		

Illustrations

7.5   Chaplain Bernard Casper, later Chaplain to the Jewish Brigade 1944–46, served 1941–46.

7.6   3780682 Pte. Leon Frank, Chindit, Burma, 13/13 Kings Liverpool Regiment, Operation Longcloth, column 7, 1943. Photo taken Sangor 16 August 1942. He was a POW.

7.7   233237 Major Joseph Crowne, MBE 'for gallantry' with the Chindits, 2nd Expedition 1944.

8.1   The SIG – left to right in Tel-Aviv whilst on leave, Dov Cohen, Rosenzweig, Maurice Tiefenbrunner, Walter Esser (the German traitor).

8.2   Egypt 1942 on leave with the SIG – left to right, Tiefenbrunner, Cpl Drory/Drori, Goldstein and Rohr.

9.1   Sgt Jack Nissenthall/Nissen, just after returning from the Dieppe Raid; note the rare Parachute wings proving his training as a paratrooper with the RAF.

9.2   Pte Murray Irving Bleeman, Royal Hamilton Light Infantry of Canada, died of wounds received at Dieppe, 21 August 1942.

10.1 Special Operator Sgt Leslie Temple, 101 Sqdn Bomber Command, front 2nd left at Ludford Magna with his Lancaster crew. Rear left to right – Fl. Eng. Sgt James, Navigator Sgt Hall, Bomb Aimer Sgt Morgan, Mid Upper Gunner Sgt Ross. Front left to right – Rear Gnr Sgt Rook, Spec. Op. Sgt L. Temple, W/Operator Sgt Bailey and 'Skipper' Pilot Officer E. Neilsen (later Deputy PM of Canada).

10.2 At Ludford Magna, Sgt Reuben 'Herky' Herscovitch (centre) with Macleod, left and Dockerty, right.

11.1 The 1977 Bruneval reunion with left to right, General Frost, Peter Nagel and Sgt Cox (with white hair).

11.2 Peter Nagel just before the Bruneval Raid.

12.1 Frederic Berliner aka Michael O'Hara, killed as an SOE agent in 1945 (SOE Archives, TNA).

12.2 SOE agent Stephen Dale aka Heinz Guenther Spanglet.

13.1 No. 3 'Jewish' Troop member L/Cpl Gordon Sayers, aka Gyula Sauer/Szauer, with the Commandos on D Day, bicycle Troop disembarking behind (courtesy Peter Masters/Arany).

13.2 The detachment from No. 3 'Jewish' Troop that landed on D Day with No. 6 Commando, left to right standing – Cpl Nichols (Heinz Nell), Cpl Drew (Harry Nomburg), Cpl Masters (Peter Arany); front, left to right – Cpl Mason (K. Weinberg), Cpl McGregor (Manfred Koury).

14.1 Muriel Byck, died on operations with SOE (photo courtesy Special Forces Club, London).

14.2 Denise Bloch, SOE agent murdered at Ravensbruck Death Camp (photo courtesy of Special Forces Club, London).

Unless stated, all photographs are from the AJEX Jewish Military Museum and Archives, with their kind permission.

Ha Gedud Ha Sinit:
The Jewish Company of the Shanghai Volunteer Corps

Established in 1853, the Shanghai Volunteer Corps was set up as a voluntary international militia to protect the foreign trade missions, established at that time in Shanghai, by various imperialist nations from Europe, as well as Russia, Japan and the USA. Frequently there were local civil wars and general disorder swirling around Shanghai in nineteenth- and early twentieth-century China, and some kind of defence force was necessary. At one time the SVC represented over twenty different nationalities. It was usually mobilized in response to riots (internal security), for example, or to augment regular foreign garrisons in the city (a strategic reserve), or expeditionary forces – such as during the Boxer Rebellion in 1900. For most of its existence, the force was funded by the Shanghai Municipal Council, but volunteers received no pay at any time.

The SVC's roll, at its peak in the late 1930s, was 2,300 men, and it comprised twenty-three different units, including Light Horse, Artillery and Air Defence, as well as national units such as Portuguese and Chinese – and, in 1932, a Jewish Company.[1] Its longest mobilization was in August 1937 during the Sino-Japanese War. Even though the Japanese surrounded the city from 1932, its policy was to keep out of Shanghai, and the SVC helped patrol the entry points facing the Japanese Forces. In 1940, the SVC took permanent control of the so-called 'International Settlement' (the area within the city where most of the foreign residents lived and worked) when the British formally withdrew. The SVC was finally disbanded by the Japanese occupation forces in early 1942, following Pearl Harbor in December 1941. Its last albeit unofficial reunion was the centenary celebration after the war, held at the Royal Yacht Club in British Hong Kong, in April 1954.

Socially, the SVC was – typically for its time – not racially integrated. The commandant was always a Briton. Whilst the White Russian Company was professional and paid, the remaining Companies were all civilians. The British 'A' Company was, for example, mostly European, and exclusively white, but 'B' Company was Eurasian, and never the twain did meet.

Jews had lived in Shanghai for decades. After the Treaty of Nanking (in 1842, between Britain and China), merchants from all over the world came to Shanghai to set up profitable businesses, and the Jews were represented by families such as the Sassoons, Hardoons and Kadouries – mostly Sephardim from Baghdad and Bombay. In contrast to the British, however, whose profits were repatriated to the UK economy, the Jewish community was very much part of Shanghai and integrated into the local business scene, to whose growth and development it was committed. Many Jews, however, took British nationality. After the 1917 Russian Revolution, a second group of Jews from Russia fled pogroms and many came to Shanghai, boosting the Jewish population, which was enlarged in the 1930s by a third group – German and other European Jews fleeing the Nazis.[2] Most of the latter two groups were not as financially well off as the first, but were communally well organized.[3] By 1939, there were almost 30,000 Jews in Shanghai.[4]

As early as 1914 there had been talk in the Jewish community and the SVC of forming a separate Jewish Company. It was regarded as a way in which Jewish identity could be reinforced, and an important and dignified way for Jews to play a part in protecting the foreign enclave, and to be seen to be 'doing their bit'. However, some important communal leaders – notably Edward Ezra – spoke against it, arguing that it would give the impression that 'Jews had too exclusive a life.'[5] Continuing the age-old discussion and dilemma, he maintained that it was beneficial for Jewish youth to mix with others and join existing units of the SVC to 'broaden their horizons'. His argument appears to have won through.

Protective sectors of the boundaries of Shanghai were allotted to various units. Following fierce fighting in 1931–32 between Chinese and Japanese forces in the area, security concerns and the generally strong desire to play a more significant role in promoting community welfare prompted the leaders of the always civic-minded Jewish community to advance plans to contribute a Jewish unit to the SVC. And so it was.[6]

The Jewish Company's first and only commander was the charismatic Noel S. Jacobs (1898–1977). A Methodist, born in Hampshire, England, he was brought up in India and Hong Kong (serving in the Hong Kong Volunteer Defence Force in the First World War), moving to Shanghai in the early 1920s, where he worked for the British–American Tobacco Company. Here he met a Russian Jewish girl, Dora Bogomolsky, and converted to Judaism to marry her. In 1923 he took over the 5th Shanghai Jewish Boy Scout Troop – made up mostly of Jewish immigrants from Russia – and instilled in them such a sense of discipline, *esprit de corps* and pride that they became the core of the soon-to-be-formed Jewish

Company of the SVC. Jacobs was at one time the president of the local B'nai B'rith (a worldwide Jewish cultural association) and also deputy commissioner of the British Shanghai Scout movement.[7] Until he left Shanghai in 1949, Jacobs remained deeply involved with the Jewish Community.

In the summer of 1932, some former members of the Jewish Scouts and members of the Shanghai branch of the Zionist movement, Betar, met at 722 Bubbling Well Road,[8] to propose the forming of a Jewish unit of the SVC.[9] The SVC commandant at the time, Colonel N. Thoms, readily agreed and it was proposed that the first platoon should become part of 'H' Company of the SVC, under Captain C. Todd, with the by now well-known Jacobs as platoon commander. Volunteers would serve for three years. Robert B. Bitker (a Russian war veteran, then a member of an American company of the Corps) and Emmanuel M. Talan (from the Artillery Company) were made platoon sergeants, and it became active on 22 September 1932. Jacobs was appointed 2nd lieutenant on 30 September. On 3 December, a second platoon was formed, and Bitker was promoted to command it as 1st lieutenant[10] on 26 May 1933. At that time, this made the Jewish Company of the SVC the world's sole legal Jewish regular force, with its own insignia and flag, the latter being what has since become the national flag of Israel.[11]

Their first drill took place in the grounds of the Jewish School in Seymour Road,[12] and the first mention of the Jewish Company came in the *North China Herald* (*NCH*) on 22 March 1933 (p.454). Strangely, the London-based *Jewish Chronicle* had picked up the story earlier.[13] The Jewish Company was inspected by British Brigadier Fleming, who wrote: 'considering how recently this company has been formed, great credit is due to the officers and NCOs responsible'. Ironically, the same issue carried a long article, with photograph, of the forming of a jack-booted Nazi paramilitary group centred on the German consulate.

On 22 May 1933, the non-Jewish personnel of 'H' Company were transferred to 'B' Company, and the Company became officially all-Jewish on 1 July – commanded by Lieutenant Jacobs – and part of 'A' Battalion of the SVC . This was announced in the *NCH* on 31 May (p.335). Talan was promoted to CSM and later (15 September) to 2nd lieutenant, and Sergeant H.V. Engberg to CSM. There was a celebratory dinner held to mark the occasion, at the Shanghai Jewish Club on 18 June,[14] attended by over sixty members of the Company.[15] The Company motto was allegedly 'No Advance without Security'[16] and its chaplain was Reverend Mendel Brown, the spiritual leader of the Sephardi Community in Shanghai.[17] They wore British-style uniforms, used English military commands and orders, and the chaplain wore a

Roman collar, which was customary at the time. Veteran Alex Katznelson described the uniforms to the author.[18] Officers and Senior NCOs had .38mm Webley revolvers, and officers had decorated swords for parades. All ranks had the Lee-Enfield .303 rifle and long bayonet with box magazine, kept at home or in the armoury, with five rounds (called a 'Peace Pouch') to enable them to reach an assembly point in an emergency with a loaded weapon. They also wore the First World War British-model steel helmet, and there was a winter and summer uniform (the latter including a topee). Every platoon had a Lewis machine-gun section, equipment being kept in the armoury. In a peculiar diversion from regular British army practice, their British-issue boots had no colour and had to be stained black, involving many hours of applying, brushing and shining for new recruits.

They wore the bronze cap-badge of the SVC, but on their collars they wore the Star of David with SVC superimposed. Officers had a more elaborate coloured enamel version[19] as well as an enamelled lapel-badge of the Shanghai Municipality. At its peak the Jewish Company numbered about 120 men organized in three platoons. Most were of Russian origin, with some Poles, Rumanians and British. Some of the British were actually passport holders from India, Singapore, Hong Kong and even Iraq, but the Company 'ethos and cuture' was British, as were its marching songs. In 1938, however, they added a Hebrew hymn to their repertoire – 'He is Lord of the universe, who reigned ere any creature yet was formed' – taken from the Mussaf (additional service) of the Sabbath prayers.[20] The *NCH*[21] records the strength of the Jewish Company at 1 September 1937 as three officers and sixty-nine men for peacetime service and a further twenty-four men on call for emergencies, totalling ninety-six; this was larger than some units (the Philippines Company had seventy-three) and smaller than others (the Portuguese had 140).

Quite lavish praise was heaped on the Jewish Company. In the *NCH* on 11 October 1933 (p.76), a high-ranking British SVC officer wrote: 'The Jewish Company are good, thoroughly good, and they are keen, thoroughly keen, and take it from me they will make you chaps sit up.' The reporter continues:

> why there has not been a Jewish Company before is something of a mystery. A peaceable race, they brought off some pretty big military business under Moses and some first class work under Allenby [in the First World War] … considering numbers, the Shanghai Jews have as fine a recruiting ground as any … they must succeed. There will be jests innumerable [about them] and none know better how to take a good joke than themselves … and they

have decided to march behind the Shanghai Scottish so as to get the free benefit of the music of that lost tribe!

In the *NCH*, 2 May 1934, there is a description of the SVC Annual Inspection Parade. The Corps marched to the cathedral for a service, but the report mentions how the Scottish and Catholic personnel 'broke away' for their own services; curiously it does not mention what the Jewish Company did.

On 29 June 1934, Jacobs was promoted to captain, Bitker to 1st lieutenant on 26 May and Talan on 15 September 1935. The Company drilled with the SVC in a building on Foochow Street known as the Drill Hall; this was a huge building which included a club, weapons store and rifle range. They practised marksmanship on the range at Hongkew Park. Here there were whitewashed barracks where they trained in shooting, bayonet drill, crowd control, and setting up barbed-wire and sandbag defences. In May 1936, at the SVC shooting competition, the Jewish Company finished third out of thirty-three in the Lewis machine gun heats,[22] and in February 1937 they were fourth out of twenty-four in the SVC speed test for stripping and reassembling, in teams of three – blindfolded – the Lewis machine gun, being beaten only by the three Russian teams who were regular soldiers.[23] Alex Katznelson wrote:[24]

> Shooting competitions between the Companies of the British ('A') battalion were customary during the summer; the Jewish Company took an active part in this. Each company supplied thirty men of mixed ranks and each man received fifty rounds. The rifle range at Hongkew was the location, at the northern end of which was a hill where mechanically operated targets were situated. Firing was from a ten- man cement lined trench with sandbags, at 300 yards range. Points were allocated per Company and the Jewish Company always did well.

In fact the Jewish Company had its own shooting competition, where participants vied for ownership of the Kadoorie Cup.[25] The local Jewish newspaper, *Israel's Messenger*, published a remarkable photograph of members of the Company posing after just such a competition at the firing range, with Lieutenants Gaberman and Bitker in the front row.[26]

In March 1936, the Jewish Company was mobilized in a practice with 'A' Company, to simulate how they would prepare in case of the withdrawal of International Forces from the International Settlement.[27] In February 1937 they took part in extensive police liaison exercises to test readiness in case of a breakdown in law and order.[28] On 31 October 1935,

Talan resigned and left for Hong Kong[29], and Bitker for Palestine on 19 October 1936; so sergeants Simon Godkin and William Goldenberg (formerly Artillery) were commissioned in their places as 2nd lieutenants on 24 and 26 October 1937, respectively.[30] Exactly one year later they were both promoted to 1st lieutenant. When Bitker returned from Palestine on 10 August 1938 he became again a 1st lieutenant and Godkin became second in command.[31]

When fighting flared between Chinese and Japanese forces in August 1937, the SVC was mobilized for three months on 12 August, and assisted the British forces in their pre-assigned sector 'B' of the Settlement. Together with the Scottish Company and the Air Defence unit, the Jewish Company were stationed in the Union Church and billeted in the Rowing Club.[32] These adjacent buildings stood at the confluence of the Soochow Creek and the Whangpoo River, opposite the Garden Bridge; this bridge was the symbolic traditional gateway to Shanghai City and thus a major potential flashpoint with the surrounding Japanese armies. It was, therefore, a complimentary sign of confidence in the Jewish Company's military capability, that the British commander placed it at this particularly volatile and strategic point.[33]

The SVC Mobilization Orders[34] show that transport allocated to the Jewish Company was '1 hired lorry and one cook's lorry with hired drivers', and stores to be carried were '2 cartons of pistol ammo., .45 calibre – 60 rounds; 60 boxes of rifle ammo. – 6,000 rounds; 3 boxes of automatic ammo. – 2,256 rounds; various stores'; these were to be collected by '1 CQMS, the Mess NCO, and 2 privates'.

The Rapaport incident occurred at this time. As Alex Katznelson wrote:

> Private Rapaport appeared for duty with the Jewish Company, but without permission left his position and wandered into the area of defence assigned to 'B' Company. Here he was stopped by a sentry and asked to leave; he refused and the sentry repeated his warning. Again Rapaport refused to go and the sentry raised his rifle and warned him yet again. He is alleged to have dared the sentry to shoot, and he did. Rapaport died of his wound and is the only known fatality of the Jewish Company.'[35]

The matter appears to have been hushed up and the Municipality agreed a financial settlement with the family, who soon after left Shanghai and settled in San Francisco.

With the Japanese land forces, there was never any confrontation, only mutual guarding of key border points.

An article in the *Jewish Chronicle* of London, on 3 September 1937 (p.34), stated that the Jewish Company also kept guard over the Jewish quarter in the Shanghai International Settlement and provided assistance to Jewish victims of the Japanese bombardment, moving them to the British and French quarters where necessary. Jews living in the Chinese areas were particularly at risk of both losing lives and property, and an appeal was made to supply Jewish Relief from abroad to several hundred destitute Jewish families in the city. It is interesting to note that in the north China city of Tientsin, White Russian Guards fighting with the victorious Japanese forces there attempted a pogrom among the local Jews, and that the local Jewish Defence Volunteer Organization prevented this and moved Jews to the protection of the British and French quarters in the city; perhaps there is another story to tell here of a Jewish Fighting Company in China.

In the *Jewish Chronicle* on 29 October 1937 (p.20), a photo appeared of a defensive sandbagged gun emplacement of the Jewish Company, outside the Sassoon Cultural Centre on the Bund (the main riverside and business thoroughfare in the centre of Shanghai), and this was followed on 5 November (p.28) by a report on the bombing of the city by the Japanese and the damage done to the city, with its major effects on the Jewish community.

On 5 May 1938, the Jewish Company celebrated its fifth anniversary,[36] and Sir Elly Kadoorie presented cups for the annual Lewis gun and rifle competitions to the winning teams; a dinner was followed by 'community singing and witty parodies'. Eighty-five members of the Jewish Company received the Shanghai Municipal Council Emergency Medal for 1937 and these were presented to most members of the Corps in a huge ceremony held on the racecourse in July 1938.[37]

It was often necessary, as the Japanese grip around Shanghai tightened, for the SVC and the various foreign allied garrisons to occasionally 'show the flag' and also attract more recruits; so on 27 February 1938, the Jewish Company, with the rest of 'A' Battalion, took part in a route march around the city in full kit with fixed bayonets.[38] (A similar march took place on 31 March 1940, as reported in the local press.[39]) The march began from Jessfield Park and was led by the band of the Second Loyal Regiment from Britain. On 11 August 1938, the Company was again mobilized for four days in case of hostilities due to the anniversary of the Sino-Japanese War. Often there were local riots and disorders among rival Chinese political factions and the Jewish Company took full part in day and night policing operations on many such occasions.[40] There was always time for recreation, however, as when the *NCH* reported on the shooting competition between 'A' Company and the Jewish Company, who lost narrowly by 1,029 points to 964.[41]

On 15 October 1938, a third Jewish platoon was formed and CQMS A. Gaberman was promoted to 2nd lieutenant on 28 October and one year later to 1st lieutenant. Sergeant B.A. Slossman then became 2nd lieutenant. Meanwhile Noel Jacobs was officially gazetted captain on 19 October.[42]

Throughout that year the SVC was on constant call and very active, working alongside the Municipal Police and the British and USA Garrisons, engaged in search operations, riot control, patrols, training exercises, route marches and parades. There was a pick-up in recruitment as the local situation deteriorated and the foreign population wanted to 'do their bit'; the Jewish Company especially attracted more members during this period, helped by the increase in the number of able-bodied male Jewish refugees flowing into the city.[43]

As the British and USA Forces gradually withdrew from Shanghai to other bases throughout 1939 and 1940, as the European war got underway and as the Japanese threat grew, there was naturally more and more work for the SVC, especially around their sector of the Garden Bridge, where they faced the Japanese naval landing forces;[44] they also stood guard over the Mixed Court (which arbitrated where mixed nationals were involved), and stood street patrols, especially at night.

As Nazi persecution of Jews in Europe increased, more and more Jewish refugees made their way to Shanghai. On 17 March 1939 the *Jewish Chronicle* reported:[45]

> The Jewish Company of the SVC ... have been most helpful in meeting new arrivals at the wharf, shepherding them into waiting vehicles and helping them ... settle into their temporary quarters at the Embankment building ... camp beds were lent by the military authorities; the Company also gave their services in the Museum Road soup kitchen and do much to cheer up those whose spirits are broken by tragedy and hopelessness.

On 27 April 1939[46] the Jewish Company held its seventh annual dinner, where Captain Jacobs reported in his speech that there was in fact a waiting list to join the Company.[47] In a 'Secret Cipher Telegram', dated 29 November 1941, from the Deputy Director Military Intelligence (DDMI) to the War Office in London,[48] in describing the strength of the SVC it was noted that among the strength of the Corps at that date stood seventy-five German Jews, but it was not made clear in which Company they were.

The Japanese takeover, when it came in early 1942, was calm but for one small skirmish on the river, and the SVC HQ was sealed, and various silver trophies disappeared. All Allied 'enemy' nationals had to wear a red armband but were at first free to move around; later they were segregated into guarded areas on the city edges. The peaceful nature of the takeover appears to have been amicably agreed by the

Shanghai Municipal Council (SMC), the British and the Japanese authorities, to avoid bloodshed.[49] The SVC weapons were quietly collected up by the Japanese from members' homes. The now promoted Major Jacobs returned to Shanghai (his wife and three daughters had been evacuated previously to San Francisco[50]) and he was interned with many others – including Reverend Mendel Brown – some time early in 1944, in a camp on the east bank of the Whangpoo River, reserved for single men. Alex Katznelson saw him off as he gallantly marched into captivity. He remained a source of inspiration for many POWs throughout their incarceration.[51] Among others interned was Sergeant Marguleff, with his wife and child (they survived and went to live in Israel after the war). Escape was virtually impossible as Europeans were so easily identified; certainly Katznelson knows of no examples. Many members of the SVC had tried earlier to leave for Palestine but very few immigration certificates were available owing to the pro-Arab policy of the British Mandate.[52]

At the last gasp, as the atomic bombs fell on Japan in 1945, large-scale looting began in Shanghai among the Chinese population on 16 August. There were thoughts of calling upon the disbanded SVC to mobilize (it is not clear by whom – probably the Municipality) to contain the situation. But only the Japanese were armed and in any position to act; within hours the looting stopped.[53]

During its existence, the Jewish Company held the usual social functions and there are photographs of annual awards dinners and similar occasions. In the memoirs of its members there was no evidence of any anti-Semitism at all in the SVC or in the wider European community.[54] Indeed, Alex Katznelson testifies that the whole city and the Chinese and European communities were free of such prejudice, although he admits that all the various communities had their own clubs, sports societies, schools, hospitals, places of worship, and so on, and thus met only in restaurants, at social events or on tramcars.

In 1949 Noel Jacobs returned to England, where he continued working, as in Shanghai, for the British–American Tobacco Company, retiring in 1956 to New Milton, Hampshire. In 1967, Israeli veterans of the Company sponsored a very emotional visit to Israel for him and Dora. Caught up in the Six-Day War, he was found filling sandbags outside a school in Tel-Aviv.[55]

He died in England in 1977, aged 79, and his wife died a few years later. He was cremated in Bournemouth following a service at New Milton church, where his ashes were later buried – but the local news report said nothing about him being Jewish.[56] On 18 May 1980, over thirty-five veterans and their families from Israel and the USA planted a grove of 3,500 trees in his name, with a stone marker in Hebrew and

English, at Modi'in near Jerusalem – appropriately the home of the Maccabees. His wife and eldest daughter, Lorna, each planted a symbolic first tree[57] and Mrs Jacobs received a certificate commemorating the planting; veteran George Miller unveiled the plaque and Anthony Gaberman delivered a moving speech. The reception was held at the home of Dr Alex Katznelson.

Appendix 1

Other Jews served in other units of the SVC (see note 50 below). I give here, for the reader's interest, further sources which may be followed up. In a booklet, *'A' Company SVC 1870–1930*, published privately in Shanghai in 1930 by an unnamed officer and kept at the National Army Museum (NAM), several probable Jewish names are mentioned, as well as in a photocopy of an article in German, 'Feldgau' (NAM, 1956). In a history of the engineers of the SVC by Lieutenant Colonel E.H. McMichael (NAM), he names Major H. Behrens, although Alex Katznelson says he was a Scandinavian non-Jew.

Appendix 2

Members of the Jewish Company, SVC
These names are gleaned from various sources, not necessarily in the text, but especially from the amazing archive of Alex Katznelson's photographs. 'N' indicates that they were also in the experimental Jewish Naval Unit, 'Yamit' (see below):

Major Noel S. Jacobs, Commanding Officer – POW of the Japanese.

Reverend Mendel Brown, Chaplain – POW of the Japanese but later exchanged.

Private Ezekiel Abraham, USA – interned in the Second World War by the Japanese.

Private Elias Altshuler – N.

Private David Arzooni, aka Jacob

Private W. Beck

H. Bernfield

Lieutenant Robert Boris Bitker

Private Bleiman

Lance Corporal Robert Brinberg – KIA MN Red Sea 1941? – N.

Corporal Moses Cohen – Marksman.

Corporal Eager

Private J.A. Emihovich

Sergeant Major Harry Engberg – Marksman and Lewis gun.

Corporal Alex 'Alexisiso' Feldman

Corporal Julius Feldstein

Corporal Isaac Finkelstein

Private Fodor/Fellor (?)

Private E. Fomil – N.

Private D. Frank – N.

Private I. 'Sam' Frank – N.

Sergeant Freddie Fuchs – Marksman, served Second World War.

Private A. or I. or N. Furman – N.

Lieutenant Anthony Gaberman – Marksman.

Sergeant Mackee Gaberman – brother of Anthony.

Lance Corporal Eric Gabriel

Lieutenant Simon Godkin/Goetkin – SVC Ten Year Long Service Medal, later lived Israel and New York.

1.1 Part of the Jewish Company, Shanghai Volunteer Corps on manoeuvres. Sgt. M. Marguleff squatting centre front row. Note the flag, reading 'Jew. Coy.'

1.2 Jewish Company, Shanghai Volunteer Corps advancing with a Lewis Gun 1938 camp; left to right – F. Fuchs, E. Hasser, Isaac Miller, M. Gaberman, Alex Katznelson.

Private Raphael Gold

Lieutenant William Goldenberg – SVC Ten Year Long Service Medal, later POW of the Japanese.

Corporal Ike Goldfield/Goldberg (?)

Private P. Gordin

Private Sammy Greenberg

Private Louis Greenberg – brother of Sammy – they went to Israel, then Australia.

Private Gruenberg

Private Grumber

Private Serge Haimovitch

Corporal David Hanin

Corporal Leo Hanin – brother of David – Marksman.

Private Harringstock

Private Eric Hassar – N.

Private Henkin

Private Hertz

Private David Hirschorn – settled in Nahariya in northern Israel, most of his family were murdered by PLO terrorists in an attack in the 1980s.

M. Elias Jacob(s)

Private Lolia Katovitch/Katowitz

Private Mark Kaptzan

Private S. Karlikoff

Private J. Karman

Katzman

Lance Corporal Dr Alex Katznelson – later Lieutenant Colonel, IDF Medical Corps, lives in Tel-Aviv – N.

Private Dr Daniel Katznelson – brother of Alex, Company bugler, both brothers served in Israel's War of Independence – later major, IDF Medical Corps.

Private Yonah Kligman – born Harbin 1914, lives in Jerusalem.

Private Joseph Krupnick

Private W. Kurz

Private Abraham Laevsky

Private Isaac Laevsky – brother of Abraham – they later emigrated to Israel.

Private Isaac Ladar

Private B. Levinsky

Private Alex 'Shura' Levitin

Sergeant Zelic Levoff

Corporal M. Leymanstein – Marksman.

Private E. Luftig

Private Henry Maitland

Sergeant Mara Marguleff/Margulev – Marksman and Lewis gun, born in Baku, emigrated to Israel and served in Palestine police, was security officer for exiled Emperor Haile Selassie, from whom he received a Gold Medal in 1938. He returned to Shanghai and was a POW there, then returned to Israel in 1945 and was in the Israeli Army in the War of Independence, 1948.

Private Mike Medovoy – N.

Private Isaac Miller – bugler – N.

Private Mischa 'Paul' Miller

Private Leo 'Leonard' Miller (three of six brothers, and brothers of Abe and David listed below).

Private Grinka Nissenbaum – brother-in-law of Isaac Shor, listed below – lives in Hadera, Israel.

Private Hania Nissenbaum – brother of Grinka.

Private Elijah Olmert – uncle of Ehud, Israeli statesman.

Private Joseph Ozer

Private David Ozeriansky – lives in Hadera, Israel.

Sergeant Monty Palmer

Private A Perleman – KIA Malaya in Second World War – N.

Private Yvsei Polatska/Poltoski (?) – N.

Private Ezra Piasetsky

Private Gabriel Rabinovitch

Private Rapaport – Killed on active service.

Corporal Pana Samsonovitch – Marksman, emigrated to Israel in 1949 and his son was KIA in Sinai in the Six-Day War, 1967. Pana had learnt Japanese when he worked on Japanese merchant ships pre-war, and so during the Occupation he was the official interpreter for the Jewish Community.

Private Moses Sakker

Private Boris Ben 'Zion' Schafran – N.

CSM Samuel Israel Sheflan/Sheiflan – Marksman.[58]

Private Sherman

Corporal Isaac Shor – N

Private Sam Shornick – N

Private Max Shussle

2nd Lieutenant Benjamin A. Slossman/Slessman – Marksman and Lewis gun, later served Burma in the Second World War in SOE.

Corporal Reuven Slossman/Slessman – brother of Benjamin – KIA Second World War, Rangoon/Singapore (no more known), also commander of Naval Unit.

Lieutenant Emmanuel Monia Talan/Jalan – POW of the Japanese as member Hong Kong VDC, escaped and later served in SOE, awarded MBE (Mil.), later lived in Israel and Australia.

Private A. Tesler – NCH, 26 October 1938, p.146.

Private V.F. Tishler

Private Tsipiris

Private M. Tzatskin

Lance Corporal Abe
Ulanovsky

Private Naftali Uvadieff

David Volovick/Volvik, aka
Vardy – lives Jerusalem.

Private G. Weissenberg

Private Idel E.J. Whitgob –
Medical Orderly/Marks-
man, Australian.

Private Wilner

Private Boris Zats/Zatz – SVC
middle-weight
boxing champion.

Private A. Zunterstein

Private Zinkewitch.

Naval Unit only
Mike Klebanoff

Abe Miller

Victor Schneerson.

*Other Names of Jewish Members
of the Other SVC Companies*
These names were submitted
by Alex Katznelson, or from
other sources (see note 50
below). There were also many
Jewish-sounding names in the
American Company by 1938–
39, as per the *NCH*, and in the
SMP (Shanghai Municipal
Police) – e.g., S. Greenberg, in
a photograph in the *NCH*, 17
May 1939, p.207:

A. Adel – Transport Coy.

A. Adler – Transport Coy.

O. Beer – 'A' Battalion, 'B' Coy.

Driver D.W.G. Belkin – Transport Coy.

Victor Berch

B. Bergman – Transport Coy.

Lieutenant H.H. Cohen –
Ten Year Long Service
Medal, *NCH*, 18 June 1941,
p.453, and 25 June 1941,
p.490.

Bob Drisin (?)

D. Ezikiel – Signals Coy.

J. Fried – 'A' Battalion, 'B' Coy.

Jackie Goldenberg – now Yaa-
cov Guri; Armoured Car
Coy; founder Israel Tank
Corps.

John Goldenberg – father of
Jackie.

Major G.T. Goldschmidt

Sergeant M. Gotfried – Transport Coy.

L.K. Hammerstein – Trans-
port Coy.

Eli Hirsh – US Coy.

C.W. Jacobi – Transport Coy.

Private M. Katz – Transport
Coy; *NCH*, 26 October
1938, p.146.

R. Klingenberg – Transport
Coy

W. Kosterlitz – Transport Coy.

Private B. Lipkovsky – Transport Coy, *NCH*, 26 October
1938, p.146.

K.P. Loewenberger – US Coy.

Abraham Miller – Transport
Coy.

David Miller – Transport Coy.

M.R. Nissim – Signals Coy.

Private P. Ornstein –'A' Battalion, 'B' Coy.

F.T. Pressburger – 'A' Battalion, 'B' Coy.

G.P. Rosenbaum –
'A' Battalion, 'B' Coy.

P. Rosenthal – Signals Coy.

Alex Sampson – American MG
Coy.

A. Schleier – Transport Coy.

L. Schlesinger –
'A' Battalion, 'B' Coy.

J. Seba

I. Seelig – Transport Coy.

Walter Shriro – Light Horse
Coy, later interpreter to the
British
Mission in Murmansk in
the Second World War.

Lieutenant V.A. Sokoloff –
NCH, 19 October 1938,
p.110.

A. Sonnenfeld

Joe Spunt – US Coy.

Eddy Weideman/Weidner (?)
–'A' Battalion, 'B' Coy.

E. Weingart – Transport Coy.

G. Weinstein – US Coy.

W. Wertheimer – US Coy.

Appendix 3

The following names are from the archive of George (Jiri) Pisk of the
Czech Jewish Scouts; these scouts joined the SVC en masse after fleeing
Europe (see above); with thanks to George and Andrew Jakubowicz.
These men all appear to have been in 'B' Company:

Sergeant C.G.
Aschenbrenner

Private P.L. Bahr
Private K. Bock

Lance Corporal Pavel V. Do-
nath
Private O. Dub

Private D. Feder
Private P.E. Fedorovsky
Private E. Frank
Private J. Fried
Lance Corporal E.
Friedberger/Freiberger (?)

Private Z./E. Grossman/Grosz-
mann

Private V. Herz

Lance Corporal H. Klein
Private R. Kroha
Lance Corporal E. Kulka
Private A. Kanterek
Private V. Kanterek – brother
of A. Kanterek?

Private M. Loewy
Lance Corporal J. Lux

Lance Corporal B.
Markitant
Corporal F. Muller

Private Jiri/George Pisk – lives
in Australia.

Private F. Popper
Private N.G Poumbura (?)

Lance Corporal R. Rebhun
Private K. Reitler
Private P. Resauer
Private E.P. Rosenfeld
Private O. Rebenfeld

Private V. Saxl
Private M. Schneider
Private E./K. Schultz
Private M. Schwarz
Lance Corporal J. Soffer
Private F. Soyka
Lance Corporal J. Steiner
Sergeant M.J. Stembera
Private E. Stransky
Lance Corporal S. Subert

2nd Lieutenant V.G. Taussig

Private R. Uhlick

Private V. Wltzek
Private R. Weinstein

Private N. Zahowsky

*From PRO 30/26/158 (A Roll of
the SVC 'B' Company kept by
Captain D.W. Mortlock)*
CQMS W.C.A. Wolnizer – Coy
HQ.
Private E. Grundt –
3 Platoon.

Lieutenant F.W. Schlobohm –
Battalion HQ.
Sergeant Louis E. Schus-
terovitz – top 'B' Coy
Marksman, *NCH*, 19 April
1939, p.117.
Lance Corporal S. Subert – 4
platoon.

Lieutenant H. Winburg – Bat-
talion HQ.
B.A.F. Wolnizer – 3 platoon –
brother of C. Wolnizer?
C. Wolnizer – 3 platoon.
J. Wolnizer – 3 platoon.

4 Platoon
Private J. Gohwald

Private H. Klepetar
Private P. Kohn
Private W. Kurz

Private O. Lustig

Private B. Mandel

Private G. Neubauer

Private W. Pollack

Private J. Schulef

Private R. Winter

Shanghai Special Police Unit
Sergeant Cyma Velinsky

Appendix 4

The Shanghai Jewish Naval Unit, 'Yamit'

Some time around 1935, the Betar movement had a vision of forming a Naval Unit, probably with the view of assisting in secret Jewish immigration into Israel. But Shanghai was a most unsuitable place to train such a unit, as it was far from the sea and nobody in the Jewish Community at that time had any knowledge of sailing or navigation. Furthermore, there were strict licensing laws about use of the river in Shanghai by the Chinese Government.

Nevertheless, instructed by the Betar leader then based in Paris, Vladimir Jabotinsky himself, plans went ahead. A strip of reclaimed land was rented, near the electric power plant on the Shanghai river at the north shore of the International Settlement. Reuven Slossman was made naval officer in charge and Eric Hassar as senior NCO. In August 1937 a heavy riveted steel-plate lifeboat, with heavy oak decks and heavy oars, was purchased and naval uniforms were made by a local tailor; the naval cap had a black band printed in gold with the name *Brit Trumpeldor* (Hebrew for 'Covenant of Trumpeldor', the famous Zionist leader of the first part of the twentieth century) and the Menorah badge as used by the Jewish Legion in the First World War.

The group met at the boat one sunny Sunday morning, and boarded it (their names are denoted by the letter 'N' in Appendix 2 above). The vessel, however, was so heavy that it could not be handled, especially against the river tide, and after hours of struggle, the crew returned the boat to shore. Soon afterwards, the Japanese captured the mooring area, and the Betar Shanghai Jewish Naval Unit was never to return. Only a photograph remains.[59]

Acknowledgements

I would like to thank the staff of the Imperial War Museum Reading Room and Department of Documents; the staff of the Reading Room of the National Army Museum and the British Library in Euston; author Ben Frank in the USA; the Colindale British Library Newspaper Archives; the staff of the Tower Hamlets Local History Library; the Library of the School of Oriental and African Studies (SOAS), University of London; Peter Nash of the Australian Genealogical Association in NSW; Paul Kaye of Leighton Buzzard (former British member of 'B' Company of the SVC); Detective Superintendent Karl Spencer of the Hong Kong Police Force; Professor Andrew Jakubowicz of the University of Sydney, Australia; Dr Robert Gohstand of the Old China Hands Archive, of California State University; Zvika Ma'oz in Jerusalem, Israel (daughter of Yonah Kligman); Dr Nancy Pine of the Claremont Graduate University, California; Peter Salinger of the SOAS Library of Judaica and Semitics; and George and Dennis Pisk in Sydney, Australia.

I especially wish to thank Dr Alex Katznelson, MD, from Ramat Gan in Israel, a former Jewish Company member, who provided the most amazing photographs and list of names of Jewish Company members from the legacy and archive of Lieutenant Anthony Gaberman, as well as never-published material on the Jewish Naval Unit. The AJEX Jewish Military Museum has a display of the Jewish Company insignia and uniforms of Lieutenant Gaberman, donated by Dr Katznelson.

Notes

1. See The Shanghai Volunteer Corps website for fuller detail on this and other aspects of the Corps (www.talesofoldchina.com).
2. 'The Jewish Company of the SVC compared with other Jewish Diaspora Fighting Units' by 'Ben' M. Frank, 1992 (www.lib.byu.edu); paper given at 1993 Harvard University seminar on Jews in China.
3. Letters from Alex Katznelson, 2004–05.
4. P. Guang, *The Jews in Shanghai* (Shanghai: Shanghai Pictorial Publishing House, 1995), p.3; however, the *North China Herald* (*NCH*), 26 July 1939, p.166, says 50,000.
5. From *Israel's Messenger (Mevaserret Yisroel)*, Shanghai Jewish Sephardic newspaper, 18 October 1938, p.25, quoted in Maisie Meyer, *From the Rivers of Babylon to the Whangpoo* (University Press of America, 2003), p.141.
6. Marcia R. Ristaino, *Port of Last Resort* (Stanford, CA: Stanford University Press, 2001), p.63.
7. *NCH*, 19 May 1937, p.275.
8. M.R. Ristaino, 'White Russian and Jewish Refugees in Shanghai 1920–44, as recorded in the Shanghai Municipal Police files, National Archives, Washington, DC', *Republican China Journal*, 16 January 1990, pp.51–62.
9. Fifty-five Jewish Czech citizens who escaped the Nazis also joined the SVC in the 1930s but not all were in the Jewish Company (see P. Meyer, and Google on 'Czech Republic Jews in Soviet Satellites'). Most of them had been Czech Jewish Scouts and founded their own Company with the Czech colours worn as a roundel on their shoulders; virtually all of them were Jewish (interview with Professor A. Jakubowicz in London, August 2004). There is a Jewish Chaplain Card at the AJEX Museum naming Major G.T. Goldschmidt as a member of the Shanghai Defence Force in 1927, 1929 and 1939, but it is not clear if he was in the Jewish Company. An article in the *Jewish Chronicle*, 3 September 1937, p.44, says several Jews serving in the SVC had been killed in action in various other Companies during the Sino-Japanese disturbances of 1932, but Alex Katznelson was unaware of this fact.
10. I. Kounin, *85 years of the Shanghai Volunteer Corps* (Shanghai: Cosmopolitan Press, 1938), *passim*. Bitker was born in Russia in 1907 and had won three Crosses of St George as a Russian soldier; he later became an American citizen.
11. Recorded in the Shanghai Municipal Council Annual Report, 1933, p.68, as quoted in Pan Guang, 'Zionism in Shanghai', *Studies in Zionism* (London) (now *Journal of Israeli History*), XIV, 2 (1995), p.73.
12. Email from Alex Katznelson in Israel, March 2005.
13. *Jewish Chronicle*, 13 January 1933, p.21.
14. The Club was in Route Pichon, now Fenyang Road (Guang, *The Jews in Shanghai*, p.15).
15. *NCH*, 28 June 1933, p.496.
16. This may be apocryphal as it was also the joke 'motto' of the Jewish battalions of the Royal Fusiliers in the First World War. This 'motto' for the Jewish Company was apparently suggested by Colonel Thoms. According to Alex Katznelson, Noel Jacobs composed a ditty, sung to the tune of 'Clementine': 'After the Scottish come the Jewish, getting Scottish music free, and their motto is no advance sir, not without security.'
17. Brown – a graduate of Jews' College, London – had come from London in the early 1930s to be head teacher of the Shanghai Jewish School and Minister of the Ohel Rachel ('Tent of Rachel') Synagogue in the city. He later married Annie Horowitz.
18. Letter, 5 January 2005.
19. Telephone interview with Alex Katznelson, August 2004. Dr Katznelson was born in Tomsk, Russia, on 23 September 1919 and his family left for Shanghai after the Civil War in Russia. He was in the Shanghai Jewish Boy Scouts from 1930–40 and the Jewish Company of the SVC from 1938–42. After the Second World War he went to live in Israel where he served as a doctor in the War of Independence in 1948, and was a senior orthopaedic surgeon (lieutenant colonel) in the IDF and various Israeli hospitals for many years; he is much published.
20. Correspondence from Alex Katznelson, August 2004. The music for this hymn was composed by a young Palestinian Jew, Uzi Hitman (died 2004). The Company always ate kosher food on duty and at the Jewish Club.

21. 19 January 1938, p.95.
22. *NCH*, 13 May 1936, p.289.
23. *NCH*, 17 February 1937, p.282.
24. Letter to the author, 1 March 2005.
25. *NCH*, 8 March 1939, p.426; see also book by Meyer, *Rivers of Babylon* (see note 5).
26. 5 July 1935, p.12 – thanks to the British Library Oriental and India Collection.
27. *NCH*, 11 March 1936, p.442.
28. *NCH*, 17 March 1937, p.452.
29. He later became a lieutenant in the Hong Kong militia, fought against the Japanese and was a POW. He was awarded an MBE in 1954 (information from Detective Inspector Karl Spencer, Hong Kong Police) and later lived in Australia.
30. *NCH*, 8 December 1937, p.381.
31. See Kounin; Bitker had been sent to Mandate Palestine by the Revisionist Zionist leader Jabotinsky, to help set up the Irgun (Jewish Fighting Underground) but he was not sufficiently proficient in Hebrew or local knowledge and he was released to return to Shanghai. He died in San Francisco in 1977 (letters from Alex Katznelson in the author's possession). See also *NCH*, 24 August 1938, p.339.
32. Harriet Sergeant, *Shanghai: Collision Point of Cultures 1918–39* (New York: Crown Publishers, 1990), p.297.
33. PRO 30/26/157.
34. Ibid.
35. Letters from Alex Katznelson, August 2004–June 2005.
36. *NCH*, 18 May 1938, p.279.
37. *NCH*, 20 July 1938, p.104.
38. *NCH*, 2 March 1938, p.334.
39. *NCH*, 10 April 1940.
40. *NCH*, 24 August 1938, p.326.
41. *NCH*, 20 July 1938, p.118.
42. *NCH*, 19 October 1938, p.110.
43. *NCH*, 1 February 1939, p.193.
44. Letter from Alex Katznelson, August 2004.
45. *Jewish Chronicle*, p.41.
46. *NCH*, 31 May 1939, p.202.
47. At the dinner, Lieutenant Godkin was presented with a pair of gold cufflinks with the Jewish Company insignia; the author wonders where these are today? *NCH*, 2 October 1940, p.26, also notes Jacobs' promotion to major as of 11 September 1940.
48. WO 106/2393.
49. Ibid.
50. Many local Jews served in other SVC Companies too, and Jewish names crop up frequently in the chapter on the SVC in A. Harfield, *British and Indian Armies on the China Coast, 1783–1985* (London: A. & J. Partnership Press, 2000), pp.371–434 and Appendices. In Kounin's book, the following names appear (often with photographs), as serving in other Companies during the early twentieth century: CQMS (later Staff Officer) Henry Harold Cohen, Light Automatic Company, p.219; Lieutenant V.A. Sokoloff and Lieutenant V.L. Kuzmin, Russian Company, p.259; Captain E. Gumpert(z), CO of 'A' Company (British), pp.58 and 201, with Lance Corporal M.L. Lessner, Private B.B. Joseph and Private F.H. Moysky, p.196; Captain A. Hertzberg, CO Signals Company, p.170, and as a bugle boy earlier on p.49; Troopers A.L Moses, Hayim, Kenneth Dabelstein (committed suicide, 2 October 1935, *NCH*) and Cohen, and Corporal Goldsack and Lieutenant Dr Karl C. 'Mosey' Mosberg, CO of the Shanghai Light Horse, p.160 and passim, before the First World War, and also in a letter to the *NCH*, 13 September 1933, p.424; Lieutenant F.W. Schlobohm of the US Company, p.125; Sergeant Major F.C. Feltz of the HQ Company, p.123; Lieutenant C. and Lieutenant L.H. Koch of the German Company (later 'B' Coy – *NCH*, 19 October 1938, p.110).
   In the *NCH* of 9 August 1933, p.218, mention is made of Private Aaron Levoff, a Shanghai resident serving in the US Marines, receiving the Yangste Service Medal from Washington HQ; there were also many other Jewish-sounding names in the Russian Company, but names alone

are not always conclusive, of course. Alex Katznelson said that no Jews ever served in the   Russian Companies. See Appendix for further names discovered.

51. Letter from Katznelson, August 2004.
52. Article quoting a visit to Shanghai by the US Delegate to the Far East from the United Pales-
    tine Appeal (UPA), Mr Samuel Ben-Ami, in *Jewish Chronicle*, 3 September 1937, p.44. In the same
    article, Ben-Ami notes that most of the active Jewish Company men were Betar members (Brit
    Trumpledor, a Zionist revisionist movement founded by Jabotinsky) and that the Company was
    the pride of the Shanghai Jewish community, upholding Jewish honour in times of unrest and
    emergency.
53. Marvin Tokayer and Mary Swartz, *The Fugu Plan* (London: Hamlyn, 1979), p.268.
54. See Frank, note 2 above.
55. Benis Frank Archive, School of Educational Studies, Claremont Graduate University (CGU),
    California; with thanks to Nancy Pine.
56. CGU Archive.
57. *Igud Yotzei Sin* [journal] (Israel), 1980, p.13, from CGU (see previous note).
58. Sheflan was an orphan cousin of Alex Katznelson and adopted by his family; he died in Israel in
    2003.
59. Letter from Alex Katznelson, who was a member of this short-lived and unique Jewish naval
    experiment; a photograph appears in Guang, *The Jews in Shanghai*, p.49.

Against Fascism: British and Palestinian (Israeli) Jews who served in the International Brigade in the Spanish Civil War

For reasons best known to themselves, most adherents of the Left – both old and new – and the mainstream Jewish community itself have been, until recently, loathe to acknowledge and recall the dominant Jewish role in the International Brigade's (IB) struggle against fascism in the Spanish Civil War. Stereotyped as timid and submissive, the reality is that thousands of Jews from fifty-three countries went to fight and die opposing Franco, firing the first shots against fascism. Some went openly as Jews, others took aliases; some fought in the battalions of their country of birth, others with other national groups; some went via a third nation, others went direct to Spain; some were refugees from anti-Semitism or political oppression already, others went freely from the democracies. In addition thousands more Jews worldwide were active in solidarity campaigns, fundraising and refugee rescue, on behalf of the Republican Democrats. Most non-Jewish students of the conflict, however, have no problem emphasizing the major part played by Jews in the International Brigade,[1] and the Black actor Paul Robeson even sang and recorded Yiddish songs for the Jewish soldiers in Spain (see reference to O'Riordan, below).

It is my personal belief that the marginalization of the huge part played by the Jewish fighters in Spain is due to the tight grip held by old-fashioned Stalinists who have been the 'Keepers of the Memory' of the IB in the post-war period, and right up to the twenty-first century – especially in the UK and the USA. To acknowledge the incredible role of the Jews is to have to admit that many went to Spain as proud Jews as much as proud socialists, and that many were also Zionists, especially the large number – proportionally the largest from any country – who came from Mandate Palestine/Israel.

For those on the 'Hard Left', this somewhat explodes the myth that everyone who went was a certified member of the Communist Party or was totally imbued with communist ideals. This was most certainly not always the case, as the author heard at first-hand from Jewish veterans whom he interviewed. Indeed, Peter Fry openly says in an interview in the film *Forever Activists* that he went to Spain primarily because he was Jewish, and this was because of his strong Jewish sense of social justice, which he felt all the Jewish volunteers had. It is also interesting to note that after the

Second World War, most of the Jewish fighters returned to Jewish communities and the cultural life with which they were familiar; they were by no means estranged from Jewishness or even Judaism. Some visited Israel many times and others have children living there to this day. They also said they sensed a strong strand of anti-Jewish feeling in some of the non-Jewish veterans' leaders, and this naturally fed into the tendency by modern writers on the Spanish Civil War to ignore the Jewish contribution to the IB.

Stalinist opposition to Zionism, especially after 1948 and the rebirth of Israel, has meant that the Left has to denounce and to make invisible any overt and separate recognition of the massive Jewish contribution to the IB and the Republican struggle, in order to fit in with its perverse and passé Marxist view of history. Hence it can justify celebrating – quite rightly – the part played by Irish and Black volunteers, for example, but not the part played by the Jews. Not to give Jews the credit they so richly deserved, for firing the first shots against European fascism, can thus be justifiably described as anti-Semitic, as it appears that national liberation is all right for everyone else – Ireland, Black Africa, Asia, the Arabs – but not all right for the Jews of Israel. This is open discrimination against Jews, and the Left needs to now revise its attitude to this issue. Thus, until now, one will not find any reference to the contribution of the Jews to the IB in any book on the IB in the Spanish Civil War, except a moderate mention in Richard Baxell's PhD thesis and later book.[2] This article now redresses the balance.

Introduction

It is estimated that up to 25 per cent of all the IB fighters were Jewish – see Alberto Fernandez, *Judios en la Guerra de Espana* (Madrid: Tiempo de Historia, September 1975); Gina Medem, *Los Judios Luchadores de la Libertad* (Madrid: 1937) and Josef Toch, *Juden im Spanischen Krieg 1936–39* (Vienna: Zeitgeschichte, April 1973) – up to 10,000 men and women. Whilst twentieth-century history documents well the mass murder of Jews, Jewish resistance is feebly recorded by comparison. This included in Spain the following approximate numbers – certainly an underestimate – of Jewish fighters and participants in the IB:

Poland: 2,250 (of 5,000 Poles, 45 per cent – Jews 10 per cent of Polish population).
USA: 1,250 (38 per cent of total USA volunteers – Jews 4 per cent of USA population).
France: 1,043 (15 per cent of French volunteers – Jews 0.5 per cent of population).
Britain: between 200 and 400 (11 to 22 per cent – Jews 0.5 per cent of population (from David Diamint's book, mentioned below).

Israel/Palestine: 350 to 500, proportionately the largest group.

Hungary, Austria: 120–150 volunteers (based on research by Hans Landauer and others in the *Leo Baeck Year Book*, 1995, p.17, footnote); Czechs, Yugoslavs: thirty-four – probably a huge underestimate); Bulgarian: seventeen; Canada: seventy-one – in the Mackenzie-Papineau Battalion; Italy, Scandinavia, Germany – totalling 1,095 (work by Arno Lustiger in *German and Austrian Jews in the International Brigade* published in Frankfurt in 1989, and also *Schalom Libertad: Juden in Spanischau Burgerkrieg*, also published in French. The *Leo Baeck Year Book*, 1990, shows that at least 400 to 500 German Jews fought in Spain).

Belgium: an article by Rudi van Doorslaer, 'Belgian Jews in the International Brigade', is in the IB Archives at the Marx Memorial Library (MML), box D4, 17 July 1986, and is in the AJEX Archives. It describes 200 Belgian Jews in Spain (thirty of them women), thirty-one of whom were killed in action and a further twenty more killed in action in the Belgian Resistance in the Second World War. It is important to note here that most of the European volunteers went on to fight in the Resistance groups in the Second World War, many of them being captured and murdered by the Nazis.

Soviet Union: fifty-three. This is a vast underestimate and current researches into newly available files in Russia have yet to yield new information on Jewish participation.

Virtually all the Romanians (see the article by Lending in the Jewish Workers' Circle (JWC) journal, *Horizons*, mentioned below).

Forty other countries: 1,602.

Fifty-nine of the American medical team of 124 were Jews (48 per cent – Prago's article mentioned below) and virtually all of the forty Polish doctors. Of the estimated sixty-six American Jews from Brownsville in Brooklyn, for example, who went to Spain, only twenty-five returned (Prago).

The Polish Dombrowski Brigade (part of the 13th IB) formed a Jewish Company from the 2nd Palafox Battalion (Palafox was a Spanish patriot from the Napoleonic invasion), called the Botwin Company, on 12 December 1937 at Tardadientes, named after Naftali Botwin, a famous Polish Jewish radical, executed in 1924 for assassinating a Polish Secret Police agent. Their orders and banner were written in Yiddish, Polish and Spanish and they issued a Yiddish written newspaper (*Botwin)*, first published on 30 December 1937. The first edition of a Yiddish newspaper, *Der Freihaits Kempfer* (Fighters for Liberty), appeared at the Front on 7 August 1937. Jews spoke Hebrew and Ladino as a lingua franca among themselves within the different national groups. The Republic also allowed radio broadcasts in Yiddish. The Botwins included the only two Arabs in the IB, one of whom was from Jerusalem and spoke Yiddish. The last stanza of the company hymn was: ' ... how Jewish Botwin soldiers drove out the fascist plague! No Passaran!' (see J. Rothenberg, 'The Jewish Naftali Botwin Company', *Jewish Frontiers Journal* (USA), date unknown, at IB archive, MML; it includes references to several books written in Poland by Botwin and Dombrowski Jewish veterans).

Trained at Albacete, the Botwins went into action on 12 February 1938 in the Sierra Quemeda near Belal Alcazar, then fought at Belchite 12–16 March 1938. They were virtually wiped out at the battles of the Ebro/Estramadura at Hill 281 (eighteen out of 120 survived) and received the Medalla de Valor from the government (see Hirschmann, below). All four successive commanders were killed in action – including Carol Gutman on 13 February and Moise Micha Sapir on 2 April at Lerida. Hirschmann also provided extracts from the books, *Poles in the Spanish Civil War* (Poland: Ministry of Defence [n.d.]) and *International Solidarity with the Spanish Republic* (Moscow: Progress Publishers, 1975), containing numerous references to the Botwins. The newly reinforced Botwins later formed the rearguard for the IB as they withdrew into France as the fighting ended.

It is ironic that the first IB casualty was Jewish (Leon Baum, from Paris) and also the last (Haskel Honigstern; the Spanish poet Jose Herrera wrote of him: 'Haskel Honigstern, Polish worker of the Jewish Race, son of an obscure land, killed in the light of my homeland.' He was given a state funeral in Barcelona on 6 October 1938). Later, most Botwins joined the Maquis and other Partisan groups in the Second World War, many dying in fighting the Nazis. In Poland, however, after the Six-Day War in 1967 and the anti-Jewish purges, all the memorials to the Botwin men that had been erected were destroyed.

As Simon Hirschmann said in an interview with the author, Jewish youth of this period – especially in eastern Europe – were living under anti-Semitic regimes and chose to fight back by becoming either Zionists or communists; many chose the latter and Spain gave them a chance to take up arms in the cause of working people and democracy, with much heroism and self-sacrifice. They are a group much to be admired. But Zionists were equally anti-fascist and many of the Jewish volunteers from Europe and Palestine/Israel were Zionist Socialists.

Joe Garber, Intelligence Officer to the British Battalion, testified in an interview with the author to the fact that there were hundreds of Jews in the German and Austrian Thaelmann Battalion, and hundreds with the French.

Listed below are some of the known British Jews who went to Spain. The figures are far from complete, as many did not identify as Jews and used aliases, but made themselves known as Jews to other Jews once they were in Spain; most witnesses have died before being able to testify just who was whom. On this issue Joe Garber was an inestimable source of information and I thank him enormously.

Abbreviations and Sources

MSCW refers to the book *Memorials of the Spanish Civil War*, by Colin Williams, Bill Alexander and John Gorman (Stroud: Sutton, 1996). *BVFL* refers to *British Volunteers for Liberty* by Bill Alexander (London: Lawrence and Wishart, 1982). *CTC* refers to *Cheetham to Cordova*, by Maurice Levine and Neil Richardson (Manchester: Manchester Jewish Museum, 1984). MML is the Marx Memorial Library. PI refers to personal interviews carried out by Martin Sugarman with Jewish veterans whilst at the sixty-second anniversary of the start of the war reunion at Jubilee Gardens, London on 18 July 1998, or to those whose names were given to him at the reunion by other veterans. Lou Kenton also sent names from the roll in Bill Rust's book, *Britons in Spain* (New York: International Publishing 1939). *LBYB* refers to the *Leo Baeck Year Book*, which has contained articles about Jews who fought in Spain and is published by the Leo Baeck Institute in London. KIA means killed in action; WIA means wounded in action.

Other important works on this subject include *Combattants Juifs dans l'Armee Republicaine Espagnole* by David Diamint (DD) (Paris: Editions Renouveau, 1979), which describes the massive contribution of Jews in the IB and contains lists of names, numerous first-hand accounts by Jewish fighters, and a section on women fighters. Also excellent is Alfred Prago's 'Jews in the International Brigades in Spain', *Jewish Currents* (New York), February and March 1979; G.E. Sichon, 'Les Volontaires Juifs dans la Guerre Civile en Espagne', *Les Temps Modernes* (Paris) October 1988; and A.S. Rockman, 'Jewish Participation in the IBs in the Spanish Civil War', MA thesis, California State University, Fullerton.

Much information and several photos were found in *The Book of the 15th Brigade*, published by the Commissariat, Madrid 1938, and republished by F. Graham, Newcastle, 1975 – abbreviated as '*B15B*' below. More details came from Alek Szurek, *The Shattered Dream* (New York: Columbia University Press, 1989), abbreviated as *TSD*, and J. Cook, *Apprentices of Freedom* (London: Quartet, 1979), especially on George Nathan and Maurice Levene.

Mentioned also in the latter book is the brief description of discrimination made against Jewish POWs; Bob Doyle (p.119) noted that after his capture (with Maurice Levitas, Dave Goodman and others) at Calaceite near Gandesa, on 31 March 1938, Italian and Gestapo guards 'ordered all Communists and Jews to step forward'. This is described in more detail in a long article, 'Irish and Jewish Volunteers in the Spanish Anti-Fascist War: 50th Anniversary Lecture' by M. O'Riordan of the Irish TGWU, at the Irish Jewish Museum in Dublin, November 1987, found in the MML Archive (pp.25–28). Gary McCarthy noted that 'at San Sebastian prison in 1938, Spanish and German guards took photos of those lads who were obviously Jewish, and

of Negroes too and when Jimmy Goldstein/Goldsmith was singled out I
stepped forward too!' (Cook, *Apprentices of Freedom*, p.123). In fact Jews were
constantly slandered in Spanish fascist radio broadcasts and newspapers –
even though virtually no Jews lived in Spain. Their large presence in the IB
was often a target for fascist newspapers all over Europe.

The list of known British Jewish KIA is included in the Appendix of
MSCW – there are forty-three of them and another seven probables. Many
others had non-Jewish aliases (as Joe Garber and others have testified)
and we may never know their religious affiliation or origin because of this.
Spellings, especially of Polish names, may have lost accuracy in the
transliteration. It is also interesting to point out how many of the Jewish
volunteers came from the East End of London, especially Hackney,
Stepney and surrounding boroughs. Finally, some further details have
come from a London School of Economics PhD thesis, by Richard Baxell,
now a book on the British Volunteers (see note 2), which he kindly sent
to me. It includes some of the actual ID numbers issued to the men and
women who went to Spain and I have included these where known.

Acknowledgements

I would like to thank especially the late Joe Garber, Sol Frankel, Lou Kenton, Simon 'Simmy' Hirschmann and Major Len Crome, MC (all Jewish
veterans of the Spanish Civil War) and Bill Alexander (former commissar
of the Attlee Battalion), for their help and encouragement in compiling
this list.

Dr Saul Issroff of the Jewish Genealogical Society of the UK was also
very helpful. Fred Dellheim – a former Jewish *Kindertransportee* and Second
World War D-Day veteran, and former secretary of the German Anti-Fascist
Association and Veterans of Anti-Fascism – presented to the author, at a
meeting with him in London in June 1999, a list of names of hundreds of
German veterans of the Spanish Civil War. A vast number were Jews. This
list exists separately at present in the AJEX Archives.

The amazing Sir Martin Gilbert was as ever of inestimable assistance
to me in my work.

I was able to add considerable detail and names by consulting many
files in the IB archive at the Marx Memorial Library in Clerkenwell,
London, and thank the librarian (Tish Newland) for her assistance. One
particular list in these files was compiled by either Peter Kerrigan or Ted
Edwards, the Attlee Battalion secretary, during or soon after the war, and
contained many British Jewish names not found elsewhere.

Special thanks also goes to James Carmody who supplied me so
generously with extra material from his own researches on the IB over
many years at both the National Archives and with correspondents abroad,

2.1 Original International Brigade (IB) Volunteer pay book of Stanley Brentman/Harrison from Portsmouth (courtesy of his daughter Rosalyn).

2.2 Palestinian Jewish IB Volunteers in Spain – Centre rear, Robert Aquist from Haifa, killed on the Ebro 22 July 1938. Sitting left, Arie Lev aka Moishe Goy, from Tel-Aviv; sitting right Israel Centner from Tel-Aviv.

including many names from David Diamint's rare book, which I also consulted at the British Library. James Carmody also directed me to a book by Marcel Acier, *From Spanish Trenches* (New York: Modern Age, 1937) at the MML, containing many personal memoirs of Jewish Brigaders.

Thanks also go to Paul Phillipon of the University of Stirling; Professor Stellan Bojerud, Royal Staff College, Stockholm; Robert Llopis of Benissa, Spain; and John Kralijic of New York.

A specific memorial to the Jewish fighters of the IB was unveiled in Barcelona in October 1986, by President Chaim Hertzog of Israel, himself a Second World War British Army major veteran. It is located near Montjuich and a photograph of it is in the AJEX Jewish Military Museum in Hendon, London, which also has a permanent display on Jews in the Spanish Civil War.

The British Battalion

The British Battalion consisted originally of 145 men and was formed between December 1936 and January 1937 at Madrigueras as No. 1 Company, of the French 14th Battalion (La Marseillaise), part of the 14th IB. As new arrivals came, the British formed their own battalion in 1937, of four Companies (three Infantry and one Machine Gun). No. 1 Company, the longest serving, were then named in honour of Labour leader and later Prime Minister Clement Attlee. Of the approximately 2,000 volunteers, as many as 300 to 400 were Jewish (11 to 22 per cent, as described by David Diamint), yet Jews have never been more than one-half of 1 per cent of the UK population.

Some other nationalities are included here due to the order of the original interviews with Joe Garber and others and/or because they were at some time associated with the British Battalion.

736 Maurice Chaim Aaronberg, born Lithuania 1897, served Russian Army 1917–18, then sergeant in British Army 1919 in Archangel; then to Sheffield, 43 Wolstenholme Rd; KIA 27 February 1937 Jarama.

1056 Sergeant Samuel/ Sydney Aarons, Melbourne, Australia.

1309 Basil Abrahams, aka David Minsk, 15th Brigade Staff, POW 13 February 1937 and repatriated May 1937, later returning to Spain to fight again. From 187 Mare St, Hackney, London/3 Cecil St, Mile End, London; a baker (*BVFL* p.185), died 1 June 1995.

Abraham Abrahamson, KIA Brunete, hero of the Soviet Union (Prago).

Paul Abrams, POW February 1937 for three months, exchanged for fascist POWs.

Nathan Abramson, Bow, London, KIA April 1938 Gandesa/Calaceite.

201 Joseph Albaya (?)

Jack/Jacob Alexander, Bethnal Green and Australia, POW March 1938.

175 Lieutenant Harry Aubrey/ Horbury (*B15B*).

Sidney Avner, more than six foot tall, from 55 Clapton Common, Upper Clapton, London; attended Davenant Foundation School; KIA 20 December 1936 Boadilla.

Louis Babot, Shoreditch

Nicholas Barblinger, possibly born Russia, later fought in French Foreign Legion, interned Oran, then joined Pioneer Corps in British Army and fought in North Africa, Italy and at Arnhem with 21st Independent Paras.

Sam Baron, newspaper correspondent (Crook diaries at MML).

David Baumgartner/ Baumgarten, aka Bennett, Manchester.

Harry A.G. Bayer/Beye, 16 Barclay Street, St Pancras, London (MML).

Reginald Bayer, Highbury, north London.

Else Behrens, photographer (MML).

Alec Bernstein, Manchester.

Captain Dr Bernstein/ Berstein (MML).

Emeric Biederman, born Romania; 44/4a Birch Lane, Longsight, Manchester (MML); after Second World War lived in Romania.

1445 Thomas Arthur Bielstein, Scunthorpe (MML).

1141 Arthur Blackson/ Blackman, London and Winchester, repatriated May 1938, possibly not Jewish.

David Blick/Black (MML), aka Block/Bloch, pilot, KIA Second World War on first 1,000 bomber raid on Cologne; Runnymede memorial. His brother Sam also KIA, RAF, Second World War.

Charles Sewell Bloom, 54 Imperial Avenue, Stoke Newington, London N16, served Badalona Hospital (MML).

Cyril/Charles Bloom, London, WIA Jarama (PI Joe Garber).

Karl Boden, Salford, Signals (MML).

598 Cyril Bowman, Cheetham, Manchester.

L. Boyarski, Johannesburg, South Africa.

O. Brinckman (?)

105 Jack Braverman (PI), 44 Cromer Street, Kingsland Rd, Shoreditch, London E2 (MML).

Stanley Israel Brentman, aka Harrison, Southsea, Hants, born Southwark.

Bill Briskey, Hackney, east London, KIA 12 February 1937 Jarama.

43 Zelig I. Bronstein, Paris (MML), mechanic with 15th Brigade.

Dave Buffman, Leeds, KIA September 1938 Ebro.

Ronald Burgess, son of Charlotte Haldane, née Franken, second wife of Professor J.B.S. Haldane (PI Joe Garber). Charlotte Haldane was a war correspondent in Spain and her first husband was a Burgess, hence her son used this name.

Ralph C (K)antorovitch/ Cantor, 142 Waterloo Rd, Manchester, KIA July 1937 Mosquito Hill, Brunete.

Phil Caplan, aka Richards, 83 Shirland Gardens, Maida Vale, London W7, boxer by profession; KIA July or February 1937 Brunete (Joe Garber says Jarama).

Alfred Capps, Hackney, east London, KIA 20 January 1938 Teruel.

H. Carrass (?)

Harold Ceiternbaum aka Bourne/Sittingbaum, from Westcliff-on-Sea.

Sidney/Solomon Chaginsky, aka Moreland, from Hackney, east London, POW March 1938, repatriated October 1938 (PI).

Fred Chaike, WIA July 1937 Brunete (MML).

Cochrane, alias (PI Joe Garber).

A. Cohen (?)

Jack Cohen, Manchester/Leeds, WIA.

Jack Cohen, Old Haymarket, Liverpool, KIA by a strafing aircraft, February 1937 Jarama.

Larry Cohen, aka Collier, ambulance driver and also served Second World War.

Leon Cohen, Liverpool, KIA (MML).

Sergeant Max Cohen/Colin/Collins, aka Myer/Meir Cohn (BVFL p.138); born 1912 in Stepney, of 82 Kyverdale Rd, London N16 and 73 Wigan House, Warwick Grove, London E5; ambulance driver and mechanic. WIA by Italian planes at Brunete and evacuated, then returned for a second tour. Drove ambulance from London to Barcelona. Detailed diaries at MML.

893 Myer Cohen, 1 Gold St, Stepney, east London.

Nat Cohen, from Streatham, south London (PI) (MSCW, pp.126–7).

1311 Nathan Cohen, Stepney, Tom Mann Centurion.

Ovadia Cohen, Greek Jewish.

752 Percy Cohen, 83 Cotswolds Gardens, Hendon, ambulance driver (Joe Garber).

Pincus Cohen, London.

Ramona Cohen, wife of Nathan, above.

Reuben A.C. Cohen, 43 Dunk St, London E1, furrier.

S. Cohen, 2 Overton St, Liverpool, builder, WIA in head (MML).

748 Sidney Cohen, 51 St Thomas Rd, Hackney, London E9 (MML). Fought with Macpaps.

101 Simon Cohen, 2 Leander St, Mount Pleasant, Liverpool (MML).

Vic Cohen (MML).

Edward Coleman, Manchester.

492 Julius Jud Colman, 3 Lytton Ave, Cheetham, Manchester (CTC, p.30), served on Cordoba front (information from K.R. Bradley, author of International Brigades in Spain, (Osprey, 1984). With Nathan in 14th Brigade at Lopera where Cornford was killed, and at Jarama in the 15th Brigade at Morata De Tajuna. Booklet by him in MML Archives, Memories of Spain, 1995.

Stafford Cottman, alias, from London.

Major Dr Leonard Crome, MC (Second World War, Colonel RAMC, Cassino); CO Medical Services IB, later 5th Army (MSCW, p.24) (PI). Russian, born in Latvia, educated in UK, WIA.

David Crook, lived in China with his two sons (PI Joe Garber). Spent seven years in solitary during Cultural Revolution and in 1990 was still in Beijing. Detailed diary in MML Archives.

Richard Nigel Cullen, born Australia, lived Putney, later RAF pilot awarded DFC, KIA May 1941 Greece.

Leslie Daikin, named by Levitas in O'Riordan article.

Danielis, Czech medic (MML).

R. Daniels, 92 Ernest St, Stepney, east London (MML).

243 Henry Daniels, c/o Mrs Bellow, 24 Barnsbury Pk, London NW1 (MML).

753 Moishe Davidovitch/Maurice Davis, of 24 Teesdale St, London E1/638, Seven Sisters Rd, Tottenham; KIA 12 February 1937 Jarama; brother-in-law of Max Lewis. He was: Leader of the 1st Aid Section, a hero throughout that terrible

day of Feb 12th ... up, down and across shell-scarred and bullet swept slopes, he and his men carried the wounded in stretchers ... and when they gave out, blankets. He escaped death a hundred times until in the late afternoon, while running to help a wounded man, he himself was fatally wounded. [B15B, p.62.]

Gustav Daubenspeck, Hackney.

Joshua Davidson, Salford/Manchester, upholsterer.

Ted (Edward) A. Dickinson/Dickenson (an alias, originally Austrian or Australian? Probably Jewish), from Forest Gate, London. Murdered as POW on 2 February 1937, Jarama, after protesting the murder of two other Jewish POWs, Elias and Stevens. He was tied to a tree and shot through the head. He had calmly shouted to his men, 'Salud Comrades', as he fell. Joe Garber says he was Jewish but there was also an Australian with the same or similar name.

Andre Diamint/Diamond, Anglo-Egyptian French Jew; 17 Antikhane el Masrich, Cairo, (BVFL, p.98); lost his leg but served in French Resistance in Second World War and was executed by the Nazis. His diary in MML archive.

John Diamond, MML, Canada (?)

Sam Dobralski from Camden, c/o Alec Horlich, Quebec; POW.

420 Sydney Edelman, 17 Wellington Row, London E2, KIA/died of wounds April/August 1938 Aragon/Tarragona.

424 Lieutenant Herman Ehlert, aka Theo Edward Mann, German-born anti-Nazi refugee, c/o Toynbee Hall, Whitechapel (MML). He also fought with Lincolns.

Ilya Ehrenbourg (MML), famous Russian writer and war correspondent in Spain, spoke to and met many of the British Battalion.

Hans Eisler, Crook diaries.

Sid Philip Elias, 17 Camp Rd, Leeds, murdered by machine gun with Stevens as POW, 13 February 1937 Jarama, when he asked permission to smoke and lowered his hands.

Vera Elkan, 14a Manchester Square, London W1, nurse, b. South Africa, served all over Spain; details MML.

421 Jack Ellis, 116 High St, Whitechapel, east London (MML).

Elstob (MML) pilot, arrested, released; may not have been Jewish.

Emrich (MML).

Willy Engels, a Thaelmann Intelligence Officer, att. Attlee Company (?).

Joseph Epstein, WIA, French, fought in partisans in Second World War, shot by Nazis.

1298 Samuel Epstein, South Africa (MML).

Lewis Emmanuel, 102 Clapton Common, London, arrested July 1937 entering Spain illegally but returned later.

1103 Lieutenant Otto Esterson/Estenson (MSCW, p.xxv). German seaman from various addresses in Stockton/Halcroft, Redcar Rd/ Ormsby/Middlesbrough? Cited for bravery at Belchite.

Joseph Farber, Polish, later in uprising at Birkenau Auschwitz (Prago).

Penny Feiwel, nurse, born 1910, wife of Michel Feiwel. She was not Jewish but her husband was; active in fundraising for the Hebrew University until 2006.

Louis Feldman (MML), born Bethnal Green, lived Israel and NY City, British Machine Gun company.

1580 Sydney Fink, Salford, KIA 10–17 November 1938 Aragon.

Dr Louis Fischer, German; Crook diaries.

Ziloman Wolf Fishel, born Stoke Newington, lived Antwerp/Israel.

Jacob/Jack Flior, from Johannesburg, South Africa, born Latvia, POW March 1938, repatriated February 1939.

Ronald Frankau.

1514 Solomon Frankel (PI 9 May 1999), tapes and photos at AJEX archive. Born Rothschild Bldgs, London E1, 31 March 1914, son of Rose and Philip; Portuguese Jewish Primary and Jewish Free School – usual route to Spain arriving December 1937 – details and tapes at AJEX Museum. As a sergeant at Brunete, saw first action against tanks with British Battalion, almost being decapitated when a canon shell took off his forage cap! On 27 July 1938, whilst attacking at Ebro crossing, was seriously wounded and invalided home December 1938.

Frank Frankford/Frankfort/-Frankfurt, born 1913 in Slough and then moved to Hackney (Paul Bagon, *Manchester University Papers on Economic and Social History*, No. 50: study on Jews and the IB, October 2001).

Fred Freedman/Frieman, 28 Duckett St, Stepney, KIA 20 January 1938 Teruel with 57 Battalion 15th Brigade.

1414 Joseph Fuhr (*MSCW*, p.xv), Walworth, London; WIA.

426 Joseph Garber, born Bethnal Green 19 September 1911, lived 7 Dunk St, Whitechapel, attended JFS School. In 1925, aged 14, was awarded the Royal Humane Society Medal for saving the life of a man who fell in the Thames at Tower Bridge (PI). Served in Merchant Navy 1928–31. Later an Intelligence officer of the IB and source of much information about Jewish lads in the IB. Manned a Heavy MG with Yank Levy at Jarama, where he was wounded twice. Knew the enigmatic George Nathan and Churchill's nephew Giles Romilly. Sadly witnessed the deaths of Phil Morris and Nathan Steigman at Jarama. In Second World War served RAMC and RASC (3 Coy, 6th Battalion), no. 7406801. Due to maritime experience was in SOE smuggling arms to Balkans and Albanian partisans 1943–44 with allied Italian Commandos, working from Monopoly with FANYs assisting. Helped smuggle weapons to the Haganah during RASC service, and a member of Trepper's 'Red Orchestra' spy ring, giving information to Russia from Nazi sources. Memoirs recorded at IWM and AJEX, photo and Jewish Chaplain Card.

Charles Gavatzman/Gautzman, aka Boyd, Stoke Newington.

David Tony Gilbert, from Bethnal Green, POW March 1938, repatriated October 1938.

W. Gilman.

Reuben Ginsburg, aka Gainsborough, London and Carmarthen.

1805 Ben Glaser, 25 Wellclose Square, London E1, KIA 6 September 1938 Ebro/Sierra Caballs. His letters at MML.

Kurt J. Glaser, aka Captain James K. Griffith, born 3 September 1918, KIA 11 April 1945 Germany, in No. 3 ('Jewish') Troop, No. 10 Commando, at crossing of Aller River.

Alfred H. Gold, 8 Spelman St, London E1/98 Bourne Hse, Shepard St, London E1, KIA 27 February 1937 Jarama.

M. Goldberg, from Russia, 41 Clack St, Stepney (Joe Garber PI).

260 Maurice Goldberg (*MSCW*, p.17); from Southern Rhodesia; POW, sentenced to death at a Spanish trial, commuted; held hostage with Leeson until after war (*B15B*, p.199). Lived Bethnal Green and 120 Clarence Rd, London E5. Born Merthyr Tydfil?

767 Benny/Bernard Goldman, 2 Brewery St, Strangeways, Manchester, upholsterer, WIA (MML). He was cited for 'displaying untiring work whilst Battalion Commissar'.

Jimmy Goldsmith (*Apprentices Of Freedom*, p.123).

80 Jack/John Goldstein, 17 St Cuthbert's Place, Gateshead/5 Smith St, Amble, Northumberland.

Harry Gomm (probable), 35 Amberley Rd, west London, KIA February 1937 Jarama.

Alfred Goodman, 3 Kenmure Rd, Hackney (MML).

Ben Goodman, Manchester (MML).

673 Bob Goodman, boxer from Manchester (*CTC*, p.39). Believed MIA/thought KIA 12 February 1937 Arganda Bridge olive groves, Jarama, or a POW. Other sources say he survived and was a tank commander at Alamein, Second World War.

Charlie Goodman, 8 Eagle Place, Stepney.

Dave Goodman, 14 Rockliffe Rd, Middlesborough, POW March 1938, repatriated February 1939 (*MSCW*, p.74).

760 Phillip Goodman, 20 Mabfield Rd, Fallowfield, Manchester/Nottingham (MML).

Phillipe Goodman, Anglo-French Jew, Second World War Royal Fusiliers, captain attached Parachute Regiment; later met Joe Garber in Balkans – SOE work (PI Joe Garber).

R. Goodman, 10 Newton Rd, The Park, Nottingham, KIA February 1937 Jarama.

W.R. Goodman, 18 Briggs St, Salford, KIA February 1937 Jarama.

Leo Green, KIA February 1937 Jarama.

Maurice Green, Manchester (MML), KIA March 1938 Aragon.

George Albert Gross, Hammersmith.

Henry/Harry Gross/Groeser, 346 Commercial Rd, London E1, WIA 12 January 1937, KIA 16 July 1937 Brunete. Cousin of Louis Stoller of Leeds. His father owned a small sweetshop. Was active in Jewish Lads Brigade and YCL. When his family discovered he was going to Spain they took and hid his clothes. He went anyway.

D. Grossart, Glasgow, died of wounds April 1937 Jarama.

Edward Guerin, Hackney, KIA Quinto 25 August/October 1937; possibly not Jewish.

David Guest, KIA 26 July 1938 Ebro/Gandesa; lived at 12a Charing Cross Rd, London WC1, educated Oundle and Cambridge (maths, first class), son of Islington Labour MP Dr Haden-Guest. His mother Carmel was Jewish, daughter of Colonel Albert Goldsmid, founder of the Jewish Lads Brigade.

Gunel/Gunal.

A. Gunter, Kennington.

Mark Gura, 18 Sigdon Rd, Hackney, London, KIA February 1937 Jarama.

Angela Haden-Guest, St Agoio Hospital, 199 Sloane St, London SW1, sister of David Guest.

Sid Hamm, 32 Lisvane St, Cathays, Cardiff Labour Party, KIA July 1937 Brunete.

Alan Harris, Leeds (PI).

Augustus Harris, Bootle, KIA July 1937 Brunete.

Jack Harris, Leeds (MML).

Sidney Harris, POW (MML), Leeds.

L. Hart, 1 Stanmore Rd, Burley, Leeds (MML).

Dr Tudor Hart (*TSD*), 16 King St (?), London, chief doctor at Motoro Hospital.

427 William Harvey/Horwitz, USA (Prago).

763 Martin Hempel, Leyton, London, KIA July 1938 Ebro.

Willy Heriberg, South Africa, POW.

Simmy/Simon Hirschman/Hirshman (Simanis Hirsmanis), born 14 February 1912 in Auce, Latvia, son of Wolf and Lily, née Weinberg. His memoirs recorded by Cyril Silvertown and Martin Sugarman (PI). Lost all his family in the Holocaust when Latvia was overrun. Served Latvian artillery 1932–33. Served in Spain in a Balkan heavy artillery group (Kolarot), completed officers' and commissars' training, then in a German 11th Brigade anti-tank battery. Eventually served in Polish Dombrowski Battalion and witnessed the Ebro battle where most of the Botwin Company were virtually wiped out; wounded four times; crossed into France with many refugees on 14 February 1939 – his birthday. From 1940–47 served in British Merchant Navy, as many IBers were refused service in the Armed Forces, and regards himself as British veteran. Separate information and tapes in AJEX Archives, with photos.

'Jock' Charles Hyman, 123b South Portland St, Glasgow, KIA 30 March 1937 Jarama.

Jacob Hyman/Hyman Jacobs (?) (MML).

Morris Isaacs, Stepney, London E1, WIA Madrid (MML).

460 Lazarus Jacks, lived at same address as Davidovitch, 638 Seven Sisters Road, London.

Jacobs, South African pilot.

Hyman Jacobs, aka Harry Jackson, born 1913, Stepney, and described in his brother Joe Jacobs' book, *Out of the Ghetto* (London: J. Simon Pubs, 1978) (MML). POW March 1938, repatriated February 1939. Witnessed many atrocities committed on Republican POWs.

1393 Lionel Jacobs, Nottingham, c/o 5 Aspland Rd, Hackney, London E8, POW March 1938, repatriated February 1939, Gandesa; exchanged for Italian POWs (*MSCW*, p.105).

431 William Frank Jacobson, 44 Winsford Terrace, Edmonton, London E18.

Arnold Jeans, aka Geenes/Genis, Manchester, KIA 19 December 1936 Boadilla.

Emmanuel 'Manny' Julius, London, killed at Aragon/Alcubierre, born 25 May 1912, Westcliff-on-Sea; moved in 1925 to Brondesbury, London NW2; attended Kilburn Grammar School. Went to Spain in late 1935 as driver and correspondent for *News Chronicle* Ambulance Volunteers; joined the militia who went on raids behind enemy lines and was KIA August or October 1936. Letter from sister Faiga Olins, 4 January 1999, with photo.

Kagan, WIA Brunete, July 1937.

Kahn? KIA, PI at reunion 1998 (not in *MSCW*).

Dr Kahn (MML archive).

Joe Kahn, Warehouseman, 37 Wellington Ave, Stamford Hill, London N16. Information from Cyril Silvertown.

Joachim/Joseph Kalkstein, born 21 July 1920 in Berlin of Polish parents. Fought in Spain, later joined Palestine police, Czech Legion and then the British SAS. KIA 27 August 1944 France 27, buried at the CWGC emetery at Recey in southern France. A sister lives on a kibbutz in Israel, a brother in New Zealand. His grave originally had a cross but a non-Jewish comrade had this changed at a ceremony in 1999. Kraus, London PI.

Jacques Kaminiski, Polish/French (Prago).

Stephen Kaminiski, London (MML)/Glasgow.

Sam Kaplan, KIA at Fuentes de Ebro, rescuing a wounded comrade; also Lincoln Brigade.

'K' Kavetsky, USA (?)

Alfred Asher Keffenbaum/Kaffebrum (*TNA* index, Foreign Office 1937), Israel/London.

Arnold Kellan/Kallan, ambulance driver (MML).

Lillian Kenton, wife of Lou, below; physiotherapist.

Lou Kenton, Second World War Merchant Navy; PI Holborn, WIA as medic (see AJEX Archives for detail).

Dr Richard Kisch, London, WIA September 1936 (*BVFL*, p.51). Tom Mann Centurion.

General Emilio/Emile/Grigori Kleber, aka Morris or Manfred/Lazar/Stern/Feteke, CO International Brigade, born Czernowitz, Russia 1896/8 (?), where there is a street named after him. He was captured as an officer in the Austro-Hungarian cavalry in 1916, then fought against Whites in Red Army as commissar of a partisan unit 1921; WIA several times. Then fought Japanese and Czechs in Soviet Far East; advised Chinese 1933; was Chief Soviet adviser to Spanish High Command. Later lived in Canada; charismatic defender and saviour of Madrid, commanding 11th International Brigade and later 45th Division, June 1937. Possibly murdered in Stalin's purges 1938/54(?).

Herbert Klein, became US news correspondent for *New Masses* (Crook diaries).

Arthur Koestler, famous Hungarian-born British writer and journalist, POW.

Isidore Konigsberg, 106 Cheshire St, Bethnal Green, POW March 1938, repatriated October 1938 (MML).

P. Kop, KIA July 1937 Brunete (DD, p.392).

1584 Jack Kramer, aka John Kremner, salesman from Manchester/Bolton and Birmingham (MML).

Peter Kroger, aka Israel Altman, aka Morris Cohen, born 1910 New York of Russian-Polish parents; 1226 Sherman Ave, NYC. Served 15th Abraham Lincoln Brigade/USA and with British. Fought in Second World War in US Army in Europe, WIA 1937 Aragon. Part of the notorious Portland spy ring in 1961. Fled to UK after Rosenberg trial, exchanged for UK spy in Russia. Died 1995.

M. Kuhen, Liverpool, KIA February 1937 Jarama (*DD*).

Issy/Isidore Kupchick, Canadian, KIA June 1937 Segovia, 14th IB (*BVFL*, photo p.81).

Bernard Lampert.

M. Landau, London.

Samuel R. Lee, aka Levy, 29 Norcott Rd, Stamford Hill, London N16, KIA 23–27 February 1937 Jarama, with Lincoln Battalion. Only son of Mr and Mrs Levy of Hoxton Rd, London, N1. *Jewish Chronicle*, 28 February 1941, p.3. Other sources say with Irish Connolly column.

George Leeson (*MSCW*, p.17), POW Jarama, tried in Spanish court, sentenced to death, commuted, hostage with Goldberg until after war (*B15B*, pp.194–95). From Dalyell Rd, Brixton, London SW9; Bill Alexander says he was Jewish.

Arthur Lerner, Stoke Newington/Canada, POW March 1938, repatriated 5 February 1939.

1241 Lieutenant Frank/Ernest/Ephraim Lesser (PI), Hackney.

Sam/Manassa Lesser, aka Russell, WIA ankle and back 28 December 1936 (*MSCW*, pp.23–4); 39 Lauriston Rd, Hackney, London E9, brother of Frank, above.

Mathew Levin/Levine (MML), Caerphilly.

1207 Ariel Levine, Hampstead, London, KIA 31st March 1938, Aragon/Caspe.

436 Conrad Levine, 22 Shore Rd, Hackney (MML).

601 Maurice Levine, 63, Kings Rd, Prestwich, Manchester, a tailor's cutter, subject of *Cheetham to Cordova* (Manchester: Manchester Jewish Museum, 1984), by Neil Richardson. Levine was a veteran of the Kinder Scout Trespass, was twice WIA in Spain (firstly at Brunete) and was in the Second World War (*MSCW*, p.80). Was guard over Colonel Delasalle the night he was shot for treason. Also saw Josip Broz (Tito) in Spain, though Tito denied being there.

Morry Levitus/Levitas, POW March 1938 by Italians at San Pedro Camp, repatriated February 1939 (PI), 3 Durward St/78 Brady St Mansions, London E1. Originally from Dublin, only Irish Jewish volunteer from a tiny community. Son of Harry (born Kovno, came to Ireland 1912) and Leah, née Rick, born 1 February 1917, 8 Warren St, Dublin, educated at St Peter's Church of Ireland School. Family went to Glasgow 1927 and London 1931. Morry served Second World War, RAMC, Burma, became a plumber after and then lecturer, then taught in East Germany.

434 Alf Levy, 123 Stepney Green Bldgs, London E1 (MML).

B. Levy, 319 Glengarry Ave, Windsor, Ontario.

1395 Maurice Levy, Dalston (MML).

Moritz Levy/Loewy, born 13 September 1921, Czech,

fought in No. 3 ('Jewish') Troop, No. 10 Commando as Maurice Latimer and fought at Dieppe, Normandy and Walcheren.

Reuben Lewis, Stepney (MML).

Paul Lewis, aka S. Silver, 36 Hallswell Rd., Golders Green, London (PI), veneer worker. Mother was French; he later lived in Australia.

Sydney Lewis, London, MIA July 1938 Gandesa (MML).

1420 Alfred Litchfield, alias, KIA 7 July 1938 Gandesa.

679 J. Lobban, Alexandria (Egypt), Glasgow, KIA September 1938 Ebro.

600 Cecil M. Louis, 14 Sandringham Rd, Golders Green, Air Force air mechanic (MML).

Pincus Percy Ludwick, chief engineer of 5th Brigade, born London October 1908, lived Manchester. His father was born Minsk, returned to Russia, KIA 1920 in Civil War against Whites. After Spain, Percy served in Soviet Air Force in Second World War; details at MML including his unpublished book. Married Sasha, lived Russia after Second World War.

Joe Maisters, Leeds (PI).

Montague Mandell, 16 Aristotle Rd, Clapham (MML) and Manchester, KIA February or July 1937 Brunete/Jarama.

1348 Alex Marcovitch, tailor, 415 Eglinton St, Glasgow (MML).

Alan Marks, aka Jacsensky, tailor, 6 Craven S., London E1, KIA July 1937 Brunete.

Bert Masky, 167 Lloyd St., Manchester (*CTC*, p.39), KIA 12 February 1937,

Arganda Bridge olive groves, Jarama, or POW – not known. Born Lithuania.
Sister married to Sam Wild.

Sam Masters, aka Morris Simon, 110 Newark St, London E1, KIA July 1937 Brunete. Cited for 'coolness and efficiency' (MML archive).

George Mayer.

Jacob Nus Mendel, pilot from Johanneburg, South Africa.

Morris Mendelson, 135 Wellington Rd South, Stockport, Manchester (MML), upholsterer.

Cecil Mennel, Canada/London (UK), 1938 KIA Teruel (PI Joe Garber).

Anton Miles, Stoke Newington, London.

1340 Maurice/Sam Miller, Hull, KIA August 1938 Ebro/Sierra Pandols, Hill 666.

David Mindline, aka Danker, Finchley (MML).

Dr Minkoff, worked with nurse Goldin/Spiegel (MML), Bulgarian via UK.

Marcel Montague, London.

Phil Morris, 33 Cambridge Bldgs, Darling Row, London E1, KIA 2 February 1937 Jarama.

1093 William Moses, aka W. Stewart (MML), 127 East Rd, London N1, plumber, army no. 143424, Canadian (?) – KIA?

1399 Max Nash, aka Nunez/Nashitz, Sephardi from Hackney, London, KIA by a sniper 1 July/August 1938 Ebro/Gandesa.

A.S. Nathan, London, KIA July 1937 Brunete.

Major George Montague Nathan, First World War Professional Guards Officer or NCO, Brigade Staff and Operations Officer in Spain; smart, pipe-smoking, with clipped moustache, Bethnal Green, London and Manchester; arrived Spain 1936, KIA 16 July 1937 Torra le Donas, Brunete; constantly exposing himself to enemy fire with his pistols, officers' riding boots and riding crop. Accused by some comrades of being with the Black and Tans in Ireland, but acquitted at an informal hearing of any misdeeds. WIA by aerial bomb shrapnel, organizing withdrawal at Brunete in Guadarrama hills, and died in Madrid. Nathan had been the first CO of the British No. 1 Company November/December 1936 (see above), Staff Officer and later Chief of Staff of 15th Battalion, CO of 11th battalion and 14th Brigade, and 1st CO of Dumont Battalion on Madrid and Cordoba fronts (Fred Copeman, *British Battalion Roll of Honour, 1939*, courtesy of Louis Stoller, Leeds). Owing to his great popularity and well-known contempt for danger, he was given a funeral with full military honours.

Wolf Nathan, aka William, POW March 1938, repatriated October 1938, seaman, fruiterer, Aubrey's Fruit Store, Newington Green, London N16/12 Challis Ct, Commercial Rd, London E1.

Alfred H. Needleman, 420 Mare St, Hackney/8 Junction Place, Amhurst Rd, Hackney, London (PI), POW March 1938, repatriated October 1938.

David Newman, Edmonton (MML).

1379 Michael Nuns, aka Emile Pezzaro, Hackney, London, KIA March 1938 Aragon.

Nurse Jeanette Opman, aka 'Jadzka' and 'Juanita', from Vilna via France (information from Len Crome, who says that there were dozens of Jewish women fighters and nurses especially from Poland and Czechoslova), KIA (PI).

Samuel G. Paesta/Paster, Stepney/Hammersmith, WIA November/December 1936 Madrid, No. 1 Coy, 3rd Section, with Thaelmann Brigade (MML); probably alternative name for Sam Masters.

Edward 'Ernie' Paul, 71 Malham Rd, Forest Hill, London, seaman, KIA February 1937 Jarama.

Elliott Paul, journalist and author of *Life and Death of a Spanish Town*.

Michael Pavlov, London (MML), possibly a Greek Jew?

Marc Persoff/Perzoff/Penzoff, Swiss, KIA 20 March 1937 Jarama (MML).

Avigdor Pickholz, born 1915 in Poland and lived in Essen, Germany, and Paris. WIA and died Gibraltar 1938/9. Two brothers lived in Israel.

Leslie Praegar, Manchester, Ambulance Unit.

866 Richard Harry Pressman, 63 Higher Carbridge St, Manchester, Anti-Aircraft Battalion (MML) .

Bert Ramelson, Leeds (*MSCW*, p.92), born Bachran/Baruch Ramelson/ Ramilevich in Cherkassy Ukraine, 22 March 1910; lived first in Canada as a child; in 1921 in Edmonton, Alberta. University law graduate, went to Spain 24 August 1937 as lieutenant and fought on Ebro and Aragon fronts in Canadian McKenzie-Papineau Battalion (Macpaps), twice wounded. Returned to UK,

March 1939, to Royal Tank Corps in Second World War, POW at Tobruk in 1941 and in Italy; escaped after two years and then served in army in India. Later, executive of British Communist Party. Died 13 April 1994.

Phil Richards, an alias, after Richard St, off Cannon St Road, London E1, where he lived; information from childhood friend, Louis Stoller of Leeds (letter September 1999). A lightweight boxing champion; KIA in Spain.

David Rosenberg, joined from Belgium, family in UK.

Louis Rosenbloom, possibly from Manchester; one of five brothers who also served in the Second World War – information from family.

Monty/Maurice Rosenfeld/Rosenfield (*BVFL*, p246), Cheetham, Manchester, KIA in Italy in Second World War, won MM in Italy.

A. Rubens, Cheetham, Manchester.

1426 Alf Salisbury, born 1907, Stepney, parents refugees from Riga, booklet at MML archive.

David Samson.

Joseph Samson (MML).

R.L. Samuel.

Julian Sanders/Saunders, Clapton, London, POW March 1938.

Rafael Schaltz, WIA (MML), USA? Survived sinking of SS *City of Barcelona* 30 May 1937.

Paul Schuster, South Africa, Thaelmann Battalion.

J.G. Schwitzer, Czech, born 8 March 1920, fought No. 3 ('Jewish') Troop, No. 10 Commando in Second World War as Tommy Swinton.

Nathan, aka 'Nicholas', Segal or Cohen, 7 Connaught Rd, London E17, KIA 27 December 1936/37 Cordoba/Lopera, cut down by aircraft machine-gun fire.

547 Victor Shammah, 116 Burton Rd, Withington, Manchester, KIA March 1938 Aragon; letters at MML archive.

917 Jack Shaw/Schukman/Shore, of 47 Fieldgate Mansions, Myrdle St, London E1 (PI), born 1917, Stepney, retired cab driver.

Alan Sheller/Alick, Stepney, Tom Mann Centurion.

Vladimir Sheraman, London.

Alfred (later Sir) Sherman, aka Theodor Vladimir Carmel, born 19 Median Rd, Clapton, London, 10 November 1919; POW March 1938, repatriated October 1938; married to Zahava, née Levin; also fought in Second World War; journalist for *Jewish Chronicle* and *Daily Telegraph* post-war; economic adviser to Israeli and British governments; fellow of London School of Economics; member of the West London Synagogue. Died 2006.

Jack Sherpenzeel/Sherpenell, London, from Maaschavenbib, Rotterdam, KIA 31 July 1938 Ebro.

Louis Shine, 4 Gardiner Ave, Cricklewood, London, POW (MML).

Gordon Siebert, West Ham.

Robert Silcock, Liverpool, POW with M. Goldberg and G. Leeson; Bill Alexander says he was Jewish.

450 Alec 'Tiny' Silverman, 4 Beaumont Square, London E1 (MML).

Terry Silverman (MML).

Louis Silverstein, Hackney (MML).

G. Silverstone, Norveegan St, Copenhagen, Denmark.

718 Sidney Silvert/Silver, 26a Hewitt St, Manchester (MML).

C. Simmons, aka Charles John Fairbank, born Portsmouth, KIA 27 February 1937 Jarama (?); possibly not Jewish.

Solomon Simon, 17 Broughton St, Cheetham, Manchester (MML), tailor.

Conrad Singer/Chuna Zhinger, served Rumanian Army, Anna Paulker Battery at Belcite in Spain. WIA battle of Teruel, later served in Second World War, French Foreign Legion. POW, liberated and joined British Army; lived in Blackpool after the war (MML), died October 2006.

J. Slavenberg.

333 Andrew Sloss (?)

Sam Smil, WIA Jarama, Romanian, lived in London. Interned in France, then offered French nationality by General Weygand to join Foreign Legion, as did many Spanish Civil War veterans. Fought at Narvik in 1940, escaped by boat to UK and joined British Army.

David Smulevitch, Polish, took part in Auschwitz uprising of October 1944 (Prago).

General Yaakov Vladimirovich Smushkevich ('Douglas'), Senior Air Force adviser and de facto commander (Russian). Stern/Shtern and he were later recalled to Moscow and executed by Stalin.

Jacques Sokel/Sokol, 112 Carleton Rd, London N7, KIA Barcelona (MML).

Dr Randall/Randolph Sollenberger, from Baltimore USA and Highland Falls NY, working at St Mary's Hospital, Paddington, London; Bury Infirmary, Manchester; and USA. In 11th Brigade,

Edgar Andre Battalion, surgeon and anaesthetist; short, stout, bearded, with a slight speech impediment. Refused to stay at base but kept in the front line with his men, often taking up arms to fight. Later served 15th Brigade, dressing many wounded in exposed positions at Mosquito Hill, Brunete. KIA tending wounded in his truck after running back and forth all day, rallying men all the time to fight, July 1937. Pioneered use of mobile operating theatre.

David Solomon, aka Lomon, POW March 1938, repatriated October 1938, salesman of 60 Gore Road, Victoria Park, Hackney, London E9.

John Sommerfeld, aka Sommerfield, London, Commune de Paris Battalion, 125th Brigade, Madrid.

Isidore Sonin, husband of Natalie, of Whitechapel; see obituary of David Sonin, *The Times*, 11 June 2008.

Stephen Spender, Jewish writer and poet – Google for details.

163 Ernest W. Spenger/Sprenger, Muswell Hill, London; MIA/WIA (MML).

1171 Sam/Charles Spiller, London (PI Joe Garber).

Isidore Springer, Polish, later in the 'Red Orchestra' spy ring against the Nazis (Prago).

Frank Squires, aka Antrim.

Arthur Stakewski/Stashevsky, Polish/Russian; economic adviser to Republican Government, later executed by Stalin.

Moses Stang, Brixton (MML).

638 Lewis Stansfield, Newton, Manchester.

1274 Leslie Edward Starr, 41 Fairey Lane, Bury New Rd, Manchester 8 (MML).

Nathan Steigman, baker, 65 Greenfield St, London E1, KIA 27 February 1937 Jarama.

Alf Sterling/Stirling – East End.

John Stevens, aka Moses Myer Nagelman, Norwood orphan, engineer from Islington, murdered whilst POW, February 1937 Jarama, with Elias, 381 Mile End Rd.

Jack Stone, aka H.G. Levenstern/Levenstein, London.

Jack/George Stone/Silverstone, London (Crook diaries, MML).

Maurice Stott, Rochdale; KIA 12 March 1937 Jarama.

Maurice Swindells ('Eddie'), Manchester; KIA February 1937 Jarama.

Jack/John Sylvester, aka Silverstone, 60 Church St, Bethnal Green, London, student at Shoreditch Technical College, KIA February 1937 Jarama.

Ronald A. Robert Symes, London, died of wounds Casa de Campo, November/December 1936 Madrid; from Hants; possibly not Jewish.

Victor Tabbush, London.

Phil Tammer/Tammar, 134 Vallance Rd, London E2, POW March 1938, repatriated October 1938 (MML).

Louis Tanklevitch/Tankovitch, Liverpool, KIA March/July 1938 Ebro/Gandesa with Lincolns/Washingtons. From 15 Dardew Court, London N12.

873 J.(?) Samson Tobias, 6 Cricketfield Rd, Clapton, London E5.

Abraham Trauber, Bethnal Green, KIA September 1938 Ebro.

Ena Vassie, Czech nurse (PI).

Sam Wagenheim, Leeds (*MSCW*, pp.92–3).

Albert Wallace, an alias, Cheetham, Manchester.

Claude Warsaw/Warson/Warsow, born 9 October 1906 or 1903, Southsea, Hants; RAF 1926–31, FO 101 Bomber Squadron in Palestine and Egypt; c/o Hampden Club, London NW1. Served in Andre Malraux Squadron in Spain, KIA 26 September 1936 Toledo/Taluvera, given full Jewish funeral. Left a father, widow and daughter – see AJEX files from *Daily Express* and Foreign Office.

Son of Joshua Warsow, Turkish national.

George Westfield, an alias, Liverpool/Manchester 8 (?), KIA October 1937 Aragon/Fuente del Ebro.

Jack S. White, 52 Myrdle St, London E1, KIA 13 February 1937 Jarama.

Mick White, brother of Jack above, 10 King John St, London E1, tailor.

Bernard G. Winfield, Notts., KIA 19 January 1938 Teruel.

1055 Wilfred/Alfred Winnick, machinist, 8 Eastham Ave, Fallowfield, Manchester (MML).

H. Wise, London, KIA 12 January 1938 Las Rozas.

H. Wise, London, KIA January 1937 Cordoba.

Jack/James Wolfe, Hillingdon, London, KIA August 1937 Belchite.

P. Zachriov, London (MML), Greek (?).

501 Doumont Z(S)ubchaninov, 15 Sandcroft Abbey, London SE2 (MML), aka Jim Ruskin, IB interpreter from Russia, linguist and transmissions officer.

Palestine/Israel

The first group of sixty arrived on 17 November 1936 (DD, p.34) and made up the highest proportion of the IB by population from any country. Between 350–500 fought (mostly in the Botwins) and about seventy were KIA, and a further fifty KIA in the Second World War. There is a JNF (Jewish National Fund) Forest in Israel in their memory:

Zundel Abine
Daniel Abramovitsh, KIA Gandesa.
Trojan Haim Adler, Dizengoff, Tel-Aviv.
Noah Aloni
Max Amram, aka Moshe Aram, KIA by Nazis, Second World War.
Miriam Amram
David Ansrowski

Moshe Antler
Sonia Antler-Zeidman, Toulouse Resistance.
Robert Aquist, Coy Commander, KIA. (He married Patience Darton, an English girl, who sadley died in Madrid in 1996 during the 60th anniversary commemorations)

Arie Baker, mechanic, aged 26.

Moshe Ben-Ari
Samuel Ben-Mordechai
Samuel Ben-Yakov
Israel Bober
Boim
Adela Botvinska
Josef Brikner
Captain Misha Bron, aka 'Michal', Ops. officer 129th Brigade.
Dr Pini Bronstein

Micha Bronzstein
Israel Bryn/Brin
Marian Burstein
Ariyeh 'Liova' Bursuk, KIA
Ebro.

Israel Center, born Poland, 25
December 1898.
Mark Centner
Pinchas Cheifetz

Raoul Danine
David Degani
Maximilien Derewski
Mordka Dusiany
Isaac Duyts

Haim Ekstein, KIA Estra-
madura.
Chaim Elkon, KIA August
1936.
Boris Israel Epelbaum
Eliyahu Erlich
Adolbert Ernester/Aruster
Moise Estreicher

Munia Faingelernter
Joseph Farber, fought in Re-
sistance at Auschwitz.
Adama Fasht
'Arab' Fawzi (?)
Angela Feiro
Yehezchiel Fikkur, born Poland,
lived Israel (Haifa), air
force mechanic.
Ruth Fuks
Moshe Fuks, KIA Second
World War.

Shaike Garber
Jonas Geduldig, shot by the
Nazis.
Abraham Gelman
Zvi Ginzer
Max Godet
Haim Goldstein
Ze'ev Gotesman, KIA
Toulouse French Resist-
ance.
Gotlib, murdered by Gestapo,
Paris 1944.
Itslele Gruber
Aharon Arnold Guinsberg

Moise Maurice Haft
Pepi Halpern
Dr Hamerman
Yacov Hariri 'Kiru'
Chaim Hech
Shula Heiman
Abraham Helfant
Dr Yosef Heller

Heniek Hercberg
Sender Herskovic
Ari (Henry) Hollender, born
Berlin, 28 December 1917.
Huber, Polish.

Jacobi
Maria Jacubovski
Emir Jaffe
Chaim Jurkowski
Adam Jurski
N. Kali
David 'Dodo' Kamy, aka Ka-
menomotsky, aka 'Camille',
Russian adjutant to 15th
Brigade, via Belgium; engi-
neer, emigrated to Palestine,
served Second World War in
French Army and 'Red
Orchestra', winning Croix
de Guerre avec Palme;
captured and murdered by
Nazis in Belgium (*TSD*).
Morris Kawer, also with Mac-
paps.
Joshua Keselman
Sounia Keselman
Kohen
Hans Kohen
Isaac Korin, KIA.
David/Judko Karon/Korin
Korenbaum, born Poland, 29
September 1915, died Is-
rael, October 2001; lived in
Israel from 1931; fought
with Dombrowskis in
Spain; fought in Israel's
War of Independence;
founder Kibbutz Kfar Men-
achem, where he died.
Angele Kot
David Kozak
Boris Kraselnik
Kopel Kraselnik
Arek Kubalski

Yohan Lamers
Zioma Lechtmann
Arie Lev, aka Moishe Goy –
author of the book "Madrid
to Berlin" about the Palestin-
ian Jewish volunteers
Moshe Levi
Nurse Dora Levin
Yankel Levine
Meir Levy
Arnold Linker
Lipman
Simon Lipschitz, WIA,
repatriated London
December 1938.
Levi Litwak

Jankele Lurie

Abracha Margoules
Levi Mayer
Isaac Meirovici, Rumanian,
POW 1938–43 in Spain.
Fred Meisuer
Ruth Meitis
Dr Anita Meyerovitch
Moniek Milenband
Munia Milband
D. Milgrom, Polish.
Ebraim Miller
Mordechai/Mark Milman/Mill-
man, KIA at Ebro.
Felix Montreuil
Diego Mula

Maurice Najman, pilot.
Shlomo Natan
Zippora/Cypora Nilar
Nizan

David Ostrovsky, later French
Resistance, died 2005.

Jaques Penczyna, one of thir-
teen members of Palestine
Jewish Hapoel who fought
in Barcelona in June 1936;
they were in Spain for the
Workers' Olympiad, a
protest against the official
Nazi Berlin Olympics;
when hostilities began they
joined the Barcelona Militia
(Prago and Jewish Workers'
Circle).
Dr Perelman
Alexandre Pieschanski
Yehezkiel Pikar, Haifa, pilot,
Andre Malraux Squadron
(Prago), later fought Israel
War of Independence.
Felina Pintchuck

Israel Radwanski
Maurice Riba
Gricha Roitman
Major Valter Roman, born Ru-
mania, CO of all IB artillery.
Mordechai Roth
Boris Dov Rudayev
David Rutenberg
Israel Rzelkowitch

Nicolas Sama, POW France
February 1939.
Franciszek Schafer
S Schlein
Joske Schnitzer
Max Schwartzenberg

Rachel/Rochelle 'Angelka'
Schwartzman

Samuel Segal, Sivkin St 26,
Tel-Aviv, served British
Army in Second World War.
Shalom Shiloni
Josef Silberman
Samuel Smuel (?)
David Smulevich, fought in Re-
sistance at Auschwitz.
Nahum Sofer
M.L. Solomon
Joseph Srolevsky
Hana Srulewicz
Samuel Stamler, KIA.
Micha Stelianu
Bernard Stern
F. Sternberg
Adolf Stipel
Naum Super
Wolf Szapiro
Nathan Szenker
Shlomo Szlayer
I. Sztein

Marcel 'Koth' Szteranzis

Max Maciej Technitchek,
Czech Coy, Polish origin.
Yakob Tvardowski

Matyss Ulman
Emile Urmish, KIA Ebro.

Volodia
Bernard Volkas, born Kovno,
Lithuania 1916, Palestine
1934, after Spain joined
Red Army Paras, POW,
Auschwitz Resistance
group, lived California.

Nachum Weiss, KIA November
1936.
Baruch Wilder
Rose Wlopolska
Isidore 'Ernst' Wolfson
Bernard Wolkas, Lithuanian,
born 1916, to Palestine 1934,
via Paris and Marseilles on

SS *Ciudad Barcelona*, torpe-
doed 30 May 1937 by Italian
submarine, only three sur-
vivors out of fifty-six volun-
teers aboard, including
Wolkas who later lived in
USA, Isaac Kupietz and Abe
Osheroff of the USA. In the
artillery of IB, WIA, fought
with Soviet partisans Second
World War, POW, survived
Auschwitz and Buchenwald
(DD, pp.393–4).
Zippora Wolfson
Ephraim Wuzek

Imrou Yakobi

Zelman/Zalman Saltzman/Zalts-
man, died 2005, US Army
Second World War.
Feivl Zavodnik, aka Bar Akiva
Samuel Zoltan, KIA French
Resistance.

Appendix

For the interest of readers, appended below are the introductory paragraphs of the other national group sections in which Jews served, taken from the fuller survey by the author.

The Jaroslav Dombrowksi Brigade

The list of Polish Jewish Volunteers was extracted mostly from *No Passeran: Polacy w Wojnie Hiszpnskiej* (Polish Participation in the Spanish Civil War), published by the Ministry of Defence, Warsaw, in 1963, and provided by Simon Hirshmann; and from the book by DD. Other names come from Szurek's book, *The Shattered Dream*. The Polish battalions were the last to leave Spain. The first Polish and Italian Jewish volunteers fought at Irun on 28 August 1936 (DD, p.33).

Four of the twenty-two committee members of the surviving 500 Polish Brigade after the war, which gathered in February 1939 at the beaches of St Cyprien in Southern France, with the survivors of the IB and the Republican army, were Jews.

The American Volunteers: Abraham Lincoln/Washington Brigade

The American veterans were among the first to publish a list of their volunteers in the early 1980s. Compiling the list was fraught with difficulties, as during the McCarthy era many records were hidden and lost, whilst many volunteers used aliases and nicknames, often misspelt. Using their own written and oral archives as well as a passport study by the Subversion Activity Control Board, ship passenger lists and US Military Intelligence

records, the project was completed by the Veterans of the Abraham Lincoln
Brigade (VALB) after three years. Most of the addresses came from copies
of *Scope of Soviet Activity in the USA: Hearings before Congress, February 1957*,
copied for the author by James Carmody.

So far as Jews are concerned, numerous obviously Jewish names were
extracted by the author from the list, but there are many Jewish-sounding
names as well, of those who may not be Jews. These have been included,
as VALB researchers quite rightly say that equally there are many Jews,
who used Anglicized or Spanish aliases, whose Jewish background we may
never know, and those of course could not be extracted; so the one
balances out the other.

I am most grateful to Moe Fishman of the Jewish VALB in New York,
USA, for his help in supplying me with a copy of the list of American
volunteers. The MML archive of the IB revealed a newspaper cutting of
21 February 1939, listing the American KIA, and a book by Adolf Ross
included the list of the American volunteers, dated 1993.

*Mackenzie-Papineau Battalion, Canada, named after the 1837 Leaders of the
Canada Rebellion*
Of the approximately 1,500 men in this battalion, there were fifty-eight
Canadian Jews (average age 30) and thirteen American Jews – seventy-one
in all or approximately 5 per cent. Their contribution is fully described in
'Canadian Jewish Boys in Spain', by Myron Momryk (unpublished manu-
script, 1995) and his *Jewish Volunteers from Canada*, (Montreal: Canadian
Jewish Historical Association, 1995), but only since the opening of the IB
Archives in Moscow in 1994 has anything much been discovered about the
Jews in the Macpaps, or indeed about this battalion at all. Further details are
available in Goldberg's 'Mit Der Kanader Yiddisher Volunteer Fun
Shpania' in *Der Kamf* (a Canadian Jewish magazine published in Yiddish,
year unknown). All the Canadians were in violation of the Foreign Enlistment Act, designed to prevent Canadians serving in Spain. Many of the Jews
assumed aliases; see G. Tulchinsky, *Branching Out: The Transformation of the
Canadian Jewish Community* (Toronto: Stoddart, 1998). Whereas only 25 per
cent of the Battalion were Canadian born, 65 per cent of the Jews (forty-six)
among them were Canadian-born – and there were, among
others: a lawyer, two doctors, two pharmacists, a social worker, a writer, a
male nurse, an aviation mechanic, a furrier, a miner, two students, a musician,
a warehouseman, two painters, two salesmen, two clothing workers, a driver,
two seamen and a barber.

Most left for Spain in the spring or summer of 1937, travelling by bus to
Detroit, New York, then Europe by ship, sailing from Montreal or Quebec
City. From Le Havre they went to Paris, then to Spain via the Pyrenees.
Eight were non-combatants; seven had military experience including four

who served with the CEF in the First World War in France. Of those whose fate is known, twenty returned from Spain (seventeen to Canada and the USA), two were POWs, eight were WIA – some twice – and eight were KIA, and one was missing. One rabbi volunteered as chaplain but was turned down, later becoming minister at the Holy Blossom Synagogue, Toronto.

A memorial to the Macpaps was unveiled in Queen's Park, Toronto on 4 June 1995.

The Latvian Volunteers

Simon Hirschmann provided much of the biographical information from his personal experiences and a Latvian language book in his possession, published by Liesna publishing in Riga, in 1965, about the volunteers for Spain, many of whom he knew as Jewish. They mainly fought with the Polish Dombrowskis but like Simon were often merged with other units. Other names came from Diamint's book. Most of the Jews later became partisans in the Second World War and most were from Riga.

Franco-Belge Brigade

These also included volunteers from Luxembourg and Holland. Of the 1,600 Belgians, 196 were Jews, many originally from Poland. The first French group of volunteers left Paris for Spain on 8 August 1936 (DD, p.33). On 18 August 1936, the first French and Belgian Jewish volunteers among the Workers Olympic team arrived in Barcelona. Jewish and the first Parisian KIA was Leon Baum. On 11 September 1937, a large exhibition in Paris was devoted to the Jewish participation in the IB (DD).

Georges Dimitrov Brigade

Named after the Bulgarian international Socialist, this group contained Jewish fighters from Yugoslavia, Czechoslovakia, Roumania, Bulgaria and other east European nations, mostly Sephardim; seven were KIA (two Bulgarian) and six WIA (two Bulgarian); eleven died in the Yugoslav Resistance against the Germans in the Second World War. Of the Yugoslavs, there were eleven labourers, five students, four doctors, two nurses, two businessmen, two journalists and one office worker; twenty-nine were men and five were women. These numbers are almost certainly a considerable underestimate (see original survey).

The Germans – Thaelmann Battalion

Approximately 500 IBers were from Germany, many already having been in Nazi camps, and were later murdered after the war in Spain when they fought in the Resistance in various countries in the Second World War. They have in many cases left no trace except their index cards in Soviet and Gestapo records. Many were in fact the first defenders of the

Republic, as they had gone to live in Spain from Nazi Germany or Austria and fought with the first of the international combat units, Gruppe Thael-mann – but as fourteen of the eighteen founders were Jews, it was known as the Judische Gruppe Thaelmann, founded 24 July 1936 in Barcelona, and first went into battle on 22 August at Saragossa.

Many of the names come from Diamant's book, but others have been added by a list supplied by Fred Dellheim in Germany, from which Sydney Goldberg of AJEX UK helped pick out Jewish names. This is not the most accurate way of finding the Jewish fighters from Germany but the only recourse, given that we have no information on religious affiliation except from Diamant.

The Austrians

I was greatly indebted to Hans Landauer of the Vienna Documentation Centre for so generously supplying me with details on more than one hundred Austrian Jewish veterans.

The Garibaldi Brigade

Many Jews fought in this group but names have been extremely difficult to find in any sources.

Miscellaneous

Further Jewish names were taken from lists of medical personnel who served with the Republican Forces, kept at the Archivo Generale Militar de Avila, in Spain, supplied to the author by James Carmody. The nationalities were not known.

More names came from the list of approximately 1,600 contained in the final volume of *Spanja* (from p.505), published in Belgrade in 1971, and consulted at the MML, about Yugoslavs who fought against Franco. These are in addition to the Dimitrovs listed by Diamint (above) and were only inspired guesses by the author using the surnames.

This chapter is extracted from the original and much longer survey by the author, of Jews worldwide who fought in Spain against Franco. This survey is available at the AJEX Archives of the Jewish Military Museum in Hendon; the Marx Memorial Library (MML) in Clerkenwell; the Imperial War Museum Library; The National Archives at Kew; the British Library; the SOAS Library at the University of London; the London School of Economics Spanish Studies Library; the Jewish Historical Society of England Library; the Jewish Studies Library at University College, London; and The Wiener Library – all in London; Manchester University Library; The Hebrew University Library in Jerusalem; The Virtual Jewish Library website; VALBA (Veterans of the Abraham Lincoln Brigade) website; and Brandeis University Library in the USA.

2.3 The memorial in Barcelona to the Jewish Volunteers of the IB, unveiled by Israel's President Chaim Herzog in 1986.

Notes

1. Members are affectionately referred to as 'IBers'.
2. *British Volunteers in the Spanish Civil War* (Oxford: Routledge, 2004).

The Man with a Hundred Lives:
Wing Commander Lionel Cohen,
DSO, MC, DFC[1]

Wing Commander Lionel Frederick William Cohen, DSO, MC (First World War), DFC (Second World War) was known as 'Sos' or 'Sausage' to all who knew him, and 'Evergreen' to his RAF comrades. He was born at Tankerville House, Tankerville Terrace, Newcastle-upon-Tyne, on 7 June 1875, son of the distinguished Anglo-Jewish family of Andrew J.F. Cohen, shipowner, and was one of six brothers and five sisters, all of whom attended the Singleton House primary school.

In the 1880s the family moved to Highbury New Park in north London after the father died, and at 14 years old, Lionel was sent to work at Lewison's (general merchants) in Charterhouse Square, Aldersgate, in the City. Lionel was always an adventurous and restless boy, and was soon bored with his life as a clerk. Without a word to his family, whilst walking past a recruiting office in Trafalgar Square, he enlisted for twelve years and two years Boys' Service in the Royal Marines Light Infantry, and was shipped off to Deal barracks near Dover as 729371 Marine Cohen.

After many experiences as a soldier for three months, and thoroughly enjoying the life of drill, musketry, bayonet instruction and boxing, he was finally tracked down by the police, and his mother and uncle Jacob arrived and bought him out for £20.

Outraged at such behaviour, the family sent Lionel to work for his uncle Harry Freeman Cohen in Johannesburg, and he sailed to South Africa on the *Pretoria Castle*, where he was given work again as a clerk. Dissatisfied still, he left this job too and after a short time as a hotel waiter, he enlisted, now penniless, as a guard in the mines on the Johannesburg Reef. He was 17 years old.

Young Lionel soon heard of the great happenings further north as the British Imperialists were surging ever outwards to take more and more control of the Southern African Territories. So Sos joined up as a volunteer with F.C. Selous and Dr Jamieson in the campaign against Chief Lobengula's impis of Matebele tribesmen, centred on the royal kraal at Bulawayo. His column, under Major Wilson, left Fort Victoria to join up with the Salisbury column at Iron Mine Hill.[2] In October 1893, as a trooper aged just 18, the youngest serving, he took part in the battle of the Shangani river. Sos was in No. 5 Troop, commanded by Captain Delamore, and they were ordered to fix bayonets and engage the enemy in the bush. A Jewish friend from Manchester whom he had met, named Walters, was killed right alongside him in the fighting. The column chaplain asked Sos to conduct the Jewish burial service.

Conditions were extremely harsh – difficult climate, poor communications, poor food and medical supplies, and a high mortality rate among the all-important horses. But by December, the Matebeleland campaign was over, and Sos, now suffering from malaria, returned south to his uncle and worked for him as a mine manager for the next five years. Yet he again became restless and left once more, this time to work in Delagoa Bay in Portuguese East Africa (now Mozambique), first as a butcher and then as a mine recruiting agent. In one incident he barely survived being bitten by a deadly green mamba snake while asleep; in another he narrowly missed being executed for treason by the Portuguese authorities, when he was mistaken for a rebel leader who fitted his description. He also had the dubious pleasure of meeting Roger Casement who was the British consul general in the capital of Lourenco Marques (now Maputo), later shot in the First World War for treason with Germany.

In October 1899, the Boer War began, and because of his experience of the Bush and knowledge of the people, Sos was asked by the British consul in Mozambique to act as a special force commander operating behind enemy lines. He was to take about hundred askaris and patrol the Mozambique frontier to prevent gun-running to the Boers by sympathizing countries such as Germany and Holland, as well as intercepting Boer messengers operating from Portuguese neutral territory. As an Allied national, he would report to the Portuguese authorities, who would pass information on to British Field Intelligence.

Living rough for months on end, Sos and his men had many skirmishes with the Boers, on one occasion arresting two German spies masquerading as prospectors, and on another eliminating a Boer Commando. The Boer General Beyers swore he would catch Sos and bury him in an ant-hill covered with honey[3] – but he was never captured.

When the war ended, Sos returned to civilian life, inheriting a newspaper (the *Rand Daily Mail*) with his brother Jack, from his uncle Harry. They soon sold it, however, and Sos went into the Stock Exchange. In 1903 he ventured in a balloon with Spelterini, daring the flyer to go as high as he could. During the ascent over the Drakensberg mountains, the gas release cord broke and they were in danger of freezing. Sos climbed out of the basket onto the rigging and in the most perilous conditions, retrieved the cord. 'Now pull the plug and lets go home', he said. And so they did.

Sos was not, however, successful in his business dealings and lost his money speculating; instead he went to work as a mining foreman, almost losing his life in a mining accident which left eighteen dead around him.

A week later the First World War began.

Lionel joined the 1st South African Horse ('B' Squad, 1st Mounted Brigade) in Pretoria as a 2nd lieutenant in 1915,[4] now embarking on his third war. He was a troop commander serving under General Van Deventer, a Boer officer, and would be up against the formidable German soldier, General Von Lettow-Vorbeck.

Sailing to Mombassa and thence riding overland to Nairobi, Lionel's brigade moved south into German East Africa to harass the Germans. His first action was at Kahe near the Pangane river, followed on 3 April by the attack on Lol Kisale hill near Arusha. With his batman – a fellow Geordie – in attendance, Sos alone with his troop managed to convince three German officers with three machine guns and 430 askaris, that they were surrounded, forcing them to surrender the hilltop post.

He was later ordered to take his troop behind the lines to act as scouts for the British main force. Now a temporary captain ('Special Service'),[5] he was involved in many skirmishes with Von Lettow-Vorbeck's men, sending back valuable information to Van Deventer. He enjoyed such work because he was his own master and was able to use his own initiative.

In May 1916 he was detailed to prepare an airstrip for eight Royal Navy Air Service (RNAS) aircraft which were to join them and act as reconnaissance. Sos immediately volunteered on 7 June 1916 as an observer and was seconded to the RNAS No. 7 Squadron, serving as No. 2 to Flight Lieutenant Leslie Brown. He flew in BE2Cs and Voisins and was involved in several skirmishes and crash-landings as well as anti-aircraft and artillery attacks from the Germans, until his transfer out on 21 February 1917. In his report, East African Air Commander Eric R.C. Nanson described Sos as a 'very capable and zealous officer'.[6]

Gradually, Von Lettow-Vorbeck retreated into Mozambique and Sos was ordered to British Field Intelligence Force from 21 February 1917, forming his own unit called 'Co-Force'[7] with forty askaris and one European officer, their job to harass Von Lettow-Vorbeck's camps and depots behind his lines. In one episode he carried out a brilliant commando-style raid, crossing the Ruvuma river on rafts, in complete silence at night, whilst it was in full flood, and when least expected, falling upon a German post and taking twenty-five prisoners.

Sending the prisoners back under escort, Sos then fortified a nearby kopje (hill) and dug in to await an approaching German column under Colonel Tafel, who he had been warned was on his way to the area trying to escape into Mozambique. Hugely outnumbered by Tafel, Sos decided that the only solution was a full-scale bayonet charge, before the hill was surrounded. So surprised by such impudence, and in hand-to-hand combat, the German force broke and ran as Sos and his men hurtled down the hill at them.

Sos continued his 'Offensive Reconnaissance' forays until his force was

3.1 Capt. Lionel Cohen (rear) in a Voisin aircraft in East Africa in 1917 in the RNAS, where he won his MC and DSO.

3.2 Wing Commander Lionel 'Sos' Cohen, after receiving his DFC in 1944.

disbanded in late 1917, whence he was appointed liaison officer to Portuguese HQ in Mozambique. During this period, Colonel Gore-Brown's unit of the King's African Rifles was cut off and short of ammunition in the bush. The Portuguese, now officially allies, refused to move, however, so Sos took his Sudanese sergeant and a motor launch full of supplies, up the Nyamakura river to relieve them, sailing back at night to his base at Quelimane. Unfortunately, Gore-Brown's force was attacked the next day and wiped out.

For his work in East Africa, Lionel received the MC on 1 February 1917 (*London Gazette*), 'for valuable services rendered in military operations in the field' (announced in the *Jewish Chronicle* on 9 February). He was promoted to captain on 6 January 1918 and major on 16 February 1918, and later was awarded the DSO (*London Gazette*, 27 July 1918)[8] for 'valuable services rendered with military operations in East Africa'. He was also Mentioned in Despatches on 11 October 1917 ('for meritorious service in the field'), 31 January 1919 and 8 December 1920 ('for distinguished service during operations in East Africa').

After the war, and now in his mid-40s, he married Victoria Maud Shepherd in Durban in 1920[9] and later, with their two daughters, returned to England as a stockbroker. Soon, however, he was persuaded to return to Mozambique as mine manager, on one occasion having to hunt down a man-eating lion that was terrorizing a mining camp, and on another falling into an animal pit already occupied by an angry lioness. On both occasions he narrowly escaped with his life.

Eventually the mining programme failed and Sos returned to England in 1926 to live at Hill House, Slinfold in Sussex, where he farmed as a hobby, also owning a racehorse.

War clouds gathered in the 1930s, and in 1937 he single-handedly founded the Royal Air Force Volunteer Reserve (RAFVR) from among ex-RAF, RFC and RNAS officers to help in case of war.[10] He successfully persuaded Lord Trenchard, father of the RAF, to be its president. He managed to get a commission as a pilot officer (no. 72629) in the RAF in February 1939 and when war did break out he was aged 64. He served, now in his fourth war, as RAF Coastal Command liaison officer with the Admiralty, volunteering to take part in seventy operational flights as observer and air gunner (always carrying his lucky gold sovereign with him), in over 500 hours flying in the Atlantic (convoy escorts); Iceland (ice reconnaissance – where on one Liberator sortie, when the heating failed, he insisted on doing his stint in the turret round Bear Island, and on landing at Reykjavik, it took two crew members to prise him out of his seat);[11] North Africa and Spain (anti-submarine patrol); Bay of Biscay (light aircraft patrol); and over north-west Europe, including a stint with the RAAF (Australians). Promoted to wing commander, he took part in the attacks on the German battleships *Scharnhorst* and *Gneisenau* over the port of Brest on 23 April 1941. In the same year, during a shipping attack off Norway, his aircraft was chased by three Me (Messerschmitt) 110s and a Ju (Junkers) 88, and on another occasion his Sunderland aircraft took part in a four-strike attack on U-boat over the Atlantic, and claimed it sunk. Over the North Sea on 19 May 1942 he was wounded in the head by anti-aircraft fire in the attack on the German pocket battleship *Lutzov*.[12] His longest patrol was in a Catalina – twenty-one-and-a-half hours over the Atlantic in July 1941. His penultimate sortie in a Halifax, hit by flak, resulted in a crash-landing from which he walked away unscathed.

When asked why he insisted on flying, he told First Sea Lord Admiral Dudley Pound: 'without practical experience I could not offer solutions to problems' and that 'it was good for morale to have senior officers sharing watches with the young air crew'.

An Air Ministry spokesman, describing Sos as 'a grand chap', announced on 1 February 1944 that for 'Gallantry and devotion to duty in the execution of Air Operations' and 'setting a magnificent example to all by his untiring energy and courage', Sos was to receive the DFC, aged 69, and that he had been the oldest aircrew member of the RAF – an unparalleled achievement in military history. He was invested by the king at Buckingham Palace in November 1944. He was also Mentioned in Despatches in 1941 and on 2 June 1943 – making five times in all in two world wars – and was awarded the American Air Operations Medal 'in recognition of valuable service', conferred by the president of the United States (*Jewish Chronicle*, 15 November 1946).

In recommending him for his DFC, RAF Marshall Sir John Slessor said: I have never put up a recommendation that I thought so well deserved than for old Sos in his 70th year ... few if any Commanders can have had a junior officer with a campaign ribbon [Matabeland] won before the CO was born!' Sos's reaction to his award was that he accepted it 'for those incredible youngsters of Coastal Command with whom I fly. I have been sufficiently honoured simply by being allowed to keep such company ... they are the salt of the earth.'

In addition to all this, his daughter Aileen Broadbent was a senior company commander in the ATS, and ATS provost marshall for Scotland; daughter Elizabeth a section officer in the WAAF; and his wife on the HQ Staff of the WVS in London.

Sos Cohen died in August 1960, aged 85 (announced in the *Jewish Chronicle* on 2 September). He never denied his Jewish roots and never changed his name; whether he ever suffered because of this we will never know. He was cremated at Balcombe Road crematorium in Crawley on 1 September and his ashes scattered in an area known as 'The Glade'.[13] In correspondence with the author, Sos's son-in-law Christopher Buckle (Deputy Lieutenant of the County of Sussex), stated that as Lionel

Cohen was not survived by any Jewish relatives (grandchildren Ann and Susan Buckle are not Jewish either) and at the request of his widow, Sos's cremation was private with no memorial service at all. His daughters (one now deceased) were educated at a convent school.

His obituary pointed out that he had served in all three Armed Services, and gave his nickname as 'the man with a hundred lives'. He was a member of the Association of Jewish Ex-Servicemen and Women (AJEX) and took part in many of its annual parades at the Cenotaph, in the Wreath Party. He was also a life member of the RAF Association, RAF Club and RAFVR Club as well as the Matabele Campaign Society. He returned only once to Africa, in 1945, to receive the Freedom of the City of Bulawayo.[14] As the SS *Athlone Castle* approached Durban, the captain ran up the Rhodesian ensign in Sos's honour – the first time it had ever been flown at sea.[15]

Lionel Cohen's twelve military decorations were as follows: DSO; MC (First World War); DFC (Second World War); Matabeleland Campaign Medal; Queen's South Africa Medal (Boer War); 1914–15 Star; War Medal; Victory Medal with MiD (First World War); 1939–45 Star; Defence Medal; War Medal with MiD; American Air Medal (Second World War).[16]

Sources

London Gazette, 1 February 1917; 27 July 1918; 1 January 1941; 2 June 1943; 1 February 1944; 15 October 1946.
Jewish Chronicle, 9 February 1917; 2 August 1918; 4 June 1943; 4 February 1944; 10 November 1944; and 2 September 1960. Undated review, *Jewish Chronicle*, 1952.
Thanks for all their help to Aumie and Michael Shapiro of Springboard Productions; the RAF Museum in Hendon; RAF Innsworth (Gloucester); Mr C. Buckle (son-in-law of Sos): Association of Jewish Ex-Servicemen and Women (AJEX), Military Museum Archives, Hendon.

Notes

1. See the biography of Sos by A. Richardson, *The Crowded Hours* (London: Max Parrish, 1952).
2. Cohen archive at the West Sussex County Archives, Chichester.
3. Cohen archive.
4. South African Defence Force Archives for the First World War (SADFA).
5. SADFA.
6. Cohen archive.
7. SADFA.
8. Directory of the DSO, Imperial War Museum Library.
9. *The Chronicle* (Bulawayo), 25 October 1947, Cohen Archive.
10. Cohen archive.
11. C. White, 'Horsham: The War Years', West Sussex County Archives 1995; this was with 120 Squadron on 30 July 1943 in III N/120 with Captain F.O. Turner over the Arctic – WW2 Forum website.
12. C. Bowyer, *Guns in the Sky* (London: Corgi, 1979).
13. Records of the Worthing Crematorium, Sussex.
14. International News Agency photograph, Cohen archive, dated 4 November 1949.
15. Cohen archive.
16. The *London Gazette*, 37776, 1 November 1946, apologized for not mentioning Sos's DSO, DFC and MC when announcing his USA Air Medal in issue number 37758 of 11 October 1946 (source: RAF Commands website).

'Stand By! Alert!': Jews in the Fire Service in the Second World War

Stephanie Maltman ('Firemen Remembered' Remembrance Group)
and Martin Sugarman (Archivist, AJEX Jewish Military Museum)

Before 1941, there were many types of fire brigades around the country, run by local councils, varying in size, equipment, methods and efficiency. Because the danger of fires from aerial bombardment was realized in the First World War, in the 1930s the government decided to take action to reorganize the Fire Services of the nation and so, in 1938, the Auxiliary Fire Service (AFS) was established to assist the regular Fire Service. The National Fire Service (NFS) was not set up until August 1941, but the AFS was already ten times their size.

By the time of the Blitz, 5,000 women had been recruited in the UK for the AFS – a first for the NFS – together with 25,000 men. The London Fire Brigade (LFB) alone had 2,500 men. An article in 1941 in the *Jewish Chronicle*[1] announced that the Women's AFS required 1,300 more women, aged 20 to 50 years, to act as telephonists, watchroom staff, etc, at '£2 and 7 shillings [thirty-five pence] per week with free uniform and certain free meals', and applications should be made to the London Fire Brigade HQ on Albert Embankment or the WAFS training offices in Compton Terrace, Highbury.

This study is an attempt to record those Jewish men and women who served in the Fire Service in the Second World War, including those in re-lated units such as firewatchers, fireguards and Street Fire Patrols. Not only were many of those who served in these latter organisations also ca-sualties, but they did crucial as well as dangerous work, exposed and vul-nerable especially atop buildings during raids while bombs were falling. Even though they were not full members of the AFS or NFS, many were trained by them. During bombing, they would help spot fires and report them, and also begin the extinguishing process with sand, stirrup pumps and water buckets, in very hazardous conditions, often succeeding alone, or when necessary coping as best they could during air raids, until the Fire Service arrived to take over. As the war progressed, and particularly after the devastating raid on the City of London on the night of 29 December 1940, when the consequences of their absence were only too apparent, these subsidiary units were equipped with more and more so-phisticated machinery. Their status was acknowledged as such when the press, for example, often publicized cases where members of such units were given severe fines in court if they did not appear for their duties on time, a sure official indication of the importance of their work.

To complicate matters, other personnel were often drafted in from unlikely places to act as firewatchers, including regular troops.[2] In the following lists, we have also included those who said they did other jobs at the same time, such as Air Raid Precautions (ARP), with firewatching duties as well.

We know that many more Jews served in Aldgate and Whitechapel (it is estimated that 85 per cent of the Civil Defence (CD) as a whole, were Jewish in the East End) and in London as a whole, as many as a third of the CD may have been Jewish; also that at AFS substations such as Well-close Square and Fairclough Street, as many as 90 per cent of the personnel would have been Jewish.[3] An article in the *Jewish Chronicle*[4] noted that there was 'a big number of Jewish ARP, AFS and other Civil Defence workers' in the Clydeside area. Another[5] described how Reverend M. Spira of Willesden Synagogue organized a service for Jewish Willesden Civil Defence workers, which included over eighty in ARP and AFS uniform as well as the commander of the local AFS, Captain White-side, who was not Jewish. Many of these Jewish volunteers were First World War veterans, others simply too old or unfit for the military.

Completing this task is a question of researching in archives and obtaining evidence from surviving relatives. Fire Service records are notoriously inaccessible and have often been moved around, and those that do survive are also widespread in different archives around the country. Many have sadly been lost or destroyed and so our record will never be totally correct. Where we obtained lists, we used surnames and sometimes first names, for example Hyman, to indicate those with a Jewish background. We know this is unreliable as, for example, when Jewish families called Turner and Wilson contacted us to say they served, names which we as authors would never have extracted from a list as being Jewish. Nevertheless, we firmly believe the method wholly justified and worthwhile, not least to show our detractors, as well as sceptics, just how many Jews served in the fire brigade. It may be in the end that the reality in terms of numbers of Jews who served in the Fire Service nationwide is as much as a quarter again of those we have recorded, because their names have been impossible to recognize.

The authors also became aware early on that family names would frequently crop up two or three times in the same fire station, a sure indication of members of the same family from the same area joining up to serve together, reminiscent of the famous 'Army Pals' battalions of the First World War. This surely reflected both the close-knit nature of the local Jewish communities, and the community nature of the AFS, as well as a patriotic determination 'to do their bit'. But it could also have equally tragic consequences, as when the Aaron and Jacob Heiser siblings were both killed in the same incident in May 1941 (see below).

Jim Barnard, born in Lowestoft, was a senior London fireman and later deputy fire chief of Essex, who trained auxiliaries and he has testified in his memoirs that of the 400 men he trained in Whitechapel for the AFS, most were Jewish, and he remembers them with respect and affection. Many were Petticoat Lane stallholders and taxi drivers.[6] In common with other schools the Jewish Free School (JFS) in Bell Lane was used as a fire station after the children were evacuated from London from 1940.

Very few Jews are known to have served in the Fire Service in Britain until the formation of the AFS. However, surviving records from the early days of recruitment in 1938,[7] when war was still distant but some believed inevitable, show that many Jewish men and women were among the first to enrol giving the lie to the belief that Jews saw it as an easy option. It is well known that even before the outbreak of war and up to the beginning of the Blitz, there was often resentment and hostility between regular firemen and members of the AFS. What is not so clearly recognized is that Jewish AFS personnel, in addition to the normal dangers of the job, had to contend with the usual endemic anti-Semitism of the time as manifested within the Fire Service. Personal research and interviews by Stephanie Maltman show clearly that anti-Semitism was a constant background to life on many fire brigade stations and substations, laced with the extra portion of British Fascist anti-Jewish propaganda that pervaded society at all levels in those days. In the same way that BUF (British Union of Fascists) members joined the military, many also joined the Fire Service; the notorious Nazi sympathizer and convicted spy, Anna Wolkoff, who joined the AFS, is one perhaps extreme example.[8]

Maurice Richardson, the journalist and novelist, in his book *London's Burning*,[9] a contemporary account based on his time in the Fire Service in 1940, describes the anti-Semitism latent at his station and points out that it was constantly the subject of discussion and often the cause of heated arguments. Many members of the AFS were usually allied with one end of the political spectrum, whilst many regular men and officers were recognised as Blackshirts and seemed happy, if not in some cases proud, to be so. In *The Bells Go Down: The Diary of an AFS Man*, published in 1942, the author,[10] who deliberately dedicates the book to 'the men of the London Fire Service and particularly to those who served east of the fire alarm at Aldgate Pump' – which clearly implies the predominantly Jewish area round Whitechapel – refers to 'N—, the Company Officer who is a Fascist. He spent a long time telling me about Mosley this morning, while I was washing down one of the taxis.'[11] Later on he adds, 'it was nice to get away from N—, strutting about in his leather boots and his specklessly clean respirator case. I believe that the cleanliness of a respirator case could be taken as a measure of Fascist tendencies ... The cleaner the respirator case the more Fascist the wearer.' Jim Barnard remembered being appalled when one of his fellow officers at Whitechapel bragged that he was a fully paid-up member of the Blackshirts.[12] Such single-minded dedication to the humiliation of Jews could, in those with power, make life uncomfortable in practice, as in the case of Renee Donn; she remembers being made, by one of the officers on her station, to return again and again to clean the same toilets she had already cleaned because, he said, 'they had not been cleaned properly'.

Added to this was the general insecurity of working-class non-Jews who met, often for the first time, generally intelligent, capable and educated working-class Jews. Stephanie also concludes that dozens of those internationalist left-wing Jews and non-Jews, who fought in the Spanish Civil War against Franco, joined the AFS on principle as they refused at first – until Germany invaded Russia – to serve in the army of a capitalist country. Expressing such views would also have brought hostile accusations of disloyal Bolshevism against such thinking and principled Jewish volunteers. In any case there seems to have been an all too ready willingness to blame 'the Jews' for many of the pre-war social and economic difficulties that particularly affected working and lower middle class families. These Jews made easy targets for right-wing agitators, and George Wheeler (see Appendix 2), who was born and brought up in the East End and served as a Fire Service messenger in Bow, suggested that once men had a bit of drink inside them it was not difficult to stir them up into believing that all their ills were the fault of 'the Jews'. With such prejudice came the usual accusations, that all Jews were 'Windy Yids', that when the bombing started they would run away, and so on. Although it would seem that direct politically-motivated anti-Semitism was at its most virulent in the areas where Jewish communities prevailed, Alf Breck, a non Jew who served in Penge, a small independent brigade on the borders of Kent, spoke of incidents in which Jews at his substation were regularly served with bacon and eggs by their non Jewish colleagues, which he defined as 'horseplay'. It would seem however, that further out of London less anti-Semitism was apparent, as indicated by Martin Hichberger who served on the outskirts of Croydon, and Sylvia Kay who served in Nottingham. Neither experienced any form of anti-Semitism at all and found most people 'very kind'. In the case of Martin Hichberger, a refugee from Germany just before the outbreak of war, he found that it was his German origin that drew more comment than his being Jewish.

Equally interesting is the fact that from the nineteenth century through to the late 1930s it was traditional to recruit London firemen from the ranks of ex-naval and seafaring men, not least because several chief officers had been in the navy, 'as they are taught to obey orders, and night and day watches and the uncertainty of the occupation are more similar to their former habits than those of other men of the same rank in life'.[13] If we remember that 'anti-Semitic views were then common in the officer class of the Navy',[14] then the link is not difficult to make.

Author Michael Wassey[15] points out that racial stereotypes were broken down when he described how firemen encountered the kindness of East End Jewish families, who often brought them tea and sandwiches during incidents, even though they were themselves clearly poor with very little to spare.

There can be no doubt from contemporary accounts and later testi-monies that anti-Semitism was an issue within the Fire Service, in London at least, and that this was a reflection of the wider culture of which it was a part. Based on interviews with many who served in the Armed Forces it would seem that the unfamiliar circumstances which they were called on to deal with and adjust to absorbed a great many of the tensions that led to resentment and conflict at home. It may be argued, therefore, that on one level the Fire Service was far from an easy option for Jews. The majority conducted themselves with dignity and forbear-ance and, in the last resort, won the respect and affection of the men and women alongside whom they fought. Maurice Richardson wrote: 'much of the anti-Semitism failed to survive the first month of the Blitz. The few imbeciles who said things like "I wouldn't save a —— Yid's house from burning" learnt sense at the fires in Whitechapel.' Stephen Spender, who came into the Fire Service after the Blitz, summed it up well in reflect-ing that 'those men who had been through the worst of the Blitz seemed to have been purged in some way, and reborn into the camaraderie of the sub station'.[16]

Several contemporary accounts of the Fire Service illustrate that a common anti-Semitic jibe of the time was that Jews joined as a soft option to the Armed Forces. This unfounded accusation could be levelled at anybody, however, as many men with young families preferred to work on the Home Front if they could, and in any case the allegation could never be substantiated, as the higher than average enlistment into the Armed Forces of Jews per head of population, shows. In addition Jews joined up in 1938 in large numbers long before war was declared.

Anti-Semitism in the Armed Forces was quite rare after basic training. Many Jewish veterans have testified that once posted to and integrated into regiments and corps, or squadrons and ships, few Jews faced anti-Semitism because the overarching feeling of everyone 'being in the same boat' prevailed, especially overseas or under fire, and usually a stand-up bout of fisticuffs would settle a dispute and result in respect and friend-ship.[17] Nevertheless, being in Civil Defence was doubly difficult for Jews who faced a lot of home-grown anti-Semitism from active Blackshirts in the Fire Service, as well as the usual dangers of fighting fires under the bombs.

In addition to this, during the notorious 'Aliens' scare of 1940, there were at first purges of any foreign born Jews who had already then volunteered for the ARP, Home Guard, Fire Service and general Civil Defence units.[18] In June 1940 there were two successive removals of 'alien' Jews from the Fire Service in London and this is borne out by at least one Jewish AFS card that gives as reason for termination of duty 'Services terminated. Alien 1.7.40'; this was after the individual concerned had been twice promoted to AFS Sub Officer, even before the outbreak of war in 1939. These measures were later rescinded, as an item in the *Jewish Chronicle* of 1941, for example, stated 'that police authorities may be prepared to relax the strict curfew restrictions (midnight to 6 a.m.) on friendly aliens so that they may volunteer for fire fighting patrols in their own districts'[19] – but stipulated that they would have to be 'in company with British men or women'. A later item[20] noted that the Association of Jewish Refugees (AJR), in a leaflet, called upon even more Jewish refugees to sign up as firewatchers, 'as many had already done so'. By January 1942, local authorities such as Marylebone in London[21] began to ease restrictions that required that firewatchers and other Civil Defence workers were to be nationals of the UK, especially in the light of manpower shortages in the prosecution of the war, and so in May 1942[22] Marylebone announced that 169 Aliens had been enrolled as fire guards.

Richard Gilbert, the grandson of Fireman Morris Lustig, wrote[23] that his grandfather related to him how he was one of the group of LFB firemen sent to serve in the Isle of Wight, which had become a particular Luftwaffe target as it guarded the approach to Portsmouth. Morris became one of the few survivors of the notorious Shanklin bombing that killed several of his colleagues, including two fellow Jewish officers (see casualty list below). Nevertheless on his return to London, where he was asked to do a desk job, he faced unpleasant, anti-Jewish remarks from some of his colleagues, who 'complained' about how a Jew managed to be one of the survivors of the tragic incident, despite the fact that two of those killed were Jewish.[24]

Conversely, the *Jewish Chronicle* had earlier noted[25] that a *Kol Nidre* service (for Yom Kippur, the most holy day in the Jewish calendar) was held by Reverend S. Levy of the New Synagogue, London, at an unnamed fire station. This was with, of course, the full support of the superintendent, there being over thirty Jewish firemen under his command; he allowed the service to take place in the station so the men could be on call in an emergency. In a later issue,[26] the *Jewish Chronicle* noted that the Great Synagogue in Cheetham, Manchester, had held a service in which over 300 Civil Defence (CD) workers had attended, including AFS, conducted by Reverend Perlmann and Rabbi Altmann, after which the congregation marched to Albert Square for the March Past the Mayor, together with other CD staff.

The *East London Advertiser*[27] also noted that Stepney's ARP controller, Mr A.R. Beaumont, issued an order concerning the Jewish High Holydays of September 1941, saying: 'a Jewish Fireguard may find a substitute should his regular turn of duty fall on any of the above stated nights [Rosh Hashana and Yom Kippur]. If unable to find a substitute, she/he must carry out their duties as previously arranged.'

(which included the heavily Jewish populated Whitechapel and Stepney), who made the effort to discover the dates of all the Jewish Holydays in order either to plan to accommodate the needs of his mostly Jewish personnel, or simply to ease his problems of constantly being asked for leave.[28]

In 1942, the Ministry of Information commissioned a film on the Fire Service, *Fires Were Started*, directed by Humphrey Jennings, to especially celebrate the war work of the AFS. It told a fictitious story centred on a day and night in the life of a docklands fire crew during the Blitz, but was actually filmed at Wellclose Square Station. One character was played by real-life Jewish fireman Albert Levy (see below) and although no reference is made to the fact that he is Jewish, he very clearly is, with one remark about him 'getting the samovar going for making tea', as well as a confirmation from Jennings' assistant, who was interviewed by Stephanie Maltman on the issue. It is felt that Jennings was in a subtle way telling his audience of the sacrifice Jewish firemen were also making, and to counter some negative views about Jews from other firemen, picked up during the making of the film and from other observers.

Sadly, the losses of firemen and firewomen are regarded as 'civilian' casualties by the CWGC (Commonwealth War Graves Commission), although Stephanie Maltman does know of several killed in the Second World War who were given CWGC headstones at Mitcham and Tooting cemeteries, before the policy changed. This policy means that the graves are the responsibility of the families, and not cared for by the Commission, though civilian casualties of 'enemy action' are all recorded by the Commission on their website and in their registers. Unfortunately, therefore, some graves have simply disappeared – either the location is lost, or the plot is known but the headstone is totally destroyed or has disintegrated (for example, see Lennick in casualty list below). Also, most graves that do exist rarely say they are Fire Service deaths; Joseph Greenberg's at East Ham is an exception. Most say simply 'killed by enemy action'.

Acts of bravery were of course recognized with awards, but as in the military, they were not always fair. A current serving police officer, Bob Parker, related to us how his father Henry, a Second World War Middlesex

Brigade fireman, witnessed the courage of Fireman Greenbaum at the tragic Bounds Green Underground bombing on 14 October 1940. Many people had been trapped below ground and a local doctor managed to crawl through the rubble and reach survivors; he was later awarded a medal. However, Bob's father always told him that Greenbaum was the real hero, because, being powerfully built, he supported a large piece of wreckage on his back whilst the doctor and others crawled through his legs. His bravery and strength were never recognized.

Firewoman Charlotte Shernheim, now Stenham, tells another touching tale. Having come as a Jewish refugee to Britain, she knew from letters and Red Cross notes from her parents that her Christian former primary school teacher in Germany had tried to help her parents before they were deported to their deaths in Minsk. After the war, Charlotte asked a friend, who was stationed in the British Army in Hamburg, to trace the teacher, who had been imprisoned by the Nazis for associating with Jews, and was ill and in dire poverty by 1945. The friend found the teacher and, despite her situation, the woman had hidden and kept family photos for Charlotte, which she passed to the friend to bring to England. Charlotte, knowing of conditions in Germany at the time, immediately cut the buttons off her firewoman greatcoat and sent it to the former teacher. She was eternally grateful and they met soon after and remained friends until the teacher died some years ago. Thus a firewoman's coat helped a Righteous Gentile.

Current research so far shows that around 400 firemen and firewomen were killed on duty between 1939 and 1945 in London alone, at least forty of them (10 per cent) Jews. However, as Jews were never more than a tiny percentage of the population of London, this suggests an extraordinarily high casualty rate among London's Jewish firefighters, even when one takes into account that Jews may have made up a higher proportion of the Fire Brigade compared to their population numbers. This is an astonishingly high sacrifice and cause for sadness but also great pride.

It should also be noted that dozens of Jewish women served in the Palestine Mandate Auxiliary Fire Service in the Second World War and there are photos in archives in the USA and Israel illustrating this.[29]

Sources
Our sources for compiling this study include back issues of the *Jewish Chronicle* (*JC*) and *East London Advertiser*; personal correspondence from relatives in the files of the Jewish Military Museum; the CWGC website (Civilian Losses); and some secondary sources such as Cyril Demarne, *The London Blitz: After the Battle Magazine* (Essex 1991); Cyril Demarne, *Our Girls* (Edinburgh: Pentland Press, 1995); 'When the Sirens Sounded' (Times Newspapers, 1949); Barry Hollis, *37 Fire Force* (Enthusiast Publications, 1988); AFS records

at the London Fire Brigade (LFB) Museum/Records Office; the London Metropolitan Archives (LMA) Fire Brigade records and registers.

Acknowledgements

Stephanie Maltman obtained access to the wartime London Fire Brigade archives at their records centre in Lambeth, and from the individual record cards extracted hundreds of Jewish names. We realise that using surnames – and in some cases first names – is not the ultimate proof of Jewish ethnicity, but believe that our experience and common sense ensure it has been a fairly accurate and reliable method of determining Jewish participation. These particular records also enabled the authors to cross-reference names given to us verbally by families and extracted from the *Jewish Chronicle* and *East London Advertiser* as well as the LMA registers. We would like to sincerely thank the archivists of the LFB for their cooperation, and also point out that these cards were only for London and go only up to 1941. Were it possible to find records for the rest of the UK and after 1941, the numbers could be potentially hugely increased.

The authors would also like to thank, for their assistance, Harold Pollins of Oxford (formerly senior tutor at Ruskin College, Oxford), particularly for his work extracting the Jewish civilian deaths from the CWGC website, which can be found online;[30] the staff of the amazing Tower Hamlets Local History Library (THLHL); the editor of the *Jewish Telegraph* newspaper; the many editors of synagogue and Jewish refugee newsletters who inserted our appeal for information around Britain; the editor of the British Jewish Immigrants Association of Israel (Olei Brittania); the editor of the *Essex Jewish News*; the *AJEX Journal*; Charles Tucker of the United Synagogue Archives; the cemetery archivists of the Federation of Synagogues, Reform Synagogues and Sephardi Synagogues movements; Joseph John Samuels of Sheffield; Derek Fisher of Jewish Care, and especially the many correspondents from the Jewish Community who wrote, telephoned and emailed us the details of their relatives who served, often prompted by the indefatigable Dr Saul Issroff of the Jewish Genealogical Society of Great Britain. Thanks to them all for their huge enthusiasm.

Further detail on many of those killed can be found on the Commonwealth War Graves Commission (CWGC) website, www.cwgc.org.uk, civilian section; the graves of some casualties can be found on the United Synagogue graves website (Google). Marlow Road Cemetery is known as East Ham Cemetery.

The casualties appear to include one set of brothers, Heiser, who were firewatchers, and two other sets, one of whom died in the Merchant Navy (Millet) and the brother of Hyman Feldman, Louis, who died as a Japanese POW.

KIA means Killed in Action; WIA means Wounded in Action; tbc is 'to be confirmed'; ranks and numbers, where known, are included. If no other description accompanies a name, then the person was in the AFS or NFS. Women have been listed under their single names if they were not married at the time of service. The Sheffield firemen are named on their synagogue memorial, possibly the only synagogue memorial in the UK to do this. The AJEX Museum archives contain a 1940 fireman's helmet and axe, NFS and AFS badges, original documents, several personal testimonies and also many photographs of Jewish personnel.

The Roll of Honour: Those Killed in Action or on Active Service, with Date of Death

George Isaac Abrahams, Firewatcher Southampton, 25 February 1943.

Isaac Amiel, Firewatcher Mile End, 10 May 1941, buried Edmonton, V 75 20.

David Appleby, KIA 14 April 1940, aged 33, at AFS Station, Invicta Rd; husband of N. Appleby of 432 Bancroft Rd, Mile End. Buried 19 November 1940 at East Ham Jewish cemetery, grave O.20.643.

Eric Aronowsky, Firewatcher Liverpool, 4 May 1941.

Solomon Belinsky, WIA, died of wounds, Leeds, 1 April 1941; appears on the Fireman's Memorial website, but appears not to be on the Memorial near St Paul's Cathedral.

Samuel Berkon, Manchester, AFS Despatch Rider, 2 November 1940.

Louis Black, Firewatcher, 8 May 1941, Hull.

George William Blumson, Firewatcher, of Whitechapel, of Jewish origin, KIA 10 May 1941, aged 15, possibly the youngest Jewish casualty (see Coster below).

Louis Brilleslyper, Firewatcher, son of Rebecca, KIA 10 May 1941, of Leytonstone, killed Mile End, buried Marlow Road, I 6 377; photograph.

Abraham Carason, husband of Eva, Firewatcher Liverpool, 8 May 1941.

David Cohen (Shanklin), 3 January 1943, from Edgware.

George Leslie Cohen, of 74 South Lodge, Circus Rd, St John's Wood, born 24 October 1913, London; builders' merchant; served West Hampstead Station. Death in service 19 March 1943, buried 21 March, announced *JC*, 2 April 1943, but not on CWGC site or Fire Service memorial; buried Willesden, P 1 12. Death Certificate may show death through illness, but he was still on active service.

Isaac Cohen, Firewatcher Liverpool, 3 June 1941.

Monty Cohen, Firewatcher Stepney.

Simon Cohen, Stepney, 11 August 1940; buried Marlow Road, N 20 630.

Jacob Woolf Corby, Hackney, 25 September 1940; buried Marlow Road, O 12 368.

Albert Victor Coster, son of Harry and Alice of 70 Sheridan Street, London E1, Firewatcher and unofficial Volunteer Fireman, aged 14 (possibly youngest Jewish casualty), KIA at 71 Sutton Street, 9 April 1943; nephew of J. Marks and Joseph Harris; buried Manor Park cemetery with officiating vicar – tbc if Jewish or of Jewish origin.

Not on CWGC site, as death was attributable to an ordinary domestic fire and not enemy action, even though he was firefighting in the Blitz period as a 12-year-old. Search for grave unsuccessful.

Harry Coster, son of Benjamin and Esther; Camberwell 3 December 1942 (grave says 1943?); buried Willesden, GX 3 133.

Israel Deutsch/Deutch (incorrectly spelt as Isreal on the memorial), 8 March 1941, Cable and Backchurch Street, Stepney; a married cabinet-maker and shoe maker who lived in Richmond Rd, Hackney, and 26, Clark St, Whitechapel; buried Edmonton, grave V 70 24. Brother of Alec/Alex (also a fireman). Israel was killed on his first call-out, having volunteered to take the place of an injured comrade. C34 Shadwell.

Mrs Miriam 'Dolly' Emden, Firewatcher, Hughes Mansions, Stepney, 10 May 1941; buried Marlow Rd, I 6 380.

Hyman Feldman, of Amhurst Park, Stamford Hill, killed 19 March 1941 in Stepney; buried Edmonton, V 71 2 – gravestone disintegrated. His brother Louis was killed as POW of the Japanese.

Daniel Friedman, Firewatcher Westminster, 16 April 1941.

4.1 Fireman Hyman Feldman, killed in action on 19 March 1941 in Stepney.

4.2 Firewoman Mrs Rene Donn (Glambotsky) in action, training on her motorbike.

Benjamin Gaidelman, Fireguard Stoke Newington, 16 August 1944.

Sydney Gevelb, Firewatcher Stepney, 16 April 1941, aged 17; his cousin Morris was in St John's Ambulance and killed in same incident; buried Edmonton, V 74 19/18, in a double grave.

Harry Glantzpegel, aka Lewis (Shanklin), from Finchley, 3 January 1943.

David Gold, Dundee (tbc), 24 April 1944.

John Goldberg, Firewatcher Battersea, died 21 November 1945 of injuries sustained November 1944.

Herbert Benjamin Golden, Paddington (tbc); son of Sydney and Annie; King's Commendation for Brave Conduct; 11 May 1941.

B. Goldsmith (tbc: on Fire Service memorial but not on CWGC website).

Neil Goldsmith (tbc: on Fire Service memorial but not on CWGC website).

George Eric Goldsmith/ Goldschmitt, killed Chelsea, from Finchley, 16 April 1941.

Morris Goldstein, Firewatcher, 16 April 1941, Stepney.

Edwin Goodman (tbc: on Fire Service memorial but not on CWGC website).

Joshua Goodman, Firewatcher Leeds, 16 December 1943.

Jack Gordon/Cohen, Firewatcher Stoke Newington, 17 April 1941; KIA, Cannon St; buried Edmonton Federation, V 74 16.

Barnett Greenberg, Peckham, killed Poplar, 11 May 1941.

Harry Greenberg, Firewatcher, 19 March 1941, Stepney.

Joseph Greenberg, Stepney, 1 January 1941, buried Marlow Road, O 26 846.

Nat Greenberg, Firewatcher/Ambulance Driver Liverpool, *JC*, 7 May 1941.

Emmanuel Gush, Exeter (tbc), 25 April 1942.

Henry Harris, Firewatcher, aged 16, 10 March 1941, Flower and Dean St; possibly second youngest Jewish casualty on duty; buried Marlow Road, I 5 307 – headstone no longer exists.

Myre/Moier Harrison, (related to Arthur Lawson, AJEX), 13 March 1941 (eight Jewish AFS men acted as pall-bearers at his funeral in Glasgow).[31]

Aaron (Harry) Heiser, Firewatcher Golders Green, 11 May1941; *JC*, 16 May 1941; KIA Old Street, buried Willesden, FX 19 857.

Jacob Heiser, Firewatcher; brother of Aaron, listed above, killed same day, same incident; buried Willesden, FX 19 856.

Gilbert Hyams/Hyman, Firewatcher Liverpool; not on CWGC website.

Leslie Walter Joseph Isaacs, Wandsworth, 16 November 1940.

Leslie Alfred Jacobs, from Shanklin (tbc), 3 January 1943.

Hyman Lennick, West Ham, 18 June 1943, buried Marlow Road, P 14 440 – headstone no longer exists.

Ascher/Arthur (David) Davis Lettner/Latner, City, 17 April 1941; family say correct spelling is Latner. Brother-in-law of Jack Silver (listed below), Ascher served at Cannon Street with Jack. He was killed by a collapsing wall, on the other side of which Jack was standing, and his death was not notified for a week as his body was missing. Ascher's wife Erna was not Jewish and she had him cremated in London, but then swam out to sea herself and scattered his ashes off the coast of Cornwall, at Looe. There is a plaque on his parents' grave in Willesden Jewish

cemetery. He was the son of Marks and Shoshana (Jessie) Latner and had returned – from the safety of the USA where he had been a musician – 'to do his bit', as his nephew remembers him saying, and then gave his life in the Fire Service.

Albert Levenson, Hackney, killed Mile End, 5 November 1941.

Abraham Levy, Hull; German Refugee (tbc if killed – not on CWGC site).

Samuel Levy, Firewatcher Bristol, 13 April 1941.

Ms Hetty Lewin, Firewatcher Stoke Newington, killed at West Central Synagogue Jewish Youth Club, Alfred Place, Holborn, 17 April 1941, buried Streatham, E 26 35 (see S. Osterer, listed below).

Abraham Lewis, aka Bookatz, Stepney, 12 May 1941 buried Rainham, A 24 24; also noted in the LMA records FB/WAR 4/12, no. 1663.

Samuel Libbert, killed Glasgow, from Manchester, 19 September 1942.

Samuel Loveman, Greenock; son of Moses and Jane, husband of Rebecca; 19 October 1940.

Victor Michaelson, Wandsworth, 6 November 1940, buried Willesden, FX 13 566 – headstone totally blank/worn.

Percy Millet, whose brother Morris was also killed serving in the Merchant Navy on 22 October 1942. Percy was the first Jewish Fireman killed on 8 September 1940, in Stepney, buried Rainham, A 19 29.

Harry Morris, AFS, son of Solomon of Hackney, 11 May 1941, buried Marlow Road, I 6 388; photo.

Miss Margaret Myers, Firewatcher, daughter of Joseph of Stepney, 8 March 1941.

Issac Nyman, Firewatcher from Ilford, killed 10 May 1941, Mile End Road; not listed as Firewatcher on CWGC website; buried Rainham, A 24 23.

Sarah Osterer, Fireguard, killed 17 April 1941 at the West Central Synagogue Jewish Youth Club, Holborn, with Hetty Lewin.

Alexander Paul, Manchester, 24 December 1940.

Pizer Pearl, from Surrey, killed Tottenham Court Rd, based at Hackney Fire Station, 26 September 1941.

Manuel (Mendel) Rabinowitz, Edinburgh, posted to London, WIA and died of injuries in Edinburgh in 1941. In an accident with a bus on way to fire station; suffered serious head injuries from which he later died after returning to convalesce in Edinburgh.

Max Randal, Firewatcher Golders Green, 18 March 1941.

Jack Raphael, Firewatcher Hampstead, 20 June 1944.

Maurice Sydney Rose, Column Officer, from Surrey, killed Bradford 11 December 1943.

Hyman Roseman, from Nova Rd, Croydon, killed

Elephant and Castle 12 July 1944, previously in ARP; buried Streatham, F 28 28. Unfit for military service; a gentle and cultured man according to his niece. Killed by collapse of heavy pipework. His wife re-married after the war.

Frederick Charles Salkeld, Section Officer, son of Bessie and William, Wandsworth, 17 October 1940.

Ernest Adam Schneider, of Stepney, killed 14 October 1940, Finsbury; his remains were not found until one year after at Bonhill St, Finsbury.

Alexander Schooler, No. 891, killed 8 May 1941, Albert Dock, Hull. German refugee, first Jewish Hull Fireman casualty, buried Hull Jewish cemetery.

Israel Schwartzberg, 29 August 1943, Bethnal Green.

Morris/Maurice (Mossy) Share, killed 8 September 1940, Bermondsey, same day as Millet, listed above; buried Rainham, A 20 14.

Benjamin Joseph/John Sheldon (tbc), killed Woolwich, 11 September 1940.

Harry Thomas Simeon (tbc), Glasgow, 13 March 1941.

Harry Simon, from Scotland,

believed buried in Manchester (tbc); call from Carl Goldberg of Manchester.

Alec Slipman, Firewatcher Holborn, 17 April 1941, buried Edmonton, V 75 23 – gravestone disintegrated.

Miss Helen Sussman, killed 19 June 1944, Kensington, buried Edmonton, W 26 19.

Harold Alan Tasho, died in Hertford, 21 February 1941, aged 27; served in Southampton (*JC*, 7 March 1941 p.7, but not on Fire Service memorial or CWGC website, as he died of illness). Buried Marlow Road, 23 February 1941, O 33 1086 – headstone no longer exists.

Joseph Leonard Tobias, District Officer, lived Euston, killed 17 September 1940, Marylebone.

David Viener, Hackney, 23 December 1945; buried Rainham A 39 19.

Myer Wand, from Stepney, killed 18 September 1940, Marylebone, buried Marlow Road, O 10 313.

Herbert Thomas Wolff (tbc); Deptford, killed 28 September 1940, Camberwell.

Phillip Zagerman, Firewatcher/ARP Stamford Hill, 13 January 1941.

(A total of 84)

A list of those who served is being compiled by MS and SM and is work in progress. It will total several thousands.

Appendix 1: A Note on Other Fire Units

Stephanie Maltman writes:

Street Fire Patrols (SFP) were set up in areas where there was thought to be high industrial or other risk (dense housing for instance); these were volunteer fire parties, groups of men and women who were part of the community living on the same street or round the corner from each other who would have access to a simpler version of a trailer pump, hand-operated, located somewhere convenient nearby. For instance, the Bruce Road pump, in Poplar, was kept in the yard of the local pub. Street parties were often first on the scene at an incident and able to deal with it themselves; if not they would call on the fire brigade. Incendiaries in themselves were not particularly difficult to deal with but they fell in their hundreds and that was very dangerous. Street fire parties were a sort of self-help organization; they arose spontaneously almost from the community and were neither part of the Fire Service nor any other branch of ARP, though they were recognized as an important part of the anti-fire war effort. In the instance of Alfred Wagerman, his son Peter remembers that his father wore an official white painted helmet with SFP painted on it in large black letters.

There were also 'works brigades'. Large factories or other industrial installations (power-stations, gas works, oil refineries) had volunteer fire parties drawn from among their employees, which functioned in more or less the same way as street fire parties but with responsibility for a particular industrial site. The initiative for these came from the management. *It is important to note that both street fire parties and works brigades were given a certain amount of initial training by members of the Fire Service.*

In some very large factories or plants in outer areas, such as Ford's and in airports, for example, there existed even before the war an approximation of their own fire brigade. This was not war related but a permanent thing, and they would have had at least one motorized fire appliance. During the war they continued to function independently, only by that time probably with their own firewatchers and so on, all drawn from employees who would leave their usual work and operate in a firefighting capacity in the event of an emergency. Again they were independent organizations and did not come under any branch of Civil Defence until the formation of the NFS, to which they were eventually affiliated and so in effect joined the order of battle.

Appendix 2: Aspects of Anti-Semitism

Extracts from a talk with George Wheeler (not Jewish) who was a 14-year-old AFS messenger boy in Bow, stationed at Lush and Cooks cleaners near the River Lea. He was interviewed by Stephanie Maltman on 1 March 2006:

There was always a bit of ill-feeling in the East End between English people and Jews. The Blackshirts ... were very good at stirring up trouble. A lot of men ... liked going down the pub ... and when you've had a few drinks, if you had a few agitators ... it didn't take long to fan the flames. They said 'the Jewish boys didn't want to fight and went into the Fire Service to stay out the army' ... I say to them, 'Were you there then?' They fought fires just like anyone else. They were in the thick of it and when you're in the open, you've got no shelter, you're working at a fire, all the sky's lit up and there's bombs dropping down among you, they didn't run away, they fought the fires like the rest of us. This is the trouble ... I would support the Jewish boys all the way along the line ... we had a big complement of them, but they were the same as the rest of us. You're going out night after night, and if they were scared, we were all one way and another, but you don't show it ... certain people were trying to put the Jewish race in a very bad light. They didn't succeed. When the crunch came, when the Blitz started, the Jewish Firemen earned the respect of everyone. They were accepted like any other fireman.

The driver (... most of them were Jewish because they were mostly taxi drivers ...) was also a pump-operator ... so the crew relied on them for the supply of water ... they stood there on their own, more vulnerable. A lot of us were brought up among Jews ... if anyone starts slating a Jew we'd be very quick to stand up for them ... when it came to the Sabbath you had to ignore it, it was war. They didn't observe it ... you're on duty for 48 hours. You have to ignore it ... we all had to stick together ... the Jewish people came out of it as good as any other British person. They did what was expected of them ... which upset the agitators quite a bit!

Extracts from Maurice Richardson, *London's Burning*:

My temperamental namesake, who hated the instructor's guts – part of his hate was anti-Semitism; the instructor was unmistakably Jewish – said, 'Bunk, you're just as good as the rest of us. He's picking on you because e thinks you got money 'cos you speak educated. He's on the tap, see? If you slipped him one he'd never say another word. Them —— Yids is all the same.' [pp.33–4.]

... There was only one taint in the otherwise intensely amiable dispositions of these men; this was virulent anti-Semitism. Gizzie was so far gone that you couldn't argue with him about it. Johnny was nearly as bad. The old sub was another Jew hater. He refused to believe there were any poor Jews in England, all Yids were twisters, etc; I used to shout at him till I was quite tired, but he only shook his head like an old dog and said, 'You can say what you like, mate, you're an educated man and you may know what you're talking about, but you'll never convince me that Yids ain't bastards. Mind you, I don't say there aren't exceptions, like young Solly here and Nat.'

Solly Greenbaum, one of the three or four Jews in the station, was a brisk, lively little man who had worked in the advertising business, so gay and friendly nobody could help liking him. Nat Marks was a huge, quiet, sardonic man with a brown face and curly hair like a spaniel's. He came from Jamaica and spoke in a deep slow growl. It was a good thing that these were so popular, for there was a great deal of anti-Semitism latent in the station, especially among the men who had had small, one-man businesses of their own and and suffered competition from Jewish street-market traders. In the boxing and burgling underworld of Gizzie and Johnny, with its sporadic gang or rather mob warfare, anti-Semitism flourished of course. The Yiddisher boys had their mob and you had yours. The genuine (economically) proletarians, like Joe Whigham, who was a building trades worker, had no racial prejudice whatever, and together with myself and George Fitt, an intelligent and educated little fair man, who'd been a photographer for a sports press agency and was a solid socialist, they used to reprove the anti-Semites. Several men came from Shoreditch, a lumpenish district where Mosley's propaganda had taken some root. One or two had very likely been Blackshirts for a time. Almost certainly Jack Connor had; he was one of the leading auxiliaries, an ex-army man, Guards, I think, and he had some of the fascist patter by heart. I found him pleasant enough but he wasn't very popular. The arch Jew-baiter, Massey, a cross-eyed, hard-faced, surly fellow, had also been in the army.* There was undoubtedly rather a savage, brooding strain in this man, and the pro-Semites among us were able to turn it to advantage. We referred to him as the Jew baiter, and the name stuck so that even the anti-Semites used it; ' —— like Massey and Jack Connor talk that way. This anti-Jew stuff is all bunk, and you know it', had remarkable propagandist effect. Gizzie, Johnny and even the old sub didn't need to be taken seriously. They could be dismissed as comics. Massey's chief victim was the third Jew, an ex-taxi driver called Tasker. He was a member of one of the little extreme left sectarian bodies of the SPGB, I think. Intelligent but with something peculiarly irritating about his personality. He was the most tactless political propagandist imaginable. I once heard him say to someone: 'You've learnt quite a lot from me, you have; you wouldn't have spoken like that a week ago.' But he stood up to Massey all right and threatened to lay him out with a billiard cue if he didn't leave him alone.

... Much of the anti-Semitism failed to survive the first month of the Blitz. The few imbeciles who said things like 'I wouldn't save a ——in' Yid's house from burning' learnt sense at the fires in Whitechapel. Correspondingly, one's own feelings towards them changed. Even if you had the strongest theoretical reasons for disliking somebody, it was impossible to feel bitter about him when you were on the job together with bombs dropping. The night came when I felt a wave of friendliness towards Massey.

*I am not trying to disparage the Army in this connection. The point is that the peace-time private soldier tends to be a rather lumpen type, no fault of his own, and as such is liable to anti-Semitism. [pp.62–5.]

... After the start of the blitz the atmosphere at A became even more friendly. Anti-Semitism disappeared or was in abeyance. Political arguments lacked sting because the arguers were in agreement about so many immediately topical questions like shelters, evacuation, etc. [p.137.]

... The driver was Nat Marks, a fat, dashing driver and an expert mechanic. He was supposed to be the best pump operator in the station. Unlike some pump operators, who were content to stand by the pump and keep as far away from the fire as possible, Nat was always thinking about the rest of the crew up on the branch. If you were in an awkward place with the hose caught on something, his huge form would suddenly come looming up in the glow and get you loose with a shove and a tug. [pp.166–7.]

Appendix 3: Attitudes to Aliens

The *London County Council War Diary*, Vol. 1, 24 August 1939 to 31 July 1940 (in a private collection) contains the following entries about Aliens in the Fire Service and illustrates what at first was their progressive deterioration in status in Britain. For Aliens, read Jews, who made up the bulk of this refugee group in Britain.

4 November 1939: AFS Aliens – Home Office Circular ARP/297/1939 ... for part-time service only.

24 May 1940: Aliens – London regional circular 144 stating that no aliens of any nationality should in future be employed in key positions in any ARP (Air Raid Precaution) service. Details to be sent to DAC (Deputy Assistant Commissioner) CID Scotland Yard of all aliens in any service. Home Office circular FB 55/1940 instructing local authorities to review the position of any aliens in the AFS – *none to be employed in key positions* [authors' italics] but consideration to be given to their transfer.

Council decided to terminate forthwith services of all German, Austrian and stateless aliens. Czechs and Poles *to be watched* [authors' italics] and particulars of all aliens in the department to be forwarded to Clerk of the Council. Special watch to be kept on any officer or employee of British nationality whose loyalty is in any way doubtful.

Home Office circular FB 64/1940 stating that all aliens in AFS and casualty services should be suspended, but individuals might be reinstated if granted exemption from restrictions on movement imposed by the *Aliens Order* and subject to consultation with the police.

31 May 1940: particulars of seven aliens in AFS forwarded to the Clerk of the Council.

4 June 1940: Aliens – Home Office circular FB 71/1940 drawing attention of local authorities to the necessity of their satisfying themselves as to the reliability of individual members of the civil defence services.

5 June 1940: Ten aliens in the AFS suspended and required to return all articles of uniform and equipment.

6 June 1940: Particulars of three aliens in addition to the seven referred to on May 31st 1940, forwarded to the Clerk of the Council and Scotland Yard.

12 June 1940: Employment of Aliens – Services of aliens in the Service already reported to be dispensed with at one week's notice on 20th June, but not to be allowed to resume duty. While individual aliens may be subsequently reinstated under certain conditions, none of the above mentioned should be reinstated except under authority from the Civil Defence and General Purposes Committee.

13 June 1940: Aliens – 10 aliens given one week's notice of termination of services on 20 June 1940.

4 July 1940: Aliens – Chairman of Civil Defence and General Purposes Committee decided that aliens discharged on 21 June should not be reinstated and that aliens should not in future be employed in the fire services.

Miscellany – Other Periods

Military Fire Service

Leonard Clements, Army.

Adolphus 'Alf' Kay, RAF Glos.

Philip Rosenthal, Army.

Stanley Rosenthal, RAF.

Currently Serving or Post-War

Walter Clayton, aka Kohn, 1952–63; German refugee.

Michelle Kent, grandaughter of Joseph Sack, Second World War.

Erhard W.W. Saar, aka Edward Lees, formerly SOE, Chief Fire Officer for Neath Fire Brigade, German refugee.[32]

Jerrard Wilson, 1957–69.

John Zaktrager, Station Officer, Kingsland Fire Station,

Hackney, 1960s, seconded to Zambia as adviser.

Believed to be Jewish, Died in Service before the Second World War

Henry Berg, died 7 December 1882.

Joseph Schubert, died 11 April 1928.

Robert Schultz, died 3 July 1895 (coachman, thrown from appliance).

Served before the First World War and the Second World War

Captain Henry Edward Davis, a former mayor of Gravesend who founded the local Fire Service in the 1870s in south-east Kent.

James Goldsmith, whaler, 1888–1924 in Fire Service, London (see his son James Goldsmith, served 1930s to 1940s).

Fire Service Artists

Enid Abrahams, daughter of George and Julia, born Hampstead 10 May 1906, RA 1939. AFS driver in Hampstead and Bethnal Green. Married Charles Dreyfus 11 February 1947, one daughter. Died 19 May 1972, London.

Section Leader Balchin, No. 36 Fire Area, Stepney/Poplar.

Julia Lowenthal.

Overseas

Abraham Hort, one of the early Jewish settlers in New Zealand, set up the Wellington City Fire Brigade in the 1840s.

In 1898, 90 per cent of the Fire Brigade in Bialystock, Poland, was Jewish and most Jewish settlements in the Pale, of Eastern Europe, in the eighteenth and nineteenth centuries, had all Jewish fire brigades.

In Nachod, North East Bohemia, at the Decin synagogue museum, are two preserved leather waterskins from 1781, bearing a Hebrew inscription, 'Kehilla Kedosha Nachod' (the Holy Community of Nachod), and were used by the Jewish Fire Brigade of the ghetto.

In Sofia, Bulgaria, in the 1870s, the Jews founded their own fire brigade.

In South Central Santiago (Chile), the 'Bomba Israel' is an all-Jewish Fire Brigade Station since 1954, and it flies the Israeli flag on its engines.

On 9/11 in New York, the following Jewish firemen were killed: Steve Belson; Alec Feinberg; David Weiss. Paul Tauber survived and the Jewish chaplain to the NYFD is Fireman Rabbi Joseph Potashnik. Around the year 2000, there were 400 Jewish firemen in New York City, and in the 1950s there was a Jewish Fireman club in New York.

Notes

1. 25 April 1941, p.6.
2. In Helen Fry's book *The King's Most Loyal Enemy Aliens* (London: Sutton, 2007) she points out that the whole of 87 Pioneer Company were drafted in as Firewatchers in March 1941 in Liverpool, over 200 men. These included Colin Anson, aka Ascher, and Karl Billman, aka Bartlett, German Jewish refugees who later served in the famous No. 3 ('Jewish') troop, No. 10 Commando. Virtually all of 87 Company were Jewish.
3. From research and a talk written by Stephanie Maltman.
4. *JC*, 18 April 1941, p.12.
5. *JC*, 10 January 1941, p.11.
6. Using Jewish taxi drivers, especially in London, to use their taxis as towing vehicles, and as engine drivers, was common, as they, of course, had 'the Knowledge' of the speediest routes to take to fires, particularly in the blackout and when thoroughfares were blocked by debris and alternative ways had to be found.
7. London Metropolitan Archives, LFB Registers LFB/WAR/4 series references.
8. Google on Anna Wolkoff to see a photograph of her in AFS uniform. Another character was Adelbert H. Krugolski a London fireman detained by MI5 in October 1939 as a suspected Nazi sympathizer. He was British by birth but lived most of his life in Germany, and with a German mother, he had been leader of the Hitler Youth branch in England. He was later released as 'harmless' and there is a file on him at TNA: information taken from A.W. Brian Simpson, *In the Highest Degree Odious: Detention without Trial in Wartime Britain* (Oxford: Clarendon Press, 1992), p.74. Yet another prominent fascist serving in the fire brigade was Brigadier R.D. Blakeney (pp.116–17).
9. (London: Robert Hale, 1941); the film *Fires Were Started* is based on this work. See Appendix 2.
10. V. Flint, *The Bells Go Down* (London: Methuen, 1942), p.35.
11. Ibid., p 9.
12. Interview with Stephanie Maltman, 1 March 2006; see Appendix 2.
13. Sally Holloway, *Courage High: A History of Firefighting in London* (London: HMSO, 1992) p.46.
14. Simpson, *In the Highest Degree Odious*, pp.219–20.
15. Michael Wassey, *Ordeal by Fire* (London: Secker and Warburg, 1941).
16. Stephen Spender, *World Within World* (London: Hamish Hamilton, 1951), pp.270–1.
17. Many Jewish men had been boxers in their youth clubs and could give good account of themselves.
18. *JC*, 24 May 1940, p.17, and see Appendix 3 too.
19. *JC*, 24 January 1941, p.5.
20. *JC*, 3 October 1941, p.4.
21. *JC*, 9 January 1942, p.9.
22. *JC*, 1 May 1942, p.5.
23. Email to author, 12 August 2007.
24. Morris had left the mess hall to bring some *kierchels* (Jewish-style biscuits, sent by his sister Ginnie from London) to share with his fellow firemen. By pure chance, it was while he was out of the room that the bomb fell, killing his friends.
25. *JC*, 25 October 1940, p.14.
26. *JC*, 20 November 1942, p.10.
27. *JC*, 27 September 1941, p.1.
28. Interview, Stephanie Maltman with McDuell's son.
29. *JC*, 17 October 1941, p.22; 31 October 1941, p.18, and Colin Smith, *England's Last War Against France* (London: Weidenfeld & Nicolson, 2009), p.214.
30. There are two lists: Jewish Civilian Casualties in Stepney; and in areas outside Stepney.
31. *JC* 28 March 1941, p.4.
32. Peter Leighton-Langer, *The King's Own Loyal Enemy Aliens* (London: Vallentine Mitchell, 2006).

More Than Just A Few:
Jewish Pilots and Aircrew in the Battle of Britain

Introduction

No attempt has ever been made to describe the part played by Jewish aircrew in the Battle of Britain during that distant, hot summer of 1940. The genteel anti-Semitism of the British 'Establishment' – and that of other western societies – has always been subtly keen, at best, to play down, and at worst to ignore completely, any Jewish contribution. At the same time this lends understated credibility to the comments of those such as author Roald Dahl, who alleged he 'never saw a Jew in the front line'.

It seems to me, therefore, that this all bestows a great responsibility on Jewish historians to dispel these racist myths and prove beyond any doubt, through careful, sourced research, that Jews in Britain and other nations have always participated in the defence of the countries wherever they have lived, and always out of proportion to their numbers in the general population.

The Allied victory in the Battle of Britain was a major turning point in the Second World War. The RAF, assisted by Allied squadrons from other nations, defeated the might of a numerically far superior German Luftwaffe in an air battle that lasted (as officially defined) from 10 July to 31 October 1940. As a result, Hitler indefinitely postponed his planned invasion of Britain because he and his High Command understood that without control of the air, German losses in a seaborne and air invasion would have meant unacceptably high casualties and probable failure. This decision changed the course of the war as Churchill's 'Few' held back the tide so that Britain and its Allies could fight another day, and ultimately win the struggle. Participation in the Battle of Britain by 2,917 Allied men of seventy-one squadrons or units is defined as being awarded the Battle of Britain clasp (worn on the 1939–45 Star – or a silver-gilt rosette if medal ribbons only are worn) for having flown operationally at least one authorized sortie with an eligible unit of RAF Fighter Command, Coastal Command or the Fleet Air Arm, as a pilot or aircrew, between 10 July and 31 October 1940. Of the Allied participants (see Table 1 for the breakdown by nation), 544 were killed and a further 794 were killed before the war's end.[1]

Table 1

Great Britain	2,333
Poland	145
New Zealand	126
Canada	98
Czechoslovakia	88
Australia	33
Belgium	29
South Africa	25
France	13
USA	11
Ireland	10
Rhodesia	3
Israel	1
Jamaica	1
Newfoundland	1

Using Wynn's data (note 1), the participation of thirty-four definite Jewish airmen among the 'Few' is undoubtedly a large proportion (1.2 per cent overall and 1.1 per cent of the British contingent) compared to our numbers in the general population of Britain, which was, more or less as now, under 0.5 per cent. This is all the more amazing, because it is well known that most of the pilots of the RAF at the time were pre-war regular, commissioned officers, or NCOs who had been aircraft apprentices, tradesmen or non-pilot aircrew. As Jews have traditionally rarely served in peacetime regular military units to follow military careers, there was and is, therefore, an already in-built numerical bias against Jewish numbers participating, before one even attempts any analysis of any figures.[2]

Flying also were men of the Auxiliary Air Force (AAF), the Royal Air Force Volunteer Reserve (RAFVR) and University Air Squadrons – mobilized shortly before the outbreak of war – most of whom were spare-time 'weekend' fliers. Again, few Jews in a predominantly working-class Jewish community at that time would have had the financial resources to spend time learning to fly and undertaking the expensive associated outlay, and in addition, far fewer Jews were then at university or the public or grammar schools – unlike today – to take advantage of the opportunities to fly even if they could find the financial resources. A generally lower level of formal education in the sciences and mathematics in the Jewish male population of enlistment age – owing to the social conditions of the Jewish community in Britain at the time – was also an obstacle at interviews for the RAF and RAFVR pilot training, which then, as now, was more technologically demanding than that required for entry into the more ordinary non-flying trades of the army and navy.

After the Battle of Britain, when conscription for all the armed forces really got under way, thousands of Jews volunteered for the RAF, and even those with only very basic schooling could get onto flying courses – if fit – so long as they showed what was then called an aptitude for learning. But in 1940, the core of the RAF/RAFVR pilot elite were basically highly educated middle- and upper-middle-class non-Jews – rather like an exclusive club where everybody knew everybody else – among whose ranks Jews were disproportionately poorly represented. The same can be said of Jewish representation among the Australian, New Zealand, South African and Canadian contingents.

Concerning the large (5 per cent) Polish contribution to the Allied pilots of the Battle, there are other more sinister issues surrounding the lower Jewish participation. Blatant anti-Semitism can be added to the class and education barriers explained above, and made it particularly difficult for Jews to get into the Polish Air Force, or indeed obtain a commission in any of the Polish Forces at that time. There were of course Jewish officers as well as thousands of Polish Jewish other ranks in all the Polish Forces in 1939, but promotion and entry to the more glamorous positions such as flying was excessively difficult for Polish Jews. Added to this, we must be clear that many Polish Jews hid their religious affiliation on enlistment and changed their names as well (both because of Polish anti-Semitism – and German, if they were captured) so that even searching through records of religious denomination gives no real picture of which Polish pilots were Jewish; in effect, we will never know.

The same may be said of the French (0.03 per cent of the Allied pilots), Czech (3 per cent) and Belgian (0.1 per cent) Air Forces. But these matters are difficult to prove, although based on the well-known general discrimination that existed against Jews in most, if not all, European countries, at all levels, at that time and especially in the armed forces.

Benjamin Meirtchak's seminal work on Polish Jewish casualties[3] is an amazing contribution to our generally known high level of Jewish participation in the Polish forces – but it is also just that – casualties only – and so missing are all the Jewish Polish pilots who had survived the battle.

Given all these factors it is even more remarkable that so many Jewish airmen have been identified by this research as being in the front line of pilots and aircrew in the Battle of Britain.

The author's research, however, at the Imperial War Museum Library in Lambeth, uncovered another and official study – *The Battle of Britain Roll of Honour*, published by the Air Ministry in 1947, of those who were killed during the battle or who died of wounds later. Here were found more Jewish names not published in Wynn's book – either because the ministry used a different definition of the timescale of the battle, or a different definition of the term 'operational flight' or both – and also

5.1 Battle of Britain RAF pilot Wing Commander Eustace Holden.

5.2 Battle of Britain Polish RAF Pilot Officer Zygmunt Klein, killed in action November 1940.

included were the names of a large number of Bomber Command and Coastal Command crew killed in action but not included by Wynn in his study. There is by no means universal agreement among historians about either the dates of the battle or the squadrons that took part. Again, this Air Ministry list contains only those killed and so excludes many more who took part, but survived. If these Air Ministry names are included, then the percentage participation of Jewish pilots and aircrew is greater still. I discovered ten Jewish men (plus one – Bardega – not in either source) out of an approximate 1,000 names *not* included by Wynn – a 1 per cent participation – which, as the figures above show, is a higher than proportionate representation from the British Jewish community by a factor of two at least. The names of these men I have indicated in the text as 'Air Ministry Roll'. Clearly the forty-six Jewish aircrew still make up 1.2 per cent of the new 3,917 participants – again over twice the Jewish numbers in the general population .

But the problem is further compounded by other lists in two books: F. Mason, *Battle over Britain* (London: Alban Books, 1969) – which states the period of the battle as having started on 1 July – and a further study by J. Foreman, *Battle of Britain: The Forgotten Months, November to December 1940* (London: Air Research Publications, 1988). Foreman includes even more men, declaring that the dates fixed by the RAF are incorrect and are relevant only to those entitled to wear the Battle of Britain clasp. He argues, convincingly, that the scale of the fighting on some days in November and December 1940 exceeded some of the worst days of the summer period.

Sources

The main details came from scanning the almost 3,000 biographical entries in the 595 pages of Wynn's mammoth and groundbreaking research (see note 1). These were all cross-checked for the British personnel (2,333) against the Jewish Chaplain Cards held at the AJEX (Association of Jewish Ex-Servicemen and Women) Military Museum in Hendon, London, to reveal the British Jewish airmen who took part.

Having extracted and listed alphabetically all the non-British men (full name and number) by nationality (583 entries) I sent these to RAF Innsworth,[4] where the staff untiringly – in three major sessions – looked up the religious denomination of each man. It is somewhat disturbing, however, that Innsworth's records showed Nelson (RCAF), van Mentz (SAAF) and Mamedoff (USA) as Church of England when my searches found conclusively that they were Jews (see their entries below). Also, the Polish Jewish pilot Klein is shown as Catholic, in Innsworth's records.

The Jewish Chaplain Cards added further fine detail about the men, as did information from Commonwealth War Graves Commission registers, available on their website. Issues of the *Jewish Chronicle* for the period 1940–46 were also closely scanned and revealed further pilots' names and personal details; the AJEX cards are not a complete record of all the Jewish military personnel.

Information on three of the Czech Jewish fliers came from a website: math.fce.vutbr.cz/safarik/ACES1/ww2-commonwealth-jewish.html.

Henry Morris's books[5] contain the names of those killed which were extracted from the Jewish Chaplain Cards, but also include those names submitted during his survey, by surviving relatives of those who were killed but who did not necessarily have Jewish Chaplain Cards made out for them, for a variety of reasons. Thus names of those who did *not* have cards have been found in Morris's books – thus these books are often a separate source of names of Jewish personnel killed.

The Jewish RAF participants in the Battle of Britain[6]

116515 Cyril Stanley 'Bam'[7] Bamberger was a sergeant pilot of Jewish origin (telephone conversation with author), later squadron leader, of 610 and 41 Squadrons. Born in Port Sunlight on 4 May 1919, he joined the RAFVR in 1938. He shot down two Me (Messerschmitt) 109s in his Spitfire (at Hawarden and Hornchurch). Later (in 1941) he volunteered for Malta and shot down two Ju (Junkers) 87s. He was commissioned in 1942 and then volunteered for North Africa and shot down another Ju 87 (Sicily) and damaged another (Italy, 1943) and was awarded the DFC on 28 September 1943. In Italy he shot down a further Me 109 and damaged another. On 3 July 1945 he was awarded a Bar to his DFC, by the king at Buckingham Palace. He served in RAF Intelligence during the Korean War. His Jewish Chaplain Card mentions an article on him in the *Jewish Chronicle*, 24 September 1943. Cyril featured in a Channel 4 television programme in 2002, on the Spitfire as weapon of the Second World War, and another Channel 4 programme in January 2004, 'Spitfire Ace'.

58063/46170 Pilot Officer, later Squadron Leader, Ben Bardega lived at 20 Cheyne Walk, London NW4 (AJEX Card). He joined the RAF in February 1939, No. 50 Squadron and was awarded the DFM on 14 September 1940 (*The Times*). He died on 25 May 1958 and is buried at Golders Green. He is not included in Wynn's book.

581137 Sergeant Alfred James Baum (Air Ministry Roll) was a sergeant observer in 49 Squadron. He was killed in action on 11 August 1940 and is buried at Reichswald, grave 30-B-7. No more is known about him; he is not mentioned in Morris and an AJEX card has not been found. However, his name is inscribed on a memorial to Jewish personnel from the north-east of England, killed in the Second World War.

751790 Louis Lionel Benjamin was a sergeant observer in 53 Squadron Coastal Command RAFVR (Air Ministry Roll) and his AJEX card says he volunteered on 6 June 1939. He was stationed at Hamble, Hampshire. He was son of Hyam and Bessie; his wife was Elizabeth ('Betty') and lived at 170 Cotsbach Rd, Clapton, London E5, formerly at 4 Cavendish Mansions, Mill Lane, London NW6. He is named in Morris and was officially reported by the RAF as missing, killed in action, aged 22, on 31 August 1940, and in the *Jewish Chronicle* on 28 March 1941. The *Jewish Chronicle* also published a letter on 30 September 1949 from Arthur Levy about there being a cross on his grave (plot LL-2-5); this was being referred to the War Graves Commission at Crosswijk, Rotterdam, by the Jewish chaplains.

44271 David Henry Davis, AFM, MiD February 1938, North West Frontier, India (Air Ministry Roll), was pilot officer/observer with 59 Squadron Coastal Command and was killed in action on 1 August 1940, aged 27. He was son of Albert Edward and Harriette Bertha of Thorn House, Smarden in Kent, and he is buried at St Valery-en-Caux, grave A-B. His name appears in Morris and his Jewish Chaplain Card states that his death was notified to the *Jewish Chronicle* on 5 February 1941 and published on 14 February 1941. David was a regular and had joined the RAF as LAC 562061 in 1928; he served at RAF Kohart, North-West Frontier, India, during the 1930s. Mrs A.E. Davis (his mother?) lived at 19 Haven Green, Ealing, London W5, previously at 46 West End Lane, London NW6. His card shows he attended many functions for Jewish personnel between 1928 and 1939, both at home and abroad. By 1940 he was with 59 Squadron flying missions with the BEF in France and had attended No. 1 Observer School, Northcoates, near Grimsby.

123055/759128 Frank Samuel Day was a sergeant observer in 248 Squadron and came from Chesham, Bucks. He fought throughout the campaign and was commissioned in May 1942, but was killed in action on 24 July 1942 with 86 Squadron, aged 28. He was the son of Nathaniel and Rika, and is buried at St Illogan churchyard, Cornwall, row 1, grave 20. He had been one of plastic surgeon Archibald McIndoe's 'guinea pigs'. His name is in Morris but there is no AJEX card for him.

79166 John Lionel De Keyser (Air Ministry Roll) was a pilot officer with 206 Squadron RAFVR, Coastal Command. His AJEX card says he was a former member of Stepney Jewish Boys' Club and his name occurs in Morris. He was killed in action on 15 October 1940, aged 25, and his name is inscribed on the Runnymede memorial on panel 8. He was the son of William and Asneth, of Johannesburg, South Africa. His death was announced in *The Stepnian* club journal in August 1941 and in the *Jewish Chronicle*, 13 February 1940.

81887 Pilot Officer Emil Fechtner, Czech 310 Squadron,[8] was born on 16 September 1916. He escaped the Czech Air Force on 15 March 1939 and joined the Foreign Legion in France. In September 1939 he was seconded to French L'Armée de l'Air and later escaped to England after France fell. He was posted to Duxford to form the Czech 310 Squadron on 12 July 1940. He crashed in an accident on 1 August, and on 15 August landed after a collision at Upwood. On 26 August he shot down a 110 and on 31 August a Do (Dornier) 215 in a Hurricane V3889, which was damaged. On 3 September he shot down a 110 and on 18 September a Do 215. He was awarded a DFC in October 1940 but sadly was killed in a crash-landing at Duxford in the same month, on 29 October, after a collision with Pilot Officer J.M. Maly. He was buried at Brookwood. Information on Jewish background is from the website math.fce.vutbr.cz/safarik/ACES1/ww2-commonwealth-jewish.html.

42598 George Ernest Goodman was pilot officer, later flying officer in No. 1 Squadron. His story is exceptional as he was born in Haifa, Israel, on 8 October 1920, though he may not have been Jewish. Wynn says he was British solely because he had a British passport – like most born under the Mandate – but he was in fact an Israeli sabra and the only Israeli in the Battle of Britain. RAF Museum researcher John Edwards testifies to these facts in an article in the *London Jewish News*, 22 September 2000, by reporter John Kaye.[9] Furthermore, in Mason's book,[10] Goodman is described as Palestinian (p.506); in another book[11] as Israeli, and yet another[12] also as Israeli. The author also has in his possession an official copy of Goodman's birth certificate, all in Hebrew, from the Haifa municipality in Israel and now kept at the AJEX Museum.[13] Educated at Highgate school he was the son of Sydney and Bida Goodman. He was in the OTC and took a commission in the RAF in early 1939, joining his Hurricane Squadron in France in March 1940, where he shared a kill of an He (Heinkel) 111 and shot down another later which had helped sink the SS *Lancastria* off St Nazaire. Later, flying from Northolt, he shot down an Me 109, shared in another, shot down an He 111, shared a Do 17 and shot down another 110. On 18 August he was hit in his Hurricane P3757 but managed to land safely.[14] On 6 September 1940 he shot down another 110 but was himself shot down, baling out with an injury. His plane crashed at Brownings Farm, Chiddingstone Causeway. He later shared a Ju 88, damaged a Do 17 and was awarded the DFC on 26 November 1940.

Also in November 1940 he flew the ferry route for the Middle East with 73 Squadron and stopped at Lagos where his parents were working in the diplomatic service. He saw his mother for the last time (his father was away) and as the squadron later flew out, they did a roll over the Goodman home and then were away.

In February 1941 he shot down a CR.42 in the Western Desert, and a 110 at Tobruk, but he was shot down and crash-landed behind the British lines. He then shared an Hs (Henschel) 126, destroyed a Ju 87 and shared another, all over Tobruk. In April he took leave in Haifa, Israel, with his two sisters, but on 14 June 1941 he was shot down and killed by flak over Gazala. He is buried in Knightsbridge Cemetery, Acroma, Libya, grave 10.C.21.[15]

135476 Maurice Venning Goodman was a sergeant air gunner with 604 Squadron, later flight lieutenant, born in Hendon on 13 April 1920. Educated at King's School, Colindale, he joined the AAF and was called up at the outbreak of war. He served on air operations throughout the Battle of Britain and then in 1942 on special operations over Germany, severely damaging a 110. He served on special operations in North Africa and Italy and was awarded the DFC on 12 November 1943. He died in 1988. His Jewish Chaplain Card mentions an article on him in the *Jewish Chronicle*, 12 November 1943.

81945 Pilot Officer Vilem Goth, Czech 310 and 501 Squadrons,[16] was born on 22 April 1915 and joined 310 Squadron at Duxford, 10 July 1940. On 7 September he shot down two 110s over Southend but his Hurricane V6643 was damaged, forcing him to land at Whitmans Farm, Purleigh. He joined 501 Squadron at Kenley in October 1940 and sadly was killed on 25 October when he collided with Pilot Officer K.W. Mackenzie during combat over Tenterden, crashing in Hurricane 2903 in Bridgehurst Wood, Marden. He is buried at Sittingbourne and Milton Cemetery, Kent. Information on his Jewish background is from the same website as Fechtner (listed above).

78684 Eric Stewart Issacson Hallows (Air Ministry Roll) was a pilot officer in 99 Squadron Bomber Command. His AJEX card says he was first with 79 Squadron and had been stationed at Harwell, Didcot and Mildenhall. He was the husband of M. Hallows, of Russley, Wood, Ditton Rd, Newmarket. He was killed in action on 30 October 1940 and buried at Willesden Jewish Cemetery in London in grave FX-13-554. His AJEX card states that the *Jewish Chronicle* was notified on 1 November 1940 and announced his death on 8 November, also stating that he was buried on 4 November; his funeral was officiated by Reverend Gollomb, HCF. He is named in Morris's book.

37970 Eustace 'Gus' Holden was a flight lieutenant/pilot, later wing commander with 501 Squadron. Born in Doncaster on 28 December 1912, he was commissioned in the RAF in 1936. In May 1940 in France he shot down a Ju 88, a Do 7 and an He 111. Later, flying from Croydon, he damaged a Do 17 but was himself wounded on 22 July. He was awarded the DFC on 16 August 1940. In September and October he shot down two 109s, a 110, two more 109s, damaged a Ju 88 and two more 109s. As CO of 501 Squadron, he took them to West Africa in June 1941 and then became a staff officer (Fighter Training) at the Air Ministry. In 1944 he was posted to HQ Far East, Kandy, staying in the RAF until 1964. His Jewish Chaplain Card mentions his being based at Tokoradi, and seeing Senior Jewish Chaplain Rabbi Brodie.[17]

90705 Kenneth Holden, the older brother of Eustace (see above), was a flying officer/pilot, later wing commander with 616 Squadron. He and Eustace were the only Jewish brothers who flew in the battle. He joined the AAF in 1939 and was called up at the outbreak of war. Between 28 May and 1 June 1940 over Dunkirk he shot down three 109s and in September damaged two more and shot down another. In May 1941 he was made squadron leader and later shot down three more 109s, damaged a further two and shared another. Awarded the DFC on 15 July 1941, he later moved to Staff HQ of 12 Group. Retired from the RAF in 1950, he died in 1991. No Jewish Chaplain Card seems to have been written for him.

748158 Lewis Reginald Isaac was a sergeant pilot with 64 Squadron, from Llanelli, South Wales, the son of James and Blodwen. He joined the RAFVR in May 1939 and fought throughout the battle. Sadly, he failed to return from a Channel sortie in his Spitfire L1029 after a surprise attack on his airfield on 5 August 1940. He had been shot down by an Me 109 off Folkestone at 0850hrs. He was 24 years old. He is remembered at Runnymede, panel 15. His loss is mentioned in the *Jewish Chronicle*, 25 April 1941, but no Jewish Chaplain Card appears to exist for him, although he is in Morris's book.

78685 Henry 'Jake' Jacobs was a pilot officer/air gunner and later squadron leader with 219 and 600 Squadron. He was born on 15 April 1907 in Great Yarmouth. In September 1940 he shot down a Ju 88, and in 1942 shot down two more Ju 88s and damaged another. He was awarded the DFC on 9 October 1942 (*Jewish Chronicle*, 16 October 1942). In 1943 he shot down three 110s, a Do 217 and a 110, and damaged a Ju 88. He was awarded a Bar to his DFC on 5 November 1943 (*Jewish Chronicle*, 26 November 1943) and AFC on 3 April 1945. He retired from the RAF in 1958 and died in 1978. His Jewish Chaplain Card states that his parents were Mr and Mrs J. Jacobs of The Cottage, Hingham, Norfolk, and that he met several Jewish chaplains in his post-war career. His DFC citation says: 'for valuable service rendered as chief signals instructor of 264 Squadron, Duxford; has destroyed two enemy aircraft – a source of inspiration to his men'. The citation for his bar says: 'has helped destroy six enemy aircraft; he is a model of efficiency'.[18]

1050704 Norman Jacobson was from Grimsby, and was an AC2 radio operator with 29 Squadron. He joined the RAF in June 1940 and was in an aircraft which shot down an He 111 in August. But on 25 August his Blenheim was shot down near Wainfleet and the crew were all killed. Jacobson was just 18 years old – the youngest Jewish Battle of Britain casualty[19] – and although his body was recovered by a trawler (*Alfredian*) near the Inner Dowsing, he was buried at sea on 27 August and his name is engraved on the Runnymede memorial, panel 27. He was the son of Alfred and Olive Jacobson.[20]

85010 Arthur Harold Evans Kahn was a pilot officer, later flight lieutenant observer, with 248 Squadron. Born in Sutton, Surrey, he joined the RAFVR in May 1939 and fought throughout the battle. He was killed in action on 15 June 1944 with 172 Squadron, aged 25, son of Joseph and Mai and husband of Helen Margaret. His name is inscribed on the Runnymede memorial, panel 202, and he is in Morris's book.[21]

787527 Sergeant Pilot Oldrich Kestler, Czech 111 Squadron[22] was born in Cizice on 18 March 1920, and joined 111 at Dyce on 19 October 1940. He joined 605 Squadron and on 7 April 1941 he collided in Hurricane Z318 with Spitfire P 8315 (Sergeant Martinec, Czech); both pilots were killed. He was awarded the Czech Military Cross, and was buried at Market Drayton, Shropshire. Jewish background information is from same website as Fechtner (listed above).

780685 Zygmunt 'Joe' Klein[23] was a sergeant pilot with Polish 234 and 152 Squadrons.[24] He was born on 24 August 1918 and joined the RAF in February 1940. He joined 234 Squadron at St Eval on 6 August 1940 and was later at Warmwell with 152 Squadron. He shot down one 109 and shared a 110 and damaged another 110. He crash-landed in Spitfire P9427 out of fuel near Torquay on 26 November 1940. In a Channel 4 television programme, 'Spitfire Ace', televised on 19 January 2004, LAC Joe Roddis described how his groundcrew most admired the Polish flyers, as they were determined to kill Germans, not just shoot down aircraft; their country was occupied and they hated the enemy with a vengeance. He named Klein as one of the bravest and described how on one very foggy day they were all ordered to be grounded. But Klein heard a German aircraft patrolling over the aerodrome and against orders took off and brought it down in very dangerous flying conditions. He was declared missing on 28 November, believed killed in action in his Spitfire in the Isle of Wight area, by 109s. His name is inscribed on the Polish Air Force memorial at Northolt.

118438/903367/902927 Lennert Axel/Aexel Komaroff was sergeant air gunner with 141 Squadron, flying Defiants and Beaufighters. With Flying

Officer I.H. Cosby he shot down a Ju 88 south of the Isle of Wight on 25 August 1941. Flying throughout the battle, he was commissioned in March 1942. He was killed on 19 September 1944, flying Mosquitoes with 29 Squadron, aged 26. He was the husband of Helen Komaroff of Prestwick and is buried at Bergen-op-Zoom, Holland, in grave 28.A.2. He is named in Morris's book and his AJEX card states that he had previously been wounded in action. Born in Shanghai in 1917, son of Charles and Elsa, sister of Ada.

77345/746721 Marcus Kramer was a pilot officer with 600 Squadron. A pharmacist from Thorpe Bay, Essex, he was born in Bermondsey in 1911, son of Mr and Mrs Emmanuel Kramer of 3 Marine Parade, Southend-on-Sea.[25] He was active in the local Jewish Community. He joined the RAFVR in March 1939, and was commissioned in February 1940. On 10 May 1940 he flew as gunner with Pilot Officer R.C. Haine with six Blenheims on an attack on Rotterdam (Waalhaven) aerodrome, just captured by German paratroops that morning. After the attack they were shot down by 110s but he evaded capture and was evacuated with his crew by the RN. He was awarded the DFC on 9 July 1940 (*Jewish Chronicle*, 15 May 1942, p.3, and his AJEX card), but he was killed in action on 21 May 1941 with 29 Squadron, aged 29. His name is on the Runnymede memorial, panel 29. His AJEX card states that the Jewish chaplains wrote to the father, who replied that 'his plane was seen to crash into the River Severn near Chepstow and his tunic was washed up almost immediately'; he was therefore believed to be dead. It also says that *The Times* reported his death on 31 December 1941.

83269/54454 Emanuel Barnett Lyons was pilot officer/flight lieutenant with 65 Squadron, born in London in 1918. He joined the RAFVR in June 1939, from Magdalene College, Cambridge,[26] fighting throughout the battle. He was later posted to North Africa in support of the 1st Army. In 1944 he fought in many air battles in Europe, being wounded in April 1945. He was awarded the DFC on 8 May 1945 and the Netherlands Flying Cross on 21 April 1947, for gallantry, when some of his squadron included Dutch pilots. His AJEX card shows he was the son of Mrs R. Lyons, c/o E. Barnett and Co., 27–83 Middlesex St, London E1 and 38 South Lodge, Circus Rd, London NW8. There were articles about him in the *Jewish Chronicle*, 10 March 1945 and 9 June 1947. He died in 1992.

81621 Andrew 'Andy' B. Mamedoff was a pilot officer from the USA, with 609 Squadron. An American researcher has confirmed with AJEX that he was Jewish,[27] son of Natalie and husband of Alys, née Craven, of London. He was born on 24 August 1912, and brought up in Thompson,

Connecticut. He performed in air shows and at outbreak of war he tried to fight with the Finnish Air Force and later the French Air Force, but failed and had to stowaway to the UK where he was given an emergency commission in the RAF and sent to a Spitfire squadron on 8 August 1940 with two other Americans he had met in France. They became the first three members of 71 Eagle Squadron, USA Volunteers, fighting throughout the battle. On a flight to a posting in Northern Ireland on 8 October 1941, he failed to arrive and his body was later recovered for burial at Brookwood Cemetery, grave 21.A.7.

39675 William 'Bill'[28] **Henry Nelson** was flying officer with 24 Squadron, born in Montreal, Canada on 2 April 1917, son of Henry and Sarafina Nelson of 4885 Cote St, Catherine Road. He was educated at Baron Byng High and Strathcona Academy and joined the RAF in 1937 after working his way to England. On 8/9 September 1939 he took part as captain of a bomber in the RAF's earliest operation, with 8 Whitleys dropping leaflets in north-west Germany. After other operations he also took part in raids on Sylt and over Dunkirk during the evacuation. He was awarded the DFC by the king at Buckingham Palace on 4 June 1940, and was the first Canadian Jew decorated in the Second World War.[29] His citation read: 'Nelson carried out many flights over enemy territory, always showing the greatest determination and courage. After one attack on Stavanger, Norway, he encountered a balloon barrage and sent a report to base HQ in time to warn following aircraft.' He wrote home: 'I thank God that I shall be able to help to destroy the regime that persecutes the Jews.'

Volunteering for Fighter Command and returning before his leave expired, he flew Spitfires from Hornchurch, shooting down a 109, a 110 and damaging another 110 on 11 August 1940 when he took on six 109s single-handed;[30] he also damaged a Do 17 on the 13 August and destroyed three more 109s on 17, 27 and 29 October. He was killed on 1 November 1940 by a 109 attack over Dover in a Spitfire P7312 at 1400 hrs; he crashed into the Channel. He was listed as missing on the fifty-second RAF casualty list on 14 November but officially presumed killed on 26 May 1941. He was 23 years old, and left a wife, Marjorie Isobel, and young son, and his name is inscribed on the Runnymede memorial, panel 4. He has a Jewish Chaplain Card.

42076 Reginald Tony Pareezer (Air Ministry Roll) was pilot officer with 204 Squadron Coastal Command and killed on 21 July 1940, aged 21. He was the son of Reginald and Florence of Thorpe, Norfolk, and is remembered at Runnymede on panel 9. He is named in Morris, but no Jewish Chaplain Card was found.

41735 Frederick Hyam/Hyman Posener was pilot officer with 152 Squadron, and joined the RAF from South Africa in December 1938, fighting through the battle and was wounded in action.[31] He was shot down, aged 23, in his Spitfire K9880 at 1635 hrs on 20 July 1940 off Swanage by Luftwaffe Oberlt. Homuth. His name is inscribed on the Runnymede memorial, panel 9. RAF Innsworth records show he was Jewish[32]and his death was announced in the *Jewish Chronicle*, 18 April 1941. His Jewish Chaplain Card says he was the son of J. Posener, POB 504, East London, South Africa.

40138/40404 Roderick Malachi Seaburne Rayner was flying officer/wing commander with 87 Squadron. He was born on 6 January 1918, joined the RAF in 1937 and was in France on the outbreak of war. During the battle he shot down a 110, a 109, a Do 17, another 110 and 109, and shared an He 111. Over the UK he shot down two more 110s but on 23 December 1940 had to bale out of his Hurricane in bad weather near Brize Norton. He was awarded a DFC on 11 February 1941, though his AJEX card says it was gazetted on 30 July 1943. He damaged another unidentified German aircraft in the Gloucester area in April 1941. He died in 1982.

39683 Reginald Frank Rimmer was flying officer with 229 Squadron and son of a First World War pilot. The family were living in Wirral at the outbreak of war. He joined the RAF in 1937 and on 2 June 1940 over Dunkirk damaged an He 111, later destroying a Do17 and sharing another He 111. He was shot down in his Hurricane V6782 T at 1530 hrs and killed by 109s on 27 September 1940 over Franchise Manor Farm, Burwash, aged 21. He is buried at Hoylake Grange, Cheshire (grave D79) and is remembered on a plaque at the farm where he crashed. He was the son of Launcelot and Cecilia of Hoylake. He is named in Morris's book, but there is no AJEX card for him. A photograph of his grave shows a cross, but this was a common error for many Jewish servicemen killed in both world wars where incorrect information was supplied about religious affiliation.[33]

41209 Geoffrey Louis Ritcher was a flying officer/squadron leader with 234 Squadron. He joined the RAF in July 1938, fought throughout the battle and shot down a Do 17 in France. His AJEX card says he graduated from No. 1 Air Observers' School, North Coates, Grimsby.

41472 Jack Rose was a flying officer/wing commander with No. 3, 32 and 232 Squadrons. He was born in London on 18 January 1917, attended Shooter's Hill School and then University College, London (studying science), and joined the RAF in 1938. From Biggin Hill he was sent to France and shot down three enemy aircraft in May 1940. He was shot down in his Hurricane V6547 at 1900 hrs on 25 August by a 109 over the Channel, but was rescued. He was awarded the DFC on 9 October 1942 and commanded 113 Squadron in Burma from November 1944. He was further awarded the MBE and CGM in 1946. His DFC citation says on his AJEX card: 'He has been on operational flying since September 1939. During May 1940, whilst serving with fighters over France, he destroyed three enemy aircraft. Posted to his present unit, he has led squadrons in fifteen sweeps over France. He has displayed courage and devotion to duty and rendered valuable assistance to allied wing commanders.'

900030 Maurice Rose was a sergeant (Air Ministry Roll) in 102 Squadron RAFVR and was killed in action on 29 October 1940. He is in Morris's book and is remembered at Runnymede on panel 19. His AJEX card says he was first in Hut 756, B squad, No. 2 Wing, No. 2 School, Yatesbury, and then at No. 7 Bombing and Gunnery School, Porthcawl. His father was J. Rose of 46 First Avenue, Selby Park, Birmingham.

84970 Francis Herbert Schumer was a pilot officer with 600 Squadron. He was educated at Giggleswick School and Worcester College, Oxford, and a member of the University Air Squadron. He joined the RAFVR in June 1939 as trainee no. 754291 and was commissioned in September 1940. He crash-landed in a Blenheim on 12 September, fought throughout the Battle and was killed in action on 12 July 1941, aged 22. He was cremated at Golders Green Cemetery. His AJEX card names his mother as Mrs J. Schumer, 107 Hodford Rd, London NW11, and his death was notified to the *Jewish Chronicle* on 18 July 1941.

37870 Lionel Harold Schwind was pilot officer with 257, 43 and 213 Squadrons. He joined the RAF in 1936 and was then posted to Iraq, but was flying Hurricanes throughout the Battle of Britain. He was shot down and killed over Gatwick on 27 September 1940 (the same day that Reginald Rimmer died – listed above) in Hurricane N2401 'O' at 0925 hrs, crashing on Wildemesse golf course, Seal, near Sevenoaks, aged 27. He was the son of Lionel and Florence, née Dayton, of Crowborough, Sussex, and the husband of Georgina, née Trueman. He is buried at Crowborough Cemetery, grave 1723. His brother is listed below.

581353 Sergeant Gordon Louis Schwind, RAF, was killed, aged 21, on 26 May 1940 and is buried at Comines-Warneton, Hainaut, Belgium.[34] No AJEX card was found for Lionel or Gordon, but Gordon's name was submitted to Henry Morris, *We Will Remember Them: An Addendum*.[35]

78257 Herbert Ronald Sharman was pilot officer/squadron leader with 248 Squadron. Born in Wood Green, London, on 22 October 1907, he was educated at Trinity County School. He joined the RAFVR in 1939, was commissioned in March 1940 and fought throughout the battle. He then trained in Canada and returned to the UK in 1943 as an instructor in navigation. With 297 Squadron he flew Whitleys, inserting agents into occupied Europe, and then flew VIPs to summit meetings in Casablanca, Tehran and Yalta. From March 1944 he undertook other VIP flights in the Far East and was awarded the AFC on 7 September 1945. He has a Jewish Chaplain Card.

85241 Leslie Mark Sharp was pilot officer with 111 Squadron He was the son of Mr and Mrs M. Sharp of 53 Adelaide Park, Belfast. He joined the RAFVR in August 1939 as trainee no. 758214. Commissioned on 7 September 1940, he flew Hurricanes with 96 and 111 Squadrons. Fighting through the battle he took off on the night of 28 December 1940 and crashed suddenly into the sea one mile offshore. He is buried at Carnmoney Jewish Cemetery, County Antrim. He has an AJEX card, and his photograph and the announcement of his death are in the *Jewish Chronicle*, 10 January 1941.

563391 William Gerald Silver was sergeant pilot with 152 Squadron. He was educated at Portsmouth Technical School and joined the RAF in 1929, flying Spitfires throughout the battle. On 25 September 1940 he did not return from a dogfight over the Portsmouth area in Spitfire P9463 at 1115 hrs, and is buried at Milton Road Cemetery, Portsmouth, plot U, row 23a, grave 13. He was 27 years old.[36]

79731/742006 Neville David Solomon was pilot officer with 29 and 17 Squadrons and joined the RAFVR in September 1938. He was commissioned in September 1939. Flying Blenheims, he then converted to Hurricanes, flying both types throughout the battle. He was reported missing on 18 August in Hurricane L1921, at 1.05 p.m.[37] after a dogfight with 109s off Dover when he had crashed into the sea. The incident is described in *The Hardest Day*.[38] He is buried at Pihen-les-Guines, Calais, France, row A, grave 4. He was the son of Lieutenant Colonel Archibald Baron Solomon and Ethel Betsy of 69 Woodbourne Rd, Edgbaston, Birmingham and 3 Livery St, Birmingham. His Jewish Chaplain Card states that when reported missing in action, condolences letters were sent to his family on 23 September 1940 and again on 10 February 1941, and it was reported in the *Jewish Chronicle* on 29 September 1940 (the same day as Wilk – listed below) as well as mentioned in *The Times*. The Jewish Chaplaincy continued correspondence with his father until June 1948. A photograph of him is in the *Jewish Chronicle*, 3 May 1940, noting his serving in the RAF.

749478 Aubrey H. Spiers was sergeant wireless operator/air gunner/wing officer with 236 Squadron and had joined the RAFVR in May 1939. He flew twenty-one sorties throughout the battle. No further information was found on his AJEX card. He died in 1988.

37306 Robert Roland Stanford Tuck was known as 'Lucky Tuck'[39] and was flight lieutenant/wing commander with 92 and 257 Squadrons. He was born in Catford, south London, on 1 July 1916, son of Captain Stanley Lewis Tuck (captain in Royal West Surreys in the First World War) and Ethel Clara, and educated at St Dunstan's College, Reading. He was at sea for two years as a cadet and then joined the RAF in 1935. Whilst training at Grantham, he was almost killed in a mid-air collision caused by turbulence[40] and he had to bale out, severely scarring his face. At Duxford in 1938 he became one of the RAF's first Spitfire qualified pilots.

As a flight commander, over Dunkirk on 23 May 1940 in his Spitfire, he shot down three 110s and a 109; on 24 May two Do 17s; on 25 May he shared a Do 17; on 2 June a 109 and an He 111, and two 109s damaged. He was wounded in this incident. His squadron leader at this time was Roger Bushell – of *Great Escape* fame – whom he later met again at Sagan camp after capture. When Bushell was shot down over Dunkirk, Tuck took over as squadron leader. Tuck was awarded the DFC on 11 June 1940, by the king at a special ceremony at Hornchurch, for 'initiative and personal example over Dunkirk'.

He continued shooting the enemy out of the sky, sharing a Do 17 on 8 July, damaging a Ju 88 on the 25 July, sharing a Ju 88 on 13 August, destroying two Ju 88s on the 14 August and two on the 18 August – but he was shot down that day, baling out with an injury over Horsmonden (his Spitfire crashing at Tuck's Cottages, Park Farm) on the estate of Lord Cornwallis – who then invited him to tea.

On 25 August he shot down another Do 17 but his plane was shot up and he glided fifteen miles to the coast with a dead engine off St Gowan's Head, and crash-landed. On 11 September, commanding 257 Squadron, he shot down a 110 and a 109; on 23 September a 109; on 4 October a Ju 88; on 12 October a 109; on the 25 October another 109, and two damaged; and on 28 October two more 109s. He was awarded a Bar to the DFC on 25 October 1940, *The Times* stating that 'In the face of constant death he preserved a lightness of heart which was not simply bravura but allied to precise and ruthlessly applied technical skill.'

On 19 December, now flying Hurricanes, he shot down another Do 17; on 12 December a 109; on 29 December a Do 17. He was awarded the DSO on 7 January 1941 'for leading 257 Squadron with great success ... his outstanding leadership, courage and skill have been reflected in its high morale and efficiency'. The king awarded the DSO and announced a Second Bar to Tuck on 28 January 1941, and at the same ceremony awarded the DFC to his good friend Brian van Mentz (listed below) – a unique occasion, for two Jewish RAF officers to be decorated together.[41]

He continued: on 2 and 19 March 1941 two more Do 17s; on 9 April a Ju 88; on 27 April he damaged a Ju 88 and on 11 May shot down two more

Ju 88s. He was awarded the Second Bar to DFC on 11 April 1941 'for conspicuous gallantry and initiative in searching for and attacking enemy raiders, often in adverse weather conditions' – he was only the second RAF pilot to win such a distinction.

On 21 June 21 he destroyed two 109s and damaged another, but was himself wounded and shot down in the Channel. He was picked up in his dinghy by a Gravesend coal barge after two hours. As wing leader at Duxford commanding three squadrons, he shot down three more 109s. He was then sent as a liaison officer to the USA with other aces, including 'Sailor' Malan, and then returned to Biggin Hill as a wing leader. On 28 January 1942 he was shot down by flak on a low-level strafing attack outside Boulogne and made a POW. He was interviewed by Adolf Galland and after the war – ironically for a Jewish pilot – made an honorary member of Galland's old German squadron.[42]

In various camps, he helped plan the 'Great Escape' from Sagan but was moved before the breakout.[43] He finally escaped on 1 February 1945 with Flight Lieutenant Kustrzynski, and met up with the Russians and spent two weeks fighting with them. He and Kustrzynski then made their way to the British Embassy in Moscow and were sent to Southampton by ship via Odessa. Tuck was awarded the USA DFC on 14 June 1946.

Tuck was shot down four times, collided twice, was wounded twice, baled out, crash-landed and dunked in the Channel.[44] The *Official History of the RAF*, Vol. 1, states:

> They had that restless spirit of aggression, that passion to be at grips with the enemy, which is the hallmark of the very finest troops. Some – like Bader, Malan and Stanford Tuck – were so fiercely possessed of this demon, and of the skill to survive the danger into which it drew them, that their names were quickly added to the immortal company of Ball, Bishop, Mannock and McCudden.[45]

Tuck is probably the most highly decorated Jewish Second World War pilot after Louis Aarons, VC, DFM. He is credited with thirty kills – one not added until 1982,[46] making him the eighth-ranking ace of the RAF with more victories than any other British pilot.[47] His portrait hangs at Bentley Priory RAF base at Stanmore – Fighter Command HQ in the Second World War – alongside many other Battle of Britain pilots. He died on 5 May 1987, aged 70. His Jewish Chaplain Card mentions an article on him in the *Jewish Chronicle* in January 1941. He was a great friend of Jewish Fighter Pilot Ronnie Austin Jarvis (killed in 1941) and their visit to the home of the Jewish Barnato family is well documented.[48]

70826 Brian van Mentz was flying officer with 222 Squadron. He was born in Johannesburg, South Africa, in 1916, son of Sidney and Rosine and nephew of Samuel Mence of Burghclere, Hampshire. He was commissioned in the South African RAF Reserve in 1937 and the RAF in 1938. In France he shot down a Ju 88 on 14 May 1940, a Ju 87 and an He 126 on 15 May, and damaged two 109s on 16 May. From Hornchurch he shot down a 109 on 31 August; shot down a 110 and damaged another on 3 September; shot down a 109 and shared a Do 17 on 7 September; shot down a Ju 88 and damaged a 109 on 11 September; damaged a Ju 88 on 15 September; shot down a 109 on 23 September; and damaged a 110 on 12 October. He was awarded the DFC on 25 October 1940. The *Jewish Chronicle* report in November says: 'This officer led his section with great skill and courage, and showed great determination in pressing home his attacks against large enemy formations. He has been engaged in flying operations against the enemy since the outbreak of war.' His DFC award was also reported in the *Jewish Chronicle* on 17 January 1941.

On 30 October he damaged a 109 and on 30 November shot down a Do 17. He was decorated by the king at Bircham Newton on 28 January 1941, together with Tuck (see above). On 2 February he shot down a Ju 88, and damaged an He 111, and on 18 March shared a Do 17.

Having flown seventy-five sorties,[49] he was killed on 26 April 1941, aged 24, when a bomb hit the Ferry Inn pub, Coltishall, not half-an-hour after Robert Tuck had left him to go to Norwich for a drive.[50] He is buried at Brookwood Cemetery, Woking, grave 25.A.9. [51] The *Jewish Chronicle* of 17 January 1941 says he was the son of Major van Mentz, adjutant of the Witwatersrand Rifles, killed in action in the First World War.

115547/754595 Jack Weber/Webber was sergeant pilot/flight lieutenant with No. 1 and 145 Squadrons and joined the RAFVR in July 1939. Fighting from Tangmere throughout the battle, he was shot down in his Hurricane by an Me 109 in the afternoon – but survived – over the Isle of Wight on 6 November 1940. Commissioned in 1942 he was Mentioned in Despatches whilst fighting in the Middle East. Whilst protecting Kittyhawk bombers on 15 July, he was shot down and again wounded. He died in 1988. His Jewish Chaplain Card states that his father was Mr J. Weber of 521 Finchley Rd, London NW3 and that he was seen by several chaplains.

76932/78451 Jack Wilk (Air Ministry Roll) was a pilot officer/air gunner with 149 Squadron RAFVR, Bomber Command. His name is in Morris's book and his AJEX card says he was born in 1904 in South Africa and volunteered for the RAF on 30 December 1939. He was at No. 1 Air Armament School, Manby, Lincolnshire and then No. 11 OTU at Bassingbourn. He was killed in action on 17 August 1940, aged 36, son of Abraham and Fairie Wilk, née Mindelsohn, and was a barrister (MA, LLB), living at 73 Westfield Road, Birmingham. His death was announced in the *Jewish Chronicle*, 27 September 1940, and an obituary with photograph says he was a Cambridge graduate who had served in the Civil Air Guard pre-war and was very active in the Birmingham Jewish Community. A second obituary appeared on 4 October 1940. He is buried at Durnbach, Germany, grave 6-H-6.

755989 Israel Winberg was a sergeant with 110 Squadron Bomber Command RAFVR (Air Ministry Roll) and is listed by Morris. His AJEX card says he volunteered on 5 November 1939 and was at Training School 32 in West Hartlepool, followed by Prestwick, Bicester and Wattisham. He was son of Morris and Anna Winburn, aka Winberg, of 11 The Oakes West, Sunderland, and he was killed in action on 24 July 1940, aged 28. His name is inscribed at Runnymede, panel 21. It was reported in *The Times*, 26 March 1941 and the *Jewish Chronicle*, 13 August 1940 and 4 April 1941.

749523 Ian Alexander Zamek was a sergeant with 58 Squadron RAFVR Bomber Command (Air Ministry Roll). He is named in Morris's book and his AJEX card says he volunteered in April 1939 and was at London No. 2 Centre and later at Abingdon.

The son of Mr A. Zamek, 16 Pendennis, Derby Rd, Bournemouth, he was reported as missing, killed in action, by the RAF on 2 October 1940, but deemed officially killed in action on 3 October 1940, aged 22. This was notified to the *Jewish Chronicle* on 18 October 1940 and again on 28 February 1941. He is buried in Berlin CWGC Cemetery, grave 7-K-1to4. His brother Norman Henry was also killed in action in the RAF in 1942 (see note 31).

Probable Jewish RAF Participants in the Battle of Britain

As well as the above men, Wynn's book reveals others who have Jewish names, but whose records show them as enlisted as other denominations. This is especially true of Polish and Czech pilots – for reasons given in the introduction to this article. As I cannot prove religious affiliation, I give below only brief details which the reader may follow up on some of the 'probably Jewish' pilots of the Battle:

76568 Pilot Officer Jack Henry Bachman, 145 Squadron, killed in action 9 April 1943 in Burma.

81884 Pilot Officer/Squadron Leader Vaclav Bergman, 310 Squadron, Czech, DFC, MiD.

111486 Pilot Officer Derrick C. Deuntzer, 79/247 Squadrons.

P1296 Pilot Officer Franciszek Jastrzebski, 302 Squadron, Polish, killed in action, VM, KW with three bars, Croix de Guerre.

745292 Sergeant Pilot Stephen Austin Levenson, British, 611 Squadron, killed in action.

76728 Flight Lieutenant Jan Piotr Pfeiffer, Polish, 32/257 Squadron, killed in action.

78256 Pilot Officer Edward C. Schollar, 248 Squadron.

84299 Flying Officer David Stein, British 263 Squadron, killed in action.

There are many others. Furthermore, in Morris's book,[52] four Polish Jewish pilots are listed as having fought in the battle, but they are not in Wynn's book:

Navigator Ryzrad Bychowski, killed when plane crashed on landing.

Navigator Zygmunt Glass, killed in action over Holland, 1943.

Navigator Rubin Lipszyc, killed in action on the last day of the war when in action over Holland.

Navigator Eljasz Posner, killed in action over the Channel, 1942.

Conclusion

This study is a tribute to the Jewish pilots and aircrew who served and those who died during the Battle of Britain, a momentous struggle that has become almost mythical in its re-telling in many books and films. For those historians with the drive, patience and determination, similar stories can be told of the Jewish contribution for all the epic battles of the Second World War – on land, sea and in the air. Let it never be forgotten.

Summary of Second World War Awards to Jewish Battle of Britain Aircrew

DSO	1
DFC	12
DFC and Bar	2 (2)
DFC and Two Bars	1 (2)
DFM	1
AFC	2
AFM	1
Czech MC	1
Netherlands DFC	1
Polish KW and Bar	1
MBE	1
CGM	1
MiD	2

Acknowledgements

AJEX Jewish Military Museum, London; Staff of the Imperial War

Museum Library, Lambeth, London; Staff of the Tower Hamlets History Library, Stepney, London; Staff at RAF Innsworth, Gloucester.

The author would welcome any further information about the men described below, and especially any information about other Jewish Battle of Britain pilots not named here, by contacting him at AJEX HQ.

Notes

1. K.G. Wynn, *Men of the Battle of Britain* (London: Gliddon, 1999), pp.i–x.
2. In an article in the *Jewish Chronicle*, 22 November 1996, researcher and founder of the Battle of Britain Society, Bill Bond, alleges that 100 Jewish airmen fought in the battle and that some of those are buried at Hoop Lane Jewish Cemetery in Golders Green.
3. See many sources mentioned by the author.
4. RAF Personnel Records in Gloucester.
5. H. Morris, *We Will Remember Them: A Record of the Jews Who Died in the Armed Forces of the Crown 1939–1945* (London: Brassey's 1989) and *We Will Remember Them: An Addendum* (London: AJEX, 1994).
6. These profiles are taken mainly from Wynn, with further information added where indicated.
7. See website on Bamberger, 'RAF Aces'.
8. K.G. Wynn, *Men of the Battle of Britain*, supplementary vol. (London: Gliddon 1992), p.62.
9. AJEX Battle of Britain file, AJEX Museum.
10. See the many sources mentioned above, used by the author.
11. P. Kaplan and R. Collier, *The Few* (London: Blandford, 1989), p.222.
12. 'RAF Personnel in the Battle of Britain', MoD, Imperial War Museum [n.d.]. In R.T Bickers, *The Battle of Britain* (London: Salamander, 1990), the RAF Second World War author, in this official fiftieth anniversary book, describes Goodman as Palestinian on page 197; he is also described as Palestinian in the Jubilee anniversary book *Battle of Britain* by Richard Hough and Denis Richards (p.191).
13. The Battle of Britain Society debated whether or not to include Israel/Palestine on its list of participating nations on the Battle of Britain memorial erected in London – arguing that Goodman was British. But this is a double standard, as Britons born in Rhodesia (as it then was) were counted as Rhodesians. In the end, after a flurry of letters, Israel was omitted.
14. W.G. Ramsay (ed.), *The Battle of Britain Then and Now* (London: After the Battle Magazines Essex, 1980), p.366. This was the same day that Solomon (see above) was killed.
15. *The Israel Air Force (IAF) Bulletin* of 1997 describes Goodman as 'our first Ace, born in Israel' (thanks to Moshe Dolev, IAF researcher, of Tel Mond, Israel, for this article sent to the author in 2003). In Hebrew.
16. Ibid., p.75.
17. There is an eyewitness anecdote from Holden in N. Gelb, *Scramble* (London: Michael Joseph, 1986), p.165.
18. Jacobs wrote an unpublished autobiography about his life, *Jacob's Ladder,* mentioned in R. Collier, *Eagle Day* (New York: Dutton Books, 1966), Bibliography, p.306, unobtainable by the author.
19. Ramsay (ed.), *Battle of Britain Then and Now*, p.380.
20. No AJEX card was found for Jacobson but it is known that the cards are not complete or accurate.
21. No AJEX card found – see note 20.
22. Morris, *We Will Remember Them*, p.108.
23. Benjamin Meirtchak, *Jewish Military Casualties in the Polish Armed Forces in WW2*, Vol. 2 (Tel-Aviv: privately published, 1995), p.118.
24. B. Arct, *Polish Wings in the West* (Warsaw: Interpress, 1971), p.88, spells his name anagramatically as 'Kinel', almost certainly to deliberately disguise his Jewish-sounding name – a typical act of anti-Semitism.
25. *Jewish Chronicle*, 12 July 1940, front page.
26. AJEX Jewish Chaplain Card.
27. See USA file at AJEX Museum.

28. A. Bishop, *The Splendid Hundred* (Toronto: McGraw-Hill, 1994), p.154.
29. *Canadian Jews in WW2: Part 1* (Montreal: Canadian Jewish Congress 1947), p.29.
30. *Among the Few: Canadian Airmen in the Battle of Britain* (Air Historical Section, Air Ministry booklet, 1948), p.22, at Imperial War Museum Reading Room.
31. AJEX card information.
32. Posener is also mentioned in the Roll of Honour of *South African Jews in WW2*, (Johannesburg: South African Board of Deputies, 1950), p.xii.
33. Files at the AJEX Museum testify to several other examples of this.
34. They are one of *well over 50 sets of Jewish brothers* killed in the Second World War; I am grateful to Harold Pollins for providing this information in 'Shemot', *Journal of the Jewish Genealogical Society of Great Britain* (September 2001 and later updates in that journal).
35. See Ramsay (ed)., *Battle of Britain Then and Now*, p.755, for a photograph of the special memorial to him at the crash site.
36. No AJEX card as above and his religious affiliation is to be confirmed.
37. Ramsay (ed.), *Battle of Britain Then and Now*, p.366.
38. A. Price, *The Hardest Day* (London: Cassell, 1998) p.92.
39. From an interview by Bob Cunningham with Tuck in 1986 published in *Code One*, the journal of the General Dynamics Company, Fort Worth, USA.
40. Larry Forrester, *Fly for your Life* (London: Panther, 1956/1990), describes Tuck's life and exploits in great detail: see p.24–6.
41. Ibid., p.234.
42. See Cunningham.
43. Forrester, *Fly for your Life*, dust-jacket summary.
44. Ibid., p.14.
45. Quoted in ibid., Frontispiece.
46. See Cunningham.
47. Forrester, *Fly for your Life*, p.14.
48. Diana Barnato-Walker, *Spreading My Wings* (London: Grub Street, 1994), p.139.
49. E. Burton, *Go Straight Ahead: Diaries of the 222 Natal Squadron* (London: Square One, 1996), Appendix 3; this book contains more detail on van Mentz, pp.169–73.
50. See Forrester, *Fly for your Life*, pp.254–5.
51. Van Mentz is also mentioned as von Mentz, in the Roll of Honour of *South African Jews in WW2*, pp.xiii, 177.
52. Morris, *We Will Remember Them: An Addendum*, p.52.

Breaking the Codes: Jews at Bletchley Park

If students of the Second World War were to be asked which group of people or single organization contributed most to the defeat of the Axis forces of Germany and Japan between 1939 and 1945, most would probably agree that it was the codebreakers at GCCS at Bletchley Park, forerunner of GCHQ.[1] Established in 1938 as a branch of the Foreign Office, the part played by the staff at 'BP' was revealed only many years after the end of hostilities, first and primarily in the book by F.W. Winterbotham, *The Ultra Secret*, published in 1974;[2] there is now a small library of publications on the subject; two significant movies have been produced in recent years,[3] and several television documentaries. From enemy messages decoded at BP, strategic decisions were made by Allied leaders which significantly altered the whole course of the war and saved countless lives.

GCCS was jokingly known to the staff as the 'Golf Club and Chess Society' – actually a good cover name. It was originally founded at the end of the First World War. BP was known as 'Station X' for a short time, and this term was later used to describe any listening station centres located in other places. As radio signals would have given the codebreaking school's location away to the enemy, making it a target for bombers, the radio station at BP was moved away soon after the outbreak of war.

Given the nature of the Nazi regime, it is ironic that the fifty-five-acre estate at Bletchley Park which housed the codebreakers was – prior to it being bought by the government – the Victorian home of the Anglo-Jewish banking family of Sir Herbert and Lady Fanny Leon, Bt. His coat of arms is inscribed over the main entrance to the main building to this day.[4]

After the war, the owner of BP was British Telecom and it was nearly bulldozed for redevelopment in 1992, until the Bletchley Park Trust saved it for the nation; it is now a fascinating and ever-growing museum of what took place there during those desperate years. Besides 'the mansion', which was the main administrative centre, several of the famous decoding huts, built after 1939, still stand today.

Some huts were wooden but as time went on, heavily reinforced concrete buildings (blocks) were added, with hermetically-sealed doors and windows against gas attack, and heavy window blinds against blast. It is

believed that many underground bunkers also exist but none today have
been exposed and so this cannot be verified except by some who allege
to have been in them at some stage.[5] More confusingly, some huts were
enlarged as work increased but were located in geographically different
places within BP, nevertheless retaining the original hut number. So Hut
6, for example, may have been in three parts, in three places.

It is estimated that about 7,000 to 8,000 staff worked at BP during its
wartime years, joining and leaving as needs dictated, working eventually
twenty-four hours per day in three rotating shifts. Civilians often worked
alongside military staff and all, of course, were subject to the Official Secrets Act. Many first had to go through intensive training at a nearby village school, Elmers, commandeered for the task; after close monitoring
and testing they were passed on to work at BP itself. The work could be
both arduous and tedious. Staff were housed on the estate itself as well
as being billeted in nearby villages, and in homes and hotels up to twenty
miles away. Buses would bring and take staff to and from work, and
Bletchley railway station was the main link to other cities for leave.
Secrecy was extremely strict, and not only did nobody in the area know
what was going on at Bletchley, but even within the facility, staff worked
in isolated units and huts and never discussed their work – and rarely
met socially – with those in other sections, except at the highest levels
of management. Some marriages took place during the war between
couples who were working at BP. There are well-documented cases, however, where men and women met after the war and married, but never
told each other for many years that they had both worked at Bletchley.

Throughout the war the Germans had no idea their despatches were
being read, especially as BP sent bogus messages in a deliberately simple
code to bogus agents congratulating them on the Intelligence they were
sending the Allies. Thus the enemy believed the information came from
elsewhere and not from their own secret decoded messages. Such was
the deception.

At first recruits came mostly through the academic and aristocracy old-
boy network but as the work grew, senior staff despaired and wrote directly to Churchill, urgently requesting more resources. The PM was
enthralled by what he knew of the material coming from BP and he sent
his now famous memo to his chief of staff: 'Extreme Priority. Action This
Day!' As well as the military, some were recruited through bogus speed
crossword competitions in the *Daily Telegraph*. Readers who won were invited to a tea party, followed by interviews, and ended up at BP.

Bletchley's earliest priority was the breaking of the German Enigma
codes. The Enigma machine was invented by the German electrical engineer, Arthur Scherbus, in 1918, and resembled an overgrown typewriter
with built-in electronic rotor wheels which could encode and decode

messages using millions of possible permutations, seemingly impossible to unravel without the code books, as its settings would be changed daily. It was adopted by the military but the Poles, ever distrustful of Germany's growing militarism, had already copied the machine, and one had made its way to Bletchley via French Intelligence by the outbreak of war in September 1939.[6] With it came drawings of a machine devised by the Poles to break the Enigma codes, called a Bombe; it later became the first computer and it was at BP that the world's first electronic, programmable computer was built in 1943 to break the codes[7] – not only Enigma, for the Germans invented yet more complex machines – but also the Lorenz, code-name 'Tunny', and the *Geheimschreiber* (secret writer), code-name 'Sturgeon' – whose codes were broken too.

Listening posts known as Y stations, located all over the UK, would pick up the enemy radio transmissions and send them to BP by motorcycle despatch (at peak times up to forty riders per hour were arriving at or leaving from BP) or direct cable teleprinter for decoding.[8] Once information was decoded, the details could be with Allied commanders in the field within thirty minutes. Block A contained the huge, visually impressive ocean wallcharts on which Allied and enemy naval movements – especially of U-boats – were constantly plotted. Pigeons were also used to receive messages from Europe and a special loft for them was situated over the converted stables.[9] It was no accident that BP was halfway between Oxford and Cambridge universities and on the main rail link to London, whilst being far enough away to avoid bombing; for Oxbridge was a major recruiting ground for crypto-analysts and London, of course, was the centre of government.

As the war went on, the increasing workload at BP meant that other sites – such as Wavendon House and Stanmore – had to be secretly used for electronic decoding, and dozens of staff worked in these 'out-stations' too, but they are beyond the scope of this study. In 1943, the staff at Bletchley were reinforced by American colleagues; work was also being done on breaking the Japanese codes from 1941. By the eve of D-Day, speed in getting intercepted messages from the Y stations to BP was so crucial that permission was given by Churchill himself to risk using radio transmissions to do this for a few weeks (see note 1); in the period before and after D-Day, as many as 3,000–5,000 decrypts per day were being processed at BP, approximately half of them naval.[10]

Many BP staff had difficulty obtaining work after the war in areas in which they had acquired expertise during the conflict, because their oath of secrecy required that they were able to reveal their knowledge of certain foreign languages they had learnt. Nor could they expect to receive references from superior officers, since the department in which they worked did not officially exist. These restrictions, however, were lifted by David Owen in 1976 when he was Foreign Secretary.

It is not this author's aim to rehearse here the story of Bletchley, as this is now well recorded, but rather to focus on the role of the Jewish community who served there either as military or civilian attached (CA). The author was fortunate to be able to personally interview several Jewish veterans in both categories, and these primary sources, together with other secondary ones, complete a fascinating picture of what was achieved.

1112693 Flight Lieutenant Richard Barnett

He was born on 23 January 1909, son of Lionel Barnett, a distinguished orientalist. Before the war he was an archaeologist at the British Museum and had learnt Turkish when digging in Turkey with the husband of Agatha Christie. Richard was involved in security work from the very beginning of the war in September 1939, monitoring overseas telegrams from a censorship office at Wormwood Scrubs. His AJEX card notes his address as 20c Holland Park Avenue, London W14. Recruited into the RNVR due to his yachting skills in 1940, he was then sent to Bletchley and helped break the codes used by the Turkish government in its communications with the Axis powers. By 1942 he was commissioned into RAF Intelligence and then left BP to supervise Turkish pilots training in Britain; he then served in North Africa (liaising with Greek squadrons) and Turkey (where he served in mufti, secretly on radar Intelligence) until war's end. Whilst in North Africa he had the ghastly task of identifying bodies washed up on the coast from a Jewish refugee ship bound for Palestine (Israel); this was one of the worst moments of his life. After the war he was keeper of Western Asia antiquities at the British Museum.[11] He died on 27 July 1986.

Peter Benenson

He was born in Germany in 1921 and later founded Amnesty International.[12] The grandson of Russian Jewish banker Grigori Benenson, and son of Flora Solomon, who raised him after her husband, British Army Colonel John Solomon, was killed, Peter was tutored privately by W.H. Auden and then went to Eton and Oxford. Here he studied history and was recruited to BP from the army, into which he had volunteered when war broke out in 1939. After the war he became a lawyer.

W13094/192366 Captain (later Major) Jane Bennett (later Guss), ATS

She was from 63 Brondesbury Park in north-west London, the daughter of Mrs Y. Bennett. She joined the Women's Territorials in 1938 and was called up when war broke out.[13] She was married to Captain H. Guss of the USAAF. In 1940 she was sent to Field Security training in Aldershot because she had French and German linguistic skills. Her sergeant major was the famous commentator, Malcolm Muggeridge. Prevented from going to France by Dunkirk, she was posted next to Bletchley Park in 1940. Her first job was sorting burnt and wet captured German documents for sifting for information; later she was sent to Hut 3, where she was typing in German messages that had been decoded. Later still she worked with Major Lithgow, whose job was extracting from decoded messages any clues from call signs and radio frequencies, to help actually locate the radio stations from where these messages were coming and thence deduce the positions of various enemy units in Europe. This was used to produce maps and passed on to the military planners as required. Starting with just two people, this section grew to many by the end of the war. At war's end she stayed with Lithgow's section to work in London.

One incident Jane remembers clearly was the night Coventry was bombed. She and her comrades left to go into the shelter but she fell down the two steps outside the hut and badly gashed her leg; she carries the scar still, 'wounded in action'.

Anita and Muriel Bogush

Anita and Muriel were sisters whose family left Stamford Hill in Hackney, London, during the Blitz, to live in Bletchley because their father would not send the girls away alone to be evacuated. Their father knew the family of Angel Dindol, a draper – the only known Jewish family in the town at the time.

Anita (born in 1924) worked in Block A, Naval Section from September 1941 to March 1946, and Muriel (born in November 1928) in Hut 4, Naval Section (which she remembers being called 'HMS *Pembroke V*')[14] from 27 April 1943 until 15 June 1945; such was the secrecy that neither knew what the other did until many years after the war. Muriel got the job after her older sister recommended her to BP recruiters, but unlike Anita she was not allowed to work shifts due to her age. They had to learn naval terms, so leave was 'liberty' and you got food in 'the galley'. Although not in the navy, Muriel always wore a white blouse and naval skirt to work with the WRENs around her. Her manager was Phoebe Senyard, whom she much admired and liked. Their parents, Rebecca and Phillip, often invited Jewish personnel to the Friday evening Shabbat meal at their home, 27 Duncan Street, and the Ettinghausen brothers, Joe Gillis and Willy Bloom (listed below) were frequent guests.

Muriel well remembers being shown into 'the mansion' on her first day and shown a security film, followed by a lecture and her signing of the Official Secrets Act. The sisters lived close enough to BP to be able to walk to and from work. A messenger at first, Muriel was soon promoted to the Naval Section, where she received the coded German messages and placed a cut-out template on top; what showed through she had to copy and send by electric tubes (as used in old drapers' shops) on to the

decoders. The staff sat on high stools around a long table in the centre of
the hut. She also recalls the wind-up scrambling phones used by the section leaders of the hut. Her team were taken in secret to London on one
occasion, to view the captured U-boat (U-110) whose fate they had plotted, and this caused great excitement and brought home to them the se-
riousness of their work. Muriel also knew about the entrances to many
underground tunnels and working bunkers at BP and recalls clearly the
visits of both Churchill and Anthony Eden to BP.

As the girls kept kosher, they always brought sandwiches to work.
Socially, life was quite active for them and much entertainment was provided in BP itself. Muriel recalls that as lipstick was scarce, they would
melt their remnants into a china eggcup over a saucepan of hot water, and
re-pour them back into an old lipstick case. Reckitts Blue (used as a washing whitener) was used as eyeshadow. On several occasions, American
troops invited groups of the women to their base near Bedford for dances;
she remembers being thrilled to hear the great Glen Miller in person. It
was all very proper, with total escorting to and from BP in army trucks
and a strict curfew, under guard.

After VE-Day, the sisters continued work on the Japanese codes until
VJ-Day in August 1945. In 1995, Muriel went to BP to visit the museum
and noticed a photograph of herself in the display; she asked the curator
who had sent it in, and was put in touch with a good friend of hers from
BP days, Daphne Skinner. In 1996, whilst on a visit with sister Anita, they
were in a group touring the hut where they worked and Muriel happened
to mention that they had both worked there. Before they knew it, the
guide insisted they address the group; it was quite an occasion.

RN Sub Lieutenant Laurence Jonathan Cohen

He was born in London in May 1923, son of the Jewish writer Israel
Cohen, and attended St Paul's School;[15] he recalls he was reading Greats
at Balliol in December 1941 when the Japanese attacked Pearl Harbour
and South Asia. He was suddenly asked by his college Master if he would
like to learn Japanese (as there was such a shortage of translators for the
GCCS). He had no idea what it would be for until he reached Bletchley.
They studied in Bedford six days a week under First World War Naval Intelligence Officer Oswald Tuck, a self-made and self-taught man who was
an inspiring teacher, and who formerly served as naval attaché in Tokyo.[16]
The speed of their progress embarrassed the School of Oriental and
African Studies (SOAS), who said it could never be done! Their social life
centred on Bedford pubs and the concerts of the BBC classical music section which had moved to Bedford.

Cohen recalls: 'At some stage a bomb fell on our building (at BP), a
purely accidental target ... we were sitting around the edge of this room

and the whole ceiling fell down into the middle ... it was fortunate and we weren't hit by anything.'[17] He was billeted in the small cottage of a 70-year-old railway worker's widow at New Bradwell. This was poverty compared to his upbringing in a middle-class house in London, but he says:

> We got on very well ... there were considerable class differences at Bletchley, though ... I took up with a girl who was in fact the daughter of a Countess! Being from a Jewish middle-class home, that was not the kind of person I would normally mix with. There were dances and parties and we enjoyed ourselves to a certain extent ... but you never asked questions about what others were doing ... or went beyond your own narrow field.[18]

There was also a very informal approach to rank:

> One day the military police guarding the entrance to BP saw two RAF sergeants walking down the driveway. They suddenly seemed to stop, look around them and walk very fast in the opposite direction. This looked suspicious and so they were arrested and taken to the guardhouse. It turned out they had a valid posting to BP, but did not like the look of it because all these people in and out of uniform were walking about arguing and gesticulating ... they thought it was a military lunatic asylum, and the posting was a mistake.

Cohen later served in the listening and decoding stations in Mombassa (East Africa) and Colombo (Sri Lanka).[19] After the war he became a much-published philosophy teacher in Scottish and other universities and later was a don at Queens College, Oxford, until he retired in 1990.

Lieutenant Michael Cohen, RNVR

He was born in 1924 and worked in the Japanese section at Bletchley. At the beginning of 1943 he was called up and after two weeks called for interview near Southampton in front of five very senior naval officers. One held up a sheaf of papers and said, 'You were a student of ancient Semitic languages.' Cohen said, with his strong Scots accent, he was at the Divinity School at the University of Glasgow and intended to be a rabbi. The officer handed him a page and asked him to read. '*Breisheet bara Elohim et hashamayim v'et ha'aretz*' (in the beginning God created heaven and earth), read Cohen. He was then told he would be sent on a Japanese language course. 'Yes sir', he replied.

After a six-month course in London and two weeks learning to be an officer, he was made lieutenant and sent to BP[20] where he worked with the Ettinghausen brothers on naval codes. In the book *Codebreakers* he is mistakenly referred to as a Moslem Scot called Daoud – this is apocryphal, and Ernest Ettinghausen has testifed in the taped interview with the author that this was in fact Michael Cohen from Glasgow, and his idea of a joke.

By 1948 he was coding messages between the Jewish Agency offices in London, and Jerusalem, and then sailed to Haifa, and helped found the 'British kibbutz' at Kfar Hanassi in the Upper Galilee. There he worked in agriculture and managed the metal factory. He was also an emissary for the kibbutz movement in South Africa. He never revisited Bletchley. 'When you have passed through five other wars, Bletchley is hard to recall ... if I close my eyes and think back, what I see are the two lovely WRENs who worked with me.' Good enough.

134464/1082701 Squadron Leader Nakdimon ('Naky') Shabetai Doniach

Also known as 'Don',[21] he was born in London in May 1907 to poor Russian Jewish immigrants and educated at Haberdashers' Aske's School.[22] His father Aaron had previously been arrested by the Russian secret police for Zionist activities, had worked to set up Jewish schools for girls in the East End of London and was a noted Arabic scholar at Oxford and SOAS, the first person to hold an academic post in modern Hebrew; he was scion of the ancient eleventh-century Don-Yahya family. His mother, Rahel Chaikin, was a noted intellectual, poet and playwright, and a founder of WIZO, the Women's International Zionist Organization. From the young age of 15, Naky was a brilliant student of Hebrew, Arabic and numerous other oriental and ancient languages at various London University colleges; he then proceeded to Wadham College, Oxford, winning many prizes to finance his studies. He visited his mother in Palestine (Israel) in the 1920s, and later, as a private scholar and bookseller, wrote many learned papers on Jewish history.

His remarkable linguistic skills saw him headhunted from the RAF (which he joined in 1940) to serve at Bletchley Park but very little is known of his work there.[23] The family lived at Leighton Buzzard, within commuting distance from BP. His daughters suspect he worked in Air Intelligence and translation. The only – and very typical – BP anecdote that was related by Naky concerned a late afternoon near the lake. A colleague, Arthur Cooper, was sipping tea with Naky as they were engaged in deep conversation. Not noticing that the tables had been taken away, Cooper gracefully and slowly was lowering his cup onto an invisible table top, and reached instead the surface of the lake, his eyes still on Naky as he spoke; the cup and saucer gently and slowly floated off into the sunset.

After eleven years in the RAF he was moved to GCHQ and throughout the Cold War was in charge of teaching Russian (and overseeing the teaching of Chinese) to Foreign Office officials, servicemen and others, and creating vital technical Russian dictionaries for the Intelligence Services. After retirement he moved to Oxford as a teacher and editor of

Oxford University Press dictionaries, especially in modern Hebrew and Arabic usage, and was much loved by both his Israeli and Arab colleagues in various Israeli and British universities. In 1932 he married Thea, daughter of the famous Polish Jewish artists Leopold Pilichowski and Lena Pillico; Thea died in 1986. For his scholarship and Intelligence work he was awarded the OBE in 1967. He died in April 1994.[24]

1263457 Albert Alfred Ernest Ettinghausen

He was the brother of Walter (listed below) and he came to BP from Queen's College, Oxford, via the RAF. He was born in Munich in June 1913, although his father had been educated and brought up in England. But his father was working in Munich at the time and as a result was interned by the Germans in the First World War as an enemy alien, whilst his wife and children, Ernest and Walter, lived in Switzerland until 1919. Back in England, in 1920, Ernest later went to St Paul's School and then worked in the antiquarian book business like his father, in Paris, where he learned French (he already knew German). He tried to enlist in the UK in September 1939 but only the Territorials were being called-up and he was sent away. He was again working in Paris when the 'phoney' war ended, and helped by the Brazilian Embassy consul, he went south after Dunkirk, using all manner of transport – including a bicycle – to escape the Nazis,[25] at one time sitting on the diplomatic baggage in the back of the diplomatic car. At Bayonne, the Spanish consul refused them passage to Spain but at Bordeaux they were assisted by the French to board a ship coming from West Africa (SS *Madeira*) together with hundreds of Free French, Poles and other Allies trying to get to England on a very overcrowded ship. He arrived in Falmouth in late June 1940.

His wife was Mrs H.N.R. Ettinghausen; they lived at Hornestall Cottage, Barley, near Royston; and formerly at 28 Belsize Park, London NW3, according to his AJEX card.

Albert immediately enlisted in RAF aircrew, but was sent instead to the RAF Provost (Police) section as a sergeant. Headhunted because of his languages, in late 1940 he was given a mysterious message to go and meet someone at Bletchley Railway Station waiting room. He was told he would be discharged from the RAF and went straight to the Naval Section in Hut 4 in February 1941.

He spent alternate weeks at the Admiralty Citadel (underground near the Horse Guards, Whitehall) at first, and also spent time at Scapa Flow with the battleship *King George V*, to get sea experience, as well as on a North Sea convoy and a Dutch submarine. He then later began the job of translating decoded German naval messages at BP in Hut 4 with his brother Walter, with whom he was billeted. Here he followed the same path as his brother (see below). It was convenient that his wife and

Walter's wife were both living in Oxford, and so visits home were simple, when possible.

At war's end Ernest moved with BP to Eastcote, and then Cheltenham (now GCHQ) as Intelligence librarian by the early 1950s. But there was mounting pressure to move him as his brother was now head of the Israel Foreign Office, potentially making him a security risk. So they found him a post as librarian of the Science Museum, but the union would not ratify it as he had no formal qualifications. He became librarian at the Inland Revenue and then director of the Inland Revenue Stamp Duty Office, for which he was given the MBE. He died in 2001, the same year as his brother.

Walter George Ettinghausen (later Walter Eytan, Director of the Israeli Foreign Ministry and Israeli Ambassador to France)

He was born on 24 July 1910 in Munich,[26] and was in charge of the translator's group of 'Z' watch in the German Naval Section, Hut 4. A scholar of German from St Paul's School and a don at Queen's College, Oxford, Walter had been called up in September 1940, having already been asked to do secret work when he was at university. He had been born in Germany but the BP security people knew he, as a Jew, and other Jews had a special stake in fighting Hitler. After several months' army training, as no. 7926780 (noted on his AJEX card, which shows him as living at 149d Banbury Road, Oxford), he was suddenly ordered to BP with his rifle and kit and arrived as a trooper from the tank regiment, wearing his shiny black boots and his polished cap-badge with beret in February 1941.[27] Walter was one of the first of the Hut 4 team. One of his team, Alec Dakin, describes 'his leadership ... exercised with gentleness and understanding, and all who knew him and worked with him, loved him.' It was suggested to him that he would be better to revert to a civilian as he would be dealing with very high-ranking naval officers.[28]

The watch had three teams working the twenty-four-hour cycle, led by Walter, and when Hut 8 broke a code, Hut 4 was ready to do immediate translation. In one group was WREN Officer Thelma Ziman (later MBE) who had come from South Africa to fight the war, and also Ernest Ettinghausen (listed above), Walter's younger brother and antiquarian bookseller. Ernest became head of one of the shifts.

Decrypts would arrive in a wire tray in the form of sheets covered with teleprinter tapes, like a telegram, carrying German text in five-letter groups, just as in the original cipher. The sorter, number 2, picked out those important to send to the Naval Intelligence Division (NID) at the Admiralty; number 3 wrote out the German text clearly, stapled it to the decrypt and handed it to number 1, who translated to English and stamped it with a number. This went to WAAF (not WREN, curiously) clerks who sent it by teleprinter to the Admiralty with number 1's

initials, e.g. WGE, Walter Ettinghausen. From here it went to commanding officers at sea. Secrecy was extremely tight and the fewest possible
people at BP saw the messages.

Translation was often not so simple, as many messages arrived partly
corrupted and the linguists had to make inspired guesses as to meaning,
using their linguistic skills, context and operational background to re-
constitute the message. They had to acquire a knowledge of German
'navalese' and built up a unique dictionary of such terms, and often used
the excellent library and card catalogues built up at BP to do this.

Some messages came via wireless listening stations on the coast. On
occasion Walter would visit these to familiarize himself with their work or
go to the NID in London to see how they worked and what their special
needs from BP might be. Others spent time at sea to get to know what
conditions were like. If pressure of work was great or the messages especially sensitive, Walter would operate the teleprinter himself, often at
night, for security reasons.

Before it was possible to read Enigma, the teams could still guess at
the meanings of some German ciphers and signals, enough to give warnings to the navy that certain German battleships, for example, were patrolling off Norway, and how to avoid or attack them. Often they could tell
an urgent message by acronyms the Germans used such as SSD (*sehr sehr
dringend* – very very urgent). The messages dealt with were extremely significant and included U-boat route plots, U-boat supply ship locations,
and movements of capital ships like the *Bismarck* or *Hipper*. Walter and his
team knew that thousands of lives depended on their work, especially
during the Battle of the Atlantic. Walter said, 'I knew the name of every
U-boat Commander.' His team helped re-route convoys to avoid them.
Walter also vividly recalled the last messages of the *Bismarck*, whose end
he helped bring about in May 1941.

Eventually the section branched out into reading Italian, Vichy French
and Spanish messages. As linguists, Walter remembered them having little
trouble in dealing with these.

It was Walter who set up a Zionist Society at Bletchley which quite a few
Jews regularly attended on a Wednesday evening at the apartment of Joe
Gillis. He was a Sunderland-born mathematician from Belfast University,
who later became a professor at the Weizmann Institute at Rehovot, near
Tel-Aviv. Among other things, Gillis broke the codes in which the Germans
sent their weather reports, most important to our air forces campaign. At
the meetings of the Zionist Society, they would discuss the independence
of Israel and Aliyah (immigration) which many carried out after the war
ended. Here, due to Walter, was founded the Professional and Technical
Aliyah Association (PATWA), organized to encourage Jewish professionals
to immigrate to Israel to form the nucleus of a modern, democratic nation.

They did not hold religious services at BP, but did try to get home for major festivals.

On one poignant night, early in 1944, Walter's team intercepted a message from a German vessel in the Aegean, saying they were transporting Jews from Rhodes or Cos for Piraeus, '*zur Endlosung*' ('for the final solution'); he had not heard this expression before but he wrote that he instinctively knew what it meant; he never forgot it and it left its mark on him until he died. It was thus indeed poetic justice, when Walter was in charge of the Israeli Foreign Ministry, years later, that it was he who initiated the original search for the notorious Nazi war criminal Adolf Eichmann, which culminated in Eichmann's capture by the Israeli Secret Service in 1960 in Argentina and his transport to, and trial in, Israel, leading eventually to his execution in 1962.[29]

One of the most memorable moments came when the message about Hitler's death arrived in April 1945, from German Naval HQ. It was late at night and Walter was on duty. He decided to wire this one himself to the Admiralty and not use a WAAF assistant. It was a fitting end for a Jewish soldier at Bletchley to have been the first to see and relay such a message. Small wonder he devoted the rest of his life working for the defence of Israel.

When Winterbotham's book came out in 1974, Walter refused to read it in protest at the breaking of the oath to remain silent; not even his wife knew what he had done until the book emerged, only 'that he worked at Bletchley'. Walter went to Israel in 1946 and was asked to set up a school to train staff for a Foreign Service for a new nation. He was involved during the siege of Jerusalem in the 1948 War of Independence, and at Lausanne in 1949 headed the Israeli delegation and signed the first agreement between Israel and an Arab country, Egypt. Foreign Minister Moshe Sharett asked him to become director of the Foreign Ministry, which he did for eleven years before becoming ambassador to France. He was then Permanent Secretary of the Israeli Foreign Office. Walter remained a close personal friend of Anne Ross, a Jewish BP worker, until he died in 2001.[30] Anne relates how for years after the war, he corresponded with his elderly landlady in Bletchley, right through his distinguished diplomatic career, until she died; this was typical of his sensitivity and loyalty.

Ernst Constantin Fetterlein/Feterlein

He was the son of Karl Fedorovich and Olga Fetterlein, née Meier.[31] She was almost certainly Jewish and so Ernst can certainly be counted as of Jewish origin. Ernst was a crypto-analyst under Tsar Nicholas in his 'Black Cabinet' and reached the equivalent rank of admiral. Leaving Russia for Britain after the Revolution of 1917, he was one of the earliest recruits into GCCS after the first World War, in 1919. He retired in his sixties in 1938 but was recalled to active service and worked at Bletchley on the German diplomatic code system known as 'Floradora'. He died in 1944.[32] His brother Paul Fetterlein also worked at Bletchley.

Eric Frank

He was born in Cardiff in 1907 but went to King Edward VI School in Birmingham and then read Classics and modern languages at Jesus College, Cambridge.[33] Nothing is known about his work at BP save that he was there, almost certainly as a translator. Post-war he taught for many years at Hasmonean Jewish Secondary School in London, then retired to Jerusalem in 1971 where he worked for various charities as a volunteer. He died there in June 1993.

Captain William (Wolfe) Frederick Friedman

He was born in 1891 in Kishinev, Russia, but was brought to the US as a baby by his parents, Frederick and Rosa. His father was a postal worker in Pittsburgh.[34] Friedman studied plant genetics at Cornell and then worked for Fabyan Riverbank laboratories in Chicago, where he also became interested in ciphers as a result of his employer's obsession with proving that Shakespeare's work was really written by Francis Bacon. During the First World War, he offered the US government help from his ciphers department at Riverbank and it soon became the official US Government cryptographic centre. Here he unravelled codes used by subversives in the US and trained US military officers in cryptography; he then joined the army in 1918 and served in France as General Pershing's personal code-breaker. By 1929 he led the Army Signals Intelligence Section (SIS) and was considered a world expert in the field, with published works, and was one of the first to apply statistics to codebreaking. He is considered the greatest cryptologist of all time.

In the 1920s and 1930s, he studied the weaknesses of the new generation of electronic coding machines and designed his own more complex version which was used, unbroken, by the Americans in the Second World War. In 1939, together with his Jewish colleague, Lieutenant Leo Rosen, he broke the most secret Japanese diplomatic 'Purple' code. It was Friedman's work which thus allowed interception of the notorious message from Tokyo to the Japanese Embassy in Washington on 7 December 1941, delivered direct to the State Department, which warned of impending war.

After a mild nervous breakdown, he recovered and was sent to work at Bletchley in 1941, as research director of the American SIS, and oversaw the exchange of information with Britain on the 'Purple' code for that on Enigma. This enabled the Allies also to read the coded messages between the Germans and the Japanese. Friedman was hugely impressed by what he learned at BP and was very concerned that the USA should develop its own cluster of Bombe decoding machines. He was also afraid that a few well placed enemy bombs could destroy everything at BP in one fell swoop – hence his sense of urgency.

Awarded the US Medal of Merit (the highest that can be given to civilians) in 1946, he stayed with the US government until 1956 and retired to continue his research on the 'Shakespeare codes', but still acting as a consultant to the US government. He died in 1969.[35]

Joan Enid Friedman

She was born in November 1918 in Birmingham, to Myer and Dora (née Tuchman); her father was a civil servant and they lived in Edgbaston. After King Edward VI School, she went to Girton College, Cambridge, to read Classics from 1937 to 1940, and then went on to teach German in schools in Southwold and Nottingham.[36] She was then headhunted by the Foreign Office and was sent to BP, being billeted in the nearby village of New Bradwell with a family whose son was away in the forces. Her job was in the Naval Section with Walter Ettinghausen, whom she knew well; on receiving decoded German messages, her task was to translate them into readable English before they were forwarded to the various Intelligence branches for use in the field. At the time of interview[37] Joan could not remember much of her life at Bletchley, but did say that her upbringing led her not to eat any non-kosher food, especially meat, and as a result her diet was quite plain.

After the war Joan worked as a senior librarian at the universities of Birmingham, Keele and Cambridge and then became a senior lecturer in librarianship at Sheffield from 1964 to 1980.

14426396/345201 Captain Joshua David Goldberg ('JD')

He was born in Manchester in December 1924, son of I.W. Goldberg of 222 Wilmslow Road. A brilliant pupil at Manchester Grammar, he had to repeat his last years until old enough to go up to Corpus Christi College, Oxford, to read Classics. From there he was headhunted for the Intelligence Corps and Bletchley Park Japanese translation section, where he attended the fifth course in Bedford,[38] and he was at BP from August 1943 until February 1944. His widow Hilda (born in Jerusalem) testifies that JD never spoke about his time at Bletchley, but only said that the Japanese course was so intense and pressurized that two men in his group committed suicide.[39] When the war ended, Captain Goldberg worked in Intelligence in Germany and later became a lawyer. His photograph is on display at Bletchley in the Japanese section.

6.1 Jim Rose (Joseph Rosenheim), Bletchley Park.

6.2 Rolf Noskwith, Bletchley Park Code Breaker.

6.3 Muriel Bogush at Bletchley Park in 1944.

114705761 Sergeant Samuel Julius Goldstein (Gould)

He was born in October 1924 in Liverpool. When war broke out he was at school (Liverpool Collegiate) but then went to study Classics at Balliol College, Oxford.[40] He then enlisted into the army (Intelligence Corps) and was selected from there to study Japanese, and went to BP from the army in spring 1944. Here he was translating Japanese intercepts. He was billeted in the nearby army camp and was able to walk to work. His main work at this time was dealing with what the Japanese and Germans were saying to each other via their Consulates in neutral countries and what the Japanese were then reporting to Japanese High Command in Tokyo with regard to German matters, often containing significant clues to issues of German plans, morale and strategy. On one occasion an orthodox Jewish family named Teitlebaum invited him for a Sabbath meal, but otherwise any Jewish contacts were in nearby Oxford.

Samuel remembers very much a college atmosphere in the spare time that the staff had – reading, common-room discussions, eccentric academics in college scarves and old school ties, and so on. At war's end, he stayed in Intelligence and was moved to London at the start of the Cold War – about which he would say nothing; he then returned in 1946 to Oxford. Post-war, he held several university posts in sociology until he retired.

Harry Golombeck

He was born in London in March 1911, at Railton Road, Herne Hill, son of a Polish Jewish immigrant greengrocer, Barnet, and Emma Sendak.[41] He attended Wilson's grammar school in Camberwell and studied philology at King's College, London, becoming an international chess champion in the process. At the outbreak of war he joined the Royal Artillery, but because of his maths and analytical skills he was recruited to BP. Here he often played chess with the great Alan Turing, and it was Golombek who broke the Abwehr code used by the enemy in Turkey. After the war he became the chess correspondent for *The Times* between 1945 and 1985 and was a prolific writer on the game.[42] He died in January 1995.

Irving John (Jack) Good, FRS (real name Isidore Jacob Gudak)

He was born in 1916 in Manchester to Polish immigrant shopkeepers (his father was a watchmaker), and became interested in maths and ciphers as a small boy. He attended Haberdashers' Aske's School in Hampstead. In 1938 he graduated with first-class honours in mathematics at Jesus College, Cambridge. He worked on Enigma and Tunny[43] as a cryptoanalyst.[44] Tunny/Lorenz carried messages to and from Hitler and his High Command. After being headhunted and interviewed by Hugh Alexander (a

British chess champion like Jack) and Gordon Welchman in 1940, Jack was sent to BP on 27 May 1941 (the day the *Bismarck* was sunk), to work first in Hut 8 under the great Alan Turing, breaking the German Naval Enigma codes; he was Turing's main statistical assistant and thus a main player in the game. He earned Turing's undying respect .

Early on at BP, Good annoyed Turing by taking a nap on the floor of Hut 8 during his first night shift. Turing refused to speak to him afterwards – until Jack used his statistical genius to demonstrate how an essential trial and error method of attacking Enigma traffic could be greatly accelerated ('Banburismus' – so called because the paper used was printed in Banbury) which meant weighing the probability of the accuracy of a crib – i.e. the probable meaning of a word or words in a message, which was not quite decoded. The two men were thus reconciled.

On another night shift, Good made a crucial discovery which helped to calculate which pairs of dummy letters the German encoders were adding to the twice enciphered, three-letter group at the start of each signal, telling the recipient how to reset his machine in order to decipher it. Good worked out that this was not random but from a preset table.

Further, some sensitive Enigma messages were enciphered twice. One night Good dreamt that the Germans were reversing this process, normal cipher first, special cipher second. When he woke, he tried it out and broke the coded messages. He had solved the problem in his sleep.[45]

Later, Good was moved to Hut F in May 1943 to work on Tunny/Lorenz, in a section nicknamed 'The Newmanry', after its team leader Maxwell Newman (listed below). Peter Hilton also worked here, as did Peter Benenson (both listed here). Among Jack's refinements to the Colossus machine was a system that enabled a speeding up of the code-breaking process. Post-war he worked as professor of statistics at the University of Manchester, with Newman and Turing , but also working for GCHQ until 1959; then he moved to Trinity, Oxford, and later, from 1967, to the University of West Virginia.[46] Whilst at West Virginia, he sported a car number plate, 007 IJG, a coy reference to his crucial wartime role. He remained a prolific publisher and one of the real inventors of the computer as we know it today. He died on 5 April 2009 in the USA (see obituary, the *Guardian*, 29 April 2009).

Peter Hilton

He was born in London in 1923, and at the age of 21 was in his fourth year at Oxford. Although a student of neither maths nor German, he was head-hunted and sent to the 'Testery' (named after Major Tester) at BP. He was the only one who turned up for the interview at his college. He found codebreaking very exciting – 'especially since you knew that these were vital messages'[47] – and often worked thirty hours at a stretch.[48] Peter remembers that the Germans were so sure their codes were not being read that they did not take precautions. For example, the Germans would often begin messages with '*Heil Hitler*' and once that was known, and kept being used, deductions could quickly be made about the meanings of the letters. Peter also remembers the use of '*Nieder mit die Englander*' (Down with the English), another set phrase which allowed easy decrypting. He could never understand how Rommel, for example, did not realize his codes were being read, because all his supplies were being sunk in the Mediterranean. Equally, he claims that BP staff felt that Montgomery did not trust the Intelligence information with which BP was providing him, because they were providing the military with a service that no other military had ever had in the history of warfare.

Post-war, Peter became professor of maths at State University, New York.

Morris Hoffman

He was working in HM Customs and studying languages at Birkbeck College, London, when war broke out. As he had a knowledge of German, he was referred by the college's careers officer to an interview with Commander Saunders, RN, in Broadway near St James's Park. Morris later discovered this was the HQ of the British Secret Service. Part of the interview was to test his German, and by 12 February 1942 he was at Bletchley Park, with no idea what to expect.[49]

Billeted in Leighton Buzzard, he was sent to work in Hut 3 and informed he would help translate German Enigma decodes passed to them from Hut 6, to which they were joined by a 'hole in the wall' partition. He remembers clearly the huge wall-map which showed the complete order of battle of the Luftwaffe, as BP knew it. With Morris were all kinds of other experts especially employed to evaluate messages as to level of importance (military attached), clarify technical German terms, locate tiny places on maps mentioned in codes, evaluate what the Germans knew about *our* messages, and so on. At one point he was allocated to assist F.L. Lucas (English don at King's College, Cambridge) who worked on the destruction of the convoys to Rommel in the Mediterranean, then John Saltmarsh (King's College librarian) on coded map references which gave Rommel's positions and intentions in North Africa and enabled the drawing by Morris of quite accurate maps for the 8th Army. Some of his maps were actually requested by Churchill. In late 1943 Saltmarsh fell ill and Morris had to take over. His particular mission became locating on atlas and sheet maps the names of small places mentioned by the Germans where crucial HQs might be located, and he was allocated four female staff to assist him in this. He bought old *Baedeker* guides from second-hand shops in London to assist in this, and old German telephone directories; BP repaid his expenses.

If ever Morris spotted in the enemy messages the name of someone being transferred from one place to another, known to be connected with radar or V1 research, such apparently innocuous detail might be of huge significance and it was his job to pass this to the section dealing with such Intelligence. Professor Frederick Norman was in charge of such an area, and he once said – referring to information Morris had passed to him – to one of Morris's assistants, 'Where Hoffman has trodden, no grass grows!' A rare compliment.

In early June 1944 – having now moved in with a Scots couple near to BP itself – he was visited by a senior officer asking for details of enemy dispositions for a map of the Cherbourg Peninsula. He finished after midnight and then went home to sleep. Early next morning he was woken by his landlord who told him he had best go to work, because 'the Second Front is blazing!' Morris did his best to look surprised.

On another occasion Morris managed to deduce an entry route used for Axis submarines in the north Mediterranean; it was referred to a senior committee but not used as it was considered too sensitive – it might give a clue that the Enigma had been broken.

On matters Jewish, Morris comments that kashrut (eating kosher food) was never a problem as he went vegetarian and was treated accordingly whether in digs or the canteen. He attended the Joe Gillis evenings and met several Jewish staff from BP. One evening a policeman appeared at the door and asked why there were so many people meeting at the place. Walter and Joe refused him entry, however, and afterwards he would often be seen watching the flat from the street. One evening he stopped and warned Thelma Ziman about using her car for an unauthorized purpose, when she was in fact on her way to work.

There were three Hasidic families in Bletchley itself, evacuated from London. When Morris's father died in August 1942 he went to their tiny *shtiebel* (prayer room) to say Kaddish. They became friendly but one of the young men tried to impress upon Morris he should not work on Shabbat (Saturday); Morris impressed upon him that even the Maccabees fought on Shabbat. On one occasion, Walter Eytan showed him a German book he had acquired and its binder had been made from a looted Torah scroll; this served as a sombre reminder of what they were all fighting against.

In 1944 Morris was privy to the fact that the first V2 rockets were about to be launched, following the V1 threat. Lucas warned him he must say nothing to anyone. He was unable, therefore, to warn his mother on visiting her and had to keep his peace whilst he sat with her as the last V1 and the first V2 hit London.

Captain John Klauber

He was born in London in 1917 and attended St Paul's School. He graduated in modern history at Christ Church College, Oxford. He went into the Intelligence Corps at the start of hostilities, from where he was sent to BP, but little is known of his work there. After the war he became a doctor and famous psychoanalyst, helping re-establish psychoanalysis in Germany. He died on 11 August 1981.[50]

Major Solomon Kullback

He was born in 1903 in Brooklyn and moved into crypto-analysis on a parallel course with Abraham Sinkov (listed below). He came to BP in May 1942[51] to learn about Enigma and assist with the breaking of the Japanese codes which the Americans had achieved. Shortly after his return to the USA he became head of the Japanese section. He was much liked and often did the night shift with his staff to boost their morale as 'not forgotten'. Post-war he stayed in US Intelligence but also taught maths at George Washington University. He was known as a man with unlimited enthusiasm and energy, who loved bowling. He died in 1994.

Lieutenant Arthur J. Levenson

He was one of the many American Jews who served at BP. He worked mainly in Hut 6 and later moved to Block 5. Secretly transported on the SS *Aquitania* in 1943 with about twenty members of the US Signal Corps, he was a young mathematician whose cover story was that he was a pigeon expert. It was the first time he had met an Englishman but integration was almost immediate and great friendships were made.

He remembered that the first British officers he met were suspicious of him and his men, and asked them to take an army test. Afterwards, the test marker came running up and said that the results were so good, they ought to be in Intelligence.[52]

He enjoyed a full social life and all his stereotypical views of the British rapidly disappeared: 'I had been full of stereotypes about the English ... distant, no sense of humour and these were the most outgoing, wonderful people ... fed us when it was quite a sacrifice ... real fun'. He remembers that the Germans:

> changed the [Enigma] wheel patterns infrequently until D-Day and so once you had them recovered, you were in. But after we invaded they changed the patterns every day. So we went to the boss (Edward Travis) and said we need four more of Colossus ... he went to Churchill ... so we got four more ... we could not have done without them.[53]

Levenson also told the following story:[54]

> Just before D-Day ... Rommel was appointed inspector general of the western defences and he sent this 70,000 letters message ... a

detailed description of the defences, where each unit was located and what equipment they had ... they were going to drop one of the American airborne divisions right on top of a German tank division ... they would have been massacred. They changed it [the drop zone].

Affable and much respected, Levenson was regarded as the commander of the Americans at Bletchley. In a radio programme,[55] he said:

Codebreaking was a somewhat esoteric profession. But it was not clear exactly who would make a good codebreaker. People who were recruited were asked whether they did crossword puzzles. And if they said they did and enjoyed doing them, and did them well, that was generally enough to get you in. We discovered people of a whole variety of backgrounds did very well. Anthropologists, Egyptologists, palaeontologists, and even the occasional lawyer turned out to have the knack.

Levenson also related in the same programme how surprised he was to see the Germans using a code indicator, 'TOM'; this turned out to be the cowboy Tom Mix, and yet nobody realized he had had a following in Germany. He went on to explain how the average time for a Bombe computer to decrypt a German code was fifteen minutes and this often resulted in BP beating the Germans in decoding it themselves. For example, A would send B a message and then B would reply, 'Cannot read you.' BP would decrypt the first message even before the Germans had done the repeat message. As a result it would be with Allied commanders before the Germans got it.

At the end of the war, Levenson was sent to southern Germany with a special Anglo-American team (TICOM – Technical Intelligence Committee) to nab the latest German communications technology before the Russians. The first proposal was to parachute them into Berlin with the 101st Airborne as protection. Instead they went overland and recovered a lot of equipment, including some from Berchtesgaden, Hitler's Alpine retreat, and drove it back to England in a convoy of German signals trucks. After VJ-Day, the foundations of Anglo-American Intelligence exchange was solid and Levenson, who worked for the National Security Agency (the equivalent of GCHQ), knew that this unending close relationship began at Bletchley.

7928156 Bernard Lewis

He was born in May 1916, son of Jane and Hyman Lewis (an east European immigrant) in east London. He attended Wilson College prep school and then the Polytechnic School, before going to read Middle Eastern History at SOAS, where he became proficient in Arabic, Russian, Turkish

and other south European and Middle Eastern languages. On the outbreak of war he joined the Armoured Corps (59th Regiment) and was
posted to Tidworth, and then transferred to the Intelligence Corps as a
corporal, in Winchester in early 1941. After several months he was suddenly ordered to 'an unknown destination' and told to collect a travel warrant to go to London. At Waterloo, he was told to ask the railway transport
officer (RTO) for instructions. He then received a warrant for Euston
where the RTO gave him another warrant for Bletchley. He was informed
that 'someone would meet him'. At Bletchley he was taken to digs in the
village and told to report to BP next morning. Concerned that his family
would not know where to contact him, he was told mail would be forwarded. Amusingly, he received a letter diverted from Winchester, the
following day; so much for secrecy and travel warrants to mysterious destinations.[56]

For several months in 1941, he worked on translating and decoding
and was detached from the army; he attended the Friday night Jewish
gatherings with Joe Gillis. He was later moved, in 1942, to the Foreign Office in London. Post-war he taught at SOAS until 1974, then at Princeton,
New Jersey, until 1986, when he partially retired, and where he now lives,
aged 88 at time of interview. He is much published.

2378351 Vivian David Lipman

He was born in west London in 1920, grandson of Rabbi Nahum Lipman
and son of Samuel Lipman, MBE. From a traditionally Jewish home he
went to St Paul's School and then Magdalen College, Oxford, to read history; he refused to sit BA papers on the Sabbath and arrangements were
made for him to take them on another day.[57] His address is given on his
AJEX card as Grange Cottage, Shattley, Stratford-upon-Avon. At Nuffield
College, Oxford, he worked for the Social Reconstruction Survey and was
then called up to the RCOS and Intelligence Corps from 1942–45, working at BP. Little is known about his work there, as, like many others, he
refused to talk about such matters. Post-war, he became director of ancient monuments and received the CVO. He was also a leading Anglo-
Jewish historian. He died in March 1990.

21524 Major Lionel Loewe

Lionel was the uncle of Michael Loewe (listed below) and worked at BP
in Hut 3, on the Enigma codes. With a German mother, Lionel was almost bilingual. He was a graduate of Jesus College, Cambridge, in Classics, and of Sandhurst, and he served in the Royal Sussex Regiment in
the First World War in France. He had worked in Military Intelligence in
India and Ireland before the Second World War and served in SOE in Holland, running a small spy ring near the German border until May 1940.

His language skills took him to Bletchley. His main job appears to have been translating coded messages from German, especially where the codes were incomplete and good German was needed to 'unravel' the true message. His son David testifies to him being constantly on night shifts. Little more is know about his work[58] there, but his son does remember him being in a performance of *HMS Pinafore* in one of the BP concert parties.

Michael Loewe[59]

He was born in November 1922 and was reading Classics at Magdalen College, Oxford, when the Japanese war broke out. After interview in London, he appeared for his first Japanese lesson at the Gas Company showroom at Ardour House in Bedford on 2 February 1942, with the first group of Oxbridge undergraduates, destined to work on breaking the Japanese naval codes. There being a great shortage of Japanese linguists, these young men and women were put forward as potential students for the Inter-Service Special Intelligence School at Bedford, with the object of learning enough very basic Japanese to break ciphers, build code books and translate intercepted Japanese radio signals into English. It was to be a six-month 'crash course'. This was followed by several weeks on a crypto-analysis course. Michael was then sent to BP on 21 August (others to South-East Asia) to Hut 7.[60] With him was another young Jewish student, Jonathan Cohen. As civilians, they were soon thrown in at the deep end to the secret world of naval Intelligence and ciphers; resplendent uniforms and naval etiquette; Admiralty communiqués and naval acronyms. They were even sent on a navy frigate patrol in the North Sea to familiarize them with naval problems.

The greater part of Michael's work was in 'stripping and book building' – eliminating the figures of a cipher table and determining the meaning of the underlying code groups, requiring statistical and indexing skills, usually done in cooperation with the Americans, who were either on site or in other locations around the world. Cribbing (exploiting Japanese operators' mistakes) and captured documents were also used. Large racks had to be made to hold the files being accumulated and for many years after the war, one such rack was used by Michael in his study at Cambridge.

Among Michael's personal memories are those of some around him cheating in the use of meal tickets; WRENs singing Christmas carols in the corridor; concerts by local talent; and the day the German war ended, announced at a solemn open-air meeting by deputy director at the time, Nigel de Grey. But a moment of truth came in August 1945, when a message came in clear Japanese. It was the emperor surrendering. But it was in such highly formal, classical Japanese, nobody could clearly understand it.

After the war he taught at SOAS and then Cambridge (Chinese studies) until he retired in 1990.

6108735 Sergeant Hyam Zandell Maccoby

He was born in Sunderland in 1924, the son of Ephraim Myer Maccoby, of 8 Lorne Terrace, a maths teacher and grandson of rabbis. From Bede Grammar School he went to Balliol and read Classics but after a short time volunteered to join the army to fight the Nazis. Short in stature, he was sent to Catterick as a Royal Signaller and in 1942 was sent to Bletchley Park where he worked mainly on the night shifts translating decoded messages for despatch. He spoke little to his family of his work there.[61] After the war he held several university academic posts, latterly as professor of Jewish Studies at Leeds, and was a prolific author on biblical subjects. He died in May 2004.[62]

Professor Maxwell Herman Alexander Newman, FRS, originally Neumann

He was born in February 1897 in Chelsea, son of Herman and Sarah Pike. He served in the First World War and was a mathematician from St John's College, Cambridge. He was actually one of Alan Turing's lecturers when Turing was a student. Joining BP in September 1942, he was located first in the crypto-analyst 'Testery' section and then later had his own department in 'the Newmanry' in Hut F, assisted by Jack Good. Newman was convinced that a machine could be built to break the codes and by May 1943 this had been done, by his collaboration with technicians at the Telecommunications Research Establishment (TRE) at Malvern. Nicknamed 'Robinson' – after Heath Robinson, the cartoonist designer of fantastic machines – it was a great success and became known as Colossus, the first computer (see note 7). It was Newman who broke the German Army Lorenz code. He was much liked; one staff member (American Sergeant George Vergine) said:

> Max Newman was a marvellous fellow, and I always sort of felt grateful to have known him ... we used to have tea parties ... which were mathematical discussions on problems, developments, techniques ... in the small conference room ... a topic would be written on the blackboard and all of the analysts, including Newman, would come tea in hand and chew it around and see whether it would be useful for cracking codes. It was very productive and afterwards it would be summarised in the research log.

Peter Hilton (listed above) added:

> Newman was a perfect facilitator ... he realised he could get the best out of us by trusting to our own good intentions ... and strong

motivation ... he was as informal as possible ... for example he gave us one week in four off ... we always wrote down what we were thinking in a huge book so we could use them ... he was a model academic administrator.[63]

After the war he returned to academia at Manchester University and died in 1984 in Cambridge. Displays at BP and his old college explain his contribution.

Rolf Noskwith

He was born on 19 June 1919, in Chemnitz, Germany, into a well-to-do textile-producing family who had the foresight to leave before Hitler came to power. Rolf's family name was originally Noskovitch, and his father was originally Chaim, then Heinrich, then Charles Henry. His mother, Malka Ginsberg, and father Chaim were born in Lodz, Poland. With family and business connections in England, they sold up in Germany and came to Nottingham in 1932 with his sister Alexandra, who later became a famous doctor.[64] After Nottingham High School, and whilst at Trinity College, Cambridge, reading mathematics, Rolf was interviewed with many other students in 1939, to help decide where they could best be used in the war effort. At first he was rejected, because he failed the medical for the artillery, but a year later this was put aside at a second interview for work as a linguist and decoder. He was again rejected, this time due to his German birth. Much aggrieved by this, he continued in his third year at Cambridge. Then in a third interview with the writer C.P. Snow and the famous chess champion Hugh Alexander, he was finally accepted and he arrived at BP on 19 June 1941, his twenty-second birthday.[65]

He was met and taken to Hut 8 by Alexander, where the German naval traffic was read, thanks to material captured from enemy weather ships, which had shortly before helped lead to the sinking of the *Bismarck*. Here he worked under the direct leadership of the great Alan Turing, with Alexander as deputy.

His first billet was in a rather primitive village cottage near Buckingham, which he reached late one night in the pitch dark. He groped his way into a room and found he was sharing with Bill Tutte, one of the great decoders of Bletchley. The following week he pleaded to be moved somewhere with more congenial facilities and went to stay thereafter with George and Elizabeth Bessell in Newport Pagnell; a bus was available but he had a bike too in case he missed it.

As intercepted messages came in to Hut 8, they were logged in a register, many being duplicates from several stations. The code had been broken by Turing, but many messages were corrupt and Rolf's job was to guess meanings or 'crib', from the German, and then they were run through the Bombe (decoding) machine, which could use hundreds of variables, until the message made sense and was decoded.

One German message Rolf decoded concerned the *Struma*, a ship carrying escaping Jewish refugees attempting to get to Israel, which was sunk in the Black Sea with almost all passengers killed. Rolf remembers this causing him much distress.

In late 1941, Rolf used a crib to unravel the meaning of messages about coloured flares used for identification by the German Navy, an obviously important breakthrough for RN ships to use. This enabled him to go on to break the 'Offizier' Enigma code, used between German Naval HQ and its U-boat officers at sea. This involved the intense and careful analysis of many German messages and captured ('pinched') code-books from U-110 (depicted in the movie *U-571*). Finally, Rolf had his hoped-for solution fed into one of the Bombes and then he took two days' leave, arranging for one of his colleagues, Shaun Wylie,[66] to send him a telegram at home to inform him if the crib had been successful, using the code word 'fish' to denote a result. Rolf's father took the telephone call as the telegram was read out, totally mystified by the word *'pompano'*. Rolf looked it up – it meant fish. 'Offizier' had been cracked and the effect on the saving of merchant ships from U-boats was huge, because the positions of the enemy were known and they could be hunted or avoided as resources permitted.

In 1943 when they needed more German messages for making cribs, they got the RAF to use a system called 'Gardening'. RAF mines would be laid in a known location at sea, the Germans would send warning messages in code to their navy, and Rolf and his team would decipher the messages, and thus the code, as they knew roughly what the German message had said.

His work continued through the war and in 1944 Hut 8 was moved to Block D, where he played an important part in deciphering weather-ship messages which gave urgent and crucial information useful for the D-Day landings. Rolf also remembers decrypting the message from Field Marshall von Witzleben after the July 1944 plot, announcing that Hitler was dead; it turned out not to be true, as we know. In fact, this message was passed to Hut 4 where Walter Ettinghausen and Michael Cohen dealt with it too; it began, *'Nur durch Offizier zu entziffern'* – to be deciphered by officer only; then, 'Naval Headquarters to all, Operation Valkyrie ... Adolf Hitler is dead ... the new Führer is Field Marshal von Witzleben.' The message was sent to the Admiralty, and then Cohen and friends walked to the canteen for their midnight meal. Cohen remarked, *'Der Lezte Witz seines Lebens'* (the last joke of his life), for *Witzleben* meant 'joke-life'. But the announcement of the Stauffenberg plotters was premature and by morning most were dead.[67]

Rolf remembers well the Jewish and Zionist Society, to which he was introduced by Jack Good, and Walter Ettinghausen saying he would be on the first boat to Palestine at war's end; this he did.

After the war Rolf stayed at BP for some time working on Japanese and Yugoslav and even American codes. He could not tear himself away and went with the whole section when it moved to Eastcote at the very beginnings of the Cold War period. He finally left in June 1946 and began work for his father's hosiery and lingerie firm, Charnos (from *Cha*rles *Nos*kwith), at Ilkeston and became director in 1952. He is still working there.

In 1947 he met Walter Eytan in New York , who was working to get the UN partition plan through at the UN for the rebirth of Israel. Rolf offered Walter his services in Israel as a codebreaker; Eytan replied, amusingly, 'Codebreakers we have plenty of!'

The first time Rolf attended a reunion was when the BP Association opened the museum and he met people he had not seen for over fifty years. When *Codebreakers* was launched at the Imperial War Museum he met again with veterans from Bletchley and also appeared in one of the Channel 4 documentaries. He also has a curious link with Alan Turing in that his father-in-law was Turing's psychiatrist.

88920 Squadron Leader Ary Thadee 'Ted' Pilley

He was born at 123 Boulevard St Michel in Paris on 7 March 1909, son of the famous Polish Jewish artists Leopold and Lena Pilichowski (mentioned above). When he was aged 4, his family all came to live in London at 7 Hills Road, St John's Wood, which became a famous meeting place for the Jewish intelligentsia of the day – including visits from Einstein on occasions – and many of the foremost Zionist leaders of the day. Ted went to the Merchant Taylors' School and then to St John's College, Oxford. Later he worked as a sales manager in the international textile business, using his languages, and he met his wife in Holland.

Ted and his wife had founded and managed the Linguists Club in London in the 1930s, where clients met to speak and practise in various European languages, led by a facilitator. Ted was serving at Aldergrove RAF base, Northern Ireland, at the outbreak of war,[68] as Intelligence officer for 245 Squadron protecting the port of Liverpool. His log book shows that he flew several sorties. But it was his linguistic skills that led him to be recruited to BP (his wife was also screened over tea at Simpson's by a discreet and cultivated MI5 agent, as she had been born in Holland). Peter Pilley says that it was Ted who recommended Naky Doniach – his brother-in-law – for recruitment to BP (see Doniach's entry above).

Ted worked in the watch room in Hut 3 with Jim Rose (listed below) in the Air Intelligence section, deciding on the priority and precise and concise wording of distilled, decoded Luftwaffe messages and Intelligence, and to whom, and in what wording, to pass them on to in the field.

At the end of the war, at some stage – probably in Italy – he was given the job of interrogating a senior Nazi leader or general (Peter Pilley is not sure whom) and almost as soon as they had begun, the Nazi asked Ted if he was a Jew. When Ted answered yes, the German said he should leave as he would not speak to a Jew. Ted walked out of the cell.

Post-war, he again ran the Linguists Club, was made Officier d'Academie by France, and helped found the Association of International Conference Interpreters and Institute of Linguists. He died in London in June 1982.

Lieutenant Frank Templeton Prince

He was born in Kimberley, South Africa in 1912; his father, Harry Prinz, was Jewish. After Johannesburg and Balliol College, Oxford, where he read English, he worked for Chatham House as a foreign policy analyst, but was also a published poet. When war came he went into army Intelligence and cryptography at Bletchley. After the war he became an established poet and lecturer at Southampton University. Author of the famous Second World War poem, 'Soldiers Bathing', he died in August 2003.[69]

77282 Squadron Leader, later Wing Commander, Jim Rose (US Legion of Merit)

He was aka Elliot Joseph Benn Rosenheim,[70] and was born in Kensington in June 1909, son of Ernst and Julia Levy. He went to Rugby and New College, Oxford, where he read Classics. His AJEX card notes his father's address as 9 Pembridge Place, London W2. Before the outbreak of war he worked helping Jewish refugees from Nazi Germany and then joined 609 Squadron RAF as Intelligence officer in September 1939. He was then sent to BP.[71] Rose specialized in assessment in the Air Intelligence section in Hut 3, for which he had to develop a cool appraisal of the Luftwaffe's order of battle, strengths and weaknesses, on all fronts, based on information coming from Hut 6. His main job was as head of 3A – BP's main air advisor – and he was to liaise with the air staff and the BP crypto-analysts, as well as to maintain the delicate relations between the competing needs of all three Services. As he described,[72] Hut 3 was centred on the watch room, where watch-keepers sat with the representatives of the three Services. Together they compiled the material being decoded from German into readable English information, prioritized it and then sent it for action to commanders-in-chief and commanders in the field. It was also indexed, so it could be cross-referenced with other information that had been received, which might then reveal patterns of developing enemy events or strategies: a message was not just of itself, but could be related to previous and later messages to reveal other Intelligence.

Rose wrote that Ultra severely cut supplies to Rommel, as it enabled the RAF to constantly sink his convoys from Italy. However, the aircraft were not allowed to bomb until a reconnaissance aircraft had been seen by the enemy, so that the Germans would not be able to guess that Enigma had been cracked, attributing the raid instead to discovery by the aircraft. It was information from Ultra, said Rose, that brought Rommel defeat at Alamein. Rose was also selected to deal with US liaison and flew to Washington with Colonel Telford Taylor of US Intelligence to select Americans who could serve in the rarefied atmosphere of Hut 3.

In December 1944, Rose flew urgently to SHAEF in Paris, with the military adviser at BP, Major Alan Pryce-Jones, to warn the Americans about the coming Ardennes offensive. They briefed Eisenhower's Intelligence Officer, General Strong. He doubted the Germans were capable of such an attack. Pryce-Jones, with his suede shoes and own form of battledress, sat on the corner of Strong's desk and said, 'My dear sir, if you believe that, you'll believe anything.' Three weeks later came the German attack.[73] Rose added, 'Hut 3 were asked to do a post-mortem ... and showed the SHAEF intelligence failure.'

After the war Rose became, among other things, an international journalist and a senior manager of the Institute of Race Relations.

Dame Miriam Louisa Rothschild-Lane

She was born on 5 August 1908 at Polebrook in Northamptonshire.[74] daughter of a Hungarian Jewish aristocrat, Roszika Wertheimstein, and the British Jewish banker Nathaniel Charles Rothschild. Educated informally but thoroughly at home, on the family Ashton Wold estate near Peterborough, and at the family Tring museums, she only much later in life studied formally at Chelsea Polytechnic (zoology) and Bedford College, London (literature), but her scholarly works on zoology have brought her numerous honorary doctorates and degrees. Miriam spent two years at BP[75] after being interviewed and headhunted like many other scientists at the time (she had been working on scientific war research in Plymouth). She worked mostly night shifts, translating German coded messages in the Naval Section. She disliked it intensely. She still felt bound by her oath of secrecy and so would say little more to the author about the precise nature of her work. She lived in a flat at Mentmore which was given to her by a Rothschild relative, Lord Roseberry, and would commute in her car to BP; he also gave her a housekeeper for the duration, so hers was a somewhat privileged status as far as accommodation was concerned. Whilst at BP, in 1943, she met and married a distinguished and wounded refugee Jewish/British Commando, later Captain George Lanyi, aka Lane, MC,[76] and she then asked to leave Bletchley on the basis that he was not born in the UK and was a security risk. In actual fact they asked her to stay, but she wanted to leave and did so.

All of Dame Miriam's mother's family were murdered in the Holocaust in Hungary. After the war she carried out an enormous amount of scientific research in Israel – where she spent a lot of time – and the UK, publishing over 300 papers and nine books. She died at Ashton Wold on 20 January 2005, aged 96.

Anne Ross (formerly Mendoza/Meadows)

She was born in June 1919 in Graham Road, Hackney, daughter of Mark and Mina Mendoza, and attended Wilton Way and then Laura Place (Clapton) Girls' School. Her grandmother and the grandmother of the actor Peter Sellars were sisters, and both are related to the great English Jewish boxer, Daniel Mendoza.[77] After Pitmans College and also a qualification in teaching Hebrew from Jews' College, Anne moved with her family to Bletchley to escape the 1940 bombing, and here she discovered staff were needed at a 'government office' at Bletchley Park. After applying she was interviewed by a civilian male in October 1940; he placed a revolver on the desk during the interview. He tried to tell her that as a Jew, she was not 'British enough' but she argued the case of her seventeenth-century antecedents and there was no answer to that. Her feeling at the time was that the interviewer was very anti-Semitic. However, her super typing skills got her the job and she was sent to work in the library at BP. Later she was sent to Hut 4, Naval Section, to type out decoded messages ready for forwarding.

On one occasion she had the temerity to ask a naval officer what GCCS meant on the letter headings. This caused a major whispering 'huddle' among the gold braid, as anyone asking a question of that sort was suspect; eventually it was decided it was a sensible question and she was told.

There were terrible shortages at the time, and paper and paper clips could not be had at first. Neither was Anne very impressed with the laid-back attitude, poor filing skills and slow typing of many of her colleagues. On one occasion, a long, narrow cardboard box, in which her boyfriend had sent her some flowers, was recycled by Anne to store the copies of the message slips they were typing, as it was exactly the size of the slips; it was a great success, but such was the state of penury and organization at BP that when a second box arrived a few weeks later, her colleagues in the hut were overjoyed. Later they had the carpenters make up racks of these; they christened Hut 4 'the morgue', as the boxes resembled coffins.

Another clear memory is when Walter Ettinghausen (listed above) arrived; one day a small, rotund man in large army boots marched into Hut 4, resembling – as Anne thought – a younger version of Einstein. It was the beginning of a lifelong friendship. But as he left the hut on that day, Anne's naval officer, Beasley, announced in his upper-class, pompous drawl, 'Good God, are we having kosher meat now?' Anne felt awful and still feels her skin crawl when she remembers Beasley's remark. However, Walter cared not and he had every Saturday off and ate kosher or vegetarian food for the whole five years he was there – an act of defiance. He was hugely popular with all the staff as well as an expert at his job.

In another incident, Anne was applying to return to secretarial work at BP but was constantly told she could not be spared from her job. One day a naval officer colleague, Billington, told her in confidence that some officers from the Admiralty had made it known that they did not want any more Jews in positions of authority at BP. In the middle of the war, this greatly upset her and she spoke to Walter Ettinghausen for consolation.

Anne remembers vividly the sinking of the *Bismarck*; Walter Ettinghausen and his second in command had cots put in the hut and were there for forty-eight hours during the chase. Anne remembers coming to work one morning as Walter emerged from the hut unshaven and unkempt, to announce they had got *Bismarck*. Decoded signals from Hut 4 had played a major part in tracking her down.

Anne was not on duty the night Hut 4 was accidentally damaged by a bomb from a lone German plane dumping its load as it limped back home. Next day she came to work and noticed no problems. Not until the end of the war was she told what had happened. The hut had been repaired and painted so secretly and quickly that she did not know.

Ultimately, Anne was put in charge of eighty staff, with twenty per shift[78] and twenty in reserve, and her administrative duties meant she no longer had time for typing. She was constantly having to manage the staff and juggle the shifts as some wished to go to a ball here, or Sandringham there; most clerks in the early days were debutantes and a few were friends of the Royal family. There was a lot of drinking and sleeping around among many of the officers and the female staff – all of which rather shocked an Orthodox Jewish working-class, teetotal girl from Hackney.

After some time a hostel was built on the site as the local billets had become full. They were only tiny 'monk's cells' but at least they were private without nosey landladies. Anne and her sister Belle managed to get one each on the genuine grounds that they could rarely eat the non-kosher food in a billet, but at the canteen could pick and choose. One day in the hostel, a woman had a baby and it died; Anne recalls that the woman hid the baby in an air shaft but it was discovered and she was escorted from BP; nobody knows what became of her. Anne says that the birth of illegitimate babies at BP was not uncommon, as indeed it was not in the country as a whole during wartime, and that the numbers increased when the first American troops arrived. One handsome American officer came to work at BP and married one of the English girls; when she had a baby it was Black, from some ancestral intermarriage in his family. It created quite a lot of gossip in those days.

The first Christmas, a huge traditional meal was prepared for the staff, but being kosher, Anne and her sister had to forego this and ate sardines and salad instead.

One of Anne's naval officers was ordered to sea to try and capture a German Enigma key from a German submarine or ship's captain. These were kept in the captain's pocket and a rapid capture was needed if such a 'pinch' could be successful, before the captain destroyed it. Anne's colleague spent many fruitless days at sea on a destroyer trying to carry out such a deed and suffering terribly from sea-sickness. Then one day they did force a U-boat to surface and as the captain came to the conning tower, he put his hand in his pocket, possibly to destroy the key; but a British rating thought he was going for a gun and shot him; he fell over the side and was never seen again. After that Anne's colleague refused to go to sea again.

Another story Anne recalls is about a young, rather plain woman in her hut who kept sniffing all the time; her colleagues told her about it and she was terribly offended. One day soon after, one of the very handsome senior naval officers, who was married to a very beautiful actress, saw her weeping in a corner and asked her to come and chat about it over a drink. The next thing that everyone knew was that they had run off together. He was later apprehended for leaving his post.

Anne remembers how the messages developed from German to Italian, Vichy French and Japanese, as the war progressed. As she had two brothers and her husband all at sea, she was allowed to visit the plot room where the huge map showed the position worldwide of all the navy's vessels, so she at least could have an idea where they were and if they were safe. When the Americans arrived some of the jargon had to be altered; all the rubber stamps had to be changed to read 'Top Secret' instead of 'Most Secret' in deference to US policy; Anne remembers that this annoyed the Brits a great deal.

Quite often colleagues would receive bad news about loved ones lost in the fighting and there was much consoling and tears on those terrible occasions.

There was a young woman called Ozla Benning in Anne's hut who was engaged to the present Prince Philip; she used to meet him at the home of Lord Mountbatten whenever he was on leave. Nothing came of this romance, long before his marriage to the present Queen, and it is not generally known of today. Anne and her husband were invited to dinner with Ozla (who kept photos of Prince Philip on her desk next to Anne's) and the prince (an unknown to the public in those days), but they could not go because Anne's husband had no suit to wear. Had she known who the prince was later to become ...

Churchill arrived at BP late one cold, misty, November afternoon. He had been examining documents in 'the mansion' and was about to leave. His car was parked in the circular drive. He walked into the central grass area and, knowing all eyes in the huts were on him, gestured to one and all to gather round him. Anne remembers that hundreds of staff poured out of the huts and stood around his diminutive figure, as his bodyguards held the throng back. Anne was standing six feet from him.

He looked around and then ordered his men to bring a large metal waste bin and turn it upside down, and upon it he was stood by his four minders. He gave an electrifying speech, underlining how crucial was their work, not only to the far-flung Allied Forces on land, at sea and in the air, but also in feeding the nation as more ships got through with food. After what Anne remembers was a long time, he got down and allowed many people to approach him and chat, despite the protestations of his bodyguards. He then made his way to his vehicle and Anne clearly remembers it was the first time she had seen shaded windows in a car. As he drove off she clearly saw his V for victory sign that he made through the small rear window, to the cheers of the crowd. They all returned in silence to their work.

Next day he sent his famous telegram: 'So pleased to see the hens are laying without clucking.'

Anne left BP at the end of the war and has been to reunions there. After the fiftieth anniversary of VE-Day, she took her two grandsons to see where she had spent the 1940–45 period. Previously they had watched the television celebrations with her as she explained all the different military units to them. As they went through the gates at BP, Anne said she would now show them where Granny won the war; the 7-year-old said, 'But Granny, what about those marching men we saw on TV?'

Whilst looking around the museum, Anne noticed that nobody was able to recognize anyone else after fifty years, and one grandson tore up a piece of cardboard and wrote her name on it and pinned it to her sweater; immediately contact was made and ever since, BP reunion organizers have provided name tags for veterans.

Margaret Judith Rubens

She was born in May 1920, daughter of Alex (a Mizrahi leader) and Rosamund (whose grandmother was an aunt of BP member Lionel Loewe). She attended South Hampstead School and then Newnham College, Cambridge, 1939–42, where she read Classics. Her address was 37 Lyncroft Gardens, London NW6. At some stage she was sent to BP, probably on translation work, but no more is known about what she did there. She stayed with the Foreign Office until 1948 and was at some stage a social worker and translator in Paris until 1966. She was related to the Loewe family, two of whom also worked at BP (listed above). She died in June 1996.[79]

Ruth Sebag-Montefiore

She was born in 1916 at 12 Westbourne Terrace, London, daughter of Major Laurie and Mrs Dora Magnus (née Spielman). Educated at Notting Hill High School and Burgess Hill School near Brighton, Ruth did secretarial work afterwards and then was recommended to apply for a job with the Foreign Office in 1939. After interview at Broadway Buildings, for an unknown posting, she was sent to BP in the very early days when only a few staff had been installed, and she found herself working in the main manor house itself. This was indeed ironic as the former owner, Sir Herbert Leon, was her great uncle. Later she moved to Hut 10. Ruth describes her work at BP in her book:[80]

> We were sending and receiving coded telegrams to and from agents in every war zone. Each agent and each codist had two identical books, one a paperback novel, the other filled with five-figure groups of numbers. To encode the telegram you encoded the first few words – which had to contain more than fifteen letters – of a line in the novel, indicating in figure code, the page, line and five consecutive letters – which represented numbers – chosen first – and the five-figure group in the numbers book, where you were starting the message. After turning the message into figures, agent and codist proceeded, by adding or deducting one group of figures from the other to encode or decode the telegram ... you never knew from day to day what messages would reveal. Incoming telegrams consisted of all kinds of news picked up by agents – safe houses for escaped POWs and new agents, disappearance of agents, leaks, landing zones – as well as enemy troop movements, sightings of U-boats, targets for the RAF – and the number of 'Zs' indicated urgency, three being most urgent. All was sent to HQ for action.
>
> Once I saw a short telegram enquiring about the health of my cousin Tim Cohen, seriously wounded at Mareth in North Africa, signed by MI6 head, Sir Stewart Menzies, a lifelong friend of Tim's father. This was quite a coincidence as I was one of 60 working three shifts! I added an extra Z (to two) and forwarded it! Our work was so secret that we did not pay income tax; this annoyed my bank manager when I was unable to tell him what I did!
>
> All the codists were female and from varied backgrounds, some with husbands serving, some with children – all uprooted. The early appointees were single, middle-aged and dedicated, if scatty; they formed a sort of self-appointed elite. We were younger, noisy but efficient, and regarded with some disdain. I had yet to learn how women who are otherwise pleasant and normal human beings can

behave in their working lives. A few codists left after the first month or two, unable to stand the life, but most of us stuck it out, marking time till the war was over.

Hut 10 was run by a retired general, ill at ease with 60 women, but the department head was a Miss Montgomery of the FO, whose agile mind was hidden behind a deceptively gentle Miss-Marple-like exterior. Thin and angular, she was always neatly dressed in well-cut coats and skirts so that the long paper cuffs she wore – a fresh pair every day – to protect her sleeves, struck a bizarre note in so non-descript and conventional an appearance. The other Huts were filled with brilliant minds, interesting individually, but collectively, when they poured out of the Huts for breaks, gesticulating, unkempt and bespectacalled, they looked like beings from another planet.

My first billet was in Bletchley town centre, in a tiny terraced house owned by a train driver and his wife, the Jarmans, both with a lively cockney sense of humour and very warm and friendly, who doted on their two sons who were serving. Bath water was heated with a small kettle, and rent was 10s 6d (52p) per week; I was joined later by a friend, Lillian Beresford-Peirse. Later I moved to Leighton Buzzard and stayed for the remaining 3 years.

In late 1944 Ruth was transferred to Eindhoven and the Hague as the Allies advanced, and was ordered to wear ATS uniform, in case of capture by the enemy. Conditions were very basic but the Dutch loved them as liberators. They often gave them food from their mess as the Dutch were starving at first. Here she met the Soviet spy, George Blake – then a callow youth, a most unlikely-looking traitor that he was.

In May 1945 Ruth was flown home and demobbed at Broadway Buildings where she had signed on. In 1946 she married her second cousin, Denzil, the widower of her late sister Pam. He was related to the first Jewish VC winner, Lieutenant Alexander de Passe, and had been born in the house which is now the Israeli Embassy.[81] Later Ruth worked as a sub-editor of children's books at Chatto & Windus in London.

Captain Abraham Sinkov

A USA codebreaker, he was born in 1907 in Philadelphia, son of Russian Jewish immigrants, brought up in New York, and later graduated in mathematics from City College. In 1930, together with his high school friend Solomon Kullback (listed here) he joined the US government crypto-analyst service using his linguistic and maths skills, working under William Friedman. He received his commission in the army and also his doctorate, encouraged by Friedman. In 1936 he was sent to Panama to establish the first US radio listening site outside the country. He arrived in the UK in January 1941, in absolute secrecy, with a liaison team to work at Bletchley on Enigma, with Lieutenant Leo Rosen (listed above).[82] They brought, among other things, the machine that would break the Japanese 'Purple' code, designed by Friedman, all under the aegis of the recently concluded Anglo-US cryptographic exchange accord.

In July 1942, he headed General MacArthur's crypto-analysis centre in Melbourne, and contributed hugely to Allied success in New Guinea and the Philippines against the Japanese. Post-war, Sinkov stayed in the US Intelligence service and was also professor of mathematics at Arizona State University. He died in 1998.

Phyllis Wix

She was born in July 1923 in Stamford Hill, Hackney,[83] daughter of Abraham and Edith, and went to school at Kilburn High. After evacuation to Keswick in the Lake District she went to the London School of Economics and was then simply called for interview to Broadway (she found later this was the HQ of British Intelligence) and asked about her interest in such things as chess, bridge and working in a team. She received a letter asking her to appear at Bletchley railway station at a certain time in July 1944. Billeted at Woburn Sands, one evening she came down to make tea in her digs and found her landlord drinking tea sucked through a sugar lump. This is a traditional Russian Jewish method and it transpired his father was from Russia, but she cannot remember the family name.

Phyllis worked the shift system in Hut 6, sorting the teleprinter tapes into order ready for the decoders. She was a little vague about how this was done but says her team used a mock-up of an Enigma machine to crib meanings, using known phrases, dates and call signs. One incident she recalls was receiving a letter of thanks from a senior officer in the field after D-Day, describing how they had overrun a German HQ and found messages, recently sent to German forces, that the British Forces had read that morning; the officer paid tribute to the speed with which the Bletchley staff were sending them information which the Germans had just received themselves. Socially, Phyllis remembers the Jewish meetings in the flat of Joe Gillis, and knew the whole crowd well.

Conclusion

Despite the tiny size of the Jewish community (less than 0.5 per cent of the UK population) it is clear that the Jewish input to the work at Bletchley was very significant, even excluding the US personnel.[84] The above accounts reveal the high quality, and the list in Appendix 2 reveals the high number, of Jewish participants; and this despite the clear genteel anti-Semitism which Anne Mendoza and Walter Ettinghausen were witness to on a few occasions, by those who should have known better. This chapter in British Jewry's help in defence of the realm can thus be added to the enormous part played in the regular and special forces of this country and is a part of British-Jewish history of which we can be enormously and justly proud.

Appendix 1

In a 1990s' edition of the *AJEX Journal*, the following appeared:

> Wing Commander Wally Zigmund, President of the Ruislip Branch of AJEX, played a role in one of the luckiest and most important captures of the war ... during his second tour of ops with 269 Squadron in Iceland in 1941. One day in bad weather one of his patrol aircraft spotted a submarine. He was ordered into a Hudson to find them and took off in heavy snow and low cloud south-west for the Atlantic ocean. Suddenly the co-pilot shouted 'U-boat half a mile ahead!' Wally's plane dropped four depth charges straddling the submarine which was forced to the surface after rolling completely over. They circled and used their machine guns every time any crew tried to get to the submarine's gun to shoot back. After three hours of this, the submarine raised a white shirt to surrender. The RN arrived and captured U-570. Code books found in the submarine were taken immediately to Bletchley and used for deciphering Enigma!

Jewish Personnel at Bletchley Park in the Second World War

Those considered Jewish are considered so either because Jewish Chaplain Cards were found or because the name makes it obvious.

The list of names of those who served at BP, used by the author, comes from the research list of Christopher King, archivist at the BP museum. I am also grateful to Rolf Noskwith, veteran codebreaker at BP, for his help during an interview in May 2004 at his home. There are many other Jewish-sounding names on King's list but without proof I have had to omit them for now.

Among others who gave personal testimony were Peter Hilton (USA); Michael Loewe; David Loewe; Morris Milner; Morris Hoffman; the nephew of Maurice Spector; Lena Woolstone; the husband of Doris Blustone; the daughter of Harry Horne (Valerie Serkes in Israel); Mrs Cynthia Maccoby; Mrs Ruth Doniach-Durant; Iona Doniach; Mrs Barbara Barnett; Beverley Nenk; Jane Bennett (Australia); Albert Ettinghausen; Samuel Goldstein; the Bogush sisters; Ann Ross/Mendoza/Meadows; Phyllis Wix; Gila Goldberg (Israel), daughter of J.D. Goldberg, and her mother, Hilda Feder-Goldberg; the *Jewish Chronicle* librarians; Bernard Lewis; Samantha

Chalmers (Newnham College Archives); Joan Friedman; Dame Miriam Rothschild-Lane; Wilf Lockwood; Penny Finestein; Kate Perry (Girton College Archives); Peter Willett (University of Sheffield); Peter Pilley; Alan Bath; Ralph Erskine; Ruth Sebag-Montefiore; Hugh Sebag-Montefiore; Anna Sander (Balliol Archives). Jeremy Schonfield (editor, Jewish Historical Society of England) was also a huge support and assistance in reaching several surviving Jewish participants and their families.

Some US names came from Tony Sales' website.

Many Jewish personnel served in the out-stations of BP and in the 'Y' Service, but that subject is beyond the scope of this study.

Note: 'P' indicates probably Jewish; where there is no rank, they are marked as CA (Civilian Attached – i.e. not in forces); *JC* refers to *Jewish Chronicle*; tbc = to be confirmed.

Abraham, Miss J.L.T. – P.

Abrahamson, Mr Sidney – translator.

Abramson, Mr J.L.T. – P.

Albrecht, Leading WREN S.D.M. – P.

Auerbach, Private, First Class, Herbert – USA.

Bailin, Captain William – Hut 4.

Bailin, Henry (brother to William, above).

Barfield, Dr – P.

Barfield, Miss B.C. – P.

Barnet, Cyril – AJEX file – Colossus team for two years.

Barnett, Flight Lieutenant Richard David – RAF.

Barnett, Kenneth Peter, translator – P.

Barrow, Lieutenant G.W./B.W. – RNVR, DSO.

Bass, Esme – P.

Bass, Mia – P.

Bauman, Elizabeth – P.

Bauman, Miss M.L.A. – P.

Benenson, Peter – born Germany, founded Amnesty International.

Benhamin, Miss K.M. – P.

Bennet, Captain R. – RNVR – probably Levy-Bennett.

Bennett, later Guss, Major Jane, ATS W192366.

Birley, Major Benjamin J. – P.

Bischoff, Mrs Elizabeth Grace

Blank, Mr and Mrs A. David – P.

Bloom, Army Sergeant William (info. given by M. Bogush) – from Leeds.

Blustone, Corporal Doris – ATS.

Bogush, Miss Anita

Bogush, Miss Muriel (sister of Anita).

Bourne/Henry, WREN Ruth – *JC* article.

Carter, Sidney Norman, aka Norman Chernitsky

Cohen, Captain David 'Daoud', aka Cowan – actually Michael Cohen, listed below.

Cohen, Laurence Jonathan

Cohen, Lieutenant Michael – RNVR.

Davis, M.J. – WAAF, 2174293.

Davis, WREN Ruth/Rosalind W.

De Haan, Miss S.G. (Marjorie?) – P.

de Minckwitz, Miss N.P.

Deyong, Samuel Peter – P.

Doniach, Squadron Leader Nakidmon Shabbeta

Elkins, Win – P.

Erends, Benny – P.

Esterson, Kitty, Leading WREN – London E.7.

Ettinghausen, Alfred Albert E.E.

Ettinghausen, Lieutenant Walter George, later Walter Eytan, Israel's Ambassador to France (brother of Alfred).

Fehl, Lieutenant Alfred P. – USA – P.

Fenton, Monica Wingate – P.

Fetterlein, Ernst

Fetterlein, Paul (brother of Ernst).

Fineberg, Lieutenant

Firnberg, Major – P.

Fischer-Sobell, Flying Officer – RAF – P.

Flack, WREN M.E. – P.

Flaxman, Miss F. – P.

Franco, Miss R. – P.

Frank, Eric Joseph

Frank, Private, First Class, Maxwell N. – USA – P.

Frank, WREN S.M. – P.

Franklin, C. Ruth, later Sebag-Montefiore – AJEX information.

Freedman, WREN Audrey Pamela – from Leeds 7.

Freigel, Lieutenant Alex T. – USA – P.

Fresco-Corbu, Roger – P.

Fried, Walter – P.

Friedman, Miss Joan Enid

Friedman, William F. – USA.

Frish, Miss I.M. – P.

Fulton, WREN E. Muriel – from Watford.

Gillis, Joseph – born Sunderland, 1911 – maths at Trinity, Cambridge – taught at Weizmann Institute, Israel – died 1993.

Gluckstein, Mrs E.M.

Goldberg, Captain Joshua David – Japanese section.

Goldstein, Theodore – USA.

Gollop, Miss I.S.

Golombek, Mr Harry – nine times British Chess Olympiad.

Good, Isidore Jacob/John

Goodman, Eli, RAF – information from Flight Sergeant, later Reverend, Herbert Richer – tbc.

Goodman, Miss N.M. – P.

Goodman, J.A.N. (P);

Goodman, Lieutenant R.J. – P.

Gottstein, Leading Writer R. – RN – P.

Gould/Goldstein, Sergeant Julius, aka Goold

Graff, ATS Lance Corporal C. – P.

Greiffenhagen, Mr R.

Greiner, Miss K. – P.

Habicht, Mr E.F. – P.

Hagen, Bridget – P.

Hardy, Miss E. Anita

Harman, Sergeant – P.

Hart, Sergeant Elsie B. – ATS – P.

Hellman, Miss E.P. – P.

Hellman, Miss J.K. – P.

Herman, Dr

Hilton, Peter John

Hoffman, Morris

Horne, Corporal Harry – RAF – 1617083 – from Cricklewood.

Horstman, Mrs J.O. – P. (is this Elizabeth?)

Hyman, Miss P.E. – P.

Hyman, Sergant John E. – USA Air Intelligence.

Instone, Captain Robert Bernard Samuel

Jacob, Colonel – P.

Jacobs, Technician Walter – USA – huge statistical contribution to Newmanry over six months.

Jaffe, Heather Jane – P.

Jaffee, Lieutenant Sidney – USA – Hut 3.

Judah, Miss Claire S.

Kahan, Mrs M.F.W. – P.

Kahn, Mrs M.J. – P.

Kanis, Miss Pamela – P.

Karet, H.W. – member of Lauderdale Road Synagogue.

Klauber, John

Klusman, Mrs D.O. – P.

Koppel-Palmer, Miss M.C. – P.

Kullback, Major Solomon – USA.

Lander, WREN A.P.F. – P.

Leibi, Captain – P.

Levenson, Lieutenant Arthur – USA.

Levin, SO Cynthia – WAAF – 2022972/8263 – AJEX card.

Levy, Suzanne

Lewis, Dr Bernard

Lewis, WREN P.M.G. (probably Pauline/Phyllis/Polly)

Lidstone, Miss P.M. – P.

Liebi/Liebl, Captain – P.

Lipman, Corporal Vivian D. – Japanese Section – S.J. Goldstein.

Lisser, Sergeant R.C., aka Lisner? – P.

Livingston, Mr – alias – German Jewish refugee (information given by Anne Ross).

Loehnis, Commander Clive or Joseph – Austrian origin – P.

Loehnis, Mrs R.B. – P.

Loewe, Major Lionel Louis

Loewe, Michael A.N. (nephew of Lionel Loewe)

Lyons, WREN P.L. – P.

Maccoby, Hyam (RCOS)

Mahalski, Norman – CA – P.

Marks, Miss A. – P.

Marks, Corporal Barbara – P.

Marks, Miss Barbara Ruth – ATS – P.

Massarsky, Sergeant – USA – P.

Megroz, Section Leader P. – ATS – P.

Mendoza, Belle (sister of Anne Mendoza/Ross).

Milner, Sergeant Ephraim – maths teacher, University of Swansea – born Bridgend 1907.

Miskin, Miss E. – P.

Monk, WREN Daphne

Myers, Section Leader – ATS – P.

Nagel, Miss E.C.B.

Nathan, L. – P.

Nenk, Major David – Japanese codes.

Newman, Professor Maxwell H.A.

Newman, WREN Doreen Audrey – 84187 – London NW8.

Noskwith, Dr Rolf

Oppenheimer, Miss O.D.

Perman, Flying Officer, RAF – P.

Pilley, aka Pilichowski, Squadron Leader Thadee, RAF (brother-in-law of Doniach, listed above).

Pinto-Alves, Section Officer – ATS? – P.

Politzer, Captain – information from R. Noskwith, listed above.

Prince, Lieutenant Francis Templeton – obituary, *The Times*, 8 August 2003.

Prins, Lieutenant Cornelius Arnold L. – 174568 Intelligence Corps – P.

Prins, L. George Vivian, RCOS (brother of Cornelius?) – at BP? – P.

Ramus, Arthur Nathaniel – translator.

Reiss, Mrs A.M. – P.

Reiss, Vincent – transport officer – P.

Roberts, aka Baker, WREN Sonia R.

Robinson, WREN Betty – 89073 – Cyncoed, Cardiff.

Rodrigues-Pereira, Miss Miriam – ATS W298557.

Roesler, Leading WREN J.M. – P.

Rose, aka Rosenheim, Squadron Leader Eliot Joseph Benn, aka 'Jim' – USA Legion of Merit.

Rosen, Lieutenant Leo – USA.

Rosenberg, Gordon.

Rosenberg, Lieutenant J. – USA Navy.

Rosenberg, Patricia Frances, aka Rose.

Rosengarten, Lieutenant Adolf – USA – after BP transferred to US Forces in Europe, 1944.

Ross, WREN Anne Meadows, aka Mendoza.

Rothband, Miss Margaret

Rothschild, Dr Miriam – decoder – from the unpublished book by J. Lennard, *Jews in Wartime*, interview.

Rothschild, Miss Joan L. – ATS – W242790.

Rubens, Miss Margaret Judith

Rubinstein, Joan

Salaman, Miss J. – ATS – P.

Salsberg, Lieutenant Edgar S. – USA – P.

Samson, 35327 Leading WREN M.D. – 35327.

Sampson, W.W. – CA – P.

Schaeffer, Lieutenant – P.

Schatz, Leading WREN T.H. – P.

Sebag-Montefiore, Ruth

Seligman, Miss J;

Shaw, Captain Harold R.N. – P.

Shenstone, WREN R. – P.

Shiner, Mr A.J. – P.

Shiner, Captain J.A. – P

Shipton, Leading WREN M.P. – P.

Sikora, Mrs M.W. – P.

Silver, Mr C.H. – P.

Singer, Miss M.J. – P.

Singer, Mr Norman – P.

Sinkov, Major Abraham – USA.

Slusser, Robert M. – USA – P.

Spector, Flight Sergeant Maurice Louis – from north-west London.

Stierlen, Miss Doris M. – P.

Stileman, Miss M.A. – P.

Sugar, A.L.

Tabor, Miss D.F. – P.

Taylor, 3rd Officer WRNS M.R. – 34728 – London W9.

Tcharny, Lieutenant Michael Joseph – 266688/10691878 Intelligence Corps.

Telfer, Mrs M.I. – P.

Tocher, Leading WREN A.J. – P.

Uzielli, David Rex – Jewish origin.

Uzielli, Miss Diana – Jewish origin.

Vogel, Captain Barnard – USA – Hut 3.

Weissweiller, Nadine – P.

Whalley, Mr J. – P.

Wix, Miss Phyllis, aka Bloch

Wolfe, Miss B.G. – P.

Wolfe, Richard – translator – died of illness, 1945, Ceylon – P.

Wolfson, Miss M.S. – P.

Wolfson, Miss Margaret – P.

Woolstone, Mrs Lena – Hut 4 with Ettinghausen brothers – born Notting Hill, London, 1919 – husband in FAA.

Wossorsky, Irving E. – USA Army – traffic identification.

Wyberg, WREN E.V. – P.

Yochelson, Private, First Class, Maurice – USA.

Ziman, MBE, 1st Officer WREN Thelma.

Zookrow, Leon – RAF – tbc.

Zuppinger, Miss Zoe – P.

Notes

1. Government Communications Headquarters, known during the Second World War as the Government Code and Cypher School (GCCS); search the internet for 'Station X'.
2. Among many others are Michael Smith and Ralph Erskine, *Action This Day* (London: Bantam, 2001); Robert Harris, *Enigma* (London, Hutchinson, 1995); Hugh Sebag-Montefiore, *Enigma: The Battle for the Code* (London: Weidenfeld & Nicolson, 2000); David Kahn, *Seizing the Enigma* (London: Arrow, 1996); Ronald Lewin, *Ultra Goes To War* (London: Hutchinson, 2001). The intelligence obtained from the code-breaking was called 'Ultra'. Such information was passed only to

the most senior-ranking commanders in the field, lest the Germans should realize the codes had been broken and change them.

3. *Enigma*, with Kate Winslet, and *U571*, with Harvey Keitel, both made in 2001.
4. Ted Enever, *Britain's Best Kept Secret* (Stroud: Sutton, 1994/99).
5. See testimony of the Bogush sisters.
6. The French too had begun cracking Enigma when a German agent offered them details for payment in 1932 (A. Rabinovich, *Jerusalem Post*, 22 February 1999, in an interview with Walter Eytan/Ettinghausen). The British were so impressed by the machine given to them by the French and Poles that when it was delivered at Victoria Station by General Gustav Betrand – head of cryptology with French Intelligence – the head of the British Secret Service, 'C', wore evening dress with his Legion D'Honneur.
7. Called Colossus, it was sixteen by twelve by eight feet in size; ten were made, operated mainly by highly-trained WRENs – see Enever, *Britain's Best Kept Secret*, p.38.
8. The General Post Office (GPO) engineers played an important role in setting up and maintaining the electronics at BP. Their research centre was at Dollis Hill.
9. Enever, *Britain's Best Kept Secret*.
10. One block at BP housed a huge card index library which stored every conceivable scrap of Intelligence gathered from around the UK's 'Y' stations and elsewhere; this was copied and sent to the Bodleian Library in Oxford in case a back-up should ever be required. It was often consulted throughout the war by all the various Intelligence branches of the Allied Forces, and staffed by a small army of civilian female clerks.
11. Information from Barbara Barnett, with thanks to Jeremy Schonfield. See John Curtis, 'Richard David Barnett: 1909–1986', *Proceedings of the British Academy*, 76, pp.321–45.
12. This may be L.B. Benenson, Intelligence Corps, 137318, found on an AJEX Museum Jewish Chaplain Card by the author.
13. Audiotape sent from her home in Australia in 2000.
14. Personal interview, June 2004.
15. Letter and telephone call from Mrs Gillian Cohen to author, March 2005.
16. Michael Smith, *The Emperor's Code* (London: Bantam, 2001), pp.152–5.
17. Ibid., p.182.
18. Ibid., p.183.
19. Smith, *Emperor's Code*, Index.
20. *Jerusalem Post*, 22 February 1999.
21. Interview with post-war GCHQ colleague Wilf Lockwood, October 2004.
22. Obituary, *The Times*, 16 May 1994.
23. Obituary, the *Independent*, 23 April 1994, with thanks to daughters Ruth Doniach-Durant and Iona Doniach – telephone interviews, October 2004.
24. The full and crucial contribution made by Doniach to UK Intelligence is described in Geoffrey Elliot and Harold Shukman, *Secret Classrooms* (London: St Ermin's Press, 2002), passim.
25. Personal audio interview with author, 2001.
26. Obituary, *Daily Telegraph*, 11 June 2001.
27. See Francis Harry Hinsley and Alan Stripp, *Codebreakers* (Oxford: Oxford University Press, 1993), p.50.
28. Ibid., Chapter 5.
29. David Cesarni, *Eichmann* (London: Heinemann, 2004), pp.222–3.
30. Letters in AJEX files.
31. Victor Madeira, '"Because I Don't Trust him, We are Friends": Signals Intelligence and the Reluctant Anglo-Soviet Embrace, 1917–24', *Intelligence and National Security* (USA), 19, 1 (Spring 2004), p.45, n.19 – thanks to Alan H. Bath.
32. Thanks to Ralph Erskine.
33. Obituary, *Jewish Chronicle*, 4 June 1993.
34. See William F. Friedman website.
35. His wife Elizabeth was a code-breaker in her own right and worked for various American law enforcement agencies breaking codes used by organized crime. She worked as a code-breaker during the Second World War, for the OSS, bringing to justice one woman spying for the Japanese using messages written on dolls which she sold using a mail order business. Elizabeth died in 1980.
36. Girton College Archives, with thanks to Kate Perry.
37. By telephone in Sheffield, December 2004.
38. See photograph in Alan Stripp, *Codebreakers in the Far East* (Oxford: Oxford University Press, 1995). Stripp knew Goldberg at Bletchley. Goldberg's name does not appear on the BP personnel list – there are many such errors.

39. Telephone conversation, October 2004 – Mrs Hilda Feder-Goldberg, neé Salaman, and daughter Gila in Jerusalem, Israel.
40. Interview with the author, June 2003.
41. *Oxford Dictionary of National Biography*, Vol. 22 (Oxford: Oxford University Press, 2004), pp.712–13.
42. Googl e 'Golombeck'.
43. See Hinsley and Stripp, *Codebreakers*, chapter 19.
44. Defined as a codebreaker; a cryptographer, conversely, invents the code. Cryptology is the science of both of these.
45. H. Sebag-Montefiore, *Enigma*, p.218.
46. Lewin, *Ultra Goes To War*; also the Jack Good website.
47. See note 53.
48. Michael Smith, *Station X* (London: Channel 4 Books, 1998), pp.145–6.
49. Personal account to author in AJEX files.
50. Internet site – thanks to Jeremy Schonfield; also William Gillespie, 'Obituary, John Klauber (1917–81)', *International Journal of Psychoanalysis*, 63, 1 (1982), pp.83–5.
51. Website.
52. See Nova transcripts on www.pbs.org/wgbh/nova/transcripts/2615decoding.html.
53. Smith, *Station X*, p.164.
54. See note 53.
55. See note 53.
56. Personal telephone call with Bernard Lewis in Princeton, NJ; thanks to Jeremy Schonfield.
57. Obituary, *Jewish Chronicle*, 16 March 1990.
58. Telephone call from Penny Finestein, who knew him; also correspondence with Michael Loewe and son David Loewe.
59. See Hinsley and Stripp, *Codebreakers*, chapter 26; also personal correspondence, May 2004.
60. Later to Block B.
61. Thanks to Cynthia Maccoby and Jeremy Schonfield.
62. Obituary, the *Guardian*, 31 July 2004.
63. Smith, *Station X*, p.152.
64. Interview in his London flat with the author in 2004.
65. Hinsley and Stripp, *Codebreakers*, chapter 15.
66. H. Sebag-Montefiore, *Enigma*.
67. Obituary of Alex Dakin, *Daily Telegraph*, 26 July 2003.
68. Interview in October 2004 with his son Peter.
69. Obituary, *The Times*, 8 August 2003.
70. *Oxford Dictionary of National Biography*.
71. Obituary, *The Times*, 24 May 1999.
72. Smith, *Station X*, p.164.
73. Ibid., p.168.
74. Obituary, *Jewish Chronicle*, 11 February 2005.
75. Personal telephone interview with the author, and article by J. Frazer, *Jewish Chronicle*, 23 July 2004.
76. See Martin Sugarman, 'A Well Kept Secret: No. 3 ("Jewish") Troop, No. 10 Commando', *Medals Today* (April 1996) (Token Press), pp.16–19; also on the internet, and in this book chapter 13.
77. Personal interview, 2001.
78. 8 a.m. to 4 p.m; 4 p.m. to midnight; midnight to 8 a.m; it was six days a week, one long weekend a month; one week every three months. Night shift were paid ten shillings (fifty pence) per week more and so there was a lot of competition to work nights, but for health and safety reasons it was limited in the amount allowed.
79. Newnham College Archives, with thanks to Samantha Chalmers.
80. Ruth Sebag-Montefiore, *Family Patchwork* (London: Weidenfeld & Nicolson, 1987), pp. 110–14.
81. Sebag-Montefiore, *Family Patchwork*, pp.116–19.
82. Smith, *Emperor's Code*, p.100; also website.
83. Personal interview, July 2001.
84. Of the list of 216, ninety-nine are definitely UK Jewish, plus fifteen Americans, totalling 114. If we assume 8,000 passed through BP (it was probably less), then ninety-nine is 1.23 per cent (over twice our numbers in the UK population of 0.4 per cent); 114 Jews in total is 1.4 per cent of the 8,000; 216 is 2.68 per cent – over five times. If we exclude the US men, it is still 2.5 per cent.

On Active Service: Five Memoirs

Jewish Sailors aboard HMS *Hood*

Traditionally, all naval volunteers of whatever creed had to have parents born in the UK and so, for many years, few Jews were able to serve in the Royal Navy. However, besides serving in the war in Quebec (in the eighteenth century), at Trafalgar (1805), and in the Boer War (1899–1902), about 500 Jews served in the Royal Navy (including Submarines), Merchant Marine and Royal Naval Division and Royal Naval Air Service in the First World War, in all theatres of the war, over forty being killed in action. They won a DSO, an OBE, seven MCs and MMs, a DCM and five MiDs, as far as we know. Several were also taken as prisoners of war (POWs).

In the Second World War, over 2,000 British Jews served in the Royal Navy and Royal Marines – with a further 300 Jewish women in the WRENs – and hundreds in the Merchant Navy (numbers have yet to be researched for the MN). Furthermore, a few hundred Palestinian/Israeli Jews served in the Royal Navy, and among those killed were three on the SOE naval raid – Operation Boatswain – on the Tripoli (Vichy Lebanon) oil refineries in May 1941. In total, over 200 Royal Navy Jews were killed in action. Awards won included Tommy Gould's VC (Submarines), Commander Harold Newgass's GC (Bomb Disposal), twenty-eight DSCs, thirty-six DSMs and many other cross-service awards. About twenty-five were POWs of the Germans and Japanese. British Jewish sailors have also served in conflicts since: for example, in Korea, the Falklands and the Gulf.

The 2001 discovery of the wreck of HMS *Hood* prompted the author to research the matter of Jewish servicemen who served on the British Battleship when she was sunk by a chance hit from the German Battleship *Bismarck*, on *Hood*'s magazine, off Iceland on 24 May 1941. All but three of *Hood*'s 1,415 crew perished in the huge explosion.

The author obtained a copy of the ship's company who were serving on the *Hood* on that fateful day, and compared this with the over 2,000 Jewish Chaplain Cards for the Royal Navy and Royal Marines, and the thousand or so cards for POWs and Missing Men, held at the AJEX Museum, and discovered the Jewish sailors named below. The author also searched the pages of the *Jewish Chronicle* for the three months following the disaster, but no mention is made of the *Hood* tragedy, or any Jewish sailors who were aboard.

Henry Morris's books, *We Will Remember Them: A Record of the Jews Who died in the Armed Forces of the Crown 1939–1945* (Brassey, 1989) and *We Will Remember Them: An Addendum* (AJEX, 1994), revealed only one known Jewish sailor on the *Hood*, but he had no Jewish Chaplain Card; we know that the cards are not complete, especially for the navy, which had *no* designated Jewish chaplain during the Second World War, and where particular difficulties abounded when men were at sea, perhaps for most of the war. It was different in shore establishments, where there was more chance of a Jewish chaplain meeting and recording details of Jewish naval personnel.

The four Jewish men were:

P/JX 172598 Able Seaman Leonard Goulstine, served as Benton, aged 24, son of Simon Edward and Jeanette, of Brighton; used his uncle's name, Benton. Jewish Chaplain Card spells his name as Goulston. Inscribed on Portsmouth Naval Memorial (PNM), panel 48, column 1.
P/JX 227193 Ordinary Seaman Albert Phineas Levy, son of Henry and Lula Levy of Par, Cornwall. PNM, panel 51, column 1.
Marine PO/X 4273 Henry Clifford Rosenthal, aged 18, son of Henry and Florence of Easton, Bristol. PNM, panel 59, column 2.
P/JX 158144 Able Seaman Benjamin Seivill Sterne, aged 18, son of Rudolph and Mabel Sterne of Grimsby, Lincolnshire. PNM, panel 49, column 3.

There are several other names which suggest strongly that the men were Jewish, but cards or other proof cannot be found to verify the fact:

Cook P/MX 64885 Robert Gordon Abrams
PO P/J 41701 Horace Walter Goldsmith, aged 42, husband of Gladys, of Greenford, Middlesex; son of Herbert and Frances. PNM, panel 46, column 2.
Marine PO/X 3394 Benjamin Leonard Green. PNM, panel 59, column 1.

(There are several other men with the surname Green.)

P/JX 234700 Ordinary Seaman Sydney Charles Samuel Myers, aged 19, son of Sydney and Selina, of Twickenham. PNM, panel 51 column 1.

(There is another Myers from Manchester.)
Other possible names include Daniels, Fisher, Freeman, Richer and Silk.

Jewish Prisoners of War at Colditz

The fairy-tale eleventh-century Colditz Castle, sited on a rocky hilltop overlooking the town on the River Mulde between Leipzig and Dresden in the former East Germany, is notorious for its use as a high security Nazi prisoner of war (POW) camp in the Second World War – Oflag 4C.

Allied officers who had made repeated attempts to escape from other POW camps were housed here by the Germans in the expectation that they would never get out of such an imposing fortress. However, as several books and various films have shown, 300 did escape and several made 'home runs' back to Allied lines.

The POW population was typically a shifting one, but of the thousand or so who were there it is estimated that about forty were Jewish, and it is known that there were about sixty French Jewish political internees as well. Approximately 100 Jewish prisoners out of 1,000 makes a very high percentage compared to Jewish numbers in the general population. Of the military prisoners, approximately one-third were French, one-third Polish/Dutch and one-third British/Commonwealth. Only some of the Jewish names are known, especially as many Jewish POWs used pseudonyms and new identities to protect themselves.[1]

One famous Jewish NCO, however, was cockney Fusilier Solomon Sydney Goldman, Royal Northumberland Fusiliers, who was badly treated by the Germans because of his Jewish faith but was sent to Colditz as an orderly for senior officers. He was remembered for his terrific sense of humour despite his ill-treatment (although the British officers tried to protect him). When he became ill, he was repatriated to Britain in 1943, but died in 1974 of illness as a result of his experiences in German hands.[2]

Another inmate was Private Ralph (Samuel) Cowan, aka Cohen, of the KRRC, captured in Crete in 1941 and later sent to Colditz as a barber. He cut the hair of – amongst others – Douglas Bader, Earl Haig, Lord Lascelles and Giles Romilly. His two daughters visited Colditz in 2005 and were warmly welcomed by the guides as children of a former prisoner.[3]

Anthony 'Fish' Karpf was a Polish Jewish officer born in Rzeszow; he too was ill-treated and subjected to a mock execution at Colditz. He eventually escaped and came to live in Britain after the war.[4]

The work of Benjamin Miertchak[5] made it possible for the author to cross-reference the list of POWs in Colditz, taken from Chancellor's book,[6] with Meirtchak's list of Polish Jewish POWs, revealing the following names (although this is not a definitive list, as we know that many Polish Jewish servicemen hid their true religious origins from both the Poles and the Germans): 2nd Lieutenant Franciszek Baumgart; 2nd Lieutenant Mieczyslaw Chmiel (he made two escape attempts but was later murdered at Buchenwald after the escapes of 19 and 20 September 1943); Captain Henryk Fajerman; Lieutenant Jerzy T. Grudzinski (later killed in the Dossel Oflag 'friendly fire' bombing by the RAF in 1943); Captain Mayer F. Hauptman; Lieutenant Bernard P. Jasinski; 2nd Lieutenant Adam Niedenthal (died 27 September 1944); Colonel Poznanski; 2nd Lieutenant Benjamin J. Rubinowicz; Lieutenant Bernard Stajer/Staier; 2nd Lieutenant Jakub/Jerzy Stein (Navy)[7]; 2nd Lieutenant Henryk Stiller; Lieutenant Colonel Henryk E. Szubert. It also appears that two Polish Jewish civilians were interned at Colditz – Pinkus Kurnedz and Jack Aizenberg.[8]

In addition, Anthony Karpf wrote a letter (undated) to Jack Lennard of Hull AJEX[9] in which he named two French Jewish officers, brothers called Shneizel, who were POW with him, but he could not remember their first names. Karpf also noted that on Yom Kippur in 1942, the commandant allowed the Jewish officers to hold a service, something never mentioned in the voluminous sources on Colditz.

When the French gentile officers tried to ostracize their fellow French Jewish comrades in their barrack, British officer Airey Neave (a 'home runner' and later a Conservative minister in the Thatcher government) and many of his Commonwealth comrades expressed their outrage and total solidarity with the Jewish officers and the row died down – though it was much exploited by the Germans in their propaganda.

Among the French Jewish escape attempts were Lieutenant C. Clein (two escape attempts), Colonel P. Francis Didier, Lieutenant P. Levy and Lieutenant P. Manheimer (the youngest French officer in Colditz). In Chancellor's lists (see above), the following Jewish names appear as POWs at Colditz: O. Bergmann; Corporal N. Blomme of the 1st French Paras; Captain R. Blum; G. Cahen-Salvador; Captain Dreyfus; A. Hirsch; M. Hirsch; Sous Lieutenant Klein of the Free French; Lieutenant R. Levy; Lieutenant A. Levy-Ginsburger, aka Levit; E. Rosenberg; R. Schaeffer; A. Sternberg.

On a recent visit to the museum at Colditz, the author found and photographed displayed portraits of prisoners including Captain Isidore Schrire/Schire, MBE (a Jewish officer in the South African Army Medical Corps, captured at Dunkirk).[10] There was also a very famous Palestinian Jewish Royal Engineers officer, Lieutenant Shimon Ha-Cohen;[11] he boasted to the Germans – to the great amusement of the British – that not only did he come from Israel, but had been born in Russia, and was thus thrice damned by the Germans. Ha-Cohen had been a sergeant major in the British Army in the First World War.[12] Another French Colditz POW was Baron Elie de Rothschild.

Captain Julius Green – a dental officer from Glasgow – was exceptional in that he worked for MI9 in the prison and sent coded letters to his wife.

The information was forwarded by her to British Intelligence. It included material supplied to Green by recaptured escapers about local German railway, troop and shipping movements and anything else gleaned whilst on the 'outside'. He also advised what materials useful for escape could be smuggled into Colditz via parcels from home, as well as items that officers should carry with them in battle, in case they were captured and sent to Colditz – hidden compasses, for example, that again would be useful for escape. He published a book about his experiences.[13] Green's other important act was to expose the English Nazi stooge in the prison, Purdy, who was prosecuted for treason after the war.

Rifleman Solomon Dennis Halfin, aka Halpin (KRRC – Rangers), arrived in Colditz by accident. Born the son of Israel and Edith in West Ham, London, on 1 January 1918, he was captured in Crete by the Germans on 29 May 1941, but escaped and spent three months in the mountains with the Partisans.[14] On the night of an attempted escape by submarine, he was recaptured with some other Commonwealth troop evaders when the Germans got wind of this escape plan, and ended up at Lamsdorf camp in Germany, where he became friends with a French Canadian POW, Sergeant Roger Cordeau, a dental technician by trade, captured at Dieppe. Dennis escaped from a working party at Lamsdorf but was recaptured at the Polish border. About to be sent to another camp, and not wanting to be separated from his friends, he exchanged identities with Cordeau. But his plan backfired when the Germans noticed that he (Halfin, now known as Cordeau) was a dental technician, and he was sent to Colditz to assist with the POW officers' dental care in June 1943. The first man he met on entering the castle was an old friend, 6850731 Rifleman Samuel Cohen, aka Cowen, of the same Rangers battalion as his, also at Colditz as a batman to POW officers (see above). By September the Germans, having seen Halfin and Cohen talking and meeting, discovered eventually that Halfin was not really Cordeau and he ended back at Lamsdorf.[15]

Another British Jewish inmate was Lieutenant J.M. Barnet, Royal Engineers,[16] who was captured in November 1940, arrived in Colditz (see Chancellor's list) on 4 August 1941 and was repatriated to Britain on 6 September 1944 with feigned illness; he counts as an 'escaper'.

Another probable Jewish inmate was Flight Lieutenant Josef Bryks of the Czech Squadron, RAF. A sad case is that of Commando Rifleman Cyril Henry Abram, captured with six others after a successful raid in Norway (Operation Musketoon) in September 1942. They spent two weeks at Colditz in 1944 and were then taken and murdered at Sachsenhausen Death Camp.[17] Abram, from Manor Park, was probably Jewish.

Among the Dutch escapers was a 'home run', via a manhole, in August 1941, by Commander Francis Steinmetz of the Royal Netherlands Navy, with comrade Lieutenant F. Larive. Other Dutch Jewish inmates included Captain A.P. Berlijn; Lieutenant M. Braun; Lieutenant L. De Hartog; Captain A.J.A. Pereira; Lieutenant J.G. Smit and Captain L.T.W. De Vries, the Royal Netherlands Army; and Stoker W. De Lange of the Royal Netherlands Navy.[18]

Anyone with further information and names of other Jewish POWs at Colditz should contact the author at AJEX.

Wingate and the Raid on Rommel: Captain S. Alan Shemtob-Reading: A Brief Life

> *The account below was given to me by the late Captain Alan Shemtob-Reading in October 2002, in the presence of his wife, at two long interviews in their flat at AJEX House in Hackney. Some years earlier, I had asked Captain Shemtob-Reading to tell me his wartime experiences for the archive of the Jewish Military Museum but he had refused, saying he did not wish to recall those terrible days. But in the late summer of 2002, perhaps remembering his mortality, he contacted me and said he now wanted to tell his story. The text was scrutinized and approved by him.*
>
> *There is only one endnote, contrary to what is usually found in historical articles, because I have been unable – albeit after only a cursory search at TNA – to find any reference to the Rommel raid, the section which will be of most interest to readers, in any surviving wartime records. This should not be a surprise to those – like myself – who have delved into the secret history of the Intelligence Services. Many records of such unconventional raids were either deliberately destroyed, lost or indeed never kept to begin with – the excuse being the sensitivity of the event and its repercussions, legal and personal, to those still alive, or their families. This is not to say that it is anything but the complete truth as Captain Shemtob-Reading remembered it. We know that many newspaper stories, for example, which make fantastic claims about particular incidents, doubted by many at the time, later turn out to be true when documents verifying the facts are found many years afterwards. Perhaps one day the full facts will emerge in some dusty file now buried deep in an archive somewhere.*
>
> *At the time of the interviews, Captain Shemtob-Reading was 90 years old. He died five years later, in 2007, and bequeathed his medals and much-treasured desert map case to the AJEX Museum.*

Alan Shemtob-Reading was born in London on 5 December 1912, scion of the distinguished Babylonian Iraqi Jewish family of Shemtob. In April 1936 he joined the Intelligence Corps of the British Armed Forces and, because of his language skills in Hebrew and Arabic, successfully applied to be posted to the Middle East.

Israel

In 1936 an Arab revolt was taking place in British-controlled Mandate Palestine, and Captain Alan Shemtob-Reading (no. 315996) was sent to work for the Special Service Office (an undercover unit similar to MI6) in Jaffa. The brief of this unit was to meet senior Arab and Jewish political leaders, to gather Intelligence, and especially to report on the movements of Arab terrorist gangs, such as those led by Kawoukchi. The unit was based in a large, discreet Arab house, serviced by Sudanese domestic staff attired in red fez and sash with white robes.

Unwilling to describe his work, which is still shrouded in secrecy, Alan would only say that it was very dangerous and also extremely frustrating, as there were constant murderous Arab attacks against the Jews. After a short spell in Nazareth, he was transferred to Military Intelligence HQ in Jerusalem, where he had the unpleasant duty of meeting the notorious anti-Jewish Mufti of Jerusalem, Haj Amin el Husseini. As history well records, Husseini was constantly inciting the Arab population against the Jews and later conspired with the Axis powers, spending the war years in Berlin where he planned, with Eichmann, the building of gas chambers in nearby Nablus to kill the Jews of Israel in due course. Before war broke out in 1939, a top secret order came from London to arrest Husseini. However, Alan's local Intelligence chief decided Husseini was too valuable a source of information, and instructed Alan to tip-off the Mufti about the order. With no alternative but to obey his superiors, Alan was reluctantly sent to carry out his duty. Donning a woman's clothes, Husseini escaped by car to Jaffa and thence by boat to Lebanon.

A much greater pleasure for Alan was meeting (then) Colonel Orde Wingate, the great British Christian Zionist military leader. Based at Kibbutz Ein Harod in the Jezreel Valley, Wingate was training and leading, with British officers and NCOs, the Jewish Special Night Squads, aimed at striking back at the Arab terrorists. On several occasions Alan had to meet with Wingate on matters of mutual Intelligence work, and on knocking at Wingate's hut door, would enter to find the great man stark naked, standing on his head, testing his limits of discomfort and stamina. Many other eyewitness accounts in the many books on Wingate substantiate Alan's descriptions.

The Arab Legion and the War in Iraq

In November 1940, Alan was part of the British Military Intelligence Mission attached to The Arab Legion in Ma'an, Jordan, serving on camel and horseback in the vast desert. His mission was to gather Intelligence and also to act as listening post to Cairo, Baghdad and Damascus. Again, Alan was unwilling to say much about this work, only that it was of great strategic importance to what was to follow.[19]

In May 1941, Alan was involved in much fighting during the British Army advance from Israel and Jordan to Baghdad and Damascus, to crush the pro-Nazi regime of Rashid Ali and the Vichy French. Many Jewish Haganah soldiers and scouts were used in this campaign, including Moshe Dayan, who had lost his eye in the fighting.

On another occassion, Alan was ordered to pay Sheik Shammar 25, 000 guineas to bring 1,000 horsemen to Baghdad to bluff Rashid Ali. It worked.

Rashid Ali escaped into Iran and the British reached Habbaniyah. Here, Alan heard about the anti-Jewish pogroms against the community in nearby Baghdad. In vain Alan tried to persuade the British commander to intervene to halt the massacre, not least because he had family there; he was always traumatized by his failure to do so. Alan had further to witness the Iraqi Regent, Abdul Ilah, meeting the British GOC and thanking him for defeating Rashid, but also asking him for help to stop the killing in Baghdad. He too was refused, as the General had orders from London not to enter Baghdad (this episode will be of great interest to the many Iraqi-born Jews now living as citizens of the UK and USA).

Syria

The British campaign continued into Vichy Syria, and again Alan was in action, dodging Luftwaffe strafing and Vichy artillery. At Palmyra there was intense fighting and heavy casualties; both Alan and his Intelligence chief were wounded and were evacuated to Tel Hashomer military hospital near Tel-Aviv. Alan spent six months recuperating and then transferred to 8th Army HQ in Cairo.

The Raid on Rommel and the MBE

Following the fall of Tobruk in summer 1942, Rommel's unstoppable forces inexplicably halted about sixty miles short of Alexandria. Cairo HQ received urgent orders from London to discover Rommel's strength, strategy and plans. Meanwhile, fully expecting Rommel to advance, all military offices in Cairo and Jerusalem began burning their secret documents and preparing for evacuation. At the same time the Egyptians were publicly celebrating the imminent arrival of Rommel.

Alan was immediately attached to a unit of eleven members of the Long Range Desert Group and ordered to set out in three jeeps from El Alamein – the Allied line – for Rommel's HQ at El Aghela, first detouring south into the Quatarra Depression and over the notorious escarpment and many minefields – an exceedingly dangerous roundabout distance of well over 1,000 miles behind enemy lines. On several occasions they were spotted by German aircraft and strafed, and one jeep was destroyed, resulting in the death of its four-man crew.

Alan would not say how the raid was carried out and how they entered German HQ, but using the services of a British convict who was a specialist safe-breaker, they opened the safe in Rommel's HQ, copied the required documents and replaced them so that nobody would know they had been there. It was clear from what they read that Rommel had simply run out of fuel – a tribute to Allied efforts in sinking most of his supply transport in the Mediterranean.

The return journey, it was decided, would go further south than the inward trip, to avoid the minefields, but tragically they encountered quicksand and the jeep carrying the safe-breaker with his reward of 10,000 golden guineas was gone within seconds. Only Alan's jeep and its four men made it back to Cairo with the much-needed secret report. For this courage and persistence, Alan and all his team were awarded the MBE.

Alan spent the rest of the war in North Africa, and from 1945 to 1948 he was in Israel. He would say nothing of this period but clearly he was able to be of great use to the Haganah in their Intelligence-gathering, preparing for the inevitable War of Independence when Britain left the Mandate of Palestine.

Alan's awards, besides his MBE (Mil.) and Jordanian Service Medal, were the Palestine Service Medal; 1939–45 Star; Africa Star with 8th Army clasp; War Medal; and Long Service Regular Army Medal.

Post-War
Alan was a long-serving member of the Association of Jewish Ex-Servicemen and Women and the Monash (Jewish) branch of the British Legion. The Israel War veterans awarded him their veterans badge – a gold, blue and white Israeli flag emblem which, with other medals, he wore with pride when acting as escort to the Chief Rabbi and other clergy at the AJEX Annual Remembrance Service and Parade at the Cenotaph in Whitehall.

Wingate's Boys: Jews with Orde Wingate and the Chindits

My thanks go to the Chindit OCA and all the veterans who helped me compile this list by contacting me through the various advertisements I placed in the *Jewish Chronicle*, *British Legion Journal*, *Dekko* (journal of the Burma Star Association), *Wartime News*, the *AJEX Journal* and other publications. Without their help, this work would not have been possible. I am especially grateful to Colonel Orde Wingate, the late general's son, for contacting me with some useful information. I am also grateful to the courageous American veterans of the USAAF Commando who provided names of their comrades who took part in the airlifting in and out of supplies and men.

7.1 Capt. Julius Green, RADC, at Colditz.

7.2 Capt. Alan Shemtob-Reading, right, with pith helmet and pistols, with Sheik Shammar during the Iraq/Syria campaign in 1941.

7.3 P/JX158144 Able Seaman Benjamin S. Sterne killed on HMS *Hood*, 24 May 1941.

7.4 Rabbi Dayan M. Gollop, Senior Jewish Chaplain to British Forces 1924–44.

7.5 Chaplain Bernard Casper, later Chaplain to the Jewish Brigade 1944–46, served 1941–46.

7.6 3780682 Pte. Leon Frank, Chindit, Burma, 13/13 Kings Liverpool Regiment, Operation Longcloth, column 7, 1943. Photo taken Sangor 16 August 1942. He was a POW.

7.7 233237 Major Joseph Crowne, MBE 'for gallantry' with the Chindits, 2nd Expedition 1944.

The list is clearly incomplete and this research would surely have revealed an astonishingly greater picture of the contribution of Jewish troops to the Chindits had it been completed twenty years ago when more eyewitnesses would have been alive.

Sergeant Asher. S. Staffs, KIA attack on Mogaung 23 June 1944 – see P.D. Chinnery, *March or Die*, pp.215–6. Probably Jewish; no AJEX card.

378027 Private Len Frank Berkovitch. From Manchester. 13th King's Liverpool Regiment; POW with Frank (listed below) in Rangoon Jail – information from Frank. Very orthodox and often prayed in the camp. As a tailor, he was tasked with sewing shrouds for POWs who died in Rangoon jail for the cemetery. He survived.

13091795 Acting Sergeant Private Sam Berkovitz. 2nd/13th Battalion Sherwood Foresters and SEAC Lancs. Fusiliers/Border Regiment. Served in Calvert's Chindit column as a Bren gunner. Born East End of London, 30 March 1906, tailor son of Rumanian immigrants; died 30 October 1998. Organized and took part in the Battle of Cable Street and recruitment of fighters for Spain against Franco; was an active member of the Communist Party. After Home Guard, volunteered in Darlington, aged 36, in Second World War, and was sent to the Pioneer Corps. Husband of Bessie of Cannon St Road, London E1 and 16 Helen's Terrace, Bishop Auckland. Father of Barry – AJEX Index card and photo and personal call. Sam wrote a book on his life and wartime experiences, edited by famous Jewish writer Simon Blumenthal.

6095498 Sergeant Gabriel 'Gaby' Bick. Husband of Anna, son of I. Bick of 35 Taplow Flats, Calvert St, Shoreditch, London E2; died post-war in Ramat Gan, Israel. 2nd Queen's Own RW Surrey/EssexRegiment/Chindits Signals and Intelligence, friend of Monty Rome. When Bick was passing a message to General Wingate, Wingate asked him if he was Jewish; when he said yes, Wingate said, 'You should not be here but in Israel!' Photo and AJEX Index card. Bick is named in D. Moore, *GI Jews*, p.114.

13043873 Lewis Bresler. RWF; c/o Charlisky, 36 Warwick St, Glasgow.

7369228 Private Harry Leon Broder. 180/215th Field Ambulance RAMC; served Col. 45 with Chindits; letter from comrade George Bush of Woking.

Monty (?) Broomkin/Bloomkin. Duke of Wellington's, att. Chindits. Information from B. Stupack, 15 Kingsley Court, Tayside Ave, Edgware, Middlesex.

5952706 A.L. Camp. 'D' Coy, 5th Beds and Herts – AJEX Index card. Information from M. Rome.

3780118 Private Sid Ellis Caplan. Born 23 March 1911. Address was 30 Beckenham Road, Cheetham.13th King's Liverpool Regiment; POW with Frank – information from Frank, In Rangoon Jail and confirmed by wife of J. Milgrom, listed below, in 2007. Survived and was in HQ Brigade, Operation Longcloth.

4202412 Fusilier Michael Chadwick, later aka Freedman. 10th Battalion RWF, later att. 23rd Brigade Chindits. Husband of Mrs S. Chadwick, 26 Ruskin Ave, Manchester. Letter and call from M. Cohen (listed below). AJEX Index Card.

Alfred Chester. Son of Bertha and Lou, Ellingfort Road, Hackney, London E9, husband of Rachel – call from sister Shirley; perhaps he is 14203953 Private R. Chester of the Warwicks. Regiment who lived at 200 Evering Rd, London E8?

3602186 Private Mendel/Manny Cohen. 4th Battalion Border Regiment. AJEX Index card and personal call – mother was Mrs R. Cohen of 34 Greenhill Rd, Cheetham, Manchester. 23rd Brigade Chindits under Brigadier Fergusson. Served India/Burma 1942–45.

6827042 Corporal John Denis Cross. HAC/Royal West Kent/Essex Regiment. Born 9 January 1918, died 1972, son of Mr H.B. Cross, 32 Nottingham Place, London W1, who himself served in 38th Battalion RF in First World War, Jewish Legion – brother of Michael. Denis is mentioned in the book *Jungle, Jungle, Little Chindit*, by P. Boyle (London: Hollis & Carter, 1946). He was attempting to blow a bridge on a raid with the Chindits whilst RAF Hurricanes were trying to bomb it. Call and letter from brother. AJEX Index card and photo.

Company Commander Major Joseph George Crowne, MBE for 'gallant and distinguished service with the Chindits'. Brigade Signals Officer, formerly Beds. and Herts. Regiment and 7th Nigerian Regiment/Gold Coast – WAF GHQ (AJEX Jewish Chaplain Cards). On 2nd expedition (airborne) and at capture of Wagown – information from Feldman and *JC*, June 1945 with photo. Son of Mr and Mrs Davis Crowne of 5 Thistlethwaite Rd, Clapton, London E5. Memorabilia at AJEX Museum and personal interview.

121576 Captain Darnley Peter Lamont Da Costa. 7th Leics. Regiment, KIA 14 July 44, buried Taukkyan 6 F 1, Burma, son of Darnley and Mary of Barbados, brother of Patrick in 1st Irish Guards, also KIA 30 January 1944 – AJEX Index card for Peter.

Sergeant John (Julius) Dubora. 6149595, 6th E. Surreys att. 6th Nigeria – Jack Lennard letter. 62 Thistlethwaite Rd, Clapton, London E5 – AJEX Index card.

6022982 Private Ernest ' Dave' Davis. Essex Regiment. Son of Mrs G. Davis, 56 Goodge St, London W1; served with Monty Rome; photo and AJEX Index card.

14203623 Lance Corporal Shimshon (Samson)/Simon S. Duque. 1st Battalion King's Liverpool Regiment/15th Battalion Queen's Royal Regiment – 81 column, 77th Brigade, Chindits. KIA 'Blackpool' stronghold 15 May 1944, aged 21, buried Rangoon. Son of Rabbi I.D. Duque of 2 Heneage Lane, Bevis Marks, London EC3; AJEX Index card and letter from comrade Leslie Ball of Virginia, USA. Medals and photo at AJEX Museum donated by his nephew Ian of Ilford, 2007.

0-729107 Major Charles L. Englhardt. Letter from comrade Major W.V. Radovitch, 1st Air Commando USAAF/Chindits.

3781622 Private Hyman Farber. MIA/KIA 8 May 1943, aged 32, 13th Battalion, King's Liverpool Regiment, Liverpool/Chindits – *WWRT*/CWGC/AJEX Jewish Chaplain Card; commemorated Rangoon memorial, Myanmar, Taukkyan War Cemetery, north of Rangoon, face 5; son of Jacob and Rachel Farber, Firwood, Manchester. Husband of Mrs C. Fisher, 81 Great Jackson St, Manchester.

6898926 Sergeant Abraham (Alf) Feldman. 35 Column. Intelligence NCO detached from 8th Battalion Black Watch to 7th Nigerian Regiment; son of Mrs A. Feldman, 51 Finsbury Terrace, Swansea, and Mortimer St, London W1. Born 85 Albany St, Camden, 17 October 1918. Flew in to 'White City' strongpoint on Dakotas, April 1944. Evacuated sick with typhus, jaundice and malaria to Michina and then India July 1944. Personal talk, photo and AJEX Jewish Chaplain Cards.

1090904 Gunner David Finestein. RA Batman to Lieutenant Leslie Grove whose widow attested to David being in the Chindits with her husband, 60th Field Regiment att. Chindits, 23rd Brigade column, 2nd expedition – information from Capain T. Weiler of Isleworth and Mrs B. Grove of Newcastle-under-Lyme. AJEX Index card says husband of P. Finestein, 182 Fieldgate Mansions, Romford St, London E1; photo from Mrs Grove.

3780682 Private Leon Frank. 13th Platoon, 13th Battalion, King's Liverpool Regiment; on Operation Longcloth 1943, Column 7; went in with mules and elephants; POW on his twenty-third birthday after trying to evade capture with six others, 21 April 1943; kept in Rangoon (*JIW* interview) and personal call/AJEX Jewish Chaplain Cards. Born Green Dragon Yard, Whitechapel, 21 April 1920; family moved to 131 Grove Rd, Walthamstow, London E17. Photo. Described in P. Chinery, *March or Die*.

6092321/10020606 RSM Leslie S. Franks. 46 Clapton Common, London E5. Queen's RW Surrey Regiment – information from nephew S. Rose.

Sergeant (later Major) 3781685 Ralph Franks. King's Regiment, husband of Mrs M. Franks, 15 Whalley Rd, Manchester – letter, AJEX Index card and photo from wife.

S/14269034 Sergeant Arthur Isidore Freedman, RASC. Chindits Intelligence HQ. 329 Foley St, London, W1.

4200940 Private Joseph Freedman. 2nd KOR Regiment, Lancaster, KIA 25 May 1944, aged 27; Rangoon memorial, face 5. Son of Mrs J. Freedman, Charlotte St, Salford, Manchester – AJEX Index card.

5339452 Private Harry Glassman. 1st Beds. and Herts., KIA 12 June 1944, aged 27, buried Gauhati, India, 4 C 11. Son of Abraham and Rachel, Stoke Newington, north London.

3534963 Private Hyman Gordon. 10th Battalion Loyal Regiment/Border Regiment, aged 29, – item in *JC*, 27 April 1945, announcing him WIA with Border Regiment in Burma. Son of Mr and Mrs S. Gordon of 347 Bury New Rd, Salford 7; had been in Chindits and had no contact with home for over fourteen months. Attended Southall Street School, the JLB and boxed for his regiment. Member of Higher Broughton synagogue and had two brothers serving – Harry in the Queen's Regiment and Morris in the Argyll and Sutherland Highlanders. Has AJEX Jewish Chaplain Card.

7668275/1523050 Sergeant Arthur Green. W. Yorks./RA Heavy ack-ack, 296 Battery, att. Chindits – AJEX Index card and photo. Husband of Mrs D. Green, 33 Marlborough Ave, Leeds 7/14 Kedelston Rd, St Lane, Leeds 8. (?) Letter from wife relates that he refused to leave his officer, Bruce Day, and ordered his men to go on, amputated Day's leg and then carried him across Irrawaddy River. This was witnessed by a Ghurka soldier who recommended Green for an MiD. Green and Day lost touch but in 1980 they accidentally met in the dental hospital in Leeds; Day said Green should have been awarded the MM. After this emotional meeting, Green for the first time spoke to his wife of his Chindit ordeal and told the full story. Mrs Phyllis Green was never able to contact Day again. Letter also from son Peter J. Green of Leeds.

3781716 Lance Corporal Harry Greenberg. 13th Battalion, King's Liverpool Regiment; son of Solomon and Eveline of Hightown, Salford, Manchester. Died of illness/wounds, 20 August 1943, aged 30 – buried St Mary's Cemetery, Madras.

140674 Captain Herbert 'Berty' Harris-Taylor, OBE. Liverpool Regiment/2nd Battalion Duke of Wellington's att. Chindits 2nd expedition; flew in Dakotas – information from Dr Captain Stuart Binnie, RAMC, of Southport and Major Freeman, and personal call. Son of Sol and Ray Harris, 14 Lance Lane, Liverpool 15 – information from brother's AJEX Index card.

11410057 Lance Bombardier Peter George Isaacs. RA; son of Mr and Mrs E.A. Isaacs, 11 West Park Place, Leeds 8. AJEX Index card; information and photo with Arthur Green from Peter Green (see entry for Arthur Green, above).

6479057 Private Jacob Lempert. Royal Fusilier/1st Battalion S. Staffs/Chindits; KIA 23 June 1944, aged 31 – *WWRT*/CWGC/AJEX Jewish Chaplain Card; son of Joseph and Sarah of 24 Jenner Rd, Stoke Newington, London; field burial at Mogaung, 600 yards north-east of railway station, later buried at Taukkyan, plot collective row, grave 14, grave E, 1–8; memorial plaque in the Sandys Row Dutch Synagogue, Whitechapel, London E1.

3777022 Private G./James or Josh 'Lefty' Levene/Levine, DCM. From 51 Caryl Gardens Tenements, Toxteth, Liverpool, son of a Jewish Liverpool docker; 77th Brigade under Brigardier Mike Calvert; 1st Battalion King's Liverpool Regiment; won DCM at Battle of Mogaung, Burma 1944, first town to be retaken from the Japanese in Burma. Citation written by Major F.C. Freeman of Caldy, Wirral (personal interview); mention in *Liverpool Echo*, 27 April 1945 and *London Gazette*, 26 April 1945, p.2212: 'cool under fire and in very close proximity to the enemy, he cleaned his muddy Bren gun and calmly drove off the Japanese, saving the day'. Gazetted 26 April 1945, Levene developed cerebral palsy and died in 1948 – Liverpool docks closed in his honour. DCM mentioned in *Jewish Year Book 1945/46*. Confirmed in War Diary of King's Regiment, p.129, footnote. Letter from eyewitness comrade Jack Lindo, who writes: 'Jimmy was firing his Bren gun from the hip position, blasting the Japs from the tops of the Bashas. A very brave act indeed. He just went about his business quietly, not shouting, just shooting from the hip ... he earned his medal that day. The village was holding up the 77th Brigade advance.' He says the name 'Lefty' was given to him because of his likeness to a famous American boxer of the period.

Citation in G.A. Brown, *'Register of the DCM'* by G.A. Brown (Western-Canadian Distributors, 1993), p.289:

On 3rd June 1944 Private Levene was Bren gunner on the point section of the King's Company (att. 1st Battalion Lancs Fusilier) near Loihinche. The column had halted at the base of Point 1094 where the track split into three branches. Private Levene suddenly fired a magazine at the enemy inflicting several casualties before they replied. There is no doubt that but for his quick observation and prompt action the enemy would have inflicted heavy casualties upon his platoon. He then crossed a track covered by enemy fire and drove an enemy LMG from our right flank saving further casualties to our troops. On the morning of the 18th June Private Levene's platoon was leading the assault on Naungkaiktaw. During the advance, ignoring heavy fire, he was always in the front. When his platoon was eventually halted owing to the platoon on the left being held up, he ran forward onto a bunker in an exposed position and killed six Japs as they intended to withdraw. He then remained in this position cutting off one of their two lines of withdrawal and killed several more. There is no doubt that his gallant action enabled his platoon to advance.

Later in the morning of the 18th June he and his section were sent to reinforce a platoon that was attacking and clearing Naungkaiktaw and had suffered casualties. He was quite unshaken by earlier experiences and was seen to engage and kill more of the enemy. He set an excellent example by his cool and fearless conduct throughout. He showed complete contempt for danger and exposed himself freely to enemy fire in order to use his Bren to the best advantage and was invaluable in clearing further strongpoints and eventually putting surviving enemy to flight.

James died in December 1948, aged 33, at Newton hospital near Liverpool, after three years in hospital. He was not married. Obituary in *Liverpool Echo*, 22 December 1948; buried at Allerton RC cemetery, 23 December 1948, with full military honours, Major Freeman attending. Photo at AJEX Museum.

3779294 Corporal Morris Levene. 13th King's Liverpool Regiment, son of Abraham and Rosa of 59a Soho Street, Liverpool 3 – AJEX Index card and letter from son.

L. Levy (possibly Leslie 6476761). AJEX Index card says of Ferndale Rd, London N16; 45 Recce Regiment; lived Brampton Grove, London NW4.

Jack J. Lindo. Liverpool Regiment; of Jewish origin.

6026356 Private Basil Michael Luck. Formerly 26th Hussars/2nd Battalion Yorks. and Lancs./Essex Regiment; from London; 14th HQ Brigade; WIA with bullets in both legs, 18 April 1944; wounds dressed by friend Derek Flintoff of OCA (personal call), then evacuated, discharged 17 January 1945. According to Jewish Chaplain Card, he was the son of H. Luck, 73 Buxton Rd, Luton.

Brigadier Neville Marks. KIA Special Forces, Chindits – information from Major Freeman, OCA. Marks was on HQ Coy staff in Wingate's column and is mentioned by him – see J. Bierman and C. Smith, *Wingate*, p.334.

14517215 Jacob 'Jack' Milgrom. Son of Abraham Milgrom, 101 Claremont Rd, London E7; Essex Regiment – information from cousin H. Pollins of Oxford, and confirmed by his wife in 2007; later he was a paratrooper.

4808743 Private Morry Pavlotsky. 2nd Yorks. and Lancs., died 26 April 1944, aged 36, buried Taukkyan, Burma, 14 C 10. AJEX Index card; son of Aaron and Rachel of 22 New Rd, Stepney, London.

22224506 John Jacob Pennamacoor. No. 9 RAMC, husband of Fanny Marie of 98 Central Ave, Southend; regular soldier until 1952 – information from M. Rome. AJEX Index card.

2035089 Private M Rodrigues. 1st Battalion Essex Regiment; ex-Norwood boy and boxer; regular soldier – AJEX Index card and information from M. Rome.

5953142 L/Corporal Maurice 'Monty' Rome. From Calvert St, Shoreditch; Beds./Herts./Essex Regiment; served Egypt, Palestine, Ethiopia, Sudan, Iraq, Syria, India and Burma with Chindits under Brigadier Perowne (HQ Signals section), author of *Lest I Forget*, privately published and at AJEX Museum; photo.

214106 Lieutenant Lionel Rose. Sherwood Foresters, HQ Staff Coy with Wingate and CO of the Gurkha HQ Defence Platoon. MIA 9 April to 1 May 1943, after crossing the Irrawaddy on return from 1st Chindit raid and was believed captured at Chindwin crossing later. POW Rangoon, mentioned by Bierman and Smith, *Wingate*, pp.302, 305, 335. Wingate described him in a letter to his (Wingate's) wife Lorna:

> a splendid boy who was instrumental in saving my own life on one occasion ... I felt very badly about his loss, which was perhaps partly my fault. He was missing ... on the Chindwin. I fear the worst but don't say so to Mrs Rose. If she is in any want now or in the future we must help her. I feel I am responsible to Rose for that ... he behaved with the greatest courage and unselfishness. He was devoted to his Gurkhas and owes his absence to that devotion – otherwise he would have come in my boat, as I asked him to. I often lost my temper with him ... but he understood.

Six weeks later Wingate received 'the glad news that ... Rose is a POW in Burma'. In Block 3 Rangoon jail – survived.

Rosenberg. From Leeds, 44 or 56 Column, 2nd expedition – information from L.W. Ellis of Pontefract, OCA.

5260505 Private Nathan Rosewood. 1st South Staffs., killed 17 March 1944, buried Taukkyan, Burma, 6 B 16, aged 21, son of Morris and Sophia of 14 Pitmaston St, Worcester. AJEX index card.

5979048/162342 2nd Lieutenant Neville Nathan Saffer. Killed on Active Service in a mortar training accident whilst training with Chindits, 28 August 1942 (?), 'B' Coy, 14th Platoon, 13th Battalion, King's Liverpool Regiment, witnessed by Private Frank – *JIW* and personal call. Buried Ramna Forest Pathania, India (*WWRT*). Son of A. Saffer, 256 Lidgett Lane, Leeds 7.

6023036 Corporal Alf Sampson. Artist and soldier, Essex Regiment/1st Battalion DLI, 2nd Chindit Campaign; recorded memoirs at Army Museum Sound Archives, Chelsea; author of *Bless 'em All* (ISO Publications, 1990) and appears in *The Forgotten War*, by Jon Latimer, among others. Photo at AJEX Museum. Husband of R.S. Sampson, 106 Lauriston Rd, Hackney, E9; son of S. Sampson, 52 Clifton Buildings, Bethnal Green, London E2 –Jewish Chaplain Card.

Captain Jessel Samuels. Chindit/Army HQ liaison officer.

Lieutenant (later Major) Sir Michael Samuelson MBE. HAC/Leicesters att. Chindits under Colonel Lockett; landed 'White City'. Of German Jewish origin – personal call.

R.J. Schieferstein. Of Reading, Pennsylvania – 1st Air Commando, USAAF.

Major Harry C. Segal. 23rd Brigade HQ – information from Captain Harris-Taylor.

Willy Shaw. Cousin of Londoner Hillier Wise – to be confirmed.

1092769 Private Henry Simmons. 51st Field Regiment, RA; son of Eva and Ben Simmons, 56 New Rd, London E1; WIA Tobruk, then to Ceylon and India, and to 'White City' by Dakota with Chindits, under Major Fergusson, 2nd Chindit expedition. Personal telephone call.

1111578 Gunner Bernard Sonnenfield. RA; 1st Expedition with Colonel Fergusson.

Alfred Specterman. With Henry Simmons, listed above, RA, at 'White City'; from East End. Committed suicide soon after war.

Lance Corporal 2347255 Bernard Stupack. Royal Signals; born 10 December 1919 in Rutland St, Stepney, London. Called up Prestatyn, then to Egypt (Tobruk evacuation), att. RA to Bardia; to Ceylon for jungle training, then Jansi, and marched into Burma with 51 Column under 'Mad' Mike Calvert. Evacuated by air, sick. Son of J. Stupack, 21 Alvestone Rd, Wembley Park, London. Personal talk and Jewish Chaplain Cards. Photo at AJEX Museum.

222851 Dvr Morris Summers RASC. AJEX Index card says brother of Ada, lived Autclif St, London E1, then West Bank, Hackney, London N16; also served North Africa. His father, Samuel, served 39th Battalion RF in First World War. Lived Osbaldeston Rd, London N16.

1113615 Wireless Operator/AG Basil Taylor. RAF, making supply drops to Chindits; from 11 Riversdale Terrace, Sunderland – AJEX Index card.

14517316 Joseph Werthizer. RE att. Essex Regiment; second expedition on foot with Major Lovelace. Lived at 15 Wentworth St Buildings, son of Peretz and Esther, born 24 August 1922, aka Velsizer, now Worth. Personal telephone interview.

7651768 Private Driv. 'Myer' Harry Winston, aka Winstein. Born London, 1911; RAOC/REME, att. Chindits; also served North Africa, Madagascar and India. Son of F. Godfrey, Rumanian immigrants called Weinstein from 23 Whyteville Rd, Forest Gate, London E7 – AJEX Index and photo.

Colonel C.E. Zeigler. Of Alexandria, Viriginia; 1st Air Commando USAAF.

(A total of 64.)

British and Commonwealth Fighting Jewish Chaplains

David Blake, Curator of the Royal Army Chaplains Department Museum, at Amport, drew up a list of Jewish Chaplains who served in both World Wars.[20] He describes the number as 'significant'. Further names and details have been added from our own AJEX Jewish Military Museum Archives by the author – especially the Jewish Chaplains' own record cards in our Archives – with the assistance of the late Reverend Leslie Hardman. The author has also extended the range to Jewish Chaplains from the Commonwealth/Empire, using other sources such as the First World War *British Jewry Book of Honour*[21], the *Australian Jewish Books of Honour of WW1 and WW2*, *The South African Jewish Book of Honour of WW2* and *The Canadian Jewish Book of Honour of WW2*, all in our library at the Jewish Military Museum and on the suggested reading list at the back of this book. It should also be remembered that many other Jewish religious ministers acted as part-time and informal military padres at home.

The first Jewish Chaplain in British Forces was recognized in 1889 and the first appointed was Rabbi Francis Lyon Cohen, in 1892; in the USA the first Jewish Chaplain was appointed in 1862, during the Civil War.

It is worth noting that most European armies appointed many rabbis as fighting Jewish Chaplains in the nineteenth and twentieth centuries, including Germany in the First World War and the Franco-Prussian war of the 1870s. In both world wars, French and Russian/Soviet Jewish Chaplains were casualties (scouring the *Jewish Chronicle* back issues will reveal many such reports from the battlefronts). One especially famous personality was the Polish Rabbi Major Baruch Steinberg, who was born in 1897 and was Supreme Rabbi of the Polish Army. He took part in the defence of Lvov in 1919 and was Supreme Polish Army Rabbi by 1933. Captured by the Soviets in 1939 he was imprisoned in Starobielsko camp, deported on 24 December 1939 and murdered at Katyn in March 1940. It is known that more than 450 Polish Jewish officers were murdered in that notorious massacre.[22]

I would like to thank also Janice Rosen of the Canadian Jewish Congress Archives in Montreal, and historian Harold Pollins of Oxford, for their expert assistance.

For historical completeness, the First World War chaplains have been included in this book.

1914–18

(Dates are those of Commission, and theatre of war is shown where known; trio refers to award of all three First World War campaign medals.)[23]

Rabbi Herman H. Abramowitz (Canadian), served with UK Forces.

Reverend Michael Adler, DSO, MiD twice (Senior Jewish Chaplain), 1909 Territorials; France, January 1915, trio, first Jewish Chaplain in the field.

Reverend Arthur Barnett, MiD, 30 March 1916, France (also Second World War).

Lieutenant Harold Boas, seconded from the YMCA in Australia.

Reverend Israel Brodie, 8 January 1918, France (also Second World War), later Chief Rabbi.

Reverend J. Dangton, CF (Chaplain to the Forces).

Rabbi Raphael della Pergola (Cairo), Chaplain to the Zion Mule Corps of Gallipoli, 1915–16.

Reverend Leib A. Falk, 25 January 1918, Palestine/Israel, Chaplain to the Jewish Legion/Judeans, 38 Battalion, Royal Fusiliers.

Reverend Isaac Frankenthal, 11 June 1916, EEF?

Reverend John Lionel Geffen, 21 August 1917, France (his son was KIA).

Reverend Nehemiah Goldston, 4 February 1918, Home Service, his son was KIA.

Reverend Mark Gollop, MiD, 26 March 1917, Salonika (also Second World War).

Reverend Simon Grajewsky, MiD, EEF.

Reverend David Isaac Hirsch;
14 August 1917, France.

Reverend Barnet Joseph,
minister in Hackney
synagogue, HCF (Honorary
Chaplain to Forces); also
served Second World War.

Reverend Captain Leveson.
Reverend Walter Levin, 27
October 1918, Italy, Egypt,
Palestine/Israel, attached to
Jewish Battalions RF
('Judeans').
Reverend Nathan Levine, 9
July 1918, France.
Reverend E.M. Levy, June
1917, France.
Reverend B.B. Lieberman, 16
January 1917, France.
Reverend Solomon Lipson,
MiD, 22 January 1915,
Home Service, then France.

Reverend Louis Morris, 22
January 1915, France, Italy.

Reverend Harris Lewis Price,
23 October 1917, France.

Reverend Henry P. Silverman
Reverend Vivian George
Simmons, 24 August 1915,
France, Reform Rabbi, trio.
Second Jewish Chaplain to
France.

From South Africa
Reverend E. Lyons in German
West African campaign.
Reverend I. Levinson in East
African campaign.

1939–45 and After
All titles are Reverend except
where Rabbi is known as
correct; TD is Territorial
Decoration.

Reverend Ruben Abenson,
RAF.
Reverend Alexander Saul
Amias, RAF

Arthur Barnett (Aldershot),
also First World War.
A. Berman
Myer Berman, Northern
Ireland.
Cecil Maurice 'Sonny' Bloch,

RAF, 12th Army SEAC.
Harry Bornstein, **died on
active service** 28 November
1943, buried Tripoli.
Chief Rabbi Sir Israel Brodie,
evacuated Dunkirk, Middle
East, first Chief Rabbi to
be knighted; also First
World War.
Solomon Brown, 1947–50.

Eli Cashdan, RAF, Middle
East/Far East.
Rabbi Bernard Moses Casper
(Jewish Brigade), MiD, later
Chief Rabbi of South Africa.
Rabbi Lionel Casper (brother
of Bernard Moses, above).
Henry Mark T. Chait
Bernard Cherrick
Phillip Cohen
I. Kenneth/M. Cosgrove

E. Moshe Davis

Rabbi Leslie I. Edgar (Liberal
Rabbi).
Michael Elton
Rabbi Baruch Epstein,
Italy/Israel.

Isaac N. Fabricant

Jacob Gill, aka Lifshitz (Jewish
Brigade).
Alex Ginsberg/Ginsburg,
1947–62, Europe.
Reverend Goldman
Rabbi (Dayan) Mark Gollop,
TD, 1926–44, also First
World War.
Rabbi Gompertz
B. Greenberg

E. T. Hamburger
Leslie H. Hardman, at libera-
tion of Belsen, H.C. to
AJEX.
Rabbi Cyril Harris, 1966–71,
later Chief Rabbi of South
Africa.
Reverend Heilpern
Rabbi Bernard Hooker (Liberal
Rabbi).
Solomon Hooker (brother of
Bernard, above), **died on
active service** in India, 12
December 1946, buried
Madras.

Simeon Isaacs
Jacob I. Israelstam

Maurice A. Jaffe
Reverend Dr Barnett Joseph,
also First World War.

Reverend Kahan/Kahen

Major Isaac 'Harry' Levy, TD
(later Senior Jewish Chaplain), Middle East (POW,
escaped) and liberation of
Belsen; 1939–66. Chaplain
to AJEX.
Maurice A. Lew
Reverend Isaac Livingstone
B. Lucki

S. Margulies
Alan A.W. Miller
Wolf Morein, **died on active
service** 18 September 1941,
buried Willesden.
Abraham Myerson

Reverend I. Newman

Reverend Chaim Pearl
Adas Pimontel

Harry Eliezer J. Rabinowitz
Louis/Lewis Isaac Rabinowitz,
Middle East, Normandy,
later Chief Rabbi of South
Africa.
Isaac Rapaport
Rabbi Isaac Richards, at liber-
ation of Belsen.

Reverend S.M. ('Louis')
Sanker, RAF.
Reverend Schacter
Reverend Shapiro
Reverend Silver
Reverend Dr Silverstone
Reverend Solomons
Arthur Super
Reverend Swift

Reverend Maurice Unterman
Ephraim Elimelech Urbach;
Middle East.

Reverend Vilenski, at liberation of Belsen.

M. Wagner

Malcolm Weisman (post-war to present), AJEX Chaplain.

Joseph Weintrobe

Reverend Wolfson

Australia, First World War

Reverend F.L. Cohen

Colonel Reverend Jacob Danglow, Commissioned 1908, AIF France, 1918–20; awarded Volunteer Decoration (VD) and OBE (Mil.); also served Second World War.

Reverend Leib Falk (see below).

Major Reverend David Isaac Freedman, MiD, commissioned 1911, served 1915–18 in Gallipoli and Egypt, known as 'the Anzac Chaplain'; also served at home Second World War.

Australia, Second World War

Colonel Jacob Danglow (see above)

Rabbi A. Fabian, 1962.

Leib A. Falk AIF 1935–45 (also First World War – see above – in Palestine/Israel).

Major D. I. Freedman (see above).

Major Lazarus Manis Goldman, Alamein and New Guinea.

Rabbi Louis Rubin-Zacks, served New Guinea, invalided home with illness.

Reverend J. Wolman, Home service.

Canada, First World War

Rabbi Herman Abramowitz, served as chaplain with British Forces. (See above)

Canada, Second World War

All those listed were ordained rabbi unless otherwise stated.

Flight Lieutenant B./M. Babb

Flight Lieutenant Charles Bender

Rabbi Julius Berger, RCAF.

Lieutenant Harold Boas, appointed as lay pastoral leader by Australian YMCA, assisting Jewish Chaplains. (also WWI)

Rabbi Major Samuel Cass, 1942–46, Army/Navy, Belgium.

Squadron Leader Rabbi Jacob Eisen, RCAF.

E.L. Fackenheim (part-time).

Captain Oscar Z. Fasman/Fashman

Rabbi Solomon Frank

Major S. Gershon-Levi, MBE (Mil.), France.

Captain Hyman Gevantman

Flight Lieutenant Rabbi Wilfred Gordon

Captain Morris Casriel Katz

I. Kenner (part-time).

Captain Ephraim Mandelcorn, Pacific.

Captain David Aaron Monson, UK and Normandy.

Captain Rabbi Isaac Bert Rose, Pacific, Europe.

Flight Lieutenant S. Sachs

Captain Lewis Weintraub

South Africa, Second World War

L. Dyson, Home service.

S. Ernst, 6th Division, Italy.

Rabbi I. Friedman, North Africa, Italy.

J. Green, North Africa.

I. Hickman, 6th Division, Italy.

Rabbi W. Hirsch, Home service.

Rabbi S. Katz

Isaac Levinson, Home service.

C.L. Matz, North Africa and Italy.

M. Menachemson, East Africa and Italy.

M. Natas, SAAF, North Africa and Italy.

J. Potashnik, North Africa and Italy.

R. Rechtman, 6th Division, Italy.

I. Romm, North Africa and Italy.

Rabbi Eliezer Sandler, post-war SADF.

Reverend Simie Weinstein, North Africa.

W. Yesorsky, 2nd Division.

New Zealand, Second World War

Rabbi Alexander Astor, Auckland, Pacific/Middle East theatres.

Shanghai Volunteer Corps, Jewish Company 1932–45

Reverend Mendel Brown

Of Interest

First World War: Rabbi Steinhal, German Jewish Chaplain, awarded Iron Cross 1916.

Second World War: Major Melcer, Polish Jewish Chaplain to UK forces.

Notes

1. Michael Booker, of the Colditz Society, told the author that at least two inmates called Smith were not Smith at all and were probably Jewish POWs.

2. *Jewish Chronicle*, 12 July 1974; also cuttings from the archives of the Colditz Association, with thanks to Michael Booker – copies in AJEX Museum Colditz file.

3. Emails from his daughter Lorraine in Australia, where Ralph now lives.

4. *Jewish Chronicle* obituary in AJEX Museum file and story related in several published books on Colditz.

5. *Jewish Officers and Enlisted Men in the Polish Forces who were POW 1939–45* (Tel-Aviv: Association of Polish Jewish War Veterans of Israel, 2003).

6. H. Chancellor, *Colditz: The Definitive History* (London: Hodder & Stoughton, 2001).

7. In his taped interview at the Imperial War Museum Sound Archives, reference 16974/3, Stein is asked pointedly by the interviewer about his non-Polish name, and he answers that he thinks one grandfather was German; he also says he was born in Kostrin on 25 March 1920 and that his father was a businessman in the agricultural wholesale trade – a typical Jewish occupation at the time. He interestingly says nothing about the fate of his parents, even though he came to live in the UK in 1945. He is rather typical of Polish Jews who wish to hide their Jewish identity. He was not an escaper.

8. Imperial War Museum Sound Archives, 9337/4 and 15536/3.

9. The Lennard archive was donated to the AJEX Museum by Jack's daughter in 2006.

10. Schire, I., *Stalag Doctor* (London: A. Wingate, 1958).

11. On display in the Colditz Museum is a Hebrew-language edition of Pat Reid's best-seller, *The Colditz Story*.

12. After the war he published in Israel, in Hebrew and English, a delightful collection of drawings of POWs he knew, composed whilst he was in the camp, dedicated to his comrades and his family; this is now a very rare item and a copy is lodged in the AJEX Museum Archives in London.

13. J.M. Green, *From Colditz in Code* (London: Robert Hale, 1989).

14. Personal telephone interview with the author in May 2003; Dennis lives in North York, Ontario, Canada.

15. I am grateful to Dr Andrew Caplan of Royal Holloway College, University of London, for putting me in touch with Dennis Halfin.

16. His Jewish Chaplain Card was found – over 70,000 of these are kept at the AJEX Museum, compiled by the Jewish Chaplains in the Second World War.

17. S. Schofield, *Operation Musketoon* (London: Jonathan Cape, 1956).

18. My thanks to Jelka Kroger of the Dutch Jewish Historical Museum for assistance with these names. It should be noted, however, that as with British Jews in the armed forces, Dutch soldiers often attested as Christians to avoid possible mistreatment by the Nazis if taken prisoner, and their military records often show them as non-Jews.

19. In recognition of his service at this time, in 1999 Alan was awarded, personally by King Hussein, the Jordan Service Medal, which was also awarded to ten other British soldiers or their widows.

20. 'Jewish Chaplains', *Menorah Magazine* (Armed Forces Jewish Community, London), Spring 2008, p.30.

21. Rabbi Michael Adler (London: Caxtons, 1922).

22. Adam Mickiewicz Institute, www.diapozyta.pl.

23. Michael R. Goldberger, 'An Englishman and a Jew: the Story of Vivian Simmons', *Medal News Magazine*, December 1994, pp.12–14.

Lions of Judah:
The Jewish Commandos of the SIG

(The initials MT in the text refer to an interview conducted with one of the last survivors of the SIG, 10428 Acting Sergeant Maurice 'Monju' Tiefenbrunner, aka Tiffen, formerly also of the 51st Middle East Commando and SAS, who gave a first-hand account of some of the incidents described below. The interview took place on 6 July 1997 at the home of his daughter Judy in Edgware, London, and other information came in letters exchanged with Maurice from his home in Jerusalem, Israel.)

Beginnings

The British Forces in the Second World War spawned many effective and daring 'special' or unconventional units. Some were very well known, such as the Army Commandos, the SAS (Special Air Service), and the LRDG (Long Range Desert Group). But among the most ambitious and mysterious were the Jewish Commandos of the SIG.

Charles Messenger[1] describes how Colonel Terence Airey – who ran G(R) Branch (formerly Military Intelligence Research at the War Office in London) – wrote in March 1942 that part of the recently disbanded No. 51 Middle East (Jewish) Commando – consisting of many German-speaking Palestinian Jews – was to be formed into 'a Special German Group as a sub-unit of ME Commando ... with the cover name "Special Interrogation Group". They were to be used for infiltration behind the German lines in the Western Desert, under 8th Army ... the strength of the Special Group would be approximately that of a platoon'. The letter[2] continued: 'The personnel are fluent German linguists ... mainly Palestinian (Jews) of German origin. Many of them have had war experience with 51 Commando ... it is essential they be provided with transport: a) one German Staff car b) Two 15cwt Trucks.' A second letter added, 'this issue [of transport] is of high operational importance'.

The SIG were a subgroup of 'D' Squadron 1st Special Service Regiment. Some were also recruited directly from the Palmach, the strike arm of the Jewish/Israeli underground army, Haganah,[3] and 'Etzel' (the Irgun), a semi-legal Jewish underground group, whose members included Dov Cohen (Cohen was later killed in Acre in 1947), Herbert Paul (Delmonte-Nietto) Hollander, Bernard Lowenthal[4] and Israel Carmi, who was later an officer in the Jewish Brigade and the Israeli Army (MT). Carmi had also been in the special Night Squads under Wingate. Another comrade remembered by Tiffen was Karl Kahane/Cahanna;[5] all four survived the war. Two others were Dolph Zeintner aka Zentner and Philip Kogel (aka Shrager-Iser), but neither saw action, according to Tiffen. The SIG's true strength has never been known, though it was probably about thirty-eight according to Tiffen, twenty according to Ariyeh Shai (see below, and in a letter and Israeli newspaper article sent by him to the author in May 1999). Other recruits came from Jews in the Free Czech Forces (about eight), the French Foreign Legion (two?) and German-speaking French Jewish troops (MT). Maurice Tiffen recalls their first training base as being at Geneifa near Suez. Having returned from Eritrea with the 51st Middle East Commando, Maurice and comrades were visited by a British captain looking for German-speakers, whom he knew he would find at Geneifa. In fact document WO 218 159 at TNA contains part of the War Diary of the 51st Commando, and a cryptic entry by the CO for 17 March 1942 describes the arrival at Burgh el Arab 'of a Capt. Buck, to select German-speaking personnel with a view to certain work'.

The British Commanding Officer of the SIG, who had served with the Punjabis, had once been wounded and captured by the Germans in North Africa at Gazala and escaped using an Afrika Korps uniform. Surprised by how easy it was – speaking German – to pass unmolested through Axis lines, he had the idea of the SIG. His name was indeed Captain Herbert Cecil A Buck, MC, 3/1 Punjabis and Scots Guards, and he was an Oxford scholar who, like his Palestinian Jews, spoke fluent German.

Authors to this day have been unable to agree on what SIG actually stood for. Peter Smith[6] calls them the Special Identification Group – as does Eric Morris[7] – but in his index Morris also refers to them as the 'Special Intelligence Group'.

Whatever their true title, Ariyeh Shai, aka Sheinik/Sheikin (MT), a Jewish veteran of 51 Commando and of the SIG,[8] was an early volunteer and described his training:

> situated somewhere at the far end of an isolated group of desert encampments ... we received no promises. Capt. Buck had warned that

lives would depend on our ability to wear our disguises faultlessly, to learn to perfection the slang prevalent among the soldiers of the Afrika Korps, and to drill in accordance with all the German methods. 'If your true identity is found out', said Buck, 'there is no hope for you.'

Contacts with other British units were nil, in order that they should live, eat, drill, speak and behave like Germans.

At about this time, a young British officer, Reverend Isaac 'Harry' Levy, who was senior Jewish chaplain to the 8th Army, was travelling west from Mersa on his duties:[9]

> [I] had been told that a somewhat unusual outfit was to be found in the vicinity of a vague map reference. Picking our way through a fairly clearly marked minefield,[10] my driver and I ultimately discovered ... a special Commando unit undergoing intensive training. Except for the CO, all were Palestinian Jewish volunteers. I met the men in a shed which was crammed full of German uniforms and equipment. I learned to my intense surprise and profound admiration that this unit was destined to be taken behind enemy lines for special Commando operations and sabotage ... All their activities were conducted in German, daily orders were published in that language and often in the dead of night a man would be suddenly awakened and he had to speak in German. None must be caught by surprise. These men knew the risks were they to fall into enemy hands ... denied the status of POW, they would be shot out of hand. The most painfully distressing aspect of my encounter with these superbly brave men was the confidential information transmitted to me by several of them.

In conversation with the author in April 1997, Isaac Levy, then honorary chaplain to the Association of Jewish Ex-Servicemen and Women until his retirement in July 1999, described the camp:

> [It] was even more off the beaten track than the norm to be expected in the Western Desert; at first I thought they were prisoners of war. On seeing my Jewish Chaplains' badges, however, they spoke freely to me about their concerns.
>
> They were convinced that one member of their group was untrustworthy, possibly a German who had been living in Palestine before the war and was a fifth columnist, and not Jewish. They wished me to notify the CO which I duly did, but he assured me their

doubts were unfounded. It subsequently transpired that the mens' suspicions were justified.

In fact two 'real' Germans, Walter Essner (or Esser) and Herbert Brueckner, had been conscripted from a POW camp to train the SIG. Brueckner was big, brash and fair-haired, in his twenties (MT); Essner quiet and good-natured in his thirties (MT).[11] They were former members of the French Foreign Legion before the war, professing to be German anti-Nazis. They had been captured in November 1941,[12] serving in the 361st Regiment of the Afrika Corp and recruited by the British Combined Services Detailed Interrogation Centre (CSDIC) as double agents. They were not trusted by the Jewish members of SIG, who opposed the idea of the two actually going into action with them, but Buck insisted and the orders were obeyed (MT and see below).

Each day the SIG were awakened by '*Kompagnie anfsteher!*' (Company get up!) followed by twenty minutes' strenuous physical training,[13] and they trained all hours of the day and night with German weapons, were questioned suddenly on their German 'identities' and taken to the mess room, goose-stepping; they even learned German marching songs, and whom and when to salute (MT). The strenuous training welded them into a team – handling explosives, desert navigation, unarmed combat: all skills required by a special raiding force. They were also all expert mechanics and drivers of German vehicles.[14]

Some of their earlier exploits included using captured German vehicles and going behind German lines near Bardia and setting up roadblocks. Dressed as German military police they stopped and questioned German transports, gathering crucial intelligence. On other forays unspecified by author Gordon Landsborough[15] they would carry out sabotage behind the German lines in German uniforms or simply pull in at German camps, speak to troops and gather information. On one occasion, Tiffen even lined up to draw pay from a German field cashier; he explained how he was nervous, but so caught up in his trained role as a German soldier that he hardly had time to dwell on the danger of what he was doing. On other occasions he and other SIG mingled with German POWs to gather intelligence and learn how they behaved (MT).

In June 1942 the SIG were given their first major task: to assist the founder of the SAS – the charismatic Major Stirling – to blow up German airfields on the coast, 100 miles west of Tobruk, at Derna and Martuba, which were threatening the Malta supply convoys (the Malta base being of supreme importance in the struggle to starve Rommel of the supplies he needed to defeat the Allies in North Africa).

When Buck was approached by Stirling about the raid, he was absolutely delighted; it would allow him the chance to show what his Palestinian Jews could do.[16] The SIG were to meet the SAS at Siwa oasis, work out detailed plans and leave no later than 8 June, to go in on the night of 13/14 June with fourteen men and an officer (Lieutenant Jordain) of the Free French Squadron, escorting them hidden in the back of two captured Afrika Korps trucks and a command car (MT). Cowles, however,[17] claims the SIG had four vehicles with Afrika Corps strip and insignia: a Knevelwagen (a military version of the VW), one Opel, one German three-ton lorry and a 'captured' British thirty-hundredweight lorry, and eight SIG men. Tiffen says twelve SIG men, four in each of two lorries and the rest in the command car – five of whom had been in 51 Commando, and two others who were Free Czech Jews;[18] Morris and Tiffen, however, claim they were posing as German guards openly escorting French POWs in captured Allied trucks.

Whatever the case, the raiders set out from Siwa after three days of checking supplies and weapons and gathering last minute Intelligence from 8th Army HQ, escorted by the New Zealand Patrol R1 of the LRDG under Captain A.I. Guild on 6 June (this patrol was to establish an RV (Rendezvous) and wait for the commandos after the raid, according to Cowles). After four days the SIG team changed into German uniforms; Buck was a private driving the lead vehicle[19] and next to him were Essner and Brueckner as NCOs, and Ariyeh Shai was driver 'Corporal Adolf Schubert'. Atop each truck was an SIG 'guard', posted German-style as a lookout. Each SIG man carried a Luger, machine gun, bayonet and grenades[20] and – according to Cowles – the French were dressed in khaki overalls with blue forage caps, with grenades and a .45 automatic revolver each. Each lorry also concealed two ready-mounted machine guns.

During that day, the British lorry broke down but was taken in tow by Buck's vehicle. Then Shai describes how 'we saw a roadblock with a red and white barrier and guard room, about 4 p.m in the afternoon. A skinny Italian soldier wearily waved us down and demanded the password.' Captain Buck was nonplussed for the moment. British Intelligence had not supplied them with the password for June – only for May ('*Fiume*').[21] Buck or Brueckner flourished their forged orders in the sentry's face, saying they had been on a mission before the old password was changed, but failed to budge him. Then a major arrived, suggesting they go to the guardroom to discuss the matter over a glass of wine. Buck and Brueckner went, playing their role superbly, explaining they had to deliver the trucks from Agedabia to the Derna workshops.

But the genial major would not relent as he had orders to let nobody through without the password. Buck looked at Brueckner and the German took the hint. 'You are holding us up', roared Brueckner in German. 'I'll report you to your superiors. Keep out of the way. Don't you see German soldiers are coming back from the desert?' Eventually they were allowed to pass through, but the sources do not explain how an NCO got away with speaking to an Italian major in that manner.

In the evening the convoy met another roadblock. A fat German corporal waved them through, warning that 'British Commandos reach even out here' and advised them to park in the transit camp a little further on. So as not to arouse suspicion, Buck did as advised. At the camp they filled up with fuel, chatted with the German soldiers, bought some provisions at the local canteen and 'Corporal Schubert' even stood in line to get some supper – lentils and dumplings. The French, in hiding, watched this with amusement from slits in the truck canvas sides. Shortly afterwards the convoy left unnoticed and parked overnight, several miles down the road.

Next day, 13 June, the party carried out a reconaissance of the airfield targets in the late afternoon, to be hit that night. Brueckner drove during this recce, taking Jordain and four other men. They saw one airfield with Me (Messerschmitt) 110s and the other with Stukas. The two fields at Martuba were not investigated for fear of arousing suspicion, but also had Me 110s. All returned safely by 5.30 p.m.

The commandos were parked within five miles of the two Derna airfields at a point which would be the post-raid rendezvouz. They were to split into two parties, one led by Buck and Essner in a truck with three SIG (including Shai) and five of the French to attack one of the Martuba airfields, and the other led by Jordain (the French CO) and Brueckner with the other nine of the French SAS and three other SIG, including two named Peter Hass/Hess and Peter Gottlieb (see notes below), to be taken in two parties to the two airfields at Derna. Swinson claims Buck stayed at the rendezvous point to coordinate the operation. Tiffen says no: he himself was at the rendezvous with the command car and another SIG member, to act as liaison between the two groups. Whatever the truth, so far all had gone perfectly well.

But before this, they had to get the proper password and so Brueckner and Essner had earlier in the day been sent to a nearby German post to ask – and got it. The challenge was 'Siesta' and the reply 'Eldorado'. Cowles, however, gives a different version.[22] Buck typed a letter to be given to the fat German NCO they had met earlier, requesting the password. Two SIG – again Hass/Hess and Gottlieb – volunteered to deliver it. They took the Knevelwagen and found the German, who quipped that he was not sure he even knew it; they all laughed merrily and went to look for an Italian guard who gave them the passwords by looking in an index book of some kind. They all then saluted each other and the SIG men left.

Buck with Essner took off to their target at Martuba with the first party. The other group left at 9 p.m. from a point three kilometres north of the Carmusa crossroads to Derna, in another lorry, first to drop off Jordain's group, and then the second Derna group under Corporal Bourmont. But before this could be done, whilst passing through Derna itself, Brueckner stopped the truck near the cinema on the pretence that the engine was overheating and went to a nearby German guard-room or garage. Cowles claims the French could hear the film projector running.[23] But Landsborough's source says that Brueckner exclaimed, 'Something has fallen off the truck; I am going back for it.' He then walked off into the night. One SIG man in the cab said, 'Brueckner is away a long time.' The other replied, 'I am uneasy. I do not trust Brueckner. I think he might play traitor.' Yet another source[24] claims that Brueckner waited till they were 200 yards from the airfield before betraying the raiders.

Whatever the truth, the next that the French knew was that the truck was surrounded by Germans who ordered 'All Frenchmen out!' Jordain says he heard the crunching of footsteps and when peering out to check what was happening, was dragged out of the truck by two Germans.[25]

But the commandos refused to give up without a fight and came out with guns blazing. They inflicted many casualties on the Germans, fighting defiantly until overwhelmed. In the melee, only the commander, Lieutenant Augustine Jordain,[26] escaped. Buck, having succeeded in his raid, destroying twenty enemy planes with the SIG and his French SAS, returned to the RV with the remainder of his party, receiving the news – about the second French group from Jordain – in shocked disbelief.[27] All Jordain's Frenchmen had been either captured or killed.[28] Jordain said he had seen two SIG men – one of them Hass/Hess – hurtling grenades with reckless abandon at the enemy; then on the brink of capture they blew themselves up with the truck with grenades. Tiffen and Shai, however, who remember clearly hearing the gunfire and explosions of both raids, also remember Jordain returning, badly wounded, in the pitch dark with four survivors – not alone. They also say that they learned afterwards that two SIG had been captured and then shot. Cowles writes[29] that months afterwards,

Jordain learnt that four of the French had been captured on the airfield and three more later on in the desert. Two others met up with the Martuba group but this RV had been betrayed aswell. They fought off a German attack but were all eventually captured. So Jordain was the only French evader of the raid.

After waiting for any stragglers, the handful of survivors then made their getaway towards Siwa with the lorry, and abandoned the command car. They waited for stragglers for almost a week at Baltel Zalegh, but none came. At one point they fooled a German plane into holding its fire by laying out a swastika flag on the sand (MT).

Much of the above description is supported by evidence given by two Luftwaffe Me 109 pilots – Leutnant Friederich Korner (captured 5 July 1942 at El Alamein) and Oberleutnant Ernest Klager (captured 3 July 1942, also at El Alamein).[30] In their interrogation, they claim: 'The Germans already knew that a group of English saboteurs would carry out a raid on German aerodromes in Cyrenaica dressed in German uniform ... being organised by an English Colonel. As a result a state of alarm had been ordered as from sundown on all aerodromes.'[31] Koerner continued:

> Brueckner got out [of the truck], saluted the [German] CO and stated that he was a German soldier acting as driver of a German lorry containing a party of heavily armed English troops in German uniform with explosive charges to destroy aircraft. The CO was rather suspicious at first but the driver pressed him to organise as many men as possible with all speed and as heavily armed as possible to disarm the raiding party. The lorry was immediately surrounded and the occupants forced to get out. A few seconds after the last one had got out, there was an explosion inside the lorry and it was completely destroyed. A melee developed and it was believed that all the raiders had been shot. However, on the following morning a wounded man presented himself at Derna hospital saying he was a wounded German soldier needing treatment. For some reason the doctor became suspicious and on examination it turned out that he was not a German soldier but a Jew from Palestine [this is almost certainly one of the two Tiffen says was shot later by the Germans]. Brueckner claimed to the Germans that he was a German POW who had been approached by the English to drive a German lorry for them behind the lines. He had at first refused but money had been offered which he again refused. However, the sum increased and he accepted as he felt it was the best way of getting back his freedom.

Brueckner was flown to Berlin and awarded the Deutsche Kreuze in gold (Buck later believed it was silver). Morris claims, however, that he was killed in the fighting, and in the 'Most Secret' post-raid report,[32] Buck stated this too (this incident is described in a report in the *Jewish Chronicle*, 13 July 1945). Tiffen had argued with Buck that using Germans as trainers was one thing, but taking them actually on a raid was tempting providence too much. Buck did not listen and Tiffen was proved right. In another statement in the post-raid report, Buck said Brueckner and Essner had been 'cleared' by Intelligence, and he 'considered it was a necessary risk for training purposes and initial operations to have men who had recently been in the German army and knew the ropes'. The report reminded critics that up to that point Brueckner and Essner had 'provided intelligence with very valuable information about German dispositions and had extracted information from many POWs on behalf of CSDIC'.

Essner had behaved well during the raid but was closely guarded by Tiffen on the way back to the base and then handed over to British MPs with a warning that he might try to escape. This he did, and was shot. Swinson, however, alleges Essner was later caught in Cairo trying to contact German agents and was 'shot trying to escape' by SIG men.[33]

Whatever the truth, most of these events were only revealed years after the war, with just a slight hint of the mysterious group's activities being mentioned in a very brief article in the *Jewish Chronicle* on 24 September 1943.

Authors John Gordon[34] and Bradford and Dillon (see note 5) relate yet another SIG exploit, when Stirling and his deputy, Paddy Mayne – whilst the Derna raid was in progress and hiding south of Benina – decided to attack Benghazi again. Stirling was anxious to show Mayne the havoc he and his raiders had caused the Germans at Benina. With four other SAS men and Karl Kahane of the SIG, and a Chevrolet truck that they had persuaded Captain Robin Gordon of the LRDG to lend them for twenty-four hours,[35] they set off across the escarpment. Mayne drove with Stirling next to him. They were first stopped at a roadblock at the dead of night, still in their British uniforms. Kahane, short and dark-haired, whom Stirling had brought along precisely for this purpose (and who had been an NCO in the German army before the rise of Hitler had forced him to flee to Palestine) used bluff and German slang to talk them through. But at a second Italian roadblock nearer to Benghazi, they were discovered. In a letter to his brother Douglas written six weeks after the raid, Mayne wrote:

With headlights on we passed through one Italian roadblock shouting 'Tedeseco' – Italian for German – but at a second check-post came upon a large gate and barbed wire. Kahane shouted that they were Germans, hungry and in a hurry and 'to open the —— gate'. Unsure, the guard called out a dozen heavily armed Germans with a Sgt Major, who was holding a potato masher grenade and a P38 pistol and who asked for the password. Kahane replied ' How the —— do we know the —— password and don't ask for our —— identity cards either; they're lost and we have been fighting the past 70 hours against those —— Tommies. Our car was destroyed and we were lucky to capture this British truck and get back at all. Some fool put us on the wrong road. We've been driving for two hours and you so and sos, sitting on your arses in Benghazi in a nice safe job, stop us! So hurry up and get that —— —— gate open.

But the German was not satisfied and walked to within three feet on Mayne's side of the truck whilst other guards focussed a light on Stirling and Mayne in the front seat. Mayne noisily cocked his Colt revolver lying on his lap, and all the others released their safety catches too; the German took one look and ordered the gate open; with many a '*Gute Nacht!*' the SAS drove on; clearly the German concluded that if anyone was to be hurt, he would be first, and even though it was clear he knew they were British, he had to let them through. Stirling, sitting next to Mayne, is in no doubt that the click of the Colt was deliberate, as the German's eyes met Paddy's. But the cat was out of the bag and Benghazi was now out of the question, so on arrival at Lete, just down the road, they came upon various targets of opportunity and blew up a roadblock, fuel tanks, pumps, trucks and Daimler half-tracks with machine guns and bombs. Now chased by armoured cars, they raced back five miles into the desert, having to use a different route to the one they had taken into the area, headlights blazing, the truck jolting fiercely as they and the Germans exchanged fire on the run. They eventually left their pursuers behind, the Germans not anxious to go too far and possibly meet an ambush, but the SAS team had had a narrow escape. They stopped eventually and celebrated with some whisky from Stirling's flask. The jolting, however, had set off the fuses they were still carrying, and as they climbed the escarpment to freedom they smelt burning. With a warning shout from one of the men, they all jumped off as the truck blew up. They recovered and surveyed the scene, then burst out laughing. Kahane[36] indicated that he was too old to laugh at such a thing but was so impressed with their humour that he told them he was convinced the Germans could never win the war against such spirited men.

They continued on foot and after an hour came to a Senussi village where they were cared for overnight. Next afternoon the LRDG came to pick them up after a messenger had been sent to fetch them.

The Raid on Tobruk

An audacious raid on Tobruk in North Africa to lay waste, from land and sea, the vital German Afrika Corps supply port, code-named Operation Agreement, took place on 13/14 September 1942, involving elements of the RM, RN, RAF, SAS, SBS, LRDG and a six-man Special Forces group of the SIG.

Taking part in Agreement were Captain David Stirling's SAS again; Lieutenant Colonel Vladimir Peniakoff of the Libyan Arab Force (Popskis Private Army – PPA), born in Belgium of Russian Jewish parents; and Colonel John E. 'Jock' Haselden, killed in action on the raid, the Egyptian-born son of English and Greek parents. He had guided into shore the abortive Special No. 11 Commando raid to attempt to kill Rommel in November 1941 at Beda Littoria,[37] Operation Flipper – where Colonel Geoffrey Keyes won a posthumous VC. Haselden was an Arabic linguist (who spoke several Bedouin dialects) and wealthy cotton mill owner as well as a member of Military Intelligence (MI) Research, who had been back and forth behind enemy lines since the war began. With Haselden on the Rommel Raid there had been members of the Palestinian Jewish 51st Commando, notably Corporal Drori who spoke both Arabic and German.[38] Drori had been in the house when Keyes was killed.

On this Tobruk raid, Haselden was the officer commanding the Commando group Force B, code-named 'Picture',[39] the land-based assault striking from the desert via Kufra Oasis, code-named 'Daffodil'.[40] LRDG Patrol Y1 (led by Captain David Lloyd Owen) were acting only as guides from Kufra to the perimeter of Tobruk, with eighty-three Commandos and an SIG team with eight three-ton Canadian Chevrolet trucks. (In WO 201/749, the SIG were described cryptically as 'Special Detachment G(R)' in the Battle Plan.) Afterwards, Y1 were to participate in another part of the raid. It was the Commandos and SIG who were actually to penetrate Tobruk itself by bluffing their way through the perimeter fence with the SIG posing as German guards, as they had done at Derna/Martuba, and assault the coastal guns of Mersa Umm es Sciausc east of the harbour with the rest of Force B.

The detachment of SIG were 'to play a special part in the proceedings'[41] with Buck and Lieutenant T.C. David Russell, Scots Guards, who was also fluent in German. Two other British officers allegedly attached to SIG were Captain H. Bray (4th Indian Division) and Lieutenant D. Lanark, Scots Guards. However, in 1989 it emerged that Gordon Landsborough, in his 1956 edition of *Tobruk Commando*, had – due to War Office restrictions – used noms de guerre for many of the Commandos. The true names were revealed in David List's 1989 introduction to the book. So Bray was in fact Buck, and Lanark was Russell. It also emerged that the Nazi traitor Brueckner was really called Brockmann.

Dressed in German uniform and speaking German, the SIG even carried faked love letters to ficticious wives in Germany and authentic German weapons, pay books (*Sold Buch*), insignia, cigarettes and chocolates. The letters were written by an SIG man, using forged German stamps and frankings, and copied by ATS (women) for authenticity, in Cairo. The women then dressed as civilians and posed with the SIG in their German uniforms, and then a Berlin background was dubbed on. One Jewish SIG member, Weizmann, actually called his 'girlfriend' Lizbeth Kunz, as this was the name of an actual well-known Nazi who lived in his street in Berlin before the war; this meant that if it came to it, he could claim (under interrogation if required) she was a real person. The SIG men were constantly tested on this detail in their documents – names, addresses, jobs; even German Army typewriters and stationery had been procured from British Intelligence for such use – but as Landsborough says,[42] 'the Palestinian Jews never faltered, never protested'.

The SIG were to play the role of German guards transporting three truckloads of British POWs to a camp at Tobruk. As Smith says, 'this was high bluff and indeed required nerves of steel and much courage', which the SIG showed they had in plenty. Needless to say, had their disguises been penetrated, the Germans would have shot them out of hand as spies (see Appendix 3). In fact, following the earlier betrayal, the Germans already knew of the SIG's existence. Buck suspected this and that is why he only took four or five of the SIG with him, as opposed to the dozen or so that might have been required (Buck also planned to kidnap a particular German general as booty, who was supposed to be staying in the old YMCA in Tobruk).[43] We must remember, however, the deep motivation of these men who had fled Nazi Germany as Jewish refugees, whose families had been or were being murdered in the Holocaust, and who were absolutely committed to the downfall of Nazism.

8.1 The SIG – left to right in Tel-Aviv whilst on leave, Dov Cohen, Rosenzweig, Maurice Tiefen-brunner, Walter Esser (the German traitor).

8.2 Egypt 1942 on leave with the SIG – left to right, Tiefenbrunner, Cpl Drory/Drori, Gold-stein and Rohr.

(A poor and not very accurate Hollywood movie, *Tobruk*, directed by Arthur Hiller and starring Rock Hudson, Nigel Green and George Peppard, made in 1966, portrayed the SIG role in this raid but tended to mix elements of their work on other raids too. It was filmed in Yuma, Arizona.)

The small SIG team reached Kufra in RAF Bombay Transports where they met the LRDG and other Commandos. There the SIG continued drilling in German uniform and using German commands as their British comrades looked on in amazement.[44] They were Corporal Weizmann and Privates Wilenski, Hillman, Berg and Steiner.[45] A naval signal of 12 September 1942[46] – from Commander-in-Chief Mediterranean to DCOME – stated that 'Buck and 6 ORs [other ranks] operating with Haselden may be wearing German uniform. Their recognition signal is "red handkerchief".'

They kept themselves to themselves because, despite the fact that it was known that the traitor had been a Nazi, the SIG were looked upon with suspicion, following the betrayal of the French group the previous June. One LRDG veteran, Jock Fraser, told the author of *Massacre at Tobruk*: 'We all distrusted these guys though some were very brave men.'

Again the SIG names were not real; David List gives the actual names: Steiner was 10716 Private Hillman (SAS Regiment), Berg was Rohr,[47] Weizmann was Opprower and Wilenski was H. Goldstein. There was also a Private Rosenzweig but Tiffen does not remember his English alias.

Weizmann/Opprower's father had been murdered by the Nazis and at 16 years old he had been sent by his family to Palestine. He volunteered for the British Army on the outbreak of war in 1939, but when he was given only administrative work he hitchhiked to Egypt and volunteered for active service. Three times he was charged for breaking camp to get into the front line. Eventually the SIG recruited him.[48]

On D Minus 7 (6 September) the main part of Force B left Cairo for Tobruk, which was 300 miles behind the lines but a distance of 1,800 miles by their roundabout route. Morris, however, says the raiders left Kufra on 5 September, to travel the 800 miles to Tobruk – which seems much more likely and is in any case borne out by Lloyd-Owen's report,[49] which says they left at 1706 hrs precisely on that day.

Gordon Landsborough[50] describes how they travelled south to El Kharga (500 miles inland), then west to Kufra (to meet the SIG) and then north to Hatiet Etla. Here, ninety miles from the target, they rested on the night of 10 September. Kennedy-Shaw (see below), however, does not even mention the SIG as taking part in the raid, possibly for security reasons, when writing his book. I am grateful to Captain, now General, David Lloyd Owen, for pointing this out to me in a letter (13 December 1999). The plan was for them – at 2 a.m. on 14 September – to call in Force C from seaward, if they had managed to silence the guns of Mersa Umm es Sciausc. (A Jewish British officer and LRDG survey/cartography expert, Captain Ken Lazarus, was with SAS Squadron 2 with Stirling, the same night that they launched a diversionary attack at Benghazi; an SIG man was on this raid too – see below.[51])

The Commando convoy of lorries did not attract attention from the German and Italian patrols because so many Allied vehicles had been captured by the Axis forces. On the trucks were the Afrika Corps motif, painted using captured German stencils by Steiner/Hillman, and identification marks on the cab roofs to ward off prowling Stukas. Also across the bonnet was a wide white stripe, sign of *Bentezeichen,* or booty, which the Germans painted on captured Allied vehicles, and the divisional sign ER 372, which Intelligence had discovered was a real division stationed near Alamein. Each vehicle carried thirty fake POWs instead of the usual forty, because of the need to hide the arms and uniforms they contained. The SIG carried the requisite fake passes and ID documents. Landsborough, however, says that only four trucks were used with one SIG driver in each and Buck in the front one dressed as a German officer. Then, about four miles out, just three trucks went in, with the fourth disabled by removing the distributor cap, which was buried near the front left wheel, for use in escape later should it be needed. At the drop-off point there was then an emotional parting with the LRDG as they cheered each other goodbye, for they all knew that many of the Commandos would be going to their deaths. It is interesting that Lloyd-Owen notes in his post-raid report that Haselden had *not* arranged a rendezvous with him in case of a land withdrawal,[52] which proved to be a costly mistake.

On approaching the perimeter road across scrubland they saw two German trucks coming towards them on the same course; but they simply sped by without pausing. Then a red German light spotter plane approached and circled twice just a few hundred feet above them, but it too passed on.[53]

On reaching the main metalled road to Tobruk they merged easily into the regular base-traffic flow to the perimeter fence. They were merely waved through by Italian guards, even though Buck leaned out to show his documents. The SIG men, playing their parts fully, responded as Germans did, insulting their Italian allies as '*Schweinhunds*' as they drove past.

Inside they met a fast-moving convoy coming in the opposite direction and the middle truck was struck a glancing blow by a German staff car carrying, according to Weizmann, a high-ranking officer. Nobody stopped but the German convoy halted and angry voices were heard; eventually, after a tense moment, the Germans sped away. Further on they were accompanied for a while by two heavily armed motorcycle combinations and a solo of German military police who were irritatingly inquisitive. The Commandos took the safety clips off their guns but there was no attempt to stop them and the motorcycles turned off.[54] They then came upon a rock face looming in the darkness, at about 9 p.m., and Haselden nodded casually towards it saying, 'That's the bomb-proof oil storage depot we must destroy later tonight.'

All around were tented enemy camps and lines of German and Italian troops going about their duties as the three trucks sped on. But then a further hitch: Buck's Chevrolet halted and he and the SIG driver got out and walked out of sight. Clearly there was a problem – a fence had been built across the turn-off they were meant to take. Soon Buck and his driver returned – they had found a new track further on, and the convoy continued.

After fifteen minutes, they were met with a harsh challenge in German; one of the Commando officers got out and walked into the darkness. Soon he returned with a German rifle, having silenced the enemy sentry. Another 500 metres and they stopped, de-bussed and put on full combat kit. Nearby were the few buildings they had expected – the administrative centre for the coastal defences they were to silence.

At 10.30 p.m. the RAF softening-up bombing raid began.

On reaching their first objective, a small villa to be used as their HQ, Haselden and the four or five SIG, with Buck and Russell, burst in and drove off or killed the Italian platoon holding it. One was captured but was later killed 'trying to escape'. Knocking out various German machine-gun posts, a wireless station and negotiating minefields, Force B began taking casualties, but at 2 a.m. signalled Force C to land using the unfortunate code-word 'Nigger' (the alternative 'Cloud' was never used[55]). However, under heavy fire and in darkness, only two of sixteen MTBs were able to land a handful of reinforcements.

Buck, Russell, Wilenski and Weizmann cleared several more positions alone whilst the Commandos dealt with several others. The SIG team then moved, as planned, a little inland to guard against any counter attack from that direction and captured and held four ack-ack gun emplacements. Through the night they held these positions against sustained attacks by the Italians to recapture the guns. Eventually they rolled grenades into the barrels and destroyed them.

But as the enemy regrouped, now fully alerted and prepared, as the sun came up, they closed in on Force B, now outnumbered and short of ammunition after a fierce fire-fight. Weizmann and Wilenski were met by Berg who told them that Buck had ordered them to destroy all their German documents and uniforms, find British uniforms and destroy the lorries. Haselden, from his HQ in the captured villa, had ordered destruction of all the coastal guns, and then every man for himself. It was clear that the Tobruk raid had failed, reinforcements would not be coming from the seaward invasion as planned, and they had to move fast to save themselves. Berg moved off and Wilenski and Weizmann destroyed one lorry with petrol and then moved to a cave, stripped off, burnt everything that would incriminate them, and then went, naked, to find two uniforms, which they had eventually to take from two dead Commandos.

Buck suddenly reappeared with Russell; they had apparently been on some other SIG mission, perhaps to try and release the Allied POWs in Tobruk (part of the original plan, had Agreement succeeded) or to capture the general in the old YMCA. There was also talk of breaking into the enemy garrison's strongroom and stealing the German funds. To this day it is not known precisely what the SIG had in mind.

Haselden ordered all the force remaining to re-embark on the last two trucks and try to break out (others made vainly for the sea but were then driven inland, and in small groups tried to head east back to Allied lines). Russell brought a truck up as Steiner appeared still in German uniform. Buck yelled to him to take it off even though he himself was still dressed as an Afrika Korps officer.

As they made to get away, the ever-calm and brave Haselden in the lead truck meanwhile decided to halt and cover the escape of those behind him. He led a forlorn charge single-handedly against the encroaching Italian forces with Russell, Buck, Watler, Berg and Steiner following him. Berg was wounded and Haselden was killed by a grenade. Steiner called his CO's name but there was no answer. In the melee and still half-light, Steiner grabbed Berg and dragged him away.[56] Others, however, were forced to surrender because they had no food, water or ammunition and were carrying wounded comrades.

Only six of Haselden's group escaped, and then made a run for it to Allied lines, including Lieutenant Russell and (according to Landsborough) Buck, Berg and Wilenski. Weizmann was with them but had been wounded later breaking into an Italian camp for food. After seventeen days he was unable to go on and agreed to be leftbehind. Local Arabs handed him over to the Italians, who handed him to the Gestapo. He was tortured for five days but revealed nothing. At one point they made him dig his grave and stood him in front of a firing squad. However, an Afrika Korps Officer eventually had him released to a POW camp.[57] After many close calls and terrible hardships, the rest of the group reached Allied lines on 18 November (despite every effort by Lloyd-Owen, Naval Signals testify that he lost all contact with Force B early on in the raid and was unable to search for or rescue any survivors the next day[58]).

In another escape party led by Lieutenant Tommy B. Langton of the SBS (ex-Irish Guards) were Watler and 19-year-old Private Steiner/Hillman; he had already lost his left boot in the fighting and also had a foot lascerated by barbed wire. Knowing he would be shot if caught, he changed his name to Kennedy and was known as Ken by his comrades throughout his evasion adventure. It was known that the Germans knew his identity. He was in fact a short, broad Austrian Jew, son of a Viennese butcher. Aged 16, he had been imprisoned for anti-Nazi activity and then escaped to Palestine where he joined the Pioneer Corps, thinking they were a fighting unit. He served with them in France in 1940 and then joined the tough 51st Middle East Commandos and fought in Eritrea.[59] At some time he had served in the French Foreign Legion. After several weeks dodging German and Italian patrols and being fed by friendly Arab villagers (Hillman in fact saved the group's lives several times by nego-tiating – as interpreter in his excellent Arabic – for food, and got himself a new pair of boots), Hillman and his party eventually reached Allied lines at Himeimat, 400 miles east of Tobruk on 13 November, having been marching for seventy-eight days, much of it in bare feet.[60] Hillman ended up at No. 1 South African Convalescent Depot.[61]

The failure of this raid marked the end of the SIG as a fighting force, and surviving members were transferred to the AMPC (Auxiliary Military Pioneer Corps). From here several joined No. 2 Commando and fought with them until war's end in the Balkans, Italy and the Adriatic. According to David List, Steiner/Hillman later joined the SAS as did Tiefenbrunner and others; Wilenski/Goldstein – who had fought on the Mersa Matru and Fuka raids with 'L' detachment LRDG – was captured after Operation Agreement but then later fought in the Far East SAS against the Japanese. Tragically Russell was murdered in Yugoslavia whilst working for SOE in August 1943 and Buck was killed in 1946.[62]

Smith's account of the Tobruk raid is inconsistent with Landsborough's, who actually spoke with eyewitness survivors. Smith used many PRO records but these records for that time are alleged to have been partial and contradictory. Ultimately, readers must decide for themselves. What is not in doubt, however, is that the SIG were extremely brave men who willingly threw themselves into the devil's cauldron, and were often left to fight their own way out. They should all be remembered with pride as Lions of Judah.

Appendix 1

On pages 181 and 110 in Norman Bentwich's book, *I Understand the Risks* (London: Gollancz, 1950), an Austrian Jewish refugee who fought on the Tobruk raid is identified as Captain F. Hillman/J. Kennedy, MC, MM. This is almost certainly the same man described above as a member of the SIG Team. Charles Butt, writing in the *Journal of Military History*, 50 (August 1999), p. 64, recalls:

> Captain 'Charlie' or 'Chunky' Hillman, MC, MM, originally of the Royal Pioneer Corps ... went on after North Africa to command a Field Security Section in occupied Germany in 1945/46. He hated Germans but had a reputation for personal bravery with both of his medals being earned the hard way on operations behind enemy lines. Later (1955) he commanded 147 Field Security Section in Nicosia and Famagusta, Cyprus, during the early days of EOKA ... it is thought he emigrated to Canada after retirement from long service with the British Army.

Jim French, 'The Rose and Laurel', *Journal of the Intelligence Corps* (December 1997), p.33, says: 'as an NCO with BAOR 1948–50, I was with 309 Field Security Section in Hamburg with OC Capt. Hillman, who clearly loved the pastries of his native Vienna. He had been in the Foreign Legion and SAS and won an MM and MC.' And WO Hillyer-Funke served under his command in an internment camp for Nazis in Wolfsberg, Carinthia, 1945–47, as Captain Leo Hillman (Intelligence Corps Archives, Michael Potter, 1999), and later again in Cyprus, where he described him as 'a good and crazy man! I liked him!'

Major Fred Warner, aka Werner, PC and later SOE, writes on page 39 of his book, *Don't You Know There's a War On?* (privately published):

> [Hillman was] one of the most decorated foreigners in the British Army, small, stout, with gold-rimmed glasses, looking more like a

professor than a tough paratrooper ... he had come to Britain via the
French Foreign Legion and Norway; he spoke English with a cock-
ney accent and always introduced himself as Baron von Schnitzel-
berger. He always chewed garlic, a habit picked up in the Foreign
Legion, and so always sat alone to eat. He was dropped by SOE into
Vienna in early 1945 and eventually interrogated the head of the
Vienna Gestapo.

Appendix 2

Maurice Tiefenbrunner was born on 18 December 1915 into an
Orthodox Jewish family in Wiesbaden, Germany, as one of eight
children. Maurice was something of an athlete and scholar and his
father a devout and well-known teacher. On 28 October 1938, Jews of
Polish origin, like Maurice's family, were deported by Nazi law to
Poland. He was 22 years old.

A brother in Antwerp managed to obtain papers for Maurice to enter
Belgium, which he achieved with hair-raising adventures via Warsaw,
Prague and Rotterdam. From Antwerp, he contacted Jewish agents of the
Irgun, illegally transporting Jewish refugees into British Palestine (Israel).
Via Paris and Marseilles, he made it to a ship with a group of twenty oth-
ers, and eventually set sail on the SS *Parita* with 950 Jewish refugees, on
a vessel meant to carry 250.

After seventy days – instead of the intended ten – of wanderings,
touching Rhodes, Smyrna and other ports, and begging for food from
passing liners (including twenty bottles of beer from one passing cruise
ship), his group took over the ship from the Greek crew, hoisted the
Israeli flag and then beached the vessel on the seafront of Tel-Aviv on
22 August 1939. It was a Friday night and thousands of Tel-Avivans
came out to greet them with food. Then they were promptly interned
at Sarafand army camp by the British. Two weeks later war broke out
and Maurice was consequently made a 'legal' citizen as an amnesty was
declared.

Allowed only to enlist in non-combatant units for political reasons
by the British, Maurice (and thousands of other Palestinian Jews)
joined the Pioneer Corps. He fought in and escaped from France via St
Malo with hundreds of other Palestinian Jewish troops, in 1940, fighting with the BEF. Regrouped at Aldershot he joined the 51st Middle
East Commando and fought in the battles in Gondar and Keren in
Ethiopia/Eritrea where he was wounded trying to rescue a wounded
comrade, promoted and Mentioned in Despatches. Maurice was finally

returned to Egypt with the 51st Commandos and then took part (in December 1941) on an early raid on Tobruk. They inflicted heavy casualties on the Italian garrison before withdrawing but were now down to one-third strength. The 51st were thus disbanded at Geneifa, and this is where Buck recruited Maurice and other Jews into the SIG around March 1942.

After the SIG raid with the Free French in June 1942, described earlier, Maurice took part in a few smaller raids and then was recruited with about fourteen other surviving SIG into the SAS under Stirling. He took part in one of the several Commando raids from naval destroyers, with other Palestinian Jews, on Rommel's HQ in summer 1942 in the Derna area. Rommel was not at home but he remembers many German officers were killed and his force re-embarked with no casualties.

(Before the SIG raid on Derna, Maurice and five friends were ordered by Buck to accompany him to King Farouk's royal palace on a secret mission to 'persuade' HRH not to back the 'wrong side' in the war. This was successful.)

In December 1942, Maurice, still with the SAS and now with five remaining members of the disbanded SIG following the large raid on Tobruk (Operation Agreement – in which he did not take part), went with Colonel David Stirling and Major Oldfield on a hundred-man raid behind Italian lines, with the aim also of destroying German targets on the way. Maurice was in a jeep at the rear of a convoy of fifty vehicles, and broke down. Seen by Italians, he and his driver (from Lancashire) were soon surrounded by armoured cars and, after they had destroyed any sensitive documents which may have incriminated them, they were captured on 18 December 1942. When the Italian army collapsed he was taken (as an important SAS prisoner) with eight others by Italian submarine to Bari. On the way they tried to overpower the crew but failed and were punished by being locked up. As the Allies advanced on the POW camp at Bari, he was moved to a POW camp at Udine. His cover (prepared before the raid) was that his name was Tiffen, born in Montreal but taken to Palestine as a child.

Then Italy surrendered and the POWs were about to be liberated by the advancing Americans when the Germans appeared and shipped them off, in dreadful conditions, to Wolfensgarten in Austria. A group including Maurice tried an escape en route but were recaptured and then shipped to Thorn in east Germany. As the Russians advanced, the Germans force-marched them yet again for five days to Fallingsbostel near Hanover, where Maurice met POWs from the famous 'Wooden

Horse' escape from Stalag Luft 3, and Palestinian Jewish friends he had known in 1939–40 who had been captured in Greece/Crete in 1941. He was finally liberated in May 1945 after thirty months as a POW.

When the Allies separated SS prisoners from Wermacht, the Germans retaliated and separated Jewish POWs from others for several weeks. Maurice says he suffered no discrimination other than this, as a POW of the Germans, though there are British POW eye-witness accounts of Palestinian Jewish troops who were murdered by Germans in Crete and Greece. In a letter to the author, dated 12 November 1997, Edwin Horlington, of the British Veterans of the Greek Campaign Brotherhood, wrote; 'I know of one case where 12 Jewish Pioneer Corps men were found with their throats cut in a cave just SE of Kalamata. This was attested to by the Chief Clerk to the Senior British Officer at Kalamata.'

Back in Britain, Maurice was tracked down by Captain Buck, who tried to persuade him to join the SAS fighting the Japanese. He declined. Maurice and his newly-wed wife, Friedel, spent several evenings with Buck enjoying nights out in London. Some weeks later, Buck's sister telephoned Maurice with the sad news that the captain had been killed in a plane crash on his way to Germany.[63]

Demobbed, Maurice went to Israel and fought in the War of Independence throughout 1948 (Woodside Park Synagogue magazine, September 1963, and his autobiography).

At various times, Maurice has worn the insignia of the 51st Middle East Commando, SAS, and the 'neutral' overalls of the SIG – not to mention the Pioneer Corps and the Israeli Army. For many years after the war he lived in west London and Israel with his wife Friedel and large family but is – at time of writing – in his nineties, living happily in Jerusalem. He has the 1939–45 Star, Africa Star, France and Germany Star and War Medal. He was Mentioned in Despatches for courage in the battle of Keren in Ethiopia.

I would like to thank Maurice Tiefenbrunner most sincerely for speaking with me, and writing to me, at length, and providing me with such unique first-hand accounts of his experiences as well as some very rare photographs. Thanks also go to Jeffrey Tribich and his mother Mala Tribich (a Holocaust survivor) for their help in putting me in touch with Maurice in July 1997. Equally, I thank the patient staff of the Imperial War Museum Reading Room and The National Archives at Kew for all their help, as well as Sean Waddingham, whose enthusiasm for naval history prompted me to get on and write a long-planned article on the incredible Jewish lads of the elite SIG.

Appendix 3

PRO HW 1/643: Message intercepted and received in German by British Intelligence on 13 June 1942 and forwarded to Prime Minister Churchill as file CX/MSS/1071/T6, stating:

> Most secret document – only to be opened by an officer – from Supreme Command of the Army to Panzer Army Africa – are said to be numerous German political refugees with Free French Forces in Africa. The Führer has ordered that the severest measures are to be taken against those concerned. They are therefore to be immediately wiped out in battle and in cases where they escape being killed in battle, a military sentence is to be pronounced immediately by the nearest German officer and they are to be shot out of hand, unless they have to be temporarily retained for intelligence purposes.
>
> This order must NOT be forwarded in writing. Commanding Officers are to be told verbally.

I am grateful to Dr John P. Fox for pointing out this document to me, as further evidence of what the SIG faced if captured.

Notes

1. C. Messenger, *Middle East Commandos* (London: W. Kimber, 1988), p.109.
2. 'Most Secret', WO 201/732 PRO; a letter by General Airey, 1 April 1942, also includes a sentence where the group is called 'Special Operations Group', with 'Operations' later struck out and 'Interrogation' written instead above it. I am indebted to Desmond Duffy of Welling, brother of the late Lieutenant Michael Duffy, Commandos, killed in action on the Tobruk raid with the SIG, for pointing this out to me in a letter of 16 December 2000. The SIG are mentioned in his superb memorial book to his brother, *One of the Many* (Scotland: Pentland Press, 1993), with some very rare photos taken on the Tobruk raid approach.
3. E. Morris, *Guerrillas in Uniform* (London: Hutchinson, 1989), p.85.
4. Y. Gelber, *European Jews from Palestine in the British Forces*, Year Book 35 (London: Leo Baeck, 1990), p.329. Information on Hollander is from his son Paul (Aug. 2009).
5. Kahane had an Iron Cross from the First World War, had twenty years' service in the regular German Army, and had been a town clerk in Austria until forced to flee to Israel after the Anschluss. He joined the SAS/SBS after the SIG was disbanded and fought in the Aegean Islands with the famous Anders Lassen, VC, taking part in the raid on Santorini, among others, where there was bitter hand-to-hand fighting; he was one of the oldest members of the raiding party, leading his section in the capture and killing of many of the German garrison there – see M. Langley, *Anders Lassen* (Kent: New English Library, 1988), pp.199, 210. For Kahane's SIG participation in the Benghazi raid of June 1942, see R. Bradford and M. Dillon, *Rogue Warrior: Paddy Mayne* (London: Arrow, 1989), pp.43–4 and Appendix 1; and V. Cowles, *The Phantom Major* (London: Collins, 1958), pp.156–61.
6. P. Smith, *Massacre at Tobruk* (London: W. Kimber, 1957), p.27.
7. Morris, *Guerrillas*, p.84.
8. Shai was born in Germany in 1922, emigrated to Israel aged 16, in 1938, and brought up at Kibbuitz Ginnegar. He joined the British Army aged 18.
9. Reverend I. Levy, *Now I Can Tell: Middle Eastern Memoirs* (London: published privately, 1978), p.49.
10. Levy, *Now I Can Tell*, p.50.
11. Morris, *Guerrillas*, p.86.
12. WO 201/727 PRO.
13. V. Cowles, *The Phantom Major* (London: Capital Book Club, 1958), p.135, and Collins' edition on Kahane, pp.156-61.

14. Ibid., p.135.
15. G. Landsborough, *Tobruk Commando* (London: Greenhill Books, 1956), p.31.
16. Cowles, *Phantom Major*, p.135.
17. Ibid., p.136: Shai (see note 8 above) agrees with this description but adds that there was another French officer – Gitterchen – and that the SIG team were armed with a Luger and Spandau each and several grenades, as well as a double-edged bayonet that could be used as a dagger.
18. WO 201/727 PRO.
19. Cowles, *Phantom Major*, p.137; J.W. Gordon, *The Other Desert War* (London and New York: Greenwood Press, 1987), p.105.
20. Gordon, *The Other Desert War*, says they carried P-38 pistols, Mauser rifles and Schmeisser sub-machine guns (p.106).
21. A. Swinson, *The Raiders* (London: Purnell, 1968), p.115.
22. Cowles, *Phantom Major*, p.139.
23. Ibid., pp.140–1.
24. Morris, *Guerrillas*, p.89.
25. Cowles, *Phantom Major*, p.141.
26. R. Miller, *The Commandos* (New York: Time-Life, 1981), p.85.
27. W. Seymour, *British Special Forces* (London: Sidgwick and Jackson, 1985), p.196.
28. D. Lloyd-Owen, *Providence Their Guide: the LRDG* (London: Harrap, 1980), p.99.
29. Cowles, *Phantom Major*, p.142.
30. WO 201/727 PRO.
31. According to John Bierman (letter to the author, 6 August 1999), the US military attaché in Cairo had sent coded messages to Washington about the impending raids and the Germans had deciphered them.
32. WO 201/727, headed 'Capt. Buck's Party'. Barrie Pitt, *The Crucible of War: Year of Alamein 1942* (London: J. Cape, 1982), is quoted in T. Geraghty, *March or Die: France and The Foreign Legion* (London: HarperCollins, 2001), p.213, as saying that 'Bruckler' re-joined the Foreign Legion after the Second World War and served with an Englishman, Jim Worden, to whom he told the story of his betrayal of the raiders. Afterwards, he alleges he had been personally decorated by Rommel and then posted to Tunisia, where he was again captured, this time by Americans. In May 1945 he was released by the French at Setif POW camp, Algiers, as he volunteered to re-join the Legion to fight Algerian nationalists. In the 1960s, Bruckner told Worden he still feared being hunted by the British as a war criminal.
33. Landsborough, *Tobruk Commando*, p.33, quoting Swinson. In an interview in 1999, Carmi says he and Shai were ordered by Buck to take Essner to a POW camp but to dispose of him en route. Carmi says he gave the order to shoot Essner and Shai pulled the trigger himself (John Bierman interview with Carmi in letter to the author, 6 August 1999).
34. Gordon, *Other Desert War*, pp.106 –7. I am grateful to Professor Asher Tropp for pointing this book out to me.
35. J. Cooper, *One of the Originals* (London: Pan, 1991), pp.54–7.
36. J. Lodwick, *Raiders from the Sea* (London: Greenhill, 1990), pp.141–2.
37. Smith, *Massacre at Tobruk*, p.27. Haselden, with native clothes and a beard, easily passed for a Bedouin and he knew the desert and many of its inhabitants very well. As WDLO (Western Desert Liaison Officer), he coordinated British and Bedouin agents: Gordon, *Other Desert War*, pp.78–9.
38. J. Ladd, *Commandos and Rangers of WW2* (London: Macdonald, 1978), p.123.
39. Smith, *Massacre at Tobruk*, p.54.
40. Morris, *Guerrillas*, p.125.
41. Smith, *Massacre at Tobruk*, p.55.
42. Landsborough, *Tobruk Commando*, p.68.
43. Ibid., p.51.
44. Smith, *Massacre at Tobruk*, p.60.
45. Ibid., p.81.
46. WO 201/750 File 1403 PRO.
47. A Jewish Chaplain Card is labelled 'J. Roer, 30777 – 1st Special Service Regt' (SAS?) and says he was seen by Reverend Rosenberg on 26 May 1945, at Botleys Park Hospital and was an escaped POW. This must be the Rohr who was in the SIG.
48. Langton – see note 50 below.
49. WO 201/745 PRO.

50. Landsborough, *Tobruk Commando*, p.34.
51. W.B. Kennedy-Shaw, *The LRDG* (London: Greenhill, 1989), p.25.
52. WO 201/745 PRO.
53. M. Tiefenbrunner/Tiffen, *A Long Journey Home* (Israel: published privately, January 1999), chapters 4 to 7. M. Crichton-Stuart, *G Patrol* (London: W. Kimber, 1958), also fails completely to mention the SIG role in their various raids.
54. Smith, *Massacre at Tobruk*, p.88.
55. WO 201/750 PRO.
56. Post-Raid Report – WO 201/742 PRO.
57. Landsborough, *Tobruk Commando*, p.215.
58. WO 201/750 PRO.
59. Colonel T.B. Langton, unpublished manuscript, Imperial War Museum.
60. Lodwick, *Raiders from the Sea*, pp.50–1.
61. WO 201/741 PRO.
62. Research by author John Bierman (letter to M. Sugarman, 6 August 1999) suggests Captain Buck, 1st SAS, was in fact captured after the Tobruk raid and spent the rest of the war as a POW with Yitzhak Ben Aharon – see note 63. After liberation he married and was posted to the occupation forces in Germany; he was killed 22 November 1945, aged 28, near Chard, on a flight to Germany. He was cremated on 28 November 1945 and interred at Reading, where a CWGC plaque (panel 1) bears his name, son of Lt Col Cecil and Eleanor Buck of Yately, Hants, and husband of Celia, née Wardle. However, Buck's post-raid report (see note 32) appears to have been written immediately after the raid, so Bierman's theory may be incorrect. Buck was born in India on 12 December 1916 and read German at St Peter's Hall, Oxford, where he was also a university fencer. Commissioned into the Punjabis (no. 1A1117) he transferred in 1939 to the 1st Battalion Worcester Regiment. I am most grateful to Sheila Jepps, Buck's niece, from Broadstairs, for some of the above information (letters to the author, 2001).
63. Leah Rabin, *Rabin: Our Life, His Legacy* (New York: Putnams, 1997), describes her childhood in Israel and on pages 54–5 writes:

> In 1941 whilst at summer camp ... a dashing British Officer on the Haifa-Tel-Aviv road gave me and a girlfriend a lift on a lorry loaded with Indian soldiers. Although he was British this Captain was born and bred in India. Since he loved music and opera and was a stranger to Tel-Aviv, I casually invited him to stop by and visit our home. Home hospitality to the Forces was very in vogue, but I never expected to hear from him. Well, he sent a letter two weeks later asking if he could call. I was only thirteen at the time. 'Leah, what kind of relationship have you established with a British Officer?' my parents asked.
>
> One afternoon he appeared at our door. Captain Buck turned out to be a multilingual cultural whiz. My father and mother took a shine to him, and the Captain even lost his heart to my sister Aviva – who by no means lost her heart to him. Later Captain Buck moved to the ... Commandos and was assigned to work with the 'German Platoon' of the Palmach – learning everything from German slang to German songs, gearing up for a mission behind enemy lines in the Western Desert ... when the war was over, his marriage to a pre-war sweetheart was tragically cut short as his RAF plane crashed en route to a military location. I learnt about this from Yitzhak Ben Aharon, a prominent Labour Party leader, who had been a close friend of Captain Buck when they were prisoners.

It is an amazing coincidence that the wife of an Israeli PM should have known one of the British heroes of the SIG.

Jack Nissenthall,
The VC Hero Who Never Was:
Raid on Dieppe – the Jewish Contribution

Beginnings

Flight Sergeant 916592 Jack Maurice Nissenthall was a Jewish Cockney born in Cottage Row, Bow, in the East End of London on 9 October 1919. He was a pupil at Malmesbury Road Primary School, with his sister Marie, and later at Mansford Technical School. His father Aaron was a Polish Jewish immigrant tailor from Pelots/Annapol, and his mother, Annie Harris-Schmidt, was born in Bow. When Jack was a boy, his family moved from Bow to Blythe Street, Bethnal Green, and he attended the Cambridge and Bethnal Green Jewish youth club. Many former members well remember how he held radio classes at the club.

Jack had been interested in radio and television ever since childhood and had worked at EMI from 1935, taking an advanced electronics course at Regent Street Polytechnic:

> From an early age I was obsessed with wireless. When still in short trousers I was making my own radio sets and repairing those belonging to my neighbours. I remember that when I did so for one old lady, she gave me half an apple as a reward. I never did discover who ate the other half ... I used to spend the whole day at the National Science Museum, going out to eat fish and chips and then going in again.

When Jack was working in the EMI shop in Tottenham Court Road in 1936, an RAF Officer, who was known only as Flight Lieutenant Bob, came looking for apprentices. Jack was taken on to work part-time at weekends and holidays at the first radar station at Bawdsey, on the isolated Suffolk coast, with the eminent radar expert Robert Watson-Watts.

He volunteered for aircrew in the RAF on the outbreak of war in 1939 but was posted instead to work in secret radar stations up and down the country because of his recognized knowledge and skills; from the early days of the war, the RAF made many modifications to their radars at Jack's suggestion. These ideas of his had a major effect on the ability of radar in British nightfighters to knock out German bombers, and his work on 'Mandrel' helped destroy the U-boat offensive. He was a key player in the RAF's Ground Control Interception (GCI) work at Bolt Head in Devon. He also submitted a report on the escape of the German battle-cruisers *Scharnhorst*, *Prince Eugen* and *Gneisenau* from Brest in February 1942, which was submitted to the RAF Director of Radar. The weaknesses in the British radar defences that Jack pointed out in this report from Bolt Head was extremely sensitive information and though acted upon, Jack's part in the corrective work was hushed-up and has never been revealed to this day. He had pointed out that the Germans had jammed the British radar.

Physically fit, an enthusiastic 22-year-old, unmarried (but with a steady girl, Adeline, or Dell, Bernard) he volunteered to give up leave and train in Scotland for the Commandos, including Parachute training. He came from a military family, as his father and uncles Michael, Max and Lew had all fought and been wounded in the First World War. Little surprise, therefore, that he was selected and asked to volunteer to be the radar expert to take part in the tragic but magnificent raid on Dieppe in occupied France, on 19 August 1942, Operation Jubilee.

Interviewed by the avuncular and pleasant Air Commodore Victor Tait (RAF Director of Signals and Radar) in Whitehall, Jack was told why he had been selected, but warned that as he knew so much, he would be assigned eleven soldier bodyguards on the raid, who had strict instructions that Jack must not be allowed to fall alive into enemy hands. This was clearly stated in *The Dieppe Raid Combined Report, Task 6*, now kept at The National Archives (Jack discovered after the war that this 'not be allowed' was in fact a breach of the Geneva Convention). Being Jewish was an added risk and he was told to go and think it over until the next day. Jack returned and told Tait he would go.[1]

His second interview was with the senior Intelligence officer at Combined Operations, Wing Commander the Maquis de Casa Maury – a patronizing and distant man – and a completely contrasting experience. He warned Jack of the risks and said, 'Nissenthall,' – accentuating the un-English sound of his surname – 'why should a Jew volunteer for such a dangerous operation?', adding quickly, 'You will get nothing out of this, you know!' Immediately Jack replied, 'We're not given to expect something out of everything we do, sir.' Clearly Maury's remark was a poorly disguised piece of racism (he was a close associate of Oswald Mosley, the British Fascist leader interned during the war), though he offered the excuse that 'I wanted to find out if you'd break under the pressure.' He added that Jack must accept the condition of permanent silence on the death order if he returned, adding, 'After twenty-five years, nobody will believe you anyway.'

Jack was to be attached to 'A' Company (commanded by Captain Murray Osten), South Sasketchawan Regiment (SSR – of the 2nd Canadian Division led by Major General J.H. Roberts), who were based on the Isle of Wight, training for the raid, although they had no part in the planning of the operation. The Canadians were to form the bulk of the 6,000-man raiding force. Their commanders were straining at the leash to have their men tried out. However, the raid had sixteen different objectives on five different beach sites along a sixteen kilometre front, and British No. 3 and No. 4 Commandos, with elements of No. 3 ('Jewish') Troop and other troops of the 10th Inter-Allied Commando, a Royal Marine Commando and fifty American Rangers would also be involved, as well as the navy providing bombardment and transport (327 vessels including four destroyers), and the RAF fighter cover (seventy squadrons including eight Royal Canadian Air Force). Embarkation would also take place from Newhaven (the main point of departure), Shoreham and Littlehampton, as well as the Solent ports.

Put simply, the raid was designed to fulfil three objectives:

a) to be an essential learning source about the problems of launching a surprise seaborne invasion of France in preparation for D-Day, especially with regard to amphibious Combined Operations landings at an enemy port.

b) to show the Germans that their defences could be breached and so force them to divert resources from the Russian front, thus creating Stalin's desired 'Second Front' in Europe.

c) to provide the Allies and Nazi-occupied nations with a victory and hope of liberation during the darkest days of the war, when both Germans and Japanese were advancing everywhere.

Dieppe was chosen as it was believed not to be as heavily defended as larger ports such as Cherbourg (it turned out that this was based on false intelligence), was within easy reach of British fighter cover and had worthwhile targets, such as the radar station, coastal cannon batteries, railways, petrol dumps and an airfield. Objective 13 was for the SSR to escort a radar expert to the Freya 28 radar station on a clifftop at Pourville – designated as Green Beach, just four kilometres west of Dieppe – and within a few minutes to uncover its secrets; the expert was Jack Nissenthall.

The Raid

Before leaving his last base at Hope Cove in south Devon to take part on his mission, Jack prepared his blue RAF small pack with his most precious possession, a small avometer given to him by his late father for his Barmitzvah. In his last two letters to his mother and Adeline, he included the Jewish prayer made before embarking on a journey: 'O Lord, deliver us from our enemies ... send a blessing upon the work of our hands.'

In London he reported to RAF Intelligence in Whitehall. He refused to remove his Jewish RAF identity discs; he wished to live and die with the sign of his people. He did not relate to the officer the anti-Semitic jibe he had heard from another Intelligence officer on his first visit, or his firm belief that having a crack at the Nazis would be a way of getting back at them for the murder of his Jewish relatives in Poland.

He was given an army uniform and an evader's pack, which was a small tin containing useful items to help make an escape if things went wrong. But this one included an extra item especially for Jack – a green suicide pill. He was then driven by an anonymous, armed SOE officer (wearing no badges or rank) to Waterloo and taken by train and ferry to the Isle of Wight and thence to Norris Castle, to meet Colonel Merritt, OC of the SSR. Not allowed to give his full name, the colonel addressed him as Jack.

The next day, Jack met his eleven 'bodyguards'. In James Leasor's definitive book on Jack, *Green Beach* (see note 1, below), the men are named as members of 'A' Company, commanded by Captain Mather: Graham Mavor, Les Thrussel, Charlie Sawden, 'Smokey', 'Lofty', 'Frenchie', 'Red', 'Buddy', 'Silver', 'Jim' (the last seven being nicknames, as Jack wanted everyone to know as little as possible about each other in case of capture) and Sergeant Roy Hawkins, the field security sergeant, who joined them later. They in turn called him 'Spook' because of his pale complexion gained from too many nights of work over radar screens.

The following day, Jack boarded the SS *Invicta*, which together with the SS *Princess Beatrix* was to carry him and the SSR to battle. The men thought it was a practice until the tannoy announced that they were sailing through the night and would land at dawn in France. Jack describes how there was silence for a moment and then the Canadians began to cheer and the deck trembled with the sound of men stamping their boots in delight at the prospect of action. Then Canada's General Roberts (commanding the landing) and Lord Mountbatten (Chief of Combined Operations) addressed the men on both ships in turn, and General Eisenhower visited the fifty American Rangers who would be the first US troops (under Captain Roy Murray) to face German soldiers in this war.

Next day, 7 July, the raid – until then known as Operation Rutter – was cancelled because of poor weather.

As pressure rose from the Russians to create a 'Second Front', the raid had to be remounted. Operation Jubilee, as it was now known, was set for 19 August. Jack was recalled to London from Devon, but in his haste put on a blue RAF shirt under his khaki army battledress. Further, he had still his blue RAF pack, which stood out against his army khaki, and no divisional signs on his uniform, which made him look even more out of place. In the event of capture, this would make him suspect, and mark him out as something more than a member of a raiding party. At a second talk with Maury, he was again offered the chance to withdraw, but refused. On arrival at Combined Operations HQ at 1a Richmond Terrace, London, he was handed

a tin helmet and revolver and briefed as before, and then driven to King
George V dock at Southampton by another SOE officer.

The same ships and men then set sail for Dieppe. Uppermost in Jack's
mind – beside his mission – were thoughts about home and childhood:
Friday night candles, Kiddush, chicken soup and *lockshen*, and his cheder
(religious school) teacher – a Polish rabbi who took snuff.

When he reached the SS *Invicta*, the Canadian troops were making a
tremendous din banging their tin helmets on the metal deck. The sight
of a staff car with Jack in it brought the noise to a great crescendo, for 'A'
Company knew that Jack's presence meant the raid was on; a huge cheer
went up as he went aboard.

On the journey across, Frenchie – one of his escort – blessed Jack with
his rosary. When Jack said he was Jewish, Frenchie said that 'it was the
same God and he was on our side'.

Twelve miles out in the dawn half-light, with a chill wind, the men
were transferred to the landing craft (LC). At one point a navy NCO tried
to tell Jack he was in the wrong LC with his escort. A fierce argument
ensued but Jack stayed put. There was still a two-hour journey to the
beaches.

Warned by an unlucky chance meeting between the invasion flotilla
section of No. 3 Commando with a German Navy patrol and two E-boats
from Boulogne, the Nazis around Dieppe were waiting for the Allied
troops. However, the Germans were expecting an invasion along the
Channel coast in any case, as they were perfectly aware of the Russian
pressure on the Allies, and of which tidal periods would be most suitable.

In Jack's LC a canteen of rum appeared and was passed from man to
man; then suddenly they hit land. As the SSR and Canadian Cameron
Highlanders came ashore at Green Beach in Pourville between 4.50 and
5.30 a.m., there was chaos, added to which Jack realized that they had
been landed at least a quarter of a mile too far west of the radar station
(code-named 'Study'), which was his particular target. This meant that
Colonal Merritt had to fight his way across the bridge first before getting
to his targets (see below).

With Canadian casualties mounting horrifically in bitter close fighting, Jack and his team raced up the beach and along the road, east
towards the bridge over the river Scie, to get to the clifftop radar. The
bridge was raked with fire and by then covered with Canadian dead, but
encouraged and led by the remarkable Colonel Merritt, who won his VC
here as he was constantly and fearlessly exposed to enemy fire, the men
rushed the bridge and found cover on the other side.

Three of Jack's escort (including Mavor and Sawden) by this time
were already killed, and one wounded – the CO, Osten, was also wounded
– but the group and others had reached the slope approaching the radar

and began the ascent, surrounded by wounded and dead Canadians. It was now morning and getting warm. 'A' Company's 100 men were already down to twenty-five.

A few weeks before his death in 1997, Jack saw a documentary on television which alleged that many of 'A' company had hidden in some houses near the beach, and that because they did not press home their attack, he was unable to break into the radar station. He wrote a bitter letter to Colonel Merritt about this, but no reply came back.[2]

From the roadside viewing point (there to this day) Jack was now only 100 yards away from his objective and could now see the radar station clearly, surrounded by open, short grassland and masses of barbed wire, sandbags and trenches. But the German firepower was too great and the site too impregnable for an attack and so Jack volunteered to take a narrow path a mile back again, with Frenchie and Thrussel, to the invasion HQ, which was in the casino near the beach, to try and get a radio message out, for a destroyer to shell the radar area, and extra men to rush the radar defences. Try as they might, they could not find one working radio among the fighting troops.

Blown off their feet by a mortar bomb on the return run, they somehow eventually made it back yet again up to the wounded Osten near the radar (minus Thrussel), where Jack decided smoke cannisters were needed to allow them to break in. He and Smokey rushed back down to the town, and at the bridge met an exhausted Colonel Merritt still rallying his men across the Scie. The CO gave Jack some reinforcements and they returned to the hill, losing many on the way through intense German sniper and mortar fire.

By this time the mission appeared hopeless so Jack decided he would go around the rear of the station and obtain the secrets of the radar alone. He knew British listening centres on the south coast had often picked up coded messages being sent between the German radars by radio and Morse. Cryptographers in Britain then decoded these messages and thus were able to determine the capabilities and strengths of the radar stations. However, now the stations used landline telephones which could not be intercepted. If Jack could cut these lines and force the use of radio again, then the German transmissions could again be picked up in Britain, and the latest secrets revealed, including the possible whereabouts of other yet unknown German radars.

He told Osten to give him covering fire, explaining that whatever risk he took, either the Germans or Canadians would get him. He took two grenades from a dead Canadian (he related how he was determined to blow himself up if in danger of capture), his own tool pack and pistol and rushed the rear wire, getting under it. He still had fifty yards to go and so far had not been spotted. He crawled closer over very rough, hard ground and at last saw the wires he was after, leading out of the rear of the station via a short mast on the sloping hill and thence disappearing underground. With his wire-cutters (and a spare set in his pocket), he dropped his pack – with the precious avometer given to him by his father many years before – and climbed the mast, slowly cutting all eight cables as bullets flew about him – both Canadian and German. By the eighth cable he was suspended fifteen feet by one hand and as he snipped it, he fell to earth, rolling away down the slope towards the Canadian positions. He had done it.

At that moment, interestingly, in a camouflaged caravan listening station on the Sussex coast near Birling Gap, a Jewish WAAF sergeant and her Jewish RAF sergeant colleague – both German-speaking – picked up signals from German radar stations on the French coast. At the same time, radar expert Ken Dearson, aboard the Navy Command warship *Prince Albert* offshore from Dieppe, also picked up the German signals. Jack's ploy had worked and valuable German radar information reached British Intelligence for days after.

Some Success

It was 10 a.m. and Jack decided there was one last chance – to try to get a tank, which would be coming from the landings at Dieppe, up to the radar to blast the wall and get in. He instinctively took command, and with his escort (Roy, Jim, Lofty, Smokey, Silver, Bud and Frenchie) they returned yet again to the church in Pourville – now a wrecked town – and dashed up the road to Petit-Appeville where they expected to meet some Allied tanks.

Suddenly they heard a distinct and distant rumble, but when vehicles came into view they saw to their horror that they were Panzers. With bullets flying all around them they backtracked at once for the beach at Pourville, with Germans barely yards behind them. Two more of Jack's escort were lost in the flight back (Silver and Frenchie). He himself was hit on the back of his helmet, leaving a huge dent which punched the metal onto his skull. At the church, not one minute from the beach, they met a German patrol and a firefight began as they were now shot at from both front and behind. Suddenly, in the midst of this, three elderly French First World War veterans wearing berets and their medals appeared on the road. Summing up the situation at once, one of the veterans deliberately stepped out into the line of fire, calmly walking down the road, puffing on his Gauloise.

A German officer ordered ceasefire, as shooting a French civilian could lead to disciplinary action. As the Frenchman came close to Jack and the Canadians, he glanced at Jack, as if to say, 'I am holding their fire; now get out!' Within a few minutes they had reached the beach HQ safely, thanks to the great courage of a gallant ally.

In and around the casino – now the casualty clearing station – Jack and his escort joined in a desperate last stand in order to gain time for landing craft to come and take them all off. Here Lofty was killed. Dozens of wounded Canadians littered the building and the courtyard outside whilst dozens of others fired at the advancing Germans. Jack himself was firing a Bren gun and then, when the magazines ran out, an anti-tank rifle, especially at the German machine guns on the cliffs above them. Added to this cacophony, the RAF and navy were shelling German positions, trying to give support and covering fire to the survivors in the beach area.

It was now 11.30 a.m. Putting the cyanide pill in his pocket ready for use, just in case, Jack, with Roy Hawkins, decided after a long discussion with the officers and men in the casino, to make a run for a landing craft laying several hundred yards off the shore. Smokey, one of the escort, at first threatened Jack with his knife if he tried to leave, but Jack convinced him that they, with Bud, Jim and Roy, could form a group and make a run for the LC. At that moment a navy smoke-shell landed nearby and Jack knew this was the moment. The group, plus several others, on Jack's command, amid all the chaos and smoke and debris, vaulted through a rear window and were away, racing towards the sea-wall and the shingle, and jumping barbed wire as bullets whined all about them. Smokey and Bud disappeared. Jim was killed on the wire but Hawkins kept up with Jack, who was quietly reciting the *Shema* (a Jewish prayer) to himself as he ran. He now discarded his helmet and jacket, but this revealed his blue RAF shirt and made him a particular target. Within seconds they were in the sea, half crawling, half swimming. About fifty yards ahead they saw an LC in the smokescreen. In one last great effort, they swam, exhausted, to the half-open ramp and grabbed the side; two sailors grabbed Jack and pulled him in. 'Pick up my mate!' blurted Jack. 'What do you think this is, the number 8 bus?' quipped a cockney sailor, hauling Roy in too. The LC turned north and made for England.

At Pourville, firing slowly stopped, as the Canadians ran out of ammunition and a ceasefire was agreed. By 1 p.m. it was all over. They were lined up outside the Hôtel de la Terrasse and Colonel Merritt, now wounded, watched with pride as his surviving men marched away, in disciplined ranks, to become POWs.[3]

Afterwards

Holed by Luftwaffe strafing, the LC made for a nearby flak ship and transferred all the passengers, just as the LC itself finally gave up the ghost and sank. Like the sailors on the LC, the Royal Marine crew on the ship were

Cockneys, and this cheered Jack enormously. One of them gave him an old RM jacket to keep warm. They made for home. Jack had survived, and at 2 a.m. they reached Newhaven, where he and Hawkins found a warehouse and fell into a sleep as of the dead.

Next morning Jack and Roy parted company, without knowing they would not meet again for twenty-five years. Of the eleven men who had set out for the radar station on the hill at Pourville, only these two got back to England.

Jack was taken by two MPs to Canadian Army HQ in Reigate, where he had some difficulty persuading the Intelligence debriefers who he was, with his army trousers, RAF blouse and RM jacket. German prisoners had been brought back and it was possible some could have got into Allied uniforms to pass themselves off as friends. Eventually he made his way to Waterloo, London, and thence by tube to the Air Ministry, and at last he met again with Air Commodore Tait.

There he was told of the success of his work. Professor R.V. Jones (who died in December 1997), a leading member of Air Intelligence and a radar expert, told Jack that because he had cut the wires as he did, the German radars, as expected, had communicated by radio and all the signals had been intercepted in England and analysed. As a result it was now clear that there was no second standby radar system being used by the Germans across north-west Europe, and that they used several different call signs for the same fighter squadron, thus deceiving the Allies into believing that they had far more air power than in fact existed. It was also clear how long it took them to calculate that an Allied air attack was incoming, for scrambling their aircraft – especially the night-fighters which did so much damage to Bomber Command – so giving them very early warning. In addition much was being learned about the technical capabilities of the German radar system itself which in turn meant that jamming devices could now be used to saturate the radars, undoing all the German deception work and making all future air attacks against the Germans more efficient, thus saving Allied lives and eventually shortening the war. A further result was that at the Normandy landings later, whilst the Allies could see everything with their radar, the German radar was completely jammed.

Jack would have loved to tell the Canadians that their terrible sacrifice had been so worthwhile, but he was sworn to secrecy. He and Tait shook hands and Jack left, tired but happy. He made his way by tube to his mother's home at 27 Mattock Lane in Ealing, buying a newspaper on the way. The *Daily Express* headline read: 'The Great Raid is over ... Commandos leave Dieppe in flames.' His mother answered the door, amazed at the grimy state of her eldest son. 'What happened to you?' she gasped. He handed her the newspaper, and she knew. He bathed and went to bed; within seconds he was asleep.

Of the 4,963 Canadians who had sailed, 907 (one-fifth) were killed (half at sea) but 2,210 (over two-fifths) were back safely in England. A further 1,840 (just under two-fifths) were taken prisoner. Of the others, the British lost fourteen soldiers and thirty-one Royal Marines, with 466 POWs; the RAF seventy killed; the navy seventy-five killed but 270 missing; and thirteen casualties occured among the US Rangers (on this raid, the American Colonel Hilsinger was the last man to be injured in the attack; Lieutenant Edwin Loustalot the first American to be killed in Europe; and Corporal Frank Koons the first to kill a German in Europe and win a British decoration, the MM, for bravery in action). Overall there were 4,259 casualties, of whom one in three died. Thirty-three naval vessels were lost including the destroyer *Berkeley*, and 106 aircraft – five by friendly fire.

The Germans admitted to 600 killed (but Allied estimates suggest far more), two coastal batteries destroyed, a ship sunk, thirty-seven prisoners and over fifty aircraft shot down.

After a communal burial by the Germans at Janval, the Allied dead were exhumed and buried individually at Hautot-sur-Mer, just above the Scie valley, where they lie today, surrounded by Canadian maple trees. Two years later, in summer 1944, the 2nd Canadian Division returned and liberated Dieppe.

The lessons learned from the Dieppe raid were clear: deficiencies in firepower, landing craft, harbour facilities, pre-landing bombardment by sea and air, radio communication, radar jamming and diversion landings. The correction of these resulted in the remarkably low casualties in the Normandy landings two years later.

Jack's toolkit was later found by the Germans at the radar site, but its significance was never discovered. A captured Jubilee plan revealed to the Germans that an Allied radar specialist had been ordered to examine the Freya, but despite interrogations of locals and POWs, no light was thrown on his role in the raid. The radar station was heavily fortified after the raid but its secrets were already out and just before D-Day it was heavily bombed. In spring 1974, the remaining concrete section fell to the foot of the eroding chalk cliffs where it remains to this day. Old gun emplacements around it still remain. Every August, Canadians return to Dieppe and the other landing sites to honour their soldiers who fought and died there, as well as to meet the many local people who helped them. At Pourville itself – which is little changed in over sixty years – the curator of the small War Museum related to the author in August 1996 how he had met Jack on one of his visits in August 1994.

The site of the casino is today grassed over, the church and Hôtel de la Terrasse remain as they were. The town has several moving memorials, easy to see and visit, scattered along the streets and promenade.

Jack's part in the Dieppe raid is well known in Canada and something of a legend, but it has never been recognized by the British authorities. Many Canadians he knew were decorated, including Hawkins who received the MM. Colonel Merritt knew very little about the importance of Jack's objective until after the war. In an interview he said that had he been properly briefed, he would have got Jack into the radar station.

Professor R.V. Jones, who was also a leading adviser in Scientific Intelligence to the government during the whole war and for decades after the war, wrote: 'Jack was a man who willingly went into the hard, savage clash of Dieppe, spurred by patriotism and an enthusiasm for electronics, and knowing that if things went wrong – which they did – he had a peculiarly slim chance of returning ... His own deeds speak for themselves ... I only wish that I had such a tale as his to tell.' Despite such praise, Jack always felt a deliberate barrier had been erected between the 'professional' university scientists on the one hand and the self-made radar technician from Bow on the other, who actually outclassed them. In private, unkind things were said about the Jew from the East End.

Lord Mountbatten said that because of what was learnt at Dieppe, for every one man killed, a dozen were saved at Normandy two years later. But he had no idea of the orders to shoot Jack if he was in danger of capture, or even that he was supposed to enter the radar station, or indeed was a radar expert. The danger that he may have been caught and tortured, to give away top radar secrets known to him, horrified Mountbatten, who said that had he known the truth, Jack would not have been allowed to go, especially as he was Jewish and in particular danger without being given a false identity. Nor did he know that Jack had returned safely: 'If I had been told, he would most certainly have been decorated on the spot ... his action may have shortened the war by two years.'

In Nigel West's 1998 book, *Counterfeit Spies*, however, he points out that Professor R.V. Jones wrote in 1978 that the order to shoot Jack, had he been captured, had been given in error:

> Actually there was no more reason for him [Jack] to be shot than there would have been for Cox [the RAF flight sergeant radar expert] in the Bruneval raid (six months before), since they knew comparable amounts about our own radar, and only as much about German radar as was necessary for dismantling captured equipment. It was a misapprehension regarding my own (possible) presence [i.e. Jones] on the (Dieppe) Raid that resulted in [this] dramatic order.

After Dieppe, Jack turned down a Commission but was sent to work on mobile radar development in the Middle East. At the war's end he married Dell and then accepted a place at the RAF College, Cranwell. There he was advised to change his name to Nissen to avoid any post-war hostility from Germans who may have discovered his role in the radar war and its effects on the bombing of German cities. In 1948 he was invited by the Smuts government to plan radar installations in South Africa, but then the incoming Nationalist government refused him a position. He stayed, however, and opened a television and hi-fi business, but fell foul of the regime for teaching Black students at his training school. He faked an assembly line so that when the authorities came to check, he could pretend it was a factory; when they left it became a school again. Finally he had to leave, and in 1978 he went to Toronto in Canada, where he lived until his death on 8 November 1997, survived by his wife, daughter Linda, son Paul and three grandchildren.

In August 1967 Jack had returned to Pourville for the twenty-fifth anniversary of the landings, and met many old and decorated friends, including Les Thrussel. Les had always told friends the story of how he had orders to shoot a top British scientist on the raid had he been in danger of capture, but nobody believed him. Now he met Jack and told him to tell Les's friends the truth.

In a café in Dieppe that evening Jack sat reminiscing with the three VCs of the raid – Merritt, Porteous and Foote. There was a loud knocking on the door and several young Canadian soldiers serving with NATO walked in. 'We heard Jack Nissen was here and we want to shake his hand.' Jack recalled afterward: 'There I was sitting with three VCs and these young men wanted to shake ME by the hand. I was in tears. This was my reward and the highlight of my life.'

Epilogue

In 1991 the first reunion of Second World War radar personnel was held in Coventry. Jack Nissenthall was an honoured guest, but he did not even receive a mention in the souvenir programme which marked the event, and few even saw the presentation made to him – a replica of the precious avometer his father gave him for his barmitzvah, which he lost in his toolkit on the Dieppe raid.

Ken Dearson, who was a member of the Mountbatten briefing team for the raid and presented the replica to Jack, had always been aware of his outstanding courage and remarkable achievment at Pourville, and for several years had been campaigning to get Jack the VC. Jack went to Dieppe 'under a sentence of death', Dearson wrote. Mountbatten had personally told Dearson after the war that Jack should have been given the VC. But this means overturning a 1949 directive ending the issue of Second World War medals. Dearson argued that some events, however, were so secret that little could be known about them until many years later. Jack's identity had been concealed for years by the Official Secrets Act, and only recently have Mountbatten's archives and other documents been released for public scrutiny, revealing Jack's crucial achievement. In fact it was Mountbatten's publicity section which put out the story that a scientist called 'Profesor Wendall' had been on the raid; this was in fact Jack.

Appeals to Prime Minister John Major and the Honours Committee in 1991 and again in 1997 were fruitless, and to this day Jack Nissenthall's deeds remain officially unrecognized. His daughter Linda, who lives in north London with her family, says this is scandalous. Jack said his main reward was helping to destroy Hitler: 'I still feel that way', he said. Actors Michael Caine and Roger Moore have both said they would like to play him in a movie, and such a film has been long contemplated.

At his funeral in the Jewish cemetery in Toronto on the '11th of the 11th' 1997, there was a huge escort of ex-servicemen from the Jewish and Canadian Legions, and many young people. Jack had been a legend in his own lifetime – truly the unknown hero of Dieppe.

Afterword

In July 1997, the author spoke to Jack's daughter who described how after the war Mountbatten and Prince Philip wrote to Jack expressing their admiration for his achievments at Dieppe, Mountbatten agreeing that a gallantry award should be made. Both Prince Philip and Prince Charles had also met Jack at Dieppe reunions, asking to speak to him privately after the official proceedings and repeating their praise for his work and great courage on the raid.

After the war, Jack met the German engineering officer, Willy Weber, who had been in charge of the Pourville radar station, and they became friends. It was Weber who had first spotted the invasion flotilla at Dieppe, but he had been told he was imagining it. Weber also discovered the wires cut by Jack after the raid but reported it as shell damage. Little did he know. At one reunion at the Canadian cemetery, Weber was refused entry because he was a German. Jack saw him, however, and personally brought him in and stood next to him during the ceremony.

Sadly, Ken Dearson died in 1995 but the struggle to get Jack his award went on, even though Jack himself remained indifferent. Canadian ex-servicemen, British MPs and former MPs and the Association of Jewish Ex-Servicemen and Women (AJEX) continued to press for recognition for him.

After the war, Dearson continued working for Mountbatten and whenever any failure occurred in the communications system, the First Sea Lord would shout, 'Send for Nissenthall!'

9.1 Sgt Jack Nissenthall/Nissen, just after returning from the Dieppe Raid; note the rare Parachute wings proving his training as a paratrooper with the RAF.

9.2 Pte Murray Irving Bleeman, Royal Hamilton Light Infantry of Canada, died of wounds received at Dieppe, 21 August 1942.

Canadian and Allied Jews at the Raid on Dieppe, August 1942

Sources

Information for this list has come mainly from *Canadian Jews at War* (hereafter *CJW*) – two volumes published by the Canadian Jewish Congress in Montreal in 1947–48; other sources include a personal visit by the author to the Canadian War Cemetery at Dieppe. The Congress volumes, however, give only those killed in action, wounded in action, and prisoners of war – not those who served at Dieppe. The list is, therefore, very much incomplete; it does not include, for example, Jewish Canadians who died of wounds after the raid and were buried at various locations in Europe where they happened to be imprisoned, or in England where they were in hospital, or all those who returned safely, or who evaded capture and escaped much later after the raid but are not recorded as having been connected with the raid.

Further details came from requests for help in various journals and newspapers in the UK and Canada, as well as from organizations such as the Commando Association; many veterans – Jewish and non-Jewish – and their families responded. Their help was inestimable.

'Photo' or 'letter': these are at the AJEX Museum in London. KIA: Killed in Action; MIA: Missing in Action; WIA: Wounded in Action; *JC* refers to the *Jewish Chronicle*; *LG* refers to the *London Gazette*.

Buried at Dieppe Canadian War Cemetery at Hautot-sur-Mer: Killed on 19 August unless otherwise stated:

A22530 Private Samuel Berger, Essex Scottish/Commandos, 354 Langlois Avenue, Windsor, Ontario. Born Poland, 24 November 1919, son of Mr and Mrs Osias Berger. Photo and letter from friend.

B37297 Private Murray Irving Bleeman, 22 Lippincott St, Toronto. Died 1.15 a.m., 21 August 1942, aged 27, of wounds received at Dieppe; RHLI; buried at Brookwood, Surrey. Born Drilz, Poland, 18 December 1914, son of Mr and Mrs Hyam Bleeman. Letter from brother and photo.

Lance Corporal B66596 Meyer Bubis, Royal Regiment of Canada (RRC), son of Solomon, 1077 Gerrard St, Toronto; buried at Dunkirk having died of wounds after Dieppe.

B67270 Private Lionel Cohen, RRC/Commandos, aged 31, from Toronto. Son of Mr and Mrs Nat Cohen; wife lived at 14 Kensington St, Toronto. Photo and letter from stepson Jerry Richmond.

D61382 Private Louis Goldin, Les Fusiliers Monte Royale, aged 27, Montreal, killed at his machine-gun post covering the evacuation of wounded comrades, witnessed by Catholic priest Chaplain Major J. Sabourin, MiD, OBE, and CO Captain Antoine Masson. Son of Mr and Mrs Joseph Goldin, 5338 Waverley St, Montreal.

B37321 Private John M. Grallick/Gorelick, RHLI, from Toronto, killed at Dieppe, no known grave. Born 1921, son of Mr and Mrs John Grallick, 168 Euclid Avenue, Toronto.

B68182 Private Simon Green, RRC; from Toronto; died of wounds sustained at Dieppe whilst a POW; buried at St Inglevert, Calais. Son of Mrs Gittel Green, 296 Rushton Rd, Toronto.

B66977 Sergeant Morris Greenberg, RRC, aged 24, killed evacuating wounded. Photo. Yiddish poet from 50 Oxford St, Toronto. Born 9 November 1917, son of Mr and Mrs Samuel Greenberg.

B37663 Private Leizer Heifetz, RHLI, from Parkerview, Saskatchewan; missing presumed killed at Dieppe; no known grave. Born Vetka, Russia 1909, nephew of Mrs Malka Lowe, Melville, Saskatchewan.

B68130 Private Morris Lozdon, RRC/Commandos, aged 32, from Toronto, husband of Mary and father of Barbara, Stanley and [?] of 61 Huron St, Toronto. Born 16 May 1910, son of Mr and Mrs Hyman Lozdon.

B37320 Private Paul Leon Magner, RHLI, aged 23, from 99 Dundas St, Toronto. Letter from cousin in North York, Ontario. Born 19 April 1919, son of Mr and Mrs Morris Magner.

Jewish Commandos of No. 3 ('Jewish') Troop, No. 10 Inter-Allied (IA) Commando, attached Canadians at Dieppe – Rice, Bates and Smith – all KIA at Dieppe on SOE mission to obtain records from the town hall at Dieppe. No further information known – see list of Jews who served in SOE. and No. 3 Troop.

A total of fourteen.

Wounded and POWs
Captain Ben Brachman, Cameron Highlanders of Winnipeg/RCAMC; WIA, in *JC*, 30 October 1942; MiD for gallantry. Photo and citation in *CJW*.

A22304 Private Joseph Brenner, Essex Scottish from Windsor, Ontario, WIA, POW Stalag 9C.

B67829 Private Jack Clausner, RRC, from Toronto, POW Stalag 2D and Oflag 7B.

A22474 Private Louis Kline, West Ontario Regt/Essex Scottish, missing, believed KIA, later found POW Stalag 8B and 2D. From Memphis, Tennessee. Born 1918, son of Harry Kline.

B37392 Private William A. Korenblum, RHLI, from Hamilton, POW Stalags 8B and 2D.

6436346 Corporal Maurice Latimer, aka 13801850 Moritz Levy/Loewy, Czech Jew who fought against Franco in Spanish Civil War; No. 3 ('Jewish') Troop, No. 10 IA Commando, wounded and escaped.

B37098 Sergeant Arthur Liss, WIA, from Toronto, RHLI/Commandos, penetrated into town with a small group and then forced to withdraw. Born 1917, son of Mr and Mrs Nathan Liss.

B66859 Private Maxwell London, RRC, POW Stalags 8B and 2D.

D62895 Corporal Manuel Manis, Les Fusiliers Monte Royal, POW Stalags 8B and 20A. Photo and personal letter.

B67597 Private Joseph Samuel Moskowitz, WIA, RRC, from Toronto, POW Stalag 8B. As a medical orderly he saw many strange incidents in the camp, detailed in *CJW*. Born 1906.

Private 'Bubi' Platt, aka Platteck, No. 3 ('Jewish') Troop, No.10 Commando, WIA, escaped to England, and one other, unidentified, mentioned in Nigel West, *Counterfeit Spies* (London: St Ermin's Press, 1998), p.261.

B25128 Sapper Paul Shusterman, RCE, from Toronto. POW Stalag 8B and 2D. Born 1918, son of Mr and Mrs Alex Shusterman. Photo.

Lieutenant Colonel Bert Sucharov, Second in Command, Royal Canadian Engineers of Winnipeg, OBE (Mil.), gazetted 1 January 1943, for courage at Dieppe and ED (Efficiency Decoration); WIA and hospitalized in Sussex; known as 'the Mad Major' on account of his recklessness under fire at Dieppe. Son of Mr M. and Mrs

Manya Sucharov, pioneer dairy farmers of Transcona, north Winnipeg. Graduate of engineering, University of Manitoba, 1937. Brother Jack in RCAF and Harry in RCOC. Photo.

H20180 Trooper Louis Todros, Cameron Highlanders of Ottowa, WIA.

L12079 Private Maurice Harold Waldman, SSR, POW Stalag 8B and 8A.

A total of sixteen: one MiD, one OBE (Mil.), one ED.

Served and Escaped
6471801 Sergeant/Trooper John Cyril Abrahams, No. 3 Commando under Major Young, landed at Bernaval east of Dieppe; formerly of RA, King's Own Royals, 12th Battalion S. Staffs, then trained at Largs in Scotland for Commandos. Took part in Lofoten raids in Norway, Dieppe and Sicily, where he was POW. Son of Mr Abraham Connie Abrahams (RNAS First World War) of 129 Myrdle Court, Myrdle St, London E1, later at 26 Highfield Terrace, Collingsworth, Bradford. Married Frances in 1945; father of Linda Hart and Alan. Died in 1967. Commando Association lists him under assumed name of Baler, and POW at Markt Pongau. AJEX Jewish Chaplain Card and information from brother-in-law Cyril Haring and daughter Linda.

R19589/H19489 CSM/WOII Abram Arbor, fought at Dieppe, Queen's Own Cameron Highlanders of Winnipeg, KIA at Falaise 23 August 1944, buried at Breteville-sur-Laize; awarded MC. Born 1918 at Narcisse, Man, son of Mrs Etta M. Arbor (citation *CJW*, p.23); married Clarice, has a daughter in England.

Lieutenant Harold Bergman, returned safely – *JC*, 30 October 1942.

Captain Elliot Cohen, OBE (*LG*, 14 December 1945), Essex Scottish; served at Dieppe.

Sergeant (later Lieutenant) David Lloyd Hart of Montreal, RCOS; MM for gallantry at Dieppe, gazetted in *JC*, 1 January 1943; citation, *CJW*, p.54; first reported MIA. Born in 1918, son of Hyman S Hart. Photo.

G. Leigh, RM (PLY105943) in LCF4. Later served in Italy and D-Day.

13801849 Private Richard Lehniger, aka Leonard, Small Scale Raiding Force/SOE/62 Commando, killed several weeks later

on a raid on Normandy with SSRF, buried St Laurent-sur-Mer.

Major (later Lieutenant Colonel) Mervin Mirsky, served at Arnhem, OBE (Mil.), MiD, Staff Officer at Dieppe raid. Photo.

916592 F. Sergeant Jack Maurice Nissenthall, RAF, British radar expert sent in at Pourville to get into the Freya radar station, recommended for gallantry award (never given). Born Bow, London, 1919. Photo (and see preceding section of chapter).

Corporal Michael Poplack, Canadian Tank Regiment, aged 24, from Vancouver; returned – *JC*, 30 October 1942.

Lionel B. Shapiro, OBE (Mil.), *LG*, 30 June 1946, for gallantry at Dieppe and on other operations. War correspondent from Montreal. Born 12 February 1908, son of Morris and Fanny Berkowitz Shapiro.

LT JX109920 Lieutenant David Benjamin Shaverin, RN, MiD raid on Dieppe, *LG*, 2 October 1942; Jewish Chaplain Cards.

Dr Surgeon Lieutenant Richard Wadia, RNVR, MiD raid on Dieppe, *LG*, 2 October 1942; AJEX Jewish Chaplain Cards.

A total of thirteen: three OBE (Mil.), one MC, one MM, three MiD.

A combined total of forty-three.

Notes

1. Document WO 106/4196 at TNA, Appendix L, p.3: 'RDF expert [Jack] to examine and search RDF station ... with assistance of one Field Security Other Rank as detailed ... travels with SSR on *Invicta* to provide adequate protection as RDF expert MUST UNDER NO CIRCUMSTANCES FALL INTO ENEMY HANDS.' [M.S.'s capitals.] Also: 'SOE to assist RDF expert.' (p.4).
2. Source: Linda Samuels, née Nissenthall.
3. J. Leasor, *Green Beach* (London: Heinemann, 1975), contains many references to other sources but is based on several personal interviews with veterans and especially Jack Nissenthall.

   Other sources used included *Saga Holiday Magazine* (Folkestone) 1991; L. Dumais, *The Man Who Went Back* (London: Leo Cooper, 1975); *Jewish Chronicle*, August 1991 and February 1992; M. Glover, *Battlefields of Northern France* (London: Michael Joseph, 1987); Ville de Dieppe information leaflet; P. Lund and H. Ludlum, *The War of the Landing Craft* (London: Foulsham, 1976); G. Brown, *Commando Gallantry Awards of WW2* (London: Stamp Exchange, 1991); D. Roxan, article in the 'New Cambridge and Bethnal Green Old Boys' Club Report', 1987/88; J. Nissenthall and A. Cockerill, *The Radar War* (London: Robert Hale, 1989); and N. West, *Counterfeit Spies* (London: St Ermin's Press, 1998).

   My deep thanks to Linda Samuels, née Nissenthall, whose many anecdotes about her father's life were passed on to me, that had come from Jack himself, and have never been published before, and to Cyril Silvertown, historian, for their help. Jack's decorations are the 1939–45, Africa and Italy Stars, Defence and War Medals.

   Jack is commemorated not only at the Pourville Museum, AJEX Museum and Combined Operations Museum at Inverary, Scotland, but also on the RAF Hope Cove/Bolt Head memorial near Marlborough village, Salcombe, in Devon.

Confounding the Enemy: The RAF Jewish Special Operators of 101 Squadron, Bomber Command

The sacrifice of Bomber Command in the Second World War was horrendous – 55,000 killed, almost 50 per cent, the highest of any Service branch – and 101 Squadron had the highest casualty (killed) rate of the RAF. From our Jewish Chaplain Cards at the Jewish Military Museum, we know that about 20,000 British Jews served in the RAF (this excludes Commonwealth Jews, of whom there were some thousands more), and more than 900 were killed. Of these we estimate that about 600 were Bomber Command deaths. Jewish RAF personnel won 188 DFCs with forty-three more bars, sixty-four DFMs with five more bars and one VC (Louis Aaron) – not to mention many cross-service awards such as the DSO. The men included, for example, two 'Dambusters' (killed) – Abe Garshowitz and Jack Guterman – and almost fifty Battle of Britain aircrew; many pathfinder and fighter pilots; and over seventy were POWs of both the Germans and Japanese.

Many of these supremely courageous men were refused the Bomber Command medal after the war, as their service fell by chance outside of two arbitrarily chosen dates. This article is a tribute to them all.

Much of the history of the secret telecommunications war against the Germans during the Second World War is still classified and shrouded in mystery, including the Radio Counter Measures (RCM) of RAF Squadron 101. Originally founded at Farnborough in 1917 as part of the RFC, Squadron 101 served as a night-bomber squadron on the Western Front,[1] was demobilized after the Armistice and re-formed at Bircham Newton in 1928. By 15 June 1943 it was based at Ludford Magna near Louth in Lincolnshire, as part of No. 1 Group, Bomber Command, having already taken part, for instance, in the 1,000-bomber raids on Germany, attacks on Italian targets and, soon after, the raid on the V1 sites at Peenemunde in August 1943.

At Ludford a far more dangerous task was assigned to the squadron. Many Allied bombers were falling victim to German night-fighters guided by ground controllers scrutinizing radar screens.[2] An Allied countermeasure named 'Window' partially upset this, but the Luftwaffe responded by coordinating the commentaries of several controllers at different locations and delegating overall command to a single master controller who guided the night-fighters towards the Allied aircraft. The British

Telecommunications Research Establishment (TRE) at Malvern developed a response to this that was tested by 101 Squadron. It was called 'Airborne Cigar', or ABC, a battlefield version of 'Ground Cigar',[3] and its original code-name was 'Jostle'.[4] Using a receiver and three fifty-watt[5] T.3160-type transmitters, the German VHF frequency – and language – was identified and then jammed.[6] The jamming caused a loud and constantly varying note running up and down the scale of the relevant speech channel.[7]

For this purpose, a German-speaking eighth crew member was included in the crew of specially fitted Lancaster bombers. He was known as the Special Duty Operator, 'Spec. Op.', or SO. All were volunteers from various aircrew trades. Since the enemy often gave phoney instructions to divert the jammers, it was essential that they should know German reasonably well. In addition, if the Germans changed frequencies the SO would have to be skilful enough to do likewise.[8] The SO had to recognize German code-words – such as *Kapelle*, for 'target altitude' – and log any German transmissions for passing on to Intelligence at the post-flight debriefing. Jewish veteran Flight Sergeant Leslie Temple recalls the Germans trying to distract the SOs[9] by using screaming female voices or martial music. Some sources allege that the SOs were trained in 'verbal jamming' – that is, giving false information in German – but this was very little used.[10]

After trials on 4–6 September 1943, the first operational use of ABC was on a raid over Hanover on 22 September, although other sources mention the night of 7–8 October.[11] The system worked, but the first aircraft using it was lost the following night on another raid. More Lancasters were modified, and by the end of October most of the squadron had been fitted with ABC. The only signs of special equipment were two seven-foot aerials on top of the Lancaster fuselage, another below the bomb-aimer's window and a shorter receiver at the top-rear of the fuselage. Because of the weight of the radio equipment and extra crew member the aircraft had a reduced bomb load of 1,000 lbs.

The SO sat just aft of the main spar on the port side of the aircraft, immediately above the bomb bay, at a desk with three transmitters and a cathode-ray screen. He was cut off completely from the rest of the crew except for his intercom, and was in darkness with no window to observe what was going on. His nearest human contact were the boots of the mid-upper gunner, four feet away. In order to avoid distraction the intercom had to be switched off, and only a red 'call light', operated by the pilot, was available should there be an emergency.[12] Since there was no room for the SO in the heated forward section of the Lancaster, he, like the mid-upper and rear gunners, had to wear bulky electric suits, slippers and gloves, dangerous if a rushed exit were required. At 20,000 feet over

Europe in winter, temperatures often fell to minus 50° C, so the SO would have to wear gloves even though these made it difficult to operate switches. He would lose the skin of his fingers if he attempted to touch metal without them.[13] It was common to have to pull off chunks of frozen condensation from oxygen masks during the flight.[14] The concentrated work of jamming kept the SOs' minds off minor discomforts for most of the flight.[15]

From October 1943 until the end of the war all main-force attacks on German targets were accompanied by Lancasters of 101 Squadron, sometimes up to twenty-seven in one raid. The ABC aircraft were stationed in pairs at regular intervals in the bomber stream so that if one were shot down, other parts of the stream would still be covered.[16] As losses mounted it was thought that German fighters were homing in on ABC aircraft, but no definite evidence for this has been found. However, on 18 November Flying Officer McManus's Lancaster was brought down over Berlin and examined by the Germans, so it is possible that German ground stations knew enough to vector their fighters onto the Lancasters when ABC was transmitting, making them more vulnerable than other aircraft.[17] SO veteran Ken Lewis, DFM,[18] described how the SOs were nicknamed 'Jos' or 'Jonahs' by the other crew members, alluding to the storm unleashed by the biblical character on the ship in which he was a passenger. On the other hand, the losses could have been caused by the rise in 101 participation on raids.

The Special Operators included a high proportion of German-speaking Jewish refugees who were especially at risk if captured, as were any of their surviving families in the Reich. One source tells of a crew member who committed suicide when captured by the Germans,[19] perhaps for this reason. There were also British and Commonwealth Jewish RAF personnel, many of whom spoke German or Yiddish at home. Special Operator 1811224 A.J.H. Clayton was captured on the night of 30 March 1944 when his Lancaster was shot down and was probably tortured to death for information on the SOs.[20] Some allege that the SOs were never to be questioned by the rest of the crew about their work.[21]

The Squadron's casualties were enormous. Between 18 November 1943 and 24 March 1944, for example, seventeen aircraft of 101 Squadron were lost in battles over Berlin. In the Nuremberg raid, five crew members of one Lancaster were lost, including Flying Officer Norman Marrian, the SO, who was badly wounded by friendly fire from a Halifax. He had baled out, but was found dead, suspended by his harness from a tree, two days later,[22] according to a survivor, Sergeant Don Brinkhurst; mid-upper gunner.[23] Sergeant Luffman describes how an SO's parachute failed to open fully and he died of his injuries.[24] A further four planes were lost over Nuremberg, making six in all, almost one-third of the surviving squadron. An additional five were lost in the successful raids running up to D-Day over France. But only one was lost on D-Day itself, when twenty-four Lancasters of 101 helped deceive the enemy into thinking the landing was to take place in the Pas de Calais by forming an ABC barrier between the Normandy beaches to the south and the German fighter bases in Holland and Belgium to the north. Other aircraft simulated airborne landings elsewhere and jammed enemy radars. Countless lives were saved in this 'Battle of the Ether', fought by a squadron of which the motto was appropriately *Mens Agitat Molem*, 'Mind over matter'.[25]

After D-Day, 101 continued using ABC in raids on German reinforcements, V1 launch sites and German industry. Losses continued, with six Lancasters destroyed over Brunswick in August 1944. On 25 April 1945, in their last mission, twenty Lancasters helped attack Hitler's last redoubt at Berchtesgaden. From October 1943, Squadron 101 flew 2,477 sorties with ABC from Ludford Magna. They dropped 16,000 tons of bombs between January 1944 and April 1945 alone and flew more bombing raids than any other Lancaster squadron in Group 1, losing 1,094 crew killed and 178 POWs – the highest casualties of any squadron in the RAF.[26]

Jewish Special Operators[27]

Flight Sergeant (later Warrant Officer) 2209350 Peter D. Kaye, a non-Jewish SO veteran from Wirral whose tour finished on 30 June 1944, explained that at any one time there might be thirty-three SOs – one for each Lancaster in the squadron – but that many more would have passed through, as casualties occurred or tours of duty finished – making perhaps as many as 150 or 200. He told the author[28] that he knew three Jewish Special Operators. One was 1398898 Reuben (later Ron) 'Herky' Herscovitz/Herscovitch, also known as Hurst,[29] who died in August 1997, aged 75. His Jewish Chaplain Card states that he was born on 20 August 1922, the son of Mr J. Herscovitz of 53 Bellott Street, Manchester 8; he was married to Phyllis and had volunteered on 11 November 1941. Another was Flight Sergeant John Hertzog, also known as Hereford. A third was Flight Sergeant G.P. (?) Herman. The AJEX museum has 70,000 – about 95 per cent – of the cards relating to British Jews serving in the Second World War. These were compiled and updated by Jewish chaplains throughout the war, and information is still added as it comes in.

Before one mission, Special Operator J.A. Davies, a lifelong friend of Herscovitz (a Yiddish speaker at home)[30] asked him why he carried a pair of civilian shoes slung around his neck on each of his thirty-six missions, and was told, 'My friend, if you are shot down, you will either be killed or taken to a proper prison camp under the control of the Geneva Convention. I am a Jew, and as the Herrenvolk would like to liquidate my race, I aim to get away from the wreckage as soon as possible. How can I possibly do that in heavy fur-lined flying boots?'[31]

John Davies recalls:[32]

> Ron and I first met at Hixon in Staffordshire and were designated
> SOs and sent to 101 Squadron together. Seven young sergeants
> were deposited outside the guardroom at a dark, snowbound air-
> field at Ludford – Bull, Bryant, Davies, Dockerty, Fergus, Neille
> and Herky. Within a few weeks Neille left, Fergus was sick, Bull
> and Bryant were dead and I was a POW after two missions. In the
> meantime, and without any warning, one night, on 15 February
> 1944, mine and Herky's names appeared on Battle Orders for the
> big raid on Berlin, with 891 aircraft. It was frightening, but Herky
> showed no emotion and indeed injected a spirit of optimism on life
> in general.

He wrote for Davies's book:

> An hour before take-off, behind us lay the ops meal with its privi-
> leged eggs, and some stressful hard to kill hours in the hut during
> which we smoked, read magazines, talked or wrote letters, the
> while keeping private fears to ourselves. Jim Davies wrote to his
> parents ... an emotional letter of apology. Four days later on 19 Feb-
> ruary we flew to Leipzig and Jim failed to return. When it was clear
> the aircraft was overdue beyond hope ... I left the Operations
> Room, went back to hut 8 and told the others. The next day
> I posted Jim's letter to his parents in Wales and watched as two
> police Corporals packed his kit. At 2345 hours that night I took off
> for Stuttgart.

Davies continued to describe how Herscovitz volunteered for a second tour
at the height of the bomber offensive – a courageous act given the low survival rate of SOs. He was not given a medal, but was an inspiring member of
the bomber crew and, aware of the consequences should he be captured, was
determined to have personal revenge on a system he despised. He had been
in a reserved occupation on a Zionist kibbutz farm in Somerset, but went
back to Manchester to join the RAF. In Davies's words:

> he was an incredibly brave man and the only member of the
> Squadron I wanted to contact after the war. I searched but failed.
> Then in the late 1940s, on an escalator in Wood Green Under-
> ground, he was coming down and I was going up. There was instant
> recognition and shouts of joy and our friendship lasted without a
> break until he died ... After the war he became a much respected
> expert in civil aviation,[33] but, conscious of his lack of a formal sec-
> ondary education, at the age of seventy, he entered St Cross Col-

lege, Oxford, to do a Ph.D. in History. He died just before the awards ceremony. Later at the College we held a 'Celebration of his Life' and it was my privilege to speak of his wartime heroism; he was my hero in war and peace.

Jewish RAF veteran Aubrey Wilson was a close friend of Herscovitz after the war and remembers some of the stories he had recounted.[34] In a letter to the author Wilson recalled one incident described to him:

> On the way back from one raid, the crew heard an object rolling about in the fuselage. Ron [Herscovitz] was sent to investigate and discovered one of the high-powered target flares (a photoflash) rolling loose and coming apart. Ron had to cradle this in his arms for several hours and on return carry it gingerly down the steps of the Lancaster and hand it to a WAAF armourer to disarm. He described the sheer horror of ... holding a highly volatile explosive device on a long and shaky journey at 12,000 feet, which, had it gone off, would have blown the aircraft apart. Ron said that it went off minutes later on the runway, after the WAAF heard it make a strange sound and threw it away. In another incident Ron described how his intense fear over targets was amplified as he could understand precisely what the German fighter pilots and controllers were saying – they shouted that they could see a certain Lancaster and were going in to attack, while Ron would sit and await a stream of machine-gun bullets to cut him apart or a cannon-shell to explode in his aircraft. When it did not, he knew someone else had bought it. Constantly being aware that you are a target in this way must have been almost unbearable.

Herscovitz himself recounted[35] how Air Vice-Marshall Saundby once gave a handshake to each man as they entered the debriefing room after a night raid. When Ron came, the Air Vice-Marshal was so taken aback at such a small chap in flying kit that he looked down and gently patted him on the head.

Another comrade, Bruce Lewis, remembers the following:[36]

> When I had joined the RAF ... at Padgate camp with an odd assortment of fellow civilians ... the first person who had spoken to me was a little, thick-set man with black curly hair. Clutching a battered fibre suitcase in one hand he had raised a clenched fist under my nose and said: 'Greetings Comrade!' He was Ron Herscowitz ... All his family had disappeared into Nazi camps. The best way he could think of getting back at the Germans was to join Bomber Command. We had gone different ways during training, but now here he was again, a 'Special' at 101 [Ludford]. He had

already established himself as a 'squadron character' with a bois-
terous sense of humour.

Group Captain John Rees said that not only were most SOs Jewish,[37] but
that they formed a separate cohort at the base due to the secret nature
of their task, and constituted a sort of 'group within the group'. Many had
come via Palestine as volunteers and helped improve the German of the
non-Jewish SOs. Most changed their second names. Felix 'King',[38] for
example, who reached the squadron via Palestine and Canada,[39] was
remembered by a fellow crew member – 1084425 Flight Sergeant Ken
Fitton – as being nicknamed 'Happy' and of 'living up to his name'. Ken
Fitton recalls that his family had had an optics or lens business in London,
but that the crew made no effort to learn his real name, aware that in the
event of capture they would then be unable to give any information about
him or, indeed, his work.[40] King told him he had been born in Berlin, that
his father had been arrested by the Gestapo and never seen again, and
that his mother had taken the rest of the family to Palestine where he
joined the RAF as soon as he was of age.

Brookes[41] rightly points out that German Jews were 'taking a treble
risk ... They were SOs, bombers and Jewish – very brave men.' Their very
attempts to conceal their origins makes identifying Jewish SOs difficult
today, however. In addition, many remain keen not to reveal their true
background, having first been excluded, humiliated and expelled from
their countries of birth and then, on arriving poverty-stricken in Britain,
been mistrusted and interned before being allowed to serve only in non-
combatant units such as the Pioneer Corps. Only later were they permitted to strike back at their oppressors – in many cases the murderers of
their families – by enlisting in fighting units. Such experiences have in
some cases left their emotional mark to this day. Once in 101, they soon
integrated and became close friends with their crew-mates, even though
they arrived later than many others who had trained together, and had in
some cases already been training for secret work.[42] Few if any questions
were asked about religious affiliation.

1893650 Flight Sergeant Leslie Temple,[43] born in 1925 to Jane and
Solomon in Stepney, joined the RAF in January 1943 aged 18, but had served
in the Air Training Corps from the age of 14. He received initial air training
at Bridgnorth in Shropshire on De Haviland Dominees and Proctors, radio
training at Madley, acclimatization on B17s at Sculthorpe in Norfolk, and a
Lancaster conversion course at Lindholme in Yorkshire, before being sent
as a full flight sergeant, aged 19, to join 101 Squadron at Ludford. He had
learnt German at school and spoke fluent Yiddish at home, but the SO work
was so secret that he had no idea until he arrived in Ludford why he had
been sent there. He completed thirty missions between 22 June (against
the Rheims marshalling yards) and 28 October 1944 (Cologne). Other raids,

from his still-prized logbook, included Essen, Frankfurt, V1 sites, troop concentrations after D-Day, Caen, Hamburg and Scholven.

SOs worked intensely on the journeys out and home for several hours,
but over the target could only watch. Once the bombers were near the
target it was obvious to the enemy where they were going, so jamming
was superfluous. Leslie Temple explained that the rear gunners in ABC
Lancasters had heavier machine guns than usual, because the planes
were especially vulnerable transmitting over enemy territory.

His worst moment was over Kiel on 23 July 1944:

> ... a date that will live in my mind forever ... We took off from
> Ludford just before midnight, at 23.55, for the heavily defended
> German naval base at Kiel. The Lancaster was blown slightly off
> course over the North Sea, so the bomb aimer had to ask that they
> fly round for a second time over the target to ensure accuracy –
> which was always extremely hazardous. As we did not jam over
> the actual target I could watch everything from the astrodome.
> There was a solid curtain of bursting, hellish flak, a wall of search-
> lights across the sky, other bombers all around waiting to release
> their bombs and predatory German night-fighters spitting can-
> non fire. Finally we dropped our bombs on target, but were sud-
> denly nailed by a master searchlight on the way out. Immediately
> a dozen others 'coned' us at 20,000 feet, extremely heavy Ger-
> man flak opened up and we were showered with shrapnel which
> simply passed through the airframe; our two port engines burst
> into flames ... I feared the worst, as we could not bale out over
> the North Sea at night ... Our quick-thinking Canadian skipper
> (Eric Nielsen, who was given the DFC for this operation) nosed
> the Lancaster down and pulled out of the beam at 5,000 feet. The
> pilot and flight engineer managed to extinguish the flames over
> the North Sea, using the internal extinguishers, and despite no
> power for the directional equipment because of the two cut en-
> gines, our skilled navigator used his sextant and stars training to
> get us home on two engines. We crash landed at Woodbridge in
> Suffolk, a special crash-landing base, at about 4 a.m., with over
> 100 holes in our Lancaster. After debriefing I laid on my bed and
> could not stop shaking for twelve hours. The MO said the best
> cure was simply to get back up again soon – and of course we did.
> No counselling in those days.

Some of the dangers experienced by SOs were common to all fliers, as
Leslie reports:

> We were taking off for a raid on the Ruhr at Volkel [14 August
> 1944]. As we tore down the runway, our starboard outer engine cut

out. We had a full bomb bay, full fuel tanks and full boost on the engines for take off. Our pilot and engineer laid hard back on the stick together and we cleared the runway by just 50 feet. Over the North Sea we dropped our bombs and went home as an aborted sortie. Sometimes we had to rendezvous with 800 or 1,000 other aircraft over England and there were many dreadful accidents. I was horrified to witness one of my best pals from Barnsley (Jack Whitely), killed in a mid-air collision [23 September 1944]. I still have the letters from his family explaining when his body was washed up near Felixstowe. I stayed in contact with them for years after, as they treated me like a son. Over the target there was often confusion and some aircraft were hit by friendly bombs from above them. Landing at night was hazardous, as aircraft came in very close behind each other ... But we were young and fatalistic and made jokes about dying. I put my faith in the Almighty and recited the *Shema* [the Jewish creed] before every takeoff; I am sure this carried me through. I count my blessings that I survived.

After serving in 101 Leslie was told to take a long leave and thereafter worked as ground crew. He married Cynthia in 1950 and had a large family, now living in Ilford as an active member of the Association of Jewish Ex-Servicemen and Women, and the 101 Squadron Association and Bomber Command Association. Nightmares concerning his missions began some years after the war and still recur. His brother Arthur (Queen's Royals) was captured at Abbeville before Dunkirk and posted as missing for some months. He was a POW for five years.

Leslie – who has the 1939–45 and France and Germany Stars and War Medals – is unfortunately ineligible for the Aircrew Europe Medal because he, like many others, began bombing later than others in the war. The cut-off date for the medal is the beginning of June 1944, probably due to a misguided political decision connected with Bomber Harris's campaign. As a result, many veterans wear the Aircrew Europe Medal who never flew under such life-threatening circumstances as Leslie and his comrades.

Flight Sergeant Gerhard 'Harry' Heilig was born 19 April 1925 to a prominent Jewish journalist from Vienna, one of the earliest held by the Gestapo in a concentration camp following the Anschluss. He spent thirteen months in the camp and escaped to England just two weeks before war broke out. His mother was Jewish and from Hungary. Gerhard arrived on a *Kindertransport* in December 1938, went to a Quaker school in Yorkshire and studied to be a telephone engineer in Leeds and London. He volunteered for aircrew early in 1943 because, as he says, 'I was only too aware that Britain had saved my life ... and I wanted to put a nail in Hitler's coffin.'[44] As an 18-year-old 'Friendly Alien' he had to make a special applica-

tion to the Secretary of State for Air, and on 17 July was posted to the
Initial Training Wing (ITW) at Bridgnorth, Shropshire. He was trained
as a wireless operator at Madley (No. 4 Radio School) on De Havilland
Rapides and Proctors, and then sent in March 1944 with John Hertzog to
214 Squadron (100 Bomber Group) at Sculthorpe to work in Radio
Counter Measures. They were told that the whole thing was so secret
that not even the CO knew what it was about. He remembers two other
Jewish SOs, named Isaacs and Lander. On arrival he and Hereford were
called to the adjutant's office and advised that their German names would
put them at risk if they were captured. Hertzog took the name Hereford,
but Heilig was reluctant. 'First, they would have to shoot me down ...
second, I would have to survive ... and third, they would have to catch me
... I decided to follow my father's example when arrested by the Nazis ...
and bear my name with honour and trust to providence.'[45] The old hands
welcomed them as they trained-up, but when, after one month, they were
about to leave the base for some leave, they were called urgently to the
CO and told they must go on the squadron's first operational flight in its
new role, in B17 'Flying Fortresses'. His was SR386 BU-N. Heilig was
'particularly happy to be able to deliver my own worst regards in person
on Hitler's birthday', 20 April,[46] on the Paris rail-marshalling yards at La
Chapelle. The flight, which took place a day after his nineteenth birthday during the prelude to D-Day, was uneventful. The next day they took
their planned week's leave.

On 16 May he moved to Oulton, from where he took part in raids dropping 'Window' – aluminium foil – to deceive German radar and give real
raids on Germany a clear run while German night-fighters chased them.
On one raid his crew used Window to attract German fighters into an
ambush by waiting Mosquitoes. On another they forced German fighters
up in bad weather, causing many of them to crash on landing. In July 1944,
after his tenth operation, Heilig, with Hereford and RAAF SO 'Bluey'
Glick, who was also Jewish, was posted to Ludford with 101 Squadron to
fly as an SO in Lancasters. Hereford writes:

> I was friendly with Glick, and as only service personnel living in
> London were allowed there on leave, Bluey came as my 'cousin' to
> my home in Finchley ... On 19 September 1944 I flew to Rheydt
> in the Ruhr ('Happy!') Valley. The Master Bomber was Guy Gibson,
> VC, of 'Dambusters' fame. I heard his last words – 'We are going
> down to 500 feet.' The Deputy Master Bomber then lost contact.
> Gibson and his crew were killed on that raid.[47]

Heilig records that after the bombs had been dropped his crew often threw
out bundles of propaganda leaflets. He discovered only later that his father,
by then working for the American OSS propaganda department, had

actually written some of them, and was delighted with the coincidence.

Gerhard Heilig remembers bringing back from one raid two pieces of German anti-aircraft shell which had pierced the fuselage a yard from where he sat. On 18 August 1944, over Sterkrade in the Ruhr, the starboard inner engine was shot out of action. On 5 September over Le Havre they were hit again by shrapnel, and once more on 12 September over Frankfurt when the starboard inner engine was hit and cut out. On 5 September they had to return with their bombs owing to poor visibility over Le Havre, and the heavy load caused brake failure on landing. As they headed at an alarming speed for the wreckage of an old aircraft at the runway end, Heilig rolled himself up into a ball for a belly landing with the undercarriage up. On halting, the crew ran for the aft door and exited, but the plane did not explode. He later found he had grabbed two parachutes and helmets, calculating in a split second that the paperwork resulting from the loss of such items would be unbearable.

Flight Sergeants Heilig and Hereford completed their thirty missions on 25 October 1944. Heilig was posted to Transport Command in the Far East until 1947, became a pilot and returned to work in Austria in 1965, where he now lives with his family.

Graham Boytell, an SO from Australia,[48] recalls SO Hans Schwartz, a German Jewish refugee who had been ordered to change his name by the RAF before being allowed on operations, and was therefore known as Henry Blake. Graham, who met him in 1944, vividly recalls Hans's joy in the mess at Ludford at being on Battle Orders for the night of 12 August. 'I have never seen anyone so happy to be going on ops as Henry was that night. It was the Brunswick raid and his first. Sadly he failed to return.' Flight Sergeant Bob Hopes remembers Schwartz as 'a most pleasant lad with dark, curly hair', and suspected from his looks that he was 'not really a Blake'.[49]

Navigator Ken Scott first met Augustus Tomachepolsky, known as 'Tomo' to his crew mates, at the No. 2 Squadron 'A' Flight 6 ITW (Initial Training Wing) at Aberystwyth where they both graduated in May 1942. They went on to Anstey, but failed the flying course and met up again at Ludford in October 1943. In November, witnesses saw the rear of Tomo's Lancaster torn apart by night-fighter cannon shells as it plunged in flames into the suburbs of Dusseldorf. Three crew members survived as POWs, but Tomo was killed. Ken Scott describes Tomo as 'a remarkable chap ... an accomplished artist who drew amazing portraits of his comrades. His family were in the fur business. I was on the same raid; we took off a few minutes earlier at 1700 hrs. I noted in my logbook four-tenths cloud, leaflets carried, uneventful trip, duration 4 hrs 35 mins ... Such are the fortunes of war.'[50]

Pilot Officer Adrian Marks[51] (RAAF), another Jewish SO, vividly remembers the Nuremberg raid of 30–31 March 1944:

At briefing we were advised by the met. officer we would have some cloud cover to and from the target. But it was a bright full moon with little cloud cover. Our usual aircraft, G for George, was not serviceable at the time, so were allocated another Lancaster, J2, whose crew were on leave. Once airborne we found we had a real problem. The aircraft could not gain altitude at the speed of the bomber stream, so we had a choice: to keep up with the others and be well below their height, or to climb to the height of the others, but fall well behind and risk arriving over the target alone. The crew discussed the options over the intercom and agreed to gain the operational altitude of the stream rather than have bombs from our own aircraft falling around us and possibly on us, and to accept the risk of being alone to and from the target. Some twenty-five or so minutes prior to the time the raid was scheduled to begin, I picked up on my ABC receiver the message, 'Achtung Nuremberg', the target having been identified. I warned my crew that we could expect more night-fighters than usual. As usual it was a zigzag course to and from the target, and I often wondered if someone back home had been careless in their conversation and that it had been picked up by an unfriendly person and made known to the Germans. We arrived over Nuremburg some 20–25 minutes late, all by ourselves, but at the correct altitude. The city appeared to be on fire in several areas, as I could see the target once the bomb doors were open. We dropped our bombs and got the hell out of the area and headed for home. At no stage did we encounter any enemy aircraft, despite the fact that ninety-five aircraft did not return that night. It was the heaviest loss recorded by RAF Bomber Command on any one night.[52]

Of 101's twenty-six aircraft, six failed to return and one crash-landed at Welford, Berkshire. Forty-seven men were killed, eight captured and one – Sergeant Don Brinkhurst – escaped.[53]

SO Sergeant Henry van Geffen[54] mentions in his diaries an SO Sergeant, Rudy W. Mohr or Mahr, who was probably Jewish and who was killed on 7 March 1945 over Dessau while bombing the railways supplying the Junkers jet-engines testing base. Another name is Pilot Officer O. Fischel/Fischl, killed in action with the crew of Pilot Officer McConnell in Lancaster III DV-236 SR-G-George on 15 February 1944 over Berlin, five of the eight crew baling out and becoming POWs.[55] Chorley says the records show that Fischl was not one of those killed, as is confirmed by his Jewish Chaplain Card at the AJEX Museum.[56]

Another Jewish SO was 1895899 Flight Sergeant Wolf Herman Engelhardt, born in Leipzig, of Polish nationality, on 9 November 1920,[57] who escaped via Berlin to England on 3 April 1939. His Jewish Chaplain Card says he volunteered for Special Duty on 24 May 1943 as AC2, but was later promoted to flight sergeant. Details of which chaplains he met are given, and the fact that his next-of-kin was his brother at 9 Thirlecroft Road, Horsham, Surrey. It also states that he was killed in action on 28 July 1944 in Lancaster III LM462 SR-V2, having taken off at 2145 hours for a raid over Stuttgart. He is buried at Rebrechien, eleven kilometres north-east of Orleans, in a communal grave with others of the crew. When his brother, Stephen Ellis, recently asked the Commonwealth War Graves Commission to add a Star of David to the grave they declined, but they did allow him to add some Hebrew lettering.[58] The rest of the crew details are also known.[59]

Jewish Personnel in other Electronic Warfare Sectors

Another countermeasure involving German-speaking Jewish refugees, code-named 'Corona', involved the use of RAF ground listening and broadcasting stations in England from which German-speaking RAF men and WAAF women broke into German fighter-controllers' radio frequencies and broadcast false instructions to the fighters.[60] On one occasion,[61] over Ludwigshaven on 17 November 1943, a broadcast in German ordering 'All butterflies go home', caused many of the German fighters to land.[62] Only one British bomber was lost that night.

J.A. Davies describes how the ABC teams were monitored from a ground station at Kingsdown, near Canterbury, a major RCM centre, staffed mainly by German Jewish refugees.[63] Former RAF Flight Sergeant 1456538 Sidney Goldberg of the RAF 'Y' Service (Mobile Field Units) radio deception/interception teams, who served in North Africa, Sicily and north-west Europe, and is at the time of writing an active AJEX member, knows that many RAF squadrons employed German linguists in activities such as Intelligence gathering and Radio Counter Measures and that a high percentage were, like him, Jewish. They included German refugee volunteers, German Jews from Palestine – he remembers Flight Sergeants Freddie Adler, J. Rosenthal, Herman, Kon and England – and British Jews who knew enough Yiddish to understand German. Dozens of other Jews worked on Radio Counter Measure schemes.

Aileen Clayton names WAAF Flight Officer Rosemary E. Horstmann (perhaps also known as Mrs H. Waters) and RAF Flight Sergeant R. Fresco-Cuba.[64] Peter Leighton-Langer[65] names WAAF Edith Perutz (later Smith), born in 1918 in Vienna, and recalls many others. Gerhard Heilig remembers meeting a Czech WAAF sergeant while on leave at an émigré club in London who told him how false instructions in German were transmitted to the enemy at her ground interception station. One evening they guided a lost German pilot to the Woodbridge airfield in Essex and found he was flying a Junker 88 with the latest equipment – a major catch for British Intelligence.[66]

Former RAF wireless mechanic John Marks 3005273, born in Shoreditch on 28 July 1924, served with Sid Chandler, a fellow Jewish operator, at No. 80 Signals Wing at Sizewell, Suffolk (now the power station). They operated diesel-powered transmitters from horse-drawn caravans for three shifts of eight hours, recognizing and jamming German fighter-aircraft communications over the Ruhr, a major Bomber Command target. Sizewell was the closest mainland point to the Ruhr industrial area.

RAF Flight Sergeant Jack Burston[67] served in a Special Intelligence Unit (SIU) made up of German speakers, based first at Beachy Head in Sussex, then the Isle of Wight and later off Normandy on D-Day, intercepting enemy-aircraft and naval radio traffic. In his small unit alone were eight Jewish personnel, besides himself, some of them from Palestine.

Jock M. Whitehouse, historian of 214 Squadron, confirms that many other squadrons had German-speaking crew members engaged in RCM against enemy night-fighters. In the case of 214, equipped with Boeing Flying Fortress IIIs, many were Jewish.[68]

The death on active service of the British-born radar and electronics expert, Alan D. Blumlein, killed in a Halifax bomber crash on 7 June 1942 with two colleagues, was described in the *Daily Telegraph* as a national loss. Air Chief Marshall Sir Phillip Joubert described it as a catastrophe for the war effort, and Sir Archibald Sinclair, Secretary of State for Air, wrote that 'it would be impossible to over-rate the importance of the work on which they were engaged', which had undoubtedly saved thousands of lives.[69]

Professor R.V. Jones[70] pays tribute to the many Jewish refugee scientists who contributed to the electronic war against the Nazis. One of them, RAF Flight Sergeant Jack Nissenthall, volunteered to take part in the attempt to break into the German radar station at Pourville near Dieppe in August 1942 (this incident is described in Chapter 9). He was accompanied by a dozen Canadian snipers with orders to shoot him if he was in danger of capture. The raid achieved an important part of its mission, but only Jack and one other made it back to Newhaven. His courage was recognized only many years after the war, by which time it was considered too late for a decoration to be given.[71]

Among many Jewish cryptographers at SOE (including Leo Marks, *Chef de Codage* in the French Section) and code-breakers at Bletchley Park, the code and cypher centre which eventually broke the German Enigma codes, were Professor Max Newman of St John's College, Cambridge, the mathematician who developed the Colossus computer which penetrated the notorious Lorenz codes of the German High Command.[72] There was a large Jewish input in both radio interception and code-breaking at Bletchley (see chapter 6).

There is little doubt that outside the small circle of 101 Squadron veterans, few know of the important and dangerous work of the Special Operators. and their Lancaster crew comrades, less still the role of the Jewish SOs. It is to be hoped that this study will bring deserved if belated recognition to this brave band of brothers.

Acknowledgements

I would like to thank the following former SOs of 101 Squadron: Flight Sergeant Graham Boytell, RAAF (of Australia); Dr (Flight Sergeant) Jim Davies; Flight Sergeant Ken Fitton; Flight Sergeant Henry van Geffen; Flight Sergeant Peter Holway; Flight Sergeant Bob Hopes; Wireless Operator Peter D. Kaye; Pilot Officer Guy Meadows; Group Captain John Rees; Flight Sergeant Ken Scott; and Dr (Flight Sergeant) Aubrey Wilson.

I would like to thank a number of other individuals for their help and encouragement in completing this study. The staff of the Reading Room at the Imperial War Museum, Lambeth; of The National Archive at Kew; and of Battersea Park Library in Wandsworth have been particularly helpful. Gabriel Kaufman, former National Chair of AJEX, started me off on the trail of the Jewish SOs of 101 Squadron, RAF. I am grateful also to Stephen Ellis, brother of the late Flight Sergeant Wolf Engelhardt, RAF, killed in action over France as an SO on 28 July 1944. Sydney Goldberg, former National Vice-Chair of AJEX and RAF 'Y' Service veteran, put me in touch with the veterans of RCM. I am grateful for the personal contributions of Gerhard Heilig of Vienna; John Herzog/Hereford of Faversham; RAF radar veteran John Marks; Mrs Shirley de Solla (widow of SO veteran Henry de Solla) of Enfield; and Leslie Temple of Ilford.

10.1 Special Operator Sgt Leslie Temple, 101 Sqdn Bomber Command, front 2nd left at Ludford Magna with his Lancaster crew. Rear left to right – Fl. Eng. Sgt James, Navigator Sgt Hall, Bomb Aimer Sgt Morgan, Mid Upper Gunner Sgt Ross. Front left to right – Rear Gnr Sgt Rook, Spec. Op. Sgt L. Temple, W/Operator Sgt Bailey and 'Skipper' Pilot Officer E. Neilsen (later Deputy PM of Canada).

10.2 At Ludford Magna, Sgt Reuben 'Herky' Herscovitch (centre) with Macleod, left and Dockerty, right.

SOs Identified as Jewish in Chaplain Cards or elsewhere.[73]

Abbreviations/Key

Addendum – Henry Morris, *We Will Remember Them: An Addendum* (London: AJEX, 1994).

AJEX – Association of Jewish Ex-Servicemen and Women of UK.
Canadian Jews at War (Montreal: Canadian Jewish Congress, 1947, 1948).
WWRT – Henry Morris, *We Will Remember Them – A Record of the Jews who Died in the Armed Forces of the Crown 1939–1945* (London: Brassey's, 1989).

Survived

Flight Sergeant Auer, possibly 788094 H. Auer, known as 'Mish', originally of Czech 310 Squadron, for whom there is an AJEX card.[74]

Flight Sergeant R. Blitz, RAF (information from Group Captain John Rees).

J96217 Flight Sergeant Murray Cohen, RCAF, born 1921 in Toronto, son of Aaron, later of Chicago; volunteered 1941, with three brothers in the forces; captured on his fifteenth mission, 29–30 December 1943, in Lancaster III LM371 SR-T over Berlin. Crashed at Schillerslage, four kilometres north-west of Burgdorf and sent to Stalag 4B, POW no. 269756. *Canadian Jews at War*, p.120.

1800983/187083 Flight Sergeant, later Pilot Officer, Henry John de Solla, husband of Shirley, son of B. de Solla, 52 Hainault Court, Forest Rise, London E17; volunteered 6 January 1942. Information from Leslie Temple, AJEX card and correspondence with family.

169599/1457154 Pilot Officer Otto Fischl or Fischel, son of Mr Fischl of Natwood, Bowness, Westmoreland; volunteered 2 September 1941. Chaplain informed father and *Jewish Chronicle* on 11 April 1944 that he had been killed in action on 15 February 1944 over

Berlin in Lancaster III DV 236 SR-G George, five others having bailed out and been captured, but on 16 April 1944 the Air Ministry reported he was POW no. 3528 at camp L3. AJEX card says he was missing in action 15–16 February 1944, and a POW.

Flight Sergeant R277148 John O.S. Fochs or Fuchs or Fosch, RCAF. Information from AIR 27 records at TNA and *Canadian Jews at War*.

AUS 434631 Flight Sergeant Phineas 'Bluey' Glick, born Grajevo, Poland, 12 November 1923 – enlisted Brisbane; RAAF, shot down and captured, August – September 1944. Known by Heilig and Van Geffen, with whom he was posted to 101. Information in letter of 29 May 2000. Named in *Australian Jewry Book of Honour* (see note 51, below).

1892246 Flight Sergeant Gerhard Heilig, son of Bruno Heilig, 2 Windsor Court, Moscow Road, London W2; volunteered 12 March 1943. Crashed 6 September 1944 in Lancaster III ND983 SR-B after the Le Havre raid, take-off 1737 hrs, crashed 2055 hrs (Chorley, p.410). Information from AJEX card, personal correspondence and interview.

1398898 Flight Sergeant Reuben 'Herky' Herscovitch, also known as Ron Hurst, son of Mr J. Herscovitch, 53 Bellot Street, Manchester 8; volunteered 11 November 1941. AJEX card.

1868978 Flight Sergeant John Hayman Hertzog, aka Hereford, 60 Finchley Court, Ballards Lane, London N3. Information in letter and phone call to author, October 2000, and AJEX card.

Flight Sergeant Isaacs, possibly the same as 656562 Flight Sergeant, later Pilot Officer, Ralph Isaacs, and possibly killed in action. Information from Heilig's letter of 19 May 2000, *WWRT*, p.206 and AJEX card.

Flight Sergeant Felix King, also known as Flight Sergeant Felix? Probably 1282123, son of Mrs G. Abrahams, 121 Castle Hill, Reading. Information from Flight Lieutenant Guy Meadows and AJEX card.

187155/1548852 Flight Sergeant Israel L. Lander, son of Mr D. Lander, 14 Bentley Rd, Liverpool 8; volunteered 17 October 1941, Information from Heilig's letter of 19 May 2000 and AJEX card.

Flight Sergeant, Lipfriend (Chorley, vol. 4, p.367), perhaps not an SO. Three surviving RAF men with this name appear in AJEX cards, one injured in the crash on 31 July/1 August 1944 of Lancaster I LL849 SR-O, take-off Ludford 1922 hrs, which clipped treetops and crashed 0242 hrs near Litchfield, Staffs

Flight Sergeant, later Pilot Officer, Adrian M. Marks RAAF, named on Battle Order of 101 Squadron, 5 June 1944, sent by Jeff Gascoigne to author, July 2000. Without a number it is impossible to identify which of several RAF and RAAF men named Marks appearing on AJEX cards he may be.

1157751 Flight Sergeant Montague Phillips of 23 Leigham Hall, Streatham, south London, volunteered 20 June 1940. Information from AJEX card.

Flight Sergeant D. J. Rubin, crash-landed Woodbridge, 16 June 1944, in Lancaster I LL273 SR-D en route for Sterkrade, take-off 2310 hrs, hit by flak, no casualties. AJEX card not located.

533809 Flight Sergeant Joseph M. Starr, RCAF, POW, in Lancaster 1 ME613 SR-M2, 21–22 June 1944, over Weselling, take-off 2314 hrs, crashed Drunen, North Brabant, east of Waalwijk, Holland; four POW, four killed. Appears in Chorley and Canadian Roll at AJEX Museum.

172574 Flying Officer Harry Taylor, aka Doniger, son of Mrs B. Taylor, 201 East 35th Street, New York, nephew of M. Doniger, 16 Laverton Road, St Annes's; baled out and POW, 30 July 1944. AJEX card. Local French historian, Alan Charpentier, described how Harry was the only survivor of his Lancaster crew, and used to visit the village of Massey –

site of the crash – every year after the war and eventually unveiled the memorial in the village to the crew.

1893650 Flight Sergeant Leslie Temple, son of S. Temple, 7 Wellington Road, London E10. Flew thirty missions with 101 from 22 June 1944 until 28 October 1944. Information from AJEX card and interview.

1891610 Flight Sergeant M. Vangelder, son of Mr H. Vangelder of 143 Golders Green Road, London NW11; volunteered 26 February 1943, taking part in frequent raids, such as on 3, 4, 7, 10, 14, 18 and 30 April and 1, 2, 3, 7 and 10 May 1945, and also in operations such as Manna (dropping supplies to Dutch and Belgian civilians) and Exodus (returning liberated POWs to UK). Information from 101 Operations Book, AIR 27 at PRO, and AJEX card.

Killed

1864380 Flight Sergeant Monty Barss, RAFVR, of 258 West End Rd, Ruislip, son of Daniel and Lily, of Ruislip, Middx. Volunteered 10 December 1941. Killed in action 12–13 August 1944 in Lancaster III LM598 SR-M2 over Braunschweig, take-off Ludford 2120. Buried Hanover, allegedly first in a Russian cemetery. Information from *WWRT*, p.186 and *Addendum*, p.26, SO Flight Sergeant Leslie Temple and AJEX card.

164909 Pilot Officer Cyril Cousin, RAFVR, son of Julius and Rachael of Hackney; killed in action, aged 20, on 29–30 August 1944 over Stettin in Lancaster III LM479 SR-F, take-off 2130, crashed Dejbjerg, three kilometres south of Lem in Denmark. Buried Dejbjerg. Information from *WWRT*, p.192, and AJEX card.

1895899 Flight Sergeant Wolf Herman Engelhardt, brother of Siegfried Engelhardt (later Stephen Ellis) of 9 Thirlecroft/Thistlecroft Road, Hersham, Walton-on-Thames; volunteered 24 May 1943, killed in action 28 July 1944 in Lancaster III LM 462 SR-V2, take-off 2145 hrs to Stuttgart, buried Rebrechien near Orleans. Information from AJEX card and correspondence with family.

1253600 Flight Sergeant Leslie Henry Fox, son of Sydney and Sarah Fox, husband of Mrs A. Fox, of 144 Walm Lane, London NW2; volunteered 29 November 1940. Killed in action 27 November 1942, reported 12 February 1943, buried Hamburg. This information from *WWRT*, p.196, and AJEX card. But Chorley (see entry date for casualty) says he was in Lancaster III JB128 SR-U2, shot down over Berlin on 2–3 December 1943, take-off Ludford 1648, and was POW no. 269770 at Stalag 4B. This is more likely as 1942 is too early.

1396497/162792 Pilot Officer Ronald Halperin, DFC, son of Frank and Yetta née Siegler, with a sister, B. Halperin, 71 Chiltern Court, Baker Street, London W1, and an uncle P.H. Halperin, 38 Heath Drive, London NW3; volunteered 22 September 1941, gazetted 15 February 1944, detached from 156 Squadron. Killed in action 21 February 1944, aged 22, buried Rheinberg. Information in *WWRT*, p.202, and AJEX card, but not Chorley.

1897268 Flight Sergeant George Kesten, parents perished in Poland in Holocaust, cousin of B. Marguiles, 20 High Street, Waddesdon, Aylesbury; volunteered 12 July 1943, trained at Madley. Killed in action 4 November 1944, aged 22, in Lancaster 1 ME865 SR-K over Bochum, take-off 1738 hrs, buried Rheinberg. *WWRT*, p.208, and AJEX card.

1892478 Flight Sergeant Rudolf or Ronald D. King, RAFVR, volunteered 11 October 1943. Killed in action 28 December 1944, aged 19, in Lancaster III PB634 SR-U over Bonn, take-off 1522 hrs, buried Rheinberg. *WWRT*, p.208, and AJEX card. J. Van Geffen, in a letter of 3 June 2000, identifies him from the register of the Commonwealth War Graves Commission as son of Adolf and Helen Kempner, nephew of David Kempner of Golders Green, London, and of D. King, 340 Andrews Road, London NW11, buried in Joint Grave 5 D18-19.

J92571/J36315 Pilot Officer Phillip Leeds, RCAF, also known as Leibowitz, born Montreal, 28 December 1917, son of Morris and Rose Leibowitz of 2781 Hampshire Road, Cleveland Heights, Ohio, graduate of Western University, brother Ben in US Army. Volunteered at Windsor, Ontario, 19 June 1942, reached UK October 1943, member of Caterpillar Club, having once parachuted from a crashing plane. Killed in action 6 November 1944 in Lancaster 1 PB692 SR-K2 over Gelsenkirchen, take-off 1200 hrs, crashed near Wanne-Eikel, buried Reichswald. *Canadian Jews at War*, p.44.

J27285 Pilot Officer Moie Marder, RCAF, born in Regina, son of I.D. Marder, 1352 Bay Avenue, Trail, BC. His brother, Flying Officer Ben Marder, also in RCAF. Volunteered in Edmonton July 1942, killed in action 30 January 1944 in Lancaster I DV303 SR-U over Berlin, at Teltow, sixteen kilometres south-west of Berlin, buried Berlin CWGC Cemetery. *Canadian Jews at War*, p.49. A lake in Saskatchewan is named after him.

162590/1040284/1040484 Flight Sergeant, later Pilot Officer, Stanley Mayer, CGM, gazetted 1 November 1943 and *Jewish Chronicle*. Killed in action 26 November 1943 in Lancaster III DV285 SR-Q over Berlin, take-off 1715 hrs, shot down Liege, buried Heverlee, Leuven. Information from AJEX card.

J39972 Flying Officer Morley Ornstein, RCAF, son of Mrs E.F. Ornstein of 563 Euclid Avenue, Toronto. Killed in action 23 March 1945 in Lancaster I DV245, on its 119th sortie, take-off 0711 hrs. Hit by flak and exploded at 1000 hrs between Moodreich and Stuhr 7 kms east-south-east of Dolmenhorst over Bruchstrasse (?), buried Osterholz, Becklingen, near Belsen, Germany. Information from *Canadian Jews at War*, p.53, and TNA AIR 27.[75]

2220929 Flight Sergeant Heinz George Popper, son of Jules and Eugenie Popper of 165 Westrow Drive, New Upney, Barking. Killed in action 29–30 August 1944, buried Malmo, Sweden. Information from AJEX card.

1144632 Flight Sergeant Anthony Ezra Rosen, son of John Henry and Farmy E. Rosen of 35 Jamieson Road, Winton, Bournemouth; volunteered February 1941. Survived crash on 23 September 1943 in Lancaster I W4923 SR-N2 after Mannheim raid, near

Ludford, take-off 1835 hrs, returned 0335 hrs. Killed in action 18–19 November 1943 in Lancaster III LM 370 SR-K2 over Berlin, take-off Ludford 1721, buried Schoonebeek, fourteen kilometres south-east of Drente, Holland. Information from *WWRT*, p.222, and AJEX card. His parents died after the war and asked to be buried with their only child in Malmo Jewish Cemetery.

1876107 Flight Sergeant Hans Heinz Schwartz or Schwarz, also known as Henry Blake, son of Erich and Elli Schwartz of 17 Mapesbury Court, Shoot-Up Hill, Cricklewood, London NW2; volunteered 25 April 1943. Killed in action 12–13 August 1944, aged 19, in Lancaster III PB258 SR-V over Braunschweig, buried Heverlee, Leuven, Belgium. Information from AJEX card.

R151355 Flight Sergeant Samuel Lewis Silver, RCAF, husband of Violet Silver of 229 Catherine Street, Ottawa. Killed in action 24 May 1944 in Lancaster I DV389 SR-X over Aachen, crashed Olzheim, ten kilometres north-east of Prum, buried Rheinberg. *Canadian Jews at War*, p.69.

416574 Flight Sergeant Richard Maitland Singer, RNZAF, son of Richard Arnold and Dorothy, née Nicol, of Auckland. Killed in action 9 November 1944, buried Oosterbeek, Arnhem. Included in *Addendum*, p.30, by present writer from personal visit to Oosterbeek. But he is perhaps Wireless Operator R.J. or J.H. Singer, RAAF, Lancaster III JB149 SR-R2 over Berlin, take-off 1947 hrs, shot down 3–4 September 1943, POW no. 222845, Stalag 4B – the only Singer to survive as POW (see date entry in Chorley).

1309934/158600 Pilot Officer Henry Tiller, son of Herman and Esther Tiller, 66 Wellesley Street, London E1. Killed in action 2/3 December 1943, aged 23, in Lancaster III LM363 SR-P over Berlin, take-off Ludford 1641 hrs, crashed Diephulz, buried Rheinberg. Information from *WWRT*, p.230, and AJEX card.

1389282 Corporal, later Flight Sergeant, Favel Tomas, also known as Tomachepolsky/Tomachopolski, killed in action 2 November 1943 in Lancaster III DV265 SR-F over Dusseldorf, take-off Ludford 1713 hrs, buried

Reichswald. Information from *Addendum*, p.31, and AJEX card.

951320/182094/51330 Pilot Officer Aubrey Arnold Weldon, DFM, son of Bernard L. W. and Alice Weldon, 56 Lord Street, Southport and Thurcroft, Yorkshire. Had been with 150 Squadron. Chorley says he was killed in action on 2/3 December 1943 with PO Tiller (listed above). Buried Rheinberg. Information from *Addendum*, p.105, AJEX card and *Jewish Chronicle*, 5 December 1941.

J43864 Pilot Officer Benny Yellin, RCAF, killed in

action 14 October 1944 in Lancaster 1 1174 SR-U over Duisberg, take-off 0222 hrs; Runnymede Memorial. Benny was from Montreal, 5319 St Urbain Street. *Canadian Jews at War*, p.81.

J43636 Pilot Officer Bernard Zimring, RCAF, son of Samuel and Elsie of 4527 Harvard Ave, Montreal; born 1924 in Kenora, Ontario. Killed in action 4 November 1944 in Lancaster 1 NF936 SR-F over Bochum, take-off 1709 hrs; buried Reichswald. *Canadian Jews at War*, p.84.

Possibly Jewish SOs

The following names, appearing in R. Alexander's *101 Squadron: Roll of Honour* (London: 1979) and Chorley's six-volume *Bomber Command Losses World War Two* (London: 1997–98), might be Jewish, but no AJEX Jewish Chaplain Cards could be found for them. In some cases the identifications are supported by eyewitness reports. Since many Jewish fliers took aliases in case they were taken prisoner, or even claimed to be Church of England when enlisting in order to avoid being identified as Jewish on their ID tags, the roll probably does not include all the SOs of Jewish origin who were killed in action:

Flight Sergeant W.R.L. or W. F. Hart, killed in action 16 January 1945.

Flying Officer G.W. Hess, killed in action 13 March 1945.

Flight Sergeant G.P. Herman, RCAF, killed in action 18 November 1943, with A.E. Rosen.

Pilot Officer W.E.M. Kon, RCAF, killed in action 5 October 1944 in Lancaster 1 LL758 SR-A over Saarbrucken, take-off 1706 hrs, crashed at Trembleur near Liege, five kilometres east-north-east of Herstel, buried at Hotton.

Flying Officer J.M. Lyons, killed in action 29 November 1944 in Lancaster III

LM755 SR-N over Dortmund, take-off 1208 hrs, buried Reichswald.

J/95545 Flight Sergeant Rudy W. Mohr/Mahr, RCAF, son of John and Anna Mohr of Winnipeg; killed in action 7 March 1945, aged 19, over Dessau, bombing the railways supplying the Junkers jet engines and testing base, in Lancaster I PD268 SR-O. Memorial at Runnymede.

Flight Sergeant A.W. Schneider, killed in action 14 January 1944 in Lancaster III DV 287 SR-N over Braunschweig, shot down by night-fighter at 1830 hrs, crashed at Klezieraneen, Drenthe, ten kilometres south-east of Emmen, Holland.

J86922 Pilot Officer and Flight Sergeant Gerhard Edgar Herbert Schultz, RCAF, killed in action 27 April 1944 in Lancaster II ILM 493 SR-X over Friedrichshafen,[75] take-off Ludford 2140 hrs, shot down over Oberwinden near Eizbach, buried Durnbach. K. Scott, a 101 veteran from King's Lynn,[76] who knew Schultz well, relates that he joined 101 at Ludford in October 1943, sharing Hut 13 with Mr Scott and his crew. A quiet Canadian from Medicine Hat City, he was always playing 'Red River Valley' on his mandolin. He joined the crew for their twelfth mission on 8 October to Hanover, take-off 2250 hrs, returning after five hours and forty minutes. Schultz went to another crew to finish his own tour of missions while Mr Scott's crew went on leave on 24 February 1944 and, soon after this, Schultz was killed. His grave has a cross on it, but his name suggests he may have been Jewish or of Jewish origin and that, like many others, he kept this secret in case of capture. (Photo of the grave from Ken Lewis.)

Wireless Operator C.H. Woelfe, RCAF, killed in action 20 July 1944 in Lancaster 1 W4976 SR-P over Courtrai, take-off 0006 hrs, crashed over town, buried Wevelegem, Belgium.

Probable Jews who Survived, Extracted from PRO 802/3/4/5 File AIR 27

Pilot Officer Berg, RAF.

J43539 Flight Sergeant R.P. Berg, RCAF.

R180913 Wireless Operator N.M. Berger, RCAF.

Flight Sergeant A.D. Block, RAF.

R218506 Flight Sergeant M. Gorbowitsky, RCAF.

Flying Officer Grauman, RAF.

AUS429920 Flying Officer J.A. Kurtzer

J40415 Flying Officer Lobsinger, RCAF.

Flight Sergeant H. Lyon, RAF.

J42681 Flying Officer A.L. Scheafer, RCAF.

J29097 Flight Lieutenant W.G. Schenk, RCAF.

Pilot Officer Snyder

J38295 Flying Officer J.R. Weinfield, RCAF.

J41384 Flying Officer J.E. Zittrer, RCAF.

101 Squadron veteran Ken Scott wrote to the author in December 2002:

I can shed some light on the fate of PO Fischl. My crew and his were on the same raid on the night of 15 February 1944 to Berlin, take off 1720, returned 2345. At debriefing we were concerned there was no sign of his crew. After getting to bed, I stayed awake hoping I should hear them walking down the path to their hut which was next to ours. I woke with a start next morning realising I had fallen asleep on my vigil. I dashed out in my pyjamas through the snow to their hut. Opening the door, I found an empty hut with beds stripped of all their possessions. The Affairs Officer had taken them for return to stores and personal items to their next of kin … they were missing. By mid morning, a new crew to replace them were occupying the hut.

In June 1947, Cyril Thompson, who was the Flight Engineer with Fischl, visited me at my home and told me what happened. After take-off, they lost the power on one engine, meaning they would not be able to fly as high or as fast and so would arrive late over Berlin. Pilot David McConnell decided to press on – most would have aborted but he was fighting a personal war as he had lost a brother in the Merchant Navy. Last to arrive over Berlin with 10/10ths cloud cover, the fires below silhouetted them against the sky and they were soon attacked by a German night-fighter. His cannon hit and killed the rear gunner, mid-upper gunner and pilot. Cyril Thompson pulled McConnell from his seat and tried to take control with only one engine, but the Lanc. soon went in to a turn and the survivors decided to bale out. Four got out – including Fischl – but

Don Hall could not locate his parachute. He sat looking at the escape hatch with his dead friends around him. Suddenly the plane dipped and his chute slid from under the navigator table towards him! He clipped it on and out he went.

He saw the plane rear up and turn on its back carrying his three comrades. He came to earth close to an anti-aircraft battery on the outskirts of Berlin. The Germans soon relieved him of his watch, lighter, escape pack, etc, plus his cigarettes which they handed round and smoked, and he finished up at Stalagluft 7. At war's end he was surprised to have all his possessions returned to him. Strange how the Germans could be so bestial and cruel to people yet meticulous in the return of trinkets.

On PO Liersch (killed Sept. 27/28th 1943), his crew and mine were returning to Ludford from attacking Hanover. We circled the airfield in a stack – 500 feet intervals waiting to be called in to land – and we were on our final approach over the lights with flaps and wheels down. I had packed my gear and was standing behind the pilot watching the lights below. Suddenly there were loud crumps, pressure waves and red flashes converging ahead of us. A German intruder behind had obviously overestimated our speed and his cannon fire was missing us. Our pilot Ron Nightingale called out on the radio to the control tower, 'Bandits, Bandits!' and the runway lights were all switched off and we turned sharp to starboard. But the intruder went on and caught Liersch's crew; the plane exploded and crashed outside Wickenby and all the crew were lost. Years later I discovered the name of the German pilot in a book.

Notes

1. J.J. Halley, *Squadrons of the RAF and Commonwealth* (London: Air Britain Historians, 1988), pp.175–6 and P. Moyes, *Bomber Squadrons of the RAF* (London: Macdonald, 1976), pp.135–8.
2. 101 Squadron website article sent to the author by the nephew of Flight Sergeant W. H. Engelhardt, Special Operator, see below.
3. *Journal of St Cross College, Oxford* (1996), Record No. 14, pp.36–8, article by former 101 SO Reuben Herscovitz.
4. A. Brookes, *Bomber Squadron at War: 101 Squadron* (London: Ian Allen, 1983), p.97.
5. Letter from former SO R. Crafer, November 2000.
6. Moyes, *Bomber Squadrons of the RAF*, pp.135–8.
7. The Germans called this note *Dudelsack* (bagpipes); see P. Hinchcliffe, *The Other Battle* (Shrewsbury: Airlife, 1996), p.196.
8. Some reports wrongly suggest that SOs broadcast false messages, but their job was chiefly to disrupt German transmissions. See P. Otter, *Maximum Effort: Part 1* (London: Hutton, 1990), p.23; see also note 10.
9. Interview with Flight Sergeant Leslie Temple, 13 May 2000.
10. M. Streetly, *Confound and Destroy* (London: Jane's, 1978), p.22.
11. Bruce B. Halpenny, *Action Stations 2: Military Airfields of Lincolnshire and the East Midlands* (London: Patrick Stephens, 1981), pp.130–3.
12. Brookes, *Bomber Squadron*, p.227.

13. Letter from SO Sam Brookes, July 2000.
14. Interview with Flight Sergeant Leslie Temple, 13 May 2000.
15. Ibid.
16. Otter, *Maximum Effort*, p. 24.
17. Halpenny, *Action Stations 2*, pp.130–3.
18. Letter and telephone conversation, November 2000.
19. 101 website (see note 2); Brookes, *Bomber Squadron*, p.235, may refer to a different incident.
20. Telephone conversation with his brother David in Canvey, August 2000.
21. Streetly, *Confound and Destroy*, p.22.
22. Martin Middlebrook, *The Nuremberg Raid, March 30–31 1944* (London: Allen Lane, 1973), p.135.
23. Telephone conversation with his cousin, Raymond Barran, 24 July 2000.
24. Middlebrook, *Nuremberg Raid*, p.171.
25. Halpenny, *Action Stations 2*, pp.130–3.
26. M. Middlebrook and C. Everitt, *Bomber Command War Diaries* (London: Midland, 1985), p.736.
27. The PRO 802/3/4/5 records of 101 Squadron, AIR 27, give little more than crew names and brief raid reports, but many Jewish-sounding names emerge, such as Corporal G. Cohen and Herscovitz, listed in the appendices above. See Brookes, *Bomber Squadron*, p.227; R. Alexander, *101 Squadron* (London: published privately, 1979), Appendices; and the six volumes of W.R. Chorley, *Bomber Command Losses in World War Two* (London: Midland, 1997–98).
28. Telephone conversation, 27 April 2000.
29. J.A. Davies, *A Leap in the Dark* (London: Leo Cooper, 1994), pp.2–13.
30. *Journal of St Cross College, Oxford* (1997), Record No. 15, pp.40–2, Herscovitz obituary.
31. Davies, *A Leap in the Dark*, p.22.
32. Correspondence and telephone conversation with J.A. Davies, OBE, LLD, August 2000.
33. Newspaper obituary, August 1998, sent to author by J.A. Davies. Unknown source.
34. Letter to author, August 2000.
35. See note 30.
36. B. Lewis, *Aircrew* (London: Cassell, 2000), p.137.
37. Telephone conversation, 27 April 2000.
38. Also referred to by H. Guy Meadows in a letter of November 2000, who says Felix came via Canada as well.
39. This may be 1892478 Flight Sergeant Rudolf King, whose AJEX card states he was killed, according to Alexander, *101 Squadron*, Appendices, on 28 December 1944.
40. Letter to author, November 2000.
41. Brookes, *Bomber Squadron*, p.227.
42. Interview with Flight Sergeant Leslie Temple, 13 May 2000.
43. Interview at his home, 13 May 2000.
44. G. Heilig, *Cry of the Nightjar* (100 Bomber Group Museum Association/City of Norwich Aviation, 1997).
45. Ibid. and interview.
46. Letter from Heilig, living in Austria, 19 May 2000.
47. Letter to author, October 2000.
48. Letter from Queensland, Australia, August 2000.
49. Telephone conversation, November 2000.
50. Letter, October 2000.
51. G. Pynt, *The Australian Jewry Book of Honour* (Sydney: Australian AJEX, 1973), p.213, mentions thirteen airmen named Marks, but it is unclear which one is referred to here.
52. T. Boiten, *Night Airwar* (London: HarperCollins, 1999), p.137.
53. Ibid.
54. Telephone conversation, 1 May 2000. He unfortunately died in 2001.
55. H. Morris, *We Will Remember Them: An Addendum* (London: AJEX 1994), p.26. This is an addendum to his book, *We Will Remember Them: The British Jewry Book of Honour of WW2* (London: Brassey's, 1989).
56. Chorley, *Bomber Command Losses in World War Two*: see entry for casualties on that day.
57. Passport and other documents lent by the family.
58. Letter in AJEX Archives.
59. Flight Sergeant E.R. Brown; Flight Sergeant T. Crane; Pilot Officer P.J. Hyland, who lived in Entre Rios, Argentina; Flight Sergeant J. Hodgson; Flight Sergeant J.T.V. Moore; Flight Sergeant C.E. Smith; Pilot Officer A.W. Tuuri, RCAF.
60. Middlebrook and Everitt, *Bomber Command War Diaries*, p.418.
61. D. Webster, and J. Frankland, *The Strategic Air Offensive Against Germany, 1939–45*, Vol. 2 (London: HMSO, 1961), p.202.
62. Ibid., p.61, the Nuremberg Raid, 30–31 March 1944.

63. Davies, *A Leap in the Dark*, p.6.
64. A. Clayton, *The Enemy is Listening: Story of the Y Service* (London: Cressy, 1993), describes German-speaking Palestinians serving in this field, but fails to mention that they were Jews.
65. P. Leighton-Langer, *The King's Own Loyal Enemy Aliens* (London: Vallentine Mitchell, 2006).
66. Heilig's autobiography.
67. Jack Burston, 'Listening to German Fighter Control', *AJEX Journal*, November 2000, p.13.
68. Letter, 17 May 2000.
69. R. Burns, *The Life and Times of A.D. Blumlein* (London: IEE, 2000), Foreword. The plane crashed at Welsh Bicknor, Ross-on-Wye, and he and his crew are buried at Ross and Whitchurch cemetery (CWGC information).
70. R.V. Jones, *Most Secret War* (London: Hamish Hamilton,1978), Index.
71. J. Leasor, *Green Beach* (London: Heinemann, 1975) tells the whole story, updated by Martin Sugarman in a paper entitled 'Jack Nissenthall: The VC Hero Who Never Was', *Orders and Medals Research Society Journal* (London), Summer 1998, pp.155–65, republished in *Military Advisor* (California), Summer 1998, pp.16–22. See also Chapter 9 in this book.
72. Max Herman Alexander Neuman, born 7 February 1897 in Chelsea, London, son of Herman and Sarah Neuman; served in the Great War; became a Cambridge mathematics don and in September 1942 was summoned to Bletchley Park, where he developed the Colossus, the world's first programmable computer. This was used to break the Lorenz codes, an advanced version of Enigma, used between Hitler and his High Command. A display at Bletchley Park Museum and St John's College, Cambridge, explains his contribution to the war effort. He died in 1984.
73. 101 Squadron Lancasters were coded 'SR'.
74. Telephone conversation with SO comrade Peter Holway of Leeds.
75. Chorley, *Bomber Command Losses in World War Two*, p.82, says it was Lancaster III DV245 SR-S and was over Bremen.
76. Correspondence, October 2000.

Bruneval and St Nazaire: The Extraordinary Story of Commando Peter Nagel

D uring the Second World War it is estimated that about 8,000 or more German and Austrian Jewish refugees – officially labelled as 'Friendly Aliens' by the authorities – served in the British and Allied Forces. After the 'Fifth Column' scares and internment had passed, most were permitted to join the Pioneer Corps and then later the regular services, with a disproportionately high number serving in Special Forces and SOE. These men and women jokingly referred to themselves as 'His Majesty's Most Loyal Enemy Aliens'.[1] One of these was Jewish Commando Peter Nagel.

Peter's justified claim to fame is that he was the only British soldier to go on both the Bruneval and St Nazaire Paratroop/Commando raids in the Second World War.

Peter was born in Berlin on 29 January 1916, the youngest of three children of Moritz ('Morny')[2] and Margarete Nagel (née Rudiger)[3]. Margarete was a Catholic and the marriage was something of a scandal in both families at the time. The family home was in east Lichterfelde, a well-to-do suburb in south-west Berlin. Peter had a sister, Sabina, who survived the war in Italy and later married an Italian, surname Veludari, and her family eventually emigrated to Argentina, where they had one daughter, also called Sabina;[4] an elder brother, Lothar, survived the war too and later travelled east, but no more was heard of him.

Peter's daughter, Jane Jervis,[5] told the author that Peter never really enjoyed his formal education and left school aged 16, as soon as he could. But his reports, dated 1922–26, from the Protestant preparatory school[6] which he attended until aged 11 (the Hansa Vorschule, located in north-west Berlin), still survive in the family's archives. They reveal that Peter appeared to excel in sports and history, but not so much in the more academic subjects[7] – a trait that reveals itself in his later character and development as a passionate and dare-devil individual. He and his brother often had fights in school, standing their ground in the face of verbal and physical anti-Semitism from other German students. Even their principal told them, 'People like you are not wanted in Germany.'[8]

His school reports also show that he passed an examination on 24 March 1926 and was able to proceed to the very famous and traditionally

Humanist Protestant Friedrichs-Werdersches Gymnasium (secondary) school in Berlin, founded in the seventeenth century and the alma mater of many famous Germans including the Bismarcks. How he progressed there, however, is not known. Most intriguing is his Protestant baptismal certificate[9] dated immediately before. The 'conversion' was carried out at the Protestant church of St Johannes in Frohnau, a comfortable north-west Berlin suburb, on 23 March 1926, in order to gain entrance for Peter into the gymnasium. This was the way many German Jews chose to go in order to be able to progress their careers and the prospects for their children in that time. Peter was only 10 years old and clearly had no say in the matter. It must also have been an issue with his mother Margarete, as she was a Catholic. Clearly, however, Morny was very consciously Jewish, as Peter was circumcised soon after he was born, in the ancient Jewish tradition.[10]

When Morny decided to leave Germany, subterfuge had to be used to circumvent the racist anti-Semitic laws and so, in order to fool the Nazis, the family split up. Margarete went to Paris with the children, pretending to go on holiday,[11] and Morny came to Britain on (as told the Nazis) a business trip to Leicester, then a world centre of the woollen knitting industry. Beforehand, he had carefully arranged through his contacts with the distinguished English Wolsey family, well known in the woollen industry, to transfer the family savings through a bogus business deal, so that the Nagels would be able to use the money[12] to begin life again in the UK. During that time, Peter lived in Paris for a while and did all kinds of mainly clerical jobs to earn a living, and Jane still has references he obtained from his French employers.[13] He then made his way to England (probably in 1935 or 1936). But his mother was trapped in Paris and was interned by the French for the duration, probably as an enemy alien.

Meanwhile, Peter's father established a small but very successful factory in Churchgate, Leicester, called Morna Fabrics, and a dress shop-cum-showroom in Soho, London, where many European expatriates were clients. Peter worked with the firm and Jane recalls Peter telling her that Morny made him work at all the 'factory floor' jobs before bringing him into the management – as all good businessmen would do with a son or daughter – to 'learn the trade from the bottom up'.

Peter enlisted in the army at Richborough on 8 March 1940 as a private in the Auxiliary Military Pioneer Corps (AMPC), no. 13081753,[14] and he was sent to No. 3 Centre, 93rd Company at Codford near Salisbury. His address at the time was given as 35 Lowndes Street, London SW1.[15] His religion was given as C. of E., which was very typical, as European Jews in British Forces were encouraged to hide their Jewish background in case of capture by the Nazis.

In a telephone interview with Leicester resident Arthur Warrington,[16] a former wartime Royal Marine who knew Peter in the 1970s, Peter had said he was commissioned into the Royal Engineers[17] from the Pioneer Corps in June 1941. Short (five foot six) and slim, with brown hair and blue eyes,[18] well educated and speaking excellent English as well as French, Peter became an explosives expert, but was very soon head-hunted by MI5 (Department X3) for SOE. He reported to an address at 2 Fitzmaurice Place and here it appears he was 'de-commissioned' to a private again, possibly to protect him as a German Jew should he be captured on an SOE-sponsored raid. He was given the alias 'Walker' and army number 4272711.[19] He was also later known as Private Newman.

At SOE Special Training School (STS) No. 6 on 14 August 1941, Peter Nagel was described as in robust health, cheerful, slight build with fair complexion, and having good English, German and French; his occupation was given as textile designer. He was said to be good at games and fieldcraft but below average as a shot, although good with the Tommy gun and grenade. His knowledge of explosives was very good and he was clearly learning radio skills as his speed was recorded as five words per minute sending and receiving, with very clear and concise report writing. He was mistakenly described as a Protestant but, as described above, many Jews – especially if from enemy countries – hid their identities or were told to attest as non-Jews for obvious reasons. If captured they would have been executed immediately. Further remarks described him as pleasant and enthusiastic, a clear thinker with plenty of self-confidence, quick to grasp instructions (even if complicated), make his own plans and issue orders, but he appeared younger than he was and was thus not automatically looked up to as a leader by other trainees.

At No. 21 STS, Lance Corporal Hall wrote on 19 and 28 August 1941 that Nagel was 'well educated, extremely intelligent, and if not for his youthful appearance and inexperience, might be a good leader ... needs tuition in leadership. Very keen all round, extremely reliable and very courageous ... will be able to work on his own ... would always find a way out ... very good English'. On 4 September: 'He was a leader on an important scheme. He worked out everything perfectly, was very calm all of the time, but his leadership was not acknowledged by his comrades as it should have been. On a few occasions they did not even obey his orders and he was not as firm as he should have been.'

On 5 September 1941, supervisor Lieutenant Colonel Anderson wrote that Nagel had a good sense of humour, was keen at fieldcraft and very good at close combat, having worked very hard, and had a good knowledge of all the holds: very good at pistols, Tommy gun, Bren and Browning and got 92 per cent in the explosives test, albeit a bit impetuous. His Morse was six words per minute and improving, and in map reading he achieved 74 per cent; he could also ride a bicycle. Again it was noted that although cheerful and competent, it was doubtful he would make a good leader as he was impetuous and did not take a strong enough line when delegating duties to others – but would do well on his own.

In contrast, however, in mid-October, Corporal Donaldson at STS 6 wrote: 'Nagel does not impress me very much. He is effeminate in his way of talking and in his bearing generally and he seems to me to have much too high an opinion of himself ... he likes to be more English than the English themselves ... also insolent and undisciplined. His attitude on life is said to be largely due to his accident in Manchester.'[20] Perhaps Donaldson had a problem with Jews.

On 2 January 1942, Peter was returned to his unit (93rd Pioneer Corps), then at the drill hall, Redruth, having been temporarily training with the Commandos. Whilst at STS 44, a trainer, Lance Corporal Rees, had written on 3 January:

> Nagel is a socially accomplished and highly intelligent individual. By birth he is a Reichsdeutscher, by conviction a European, ideologically an anarchist, which feeds his individualism ... an intelligent sense of responsibility tempers his behaviour. He is also an inveterate and successful womaniser ... he kicks hard and consciously against injustice without caring about the [pin]pricks ... he has often found himself up against the authorities during the recent trouble here,[21] but always he has stood out and maintained his position stubbornly. He has an explosive enthusiasm and would be willing to do any job where he could work alone and use his intelligence. He has relations all over Europe including an uncle in business in Marseilles, a sister in Biarritz and a mother in Paris. He would be only too ready ... to go to France for us, where he could easily get a job in his uncle's business to serve as a cover (his uncle is violently Anglophile and Germanophobe). With Opoczinski[22] he was one of the few who understood the reasonableness of sending the group back to the Pioneer Corps, although for himself ... it would probably be a greater blow than for any of the others, for as a Reichsdeutscher he has hardly any chance of transfer from the Pioneer Corps. If it is not intended to use him in the organisation I feel that his claim for transfer to the RAF or Merchant Navy, should be very strongly backed by us.

On 6 January 1942, supervisor Major Butler at STS 44 wrote that Peter was very good all round. Then in February came Bruneval.

11.1 The 1977 Bruneval reunion with left to right, General Frost, Peter Nagel and Sgt Cox (with white hair).

11.2 Peter Nagel just before the Bruneval Raid.

The Bruneval Raid

The Bruneval Raid (Operation Biting) was a Combined Operations attack on the German radar station on the cliffs at Bruneval, fifteen miles north-east of Le Havre on the French coast, to capture components of a Wurzberg radar. Study of the radar would then enable the RAF to find countermeasures to the device which guided German bombers to targets in Britain. The raid used elements of the new 1st Parachute Brigade (part of 1st Airborne Division), namely 'C' Company, 2nd Battalion, the Parachute Regiment (120 men) led by Major (post-war General) John Frost – later of Arnhem Bridge fame. With them would go Flight Sergeant C.W. Cox, an RAF radar expert, to dismantle the required pieces to be 'pinched'. Much needed, however, was a Commando-trained German-speaking interpreter to interrogate German prisoners; Peter Nagel was detached from No. 2 Commando[23] and chosen for this role. He was given the name 'Newman'.

M.R.D. Foot [24] described Peter as 'a Sudetan German who was to confuse the enemy by shouting orders and counter orders in the dark'. This is confirmed in a letter from P.M. Lee of the Historical Sub-Committee of the Special Forces Club on 16 October 1990[25] to Jack Lennard of Hull AJEX. There is, however, no evidence that this 'shouting' ruse was actually used, and Foot is mistaken, as Peter was not a Sudetan.

One wet, cold day, into a damp hut at Tilshead (on Salisbury Plain), the CSM of 'C' Company brought before Major Frost 'a small but handsome man, dressed as a private soldier in the Pioneer Corps', detailed to report to the CO as German interpreter for a special mission. He came from Combined Operations HQ via 1st Airborne Division HQ at Syrancote House (near Netheravon) and was 'a German Jew'[26] called 'Private Newman'.[27] Only Frost, Captain John Ross (Second in Command) and Sergeant Major Strachan were to know his true nationality in case he should be captured. Frost studied Newman carefully, noting his many good points: toughness, intelligence, humour; he spoke fluent English and had lived in Paris, Vienna, London, Budapest, New York as well as Berlin. Given fears about German agents infiltrating refugee communities, Frost felt very uneasy about 'having a Hun on the strength [of his command]'.[28] Frost actually says in his book that the name and number they gave 'Newman' corresponded to that of a real soldier who had deserted between the wars. So when Peter was later taken POW at St Nazaire, the Germans cross-referenced his details with the Red Cross and were satisfied he was just 'an ordinary' British soldier. This almost certainly saved his life.

Next day the Company left for Scotland by train, to Inverary on Loch Fyne, and were comfortably billeted on board the ship HMS *Prins Albert*, but they spent many uncomfortable and wet days and nights practising embarking and disembarking from landing craft with the Royal Navy – who had no idea they were Paratroops (they had been ordered to remove their parachute wings badges). Lord Mountbatten, CO of Combined Operations, came to inspect them and took Frost aside and asked if he had any worries. Frost said he was unhappy about Newman, so Mountbatten sent for him at once. Mountbatten subjected Peter to what Frost admiringly considered to be a tremendous barrage in absolutely fluent German, standing him in front of the desk and shouting at him. Peter answered quietly and smoothly, they shook hands and then Peter was dismissed. The admiral turned to Frost and said 'Take him along; you won't regret it for he is bound to be very useful. I judge him to be brave and intelligent. After all, he risks far more than you do[29] and of course he would never have been attached to you if he had not passed security on every count.' Peter himself remembers Lord Louis's interrogation on the ship as a pleasant and gentlemanly affair, and thought the admiral utterly charming.[30]

Next day the *Prins Albert* sailed to Gourock and from there 'C' Company returned by train to Tilshead, arriving on 14 February. Here they made more training jumps,[31] travelled to and from the south coast to train on the MGBs (Motor Gun Boats), and were inspected by General 'Boy' Browning, CO of all Airborne Forces. None of the men knew what was in store for them and four times the raid was postponed by bad weather. But they suspected something important, as they had been practising on a mock-up of buildings near cliffs (in fact a mock-up of the whole Bruneval site) at Alton Friars.[32]

On the eve of the raid, the men went to RAF Thruxton, just west of Andover in Wiltshire, and sat waiting for the take-off. Here Peter was ordered to join Frost, Ross and Strachan as they passed around the small groups of relaxed men, chatting and joking to them in turn as they sat on the edge of the aerodrome on a glorious evening, checking their gear, some singing and brewing tea, waiting for zero hour.

The raiders were dropped by parachute from twelve Whitley V bombers of 51 Squadron,[33] on the night of 27 February 1942. There are books describing the raid but put simply, when the Paras landed virtually dead on target and unopposed, on the snow-covered cliff area, Peter was with Frost's Hardy section; the Company had been divided into sections to deal with planned, specific tasks and included two other Jewish participants, Lieutenant Peter Naumoff, commanding Drake section, and Parachute Lieutenant Dr Abe Baker, commanding the medical team waiting offshore to be called in to take off the raiders after the operation was completed.

Frost's five-man team, including Peter, rushed for the château (code-named 'Lone House'), where they discovered the door wide open. Blowing his whistle, Frost led the charge inside where they heard shooting from upstairs. Here a German was firing at the other sections and he was killed immediately. Leaving the house, the section then ran to the radar pit some yards away, which had already been secured, and Peter was ordered to question the badly-shaken German prisoner who had been taken there. He readily said he belonged to the Luftwaffe Communications Regiment. Radar expert Cox (later awarded the MM) then tore aside a thick, black rubber curtain that shielded the radar set and called to Peter, 'Hey Peter, this thing's still hot. Ask the Jerry if he was tracking our aircraft as we came in.'[34] The German confirmed this in answer to Peter's question.

Whilst the fighting was continuing, Peter and a comrade saw a German run towards the edge of the cliff and dive for cover on a ledge. One of the veterans, whose voice was on the soundtrack of the 1982 MOD film reconstruction of the raid, said: 'We had a young German with us as interpreter' and he (Peter) 'coaxed this German back onto the cliff top and questioned him'.[35] He wore a blue uniform and was a radar operator. 'Even if he was a bloody cleaner, he must know something', says Peter's voice, clearly recognizable with the slight German accent in the commentary. When interviewed in a film made by Yorkshire Television (YTV) in December 1976 and broadcast in January 1977 for the thirty-seventh anniversary of the raid, Peter described on camera, with his name prominently displayed as a subtitle, what happened. The German was pulled back up the cliff face and 'I tore the swastika badge from his uniform.' 'Why?' asked the interviewer. 'For my personal satisfaction', smiled Peter. 'Then I started to interrogate him about the number of German troops and their positions – we only had some information till then – and I thought he was lying. So I shook him by his lapels and said so, and my comrade said we should kill him. But I said no as we had to have prisoners and he was very young and started to cry and was shaking with fear, so I said we should take him along.' And they did.

As the Germans in the area began to respond, resistance increased, so having got what they had come for, and with the prisoners in tow under Peter's guard, the Paras made their way to the pick-up. However, they discovered some Germans in a trench defending the route to the rendezvous beach and a firefight broke out. Eventually the Para officer commanding the group decided on a frontal charge. Peter comments on the voiceover: 'They had never seen such savages [as us]; they were absolutely fabulous ... Grenades were thrown into the trenches and we quickly took more prisoners.'[36] In three hours it was all over.

The operation was a great success and the Royal Navy, with some army units for cover, picked up virtually all of the raiders; only two were killed and six wounded, with eight captured. Five Germans were killed and three important prisoners – including the technician – were taken. It was the first Battle Honour of the Parachute Regiment and Peter Nagel was proud to have taken part. General Browning's report stated[37] that Peter's 'knowledge of the German language and of the psychology of the Germans, proved of great assistance'.

The moving epilogue occurred in December 1976, when Professor R.V. Jones (the Government's chief radar expert throughout the war and head of the Air Ministry Scientific Intelligence Unit; he had conceived the raid) attended a reunion of the Bruneval Raid participants[38] in connection with the Yorkshire Television documentary.[39] Here he met some of the few survivors (many had been killed later in the war):

> [including one] whose expert knowledge and unusual bravery I had hardly till then appreciated, Peter Nagel ... he had volunteered and ... even more than Cox, perhaps, he was in a specially dangerous position if captured as the Germans would have had no mercy if they had discovered his origin; but he went, as Private Newman, and without his cool-headedness we might not have brought back the radar prisoner... after the programme that gallant man came quietly up to me and said, 'We would like you to know that if you had asked us, we would have gone on another hundred raids.'

The raid on Bruneval in which Peter played so significant a part was hugely important. Cribbing how the German radar worked saved thousands of civilian lives in Britain, as well as thousands of Bomber Command personnel, and Allied troops on the D-Day landings. It was also a huge morale boost for the Allies during the very darkest days of the war. Lord Mountbatten stated in the film that at the same time the raid also depressed morale in Germany; apparently General Student, founder of the German Paras, saw the film on German television, wrote to Mountbatten, and said he was in Hitler's HQ when news of the raid reached him. The Führer was incandescent with rage.

For his part in the raid, on the occasion of the fortieth anniversary of the Bruneval Operation, Peter received a Diplôme d'Honneur signed by France's President Mitterand, and HM Queen Elizabeth, dated 20 June 1982.[40]

St Nazaire

Not thirty days after Bruneval, on the night of 28 March 1942, Peter was volunteering again from No. 2 Commando, this time on the equally famous St Nazaire raid in Brittany.[41] He was taken along on the express orders of Mountbatten, because 'he knew how to deal with the

Germans'.[42] This raid was another Combined Operations effort, Operation Chariot, with an RAF bombardment followed by a naval and seaborne Commando attack. The aim was to destroy the great Normandy dry dock, so neutralizing the great German battleship sea-raider *Tirpitz* by depriving her of repair facilities within striking distance of Allied Atlantic convoys. In addition, damage would be done to the submarine pens, so reducing the U-boat menace.

Peter was on board the only MGB (Motor Gun Boat 314) which took part, with the HQ Company, consisting of Commander Ryder (the naval commander) and Colonel Newman (the army No. 2 Commando commander), both of whom later received the VC. Among those with Peter were also Privates Murdoch and Kelly, machine gunners and – like Peter – bodyguards to Colonel Newman; Captain Stanley Day (awarded an MC), the adjutant to Colonel Newman; Sergeant Steel with the all-important special radio; Lance Corporal J. Harrington (awarded an MM); and Captain A. Terry, the War Office representative (awarded an MC). As the task force of armed MLs (Motor Launches) and destroyers stealthily approached the Loire estuary on the final run up to the harbour targets, MGB 314 was in the van at the tip of the spear.[43] All hell broke loose from German defences and the British ships replied with all guns blazing.

Peter was renamed 'Walker' for this raid as the name 'Newman' (used at Bruneval) would have confused him with the raid commander, whose personal German- and French-speaking interrogator he was, and beside whom he was ordered to stay throughout the raid as special assistant.[44]

What follows is a first-hand account of the raid as Peter saw it, alternating with descriptions from the book sources. Peter wrote his own short version in the first person, in French, possibly for a French radio or television broadcast in France, or possibly for a BBC Radio French language broadcast – we do not know; it is not dated and is in the private collection of his daughter Jane Jervis, who translated it for this article.

> I belonged to No. 2 Commando and was the German and French interpreter and also one of the bodyguards for the officers commanding the operation. I was therefore with Colonel Newman in the gunboat which headed up the convoy to St Nazaire. It was a beautiful Spring night and the waters of the port were as calm as a lake. We glided slowly towards our objective, passing a German ship guarding the entrance to the port. I could see German sailors staring at us and the tension was unbearable. My job was to be on the bridge, helping to operate a machine gun. We waited for the order to open fire; we wondered how much longer the Germans would let us continue without resistance
>
> Suddenly they began firing. I had never seen anything like it.

The tracer bullets crossed over one another, forming a giant fire-work display. The enemy anti-aircraft guns, installed on the roofs, fired down upon us at point blank range. My gunner fired without stopping at the enemy searchlights that were sweeping the waters of the port. The firing was so intense that nobody knew exactly what was going on. Several of our launches were hit and as they were made only of wood and filled to the brim with petrol, they xploded. I then saw the destroyer *Campbeltown* charge into the lock gates with such speed that it seemed to jump like a horse leaping over a hedge! The violence of the shock threw up the stern and then the bow smashed into the gates – exactly as was planned.

This was at 1.34 a.m., as described on page 41 of C.E. Lucas-Phillips's book, *The Greatest Raid of All* (London: Pan, 1958, 2000).

My gunner, Private Kelly, was wounded and I took over the gun; after a few minutes we landed and despite his wounds, Kelly had got ashore (behind me). I tried to put him back aboard but he would not hear of it; he wanted to come with us. I wanted so much to tell his parents of his bravery, and I am sure he may have been killed as I never heard from him again. If he had got back on board he would have seen England again.

Kelly was tragically later shot between the eyes and died alongside Colonel Newman (Lucas-Phillips, *Greatest Raid*, p.215). Prior to disembarking the young Kelly had been caught donning his kilt by Colonel Newman, a matter of honour for the young Scotsman, and with a boyish, guilty look he had said, 'Can I, Sir?' Smiling, Newman agreed, saying, 'All right, if you think it will make you fight better that way.' The colonel was later glad he had granted what was a last wish to this courageous soldier (Lucas-Phillips, *Greatest Raid*, p.124[45]).

Surrounded by a blazing inferno of gunfire, Peter's MGB docked at a wooden jetty in the Old Harbour Entrance that led into the Bassin de St Nazaire, just to the west of the dry dock main target.[46] Just prior to this, Ryder and Newman had a friendly argument as to whether Ryder should first sink a nearby enemy boat or disembark Newman. Newman insisted that Ryder's job was to get him and his men ashore at once. Ryder gave way and they shook hands, wishing each other luck; they were not to meet again for three years. Then Peter, the colonel and his party, in their rubber-soled Commando boots, 'armed to the teeth, sprang over the side and away up the steps like young goats' – Murdoch and Kelly preceding the colonel (Lucas-Phillips, *Greatest Raid*, p.180 and passim). They then charged at the double,[47] unseen in the shadows, along a narrow road to a small bridge – with heavy fire pouring above their heads – near which was a building to be used as Colonel Newman's battle-raid HQ. Here they met fierce resistance and so waited for reinforcements to arrive:

> Our group hurled itself into action taking up positions on the dock side. Across the basin we could see the enormous mass of the concrete wall (submarine pens) with several submarines moored along its length. We were now in the heart of the battle as we awaited the runners with information on how the demolition groups were getting on with their tasks.

On trying to enter the building that he had chosen as HQ, Newman bumped helmets with a German as he rounded a corner, instinctively saying sorry. The astonished German thrust up his hands in surrender. Terry questioned the prisoner in German and they were all amazed to find that this building was in fact the German HQ. At that moment they came under heavy fire from a German minesweeper in the basin, and sharply took cover.

> On my right an officer fell, and I knew he was mortally wounded, but he refused to let anyone fetch help and ordered his group to continue the attack without preoccupying themselves with him. The Germans meanwhile were everywhere, running in all directions. All the same we managed to take some prisoners. We saw some trying to hide but fired on every shadow that moved and on the blockhouse on the other side of the dock. But they spotted us and the situation became more alarming. One of our prisoners took advantage of the situation and escaped into an anti-aircraft shelter. We shelled it with grenades (there must have been others sheltering in there) but at that moment I was struck by shrapnel in my arms and legs. My arms hurt me so much I could not continue my duties and Colonel Newman ordered me back to the gun boat. But as I headed back to where I thought the boat may be, I was surrounded by Germans screaming at me. Suddenly, one jumped out, pistol in hand; I fired and he disappeared. At the same time one of our launches exploded near the Old Mole and I realised our way back was now cut off.

Other Germans were no more than twenty yards away from Newman's group and lobbing grenades at them. Jovially unruffled, the colonel merely moved his team to shelter behind a shed. Having unsuccessfully tried to contact Ryder on the special radio, about re-embarking, Newman realized he must give the order to withdraw using the rain rockets (signal flares), but these had been lost at sea.

> I thus tried to rejoin Colonel Newman to let him know that nobody in this area had been able to either land or re-embark, and then,

distracted, accidentally ran into a barbed wire barrier, and was caught like a rabbit in a trap. I disentangled myself and got back to my group, which had been calmly continuing the fight. The Germans, however, were just the opposite and running round in all directions and shouting in confusion and panic. One of them, badly wounded, cried out 'For the Führer! For the Führer!' I reported to Col. Newman what I had found but he seemed already aware of the situation.

The battle raged on for hours with the Commandos holding their own against numerically superior German forces, for whom reinforcements were arriving with increasing speed. About a hundred men, many wounded, had by now rallied to Colonel Newman and, albeit radiating confidence in front of his men, he knew that with rescue from the sea now no longer possible, and the major objective achieved, the men would have to fight their way out of the town to make ultimately for Spain, 1,000 miles away (as had been envisaged in such an event) via a bridge over the southern part of the Bassin de St Nazaire dock, using 'fire and movement' tactics. Calmly, and returning effective fire at the more panicky Germans, the colonel's group moved forward, Peter with them, to both break out into the relatively safer countryside and also move away from the hidden explosives of the *Campbeltown*:

> The decision was made for us to risk everything and to make a passage across the German lines and head for the countryside. From there on it would be every man for himself ... German resistance became increasingly effective and our fire weaker; we were short of ammunition, having only what we could carry.
>
> [Lucas-Phillips, *Greatest Raid*, pp.216–27.]

About 3 a.m., the Commandos defiantly dashed through the narrow dock streets, with their wounded, many of them armed only with pistols, being fired on from windows and street corners, keeping to the shadows, halting from time to time to gather together, using covering fire, overcoming pockets of resistance, allowing stragglers to catch up, some of the lame courageously dropping out, determined not to hold the others up, with Newman calmly calling, 'Get on lads! Get on!' Light from fires, together with a bright moon overhead, suffused the area with a dim, phantom radiance.[48] The crack of guns alternated with grenade bursts and shouting voices, as Colonel Newman inspired his men forward, cracking jokes, directing fire, never taking cover.

Now they had reached the exposed Old Town Place, which had to be crossed to reach the girdered escape bridge now only seventy yards away. The whole area was covered by German machine-gun fire. 'Away you go lads', called Newman, leading the way, and they were off, with enemy bullets sparking off steel, a stirring, olden-times charge into the heart of the Germans, sending them reeling.

However, with ever-lower ammunition and with German armoured cars appearing at the last minute, and the wounded more and more in distress, and increasingly surrounded, the trap slowly closed and most of the Commandos had to stop and shelter in local cellars. From the cellars, most were taken POW early next morning.

> As dawn broke, I tried to cross the bridge [known now as the 'Bridge of Memories' – see Lucas-Phillips, *Greatest Raid*, pp.25, 220–1] but at each attempt German machine gun cross-fire forced me to retreat. I therefore decided to hide in a warehouse between some sacks of cement. [Lucas Phillips, *Greatest Raid*, pp.226–7.] I had seen some of my comrades do the same and I hoped to find some French workmen and get some working clothes, and under this disguise get out into the countryside.
>
> I have never known a moment of depression as bad as this in my whole life; I could already imagine myself ending up in a concentration camp. I knew *Campbeltown* should have exploded three hours after the beginning of the raid and nothing had happened. There I was crouching in my hole, counting the minutes, cursing that so much sweat and blood had been spilt to achieve nothing. The Germans continued shrieking and shouting till sunrise. After a few hours a German patrol started firing into my hiding place and next moment I found myself pushed with my back against a wall alongside several comrades. We were searched right down to our underclothes. I could gather from their conversation that they wanted to shoot us, but at that moment an older German sergeant came along and sent us under close guard to a boat moored several metres away. Our wounds were dressed and then suddenly an enormous explosion occurred as *Campbeltown* went up! The lock gates vaulted into the air at 10.30 a.m. The raid had been a success!

Prisoner of War

Thus Peter was captured (for some reason Pioneer Corps records show Peter as transferred to the Royal Fusiliers in October 1943 even though he was already a POW[49]). He had been wounded by a hand grenade[50] in his arms, back and legs and, unable to get away on a boat or overland, was captured just a few minutes before HMS *Campbeltown* blew up. Sadly his father received a letter from the War Office, via the King, stating Peter was 'Missing presumed dead in action'.[51]

After being gathered on one of the quays, the British POWs, in torn and blood-stained uniforms, unshaven, limping and many bandaged, were taken to La Baule emergency hospital on a very uncomfortable old French bus, under heavy guard, a few miles to the west, with many other wounded. It was located in a villa near the sea.[52] Peter had a cursory interrogation and then was moved by truck on a journey of several hours, to another hospital at Rennes,[53] and thence to Marlag und Milag Nord (actually a German Merchant Navy and Marines POW camp at Wester-timke, near Bremen, Germany) by cattle truck. Here he was interrogated two or three times more but gave only name, rank and number.

Peter told his daughter Jane that the Nazis were suspicious of his slight 'non-English' accent, but his mates covered for him and said that he came from Leicester and 'they all talked a bit like that up there'. He was also quizzed about his dental fillings and told the Germans that his dentist was a Pole who used the continental style; this explanation was almost certainly given as a ruse to Peter by his British SOE trainers, who knew the Nazis used this technique to try and pick out German and other Jewish refugees serving in the Allied Forces. The Nazis even gave him an arithmetic test, knowing that one tends to calculate and speak arithmetic in one's mother tongue, and also write the digit seven with a cross through – another trick to pick out Jewish fighters not from the UK – but he was quick enough to successfully pass himself off as a true Brit.

Peter remained with an organized POW party commanded by a colonel (perhaps it was Colonel Newman?). Whilst at Marlag he and some comrades tried to escape by tunnel but it was discovered. As a result Peter was then sent to Sandbostel Camp (Stalag 10 B) between Bremen and Hamburg for one month, then returned briefly to Marlag, and went finally to Stalag VIIIB at Lamsdorf in Silesia.[54]

From September 1942 he worked in a sugar beet factory, befriending some Czech youths who were engaged in sabotage and who later were probably – according to Peter – caught and liquidated by the Nazis. From here he was sent to work in a clothing factory at Jagerndorf camp,[55] where he met a Czech girl and approached her about organizing acts of Re-sistance. However, she dissuaded him, saying that the locals were pro-German, and that her family were already in prison and she could not put them in further peril. The manager was very pro-Nazi and for the next nine months Peter lived in the shadow of discovery, until as punishment – probably for being 'difficult' – he was sent to a bleak forestry camp in the mountains. Here he organized others to carry out minor sabotage such as damaging machinery, but already under suspicion and involved in a strike, he was returned to Lamsdorf camp.

At Lamsdorf, totally undaunted, he again became involved with the Escape Committee and, together with an RAF pilot, escaped to Jagerndorf using forged French workers papers. Here he contacted the Czech girl he had met in the clothing factory, and from her they obtained clothing. They also had some idea about which route to take across Austria from a British major who had already escaped to Italy and Yugoslavia but been recaptured in Austria.

Leaving the camp, they got to Klagenfurt in Austria within thirty-six hours, arriving on a very wet and dark night about 20 June 1944, braving the 9 p.m. curfew, after which the Germans were allowed to shoot on sight. They decided to dodge patrols and make for the railway station at Assling, but here they were caught by the military police and taken to Gestapo HQ in Klagenfurt, still pretending to be French workers. They were sent to Landeck camp and guarded by an Austrian Alpine Regiment. They kept to their story that they had stolen the clothing and were put in solitary confinement. From here they were sent to yet another camp at Pongau, and finally back to Lamsdorf. Peter testified in his post-war debrief that they had not been ill-treated at any time.

At Lamsdorf, Peter befriended a New Zealander, Sergeant Major Herd, who got him transferred after six weeks, to assist him at a hospital in Nuremburg. En route, Peter said he was shocked to witness a large column of civilian prisoners – Russians, Poles and Hungarians – being herded on a horrific forced march by the Germans, who shot several of them in cold blood every few hundred yards. After a few weeks, Peter was again shifted, this time to Moosburg camp, near Munich, where they were finally liberated by the American forces in the spring of 1945.

Peter was awarded the War Medal and 1939–45 Star.

Post-War

After the war, Peter's record shows he was in the Royal Northumberland Fusiliers, attached to the Durham Light Infantry (DLI) – from 18 June 1945 until 23 May 1946 – from where he was demobbed. But his 'Soldier's Release Book'[56] reveals that he worked for some time at German POW Work Camp 248, Cinderfield Lane, Norton, near Chesterfield, since demolished. His CO's reference states 'I have only known Nagel for one month. He has a very good appearance and has always done his job very well and is diligent. He is a most willing worker, sober and honest.'

Peter returned to Leicester, and his mother was able to rejoin the family there.[57] She became a British citizen in August 1946.[58] In the early 1940s, Peter had met Muriel Phyllis Owen,[59] a WAAF sergeant, and after he became naturalized[60] they married in a registry office in November 1946 at Barrow upon Soar, Leicestershire; their daughter, Jane Sabina, was born on 5 June 1949 in Leicester.

Before the war, Muriel attended the Froebel College of Teacher Training

and taught primary school children with the then revolutionary methods of play-centred learning, later taken up worldwide. Though quiet
and reserved, she shared Peter's pro-democratic and anti-Nazi political
views and was very committed to Women's Rights – wearing trousers and
smoking at a time when it was considered shocking for women to do so.
Jane was brought up impressed by both parents on the need to exercise
the right to vote – 'good men and women died to give you the vote' – a
message she has passed on to her family. In 1973 or 1974, Peter and
Muriel divorced and Muriel continued to live in the family home
at Waltham-on-the-Wolds. She died on 9 November 1975 in Leicester
following cancer of the pharynx; Peter had cared for her right to the end,
despite their divorce. Her ashes are scattered in Hutcliffe Gardens in
Sheffield, near to those of Daisy Jervis, who was Jane's mother-in-law.

Jane studied psychology at Leeds University, where she met a dental
student, Richard Leonard Jervis, who was studying at Leeds Dental
School. Jane and Richard married in November 1972 and followed their
respective careers of primary teaching and dentistry. Their only child,
Adrian Martin, was born in 1978 when they were living in Melbourne.
They returned to the UK in 1980 and have since lived in Leicester.[61]

Morny handed the business over to Peter in the late 1950s. The
London showroom was closed down and the business sold to Courtaulds,
makers of the new synthetic yarns, with Peter kept on as senior manager. This was the 1960s, boom-time for knitted synthetic fabrics. Business expanded and the factory moved to modern premises in Sandhurst
Street, and then Kenilworth Drive in Oadby; at one time Peter ran three
factories. He was the creative force, full of new ideas and practical business know-how acquired from experience in the more traditional knitting
trade. His PA, Peggy Snowdon, was a great organizer and provided
excellent support. Between 1950 and 1962, Peter lived in Thorpe
Satchville, then the family moved to Waltham-on-the-Wolds in 1962.[62]

At one stage after his divorce, during the late 1970s, Peter lived for
part of the time in a small flat at Elizabeth Court, Long Street, Wigston
Magna. Here he met Arthur Warrington, the caretaker, with whom Peter
became friendly as they had both seen service in the Second World War.
At this time Peter lived alone.[63] In his late fifties, he married a Yugoslav
woman, but soon afterwards she left him to go to America, which greatly
upset Peter.

Often after work, Peter invited Arthur into his flat for a glass of whisky
and they would talk about old times. Arthur said Peter told him he had
been on other Commando raids into France that were not on record, and
described Peter as an unbelievably brave 'little Jew-boy' (using the passé
pejorative term describing Jews, commonly used by some gentiles who
should know better). Peter said often that although an officer to begin

with, he had never received officers' pay.[64] Arthur also recalls that Peter was openly proud of his Jewish heritage. Despite the smallness of this particular flat it had a relatively generous area given over to his collection of religious icons and also what appeared to Arthur to be a Chanuka candelabra, because of its large size (it was actually a large pair of double-branched silver candlesticks of sentimental value, possibly brought from Germany, polished up by Jane as a child, then by Peter).

At one point there was an arson attempt on the old factory, possibly by a disgruntled employee but it may have been racially motivated. One evening, after staying late at work, Peter was attacked by a group of young muggers as he went to his car, but they were apparently shocked by his swift Commando-style and aggressive response, and they soon ran off, much to the delight of Peter's friends and staff on hearing the story from the police.

Peter retired in September 1979 but sadly fell ill with an aggressive form of skin cancer in the early 1980s, and he died of a brain tumour on 25 September 1983, aged only 67. Whilst he was ill, Ray Holt, a 2 Para veteran, wrote to Peter not long before he died, asking him if he would join the 2 Para veterans again at the coming reunion at Grantham, saying, '2 Para hold you in great respect for the risk you took at Bruneval and we would dearly like to make a little presentation to you.'[65] Sadly Peter had to reply that he was too ill, and when the veterans finally went to visit him later in the year, to award him a Paratrooper statuette (symbolizing the Bruneval Drop), he was too sedated to understand what was happening. For years Jane could not bear to look at the gift his comrades gave him, but today it has pride of place in her lounge. It is inscribed: 'Presented to/ Peter Nagel/ From/ His Comrades of the 2nd Battalion/ The Parachute Regiment./ A Brave Man and Good Friend.' As Jane has remarked, that says it all.

Peter was cremated on 30 September 1983 and his ashes were scattered in the Glade woodland area at Gilroes cemetery.[66] He had remained a member of the 2nd Paratroop Association[67] and several veterans attended his funeral, where they placed a Union Jack flag on his coffin.[68] His obituary[69] appeared in the *Leicester Mercury* on 28 September 1983 (page 5), describing him as a local war hero and showing a partially blurred photo.

Everyone who knew Peter in Leicester liked and admired him. Both he and Muriel were outstandingly generous, always ready to help others out. They were always sympathetic to fellow refugees; among their closest friends was a family of escapees from communist Ukraine (this particular family emigrated to Melbourne Australia, where Jane later remade contact). In the 1950s there were Jewish friends in London and friends amongst the local town of Melton Mowbray's large Polish community.

Jane has childhood memories of the 'Polski' shop where her parents drank real coffee and chatted before buying European food that reminded Peter of his roots – salami, *wurst* (sausages), gherkins, poppy-seed bread and, of course, *kuchen*. Peter was very modest and rarely spoke to anyone about his incredible war story, including to his daughter Jane, who has only recently really discovered just what he did. His small stature belied his incredible bravery. Jane described him as 'impulsive, always challenging authority, and passionate about whatever he did'.[70] This is certainly borne out by both his SOE training reports and his volunteering to fight with the most daring of units in the most dangerous of circumstances – Special Forces.

Although he had no formal link with the local Jewish Community, he had many Jewish friends and was always proud of his Jewish roots, as is his daughter. Jane described him as having a high moral code, due to his Jewish upbringing, to which he stuck all his life. She once asked him, when she was quite young, if he believed in God, but he said, 'Not after the Holocaust.'

Peter Nagel was one of a great but little known part of the Jewish 'Hall of Fame' of the war period, an unsung hero, immensely courageous and daring, of whom we may be justly proud.

Acknowledgements

I would particularly like to thank Jane Jervis, Peter Nagel's daughter, for all her patience and trust, and for supplying me not only with a large amount of family history but the amazing and never published account of Peter's experience on the St Nazaire Raid – 'The Greatest Raid of All'.

Notes

1. See, among others, these superb books: Helen Fry, *The King's Most Loyal Enemy Aliens* (London: Sutton, 2007); Peter Leighton-Langer, *The King's Own Loyal Enemy Aliens* (London: Vallentine Mitchell, 2006); also Norman Bentwich, *I Understand the Risks* (London: Gollancz, 1950). Note the excellent bibliographies in these books.
2. Moritz was born in Stanislau, Poland (now the Ukraine) in the Austro-Hungarian Empire, on 22 January 1878. The town always had a large Jewish population. A relative of Moritz – perhaps his uncle David – had emigrated to the USA before the war and was also in the clothing industry; the Jewish Nagel family thus survives in the USA to this day.
3. Born 1 March 1883 in Berlin.
4. Sabina (junior) married a Uruguayan, divorced and had one son, and later moved to Canada.
5. Telephone calls and email correspondence with Jane Jervis in Leicester, July 2008.
6. Jane has some of these prep school reports; copies in AJEX Museum.
7. Thanks to neighbours Astrid and Barbara of Hackney for help in translation.

8. Email from daughter Jane Jervis.
9. Copy with Jane Jervis and in AJEX Archives.
10. Email from Jane Jervis.
11. Their French ID card numbered 34-AE52065 is dated 1935, with a note of visits from Paris to England in 1934, 1935 and 1936; in possession of Jane Jervis and copy at the AJEX Museum.
12. The anti-Semitic laws then permitted Jews to take only tiny amounts of money out of Germany.
13. Copies in the AJEX Museum files. He worked as a buyer for Willy Rosambert and Zeman-Gourbaud, Paris Department Stores.
14. Pioneer Corps (PC) records, with thanks to Lieutenant Colonel John Starling of the PC Museum and Records. However, Jane Jervis's records show army no. 4279870 and his rank as fusilier. In fact Jane has a total of seven British Army ID tags for Peter (Nagel), two grey and five red; two say C. of E., four say Protestant and one is illegible. One grey and one red say 'Walker 4272711'.
15. TNA SOE file HS9 1084, with thanks to Howard Davies of TNA.
16. 11 May 2008.
17. Arthur could be confusing this with the Royal Northumberland Fusiliers.
18. AB64 Soldier's Service Book, copy in the AJEX Archives.
19. TNA HS9 1084 says 427211, but this is an error.
20. Nothing further is known about this.
21. Unrest among the ranks was possibly due to the Jews not being employed properly in Special Forces, for which they had been training; however, this failure to use the Jewish fighters soon changed.
22. Sergeant Abraham Opoczinski, aka Adam Orr, another famous Jewish Commando who was in the famous Small Scale Raiding Force (SSRF/SOE) and sadly killed in action later in April 1945.
23. In TNA HS4 Czech papers on SOE, a typed document was discovered by chance by the author in May 2008, headed 'Pte Peter Walker', stating that he was in No. 2 Commando and telling the story of Peter's time as a POW. It has clearly been misfiled or it is here due to the Czech connection in the story of him as a POW.
24. *SOE in France* (London: Frank Cass, 2004), p.166.
25. Lee was himself formerly of SOE; he said Newman passed 'through his hands' and he had 'concocted a cover story for him before going on the Bruneval Raid', adding Nagel/Newman 'was very brave'. Letter in Bruneval file of AJEX Jewish Military Museum Archives. Lee says in his letter that he carried on a coded correspondence with Peter when he was in a POW camp and then heard – mistakenly – that he had 'died of pneumonia'.
26. Major General John Frost, *A Drop too Many* (London: Buchan and Enright, 1982), p.42.
27. See G. Millar, *The Bruneval Raid* (London: Cassell, 1974), passim. Frost had been warned some days earlier that Peter was coming, by General Browning's Liaison Officer with Colonel Frost, Major Peter Bromley-Martin, saying 'I don't think I should tell you about Newman yet.'
28. From his post-raid account, quoted by Millar in his book.
29. On account of him being German and Jewish.
30. Personal interview with Peter Nagel, quoted in Millar's references; Millar met Peter before writing his earlier (Bodley Head) version of his book, and describes him on page 10 as 'no more like a private soldier now than then, but the most fascinating of companions'.
31. Peter earned his Parachute Wings in February 1942 (Army AB64, in collection of Jane Jervis).
32. Imperial War Museum Sound Archives, BBC Radio 4 programme on the Bruneval Raid, item 27282, in which Cox, Frost and others took part. The author has been unable to locate Alton Friars. It is interesting to note that in not one of the thirty or more Bruneval or St Nazaire sound archive recordings at the Imperial War Museum do any of the veterans mention the role of Peter Nagel/Newman at all; it was clearly a well-kept secret until long after the war.
33. Commanded by the famous bomber ace, Squadron Leader Pickard.
34. Millar, *Bruneval Raid*, passim.
35. DRA 1462 Film at Imperial War Museum Film Archive, made in 1982 as a re-enactment of the raid by the MOD, to mark the fortieth anniversary of the raid, viewed by the author; wartime radar expert Professor R.V. Jones narrated it and veterans' voices were used as commentary, including Peter's easily recognizable, slightly German-accented English. Peter's participation

in the film is confirmed in a letter from the film's producers (copy in AJEX files) of November 1981. Sadly, none of the veterans speaking are named in the credits; there is just a general thank-you to veterans of the Parachute Company who took part.

36. In the 1977 YTV film, Flight Sergeant Cox, who was not a Para by training but enjoying a quiet war as radar mechanic in Devon until then, described the Paras he fought alongside as 'fierce as Dervishes!'

37. TNA WO/106/ 4133, p.3, 'General Browning's Report'.

38. *Most Secret War* (London: Hamish Hamilton, 1978), p.248.

39. See note 36 above; the film was *The Secret War of Dr Jones* in the 'Wednesday Special' series, 5 January 1977, directed by Peter Jones, viewed by the author at the British Film Institute, July 2008. It starred several important veterans including R.V. Jones, Peter Nagel, General Frost, Flight Sergeant Cox, Lieutenant Vernon and Para Jim Sharp.

40. In possession of Jane Jervis.

41. 'Walker' is listed in the roll in the appendix of Commander R. Ryder's classic book, *The Attack on St Nazaire* (London: John Murray, 1947), p.116, as being in No. 2 Commando; the other two *known* Jewish raiders were Leading Seaman Monty Rakussen, RN (killed on ML 268, p.110 of Ryder – his photo and medals were given by his daughter Penny to the AJEX Jewish Military Museum some years ago, together with memorabilia of the St Nazaire Society, and are on display) and Trooper Len Scully (No. 1 Troop, 2 Commando, p.113 of Ryder), who managed to escape back to Britain.

42. C.E. Lucas-Phillips, *The Greatest Raid of All* (London: Pan, 2000), p.124.

43. J.G. Dorrian, *Storming St Nazaire* (London: Leo Cooper, 2001), p.108.

44. A number of books on the raid have been written over the years and many of these titles can be found via the internet.

45. 4467369 Private Francis Kelly, Border Regiment, No. 2 Commando, was the son of Mary and Joseph of Liverpool, and was aged 21; he is buried at Escoublac-la-Baule, Brittany, grave 2C6. This had been next to the hospital where many of the wounded had been brought, and later was made into the CWGC cemetery.

46. The explosives-laden HMS *Campbeltown* was already successfully firmly lodged in the dry-dock gates – as planned – and, unbeknown to the Germans, would later explode and destroy the dock for the rest of the war.

47. Lucas-Phillips, *Greatest Raid*, p.200.

48. Ibid., passim.

49. This is an error, as it was the Royal Northumberland Fusiliers, the cap-badge of which is in Jane Jervis's collection.

50. HS4 Czech papers of SOE.

51. In the possession of Jane Jervis, and a copy at AJEX Museum.

52. Imperial War Museum, Department of Documents, 94/7/1, testimony of Lieutenant Philip J. Dark, RN.

53. Located at Rennes from 1940 to 1943 was a German POW Camp, Frontstalag 133. Here Peter was issued with a silver-coloured POW tag, no. 18742, now in the collection of Jane Jervis. From this camp, POWs were later transferred to Germany, to other permanent camps. It was described as a place of 'indescribable filth' (Lucas-Phillips, *Greatest Raid*, p.266).

54. Now Lambinowice in Poland.

55. Now Krnov in the Czech Republic.

56. In the collection of Jane Jervis, and a copy at AJEX Museum.

57. Moritz died in the late 1950s, after his wife.

58. Naturalization paper AZ 19243. She died of cancer in September 1955, in Wimbledon. It appears Moritz and Margarete had been living in Longwood Drive, Roehampton.

59. Born in India on 11 March 1912, daughter of a British Indian Army soldier, she had been a teacher before the war.

60. Reference number of naturalization, N1426.

61. Peter's grandson Adrian is a housing officer and married Esther Ray in December 2000.

62. Much information on Peter's post-war life in Leicester is from Jane, but some comes from several of his ex-employees and colleagues, including Peggy Snowdon, Ron Simnett, Stan Jeffrey, Margaret Spencer, Trevor Walker and Gerald Whitely.

63. After Muriel died, Peter sold the family home and moved to Woodside Road, Oadby.

64. This was a source of family humour as Muriel had been a sergeant whilst Peter was only a private.

65. Copy of letter in AJEX Archives.
66. Thanks to records officers at Gilroes cemetery. Jane confessed that she wishes now that she had not obeyed her father's wishes, and had instead made some permanent memorial to him, in order that people could visit it.
67. 'Parachute 2 Club', which used to have reunions at Grantham each year.
68. He also belonged to the St Nazaire Veterans' Society and attended their reunions when he could.
69. With thanks to Yvonne Wattam and Clare Underwood at the Leicester Records Office.
70. Correspondence with Jane Jervis, July 2008.

'Set Europe Ablaze!': Jews who served in the SOE

All the hundreds of SOE files are now located at The National Archives (TNA) at Kew. However, a very large proportion of the personal agents' files remain closed for as much as the next twenty years or more. Thus searching for Jewish names is partially dependent on use of surnames – and sometimes first names – in the SOE catalogues, unless augmented by additional information, of which there is much, in the more openly available general SOE files and reports from various SOE country sections. This study is thus very much work in progress, but even then has taken many years – on and off – to compile. So significant does the author think this information is, however, that it is offered here knowingly incomplete, albeit continuing to grow. For never was an arm of the Second World War Allied forces so dangerous to work in, and the Jewish contribution so huge. It is noteworthy that the first Director of SOE was the Jewish Banker Sir Charles Hambro, a decorated WWI veteran, and that the Jewish firm Marks and Spencers gave the whole of the 5th Floor of their Baker St. H.Q. to SOE for the duration of the war.

The Special Operations Executive was established soon after the start of the Second World War, to train and send agents – men and women – into occupied enemy territory in Europe. It was said to have been the brainchild of Sir Winston Churchill; the aim was, to quote Churchill, to 'set Europe ablaze', by organizing sabotage and general resistance against the Nazis; however, agents were soon working not only in Asia (against the Japanese) but also in neutral and friendly nations the world over, to gather information and Intelligence for the Allies.

The agents were headhunted by, among other methods, examination of military and civilian files of targeted individuals who first of all were thought to have the linguistic skills and motivation to be of use to work abroad; sometimes brief and discreet adverts were placed in the press or in places where military and those considered 'trustworthy' people gathered, such as officers' messes, clubs and universities; some were recruited by government agents at social gatherings where likely types would be targeted and drawn into conversation, in order to judge their suitability for further interview; others simply openly volunteered for hazardous work to help the war effort and were sent discreetly to non-descript offices for further processing by anonymous SOE recruiters.

Once chosen, the potential agents would be briefed very broadly on the kind of work they were to do and told it was very dangerous; they were then offered the chance to withdraw; some did, most did not. Survival rates 'in the field' were low, especially among those chosen as couriers and radio operators. Training was intense.

Jewish agents were deemed most suitable for many reasons; education and linguistic ability among many was high, motivation against the enemy was profound. Many Jewish agents came from families who were recent immigrants to the UK from a variety of nations, some with families still in occupied countries, and often, therefore, had both not only a second language, but essential knowledge about the countries where their extended families still lived in occupied Europe, which would be of great advantage to a prospective agent! But they also faced a double danger, of being a 'spy' and also being Jewish, if captured. To reduce the chance of being shot if made a prisoner, all recruits were given other identities in the field, and commissioned into a regular branch of the military; most were in the 'General Service' Corps; some kept their regimental origins; women were often in the ATS, FANYs or the WAAF. Sadly such precautions had no effect on the murderous 'rules' of the Nazis, and most captured SOE agents were murdered, mostly in death camps where Jews were also being exterminated.

The Jewish agents followed the typical route of all other agents – whether born in Britain or not, they trained in special and isolated centres around the country and then were inserted into enemy territory; others were recruited in occupied countries and then extracted, if deemed suitably skilled and able, to be trained in the UK and then sent back as full agents, with military rank, to work in their country of origin.

It is not the author's aim here to recite a history of SOE; any good book on the subject contains huge bibliographies for the reader to consult, and the Imperial War Museum Sound Archives has several testimonies from Jewish agents (Dick Rubinstein and 'Yogi' Mayer, for example). But it is suggested that two of the best books from the Jewish perspective are Leo Marks, *Between Silk and Cyanide* and Sarah Helm, *Vera Atkins: A Life in Secrets*.[1] The author's own five studies of Jewish agents are also important to read as they give much SOE background material too (see the SOE agents chapters in this book).

As well as the actual agents and their trainers, many Jewish personnel took part on the fringes of SOE – for example in the insertion and extraction of agents; the aircrews of the Special 'Moonlight' Squadrons of the RAF; the MTBs,[2] submarines, feluccas, canoes and small boats of the Royal Navy and Royal Marines. Others were wireless operators, drivers or clerks at the Baker Street HQ. Sorting out the identities of these people is immensely difficult, however, as they themselves often did not know whom, for example, they were transporting, and less still, why. Some of these names I came across just by chance when interviewing Jewish veterans on other matters for our AJEX Museum archives.

Another issue is that of defining membership of SOE; some individuals were temporarily attached from other units such as the Commandos or Intelligence Corps. Others were co-members of other units such as the Jedburghs, who were a joint project of SOE, OSS[3] and the Intelligence services of occupied Allied nations in exile in the UK. Still others were 'crossover' members, as, for example, those in the Haganah (Israel underground army) who had very strong manpower links with SOE ranging from use of Haganah agents in enemy and neutral countries for gathering Intelligence, through to Haganah and British and Allied agents together physically carrying out actions against the enemy and their agents anywhere in the world.

Another category were those attached temporarily to SOE from Commando units for specific tasks or on specific raids. Jewish members of the Small Scale Raiding Force (SSRF or 62 Commando), which was informally known as SOE's 'private' commando, are included, as also are those from the famous No. 3 ('Jewish') Troop of No. 10 Inter-Allied (IA) Commando who went on, or who were considered for, SOE raids.

In addition, many Jews who were liberated from Axis POW camps in North Africa in 1942–43, were interrogated by British Intelligence to see if they were suitable for working in SOE, and a file (HS/3/70) at TNA in Kew reveals dozens of Jewish names in this category. However, there is no evidence they were actually employed by SOE in any way, so I have not been able to include them. Similarly in HS4/115 at TNA, there is a typed list of about twenty Palestinian/Israeli Jews which the author had never seen before, who volunteered for SOE service in the Balkans and south east Europe – aside from the famous 'parachutists' which included Hannah Senesh – but it is not possible to know whether they were ever chosen to participate. HS4, HS7 and HS8 also contained many Czech, Hungarian and Polish SOE members with Jewish-sounding names, but it again has not been possible to confirm if they were in fact Jews. Meanwhile, HS8/1013 contains a huge ledger entitled 'SOE Employees – not complete'. From this the author was able to extract many names of SOE secretarial and cypher staff, not found in any other sources.

Even more complex is the matter of the thousands of Jews in France, Belgium and indeed all over occupied Europe, who worked tangentially for SOE by being in their local Resistance groups. I have been able to include only some of these people in this study, where their names are obviously Jewish or of Jewish origin. Of France's 300,000 Jews, historians estimate that 25 per cent were in the Resistance, but how many were working for SOE directly may never be truly known.

In addition there is the issue of the individual agents' files at the TNA in the HS9 series. Many of these files are closed until years ranging from

2010 to 2031, yet contain, as the author knows, vital facts about the religious or ethnic backgrounds of the SOE personnel. If it were possible to access these, the number of Jewish agents would be hugely increased.

The work of Steven Kippax, on listing SOE agents, contains many Polish agents names and many could be, and many certainly were, Jewish. The author has included some of the more obvious ones but this is very much a hit-and-miss exercise; suffice to say there are many more to find, but whose Jewish background we may now never be able to prove, and whom it has been necessary to leave out as a result.

Some Jewish SOE agents who perished have not been properly recognized as such, which hugely diminishes the extremely dangerous nature of what they did and how they died. The Valençay memorial, near Paris, to 'F' (French) Section is specific to SOE, but the memorial to the missing at Brookwood says nothing about the Special Force these people served in; the Commonwealth War Graves Commission (CWGC) registers and website also often only lists SOE agents as 'General Service' or in their original regiment or corps; the Commission is very amenable to changing this but requires the researcher to furnish the proof, often not too difficult but very time-consuming. The Special Forces Club (SFC) in Chelsea is often very helpful here through its Historical Sub Committee, as is David Seaman, the former SOE specialist at the Imperial War Museum. The SFC also has a fabulous collection of framed photographs of their SOE agents, both those killed and those who survived. Indeed some SOE agents were never commemorated at all by the CWGC, especially the Israeli/Palestinian Jewish 'Parachutists', Hannah Senesh and Enzo Serini, for example. But research by the author at TNA, with the help of the Israel Defence Forces archivists, helped him to unearth the documentary proof of their enlistment in British Forces and later their SOE membership, and they are now properly remembered (in 2006, after over 60 years). Curiously, the SFC has had a photograph of Hannah prominently displayed on their wall for decades.

At the time of writing the author is working with the CWGC records section to have other Israeli Jewish agents listed as SOE (as one example, Aba Bardicev is listed as RAF), so the true nature of their courage and lonely deaths may be properly recognized. Another example is Muriel Byck, who died of illness on duty in France and as a result, unusually for SOE, has a marked CWGC war grave. Beneath the beautiful Star of David, however, it says only that she was a WAAF, with nothing about SOE. The CWGC has declined to alter this.

For many years, SOE agents' files were available only as 'distillations' from the Foreign and Commonwealth Office, keeper of SOE records; they were considered too sensitive for general use and only a privileged few were allowed access. Since 2000, however, they have been moved, and are openly accessible at TNA in Kew,[4] but many researchers suspect they have been weeded, and some agents' files are completely missing. Much of this mysterious secrecy is due to the fact that years after the war, it was slowly and painfully revealed (and both Leo Marks and Vera Atkins substantiated this to the author in his interviews with them) that many SOE agents had been betrayed by Vichy French and Nazi infiltrators, or French patriots who were blackmailed by the Gestapo who threatened their families, and who remain alive to this day. Worst of all, MI6 agents who were engaged in 'turf wars' with SOE over who should have influence over which branches of the Resistance, as being politically correct – for example, Communists, as opposed to Gaullists in France – were sometimes ordered to compromise – that is, betray – SOE operations and personnel.

There is even an unsubstantiated rumour that some high-ranking MI5/6 officers in London were actually Soviet agents, who were directed by Moscow to betray more right-wing Resistance groups in favour of left-wing groups in Europe, in what would be the post-war struggle for power in the newly liberated countries. We may never know the bitter truth, and clearly this remains to this day a very sensitive topic and political issue.

Below then follow the lists. The author cannot claim that they are exhaustive, and indeed they probably never can be. Rather, it is a determined effort to acknowledge the huge contribution – as always out of proportion – of, and to pay tribute to, the incredible courage of the Jewish SOE personnel who played such a significant role in that most amazing of Secret Armies, under the most hazardous and dangerous of circumstances.

The author has used as many sources as he could find, but no doubt new names will emerge over time, not least because so many Jews so successfully hid their true identities, even until their deaths, sometimes long after the war. I have attempted only to give birth-name and in some cases a later alias; then any awards, and sometimes nationality if it is clear. It is especially difficult to differentiate between Austrian and German agents; no mention of nationality usually means they are British, or it is simply not known. The author has also stated, where known, if they survived or died, and if the latter, where. Those readers who wish to fill in other details must turn to the many sources in libraries, museums, websites, newspapers and archives around the world. The author's own sources have been gathered over fifteen years from many such places.

Captain Arthur Radley, SOE Staff Officer for the Austrian Section based in southern France, said:[5] 'most of the 'joes' [agents] were Jewish refugees who came over to England in '38 and '39 and had been recruited, 20 or 30 of them ... they were tremendous. They were all very high calibre people ... they were intellectuals, dons. They were keen young men.'

In his Top Secret report, the head of East Mediterranean SOE, Lieutenant Colonel Anthony Simmonds, wrote (TNA HS7/172) of the Balkans section:

The agents were recruited from [Jewish] Palestinians ... and we were able to employ the underground channels and the long experience in clandestine travel, which the Jewish organisations have had to acquire in Europe since the rise of Hitler. These agents proved without exception to be resourceful, efficient and courageous ... despite unique difficulties such as no real front line enemy to work behind, no partisan groups in Bulgaria, Roumania and Hungary, and hostile local populations.

And the famous SOE agent Peter Churchill, who later married 'Odette' Sansom, GC, on responding to a letter to the Hull AJEX[6] about Isidore Newman, wrote that Newman was only one of 'a legion of Jews who covered themselves in glory in the SOE'. I can think of no finer epitaphs.

Acknowledgements

The author would like to thank all those mentioned in the chapters on five of the Jewish agents described in this book, whose names can be found in the acknowledgements sections; the AJEX Museum for use of the Jewish Chaplain Cards; Helen Fry and her book, *The King's Most Loyal Enemy Aliens*; also Steven Kippax of the SOE website chatroom; the late Peter Leighton-Langer (PLL) and his book, *The King's Own Enemy Aliens*; the late Jack Lennard Archive (Hull), *Jews in Wartime*, bestowed to the AJEX Museum by his daughter Phillipa in 2006; Peter Pirker of the Department of Government of the University of Vienna, for sharing his research on the Austrian Jewish agents; and the reader advisers at TNA in Kew, especially Howard Davies, Gareth Owen and Geoff Baxter. Lieutenant Paul 'Yogi' Mayer, aged 96 at the time of writing in 2009, and unofficial historian of 12 Force, provided detail on all his former Jewish SOE comrades.

Abbreviations

'att' means 'attached to'; 'b' means 'born'; I/C is Intelligence Corps; *JC* refers to the *Jewish Chronicle* newspaper; KIA means 'Killed in Action'; POW means 'Prisoner of War'; SIS is Special Intelligence Service/MI6; 'tbc' means 'to be confirmed'; WIA means 'Wounded in Action'.

The significance of serving at Tempsford is that this was the main SOE, and one of the Jedburgh aerodromes, for those who were parachuted or landed by aircraft, into Europe by 138 and 161 'Moonlight' squadrons.

12.1 Frederic Berliner aka Michael O'Hara, killed as an SOE agent in 1945 (SOE Archives, TNA).

12.2 SOE agent Stephen Dale aka Heinz Guenther Spanglet.

List 1

Names and Nationality – British or unknown unless stated	Awards	Place of death if relevant, and comments; European theatre unless stated
Raoul Isaac ABECASSIS (Turkish/Greek?)		
Moses ABENSUR (Turkish?)		North Africa/Spain/ Portugal
Baruch ABERBACH (Austrian)		Force 133/Palestinian Jew, not used in action.
Myer H. ABRAHAMS, RAF		Tempsford
Lt Albert ABULAFIA		Middle East
Lt Gabor/Gabriel ADLER, aka John Armstrong, aka Gabriele Bianichi (Hungarian/British)		POW executed near Rome, Italy; body found May 2007; Cassino memorial (TNA HS8/449).
Sandor ADLER (Hungarian)		Worked from Budapest.
John/Ivan AGOSTAN (Hungarian)		Assisted SOE escapers.
Jean Maurice AISNER, aka Besnard (French)		
Mme Julienne Marie Louise AISNER (French)	King's Commendation for Brave Conduct	Died 1947.
Abraham AKAVIA (Palestinian Jew)		Served with Orde Wingate in Israel and Ethiopia.
Capt. Sydney ALBUM	MC of Valour (Yugoslavian) given personally by Tito	Recommended MC and OBE – not awarded; liaison with Tito/SOE?
Miss Sima ALKALAY/ALCALAY		
Yigal ALLON (Palestinian Jewish)		2nd commander Syrian ('Fake Arab') Platoon, Haganah, with SOE – later Chief of Staff IDF and Deputy PM and FM of Israel.
Karl Otto ALTMANN (German?)		
Jakob ALTMEYER		Listed as SOE Staff Middle East.
Rudolf ALTSCHUL		
Crafts. John Alfred ALVAREZ, RN to SOE		Experiments with underwater craft – dismissed as a communist 1945.
Major Joseph Felix AMIEL, aka Joseph Zephirin Andrieu (Belgian)	OBE	
Israel/Rehavam (?) AMIR		Haganah Communications liaison with SOE; Yugoslavia (see Force 199 list). Lived Yavniel.
Hans AMOSER		
Lt Herbert Patrick 'Lofty'ANDERSON /Herbert Helmut FUERST (Austrian)		12 Force to I/C.
Andre Joseph ANGEL, aka Bernard		Arrested 12/2/44 and died Mauthausen 11/7/44.

Names and Nationality – British or unknown unless stated	Awards	Place of death if relevant, and comments; European theatre unless stated
Lt Benjamin APTAKIN		
Robert-Henri AREND (French)		W/O (Wireless Operator)– captured and survived Buchenwald.
Helene Bertha ARON (Anglo-French)		
Jean Marie/Maxime ARON, aka Allais/Joseph (French)		Captured, escaped.
Roger ARON		
A. ARONSOHN, aka Verdonck Willem (Dutch)		
Capt. Georges ARONSTEIN (Belgian)	MBE	
Miss ASKINAZY (Polish)		Russia
Ronald ATKINS (brother of Vera), born Rosenberg		SOE Turkey/Balkans/Romania
Vera May ATKINS, née Rosenberg	Croix de Guerre, Legion d'Hon.	'F' Section Senior Administrator, Baker Street; born Romania.
Heinz AUFRECHT/Michael ALFORD (Austrian?)		To I/C.
Shaul AVIGUR (Palestinian Jewish)		Haganah liaison with SOE on the 37 Parachutists.
Gideon AYAD (Iranian)		Wireless Operator
Hugo BACHER (Romanian)		
Gyorgy BALINT (Hungarian)		
Lionel BARNETT		Assisted the Meyers in Madagascar Operation (see below)
A. BARZILAY		Palestinian Jewish SOE, KIA; not commemorated by the CWGC.
Moshe BASSIN (Palestinian Jewish)		Haganah; liaison Communications with SOE.
BATE(S), possibly aka Gustav Oppelt (See PLL); possibly not Jewish	Referred to in G. Rees, *Bundle of Sensations*, (London: Chatto & Windus, 1960), pp.157–8; see Rice and Smith below.	Czech, perhaps survived in GDR after WW2; with Rice and Smith (see below) were in No. 3 ('Jewish') Troop, No. 10 IA Commando, att. 40 RM Commando, on an SOE mission to obtain military documents from the Town hall on the Dieppe Raid. Probably all KIA.
Gert August BAUMGARTEN		
Nina Irina BAUMGARTEN		
BAUMGARTNER (French)		
Zofia BAUMGARTNER (Polish)		Secretarial
Sgt Theodore BAUMGOLD, aka Jules (American)	MiD	Jedburgh/SOE
Lt Ralph Howard Michael 'Robert' BEATTY (alias) (German)		12 Force to I/C.

Names and Nationality – British or unknown unless stated	Awards	Place of death if relevant, and comments; European theatre unless stated
Sgt. Fritz BECKER, aka Frederick Benson (German)	King's Commendation for Brave Conduct (Posthumous)	SIS/SOE Force 12 – killed in action Poland after Para drop dressed as SS Officer, 29/10/44 – Groesebeek Memorial
Alfred Heinrich Hugo Julius BECKER (German)		Middle East; attested as Protestant but believed Jewish.
Lt Rudolf Phillip BECKER, aka Robert Phillip 'Butch' Baker-Byrne, aka Bosquet (German)		Operation Vivacious to destroy V2 engine factory in Berlin; POW.
Oscar/Oskar BEHRON (Austrian)		Worked in Turkey; attested as RC – tbc.
Ms Anna BEIER		
Louis BELIN (French)		Ran Dordogne escape line; captured and sent to Oranienberg camp.
Bernard BEMBERG (French)	King's Commendation for Brave Conduct (posthumous)	Captured and sent to "Dora" Nordhausen and Buchenwald; murdered by Nazis.
Jacques BEMBERG (brother of Bernard)		
BENAZARAPH		North Africa
Elie BENCHETRIT (Morocco)		b. 8/8/10
Henry BENHAMON, aka Andalou/Lafont (French/Algerian)		b. 6/1/15
W. BEN-LEVY		
Isidore BENVENISTE		
Andre BENZONI		
Pte Nick BERBLINGER, aka Allington (German)		Served Foreign Legion, 21st Independent Paras then to SOE.Field Security
L./Cpl Leon J. BERGBAUM (Canada)		
Peter 'Putz' BERGER, aka Barry		To I/C.
Suzanne Diamant BERGER (French)		b. 11/2/03 – son killed in SAS in 1944 Normandy.
BERGMAN (Dutch)		KIA in Halifax aircraft plane crash 23/5/43.
Sgt Jacob B. BERLIN, aka Ammonia (American)	MiD	Jedburgh/SOE; later became a priest.
Aron BERLINER/BERLINGER (Hungarian)		Wireless Operator – executed.
BERMAN (Palestinian Jew working in Balkans)		
BERMAN-FISCHER (German)		
Daniel BERNSTEIN (French)	Certificate of Commendation	Paris; arrested and survived.

Names and Nationality – British or unknown unless stated	Awards	Place of death if relevant, and comments; European theatre unless stated
Helena Verna BERNSTEIN		b. 31/10/17 – Secretarial.
Sgt Major J. BERSKY (Czech) ?	Certificate of Commendation	Killed 19/10/44.
L.E.D. BERTHAU ?		KIA 7–15/5/45.
Juliane BESNER ?		Courier
Mlle BETBEDER (French)		POW Gestapo, Paris; murdered Ravensbruck – former teacher in Lycée Française, London.
Rita BIEHAL		Clerical at Baker Street.
Lt Eugene BIELINSKI, aka Filip, aka Kiala/Lampart (Polish)		KIA Poland 1944 (is he the same as Bielski below?).
R. BIELSKI (Polish) ?		KIA August 1944.
Ms Lili BIER (Hungarian)		1940–41 Hungary then to Cairo.
Emmanuel BIERER (Polish) – attested as Protestant but was Jewish		SOE Turkey with GEDYE (b. 19/8/1895).
Helene BIERER (wife of above)		Turkey
Frederic BIERER, aka Bentley		SSRF on Herne raid Operation Huckaback (see Hubertus LEVIN below); also No. 3 ('Jewish') Troop, No. 10 Commando.
Thomas BINDERMAN		b. 25/2/10.
Lajos BIRO, aka Brent (Hungarian)		b. 15/11/13.
Lt William 'Billy' BLAKE, aka Bielschowski 13801201 (German)		12 Force to I/C.
Lt Peter Barry BLAKE, aka BLAU (German)		12 Force to I/C.
Rudy Albert BLATT		b. 25/10/12 – Dutch Commando.
Heinz BLEICH (German)		
Robert BLOC		b. 2/7/21.
Lt Andrei Georges BLOCH, aka Alan George Boyd	MiD	POW, executed 1942 Mont Valerieu, Hauts de Seine.
Andre George BLOCH (France)		POW, executed; former Socialist Deputy in the parliament.
Lt Andrei Pierre BLOCH, aka Peter Martin (USA)		Wireless Op. – inserted 7/9/41. Code name 'Bowtie'.
Ensign Denise BLOCH (French, FANY)	King's Commendation for Brave Conduct, Croix de Guerre, Legion d'Hon.	Executed Ravensbruck with Violette Szabo, GC.
Eileen BLOCH		b. 25/4/17 – Secretarial.
Madame Gabriella BLOCH (wife of Jean-Pierre)	King's Medal for Courage	
Jean-Pierre BLOCH (French)	King's Medal for Courage	POW, escaped.

Names and Nationality – British or unknown unless stated	Awards	Place of death if relevant, and comments; European theatre unless stated
Jean Richard BLOCH (French)		Escaped to Moscow.
Louis Albin Simon BLOCH		b. 26/2/23.
Marc BLOCH (French)		Executed 1944.
Marcel BLOCH (French)		
Michael George BLOCH		b. 12/2/24.
Capt. Paul BLOCH-AUROCH, served as P. Aguirec (French)		Jedburgh/SOE; KIA Indo-China 26/4/46.
Capt. Rene Eugene CLEMENT-BLOCH (French)		Jedburgh/SOE – b. 6/8/11.
Miss 'Timmie' BLOCH (French)		
Max BLOEMHOFF (Hungarian)		
Capt. Marcus BLOOM	MiD	Described by his SOE trainers as 'a pink yid'. Murdered Mauthausen.
Patricia S. BLOOM		b. 24/1/16.
Rene BLUM		b. 5/6/20.
2nd Lt Kazimierz BLUMHOFF (Polish)		Middle East
Col Marcelle BLUMSTEIN, aka Schwartzenfeld		Escaped to Spain.
Hand BODE (German)		
BOGOMOLETZ (Russo-Romanian)		
Capt. Robert Rene BOITEUX, aka Burdett – part Jewish (Anglo-French)	MC, Croix de Guerre, MBE, Legion d'Hon.	France and Burma
Capt. Henri BORUSH – born Stepney	MC	Two missions to France.
Lt Erich Franz BRAUER, aka BOWES (German)		12 Force to I/C.
Michel/Maurice/Marcel H.R. BRAULT, aka Jerome/James Levy, aka Barrault (French)		Spain/Portugal
Gerard Emmanuel BRAULT		
M. and Mme BRAULT (parents of above)		
Commandant Maurice BRAUN (French)	Legion D'Hon.	Survived Buchenwald/ Flossenberg.
Frank BRIGHT (Czech)		Based in Prague.
Esther BROMBERGER, aka Evelyne Benoit (Belgian)		Worked Paris with brother, Louis Tcherkoski.
Georges BROUSSINE (French)	MC, Croix de Guerre	POW, escaped.
BROZ aka TAUSIG (Czech)		
Jacques BRUNSCHWIG (French)		POW
Lt George Herbert BRYANT, aka Georg Breuer (German)		12 Force – North Africa, Italy, Austria.
Petty Off. BUCHANAN (alias), RM Commando		Att. SOE

Names and Nationality – British or unknown unless stated	Awards	Place of death if relevant, and comments; European theatre unless stated
Fritz Werner BUCHDAHL 13801956, PC (German)		Was believed by Yogi Meyer to have been killed with GILES (Yugoslavia) but TNA HO 405/2403 has his application for British nationality in 1947; he survived.
Ivan BUGARSKI		Middle East
Lt Peter BURGER/BERGER? (German) – same as Peter Berger, above?		12 Force
Section Officer Muriel Tamara BYCK, WAAF	MiD	Died of illness in France on her mission, 23/5/44. Buried Pornic, Brittany.
Lt Ted E. BYRON, aka Tamas Revai (Hungarian)		See HS4 114 – moved to Middle East.
Mme CAHEN (French)		Courier
Major CAYZER		
Sgt CHITTIS (Palestinian Jew)	MiD	Wireless Operator to Brig. Eddie MYERS in SOE ops in Greece.
Kurt CITRON		
Sgt Cyril CLAYTON		RCOS att. SOE Italy.
5466V Cpl Gunther Rene COEHN, later Cohn (South African/German)	DCM	With UDF in North Africa then to Force 133 Crete ; POW, survived.
Anne COHEN		Cypher Clerk London (?)
Capt. Gaston Armand COHEN/ COLLIN (Anglo-French)	MC, Croix de Guerre, Legion d'Hon.	SOE and later Jedburgh Trainer; nick named 'The Palestine Express' by Buckmaster, *They Fought Alone*, p.74
Lt Albert COHEN (French)		
Annie COHEN		
A. Gustave COHEN (French)		
David COHEN (Hungarian)		Wireless Operator
G.R. COHEN		Wireless Operator, Crete.
Cpl Harris Marks COHEN, RAF		Worked as ground crew at Tempsford, despatching SOE agents.
Ida COHEN		Secretarial
Commander Kenneth COHEN		Jedburgh liason with USA/agent.
General 'Two Gun' Morris COHEN		Worked as SOE observer in China; POW of the Japanese.
Ms Vida COHEN		Secretarial
Capt. William Henry COHEN		
Gerhard H.C. COSSMAN, aka Peter Crawford		
Sonia Miriam CROUCHER, née Rubinstein		
Andrew Louis D'ANTAL (Anglo-Brazilian)		TNA HS11/1
Lt. Stephen Patrick DALE, aka Heinz Guenther Spanglet, aka Turner, aka Ziba (German)		12 Force – nicknamed 'Ziegeuner baron' (Gypsy Baron) – POW, survived.
Angelo DANAIL (Bulgarian)		Turkey

Names and Nationality – British or unknown unless stated	Awards	Place of death if relevant, and comments; European theatre unless stated
Col Gordon DAVIES (Australian)		Burma SOE.
Lt Col Peter DAVIS, RM	DSC	Insertion/extraction SOE agents Yugoslavia and Mediterranean.
Capt. Edward DE HAAN		
Capt. Louis DE WOHL – tbc		Served in the USA.
Maisie DEFRIES		Secretarial
Capt. Daniel DELIGANT (French)	MBE	
Capt. Erwin Peter DEMAN, aka Irving Dent (Austrian/Hungarian)	MBE, MC	Previously in French Foreign Legion, POW 1940 escaped Stalag 12C.
Capt. H.M. DESPAIGNE (French)		
George F. DEUTSCH		
Julino DEUTSCH		
Otto Michael DEUTSCH		
Capt. Lionel M. DRAGE – tbc		
Vera DUCHNITZ, née Pick (Czech/ German)		Secretarial
Miss Mary DURLACHER		Secretarial
Major Abba (Aubrey Solomon) EBAN (Israeli) aka Aubrey EVANS		Att. SOE Jerusalem. Later Deputy PM and Foreign Minister of Israel.
Lt.Ernst Hans Carl Eduard EBERSTADT, aka David Edward Charles Eversley (German)		12 Force to I/C; also No. 3 ('Jewish') Troop, No. 10 Commando.
Rudolf EDLER (German)		
Victor EHRENFIELD		
Max EINHORN (German?)		
EINSTEIN (Polish)		May not have been on ops.
Abraham ELJARIAT (Morocco) – tbc		
Lawrence Roger ELLIOT, aka Lothar Ettlinger (German)		12 Force to I/C.
Peter EMMERRICK (alias) (German)		Balkans SOE and RSR (Raiding Support Regiment).
Keith ENOCH		Dropped into France and Germany – interrogated Kramer at Belsen.
Paul ERLICH		Killed.
Lt Dr Albert ESKENAZI, aka Martins (French)		
EXLER (?)		
Lt Hugh Peter FALTON, aka Hermann Faltitschek (German)		12 Force
Sgt Joseph Paul FRIEDLAND, aka FARROW (Austrian)	BEM	POW Germany, survived.
Lucien FAYMAN, aka Louis (French)		Captured; survived Belsen.
Hans FEBRANS (Czech residing in Stockholm)		Tbc if SOE.

Names and Nationality – British or unknown unless stated	Awards	Place of death if relevant, and comments; European theatre unless stated
Sgt Harry FEIGEN, RAF– parachute instructor		Trained SOE agents.
Robert FEIGL (French)		
Lt. Herbert FEIN, aka Razer (German)		12 Force to I/C.
Lt Adolphe FEINGOLD (Polish)		Described in HS4 as 'an intelligent little Jew'. Inserted to assassinate Rolf Muller, Head of Marseilles Gestapo; unsuccessful. Later SOE trainer and served Israeli Intelligence in War of Independence.
Lt Leon FELDMAN, aka Fantin		Wireless Operator
Zena FELDMAN		Secretarial
Guy Rene FINK		
Maxim FISCHER (Romanian)		Not used in action.
Lt Otto FISCHL/PICHL (tbc) (Czech)		KIA August 1944 with Lt Ernst HOFFMAN.
Martha Maud FISCHMANN (Russo-Greek)		Secretary/interpreter. Served in Greek mountains.
Victoria FISCHMANN (sister of above)		As above.
Jacques FISHBACHER		
Walter/Paul FLEISCHL, aka Fletcher (British, with Austrian parents)	CBE (OBE, MiD WW1)	SOE banker in the Far East.
Max FLORENTIN and Sam FLORENTIN		Brothers recommended for unnamed decorations for aiding escaped airmen.
Lt Gyorgy FOERSTNER – Hungarian Army		Worked for SOE.
Walter Leslie FORSTER	CBE	SOE sabotage of Burma oilfields as British retreated 6/11/42.
Wilhelm Georg FORTANG/William George Fort	King's Certificate of Merit	i/c SOE agents' clothing at Natural History Museum HQ.
Lt Marcel FOX (French)		Captured and murdered at Flossenberg 29/3/44.
Claude FRANCK (French, Lyons)		SOE financier.
Col Louis FRANCK, aka Vercke (Belgian/British)	CBE, MiD, Italian Partisan Medal, US Award	Head of SOE Mission to USA 1943–45 with Donovan and Stevenson; served Belgian Army (King's Courier), Dunkirk, Italy, West Africa. tbc.
E.M. FRAENKEL		
Major Jacques Henri FRAGER, aka Dupre (French)	MiD (DSO?)	Murdered Buchenwald 1944.
Ephraim FREEDENTHAL/FREEMAN		SOE driver but may have been on one mission to Norway
Capt. Anton Walter FREUD, aka French (Austrian)		Grandson of Sigmund. POW.
Fritz FREUND		
Julius FREUND (Austrian)		

Names and Nationality – British or unknown unless stated	Awards	Place of death if relevant, and comments; European theatre unless stated
Richard FREUND (Czech/German)		
Rudolf 'Rudi' FRIEDLAENDER, aka Sgt Lodge (German)	DCM (file HS9 544/10)	SAS att. SOE, KIA France 1944.
Syma FRIEDMANN, aka Willamanski		Double agent Switzerland/Palestine.
Zygfryd FRIEDMAN (Polish)		North Africa but may not have been on ops.
Elaine Marion FROOMBERG		Secretarial
Lt Dr. Henri FUCS, aka Henry Fox, aka Fournier, aka Rouneaux, aka Abel (Romanian/French)	MC, Croix de Guerre	POW French Army, escaped.
M. FUERLOSCHER/ FEUER LEOSCHER (Palestinian Jewish)		Turkey/Palestine
Elinor GALLETT		May not have been used.
Alexander GANS (German?)		
Pte Joseph GARBER		Fought in Spanish Civil War; as ex Merchant Navy, used with small boats inserting/extracting SOE in Yugoslavia.
Asher Baruch Benedict GAVRONSKY		
Mrs Litzi Alice GEDYE, née Mehler or Lepper (Austrian)		Worked in Balkans/Turkey/Israel.
Major G.E.R. GEDYE		Middle East
Capt. Emile Marc GERSCHEL (French)	MC, Croix de Guerre	
Mrs Giliana B. GERSON, née Balmaceda (Chile/France)		First female member of SOE; married to Victor of the VIC escape line.
Major Victor Haim GERSON, aka Rene, aka Vic	DSO, OBE	Served WW1 British Army.
Henry Morris GERSON	MBE	France, Greece, Israel, Syria, North Africa
Fl. Sgt Michael GIBBONS	DFM	'Moonlight Squadrons', Tempsford
Gilbert GIL-SCHWAB (French)		Scandinavia
Commandant Ernest Richard GIMPEL, aka Guimpez, aka Charles Beauchamp (French)	King's Commendation /MID	Nephew of Lord and Lady Anthony Abrahams. POW 1940, escaped; captured in SOE, escaped; captured, survived both Auschwitz and Flossenberg.
Lt Raymond Pierre GLAESNER, aka Lagarde, aka Perrin (French)	DSO	POW, escaped – tbc.
Alexandre GLASBERG (French, Lyons)		
Henri GLASBERG		
Leo GLASER (Austrian?)		
Paul GLASER		
Max GLESINGER (Austrian) – tbc		
2nd Lt GLICKMAN (USAAF)		
Major Jacques GOAR (Anglo-Egyptian)		Served also WW1.

Names and Nationality – British or unknown unless stated	Awards	Place of death if relevant, and comments; European theatre unless stated
Friedrich GOERTZ (German, Jewish origin)		Escaped to France, returned to Germany and became a political POW, and called up 1942; POW 1944 Normandy, and joined SOE; did not see action.
Eleanor GOLD		Telephonist, London (?)
Lt Israel GOLD, aka Charles Gardner, aka Goodwin/Gumley (Austrian/German refugee).		
Capt. Jack Lionel GOLDBERG		Force 136 Far East
Syd V. GOLDER		Yugoslavia (Obit., *JC*, 1/6/07).
Fl. Sgt Joseph A. GOLDING (son of Mark and Honor Golding)		138 Sqdn RAF Tempsford. KIA 3/12/44.
Mrs Maria Marjorie GOLDMAN		Secretary to head of SOE Ops Far East.
Ernest GOLDSCHMIDT/GOUNAT/ GONNOT (French)	Croix de Guerre, King's Commendation for Brave Conduct	
Gustav GOLDSCHMIDT, aka Goldschild (French)		North Africa
Konrad Levin GOLDSCHMIDT, aka Grant, aka Groves		Att. from No. 3 ('Jewish') Troop, No. 10 Commando. WIA.
M. GOLDSCHMIT-FORGEOT (French)		
Paul GOLDSCHMIDT (German)		Spain/Portugal
Walter GOLDSCHMIDT		
Stanley Ludwig GOLDSMITH		
Cpl A.S. GOLDSTEIN	Certificate of Commendation	RAMC
G. GOLDSTEIN		
Marcel GOLDSTEIN, aka Gauthier (French)		
Constan GOLOUBITSKY, aka Gardiner – tbc		
Godfrey GOMPERTZ		
Capt. Phillipe GOODMAN (Anglo-French)		Served Spanish Civil War. Royal Fus. and Paras. Knew Joe Garber in Balkans ops, Italy.
Mounya and Mischa GORDIN (Palestinian Jewish brothers)		Haganah Communications liaison with SOE.
Major (Doctor) Jean GORODICHE, aka Granville/Gautier/Gravier (French)	OBE	Served French Army, then escaped to UK, was medical officer with SOE Resistance on Massif Centrale.
E.J. GORSKI (Polish?)		Killed.
S. GORSKI (Polish)		Killed?
Lt Kurt W. GOTTLIEB (Austrian)		Sherwood Foresters, SOE Cairo.
Baron Phillipe de GOUNZBERG (French)	Legion d'Hon, Croix de Guerre, OBE	

Names and Nationality – British or unknown unless stated	Awards	Place of death if relevant, and comments; European theatre unless stated
Sig. GOULDEN-BERG		RCOS (Italy)
Ms Suzanne GRADSTEIN (French)	Certificate of Commendation	
Lt Alan Ronald Norman GRANT, aka Noe Csuppa/Czuppa/McAbe (German /Polish)	MiD	12 Force – Yugoslavia/Italy.
Lt Christine GRANVILLE, aka Goldfeder-Skarbeck, aka Grycka, aka Pauline	GM, Croix de Guerre, OBE	Murdered by stalker after WW2; worked mainly Poland and France. Buried in error in Christian churchyard in London.
Mr H. GREENBERG		
Jack GRICE (Australia)		Israel/N.Africa/Greece.
Myer GRIENSPAN		
GRIGOROV (Bulgarian)		May not have been on ops.
Capt. Albert GRINBERG, aka Robert Martin (French)		
Josiane GROS		French, killed?
Claude Emil Cesar GROS, aka Armand Lallau		
Mr Nicol GROSS		Political and Economic Warfare Dept Middle East.
Sgt Arthur GRUEN, aka Fidele (American)		Jedburgh/SOE
T. or J. GRUEN (Dutch)		Shot down, escaped, arrested, survived.
Zsigmund GRUEN		
E. GRUENFELD		
Jean GRUNEBAUM (French)		
Marcelle GRUNER (French?)		
A.R. GUBBAY		
A. GUGGENHEIM (German)		
Siegfried GUGGENHEIM (German)		
Harold GUINSBURG		North Africa/Spain
Heinz GUMPERZ (German)		
Sgt GUTTMAN, RAF		SOE staff Istanbul.
Egon GUTTMAN		
Leon GUTTMAN		
Wilhelm GUTTMAN		
Pal 275, Cpl Isaak M. GYORI, aka Michael Trent, RASC (Czech/ Palestinian Jewish)	Italian Partisan Medal	KIA Italy.
Dr Albert HAAS (husband of Sonja)		POW. Survived Auschwitz.
Paul HAAS		Physiological research section.
Mrs Sonja HAAS (Belgian/French)	Croix de Guerre, Legion d'Hon., British Medal of Freedom (?)	POW. Survived Auschwitz.

Names and Nationality – British or unknown unless stated	Awards	Place of death if relevant, and comments; European theatre unless stated
Lt Walter HACKER/HARRIS		
David HACOHEN (Palestinian Jewish)		Liaison Haganah/SOE.
Eli HAGGAR (Palestinian Jew, tbc)		Served France, Germany, Italy, Turkey – MIA.
Alec HALPERN		SOE USA
Col Sir Charles HAMBRO	CBE (MC, WW1)	First Director of SOE, Baker Street.
Elizabeth HAMBRO		Motor Transport section.
Pamela HAMBRO		Secretarial
Capt. Richard Everard HAMBRO		Brother of Charles.
Frank Alfred HAMBURGER		
Col Julius HANAU, aka Hannon, aka Caesar; served WW1 (South African)	OBE (recommended DSO for operations in Madagascar)	Balkans and West/East Africa. Believed assassinated Cairo 1943 (family interview).
Bernard HANAUER		Dutch
Gabor HARASZTY, aka Albert (Hungarian)		Murdered by NKVD post-war.
Karoly HARASZTY (brother of above)		
H. (Henry?) HARING (Brighton Rd, Stoke Newington, London N16)		
George and Jan HARTMAN (Czech)		Based in Prague.
HARTMANN (Hungarian)		SOE recruiter working in London.
Ludwig Joseph HARTSTEIN		
Joe HASSAN (Moroccan)		SOE banker in Algeria, Morocco, Spain.
Mrs Ruth HAUSMANN, aka Beasdale		Clerical, tbc?
Capt. Victor Hyam HAZAN, aka Gervais (British/Moroccan)	MBE, Croix de Guerre	France
Capt. Leo HEAPS (Canadian – 6th Airborne Paras)	MC	SOE operation to rescue survivors from Arnhem.
Heinz HECHT		Spain
Walter K. Robert HECHT		Propaganda section.
Maurice HECKMANN		
Capt. Ely HECKSHER		Force 136 Far East
Lt Oscar HEIMANN (Czech/Swiss)		Described as 'a keen yid' by his SOE trainers (HS9/688/9) – served in France.
Fritz HEINE		X Section
Major Keith Robert HEINE	MiD	SOE Selangor, Far East
Otto HESS, aka Peter Giles (German)		From No. 3 ('Jewish') Troop, No. 10 Commando/SIS; executed Yugoslavia. Groesebeek Memorial.
Joseph H. HAYIM		Middle East
Walter HELFGOTT		

Names and Nationality – British or unknown unless stated	Awards	Place of death if relevant, and comments; European theatre unless stated
Horst HERZBERG		
Leo HILLMAN, aka Georg Bergmann/ Charles Kennedy/Gerber (German)	MC, MM	Commando/SIG/SOE/SAS.
Collette HIRSCH, aka Christine (French)		Arrested, escaped.
Lt Jacques F. Gustave HIRSCH (French)	MBE, Croix de Guerre	
Mlle Jeanne HIRSCH (sister of above)		
Cpl John Edward HIRSCH		India, Field Security.
Lt Pierre HIRSCH, aka Popaul (French)	MBE, Croix de Guerre	
Rene HIRSCH (French)		
Josef HIRSCHBERG (German)		Holland/USA/Canada
Lajor HIRSCHFELD (Hungarian)		
Henri Emmanuel HIRSH		
M. and Mme Leon HIRSH (French)		
Lt Herman HOCHFELDER, aka Harriman, aka Hillman (Czech)		Israel/Egypt/Turkey
Lt Ernest HOFFMAN, aka Holzer – tbc (German)		KIA Oct.–Dec. 1944 Germany whilst on mission.
Hans Gunther HOFFMAN – aka Hobson? tbc		
LAC K. HOFFMAN, RAF (775636)		Hungarian origin.
Max (Moritz) C. HOFFMAN, aka Kaufman (French)		Ran an escape line, Portugal/Spain.
Harold Mark HOFFMAN		
Sqdn Ldr John Michael HOLLANDER		Electrical Engineer, RAF I/C radios for agents in UK and North Africa.
Major Paul W. HOMBERGER and Mrs HOMBERGER		North Africa/Spain/Portugal
Bernard HORNUNG		
Gustav HORNUNG		
2nd Lt George HOROVITZ (Hungarian)		Middle East
Claude HOROWICZ (Franco-Polish)		
Phineas HOROWITZ		USA/Ireland/Far East
Lt George HUELSMANN, aka Hulsman (German)		12 Force to I/C.
Sqdn Ldr John HUNTER	DFC, AFM	Moonlight Sqdn
Max HYMANS, aka Frederic Glen (French)	OBE	First SOE parachute drop into France; formerly Secretary of State, French government; also served in Spain.
Capt. Stanley INGRAM, aka Isaacs	Danish award	
Aaron IOUDAS (Greek)		
Juliette P. ISAACS		Secretarial

Names and Nationality – British or unknown unless stated	Awards	Place of death if relevant, and comments; European theatre unless stated
Capt. Stanley ISAACS		
Lt Col Morris (Moses) ISRAEL (Australian)	Certificate of Commendation	India/USA/South Pacific with Z Force/ Force 136, AIF. Director of Signals for all Australian Special Forces in WW2.
Pte Ruben ISRAEL (Palestinian Jew, born Turkey)		Previously 51st Middle East (Jewish) Commando, WIA, Commandos North Africa, POW, escaped; to SOE but not used in the Field.
Capt. Rene Sello ISRAEL, aka Frederic/Painter (French)		
Maurice JACOB (French)		Captured
Lt Howard (or A.M.) JACOB(S)		Polish/Czech liaison.
Major Gideon JACOBS, RM (South African)		Dropped into Sumatra 1945 to persuade Japanese to hand over POWs.
Gordon JACOBS (Anglo-French)		
Major Joshua M. JACOBS		SOE Psychologist.
Montague JACOBS		
Peter John JAFFE		
Fl. Lt JAFFE		Tempsford aircrew.
Mirkea JAKOB (Romanian)		Boat Captain and SOE agent on Danube.
Capt. Horace Ben Rosenthal JAMES		Technical section SOE
Andrew and Miklos JANOVITZ – brothers (Hungarian)		See HS4 116.
Robert Peter JELLINEK	MBE	Served Switzerland.
Daniel KAGAN (Polish)		May not have been used on ops.
Eugen KAGERER-STEIN, aka Sgt Eugene 'Didi' Fuller		From No. 3 ('Jewish') Troop, No. 10 Commando – KIA.
Capt. Paul KAHAN (French)	Cert. of Commendation	
KAHN (Romanian)		Danube shipping.
Ernest KAHN		Spain/Portugal
Hazel KAHN		Secretarial
Louis KAHN (French?)		
Leonide KAHN		
Roger Jacques KAHN, aka Pierre Chenu		
Lt Charles Karl Egon KAISER (Austrian)		Force 12. Inserted Austria/Germany.
Andras KALMAN (Hungarian)		Trained to parachute into Hungary but cancelled owing to betrayal.
John Eugene KALMAN		
B. KAMINSKI (Polish)		KIA May 1944.
Lt Henri KAMINSKI (French)		Jedburgh/SOE
Henri Jean Pierre KAMISKI		
Sgt Fritz KANNITZ, aka Jonson (Austrian/German refugee).		

Names and Nationality – British or unknown unless stated	Awards	Place of death if relevant, and comments; European theatre unless stated
KANSKI (Polish) – tbc		
Capt. D.J. KAPLAN, RAF		Debriefing officer, SOE/Jedburghs.
Vladimir KAPLAN		
Major Alec Louis KAPLOWICH, aka Kay		Spain/Portugal
David KARMEL		
Lt Otto 'Putzi' KARMINSKI/SIMON	MiD	12 Force Italy
M. KARSENTY/KASRSENTI		Jewish journalist working in Oran, Algeria
Sgt Yechiel Asher KASAP/KASSAP/KASP	DCM, MM	KIA with SOE, 21/11/43, from Palestine Regiment No. 12300/Commandos; remembered Athens Memorial, face 10 (see HS7/173 TNA reference).
Lazlo KASTNER		Spain
Benedicine KATZ, aka Etienne, aka Bennet (French)		
Dr Conrad KATZ		Mexico?
Jean KATZ, aka Castel		
Lazlo Namenyi KATZ		
Peter KAUFMANN (German)		
Ray KAUFFMAN (USA)		Liaison with SOE Java.
Robert KAUFFMAN (French)		
Jacques and Roland KAUFFMAN (sons of Robert)		
Mrs Josefne KELLNER, née Rosenblatt (Hungarian)		
Leopold KELLNER or GELLNER (Austrian)		Turkey? May not have been on ops.
Lt Paul KELLNER		Caribbean?
Lt C.V. KENNEDY (alias)		
Pte M.K.S. KHOURI, PC, Pal 12771	MM and Bar	Force 133 Balkans.
John KIMCHE		Worked in Switzerland.
Maria KIRCHNER (Polish)		Courier
Henry KIRSCHEN (Romanian)		
Andrew KIRSCHNER (Hungarian)		Not used by SOE – transferred to Commandos.
Armand KIRSCHNER (French)	King's Medal For Courage	POW, escaped to SOE.
Alfred KISS (Anglo-German, Bristol, tbc)		
Major George I. KLAUBER	MiD	Force 139 (Polish origin).
Lt Arnost KLEIN		Czechoslovakia
John G. KLEIN		Planning section
Joseph KLEIN		
Julian KLEIN		Spain/Portugal
Robert KLEIN		

Names and Nationality – British or unknown unless stated	Awards	Place of death if relevant, and comments; European theatre unless stated
Harry KLEY (German)		SOE ?
281835 2nd Lt Charles (or K.K.), KLINGER Czech att. SWB Regt, formerly Czech Army and Pioneer Corps		Czechoslovakia
Lt Col James (Norman John) KLUGMANN	MiD and Yugoslav award	Deputy Dir. Yugoslav Section SOE in Cairo and Bari.
Henri and Paul KOCH		
Lt Franz Josef KOENIG/KING, aka Frank John Kelly (German)		12 Force
KOENIG, aka Gerhard KOCH?		
Dr Eugene KOGON (Vienna/France)		Buchenwald – survived (?).
Albert KOHAN (French)		
Marcelle KOHLER (French)		
Jean KOHN (Franco-American)		Joint Jedburgh.
Paul/Pavel KOHN (Czech)		
Teddy KOLLEK (Palestinian Jewish)		Cairo; later mayor of Jerusalem in Israel.
Adolf KON (Polish)		South America
L./Sgt Jack KOPS		Parachuted into Macedonia 9/8/44.
Cpl J.R.P. KOPPS (is this the same man as Kops?)		'Mission Triatic'.
Vincent William KORDA, aka Kellner (Hungarian/British)		Film magnate
Claus KOREN		
Moritz KORNFIELD		
J. KOSLOWSKI (Polish)		KIA 18/8/44.
Szama Hersz KRAKOWIAK (Franco-Polish)		Served Foreign Legion. Son of Lazare and Mirla.
KRAMMER (Hungarian)		
Leonard KRATZOFF		SOE Field Security
Harry KRAUS (Czech)		Pioneer Corps – SOE translator.
Lt KREBS (Polish)		Operation Dunstable.
Bruno KREISKY (Austrian)		Later Austrian Chancellor. SOE contact in exile in Sweden.
Lt Marcel (Marks) KRUMHORN, RA		
Otto KUDERNATSCH, aka Johann Kreiner (Austrian)		Post-war to IC.
Haim KUEN (Yugoslav)		Bulgarian courier.
Jules KUGENER		
Joseph KUGLER		
Henri LABIT (French)		
W. LAMM (Belgium)		
Sqdn Ldr Stephen W. LANDA, aka Lawrence		Polish liaison section.

Names and Nationality – British or unknown unless stated	Awards	Place of death if relevant, and comments; European theatre unless stated
Capt. John Joseph LANDAU, PC, Intelligence Corps, to SOE – No. 333733/13806150		Born 1918, Hungarian refugee to UK in 1938, dropped into Yugoslavia (interview with family).
Vivienne Regina LANDAU		Secretarial
Lt Harold LANDER		
Capt. Roger Charles LANDES (Franco-British)	MC and Bar, Croix de Guerre, Legion D'Hon.	Died July 2008.
George LANE/LANYI (Hungarian)	MC	No. 3 ('Jewish') Troop, No. 10 Commando/SOE – married Miriam Rothschild.
Jeno LANZMAN (Hungarian)		Wireless Operator, executed Budapest (HS4 98).
Capt. LASAREWITZ		Jedburgh/SOE trainer ME65 School.
D.S. LASKEY		Greece
David LAVI		Research section
Sidney Steven LAVINE/LEVENE – UK born, but served WW1 CEF France		Emigrated to USA – WW2 OSS in Portugal and South America.
Wing Cmdr LAWSON, RAF		British liaison with Palestinian Jewish SOE, Israel.
Capt. Ernest LAWSON (Glasgow)		Info. from brother Arthur Lawson of AJEX.
Alfred LAYTON/LESCHZINER (Austrian?)		To I/C.
Lt LEDER, aka Leach		
Capt. Lionel LEE/LEVY, RAC (born in Hackney)	MC, Croix de Guerre	Murdered Gross Rosen 27/6/44; Brookwood Memorial.
Lt Edward LEES/Ehard W.W. Saar, aka 'Teddy di dinamitardo'/Cheney (German)		Yugoslavia/Italy
Richard LEHNIGER, aka Leonard (German)		KIA France with Small Scale Raiding Force / 62 Commando, SOE. Although he was Jewish as are his children, the CWGC grave has no religious symbol as he claimed to be an atheist.
Dr LEIBOVICI (Franco-Polish)		Worked for SOE in Paris.
M. LEIBOWITCH (French)		SOE contact.
Josef LEITNER, aka Seipl (Austrian)		
Aharonchik LESHEM/LISHEVSKY (Palestinian Jewish)		Commander Syrian ('Fake Arabs') Platoon, Haganah and Palmach with SOE.
Joel LETAC (French)		POW France, survived – tbc.
Lt Edward (Eugene) Francis LEVENE/ FELANGUE	MiD	Murdered Flossenberg 29/3/45; Brookwood Memorial.
Renato LEVI, aka Sabre (Italian)		
Walter LEVI		SOE Special Clothing Services, London.
Georges LEVIN (French)		
Gerhard LEVIN		

Names and Nationality – British or unknown unless stated	Awards	Place of death if relevant, and comments; European theatre unless stated
Lt Henri LEVIN, aka Georges (French)	DSO	2nd in command 'Vic' escape line.
Hubertus LEVIN, aka Patrick Hugh Miles		Raid on Herne, CI; SSRF (see Lehniger).
Lt LEVY, RNVR		Ran agents and supplies in Balkans in MTBs – WIA (see TNA HS7/171).
Andre LEVY		
Charles LEVY (American)		Worked in Portugal.
Frederic LEVY		
Gerard Patrick LEVY		
Gaston LEVY (French)	Certificate of Commendation	
Capt. Jacques LEVY (French)	Certificate of Commendation	
Jean-Michel LEVY, aka Remy		Wireless Operator
Lt Dr Jean-Pierre LEVY (French)		
Joseph William LEVY		
Dr Louis LEVY ('of Antibes'), aka Jovet (French)	Certificate of Commendation	Murdered Sachsenhausen, 1945.
Louis and Theodore LEVY (of Ferzensac, France)	Certificates of Commendation	
Lucien LEVY		
Madeline LEVY, aka Masson		Daughter of Emile and Lily Levy, b. Johannesburg – 'F' Section France. Died 2007, aged 95.
Capt. Michael Meyer George LEVY	MiD – died Vancouver 2007	SOE Selangor, Far East Force 136; escaped from Japanese internment in Shanghai.
Mike LEVY (German)		1945 in Germany.
Mme Roger (Jeanne Marie) LEVY (French)	Certificate of Commendation	Captured and murdered by Nazis.
Capt. Roger LEVY (French Air Force) – husband of Mrs R. Levy above	MC	
Fl. Off. Ross Victor Allan LEVY (RNZAF) – from Wellington, NZ – 161 Sqdn	DFC	Killed in action from Tempsford, 19/10/44, buried Cambridge, UK.
Lt Rene LEVY-PICARD		Not used on ops.
William LEWISOHN		Worked in North China.
Herman LEWY		
Capt. Julian Joseph LEZARD (South African)	MiD	Force 133 France and WIA.
Major Phillippe LIEWER, aka Geoffrey Staunton (French)	MC, Croix de Guerre	
Mrs LIEWER (wife of above)		Spain
Max LIPPMAN, aka Heine (German)		From Pioneer Corps 13809030, to SOE.
Major Ole/Olav LIPPMANN (Danish)	OBE (Mil.)	Head of SOE in Denmark.
LITVINE, aka Lousseau, aka Wing Cdr Simons		

Names and Nationality – British or unknown unless stated	Awards	Place of death if relevant, and comments; European theatre unless stated
Claude LIVSCHITZ (Belgium)		Captured and tortured.
Sir Ben LOCKSPEISER		SOE scientist.
Walter LOEB (Dutch/German)		Propaganda section – may not have been employed.
Major Lionel Louis LOEWE		
Max LOEWY		
Capt. LONGDEN (Austrian)		Served in China 204 Military Mission.
Lt Frederick Charles LOWENBACH (Romanian)		Germany/Switzerland escape line.
Charlotte LUETKINS, aka Mendelsohn		Czech Sudetan, Czech translator, Baker St.
13801595 Pte E. LUSTIG, PC		
Gabor MAKAI (Hungarian)		
Capt. Leopold Herman MANDERSTAM (Russian)	MBE	Head of Russian and Angola Section SOE, author of *From Red Army to SOE*.
Rudolf MANHARDT, aka Roger Minter, aka Neuman		German soldier deserted Italy 1944, stepfather Jewish, served in Austria.
Louis MANNHEIM (Franco-Hungarian)		
Lt Pierre Emile Jacques MANUEL, aka Pessard, aka Bressac (French)		POW 1940, escaped to UK, served in France 1944.
L. Cpl Jerzy MARA-MEYER (Polish)		Inserted March 1942 to Lublin rising, KIA December 1942 – tbc?
Capt. Hugh John MARKS, Yorks. and Lancs. – of Jewish origin, tbc		Escaped Norway 1940, SOE, drowned in training off Scotland preparing for ops.
Leo Samuel MARKS	MBE	Chef de Codage at Baker Street.
Fl. Sgt A/G (Nav.) Ellis MARKSON (son of David and Sarah)		161 Sqdn RAF Tempford, KIA 9/8/44.
Lt Col Eric Albert MASCHWITZ		SIS/MI6 to SOE in UK and USA.
Lt Paul 'Yogi' MAYER, aka Michael Frank (German)		12 Force and historian; to I/C.
Julius MEINL		Adviser on Yugoslav missions, Baker St.
Capt. Albert MELCHIOR (Belgian)	King's Commendation for Brave Conduct	
Capt. Charles MELCHIOR, aka Leandre	Croix de Guerre	POW, survived.
Paulette MELCHIOR (wife of Charles), aka Simone		
Albert Clive MENDELSOHN		Portugal and Angola
Lt Dominique Armand MENDELSON, MC aka Benjamin (French)		
MENDELSOHN, aka Phil Duncan		
6896702 Derek MERTON		JC obituary describes missions in Lysanders to France (tbc).
Louis METZ, aka Babriel		

Names and Nationality – British or unknown unless stated	Awards	Place of death if relevant, and comments; European theatre unless stated
Berthe MEYER	MBE	Husband and wife (see below) Wireless Operators and agents in Madagascar against Vichy French
Percy MEYER	OBE	
Lt Rene MEYER (French)		Jedburgh/SOE
Verity H. MICHAELSON		Cyphers
Lt Charles George MICHEL, aka Michot (French)		Escaped POW 1940, to SOE.
Mlle Simone-Francois MICHEL-LEVY	Cert. of Commendation (Posthumous)	Murdered at Flossenburg.
Samson MIKIECZINSKI (Polish)		Istanbul
Capt. John MILLER, aka Stephan Wirlander		N Africa, Italy, Turkey
H. MILLESTEIN (French)		
S.C. MISKIN		Secretarial
Sydney MITCHELL, RAF		Aircrew despatcher to SOE agents.
Lt O.J. MITZLER		
Andre MOCH, French Socialist MP (Deputy)	King's Commendation for Brave Conduct	KIA in France on ops.
Frigyes MOLNAR (Hungarian)		HS4 116
Jane MONNICKENDAM		Secretarial
The Hon. Lionel Samuel MONTAGU	(DSO, MiD, WW1)	'Special Duties' with SOE.
Ms Hilda MONTE, aka Meisel, aka Oldag, aka Selma Trier (Austrian)		Portugal
Origliano MONTEFIORE		Worked in France.
Peter John MORTON, aka Meyer (German)		IC/SOE killed 10/3/45; Groesebeek Memorial.
Rudolf MOSER, aka Henry		Yugoslavia
Pearl MUNTZ		
Werner MUNKSHOLM, aka Moritzen (Danish)		Denmark/Sweden
Brigadier Wolf Edmund MYERS	DSO, CBE	Greek Gorgopotomos viaduct operation; later Arnhem Chief Engineer CO, and Korean War.
Sgt David NABARRO (RCOS)	Certificate of Commendation	
Leah Sarah NADEL		
Lt Maurice NAEGEL (French?)		Murdered by Nazis.
Peter NAGEL, aka Newman, aka Walker (German)		Pioneer Corps to No. 2 Commando for raid on Bruneval (part SOE mission) and St Nazaire (POW, escaped, recaptured).Trained by SOE. Post-war lived in Leicester.

Names and Nationality – British or unknown unless stated	Awards	Place of death if relevant, and comments; European theatre unless stated
Raymond NAGEL		
David NAMERI (Israeli)		Organizer/trainer of Palmach/SOE ops.
Emmanuel Louis NATANSON		
R. NAUDEL		Not used on ops.
Georgy NEUBAUER (Hungarian)		
Gottfried NEUBAUER, aka Josef Cjika		
Hans NEUFELD, aka Harry Newman, Nuffield/Slade (Austrian)		
Henry Oscar NEUMAN		
Marcel Paul NEUMAN		
Lt Hendrick NEUMANN (Norwegian)	King's Medal for Brave Conduct	
Lt Theo NEUMANN/NORMAN – may not have been Jewish		12 Force – Austria Wireless Op.
Capt. Isidore NEWMAN	MBE, MiD, Croix de Guerre	Murdered at Mauthausen.
Julian/Philip NEWMAN		Spain
Rex NEWMAN		
Fl. Sgt Jack NISSENTHAL (RAF)		His famous role on the 1942 Dieppe raid to 'pinch' German radar was an SOE operation.
Emmanuel NOWOGRODZKI (Polish)		
Lt Humphrey O. NUNES		
Maurice NUSSENBAUM (French)		
Lt Frederick Michael O'HARA, aka Egon Friederich Paul Berliner, aka Fl. Officer Chirgwin, aka Knoll, aka Hofer (Austrian)	Recommended for MC but was KIA (see HS6/22 at TNA)	12 Force – POW and murdered by SS – Operation Evansville; Cassino Memorial 4/4/45.
Adriano OLIVETTI (Italian)		
Sub Lt Sonia OLSCHANESKY (French-Polish)		Murdered Natzweiler 6/7/44 – not commemorated by CWGC.
Herta OPPENHEIMER (Jewish origin)		Portuguese escape line for Allies.
Sgt Abraham OPOCZYNSKI, aka Adam Orr, aka Anthony James		Trained by SOE. SSRF (see above), SAS, POW, escaped, KIA 1945 in Germany, buried Durnbach.
Henry Ralph OPPENHEIM		Force 136 Far East
George OPPENHEIM		
Richard OPPENHEIM		
John ORBACH		
Feodor ORNSTEIN		
Sgt Gertrude Dorothy ORNSTEIN		Force 136 Far East – Secretarial.
Jerome ORTSTEIN (French)	Certificate of Commendation	
Winifred Bertha ORTWEILER		SOE secretarial/driver

Names and Nationality – British or unknown unless stated	Awards	Place of death if relevant, and comments; European theatre unless stated
Capt. Ernesto OTTOLENGHI, aka Ernest Ottley (Italian)		Served Africa and Middle East.
Raphael Mesod OZIEL (Moroccan)	King's Medal for Brave Conduct	
PALMER/POJU		
Leo PARDO (Austrian)		Not used on ops. but possibly in Turkey.
Cpl Woolf PEREZ, RAF	MiD	Tempsford ground crew
Capt Maurice PERTSCHUK, aka Martin Perkins	MBE, Legion D'Hon., Croix de Guerre, MiD	Murdered Buchenwald 29/3/45; Brookwood Memorial.
Pilot Officer Peter PERTSCHUK, RAF (brother of Maurice?)		
Howard John R. PETERS/Hans Joseph Pincus/Pinkus (Austrian?)		To I/C.
Capt. Adolf PILCH (Polish)	King's Medal for Brave Conduct	Home army 1941–45/SOE.
Jacques PINKASFELD		Polish, att. SOE Middle East 1940–43.
Elias PINTO		
Jacob Abraham PINTO		
Alberto PIRELLI (Italian)		
Paul POEMERL (Austrian)		IC/SOE German POW – may have been Jewish (see book, *Hitler's Jewish Soldiers*[7]) – POW liberated Mauthausen/Dachau?
P. POLACK (Dutch)		Deployed 16/8/44 to March 1945.
Lt Dr Charles POLAK, aka Mathertiuan, aka Pittard (French)		Medical SOE in France 1944–45.
Maria POLAK		
Oscar POLAK (Austrian)		Served Europe.
Lt POLANSKI (Poland)		
Erich POLLACK (German)		Specialist Printing section.
Sigmund POLLACK (Austrian)		Turkey?
Sgt POLIC – 13122241		PC to SOE.
Sgt Pilot Max POLITZER (Czech att. 138 Sqdn)		KIA Tempsford 10/3/42 – ashes repatriated to Czech republic.
Sgt Nav. Joseph Norman POLLAND, (son of Sara and Samuel – tbc)		138 Sqdn Tempsford, KIA 19/12/43.
Lt PORTHOS (alias), aka Andre Schwartzmann, aka Regnier (French)		
Col Marcel POUGATCH, RAOC		Greece 1944.
J. POZNANSKI (Polish)		KIA 10/43.
Peter Michael PRIESTLEY, aka Egon Lindenbaum/Lindenberg, aka Michael Stockner (Austrian)		POW, survived.
Valentine RAAB, aka Albert Rabenstein		

Names and Nationality – British or unknown unless stated	Awards	Place of death if relevant, and comments; European theatre unless stated
Capt Adam/Ari (Adolph) RABINOVITCH/Rabinowicz, aka Frederic (Russian/Egyptian/Palestinian Jewish)	OBE, Croix de Guerre, MiD	Escaped French POW, SOE, murdered by Gestapo Gross Rosen, 2/3/44; Brookwood Memorial.
Lazare RACHELINE (French)	OBE	Escaped POW 1940.
Maurice RACHELINE (brother of Lazare)		
Victor RACHELINE	MiD	Murdered 10/6/44 – ran an Allied escape network.
Eve RACKMAN		
A/C David Hay RAEBURN, RAF		Tempsford ground crew
John RAMENSKI/RAMEL, aka John Ramsey (Polish/Scots)		Safebreaker, possibly Jewish origin, later 30 Commando.
Major Aron RAPOPORT, RAMC	MBE	SOE Force 136, Burma.
Michael RAPOPORT, RAMC		Cousin of above (?) – served India/Burma.
Elijah RAPOPORT, aka Sam Eric		PC to SOE – killed at sea 7/6/44 – D-Day; b. Bayeux under English name – tbc.
Yohanan RATNER (Palestinian Jewish)		SOE raids with Syrian Platoon of Haganah and SOE.
David RAZIEL (Israeli)		Commander of Irgun, killed in action for SOE in Iraq in 1941. Not commemorated by the CWGC.
Ernst REDLICH (Austrian)		Appears to have worked in Greece (HS8/870 TNA).
Capt. Harry REE (father Jewish)	DSO, MC, OBE, Legion d'Hon, Croix de Guerre	Famous 'F' Section agent.
CSM Eric Lionel REE, brother of Harry Ree		SOE Security Section – died in North Africa.
Dolf REISER		SOE forger.
Geza/Gerza REISMAN (Czech)		
Major Friederich Franz REITLINGER, aka Roberts (Austrian)		Jewish origin, dismissed Austrian Army 1936, served Middle East and Europe.
Yochanan RETNER (Israeli)		Trainer/organizer Palmach/SOE ops.
Lt Eric RHODES, aka Erich Rohde (German)		12 Force
RICE – see Bate(s) and Smith – alias		Czech – alleged POW – officially MIA since Dieppe Raid 1942.
A. RIEDL (Polish)		KIA 7/3/44.
M. and Mme Gabriel RIGAL	Certificates of Commendation	
Henry RITTER		Polish refugee, member of Oxford and St George Jewish Youth Club, Stepney; SSRF (see above).
Maurice ROSCHBACH		
Maurice ROSENBACH, aka Serilan (French)		Known to have parachuted from Tempsford – photo.

Names and Nationality – British or unknown unless stated	Awards	Place of death if relevant, and comments; European theatre unless stated
Albert Israel ROSENBERG		
Alex ROSENBERG		
Johanna Emarta ROSENBERG		
Ludwig ROSENBERG		
L. ROSENBLUTH/ROSENBLUETH		
Istvan ROSENFELD (Hungarian)		
Dr Henri ROSENSCHER, aka 'Raoul', aka H.P. Richet (French)		KIA 1/8/44 Grenoble as Medical Officer to SOE.
Capt. Jean Pierre ROSENTHAL, aka Apotheme (French)	MC	
Alan Claud ROSENWALD		
Sgt D. ROTENBERG/ROTHENBERG		SOE trainer and Field Security.
Helmut ROTHENBERG (German)		Collected clothes from refugees in London for SOE.
Roger ROTHSCHILD, aka Radart		
G. RUBENSTEIN, aka Supervia		
Murray Eric RUBIN		
David RUBINSTEIN (Norwegian)		Brother of Ruth. Worked in Sweden. Arrested there
Major Richard RUBINSTEIN	MC, Croix de Guerre, MiD	France and Burma/also Jedburgh.
Ruth (Lillemore) RUBINSTEIN (Norwegian) aka Rodner		Served in Sweden.
Zinder RUBINSTEIN, aka Roger Martin		
Gustav RUDIGER (German)		Served in Balkans (HS4 116).
Walter RUHM/ROOME		Extracted safely – Helen Fry's book, p.91. Used papers of dead German soldier for seven months undercover.
Jack SAADIA		
Greta SACHS (Hungarian)		Arrested, escaped.
Mr SACHS		Clerical staff Istanbul
Palle SACHS		
Yitzhak SADE (Israeli)		Trainer/organizer SOE/Palmach ops.
Boba SADIKOFF		
Herbert SAGEL		Yugoslavia
Major Donald SALINGER	MiD	South East Asia Special Operations
Camille SALOMON (French)	Certificate of Commendation	
Frederich SALOMON		
Georges SALOMON (French)		Murdered by Nazis; former teacher Lycée Française, London.
Jean SALOMON (French)		
Luc SALOMON (French)		
Ya'acov SALOMON (Palestinian Jewish)		Haganah; coordinated training of 37 Parachutists with SOE.

Names and Nationality – British or unknown unless stated	Awards	Place of death if relevant, and comments; European theatre unless stated
Cornelio MICHELIN-SALOMON		
Vera MICHELIN-SALOMON		
Stephanie SALTER, née Wagner (German)		Israel
Capt. The Hon. Anthony Gerald SAMUEL (son of Lord Bearsted)		Courier in both neutral and occupied Europe, as well as South America.
Raymond SAMUEL (French)		
Col Walter Horace SAMUEL, 2nd Viscount Lord BEARSTEAD (MC, MiD, WW1)		Interviewer for SOE, father of Anthony, above.
James SAMUELS (Is this Capt. J.V. Samuels, Force 136 Far East?)		
Lt Eric SANDERS, aka Erich/Ignaz Schwartz (Austrian)		12 Force
Lt Giacomo SARFATTI, aka Galea, aka Rossi (Italian)		Italy
Mr SARKOZY (Hungarian)		Assisted escaping agents.
John SASSON		
Albert SASSOON		Wireless Operator
Sir Ellis Victor SASSOON, Bt.		
George Victor SAUNDERS, aka Salloschin		No. 3 ('Jewish') Troop, No. 10 Commando – attached to SOE.
Sgt Harry John SAUNDERS, aka Dietrich Holzer	MM	Germany 1945.
Josef SAXE (Belgium)		
Anna, Heinrich, Herta and Vera SCHACK (Austrian)		May not have been on ops.
Walter SCHAEFFER, aka Sanger (Palestinian Jewish)		Not used in ops.
SCHAEFLER (Rumanian)		
Peter SCHAMASCH		
Henri SCHAWB/SCHWAB (?) (French)		
Albert P. SCHEFFER(S)		MIA.
Robert SCHEIN		
Lt Oscar Gerald SCHEINMANN, aka J. G. Perkins		Austrian/German refugee; served Italy.
Lt Paul SCHERRER (French)		Jedburgh/SOE 1944–45.
Luis SCHLESINGER		
Willi SCHLESINGER		
Bernard SCHLUMBERGER (French)		
Roger SCHMALZ (French)		
J.G. SCHMALZER (French)		
Walter SCHNEK		

Names and Nationality – British or unknown unless stated	Awards	Place of death if relevant, and comments; European theatre unless stated
A. SCHNITZER (tbc)		
Herbert SCHOEN, Pal. 23173	BEM	Force 133 Balkans, captured, escaped.
Col R.C.F. SCHOMBERG (Jewish origin).		Force 136 Far East
Franz SCHONMANN (Austrian)		Survived sinking of 'Arandora Star'; not used in the field.
Lt Maurice SCHUMANN, aka Andre Sidobre (French)	Croix de Guerre (1940) and Legion D'Hon.	POW 1940, escape to UK with De Gaulle and FF and returned D-Day; later French Foreign Minister.
Hans Otto SCHWALM, aka Jan Petersen		Not used on ops.
Elizabeth SCHWARTZ, aka Ruth Koerner		
Sandor SCHWATSCKO		
Karl SCHWARTZ (Russo-Austrian)		
Rudolph SCHWARTZ, aka Raymond Sharpe		Austrian
Edward SCHWARZ, aka Hauber, aka Hammer		Wireless Op.
SCHWARZFELD, aka Thomas/Aubrey		
Francois SCHWEIGER (German)		
Lt Harry (Hans) SCHWEIGER/Harry John Stevens (German)		12 Force. Described in his SOE report as having 'a rat-like type of Jewish face'.
George Henry SCHWITZER		
Gregor SEBBA (Austrian)		SOE liaison in USA.
F.W. SECKEL (Austrian)		Portugal
SEINFELD (Polish)		Courier
Lt Cmdr Adrian SELIGMAN, RN	DSC	Commander Levant Schooner Flotilla inserting/extracting agents.
Sqdn Ldr H.I. SELIGMAN		SOE vetting officer in London.
Francis Gerard SELIGMANN (French)		
J. SERAFIN (Polish)		KIA 20/5/44.
Anton/Antoine G. SERENI, aka Casimir (French)	MBE	Wireless Operator, circuit 'Jockey'.
Sgt Ken SEYMOUR (alias?)		Jedburgh Wireless Operator, POW, survived Auschwitz.
Leon SHALIT (Anglo-Russian)		Russian section.
78257 Sq Ldr, Herbert Ronald SHARMAN. Battle of Britain Pilot	AFC	With 297 Squadron, inserted SOE agents into Europe.
Giora SHENAN (Palestian Jewish)		Trainer/organizer Palmach/SOE ops.
Ze'ev SHIND (Palestinian Jewish)		Haganah liaison with SOE.
Alex SHOKOLOVSKY (French/Polish?)		Killed.
Fl. Off. Herbert SICHEL		

Names and Nationality – British or unknown unless stated	Awards	Place of death if relevant, and comments; European theatre unless stated
Mrs Daphne M. SIEFF		Worked in SOE code room, Baker St.
Ms Jan SILVER		FANY at Tempsford.
Arthur SILVESTER, RAPC		Not used on ops.
SIMON (French)		To I/C – not used on SOE ops.
Imre/Endre SINGER (Hungarian)		
Capt. Benjamin Abraham SLOSSMAN		Born Russia, served Shanghai Volunteer Corps and British RASC to Force Z and 136 in Burma (brother KIA Burma with Glos. Regt).
Meyer SLUYSER (Dutch Socialist) – tbc		
SMITH, aka Sleigh? (see PLL) – see Bate(s) and Rice		Czech – MIA since Dieppe Raid 1942.
Alexander SMOLNIKOV		Israel/Turkey
T. SOKOLOWSKI (Polish)		KIA 6/2/43.
Fl. Off. (Nav.) Leonard J. SOLOMON		Tempsford aircrew KIA 1/6/44 – 138 Sqdn.
Margaret SOLOMON		Secretarial
Mihail SOLOMON (Romanian)		Middle East
Kurt SONNENFELD, aka Wirth (German)		
D. SPIELMANN		
Capt. Barry SPIERO		
Maurice SPIRO (Albanian)		
Lola SPITZ		
Hans SPITZER (Austrian)		Force 133
Kurt STEIN, aka Stewart (German)		Sweden
Desire STEINER (French)		
Eugen STEINWURZEL (German)		Served Hungary and Turkey – arrested; survived (?).
Artur STERN (Hungarian)		HS4 116
Capt. David STERN, aka Beau	Croix de Guerre, MiD	SOE/Jedburgh.
Lawrence STERN		
Max STERN		
Rosa STERN		
Jacques STERNBERG (Belgium)		SOE Courier.
Max STERNBERG (French)		
Lt Ronnie STEWART (alias) (German)		12 Force
Maximilian STIER (Romanian)		
Major Rudolf STUPPEL, RAMC	MiD (posthumous)	POW escaped to Yugoslvia with Tito partisans/SOE – killed 31/10/43, buried Belgrade.
Andre SUSSMAN		

Names and Nationality – British or unknown unless stated	Awards	Place of death if relevant, and comments; European theatre unless stated
August SUSSMAN, aka Gustav Simo		Was in German Army, as anti-Nazi Austrian, of Jewish origin, then deserted to Greek partisans and then to UK Army; trained for SOE.
Cpl Harry SUTTON/Heinz SOFFNER		
M. TAJCHMAN (Polish)		KIA 3/8/44.
T12329 Major Monia TALAN (Palestinian Jewish)	MBE	Force 136 SOE; formerly Jewish Company, Shanghai Volunteer Corps and Hong Kong Volunteer Force, escaped to China by MTB.
Alexander TARNOPOL		
Lt Vladimir TAUSSIG (Czech)		Not used on ops.
Jacques TAYAR (French)		
Louis TCHERKOSKI (Belgian)		See Bromberger – worked in Paris.
Birko TEN(N)ENBAUM/ TANNENBAUM		Pole serving Czech Army; trained for SOE; used Spain/Portugal?
Lt Lazar TEPNER (Romanian serving in RCAMC)		
Peter TERRY, aka Tischler		WIA, att. SSRF (see above) and 47th RM Commando from No. 3 ('Jewish') Troop, No. 10 Commando.
Lt Peter Johann ULANOWSKY, aka Peter Hall, aka Lt Brand (Austrian/ German)		Served in Slovenia.
Dr E.W. UNNA (German)		
Mario R. UZIELL		
Nino UZIELL (Italian?)		
Istvan VAGO (Hungarian)		
L. Van BLANKENSTEIN (Dutch/ Canadian)		
Jean Louis VANDERMEULEN		
Maria VECRIS (Austrian)		May not have been on ops.
Giuseppe VENANZI (Italian)		
P. VERHOEF (French)		Secretarial
Emmanuel VILENSKY/YELAN (Palestinian Jewish)		Haganah Interrogation liaison with SOE.
Adele/Ada/Anna VISNOVIZ/ VISHOVITCH, née Huber (Hungarian)		Courier – claimed RC but Huber is a Jewish name; worked in Hungary, Italy, Istanbul; captured and survived Ravensbruck.
Walter WACKWITZ (German)		
13804041 Pte J. WALDMANN		Slovak translator at Baker St.
Sgt Jack August WARNDORFER (Austrian)		IC/SOE killed 14/10/44–12/1/45; Groesebeek Memorial; nephew-in-law of Admiral Lord Cunningham.

Names and Nationality – British or unknown unless stated	Awards	Place of death if relevant, and comments; European theatre unless stated
S/Lt Marcel Abraham WARSZAWIACK (French)	King's Medal for Courage	
Max WASSERMAN (Czech)		
Bernard Henri WEIL		
Claude Robert WEIL		
Capt. Gabriel Pierre WEIL (Belgian)	Chev. de l'Order Couronne and de l'Order Leopold II and MBE	POW 1940, escaped, SOE.
Hans Hartmut WEIL		
Commandant Jacques WEIL (French)	OBE	Fiancé of Sonia Olschanezky.
Maurice WEIL		
Robert Simon WEIL		
Ms Simone WEIL		Auschwitz; survived/later President of the EU (?).
Andre Pierre WEILL-CURIEL (French)		
Rene WEILL (French)		
Alic WEIN		Radio Operator.
Frantisek WEINER, aka Frank Viner (Czech)	Croix de Guerre but from French Army 1940 before SOE	
Ernest George WEINBERGER, aka Webster		KIA SSRF att. 47th RM Commando from No. 3 ('Jewish') Troop. Cross on grave as he attested as C. of E.
Suzanne WEINSTEIN (French)		Survived Ravensbruck.
Sgt WEINSTEIN, aka 'Tom' (Palestinian Jewish)		Hungary
Lt WEINZIERL/WEINSINGER? aka Sedlak, aka Wood (Austrian?)		Pioneer Corps to SOE, Force 399 Hungary.
Dr Eric Karl WEISINGER, aka Marcus (Austrian)		
Ensign Enid WEISS/WHITE		FANY, Monopoli SOE base.
Sgt Peter WEISZ/WEISS (Austrian)	King's Commendation for Brave Conduct	IC/SOE – POW – killed Dachau 1–30/4/45; Groesebeek Memorial.
Gottlieb WERNER (Czech Sudetan)		Austrian Army WW1
Capt. Manfred WERNER, aka Frederick Michael Warner (German)		12 Force
Jacques/Jean WERTHEIMER		
Maurice WERTHER (French) tbc		
Edgar Bernard WESTFIELD/ WESTFELD (German)		Chemist, served SOE Force 133, Middle East.

Names and Nationality – British or unknown unless stated	Awards	Place of death if relevant, and comments; European theatre unless stated
Franz WIENER (Romanian)		
Major Lionel WIGRAM – writer of Basic British Army Training Text on Infantry Tactics		'Wigforce' SOE, KIA Italy February 1944.
Abraham Victor WIJNBERG, aka Winjdaal (Dutch)		Captured, executed Amersfoort camp 1943.
Major Lyell WILKES, MP, Middx Regt.	MiD	Behind the lines in Greece – *JC* item.
Sgt Norman WILLERT, aka Norbert Wegner (Austrian)		Intellelligence/SOE/OSS – KIA 1/9/44; Groesebeek Memorial.
Lt Harry WILLIAMS, aka Wunder (German)		12 Force into Germany – fought in Spanish Civil War against Franco.
Madame WIMILLE (French)		Courier with her husband, POW with Denise Bloch, survived.
Jean Pierre WIMILLE (French)		Husband of above.
Ernst WINTER		
Capt. Ernest Felix WISE/WEISS, aka White (Austrian)		Attached Rome SOE. Son of Hermione Loew; on confidential work in London and post-war German occupation forces.
Ethel Rose WIX		SOE Baker Street clerical officer.
Lt Gordon Frances WIX		Force 136 Far East – attested as C. of E.
Andre WOLF (French)		KIA Signes.
Claude Kurt WOLF (French)		Wireless Operator
Miss D.R.M. WOLF		Secretarial
Edith WOLF (Hungarian)		Arrested, escaped.
Pierre WOLF (French)		
Alex WOLFE (Hungarian Canadian)		
Emile WOLFE		
Milton WOLFF (USA)		Commander Abraham Lincoln Brigade in Spain, attached SOE in Europe until 1941, then to OSS – died 2008.
WOLOCHOFF (Russian)		
Major Ivan/Ian Justin WOOLF, aka J. Wallace, aka Jean Paul (Anglo-Swiss)	MiD	France and Burma and Jedburgh (Force 136), died 2008; wife Miriam was niece of Leonard Woolf, publisher.
Miss Mamie C. WOOLF		Wireless Operator
Cmdr V. WOLFSON/WOLSON, RN	OBE	SOE official Istanbul and Danube naval missions.
Lt Col Jean Alexandre WORMS, aka J. de Verieux (Swiss/French)	MC, Croix de Guerre and 19 other decorations	Executed Flossenberg 29/3/45;Brookwood Memorial.
Sgt Max WYSOCKI – Polish AF – att. 138 Sqdn – tbc	NOT commemorated by CWGC	KIA from Tempsford 17/12/42 – Malta Naval Cemetery, Capuccini.
Zvi YEHI'ELLI (Palestinian Jewish)		Haganah liaison of the 37 Parachutists with SOE.

Names and Nationality – British or unknown unless stated	Awards	Place of death if relevant, and comments; European theatre unless stated
Reuven ZASLANY/SHILOAH/'Raz', aka 'Jonathan' (Palestinian Jewish)		Senior Israeli Intelligence Chief in Liaison with SOE/MI6 1931–44/Turkey.
Lt Edward ZEFF, aka Zoltan	MBE, Croix de Guerre	Liberated at Mauthausen.
Lt Hans ZEILINGER, aka Linger, aka G.H. Adams		Austrian/German refugee.
Jean and Andre ZELA		
Konstantin and Vera ZERKOWITZ		Attested as RC, probably Jewish.
Peter ZERKOWITZ (Hungarian)		Turkey
Bruno ZEVI		
Hans ZUCKERMAN (Norwegian)		2nd i/c Operation Antipodes.
Otto Ludwig ZWIEBACK, aka Roger L. Stanley		
Lt Leon ZYNGERMAN	Certificate of Commendation	

The following list was found in TNA file HS4 133, made up of Hungarian Jews who were refugees in Tangier in 1941 and offered to serve for the British in SOE in East Europe:

Jozsef ELLMAN
Jozsefine ELLMAN, née GUTTMAN
Lazslo FISCHL
Lajor HIRSCHFELD
Zoltan KELLERMAN
Jozsef KELLNER
Jozsefina KELLNER, née ROSENBLATT
Gyula KLEIN
Istaven ROSENFELD
Sandor STARK
Istwan WEIL

List 2

These names come from TNA file WO 106 6155. The contents are mainly about Pioneer Corps men who changed their identities after moving into 'Special Forces', but it is not clear, except for a few, who actually went into SOE. Most appear to have been sent to Italy and the Balkans.

13041872 Private Max AZAN
13041876 Gustav BERTRAM, aka Britain/Bodo
13122238 Milos GRUBICH, aka Miles Brubich, recruited into SOE from Canada in 1942, to the Middle East, but did not see action – tbc.
13046674 Sergeant Adam HERTER, aka Herbert

13041877/13807930 Private T. NAIDENHOFF

13122227 W. PORZIG

13122260 Corporal Josef Ludwig ROTH

13122230 Sergeant Karl Heinz SCHUMACHER

13122252 Corporal Franz Carl WALLNER

13122230 Horst WEBER

13122240 Sergeant Heinz Georg WINTER

List 3

The following names, members of SOE, come from Peter Leighton-Langer's book, *The King's Own Enemy Aliens* (London: Vallentine Mitchell, 2006). Some may not be Jews, it simply is not known, but they are given here in the hope more research may throw light on the matter.

Fritz Peter ANZBOCK, aka Horak

M. BABIN 13807884

Ernest BAERWALD, aka Pierre Charleroi 13807861

E. BALLING 13806024

G. BEGICH/BEGIC 13807892

BENNETT (alias)

Heinrich BERGER-WALDENEGG, aka Henry Baum/Burleigh

Charles (1st name only known)

Manfred CHALAUPA, aka Alfred Achatz, aka Anton Kaulaut – tbc

Charles (?) CRAVEN

A. DUSCHENES 13810028

K.J.H. EISNER 13800980, aka R.H. Belgrave 6387021, aka Grant 13116381

Emil FACHS, aka Emil Blaha/Straker

E. FERRARO 13806120

K. FINK 13806115

Albrecht GAISWINKLER, aka Karl Schumacher, aka Alfred Winkler

O.C.S. GEISLER 13806041

GRAFL, aka John Green/Johann Boenisch

HABETTLER

Josef HEMETZBERGER, aka Ruzicka, aka Schmittbauer

K. HERSCHEND 13806129

Nikolas HUETZ, aka Hauber/Hammer/Heger

Harold HUGHES, aka Kirk

J./M. JENSEN

M. JURMAN

A. KNUDSEN 13806017

Blasius KOBAN, aka Bernard Kan/B. Loeffler/Kezeker

J. KOULOUKAS 13807698

KROSSMAYR, aka Kennedy

V. KROTSKY 13806113

A.T. LARSEN 13806049

H.H.P. LARSEN 13806042

P. LIZZA 13806131

P. LOK-LINBLAD

Karl LZICAR

Rudolf MANHARDT

F. MARTIN 13806116

A.D. MASTBAUM 13810022

Hubert MAYR, aka Banks/Jean Georgeau/Josef Rimmel

Johann MUELLER/MALLE/MORRIS, John

F.B. MUUS 13806063

Paul NIGGAS/NORTON, aka Paul Windisch

Ferdinad PANHOFER, aka Sokol

V.K. PEDERSEN 13806050

Georg PICK 13116506/311174

Ejar PRETZNER, aka Harold Blum/Franz Berger

Johann Sepp RASBORSCHEG

H.K. RIEMER 13802245, aka Roberts 6436359

T. RUEMAN 13046356

Herbert SAGEL

Gerhardt SIMBUERGER, aka George Stones/Huber

Roman SPREIZHOFER, aka Roman Haas/Franz Roschitz/Andrea Knabl/Hans Wieser

Karl STANDHARTIGER, aka Josef L. Roth, aka Karl Schmidt

Norbert TRAUTTMANSDORF/TAGGERT, KIA

S. TRKULJA 13806072

U. UM – anonymous.

ULLSTEIN

R. VETERS 13806132

W. WACHSMANN 13807531, aka J. Hayes 6346358

H. WERTHEIM, KIA – two brothers.

List 4: The Incident of the Non-Commemorated Palestinian Jewish Commandos of SOE from Operation Boatswain, 18 May 1941

With the assistance of Lt Col (Ret.) Neri Areli, Director of Haganah Historical Archives of the MoD of Israel

On the night of Friday 18 May 1941, the Commando boat *Sea Lion* ('Ariyeh Ha Yum'), secretly left Haifa harbour on 'Operation Boatswain'. Commanded by Major Sir Anthony Palmer, SOE, RA, with twenty-three enlisted Jewish Palestinian volunteers of the Haganah and Palmach/'Buffs', (East Kent) Palestinian Regiment. Their mission was to destroy Vichy French oil refineries near Tripoli, Lebanon. All the men disappeared at sea, without trace, before the mission could be carried out.

Despite efforts since 1945 by both British and Israeli investigators, in Lebanon, France and Britain, nothing has ever been discovered about this mystery, except copies of garbled messages unearthed in French military archives pertaining to vessels attacked that night in the eastern Mediterranean, and a British request about possible POWs in French prisons in 1941. It appears the *Sea Lion* did transmit twice before contact was lost, and later bodies were found on the Lebanese coast, including Major Palmer's.

With the exception of Palmer, the men are *not* commemorated by the British Commonwealth War Graves Commission and no satisfactory reason has ever been given for this. They are listed in our Jewish Book of Remembrance in the Palestine Jewish Volunteers section (under 'SOE, killed 18/5/41') and also, of course well remembered in Israel. The Allied Special Forces Association also remembers them at the National Arboretum in Staffordshire, in the Special Forces Grove, and on their website, as does the website of www.specialforcesroh.com.

The twenty-three are known in Israel as the Yordei Hasira or 'those who went down in the boat'.

This was the first Anglo-Israeli mission as the Haganah/Palmach became integrated within the vanguard force of the British Army invading Vichy Lebanon and Syria. The sacrifice of these men became legendary and an inspiration for the then recently formed Palmach (the strike arm of Haganah).

Allowing for spelling differences owing to transliteration of Hebrew names to English, and with the British Army numbers issued to them as per the documents found in the IDF Archives, the men are:

20. Lieutenant Zvi SPECTOR

4. Warrant Officer, First Class, Isaac HECKER

22. Sergeant Gershon KOPLER

3. Sergeant David NAFHA

19. Private Mordechai COHEN

14. Private Arieh EIZEN

16. Private Arieh GELBERT

10. Private Jacob GORDON

17. Private Sami HANOVITZ

21. Private Baruch JACOBSON

9. Private Menachem KURAKIN

5. Private Abraham NURIEL

6. Private Nerial PAGLIN

12. Private Mordechai PLONCHIK

13. Private Ze'ev ROTMAN

15. Private Ariel TEMES

18. Private Shimon UTCHITEL

11. Private Ephraim VEIMAN

8. Private Haim WEISMAN

7. Private Yehuda ZERNER

1. Warrant Officer Katriel YOFEH – Skipper of *Sea Lion*

2. Petty Officer Amiram SHOCHET – Second Hand of *Sea Lion*

23. Petty Officer Israel NORDEN/NORDAU – Engineer of *Sea Lion*

Another possible (twenty-fourth) member was Rudi Schremmer/Kremmer, but it has not been possible to verify this.

List 5: 'A' Force 199, Palestinian Jewish agents, Cairo

This unit was commanded by Lieutenant Colonel Anthony Symonds/Simmonds; there were 300 Palestinian Jewish volunteers[8] of whom 110 were selected for parachute training at Ramat David, near Haifa, and of whom thirty-two went into Europe; a further five infiltrated their target by other means of insertion. The detail for this section comes from IDF Archives In Israel, in both Hebrew and English.

Three went to Hungary; five to Slovakia; ten to Yugoslavia; nine to Romania; two to Bulgaria; one to Austria; one to France; six to Italy. Thirty-one were from kibbutzim, four from Moshavs; twenty-six served behind the lines and six never reached their destinations; thirteen returned home, and six others were POWs and survived; seven were POW and executed, including two women.

Names	Aliases	Where they were inserted and lived
Lt Aba BERDICHEV/BARDICEV, RAF	Aka Lt Robert Willis ('Anticlimax')	Yugoslavia/Slovakia – murdered Mauthausen,15/1/45; Runnymede Memorial. Bema'avak.
Yitzak BEN EPHRAIM	Aka 'Franz'/'Hail'	Romania; Shamir
Chaim BEN SASON/SHOSHAN		.
Sgt Aharon BEN YUSEF, RASC	Aka 'Chair'	Turkey; Tel-Aviv
Sgt Dov BERGER/HARIRI, RA**	Aka Jack ben Tipora, aka 'Freeman'	Romania; Beit Oren
Ms Sara BRAVERMAN (Palmach)	Aka 'Meyers'	Yugoslavia; Shamir
Liova BRONSTEIN	Aka 'Chamani'	
Yaacov CHOVER/HUBER		Egypt; Nes Ziona
Warrant Officer Reuven DAFNI, RCOS	Aka 'Gary'	Yugoslavia; Kibbutz Ein Gedi
Tsadok DORAN	Aka 'Dixon'	

Names	Aliases	Where they were inserted and lived
Sgt DOROGOYER, RAF	Aka 'Tsigane'	Romania, cancelled; Nir-am.
Dani EPHRA/ EPHRAIM/ DAFNI (?) (Palmach)	Aka George Carpenter	Italy; Ein Gev
Sgt Arieh FICHAMAN, RASC**	Aka Gideon Jacobson	Romania, POW survived – Beit Oren
Yehuda GOKOVSKY/ AVISHAR **	Aka Joseph Canany	Romania, POW, survived; Yagur (made ten escape attempts).
Peretz/Ferenez GOLDSTEIN, PC (Palmach)	Aka 'Jones'/'John'/'Lemon' – the YOUNGEST of the agents!	Murdered Oranienberg 1/3/45; Athens Memorial; Ma'agen.
Sgt Zvi Ben Yaakov, aka Jindrich GRUNHUT, RAF (Palmach)	Aka Michael Janay/Yani aka 'Uncle' and 'Leadburn'	Murdered 20/10/44; Slovakia; Alamein memorial. Achotrim
Chaim HERMESH	Aka Harry Morris ('Nuisance')	Nitzanim
Sgt Baruch KAMIN(KER), Palestine Regiment	Bernard Shool, aka 'Slave'	Balkans/Rumania; Nir-am
Uriel KANER	Aka 'Uriel'	Yugoslavia; Ruhama
Sgt KASZAS, RAF (is this Hermesh, above?)	Aka 'Morris'/'Nuisance'	Balkans
KAUFMAN	Aka 'Doiner'	
Pinchas KLEEMAN		Egypt; Kfar Chitin
Dan LERNER (Palmach)		Yugoslavia, POW, escaped; Neot Mordechai.
LEVY	Aka 'Pastor'	Romania, POW, survived; Sarid.
Arieh LUPESKO (Palmach)	Aka 'Rito'	
MACADAM	Aka 'Nutmeg'	
Sgt Yitzak MACARESCO, RA, escape commitee.	Aka 'Fiscal'	Romania, POW, survived; Avkaa
Sgt Yoel PALGI/ NUESBOECHER, RASC	Aka 'Halbert'/'Mickey'	Balkans; Ma-agen
Shalom PINTSI**	Aka 'Ben'	Yugoslavia; Gat
Ms Chaviva REICK/REICH, WAAF (Palmach)	Aka Ada Robinson, aka Martinovic ('Stickler'/'Auntie')	Murdered 20/11/44; buried Mt Herzl, Jerusalem, Israel; Kibbutz Ma-anit.
Sgt Rafael REISS/REISZ, RAF	Aka Stephen ('Rafi') Reiss, aka 'Challock'	Balkans – murdered 20/11/44; buried Mt Herzl, Israel; Huliot.
Peretz ROSENBERG	Aka 'Rose'	Yugoslavia; Beit Shearim operation "Typical"
Yonah ROSENFELD/ ROSEN (Palmach)	Aka 'Orange'/'Dickens'	Yugoslavia; Ma-agen
Pincas SASON (Palmach)		Bulgaria, cancelled; Yakum.

Names	Aliases	Where they were inserted and lived
Ms Hannah SENESH/ SZENES, WAAF – born Hungary	Aka 'Minnie'/'Georg'	Yugoslavia – murdered Hungary 7/11/44; buried Mt Herzl, Jerusalem; Sdot Yam.
Enzo Chaim SERINI/ SERENI /SYRENI, aka Symons – born Italy	Capt. Samuel Barda	Yugoslavia; murdered Dachau 18/11/44; Brookwood memorial and Mt Herzl memorial. Givat Brenner.
Yaacov SHAPIRA Chaim SHOSHANY	Aka 'Maxim'	Italy; Moaz Yam. Haganah communications liaison with SOE.
Nissim TESTA-ARAZI		Yugoslavia; She'ar Hamakim
Sgt Yeshayahu TRACHTENBERG, RA	Aka 'Theo'/'Hardy'	Romania; Nir-am
Chaim WALDNER	Aka 'Andre'	Italy; Tel-Aviv
Sgt Varon YUSEF (Palmach), RAF	Aka 'Carpet'/'Shimony'	Turkey; Bulgaria; Yakum
Rehavam ZEBLODONSKY	Aka 'Allan'	
Eli ZOHAR	Aka 'Joel'	Yugoslavia; Gat

** killed in Israel at memorial service to Pertez Goldstein when aircraft crashed nearby, after the war.

Significantly, not one of the Palestinian Jewish SOE members in Lists 4 and 5 ever received awards from Britain, when it was customary to award at least an MiD to those killed behind enemy lines. Four have locations named after them in Israel:

Alon ABA (Bardicev)

Yad HANNAH (Senesh)

Lehavot HAVIVA (Reick)

Netzer SERINI (Serini).

In addition, the following names occur in an 'F' Section file at TNA, of Palestinian Jews associated with an SOE Mission led by Major Bodington in Israel:

Yehuda ARAZI

David (Dov) HOS/HOZ (a founder of Haganah)

Yitzhak (?) LOURIE

Moshe SHERTOK (later Foreign Minister of Israel).

And in HS/173 (TNA):

Sergeant EISENBERG

Sergeant KASSAP, KIA SAS/Commandos (see List 1 above)

Sergeant RAFAELLI.

The following list was discovered by the author at TNA in file HS4 119, headed 'SECRET', with the title, 'List of names of Palestine residents who are prepared to enlist for sabotage in South-Eastern Europe, more particularly in Hungary ... collected by Mr Gaster and Dr Schwartz'. It is not known whether any of these people proceeded to training at Ramat David or elsewhere, but they are included as an indication of the courage and determination of Palestinian Jewry to fight back in whichever way they could.

In Athlit Clearance Camp

Marcel GROSS

Joseph HALMI

Desiderius KUBICZEK (not Jewish?)

Alexander LINEBERG

Ernst OPPENHEIM

Kibbutz Kfar Glikson

Franz FARAGO

Zvi HERMANN

Miscellaneous

Hadani DAVIV – Kibbutz Dan

Charles EHRENTHAL – Kfar Saba

Arnold FEUERSTEIN – Tel-Aviv

Dr Nicholas FRISCHMANN – Tel-Aviv

Paul HAJDU – Tel-Aviv

Abraham HIRSCH – Kibbutz She'ar Hanegev

Alexander ISAK – Kibbutz Merhavia

Frances JAMBOR – Kibbutz Dan

Alexander KALMAR – Tel-Aviv

Dr Ladislas MOSES – Tel-Aviv

Paul SIMON – Kibbutz Dalia

Emil VERMES – Tel-Aviv

List 6

These names from HS9 at TNA are closed files, kindly scrutinized by Reader/Adviser Howard Davies; there is no statement in the files that they are Jewish *but* they may be, on the basis of surnames only. The author will be happy to receive any feedback possible on these individuals.

Margot HOFFMAN

Max HOFFMAN

Rudolf HOFFMAN

Simon HOFFMAN

Marcel JAURENT- SINGER (French)

Joseph MEISTERMAN

Alexander SCHNEIDER

Andre SCHOCK

Theodore SCHUBAUER,   Killed on mission 24/2/41 on board SS
   aka Thomas Shearer (Austrian) – tbc   *Jonathan Holt* en route to Yugoslavia/WestAfrica

Valerie SILVER

McCord SOLLENBERGER

A. WOERTHER

List 7

In 1941 the British SOE asked for volunteers from the Haganah/Palmach (official Jewish underground forces in Israel/Mandate Palestine) for agents to work behind the lines in German-occupied Greece. Six men from the Haganah Special Sea Demolition unit eventually were chosen for an essentially suicide mission. In Israel they became known as the 'The Jewish Ghost Commando'. After three months in Greece, they returned safely but their work was neither rewarded nor recognized by Britain. Afterwards, they all joined the Royal Navy and were part of the Haifa Port Boom (defensive underwater fence) Guard Unit for the rest of the war, later taking part in Israel's War of Independence in 1947–48.

Jacob AGEYEV (Instructor) Able Seaman, RN

Shmuel BEN-SHIPRUT Able Seaman, RN

Yoel GOLOMB Able Seaman, RN

Shlomo KOSTICA Able Seaman, RN

Mordechai LISHINSKI Able Seaman, RN

Itzhak SPECTOR Able Seaman, RN

(With thanks to Ilan Guy of Israel, nephew of Jacob Ageyev, and the Palmach website).

Appendix 1

Some totals for this study

Note that some awards are multiple, i.e. one agent receiving more than one, so this needs to be kept in mind when comparing percentage figures of awards.

British, Commonwealth and British citizens and British based SOE agents who were Jewish, made up 276 Personnel, to whom the following awards were made:

GM	1
CBE	5
DFC	2
DSO	3
MBE	11
MC	12
DSC	2
OBE	6
BEM	1
MM	2
DCM	2
DFM	1
AFC	1
AFM	1
MiD	19
Croix de Guerre	13
Legion d'Honneur	6
King's Commendation	6
Other Foreign Awards	5

Total awards – 99, which is 36 per cent of these agents.

Total killed – 34, which is 13 per cent of these agents.

Israeli/Palestinian Jewish agents made up 119 personnel, with possibly nineteen others, to whom the following awards were made:

MM	3
DCM	1
OBE	1
BEM	1
MBE	1
Croix de Guerre	1
MiD	2
Other Foreign Awards	1

Total – 11 awards, which is 9 per cent of these agents.

Total killed – 37, which is 31 per cent of these agents – an extremely high casualty rate.

Non-British Jewish agents made up 662 personnel, but of whom about fifty are probables only, plus possibly twelve others, to whom the following awards were made:

DSO	2
MBE	7
OBE	7
MC	9

Croix de Guerre	12
Legion d'Honneur	5
MiD	7
King's Commendation	29
Other Foreign Awards	2

Total – 80 awards, which is 12 per cent of these agents.

Total killed – 44, which is 7 per cent of these agents.

Total Jewish SOE agents at a maximum is thus 1,088 – receiving 190 awards (17.5 per cent of the Jewish agents); total killed was 115 (or 11 per cent of total Jewish personnel). It is believed that the total number of SOE agents was about 10,000 men and 3,000 women, making 13,000; so the Jewish contribution is approximately 8.3 per cent. This is astonishing, given that Jews never make up more than half of 1 per cent of the UK population and maybe 1 per cent of France.

Notes

1. See the Suggested Reading list at the end of the book.
2. Motor Torpedo Boats.
3. Office of Strategic Service, forerunner of the American CIA.
4. If an agent is still alive, researchers have to locate them and get their permission to see their file; the writer did this with Dick Rubinstein. For some agents their files remain closed, and if they have passed away, then a member of the family still has to give permission as well as supply a death certificate of proof; this happened with John Landau.
5. IWM Sound Archives, 8775, quoted in Rod Bailey, *Forgotten Voices of the Secret War* (London: Imperial War Museum, 2008), p.295.
6. In the AJEX Museum files.
7. By Bryan Mark Rigg, published by the University of Kansas, 2004.
8. TNA HS4 91.

No. 3 ('Jewish'[1]) Troop, No. 10 Commando

During the First and Second World Wars, Jewish Servicemen and women of the British and Allied nations played a part in those struggles in excess of the proportion to their numbers in the general populations. Many will know of the Zion Mule Corps (1915–16), the Jewish Legion (38th–42nd Battalions, Royal Fusiliers – 1917–19) in the First World War, and the Jewish Brigade (1944–46), the 51st (mainly Jewish Palestinians) Middle East Commando, the SIG Commando in North Africa, the Jewish members of SOE, and other Jewish groups of the Second World War.

One of the best kept secrets of the Second World War, however, has been the nature of the existence of No. 3 (Miscellaneous or 'X' Troop) of the unique No. 10 (Inter-Allied) Commando/Special Services Brigade. The reason? They were virtually all (95 per cent) German-speaking Jewish refugees, mainly from Germany and Austria (but also some from Czechoslovakia, Hungary and other European countries).

The excellent book by Ian Dear – a seminal work on No. 10 Commando, *Ten Commando 1942–45* (London: Leo Cooper, 1987) – and another by Peter Masters, *Striking Back: A Jewish Commando Writes* (Novato, CA: Presidio Press, 1997), are the only thorough, published studies of this amazing group of men of the famous 'Jewish' No. 3 Troop. Before this, virtually nothing had been published about them. It is not my aim therefore to repeat what Ian Dear and Peter Masters have so wonderfully and ably already researched.

Suffice to say that there were French, Dutch, Belgian and other 'national' Troops (totalling at the largest about 1,000 men altogether), and then the Jewish Troop. Even now many of No. 3 Troop cannot speak of the nature of their exploits, for a variety of reasons, and others have died. But 'X' Troop were, even by the standards of No. 10 Commando, a particularly extraordinary bunch having, as well as the normal skills of all Commandos (in explosives, parachuting and so on) extremely high intelligence and education, and they were indeed by far the most highly trained group in the British Army, especially in fieldcraft, camouflage, compass marching, street-fighting, housebreaking and lock-picking – see Michael Arton, *One Day in York* (London: Hazelwood, 1989). Many were attached to the SSRF (Small Scale Raiding Force, part of SOE), SBS and SIS and most files on this aspect of the war remain closed.

Altogether 142 men passed through their ranks, of whom many became officers – commissioned in the field for specific acts of bravery – and many others sergeants. Twenty-two were killed in action and at least another twenty-two wounded (of the forty-four men from No. 3 Troop who fought in Normandy, twenty-seven were killed, wounded or taken prisoner). They won one MC, one MM, one Croix de Guerre, one MBE, one BEM, one Certificate of Commendation and three Mentioned in Despatches (MiD). The numbers of awards are derisory considering their exploits and the inevitable death sentence they faced if captured – not to mention the danger to any of their surviving relatives in Nazi Europe. Many details of the men were known to the Gestapo and reprisals would have been immediate.

But this paucity of decorations is explained by the fact that the Troop never fought as a unit; they were often detached to serve with other Special Forces in order that they could use their special skills – in silent reconnaissance, capturing and interrogating prisoners in the most hazardous of situations, often alone behind the lines and usually at night. They also were particularly knowledgeable about German military units and training, as well as weapons. For this reason, a commanding officer was loath to recommend for awards men who did not belong to his unit, especially as there was probably an unwritten 'ration' of awards per raid or per unit (letter from Lieutenant Peter Masters, aka Arany, No. 3 Troop, to the author, 25 January 1995).

However, at Ashton Wold in Northamptonshire the Hon. Miriam Rothschild planted a grove of trees in the grounds of her beautiful house in memory of those of No. 3 Troop who were killed; her husband, George Lane, aka Lanyi, was the first officer and MC of No. 3 ('Jewish') Troop, No. 10 Inter-Allied Commando.

The No. 3. Troop CO was a quiet, Welsh Cambridge graduate in Languages, Captain Bryan Hilton-Jones (later promoted to major and second in command of the whole of No. 10 Commando; he was tragically killed in a road accident in 1970), son of a doctor from Caernarvon. All his men came as volunteers from the Alien Companies of the Pioneer Corps from 24 July 1942, arriving for training at Irvine in Ayrshire (many had been interned in 1940 following the 'anti-aliens'/invasion hysteria, but later released to serve in the forces, some in France at Dunkirk). As Peter Masters wrote: 'Getting back at the Nazis was an ever present motivation' in No. 3 Troop; 'our Jewish Commando was the very antithesis of the "lambs to the slaughter" allegations'.

Volunteers reported to the Grand Central Hotel, Marylebone, for selection, and thence to No. 10 Pioneer Corps training centre in Bradford.

From Autumn 1942 they trained at Aberdovey, Wales, or Achnacarry, Scotland, then Eastbourne and Littlehampton in Sussex, men being detached as required to go on raids with other Commandos or with the SOE and SIS.

The men had to take English noms de guerre and new identities, false personal histories, regiments, next of kin, and so on (most chose to keep the same initials), to at least have a chance of not being found out if captured by the Nazis, as being Jews. The casualty officer at the War Office (Dawkins, a senior Civil Servant) was one of very few who knew their real and assumed identities and kept parallel lists of the names of No. 3 Troop.

They wore the No. 10 Commando shoulder title (or sometimes the number of the Commando to which they were attached) and the Combined Operations arm flash. On their green berets they could not wear the Pioneer Corps badge as this would have betrayed their origins, so they wore the badges of the Queen's Own Royal West Kents, East Kents (Buffs), Royal Sussex or Hampshire Regiments, or the General Service badge (letter to author from Ian Dear, 28 October 1994).

In 'Top Secret' letters from Combined Operations HQ (Defence 2/780 – PRO) Major General R.G. Sturges, GOC Commandos and Special Service Group, wrote in April 1944 and February 1945 that No. 3 Troop had been 'trained for and employed on work of a highly combatant nature and are volunteers ... their behaviour and work has always been most satisfactory ... this is a good subgroup, well able to look after itself, and has done excellent work'.

Writing a Secret Report on No. 3 Troop after the war from his home at Crug, Caernarvon, in April 1946, Major Bryan Hilton-Jones said that No. 3 Troop 'were conspicuously successful and earned high praise all round, the best illustration of which is that many were Commissioned as officers into the Commandos to which they had been attached ... They were the most interesting and worthwhile branch of No. 10 Commando.' After D-Day, Captain Griffith (aka Glaser) became the first Jewish CO of the Troop until he was killed at the River Aller crossing on 11 April 1945.

In September 1945 the whole Commando was disbanded, but many of No. 3 Troop continued in sensitive and secret work in the Occupation Forces such as tracking Nazi Resistance groups, war criminals and translating captured documents. Perhaps the last word should go to Major Hilton-Jones, who wrote: 'Despite many and serious difficulties, this band of 'enemy alien' volunteers earned for itself a not unflattering reputation, the achievement of which was in no small measure due to the sincerity and wholeheartedness put into his service by every member of the troop. For them perhaps more than for any others it was a question of self-respect and self-justification.'

Below, published for the first time, is the No. 3 ('Jewish') Troop, No. 10 Commando muster roll. Long may they be remembered.

13.1 No. 3 'Jewish' Troop member L/Cpl Gordon Sayers, aka Gyula Sauer/Szauer, with the Commandos on D Day, bicycle Troop disembarking behind (courtesy Peter Masters/Arany).

13.2 The detachment from No. 3 'Jewish' Troop that landed on D Day with No. 6 Commando, left to right standing – Cpl Nichols (Heinz Nell), Cpl Drew (Harry Nomburg), Cpl Masters (Peter Arany); front, left to right – Cpl Mason (K. Weinberg), Cpl McGregor (Manfred Koury).

I wish to specifically and sincerely thank both Ian Dear and especially Peter Masters, formerly sergeant (later lieutenant in West Africa) in No. 3 Troop and author of the definitive work on No. 3 Troop, *Striking Back: A Jewish Commando Writes*, for their generous help in compiling this list; and Michael Arton for allowing me to use his research, published in his book.

No. 3 ('Jewish') Troop, No. 10 Commando

This list was originally published in February 1995 but has been updated continually and with detail added from TNA/PRO WO/106/6155; with thanks to Tony Williams, MBE. 'PLL' refers to the book by Peter Leighton-Langer, *The King's Own Loyal Enemy Aliens* (London: Vallentine Mitchell, 2006); JL refers to Jack Lennard Archives; ID refers to Ian Dear.

Number and real name on enlistment	Nom de guerre with number and final rank	Date/Place of Birth	Notes
13802871 LANYI, Georg (Djury) H.	285687 LANE, George, MC, MM (Lt) and 1st Troop Sgt	18.1.15, Hungary	1st officer, MC Operation Tarbrush, citation ID, p.169. Former husband of Miriam Rothschild; interrogated by Rommel as POW. Lives London. Also in SOE. Olympic Polo 1936.
1380228 ARNSTEIN, Alfred Valentin	6387035/13118501 ANDERSON, A.V. (BNA 13053690)	11.1.19	RWK Regt – RTU'd England.
13804535 ARNSTEIN/ ARENSTEIN, Hans Richard	L./Cpl 6436352/ 13118502 ANDREWS, Harry, Royal Sussex	18.2.22	KIA 11.8.44 or 19.8.44, son of Max and Gertrude of Sao Paulo, Brazil; buried Ranville, Normandy – letter from mother to Jewish chaplain requesting Star of David on grave after cross was erected.***
13805191 ASCHER, Claus Leopold Octavio	6436355/13118503 Sgt ANSON, Colin Edward	13.2.22	WIA Italy, RSR; (Raiding Support Regiment) lives Watford.
13807122 ABRAMOVICZ/ ABRAHAMOWICZ, R.	Pte 6436363 ARLEN/ARNOLD, Richard George, Royal Sussex	4.1.23	KIA Franceville Plage, Normandy, 7.6.44, aged 21; son of Salmon and Berthe; Bayeux memorial, no known grave.
13807400 BAUMWOLLSPINNER, Gotthard	6305477/13118507 BARNES, Robert Gerald	4.12.18	BEM, WIA, died post-war.
13801297 BILLMAN, Karl Walter	6305473/13118508 Lt BARTLETT, KennethW/320207	21.4.12	Buffs – lives Munich.
BAUER, Georg	BOWER, George	Austrian	PLL

Number and real name on enlistment	Nom de guerre with number and final rank	Date/Place of Birth	Notes
13804390 Sruh, GOTTFRIED 'Friedl' Conrad *	6305460/13118708 Sgt BROADMAN, Geoffrey Max, aka Toni Ruh?	27.7.17	WIA Normandy; lived Lydbrook, Glos. Allegedly only survivor of abortive Vermork raid in Norway by RE (PLL); att. 4 Commando.
13805994 CARLEBACH, Peter	6305480 CARSON, Peter Andrew	27.10.19, Berlin	Dunera boy; invalided out after accident at Seven Sisters cliffs; lives Edinburgh.
COHEN, F.T.	5550156 COLLINS	2.3.23 Germany	JL
	6305489 CURTIS	23.9.23, Germany	JL
EUGEN, Litvak	DALE, Leslie		
DAIKES			PLL; Walcheren.
13802951 HANSEN, Einar Reska* (Danish)	6436367/13118602 DAVIES, Jack	10.9.20	MiD Tarbrush.
DOBRINER, Max	DICKINSON/ DICKSON, Geoffrey	16.3.26	PLL
13802948 DUNGLER/ DANDLER, K.	6305482/13118510 Cpl DOUGLAS, Keith	9.8.21	Walcheren; died post-war.
14216528 NOMBURG, Harry	Sgt DREW, Harry	17.11.23	5th PC, Denbigh; wife in Haifa, Israel. WIA Normandy; att. 12, 6, 3 Commandos; lived New York, died 1997.
HIRSCH	6387043 DUDLEY, L.A.	1.8.19, Germany	JL
	6387046 DUNN, D.	2.7.26, Germany	JL
13807299 GOLDSCHMIDT, Werner	6436360/13118517 Capt. DWELLY, Vernon J. ('Ducky')	29.10.21	Dunera boy; Walcheren; Novota (California); att. 4 Commando; unarmed combat instructor.
	Lt EMMETT, Bunny		RAF and R. Tank Reg; 4 Commando at Walcheren – PLL.
13803417 ENGEL, Hans Gunter	6436357 ENVERS, H.G. (John)	7.4.22 or 7.11.22, Breslau	WIA Normandy 19.8.44; lives Toronto; att. 4 Commando.
EBERSTADT, Ernest Karl Eduard	EVERSLEY, David Edward Charles	1922, Frankfurt	Later in SOE – PLL.
	FARLEY		

Number and real name on enlistment	Nom de guerre with number and final rank	Date/Place of Birth	Notes
13801057 FREYTAG, Ernst Herbert	6305479/13118514 Sgt FARR, E.H. ("Tommy")	26.2.19	Born Berlin; Walcheren and Op. Premium at Wassenaar.
13804661 FEDER/FETER, Ernst Wolfgang	6436370/13118511 TSM/WO1 FENTON, Bryan Leslie	20.4.21, Berlin	Maas crossing; lives Kusnacht, Switzerland.
13807080 FUERTH, Hans George	6305463/13118515 Lt FIRTH, Anthony	7.9.18, Halle	Dunera boy; lives Toronto.
13051439 FLEISCHER, F.	FLETCHER, Frederick	Austrian	1st Batt. Worc; att. 6 Commando; KIA Le Plein, 11.6.44 – PLL. buried Ranville, son of Rudolf and Hedwig of Cricklewood.
13807365 FRANK, Max Gunther	6387027/13118512 Cpl FRANKLYN, George Mack, Royal West Kent	30.4.23.	WIA Sicily; KIA D-Day. 6.6.44, aged 21. Son of Ernst J. and Carla of Huddersfield; buried Hermanville. Cross on grave – error.
13805167 FREY, Hubert Clarence	5550127/13118513 Cpl FRASER, Evelyn Harold	23.3.20	Invalided out after accident at Seven Sisters cliff; lives Auckland, NZ.
13801130 KAGERER-STEIN, Eugen Von	5550126 Sgt FULLER, Eugene 'Didi', Hants Regt, att. 47 Commando	19.12.13	Austrian, aged 30, WIA D-Day; KIA Normandy, 13.6.44; buried Ranville. Att. 47 RM Commando. Son of Alfred and Anna; husband of Cicely of Balcombe, Sussex. Cross on grave – error.
13800982 GOLDSTERN, Konstantin	6387015/13118518 GARVIN, Robert Kenneth	11.1.17	Died post-war, Wales.
ZIVOLAVA, Otto	GAUTIER, Jean	Austria	JL
13807042 GUTTMAN, Hans Julius	6387014 GILBERT, Ronnie, MBE	28.9.19	WIA Normandy; lives Norbeck, Blackpool.
13801168 GEISER, Kurt H.	Troop Sgt Major GORDON, Henry E.A.	3.4.1915	Lives Walton-on-Thames, related to Liebknecht, family of German Socialists.
13804337 GUMPERTZ, Kurt Wilhelm, Hants. Regt	5550144/13118520 GRAHAM, Kenneth Wakefield – att. 4 Commando	27.6.19	KIA Normandy 12/13.6.44, buried Hermanville, aged 24. Son of Karl Wilhelm and Else; husband of Elisabeth of Highbury, London. No religious symbol on grave in error.

Number and real name on enlistment	Nom de guerre with number and final rank	Date/Place of Birth	Notes
13805610 GOLDSCHMIDT, Konrad Levin	6387031 Sgt GRANT, Hubert Brian, aka Groves	5.8.17	WIA, lost leg fighting in Italy with 9 Commando; retired judge lived in Cumbria.
13805014 GANS, Manfred	6387019 /13118516 Capt. GRAY, Freddy (BNA 13041024), 41 RM Commando	27.4.22	RWK Regt; Walcheren, lives Leonia, New Jersey; WIA five times.
13802030 GLASER, Kurt Joachim	322333/6387018/13 118519 Capt./Lt GRIFFITH, Keith James/John, RWK – att. 45 RM Commando, later CO 3 Troop	3.9.18	KIA Germany, 11.4.45, crossing Aller River aged 26; fought in Spanish Civil War. Buried Becklingen, Germany. Son of Dr Willy and Maria Therese of Epsom, Surrey. Cross on grave in error.
13700295 REICH/WEICH/ Weil, Salo Robert	6436350/13118714 Cpl HAMILTON, Robert Geoffrey	1.8.16	Austrian, KIA Walcheren, 1.11.44 Westekappelle, att. 41st RM Commando. Buried Bergen Op Zoom, Holland, aged 28. Royal Sussex Regt. Son of Jacob and Sabine of Vienna, Austria.
13801533 HAJOS/ HAJOSCH, Hans	6380736/13118601 Sgt HARRIS, MM, Ian	1.1.20	WIA Normandy 3 times. MM 6.4.45 – citation in Peter Masters's book – att. 45 Commando – lives Reading.
13805511 KATZ, Weinhart Paul Oscar	13118608 Pte HEATHCOTE, Michael Paul		
13801503 HERSCHTHAL, Fritz	5550136/13118604 HEPWORTH, Freddy – att. 45 Commando	11.12.20	Died USA 3.2.95.
13801397 HERSCHTHAL, Walter	5550145/13118605 HEPWORTH, Walter/Douglas	16.1.18	Died post-war Australia.
13805632 NATHAN, Eli/Erich Wolfgang	6305467/13118702 Lt HOWARTH/ HOWARD, Eric William, Royal East Kent. Later CO 3 Troop	16.10.22	WIA D-Day, commissioned in the field for bravery – KIA Osnabruck, Germany, 3.4.45, aged 22. Buried Reichswald Forest, son of August Victor and Margaret Clara Elisabeth, née Gayler, of Streatham Hill, London. Cross on grave in error.
13802194 HIRSCH, Stephan	5550149/13118606 Cpl HUDSON, Steven Keith	5.6.18	Hants. Regt.

Number and real name on enlistment	Nom de guerre with number and final rank	Date/Place of Birth	Notes
13800841 KNOBLOCH, Guenther Hans	6436349/13118610 Lt KENDAL, Harold George 'Nobby'	9.12.07	Died post-war Vancouver – Sicily with Belgian Commando, Poles at Cassino, founded 8th Army ski patrol, with 2 Commando at Vis, Intelligence Chief 8th Army.
	KEREN		JL
13805755 KIRSCHNER, Andre Gabriel	6436361/13118609 Lt KERSHAW, Andrew G.	31.10.21	Died post-war USA.
13804297 LOEWENSTEIN, Otto Julius	5550146/13118620 Lt KINGSLEY, Roger James	2.2.22	OBE, MID Germany – att. RM Commandos – lives Manchester.
13800170 KELLMAN, M.	6436351 KIRBY, M.J. 'Ernest'	26.12.03	
KOENIGSWATER			JL
13807180 LEWINSKY, Max	6387023/13118619 Pte LADDY/LADDIE, Max, Royal West Kent	19.8.11	KIA D-Day 6.6.44 in landing craft with Webster, b. at Hermanville, memorial at Aberdovey where he lived with Welsh wife. Aged 33. Cross on grave in error.
13800037 LANDAU, Ernst	6436353/13118614 Lt LANGLEY, Ernest Robert F. L	18.19.03	Died in UK 1957.
13801850 LEVY/LOEWY, Moritz/Max	6436346/13118701 Cpl LATIMER, Maurice	13.9.21	Czech, fought in Spanish Civil War, WIA Dieppe Raid, Normandy and Walcheren – died post-war UK.
13801313 LENEL, Ernst Richard	6387016/13118615 Sgt LAWRENCE, Ernest Richard, Royal West Kent	26.10.18	MIA presumed KIA 22/23.6.44 – Bayeux Memorial, Normandy, aged 26, no known grave. Son of Richard S. and Emilie, née Maas.
13801331 LAUFFER, Guenther	13118806/6436365 LAWTON, B.R.		DOAS – PLL.
LIEBEL, Peter	LEIGH-BELL, Peter – AJEX card says 1st Batt. tanks RAC		
LENEL, Victor			Brother of Ernst, above.
GUTTMAN	LEWIS		
13805333 LEVEN, Peter Guenther	13118616 LONG, Peter		
13800645 LEWIN, Siegfried	13118618 LOUIS, Frederick Mac		

Number and real name on enlistment	Nom de guerre with number and final rank	Date/Place of Birth	Notes
LOWY, Arthur F.			
LUCHTENSTEIN, Hans Gunther	LUDLOW (John Hugh)	Leipzig 4.4.21	Interned, PC, Dunkirk, D-Day and liberation of Belsen.
13804473 KURY, Manfred*	6387030/13118613 MCGREGOR, Jock/Jack Fred	24.5.21 or 18.9.03?	Died post-war UK.
13803539 WOLFF, Walter L.	6387033 MARSHALL, Alan W.	3.4.22	Died post-war UK.
13803503 WEINBERG, . K.	6387028 Sgt MASON, Gary	2.1.20	R. Mass, Belle Isle raid.
13804450 ARANY, P.F.	6387025 Lt MASTERS, Peter F.	5.2.22	Ox. & Bucks., WAF, lived Maryland – author of *Fighting Back* – died 3/05.
MAYER	5550137 MELVIN, P.H.	12.3.22 Germany	JL
13801895 BLUMENFELD, M.J. Ludwig George	6387026/13118509 Lt MERTON, Michael James	21.6.20 Berlin	Att. 2 Commando and with Poles at Cassino. Appledore, Kent.
13801467 LEVIN, Hubertus	5550135/13118617 Lt MILES, Patrick Hugh	22.1.20	SSRF/SOE Operation Huckaback on Herne, CI. Pebworth, Warwicks.
	MONAHAN		
13801092 MEYER, Kurt	5550147 L./Cpl MOODY, Peter	28.9.18	Hants. Regt KIA Normandy 13.6.44, aged 25 – son of Fritz Max and Margeretta of Birmingham – buried Ranville, Normandy.
	MOSS, J. – 5550131	Germany 23.5.21	JL
	NAUGHTON		Died OAS.
13805553 ZWEIG, Werner	6436347/13118718 Sgt NELSON, Vernon	5.11.22	WIA Italy – Cert. of Commendation – 40 RM Commando/46 RN Commando.
13807201 NELL, G. Heinz Herman	6305464/13118704 Capt. NICHOLS, Gerald Peter	8.10.20	WIA Normandy – rescued Lord Lovat – Dunera boy – lives in London. I.D. p.249.
13803316 NATHAN, Eli/Ernst	6387022/13118703 NORTON, Ernest	19.8.22	RWK Regt – att. 4 Commando, Operation Tarbrush – KIA Normandy, 13.6.44, aged 21, son of Moritz and Sibilla – buried Ranville.
13800022 HENSCHEL, Oskar/Oswald (aka Ludwig Hayder?)*	6305481/13118603 TSM O'NEILL/ GREY, Oscar Roy	1.3.13	RTU'd at Normandy after WIA – with 41 RM Commando.
PEYER	PALMER		
	Sgt PIRQUET, P.		JL
	PRATT		

Number and real name on enlistment	Nom de guerre with number and final rank	Date/Place of Birth	Notes
13805787 ROSSKAMM, Stephan	6305459/13118705 L./Cpl ROSS, Stephen	28.2.22	The Buffs – lives Cleveland, Ohio – WIA Italy three times – att 9 Commando.
ROTSCHILD, Freddy			Toronto post-war – PLL.
13805183 SALOSCHIN/ SALINGER, G.Victor	6436364 L./Cpl SAUNDERS, George Victor	12.2.21	Was at school with Prince Philip – lived Moulsford, Oxon. – att. 45 Commando and recommended but not awarded MM.
13807278 SZAUER/ SAUER, Gyula Jence	6436364/13118711 L./Cpl SAYERS, Gordon Julian	9.5.15	Born Hungary, Croix de Guerre – lives Australia – WIA – att. 4 Commando and French Troop 10 IA Commando.
13801102 STEINER, Uli	Capt. SCOTT, Leslie	29.3.17	Died post-war Montreal – last CO of 3 Troop.
13805733 SACHS, H.P.	6305471 SEYMOUR, Herbert A., East Kent Regt	1.2.18	KIA with Villiers crossing Rhine on Buffalo LC, 23.3.45, aged 27 – son of Eugen and Margaret of St John's Wood London – Groesebeek memorial, Holland – no known grave.
SCHONFELD	SHAW, P.F. – 555039	20.12.23 Germany	JL
13805613 SAMSON, Alfred	6305372/13118706 Lt SHELLEY, Percy A. (P02090)	30.7.21	Att. RM Commandos – lived UK.
KARMINSKI, Otto 'Putzi'	SIMON		
	Frederick SPENCER		Austrian – had been in Dachau and Buchenwald.
13800866 STEIN, Artur	6305470/13118709 Sgt SPENCER, Tom	11.12.16	Died post-war UK – att 3 Commando.
13801207 STRAUSS, David	6305475/13118710 Lt STEWART, David (P02090)	19.1.14	Att. 45 RM Commandos – raid on Merville guns D-Day.
13805606 HORNIG, Paul	5550140/13118607 L./Cpl STREETEN, Paul Patrick – att. 41 RM Commando	18.7.17	WIA Sicily, lives Boston, USA.
13802051 BARTH, Georg Alexander	6436371/13118505 Officer Cadet STREETS, George Bryan, Royal Sussex	5.10.17	Killed motorcycle accident after serving Normandy, on OCTU course UK, 29.6.44, aged 27, buried Barmouth, Merioneth, WWRT, p.268 – son of Josef and Leopoldine, husband of Lici of Paddington, London. Cross on grave – error.

Number and real name on enlistment	Nom de guerre with number and final rank	Date/Place of Birth	Notes
	SUTTON, Lt Francis George	Austria	JL
13802309 SCHWITZER/ SCHWEIZER, J. Tamas Gyorgy	6436368/13118707 SWINTON, Tommy G.	8.3.20	Lives Spain, fought in Spanish Civil War – WIA. 41 RM Commando.
13804028 THEILINGER, Jan	6305478/13118712 TAYLOR, John Robert	25.9.16 – 8.2004	Czech – invalided out after grenade accident Littlehampton – served IB in Spain – Jewish origin – conversation with his son in Portsmouth, October 2004.
13807275 TROJAN, Richard Walter	6305469/13118713 TENNANT, Richard William John	14.5.22	Lives London and Goeriach, Austria.
13807650 TISCHLER, P.J.	6436366 Cpl TERRY, Peter J.	21.6.24	SSRF/SOE, WIA twice Normandy, lives Bridgehampton, NY – att. 47 RM Commando.
13805471 ZADIK, Walter Gabriel	5550141/13118717 Sgt THOMPSON, Walter Gerald	23.8.19	POW 20.6.44 Normandy – att. 4 Commando.
	THORNTON		
13805027 BAUM, Hans	6387020/13118506 TREVOR, Charles Leslie	14.7.22	WIA at Normandy – died London, August 1995.
13801460 POLLASCHEK, O.	6436369 TURNER, A.C.	13.5.19	Dachau/Buchenwald – att. 3 Commando – lives Eastbourne.
13807326 VOGEL, Egon	6436356/13118714 VILLIERS, Ernest Robert, Royal Sussex	7.9.18	Dunera boy – KIA Rhine crossing with Seymour, 24.3.45, aged 25 – buried Reichswald Forest – att. 46 RN Commando.
13804308 WEIKERSHEIMER, L	5550141 Sgt WALLEN, Leslie	2.7.20	Died post-war UK.
13800419 WASSERMANN, O.	5550130 WATSON, William/Walter J.	1.6.14	Dachau, wife and children murdered, WIA Walcheren, lives UK.
WACHSMANN, Wolfgang	HAYES, John, aka Waxman	1.5.24	Transferred to 9th Batt. Paras, 6th Airborne; D-Day, WIA, lives Australia (Helen Fry, *The King's Most Loyal Enemy Aliens*)
13801574 WEINBERGER, E.G.	6306466 WEBSTER, Ernest George, Royal East Kent Regt	11.8.16	SSRF; KIA Normandy with Laddy, att. 47 RM Commando 6.6.44 aged 28 – husband of Gerda – buried Bayeux, Normandy. Cross on grave in error.

Number and real name on enlistment	Nom de guerre with number and final rank	Date/Place of Birth	Notes
13807570 WILMERSDOERFFER, Hans Johann Max	6305465/13118716 Capt. WILMERS, John Geoffrey	27.12.20	Att. SAS, Operation Forfar, died post-war Guernsey.

Most of these above 111 names are from the PRO file on No 10 Commando, drawn up by the first CO, Capt Bryan Hilton-Jones on 19.4.44 as a request for Naturalisation for the men. Some names come from the Jack Lennard Archive. The notes and ranks are taken from Ian Dear's book, *Ten Commando* (1987), Peter Masters, *Fighting Back* (1998), and the Commonwealth War Graves Commission Registers for the killed. Other names are from Peter Leighton-Langer's research.

***On 21 January 1957, Mrs T. Arenstein wrote from Sao Paulo, Brazil to the British Jewish Army Chaplain, Rev. Isaac Levy, asking him to arrange the Star of David on the grave. This was carried out. Letter at AJEX Jewish Military Museum.
* means not Jewish.

Supplementary List A
The first 3 men were probably on an SOE operation to obtain military documents from the Town Hall in Dieppe and all KIA at Dieppe.

Number and real name on enlistment	Nom de guerre with number and final rank	Date/Place of Birth	Notes
	RICE – 5550123? – PLL		Czech – action referred to in G. Rees, *Bundle of Sensations* (London: Chatto & Windus, 1960), pp.157–8 – first 3 Troopers to be killed with attempt to occupy Town Hall at Dieppe with 40 RM Commando (PLL). Alleged POW – MIA since Dieppe.
OPPELT, Gustav? PLL	BATES/BATE		Czech; perhaps survived post-war GDR.
SLEIGH? PLL	SMITH, F.J. ?		Czech att. 40 RM Commando.
FARAGO, Viktor	FORD – Hungarian		RTU'd
HESS, Otto 6387034/13802070	GILES, Peter	Wiesbaden	RWK; KIA Yugoslavia (SOE?), 1.10.44, aged 23, but CWGC commemorates him at Groesebeek, Netherlands.
JESSEN/JENSEN, R.	Cpl ROLF, James		

Number and real name on enlistment	Nom de guerre with number and final rank	Date/Place of Birth	Notes
BIERER, Frederic	Sgt BENTLEY, Frederick		30.3.43, to 62 Commando and SSRF; Operation Huckaback (Herne); lives New York.
ROSENBERG, Stefan	RIGBY, Stephen ('Nimrod') – D-Day deception Commando		Austrian Jewish, 'Unknown warrior' of Leasor's book; did he exist?
GOLDSCHLAEGER, K.T. – 13801160 – PLL	Cpl CLARKE, E. – 13118804/5550135?		MiD Osnabruck. Died post-war UK.
13802873 KOTTKA, Vladimir	13118611 Cpl JONES, Jack		Russian-born; Operation Hardtack; POW.
13810017 LEVY, Karl Ernst	BEM 6436377 LINCOLN, Ken		
JACOBUS, Peter	55550143 JACKSON, Fred	25.11.21, Austria	Interrogated Hoess at Auschwitz; died post-war UK.
PLATECK/ PLATSCHEK	PLATT/PRATT (?) ('Bubi')		WIA Dieppe; lived Canada – died South America?
13802608 AUERHAHN/ AVERHAHN, Werner	5550132/13118504 L./Cpl WELLS, Peter Vernon Allen		Hants Regt; KIA 19.1.44, Italy, aged 26; buried Minturno, Italy; son of Arthur and Erna of Cricklewood, London. No religious symbol on grave in error.
13805629 KRAUSMANN/ KRAUSEN, Hans/Heinz	13118612 AITCHISON, Harry		Died post-war NY.

These above fifteen names are from Dear's and Masters's books and not the PRO list – so must have passed through the Troop by the time Hilton-Jones's list was written. Of these two totals, twenty-two were KIA.

Supplementary List B

Number and real name on enlistment	Nom de guerre with number and final rank	Date/Place of Birth	Notes
BERLIN, Ludwig Carl	14400852 Lt BURLEY, Leonard Charles		Dorsets, 9th Commando, attached to 3 Troop in Germany.
Son of F. INDLANDER, 33 Greencroft Gdns, London NW6	13117462 Pte BURNETT, Walter, aka INDLANDER		Royal Fusiliers/156 Field Battery and 173 Field Regt, RA (AJEX Card).

Number and real name on enlistment	Nom de guerre with number and final rank	Date/Place of Birth	Notes
	16001269 Pte FOSTER, R.		REME
	BNA13053609 Pte MARTIN, W.		RWK
	14727794 Pte MINES, J.		RWK
	11316230 Pte PETERS, H.		Black Watch
SCHLOSS, Jakob	BNA13041025 Pte SCOTT, Jack	1924	RWK; Italy, Island of Vis, Yugoslavia.
	14437220 Pte SMITH, J.		Ox. & Bucks. LI.
	PAL Driver SPIELMAN, E.		RASC
	13053667 Pte STEVENS, J.		RWK
	BNA13053600 Pte STEVENS, T.		
	BNA13053667 Pte STEWART, J.		RWK
WOOLF – 6436380	14430010 Craftsman WARD, G. or E.A.	12.2.25, Germany	REME
	BNA13041047 Pte WARREN, H.		RWK
	ME14041045 Pte WARWICK, R.		Essex Regt.
WEISS, Adi	13106924 Pte WHITE, Alan		RWK; died post-war London.

Except for L. Berlin, the above list of sixteen men is from Arton, *One Day in York*, and comprises men recruited in Italy to No. 3 Troop in 1945 by Lieutenant Bartlett, as part of CMF att. No. 2 Commando.

Note

1. The title 'Jewish' Troop is an unofficial one and coined only after the war, when it was safe to offer this apt description of this unit after the real facts became known on the release of papers at The National Archive (formerly the Public Records Office). To have called these men the 'Jewish' Troop in wartime would of course have been fatal for any captured.

14

Daughters of Yael:
Two Jewish Heroines of the SOE

Jewish participation in the hazardous war of the Special Operations Executive (SOE) during the Second World War was – as in all theatres of the war – far out of proportion to the community's numbers in the general population.

Some of the Jewish SOE agents are quite well known; Captain Adam Rabinovich, Croix de Guerre (code-name 'Arnaud'), murdered by the Gestapo; Captain Isadore Newman, MBE ('Julien'/'Pepe'), murdered at Mauthausen Camp; Captain Maurice Pertschuck, MBE ('Martin Perkins', aka 'Eugene'), murdered at Buchenwald Camp. In addition, hundreds of other Jews fought with SOE agents in the Resistance groups of occupied countries, especially in France and Poland.[1] Much less well known, however, are two of the Jewish women who fought the secret war in France – Denise Bloch, Croix de Guerre (who was French but served in the British Forces) and Muriel Byck, Mentioned in Despatches, who was British.

The SOE was a British secret war department formed in 1940 to 'Set Europe Ablaze' by organizing and supplying the underground Resistance movements against the Nazis (and later the Japanese) in all occupied countries. It was one of several Secret Armies commanded from London by General Colin Gubbins, who was vice-chair of its council; the chairman was the Jewish banker Charles Hambro, until succeeded by Gubbins in September 1943.[2] The French section of SOE was commanded by Colonel Maurice Buckmaster, a Dunkirk veteran, working from secret offices at Marks and Spencer's HQ in Baker Street, London.

This section infiltrated thirty-nine women into France by plane, boat, submarine and parachute between May 1941 and July 1944. Whichever Service they were recruited from – WAAFs, ATS and others – the women were often enlisted into the FANY (First Aid Nursing Yeomanry) in order to go some way towards complying with the Geneva Convention that women in the Services should not bear arms – though this was not consistently practised by SOE. Of these thirty-nine, fifteen were captured and only three of these survived. Of the twelve murdered by the Nazis one was the Jewish agent Denise Bloch[3] and a thirteenth girl, Jewish agent Muriel Byck, died of meningitis after six weeks of intense work in the field, on 23 May 1944.[4]

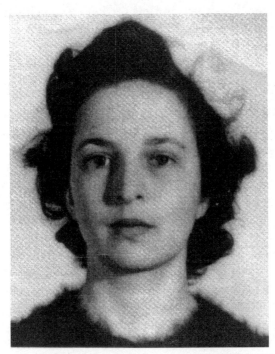

14.1 Muriel Byck, died on operations with SOE (photo courtesy Special Forces Club, London).

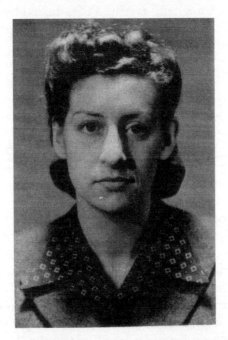

14.2 Denise Bloch, SOE agent murdered at Ravensbruck Death Camp (photo courtesy of Special Forces Club, London).

The Free French section sent in a further eleven girls from the Corps Auxilière Féminin or French ATS, all of whom survived, making a total of fifty women in all who served in France.

DENISE MADELEINE BLOCH –CODE-NAMED 'AMBROISE'

Ensign F/27 Denise Madeleine Bloch – code-name 'Ambroise' – First Aid Nursing Yeomanry, SOE, received the King's Commendation for Brave Conduct, Legion D'Honneur, Croix de Guerre avec Palme and Medaille de la Résistance avec Rosette. Denise was murdered by the Nazis at Ravensbruck death camp near Mecklenburg, together with Violette Szabo, GC, and Lilian Rolfe, Croix de Guerre, sometime between 25 January and 2 February 1945. Denise (who had three brothers) was aged 29, the daughter of the Parisian Jewish family of Jacques Henri and Suzanne Barrault, née Levi-Strauss.[5] She is commemorated at Brookwood Commonwealth War Graves Cemetery, Surrey, panel twenty-six, column three, and on a separate plaque with Szabo, Rolfe and agent Lefort; also on the FANY memorial on the wall of St Paul's Church, Wilton Place, Knightsbridge; on a plaque at Ravensbruck death camp itself[6] and on the 'F' Section memorial at Valençay in France, unveiled in May 1991 by the Queen Mother.[7]

Denise has been described as being 'broad shouldered and blonde'[8] but her Service photograph[9] reveals a dark-haired beauty. She dyed her hair blonde in France,[10] as the police had raided her flat in Lyons and stolen photographs of her with black hair.[11]

In 'F' Section of SOE, Denise enlisted under the assumed name of Danielle Williams,[12] though some SOE documents[13] insist on spelling her real name as 'Block'. Vera Atkins[14] – the Jewish squadron and Intelligence officer in SOE 'F' Section, and personal assistant and number two to Buckmaster – remembers her[15] as tall and sturdy and also argumentative, but explains this trait as being due to the fact that she had already had a lot of experience in the Resistance in France before her exit to England, and thus knew better than her trainers what Nazi occupation really meant.

The archives of the Special Forces Club in London[16] and the SOE files[17] reveal that Denise and her family were living in Lyons where she worked as secretary to Lieutenant Jean Maxime Aron (code-name 'Joseph') an employee of Citroen and Jewish Resistance leader. She was engaged to M. Mendelsohn (himself an agent) but this was allegedly an engagement of convenience to assist her work.[18] She was recruited in July 1942 in Lyons by M. Rene Piercy (code-name 'Adolphe'/'Etienne')[19] and in turn she recruited her 'fiancé'. Denise worked first in the 'Detective' circuit (or *réseaux*) commanded by Captain Henri Paul Sevenet (code-name

'Rodolphe')[20] with the wireless operator (WO) Captain Brian J. Stone-house (code-name 'Celestin'), who died on 2 December 1998. As well as being a courier, she was meant to look after and accompany Stonehouse, whose French was not very good.

In her London debriefing on 11 June 1943,[21] Denise described how she saw Stonehouse in the street in Lyons with two men on 24 October 1942; she followed them and saw that he was taken to a police station, and she realized that he had been arrested. Stonehouse was good at drawing and always had his sketchbook (which Denise often carried) despite Denise's warnings to him not to carry such incriminating items with him. He once addressed her loudly in the street in English and said, 'After the war you must come to Scotland to see my house.' Denise alleged he was homesick and too young for his job. Curiously, Stonehouse's debrief document[22] does not mention Denise at all for some inexplicable reason, and yet clearly he worked closely with her for some time.

Being in danger, following Stonehouse's arrest, she left for Marseilles on 26 October. Whilst there she was sent to a rendezvous at her hotel to receive secret papers about landing grounds and other matters from agent 'L'Allemand' at 7 p.m. on the evening of 31 October. The next day he was arrested but she could not explain to her debriefers why this had happened.[23]

From Marseilles she volunteered to return to Lyons with the papers she had been given, instead of Aron, but he and Sevenet insisted on accompanying her because she was a woman alone. However, unbeknown to them they had been betrayed to the Gestapo and Aron was arrested at the station, near the small entrance, by a Gestapo group that had his photograph from a raid on his flat (he later escaped and got back to Britain on 26 July 1944). Sevenet was right behind Aron but slipped through. Denise also evaded capture by accidentally leaving by the main exit, and she and Sevenet were met by Amedee Contran; all three then went into hiding in St Laurent de Chamousset near Lyons on 3 November 1942, in the house of Mme St Victor.

Denise admitted to having sent a cable to her mother (which had been intercepted by the police) in Lyons. The police had searched the mother's flat, finding nothing, but the cable may have been the reason why the police were waiting at the station in Lyons for her and her two comrades. However, the Gestapo were expecting Denise to arrive with Aron and so missed her – by sheer good fortune – when Aron left the station alone.

Denise then moved to Villefranche-sur-Mer on 10 November, remaining in hiding and out of action until January 1943. She made only one trip – to Nice to get her hair dyed. She then moved to Toulouse, and Sevenet introduced her to Sergeant Maurice Dupont of circuit 'Diplomat',[24] who was to help her cross from Oloron into Spain and out of danger, but deep snow and enemy patrols prevented this and they had to return to Toulouse.

In Toulouse they met Colonel George Reginald Starr (code-named 'Hilaire'/'Gaston'), of circuit 'Wheelwright', who took her to work in Agen with Phillipe de Vomecourt (later commanding officer of Muriel Byck). After two other Jewish SOE agents, Lieutenant Maurice Pertschuk ('Eugene') and his WO, Lieutenant Marcus Bloom ('Urbain'), were arrested in April 1943, Starr decided to send Denise to London as his courier, with Dupont, as they now had no wireless transmission facility. Denise knew and had met Pertschuk several times whilst carrying messages between Toulouse and Agen, and described him[25] at their meetings as often dishevelled and worried, seeing him last on 12 April for their usual lunch together. The following week Pertschuk never arrived for his lunch appointment. She and Starr waited in vain at an agreed safe address and made inquiries, but later they discovered that Pertschuk had been arrested the next day, 13 April. Yet again Denise had had a very close shave.

In her London debrief, Denise gave much useful information describing, for example, how there were many young men who were constantly picked up on the street by gendarmes and Gestapo for labour work in Germany, and warning that because of this, agents sent to France in future should not look too young, or they would often be stopped automatically and arrested. She also emphasized to SOE that future agents must speak excellent French, for anyone suspected of having a foreign accent was deported at once to Germany. In addition she described how the Gestapo agents spoke such good French – many having lived there for twenty years or more – that you did not know if you were talking to a French national or a German.

Denise went on to describe graphically how on one occasion she was carrying her radio in the usual suitcase pack when about to travel on a bus. She saw a Gestapo inspection in progress at the bus stop, so she engaged one of the Gestapo in poor German, causing him some amusement, and asked him to hold her case whilst she bought a newspaper. She then showed her papers to a civilian inspector, returned for her case and got coolly on the bus with no trouble – like something from a wartime movie![26]

She also related how she and Sevenet found by chance a sympathizer contact in the Deuxième Bureau (French Internal Security) who would issue agents with forged *cartes d'identité*.

Exit to England

Denise and Dupont finally left Agen on 29 April via Toulouse, Montrejeau (where they spent the night) and then travelled for three hours by train, seventeen kilometres to Cirs de Luchon, on the first stage of the journey to get to Britain. Starr had promised her a route out of the country of only three kilometres on flat ground. At Cirs, she told the *chef de gare* she had urgent papers to get through to Britain. He said she was mad and there were six hundred yards and several patrols to pass before reaching the hotel where she could get 'help'. But they went on and met no Germans; the proprietor of the Hôtel des Trois Ormeaux found her a room for the day until he arranged two *passeurs* for the price of 5,000 francs[27] to get her over the Pyrenees. She left half-an-hour after midnight, and after fifteen hours hiking across the Pyrenees at 3,300 metres, with bare legs and a half-length coat (at one point her guides stopped and made her a fire, to warm herself), they reached Bausen at 3 p.m. on a Saturday. Here she had to wait three days for the bus, but was glad to be able to rest. The Spanish police, meanwhile, confiscated all her papers including Colonel Starr's report. She then proceeded via Veille to Lerida, arriving on 5 May, where she met the British consul from Barcelona and had dinner with him. He gave her documents to proceed to Madrid (8 May) where she stayed for five days, and in her hotel met four Allied escaped airmen (two American and two British). From Madrid, Denise continued to Gibraltar (15 May) for three days, then Lisbon and ultimately to London, arriving on 21 May 1943, after a twenty-two-day journey.

There she gave her report verbally[28] to SOE underlining the lack of arms, money, wireless transmitters and general stores such as clothes and food, of which Starr was especially short. She also warned that Starr asked that the SOE should be careful to whom they supplied arms as some Resistance groups were left wing and might attempt to take power after the Nazis were ejected.

Denise's debriefers[29] commented afterwards that she was very anxious to return to Lyons to work, but SOE warned her that she was almost certainly by now known to the Gestapo. She disagreed, but said that if it was so, then Starr also needed to be brought out, as they were often seen together. She added that as she had been at the same address for months, the Gestapo would have picked her up by now. She also told her debriefers that she had managed to meet her mother for a meal three months ago, and that she had alternative *cartes d'identité* in the names of Katrine Bernard and Chantal Baron.

Training

Denise now proceeded to formal training for ten months as a WO and parachutist with SOE in Britain, and was enlisted as a FANY Ensign.

According to B.E. Escott,[30] 'F' Section training began at Wanborough

Manor near Guildford for those who had passed the first stiff interviews
in London. From here they continued to Arisaig House in Inverness-shire
for training on arms and explosives. Those requiring very specialist
instruction (including industrial sabotage and wireless) continued to
specified specialist centres round the country. Then came parachute
training at Ringway, near Manchester, whilst living at Tatton Park, and
finally security training (including the use of safe-houses and letter boxes)
at Beaulieu in Hampshire. For SOE in general, however, there were as
many as fifty training schools up and down the country, mostly in isolated
country houses.[31]

At her initial training school, the following comments[32] were written
about Denise's progress:

> An experienced woman with knowledge of the world. She has
> courage and determination and a thorough understanding and
> hatred of the Boche. Has complete self-assurance and is capable of
> handling most situations. Has a feeling of physical inferiority which
> limits her athletic activities. Keen to get back into the field and
> under a good male organiser would make a very good W/T operator
> [WO] or courier. Is not physically suited to the training of Group A
> (i.e. para-military training).

Vera Atkins recalls one of Denise's final pre-mission briefings at a
commonly frequented secret location used on such occasions, in an SOE
flat at 6 Orchard Court, Portman Square[33] as well as the final kitting-out
in authentic tailor-made French clothes.[34] Denise also met Leo Marks,
MBE (the Jewish chief cryptographer – *chef de codage* – at SOE throughout most of the war), in February 1944, for a code briefing and was given
her 'code poem' by him, which he had composed.[35]

Return to France

Denise returned to work in France on the night of 2/3 March 1944 with
Captain Robert Benoist (code-name 'Lionel'), landed by an RAF West-
land Lysander at Soucelles, ten kilometres south of Vatun and two-and-
a-half west of Villeneuve, near Nantes. The secret drop was code-named
'Laburnum'.[36] Her circuit, 'Clergyman', was a large one consisting of 2,000
armed members of the FFI (Forces Françaises de l'Intérieur) which had
to be re-established after its collapse the year before. One source[37] alleges
that the plane was met by Resistance leader and former pilot Clement
Remy, code-name 'Marc'. Denise had returned to France now running the
double risk of being both an official SOE agent *and* Jewish.[38]

Her orders were to act as courier, encoder and WO and to assist in the
attack on high pylons over the River Loire at Île Heron and cut railway

and telephone lines converging on Nantes, before D-Day, to disrupt German communications. Benoist's orders were that Denise 'will be under your command but it must be understood that she is the ultimate judge in all questions regarding the technicalities and w/t and w/t security. She will encode the messages herself ... and it is of the utmost importance that her time on the air should be reduced to the minimum.'[39] She contacted London within two weeks, on 15 March[40] and worked for three months, sending thirty-one messages and receiving fifty-two.[41] Benoist, a wealthy racing driver, was sadly captured on 18 June 1944 in Paris, visiting his dying mother, and later hanged at Buchenwald death camp. Denise was captured the day after, following a Gestapo raid on a château belonging to the Benoist family (Villa Cecile) in Rambouillet at Sermaise,[42] west of Paris, where she was based, with agent Jean-Paul Wimmelle (who managed to escape). Vera Atkins[43] said that it was clear there had been a betrayal – and they knew immediately she was captured by a message from their agents – but it would never be known who was involved unless it was possible to scour the German documents on the issue. Nazi spies and sympathizers were rife in France at the time and so such incidents were commonplace. Only the German archives might reveal how the Gestapo knew of the presence of the SOE agents at the château, and who the informers were, but SOE then had neither the ability or time to get to the truth whilst the war had to be won. After the German surrender, SOE was wound up very quickly (1 January 1946) and it was felt that no good could come of finding the traitors; with the turmoil in post-war Europe, matters like these were often left uninvestigated and unsolved.

The Beginning of the End

As the Allies approached Paris, the Germans were forced to move all their prisoners further east and into Germany. Imprisoned at the infamous gaol in Fresnes, twelve miles south of Paris, Denise was taken to Gare de L'Est by coach on 8 August with Szabo and Rolfe. They had all been in Fresnes prison at the same time, but unbeknown to each other. A report written by Vera Atkins – when seconded to the Judge Advocate General's Branch HQ BAOR, 13 March 1946[44] – mentions that Denise had also been seen in interrogation centres at both 3 Place des États-Unis and the notorious 84 Avenue Foch, in Paris, Gestapo HQ.

Each prisoner was given a small parcel by the Red Cross, enough to last for two days. Their third-class railway wagon was attached to the end of a heavily guarded train carrying 300 German wounded as well as male prisoners. The women prisoners – separated from the men, who included Wing Commander Yeo-Thomas, 'The White Rabbit' – were chained by the ankles in pairs. Vera Atkins's report[45] states that other SOE agents on the train with them included Major Peuleve and Squadron Leader Southgate, en route to Buchenwald. After many hours' delay, the train left on that hot August late afternoon on its way to Germany.

The following day the train was attacked and damaged by the RAF, so they had to continue the journey on trucks later that night. During this attack a famous incident occurred, when Violette Szabo crawled into the male prisoner section to bring them food and water. On reaching Metz, they were billeted in stables for the night; agent Bernard Guillot alleges he saw many women prisoners at this time whilst he was being moved between prisons and especially mentions Denise in his debrief of 12 April 1945.[46]

The girls were then sent on to Gestapo HQ in Strasbourg. Later they reached Saarbrucken; here the three girls were seen by Mlle Monique Level, a French prisoner, as they arrived, with Lilian looking quite ill.[47] Finally, they arrived at Ravensbruck (the world's largest prison for women ever known) after a week's appalling journey. The date was 22 August 1944.[48]

Details of Denise's imprisonment and death are described by E.H. Cookridge in *Inside SOE*.[49] The three SOE girls managed to share the same bunk in their hellish prison hut. Here they were seen by SOE agents Yvonne Baseden and Eileen Nearne.[50] But after three weeks at Ravensbruck, on 3 September, Denise, Szabo and Rolfe, with Nearne, were taken to Torgau, a labour camp 120 miles south of Ravensbruck, where conditions were slightly better and they worked in a factory. Nearne said they were in good spirits, especially Violette, who was constantly planning an escape.[51] Lilian, however, was unwell.[52] Later, Nearne was sent elsewhere and never saw them again.

Several weeks later, on 5 October, they were returned to Ravensbruck. After two weeks there they were moved,[53] on 19 October, and sent east to join an *Aussenkommando* – 300 miles away, near Konigsburg – labouring in heavy forestry and building work at an airfield. They travelled by truck, arriving in November 1944, and worked for three months in the harshest conditions of an East European winter, mainly with Russian and Polish POWs.[54] Both Lilian and Denise were very unwell as a result of the ill treatment here whereas Violette had stood up to it better. Witnesses described how all three always stuck together and showed remarkable spirit.[55]

Violette became particularly friendly with Solange (see note 54), whilst Lilian (who was increasingly ill and in the hospital) was befriended by Renee Corjon (see note 52). Then, on 20 January, the three agents were again returned to Ravensbruck; Solange and Corjon speculated that it might be for repatriation via Sweden or Switzerland. Little did they know that it had been decided by Berlin to carry out systematic mass executions; the Allies were fast approaching and the Germans wanted to kill prisoners who had witnessed atrocities or who were considered 'important' and constituted a 'danger' to the German state.[56]

At Ravensbruck, Baseden saw them yet again and was shocked at their much deteriorated health. They told Baseden that they had managed to contact some male POWs on their transport back and given them a list of agents they had seen imprisoned, hoping it would get back to London. Baseden alleges they were optimistic about getting onto another transport, perhaps to perform lighter work outside the camp, and that a French prisoner, Mary de Moncy – who worked in the infirmary – had been able to get them some food and clothes.[57] It was de Moncy who told Yvonne Baseden later that one day the girls had been taken to the punishment cells for solitary confinement, all three being in a poor state and Lilian unable to walk. After a further three days they were moved to an L-shaped block of cells called the bunker (a kind of prison within the prison) and were seen by an unnamed Czech woman.[58] Odette Churchill, GC,[59] describes this abominable place:

> A short passage with a barrel gate at the end with spikes leading to the floor and ceiling, had on one side the cheerful rooms of the SS ... the gate swung on a spring hinge and led to a flight of stairs descending to a stone underground second passage with white electric light, and cells on one side, which were all in darkness inside ... the cell doors had hatches through which food was passed.

A day or two later all three agents disappeared.

After the war, it was discovered that the three women were taken from their cells to the yard behind the crematorium at about 1900 hrs one evening. Denise and Lilian had been badly treated and were on stretchers; only Violette was able to walk. Camp Commandant SS Sturmbannführer Fritz Suhren read the death sentences ordered by RSHA (SS Security Section) in Berlin, with Second in Command Schwartzhuber also present. SS Sergeant Zappe guarded the girls whilst this was done. SS Scharführer Schulte (or Schulter) – a block leader from the men's camp – then shot each girl in the back of the neck, as they knelt down, with a small-calibre gun, as SS Corporal Schenk (in charge of the crematorium) brought them forward and held them. Camp doctor SS Sturmbannführer Trommer certified the deaths and the clothed bodies were removed singly by internees and immediately cremated. The camp dentist, Dr Martin Hellinger, was there to remove any gold teeth.

Suhren was arrested by the Americans on 3 May whilst bringing Odette Churchill, GC, from Ravensbruck to the American lines as a mitigating offering. He escaped, was recaptured, escaped again for two years, was recaptured again in 1949 by the British when he was found working in a brewery, and then handed over to the French. They, as Peter Churchill wrote,[60] 'had no foolish sentiment about these murderers' and tried and then executed him in – ironically – Fresnes prison. The dentist received fifteen years in prison, was released in 1951 and practised in Germany for years afterwards.[61]

The Truth

For months after the war, it was unofficially believed that the three girls had been liberated by the Russians and that they were possibly on their way home via Siberia, or even Sweden. This had happened before to some survivors of the German camps. A document in the SOE files, however,[62] dated 28 April 1945, shows that SOE believed the three girls were still at Ravensbruck. In April 1946 a newspaper story about the missing girls was seen by Mrs Julie Barry living at Joyce Grove, Nettlebed in Oxfordshire. She was a Guernsey woman who had been deported to Ravensbruck and allegedly forced to become a Kapo (no. 39785) in the Strafeblock.[63] Barry was in fact a Jewish refugee who had arrived in Guernsey in July 1939 as Julia Brichta and in April 1942 married a local man, Jeremiah Barry. However, she was denounced by local Guernsey residents and deported to Ravensbruck via France on 5 May 1944.[64]

When interviewed by two War Office officials, Barry's story was that she saw the three girls at Ravensbruck in rags, faces black with dirt and hair matted, spoke to them and gave them food and clothing. She especially remembered Violette Szabo. But her story cannot be confirmed. Another British POW at Ravensbruck was Mary Lindell. Escott quotes her[65] as affirming that the usual method of execution there was by hanging, and she had it on reliable authority from others in the camp that the girls' clothes were returned to the stores intact after execution. Baseden,[66] however, disputes this based on information from Mary de Moncy, who said their clothes were never returned. We will probably never know the truth of the manner of their death.[67]

Meanwhile, Vera Atkins went to Germany on her own initiative and became attached to the Nuremburg War Crimes Investigation team.[68] She began conducting inquiries in Germany on all missing agents. At Minden prison she found Obersturmführer Johann Schwartzhuber, SS, the second in command (*Schutzhaftlagerführer* or Camp Overseer) at Ravensbruck, and previously a prominent prison guard at Auschwitz, and interviewed him on 13 March 1946.[69]

After some strong words from Atkins, a guilty-looking Schwartzhuber admitted that the three women had been brought back from Konigsburg and put in the cells at Ravensbruck. He then confirmed how the girls were killed, adding that a female overseer (possibly Barry) escorted them to the crematorium yard but was sent back before the execution. He said:

All three were very brave and I was deeply moved ... we were impressed by the bearing of these women ... and annoyed that the Gestapo themselves did not carry out these shootings ... I recognise with certainty the photograph of Danielle Williams (Denise Bloch) and I think I recognise the photograph of Lillian Rolfe. I know that the third had the name of Violette.

The translation was confirmed by a German linguist, Captain A. Vollman.

Schwarzhuber also confirmed that Lilian Rolfe was unable to walk and had to be assisted to the place of execution; this was a long trek, from the cells via the kitchen, through the main gate, past the garage, to the crematorium itself. Barry insists that only Violette walked and the other two were on stretchers. Violette was shot last and had the final agony of having to watch her friends murdered in front of her.

Like Suhren (who also testified to the supreme courage and cheerfulness of the girls), Schwartzhuber was sentenced to death after his trial in Hamburg and hanged. Thus, the indefatigable Vera Atkins was able to write letters of condolence to the girls' families only in the spring of 1946, and only after this evidence from Vera Atkins was Whitehall able to issue death certificates for the three agents – over a year after the murders. They have no known graves.

Thus was Denise Bloch's short, brave life. Like many others her name is proudly carved on four memorials – lest we forget.

Postscript

In 1968, Alan Rolfe, brother of Lilian Rolfe who was murdered with Denise, saw an announcement in the *Daily Telegraph* of 24 May in memory of Denise Bloch, signed 'Dave'. After enquiries at the newspaper, Dave replied to Alan Rolfe, and turned out to be Flight Lieutenant David Lomas, who knew Denise when she was training in England. He was lobbying Lambeth Council to name a block of flats after Denise Bloch, as they had done for Rolfe and Szabo on the Vincennes Estate at Norwood, south London. However, he never succeeded – Lambeth Council claimed that all the flats had been named already, and in July, Lomas was killed in an aircraft crash, in the Far East, it is thought. The matter was never pursued. Perhaps it was because Denise was French – or Jewish – or both; we will never know. But Vera Atkins does confirm that perhaps there had been a romance (interview, 25 April 1998, East Sussex), though she pointed out that the private lives of the agents, in their free time on leave from training, were their own.

This original correspondence was donated by Alan Rolfe to the AJEX Jewish Military Museum.

MURIEL TAMARA BYCK, SOE, MENTIONED IN DESPATCHES

Honorary assistant section officer 2071428 WAAF/SOE agent 9111, seconded to FANY, Muriel Tamara Byck, MiD, code-names 'Violette' and
'Michele,'[70] was born on 4 June 1918 in Ealing, London, daughter of
French Jewish parents, Luba Besia, née Golinska, and Jacques Byck, who
had both taken British nationality. Her parents were divorced; in 1943,
Jacques (born in Kiev, Russia) was living in New York; Luba (born in Lvov,
Russia) was living at 2 Bayfort Mansions, Warren Road, Torquay, having
remarried, now Mrs G.E. Leslie.[71] Muriel joined the WAAF in December
1942[72] and became a full member of the SOE in July 1943.

Muriel's background information file[73] reveals that she spoke fluent
French and moderate Russian and in 1923/24 had lived in Wiesbaden in
Germany. She went to school from 1926 to 1930 at the Lycée de Jeunes
Filles, St Germain in France, and from 1930 to 1935 attended the Lycée
Française in Kensington, London SW7, where she took the Baccalaureate
and then went on to university in Lille, France.

Recruitment into SOE

From 1936 to 1938 Muriel was a secretary in London, and from 1937 to
1939 an assistant stage manager at the Gate Theatre. Muriel had a strong
sense of duty and from 1939 to 1941 was a voluntary worker in the Red
Cross and WVS, and an ARP warden in Torquay. From 1941 to 1942 she
worked as a national registration clerk in Torquay and then joined the
WAAF as a clerk in December 1942, pending a Commission. She was
recruited into the SOE in July 1943 because of her excellent French, and
began initial training in September 1943 at Winterfold, Cranleigh, in Surrey. From here she proceeded to paramilitary training at Meoble Lodge,
Morar, Inverness-shire until October, and wireless transmission training
at Thame Park, Oxfordshire in November/December 1943.

Whilst in training she was graded average as a general agent, but with
a high intelligence rating (eight out of nine), with a high grade for Morse
and mechanical aptitude. She was described as:

> a quiet, bright, attractive girl, keen, enthusiastic and intelligent.
> Alert but not very practical and as yet lacks foresight and thorough-
> ness. She is, however, self-possessed, independent and persistent,
> and warm in her feelings for others ... a girl of considerable promise
> who will require much training to help her to overcome her lack of
> experience, her complete ignorance of what the work really involves
> and her general guilelessness. Her temperament would appear to
> be suitable for work as a courier, or possibly propaganda.[74]

Vera Atkins remembers her as being very self-assured and being committed completely to wanting to go into this very hazardous work, to defeat Nazism and all it stood for.

At Meoble she showed little aptitude for paramilitary training (close combat, fieldcraft, weapon training, explosives and demolition), except for signalling. She was not physically very strong, though successfully completed parachute training. She was commissioned (WAAF honorary assistant section officer) on 1 April 1944.

Into France

Muriel – petite, dark and aged 25 – was engaged to be married to a French agent in the offices of the OSS (Office of Strategic Service, forerunner of the CIA, now the American Secret Service), a Lieutenant Morange (an alias) whom she had met whilst training,[75] and he had given her a leather-covered powder compact. When her circuit leader, Major Phillipe Albert de Crevoisier de Vomecourt, DSO (code-name 'Antoine') met Muriel in London and was security-checking her possessions before her jump, he told her she could not take the gift with her as it was too new and nothing like it could be bought in France. If she were caught with it, it would give her away as a foreign agent.[76] Muriel insisted on taking it but he agreed only if he could make it look old, which he achieved by rubbing it with ammonia.

Muriel was given three sets of identity papers with photographs that differed only by her arranging her long black hair in different styles. Her operation was code-named 'Benefactress' and her forged papers named her as Michele Bernier.[77] She was told that if for any reason she had to change identities, she should inform London of the details immediately. In fact SOE were so concerned about her youthful looks, they gave her special training with a make-up artist in London on how to look older by using a pencil under her eyes.[78]

Her flight took off from Tempsford aerodrome near Bedford after four nail-biting delays due to bad weather, and she parachuted into France on the night of 8/9 April 1944, with agent Captain Stanislaw Makowski, code-name 'Dmitri'/'Maurice'[79] and two other agents, Captain C.S. Hudson ('Marc'/'Albin') – who was her CO until de Vomecourt arrived by plane – and Captain G.D. Jones ('Lime'/'Isidore'/'Gaston'). Muriel was to work as a wireless operator with Resistance leader de Vomecourt of circuit 'Ventriloquist' in the Orleans-Blois area and train any wireless operators whom it was possible to recruit locally.[80] She was then to supply London with the details about these new recruits so they could be given code-names and status. She was also to establish postboxes for contact should wireless transmission break down. Although under the command of 'Antoine', she was ordered to be as self-reliant as possible on all wireless transmission matters. She was to take 100,000 francs and for security reasons keep expenses as moderate as possible.

Interestingly, part two of Muriel's orders[81] mentions an emergency address – handwritten in contrast to the typed order sheets – for her to contact should she become separated from her dropping party and the reception committee on landing; it was Bureaux Agricoles, 10 Place de L'Hôtel de Ville, Chalcauoux. She was – in true cloak-and-dagger style – to ask for M. Chabena or M. Monesher using the password, 'Je viens de la part de Philippe voir si vouz pouviez m'aider', to which the reply was to be 'Veuillez attendre un instant.' Curiously, written next to this instruction is the word 'Blown', suggesting this address had been compromised.

After landing at Issoudun she was taken to Salbris to the home of Antoine Vincent, a member of the circuit. Here she again met de Vomecourt and the two men took her to a meal at a small restaurant by the level crossing just outside town. It was used almost exclusively by Germans and when they arrived, Muriel was terrified. 'We can't stay here', she whispered, 'let's get out while we can!' But Vincent explained that she had been brought here deliberately to get used to the sight of Germans and that once she was, she need not worry too much about them. She did not enjoy her meal that day.[82]

Her circuit had four transmitters in different locations, covering a wide area within a ten-mile radius of Vincent's house, and – in accordance with her orders – they were constantly moved about to avoid detection by the Germans, with transmissions being as brief as possible.[83] Her first transmission was on 7 May 1944 and she subsequently sent twenty-seven messages and received sixteen.[84] She never used the same set consecutively or at the same hour on any day. She was thus continually cycling from one to the other, and although many a man's health and nerves degenerated under the stress, Muriel remained cheerful and buoyant despite her frail and youthful looks. Rushing from location to location, she would encode, send, receive and decode messages, always on schedule, and on her own initiative she would often do this for other circuits as well, so messages would not ever be delayed. She also acted as a courier, alerting sabotage teams over a wide area.[85]

Her base was in Vincent's junkyard, twenty-five yards from his garage which was used as a repair shop by the Germans. Her station consisted of a rickety hut with a rusted corrugated iron roof, with light filtering through cracks in the wall. She was surrounded by old tyres and car parts and the reek of oil and petrol. She had a box and table to work at. Whilst she was transmitting, a guard was posted at the yard gate to give her warning if need be.

One day in late April, (this date of de Vomecourt's conflicts with the

SOE file date) whilst transmitting to London, she noticed an eye looking through a hole in the shed wall. Her stomach lurched but she quickly switched to plain language to tell London she was being watched. Continuing to send, she picked up the set and approached the hole, in time to see a German soldier leaving the yard. Full of fear, and not understanding where her lookout was, she packed her equipment, threw dust over her box and table to disguise the fact that anyone had been in the hut, and slipped into Vincent's house and told him what had happened.

He decided at once to get her away in a car after consulting de Vomecourt, who came to collect her. When the Germans arrived – forty of them – they were already sceptical that their soldier had actually seen a pretty woman with a transmitter in a junkyard shed. They searched and found nothing and the soldier was given ten days' detention for wasting his officer's time.

Securely relocated in a new safe-house (with the help of the Resistance doctor Andrieux), Muriel returned to work; her story was that she was recovering from an illness and had come from Paris to recuperate. She had to take medicine during the night and her hosts should not be worried by her alarm going off at strange hours (this was, of course, to cover her wireless operations) or visits from her 'uncle', de Vomecourt.

The Last Days

In early May it was decided by London and the circuit to bomb the nearby German ammunition dump at Michenon. At 2 p.m. on 7 May, Muriel received a message from London saying that the dump would be hit the following night.

The raid was a great success but Muriel had been shaken by the terrific explosions to which she had been quite near. She later became very tired and listless and was moved to the house of circuit member Dede and his wife and three daughters at Nouan-le-Fuzelier; later still she was moved to the house of blacksmith Jourdain at Vernou, thirty miles to the west. De Vomecourt had been away but returned when he was told Muriel was ill, and told her there was a plane leaving soon for England and she could write to her parents. These two letters[86] were later delivered by de Vomecourt when he wrote – describing Muriel's death – to her father on 6 December 1944.

But Muriel deteriorated seriously and collapsed at Jourdain's home. A physician was called – in his letter to her father, de Vomecourt says three doctors[87] attended her – and diagnosed meningitis, saying she must be taken immediately to hospital. This was a great risk but de Vomecourt decided it must be taken; she was heavily involved in her work and much admired by all her comrades.

He went alone with her in the ambulance to the hospital at Romorantin, saying he was Muriel's uncle, M. de Courcelles, and that they were evacuees from Paris. Whether the nuns believed him or not, they admitted the patient and did all they could to save her. An operation was performed at 10 a.m. but she died in Phillipe's arms at 7 p.m. on 23 May 1944. De Vomecourt described how he 'assisted personally at all the duties generally assumed by the family' after Muriel had passed away[88] and said that she was buried secretly in a temporary vault, under a false name, in a zinc coffin, so that 'you will be able to transport her later if you wish'.[89]

De Vomecourt attended her funeral and had great difficulty in persuading her many friends to keep away for fear of arousing Gestapo suspicions. He followed the hearse alone through the town to the cemetery, just escaping the Gestapo – who had come for him there – by jumping the cemetery wall where a car awaited to whisk him away.[90] Gleeson[91] alleges that after the war, Muriel's family had her body brought back for burial in England. However, Escott rightly says she was re-buried in the Commonwealth War Graves Commission Cemetery at Pornic, twenty kilometres south-east of St Nazaire. She lies in plot two, row AB, grave eighteen.[92] When the author visited the site he discovered that the poignant inscription reads: 'Here rests in peace Muriel Tamara Byck, our only child and beloved daughter.' In her will she left her savings of £42 to her beloved fiancé.

It emerged subsequently that Muriel had meningitis as a child but she told nobody for fear of being refused enlistment in the SOE, as there is a risk of recurrence. Such was her courage, and determination to take part in the struggle against the Nazis.

In his letter to Muriel's father, de Vomecourt added that he would be happy to introduce him to all Muriel's many friends in France as soon as it was possible for him to come, and that a lady who had lost her only son in the Maquis, and at whose house Muriel had once stayed, was writing to him and Muriel's mother to express her appreciation of Muriel's great work and sacrifice for the liberation of France. This very moving letter, in French and written in March 1945, is a long tribute to Muriel, full of praise for her wonderful personality and beauty, her sense of duty and hard work, her laughter and gaiety, and describes her as a unique person, who died as a soldier, giving her life, like the lady's son, for right and justice.

Muriel never abandoned her Jewish faith and spoke often of her devout family in England, but she nevertheless wore, as a good luck charm, a little gold cross which was given to her by a Resistance man who had met her at the parachute drop at Châteaurenault. To this day, Resistance members and their children as well as other local people of the Sologne area visit her memorial at Romorantin, Loir et Cher, to lay flowers at Remembrance ceremonies.[93]

Muriel is also commemorated – like Denise Bloch – on the Knights-bridge and Valençay memorials as well as the war memorial at the Lycée Française in Kensington. These courageous women followed in a long and great tradition of Jews fighting back, helping dispel the anti-Semitic myths that all went like sheep to the slaughter – or worse, avoided fighting at all.

Long may they all be remembered.

Acknowledgements

This chapter could not have been written without the help, encourage-ment and advice of the following individuals and organizations, to whom I am greatly indebted:

Vera Atkins, CBE, Croix de Guerre., Com. de Leg. d'Hon., former SOE 'F' Section squadron and Intelligence officer, East Sussex. Gervase Cowell, then chair of the Historical Sub-Committee, Special Forces Club, London. Leo Marks, MBE (Mil.), *chef de codage*, SOE. Alan Rolfe, London, brother of the late Lilian Rolfe, SOE agent. Duncan Stuart, CMG, SOE former adviser at the Foreign and Commonwealth Office, London. My wife, Jane Sugarman, for technical advice and putting up with my many absences from home. The staff of the Commonwealth War Graves Commission, Maidenhead. Mark Seaman and Nigel Steel, research staff at the Imperial War Museum, London, and other library staff in the Reading Room. Staff at TNA, Kew, London, and Battersea Park Road Library, London.

Notes

1. M. Sugarman, research – a growing list, published in this book, chapter 12.
2. Nigel West, *Secret War* (London: Hodder & Stoughton,1992), p.9.
3. J. Gleeson, *They Feared No Evil* (London: Corgi, 1976), Preface.
4. Ibid., pp.57–8.
5. Foreign and Commonwealth Office files of the SOE adviser, Sir Duncan Stuart, unnumbered pages (hereafter FCO), now at TNA.
6. The ceremony at Ravensbruck took place on the morning of 10 June 1993, organized and led by Gervase Cowell of the Special Forces Club, with representatives of the Foreign and Common-wealth Office, the British Embassy in Berlin and the Ravensbruck Museum. The plaque was unveiled by former agents Odette Hallowes-Sansom, GC, MBE; Eileen Nearne, MBE; and Yvonne Baseden, MBE. Present were Vera Atkins; Francis Cammaerts, DSO (senior SOE officer in France); Brian Stonehouse; Leo Marks (SOE *chef de codage*); with representatives from the FANY (WTS), WAAF (WRAF), the sister of Lillian Rolfe, the daughter of Violette Szabo, Judge John de Cunha (a prosecutor at Nuremburg) and several former members of the French Resist-ance. There was a large article in the *Daily Mail* on the following weekend.
7. J.D. Sainsbury, *The F Section Memorial* (London: Imperial War Museum Library, 1991).
8. R.J. Minney, *Carve her Name with Pride* (London: Portway,1988), p.160.
9. Irene Ward, *F.A.N.Y. Invicta* (London: Hutchinson, 1955), p.240.
10. FCO photograph.
11. FCO debrief of Denise Bloch.
12. PRO/TNA HS6/422 notes that Denise had the following noms de guerre: Denise Madeline, Ka-trine Bernard, Danielle Wood and Chantal Baron.
13. PRO/TNA (Public Record Office/National Archive, Kew, London) files, HS6 Series (hereafter TNA).

14. Née Rosenberg – her parents were Romanian Jewish (obituary, *Independent*, 3 July 2000). See Sarah Helm, *Vera Atkins: A Life in Secrets* (London: Random House, 2005).

15. Interview, 24 April 1998, East Sussex. The charming and forthright Vera Atkins (CBE, Croix de Guerre, Com. de Leg. d'Hon.) kindly agreed to meet me on 24 April 1998 at her home in East Sussex. She was at the time in her ninetieth year but her memory was as sharp as it ever was. She was squadron and Intelligence officer to SOE 'F' Section and personal assistant to Buckmaster and had known all the agents over the war years who had passed through the SOE offices in London. Her job was multifaceted and included briefing agents on the latest rationing regula-tions in France, obtaining French tailor labels for clothing, supplying bogus travel documents and photos of bogus husbands or wives – see J. Tickell, *Odette* (London: Pan, 1949 and1955).

16. Letter from Gervase Cowell, then chair of the Special Forces Club Historical Sub-Committee, to author, 13 February 1998.

17. FCO.

18. FCO debrief of Denise Bloch, 11 June 1943. Mendelsohn was arrested on 30 October 1942 and imprisoned for a year, during which Denise's father tried to get him, Aron and two others out, by bribing the Germans through a lawyer for 1,500,000 francs. Eventually Mendelsohn escaped from France on 31 December 1943 and reached England on 17 April 1944 (FCO debrief, p.3). It seems the Bloch family were all active in one way or the other in the Resistance.

19. FCO.

20. Ibid.

21. Ibid.

22. PRO HS6/437, 6 June 1945.

23. Ibid.

24. Ibid.

25. Ibid.

26. Ibid.

27. Ibid.

28. Ibid.

29. Ibid.

30. B.E. Escott, *Mission Improbable* (London: Patrick Stephens, 1991), pp.31–4.

31. West, *Secret War*, pp.267–9.

32. FCO.

33. Interview, 24 April 1998, East Sussex.

34. A group of German refugee Jewish tailors working from a secret workshop near Oxford Circus pro-duced these items, scouring London's synagogue worshippers for authentic French and German labels and either buying the clothing or borrowing items to copy for SOE agents about to be dropped into France. Vera Atkins named a Captain Ken More who was in charge of procuring items of this kind for SOE and other relevant agencies. The Jewish leader of the tailoring group itself was made an honorary captain in the SOE (Gleeson, *They Feared No Evil*, p.25).

35. L. Marks, *Between Silk and Cyanide* (London: HarperCollins, 1998), p.474:

> Make the most of it
> A coast to coast
> Toast of it
> For what you think
> Has been God-sent to you
> Has only been lent to you.

36. H. Verity, *We Landed by Moonlight* (London: Ian Allan, 1978), p.220.

37. J.O. Fuller, *The German Penetration of SOE* (London: W. Kimber, 1975), p.137.

38. L. Jones, *A Quiet Courage* (London: Bantam, 1990), p.127.

39. M.R.D. Foot, *SOE in France* (London: HMSO 1966), p.88.

40. FCO.

41. G. Cowell, from Special Forces Club files.

42. FCO.

43. Interview, 24 April 1998, East Sussex.

44. Vera Atkins, FCO (hereafter VA FCO).

45. VA FCO.

46. PRO HS6/439 (Odette Churchill, GC, in WO/309/282, alleges she saw Denise in cells at Karl-sruhe and when seen talking, Denise was badly beaten by a female SS guard Becker: statement to 2nd Lieutenant A.W.H. Nicolson, 14 December 1946, in Hamburg).

47. Her report in PRO HS6/440.

48. Mlle J. Rousseau, Sancellemons, Haute Savoie: VA FCO.

49. E.H. Cookridge, *Inside SOE* (London: Arthur Barker, 1966).
50. PRO HS6/437, 20 June 1945 and 15 June 1945 respectively.
51. Minney, *Carve her Name*, p.168.
52. Mme Renee Corjon, Bellve, Nogent sur Vernirsson, Loiret: VA FCO.
53. Mme Renee Rossier, Allegre, Haute Savoie/3 Villa Montecalme, Paris 18: VA FCO.
54. Mme Solange Rousseau, St Maur, Seine & Marne: VA FCO.
55. VA FCO.
56. Jones, *Quiet Courage*, p.85.
57. PRO HS6/437.
58. VA FCO.
59. Tickell, *Odette*, pp.266–7.
60. P. Churchill, *The Spirit in the Cage* (London: Hodder & Stoughton, 1954), p.234.
61. Cookridge, *Inside SOE*, p.173.
62. PRO HS6/438.
63. Minney, *Carve her Name*, chapters 19 and 20.
64. F.E. Cohen, 'The Jews in the Islands of Jersey, Guernsey and Sark during the German Occupation 1940–45', *Journal of Holocaust Education* (London: Frank Cass) 6, 1 (Summer 1997), pp.34–5. I am indebted to Stephen Stodel, London (nephew of former Jewish POW, the late Morris Stodel, Royal Signals), for pointing out this article to me.
65. Escott, *Mission Improbable*, p.208.
66. PRO HS6/437.
67. In an unsigned leaflet in the museum's possession, apparently produced by the PRO on 20 July 1998 when new SOE papers were released for public scrutiny, and found at the PRO itself, it states that at least 87 per cent of SOE files were deliberately destroyed between 1945 and 1950, some by SOE and some by the SIS (Secret Intelligence Service); many others have simply not been released. The debrief document on the fate of Violette Szabo is missing, as are many on other operations and allegedly unfounded allegations of treachery, as well as on the assassination of alleged traitors in the field. Other documents were lost in a fire at Baker Street HQ, including most of the files from the Polish section.
68. Interview, 24 April 1998, East Sussex. After the war ended, Vera Atkins felt strongly that she should investigate what had become of all the agents who had disappeared whilst on active service. Against the wishes and advice of her superiors, and facing some hostility, she went to Germany in November/December 1945 to assess whether she could begin to discover the truth of the fate of the missing agents, and who exactly in the Allied Occupation Forces would or could help her.
69. VA FCO. After approaching agencies such as the Red Cross, Military Intelligence and others, Vera Atkins finally spoke to Group Captain Tony Somerhough, the commanding officer of the legal department of the British War Crimes offices in Germany at Bad Oynhausen near Hanover (then HQ, BAOR). He allowed her to interview some imprisoned Nazis; she realized after this experience that she might make some headway in her own investigations. Even though she was not legally trained, and although there were no vacancies in the War Crimes offices, the CO allowed her to stay. MI5 paid her army salary and she stoically continued with her work – as a matter of honour – until the end, driven by her determination to get to the truth, both for herself and for the families of the agents whose whereabouts had not been known after they disappeared, and most of all in memory of the agents themselves.
70. Cookridge, *Inside SOE*, p.633.
71. PRO HS6/467.
72. Jewish Chaplain Cards, AJEX Jewish Military Museum, London.
73. SOE Foreign and Commonwealth Office files on Muriel Byck, courtesy of Sir Duncan Stuart (hereafter FCO Byck), now at TNA, Kew.
74. FCO Byck.
75 Ibid.
76. P. de Vomecourt, *Who Lived to See the Day* (London: Hutchinson, 1961) p.170.
77. FCO Operation Instruction No. F95, 26 March 1944 (hereafter FCO 95).
78. PRO HS6/582: report by de Vomecourt, 11–19 January 1945.
79. Foot, *SOE in France*, p.468.
80. FCO 95.
81. Ibid.
82. de Vomecourt, *Who Lived to See the Day*, p.186.
83. FCO Byck.
84. Ibid.
85. Escott, *Mission Improbable*, chapter 14.

86. FCO.
87. Ibid.
88. Ibid.
89. Ibid.
90. Foot, *SOE in France*, p.383; de Vomecourt, *Who Lived to See the Day*, pp.202–10.
91. Gleeson, *They Feared No Evil*, pp.57–8.
92. Letter from Commonwealth War Graves Commission, 20 February 1998.
93. Cookridge, *Inside SOE*, p.377.

15

The Hero of Mogadishu:
Captain Simmon Latutin, GC

The King has been graciously pleased to approve the posthumous
award of the GEORGE CROSS in recognition of most conspicuous gallantry in carrying out hazardous work in a very brave manner to Captain
Simmon Latutin 242974 Somalia Gendarmerie (Harrow Middlesex.)
London Gazette, 6 August 1946.

*(The George Cross – instituted by King George VI in September 1940 – is only
awarded to soldiers or civilians of Britain and the Commonwealth for acts of the
greatest heroism and conspicuous courage in circumstances of extreme danger, but not
necessarily in the field of battle; it is equal in stature to the Victoria Cross as the
highest and most prestigious award.[1])*

Simmon Latutin was born at number 20, North Villas,[2] off Camden
Square, Camden Town, London, on 25 July 1916.[3] His father was
Moses Vlatutin, born in Riga[4] in 1887, distantly related, so the family history has it, to a famous Russian Jewish general of the same name who had
later lifted the siege of Kiev – his home town – during the Second World
War, and died there after the war. The father of Moses Vlatutin was a regimental tailor who travelled, with his family, as the regiment was posted
from place to place. When his first wife died (she was the mother of
Moses) he remarried and had a second family. At least one of Moses's
stepsisters fled Russia to Israel, where relatives live to this day.

Moses himself had become a master tailor at the age of 16, and had
thus earned the right – under the anti-Semitic laws of the time – to move
from village to village for work in Czarist Russia. He made his way to
Odessa and later to Romania, where he stayed for some years working hard
to save for his emigration to America. Around 1912, he arrived in London,
having crossed Europe in stages by train from city to city. Here he met and
fell in love with Fradel Kraftcheck[5] (who later shortened her name to
Frieda/Freda Kraft), born in Warsaw in 1895, but brought to England with
her brother and parents when she was 3 years old. Moses became Morris
and the couple married in 1913.

15.1 Acting Major Simmon Latutin, George Cross, SLI, attached Somalia Gendarmerie; taken in 1944. He is wearing the SLI collar badges and the cap badge of the Gendarmerie.

15.2 Margaret Latutin, newly widowed, with her two daughters Anne (left) and Elisabeth, in Harrow just after the GC investiture. Note Simmon's photograph on the left.

An orthodox Jewish working-class family, they first lived in Stamford Hill, Hackney, and later moved to a rented house in Camden Town, where Shimeon (later Simmon) and his younger sister Blanche were born. Simmon's mother did not enjoy good health and for many years his father, with his European accent, worked in his tailoring shop in the basement of their house, so he could be near to and care for his wife at home.

Sheila Gaiman, a first cousin and daughter of Pearl (Simmon's aunt) recalls[6] that after Simmon had shown his musical talent (on the violin and later viola, at the age of 7) his parents tried to shelter him from the normal rough and tumble games that other boys got up to, for fear he would damage his hands. How successful this was remains a mystery. She remembers that he practised intensely and often, according to a strict timetable his parents laid down; they were enormously proud of his skill and had high hopes for him as a top musician in the years to come. Sheila recalls how Simmon's bedroom faced over the back garden in Camden and when they went round to visit, they would secretly play ball with him from the garden, throwing the ball back and forth to him in his first-floor room.

Simmon attended the North London Polytechnic School between 1931 and 1933, attached to the nearby college which stood as now in Holloway Road;[7] he was very bright and the head teacher advised the family that he should apply for a mathematics scholarship at Oxford University. But Simmon, the gifted and sensitive musician, loved to listen to music whenever he could – there was never enough money to attend concerts – and had his heart elsewhere. Three years after his barmitzvah, at the age of 16, he won the Westmoreland Scholarship to the Royal Academy of Music to study violin.[8] He was a student of piano and violin from 1932 (when he won the four-year Sainton Scholarship for violin in September of that year[9]) until 1940. His student record shows that he won first the bronze and then the silver medal for violin, culminating in the Certificate of Merit, the highest award possible in that instrument. He was awarded various bursaries as a result of his talent, including the Bache Scholarship in 1935.[10]

Still aged only 16 he was approached by Sir Henry Wood's assistant to apply for a post in Brighton to play the viola; he borrowed a viola, played it that evening, and auditioned for the job next morning and got it.[11] Within four years he was playing for the London Symphony Orchestra, at 20 years old, one of its youngest players, having beaten off very stiff competition.[12] As an honour, he was loaned the RAM's Stradivarius viola to play for several years up until the war.

Archives at the London Symphony Orchestra offices in the Barbican first mention Simmon in the programmes of the thirty-second series of concerts of the 1937–38 season – specifically on 25 November 1937, where he appears in the viola section playing at the Queen's Hall[13] in Elgar's 'Dream of Gerontius', conducted by Adrian Boult.[14] His name appears consistently up until April 1940,[15] after which the names of the orchestra members stop appearing and archive programmes peter out, perhaps due to wartime paper shortages. Simmon is also mentioned once in the minutes of the board of the LSO in August 1939, where he was refused permission to play with the English Opera Company as 'it was not in the best interests of the Orchestra'![16]

At the RAM Simmon met Margaret Liebet Jacob, a woodwind student and daughter of a long established and observant Anglo-Jewish family, George and Phoebe Jacob (née Green). Their origins in Britain dated back to the seventeenth century. Margaret had been born on 6 December 1917, at 129 Hamilton Terrace, St John's Wood, one of three children, with an older brother and younger sister. She went to St Paul's Girls' School in Hammersmith and attended the Hampstead Synagogue in Dennington Park Road. She was a diligent student and learnt Hebrew, Bible studies and religious studies (privately at home from a Miss Manville) with enthusiasm and ability, from the age of 4, passing the Chief Rabbi's confirmation tests when she was in her teens.

Margaret and Simmon, with their obvious mutual interest in music, fell in love. He was tall, broad and muscular, well spoken, with curly, dark brown hair and brown eyes. Classical music was his life – he had little time or money for other pursuits – and had he lived longer, he would certainly have become assistant conductor to Henry Wood; with a well developed sense of humour, he was at the same time very serious.

They became engaged and after they were married bought a diamond for £49 from a street trader in Hatton Garden, which they had set in platinum for £3, for Margaret. It became their engagement ring.

Parental relationships were, however, strained, for Margaret's parents – especially her domineering mother – were unhappy, and totally disapproved of her relationship with the son of an orthodox Jewish family of recent East European origin. Margaret also found visits to Simmon's parents quite difficult as the family were strictly kosher and pious. In addition, Simmon's parents seemed not to be pleased that his work took him away from home on Sabbaths and Holydays, nor that work in his field was so hard to come by, especially when war first broke out. Simmon consequently lived away from home. Margaret too felt the need to leave home but Simmon would not agree without them first being married, since many people knew about their relationship – and Simmon refused to risk any chance of scandal for her. They decided that this was the opportunity for them to marry, sad though it was for them to do so without telling their parents beforehand. Not being able to face two sets of parents who had never met, at an orthodox Jewish wedding, they were married in a private ceremony at Marylebone Town Hall Registry Office on 15 March 1940, with two casual acquaintances for witnesses, and told their parents later. They used part of an old gold watch chain to make a wedding ring as they could not afford anything else, and had the rest of the chain made into a bracelet for Margaret.

Following the marriage, Margaret's parents became even more estranged, but Simmon's parents – especially his mother – were always very kind and supportive, and Freda always referred to Margaret as her daughter. Simmon's sister Blanche was also very close to Margaret and they were firm friends.

They lived in a bedsit at 94a St John's Wood High Street, NW8.[17] Margaret was working in full-time Civil Defence, earning under £2 per week,[18] involving stressful and long shift work as a first-aid auxiliary; also practising setting up a mobile hospital should the need arise; and staffing tube station first-aid posts during the Blitz. Simmon, meanwhile, did voluntary unpaid Civil Defence work and also had some weekend work playing at concerts. There was little time for visiting family and friends; life consisted of work, sleep, housekeeping and staying alive during the bombing.

One of Simmon's younger cousins, Marlene Malnick (née Tobias), is related to the author,[19] another amusing story. Her father, Simmon's uncle Mick (aka Myer), was recovering from an operation in the London Clinic near the Royal Academy of Music around 1938. On a number of occasions, Simmon visited him and played his viola to cheer him up. After some time, Mick told Simmon that whilst he was welcome any time, he should not bring his viola in future – because there were complaints from matron that the young nurses were distracted from their work, by constantly going into his room to see the handsome young man who was playing such divine music.

Then in July 1940 Simmon was called up into the army.[20]

War Service

Simmon was a tall (five foot eleven), robust and physically strong man with the build of a rugby player, but his eyesight was very poor; consequently, at his medical he was graded B3 and sent to the Primary Training Company, No. 4 Centre, Auxiliary Military Pioneer Corps (AMPC) as Private 13052358, at Clacton.[21]

In March 1941 he was promoted to lance corporal and in June attached to the 20th Company of the Pioneer Corps. Through July, August and September, he attended and passed cadre courses at No. 23 Pioneer Company Group at Donnington, where he was described by his commanding officer as 'very keen, thorough and intelligent … [especially] in squad control'.[22]

But he loathed this period and was determined to apply for a commission for a fighting regiment, as he wanted desperately to confront the Nazis; the first time he failed, but on the second occasion, he was able to memorize the reading card whilst waiting for the eye test. Bluffing his way through, and possibly with the connivance of a friendly medical officer, he was graded A1, much to his delight. In January 1942 he was selected as a candidate for OCTU and in March proceeded to No. 3 Infantry Training Centre for a pre-OCTU course of instruction. In April 1942, he was sent to 'C' Company, 163 OCTU, at Heysham.

During his OCTU, he was described by his officers as 'above average intelligence, with evident powers of leadership, initiative and resourcefulness when in command ... leadership comes easily to him and he can be a "tough" as well as a thinker ... I have no hesitation in recommending him as an outstanding cadet with wide knowledge who with experience in a battalion, will be one of its most useful and promising officers.'[23]

From here he was posted to the IXth battalion, the Somerset Light Infantry at Donnington.[24]

His Jewish Chaplain Card notes that he had a spell in Colchester military hospital in August 1940, where he was visited by a 'Rabbi R.', military chaplain, and given the usual *Jewish Military Prayer Book*, *Book of Jewish Thoughts* and *Psalms*. He also met Senior Jewish Army Chaplain Dayan Rabbi Gollop on 13 July 1941, Rabbi Edgar in August, and in May 1942 Reverend Lew.

Margaret lived through the Blitz in London in various bedsits near her parents' home. When she fell pregnant, she contacted her old synagogue and asked if she and Simmon could arrange to be married in the proper Jewish tradition before their child was born; but the cost was so exorbitant, and the response so hostile, she abandoned the idea. At around this time she sought some financial help from the Officers' Family Fund and received a small loan and grant which she eventually paid back.

Afterwards Margaret was evacuated to a flat in Park View, West Road, Berkhamstead, a town where members of her parents' extended family were in any case living; and on 5 January 1942 their first daughter, Anne, was born at the Grange Nursing Home in Berkhamstead. Relations with Margaret's parents considerably improved after this happy event, joyful as they were to have a grandchild.

During October through to December 1942, Simmon attended the Tactical Training School at Aldershot and also managed to be the concert/entertainments officer for the officers' mess with the Somersets.

Among Margaret's first cousins in the area were brothers Jack Green (aged 10) and David (aged 8).[25] Jack has very fond memories of his 'uncle' Simmon – who first taught the boys to ride their bikes – coming home on leave on a number of occasions during 1943, in uniform. He would telephone them and off they would all go cycling into the surrounding countryside, walking on the golf links and visiting a ruined castle, returning hours later for tea, with David riding piggyback. They remember him as a kind, avuncular and charming man, to whose visits they looked forward. By an amazing coincidence, when Jack was at Clayesmore School near Blandford, in 1950, as a member of the CCF (Public School Combined Cadet Force), he trained for three weeks with the Somerset Light Infantry, Simmon's old regiment.

Simmon's cousin Sheila Gaiman recalls vividly how the family were enormously honoured about Simmon's membership of the LSO and when he came home on leave he would often go to play in their radio concerts. They would all gather around the radio and Paul Beard, a famous leader of the BBC Symphony Orchestra, with whom the LSO frequently played,[26] would announce that Simmon Latutin was playing with them that evening, as the family swelled with collective pride.

Margaret recalls one charming incident when Simmon – as a new and very proud parent – was wheeling daughter Anne in her pram. He was newly commissioned, smoking his pipe, when a private approached the young family and smartly saluted an officer. With one hand on the pram and the other on his pipe, Simmon rapidly appraised the situation and whispered loudly to Margaret, 'Grab the handle!' whilst with his now free hand he returned a crisp salute to the soldier.

By January 1943, Simmon had been posted with his battalion to Northern Ireland and Margaret went on a visit to County Down for three months with Anne to be near his army base. She was in digs, firstly on a farm close to his camp, and later in Downpatrick. But Simmon was able to get frequent passes to spend time with his family. Between 10 February and 10 March 1943, however, Simmon attended a Battle Course at Barnard Castle.

Not wanting to have an only child, soon Margaret fell pregnant again and returned to Berkhamstead. By the time she was four months pregnant, Simmon came home to Berkhamstead in April 1943, on embarkation leave, pending posting to former Italian Somaliland, in East Africa. Simmon was very disappointed, as he wanted to stay with his regiment who had started rehearsing for D-Day. Both he and Margaret believed that he was posted away to avoid having him in action with his poor eyesight, a disability that the other officers had obviously noticed.

On at least one occasion Simmon went to Haslemere to visit a much loved aunt, Pearl (Freda's sister) and his cousins. His cousins, Rhoda Zeffertt and Sheila Gaiman (Pearl's daughters), who were small children at the time, remember Simmon as such a gentle and kind man; they recall clearly that the visit was during his embarkation leave and he had come to say goodbye.[27] There was great excitement as he came to the garden

gate in his smart officer's uniform. Pearl was especially excited but had
accidentally put on her dress inside out and Rhoda recalls how she would
not change it in case it brought bad luck. Pearl adored Simmon; although
his aunt, she was only about ten years older and they had been playmates
when Simmon had visited them in Mile End as children. She had spent
many hours with him as a baby and in effect helped partly to bring him
up.

East Africa

On 9 April 1943, travelling the usual troopship route via West and South
Africa, around the Cape, Simmon left the UK and arrived in Durban on
21 May, then proceeding to Mombassa, arriving on 10 June. Simmon was
first sent to the border with Abyssinia, commanding African troops who
were engaged in trying to stop Arab slave traders transporting their
appalling 'cargo' from the Abyssinian border to the Cairo markets. In his
letters home he described to Margaret some of his adventures.[28] On one
occasion a runner came to him with urgent news, which Simmon thought
had to be about the arrival of his second child; instead it was about the
surrender of Italy on 8 September. Soon after, another runner arrived, this
time with the glad news of the birth of his second daughter, Elisabeth.[29]
The only European for 400 miles, he was asked to give all kinds of advice
and show leadership to local people on many occasions – once having to
oversee the birth of an overdue baby in a village.[30]

Rhoda Zeffert recalls that just before the Christmas of either 1943 or
1944, when Simmon was in East Africa, his toddler daughter Anne was on
the British Forces Radio to recite a popular nursery rhyme song of the
day, for her dad; Rhoda clearly remembers all the family in her house
gathered around to hear Anne perform[31] and also recalls Anne saying hello
to her daddy, and Captain Simmon Latutin's name being mentioned by
the compére; all the children were allowed to stay up and listen.

In late summer of 1943, Simmon was posted to Mogadishu to command the infantry training school for Swahili-speaking Kenyan African
troops[32] and troops of the Somalia Gendarmerie about to go to Burma to
fight under Wingate. He was promoted to acting major (he was promoted
captain on 1 August 1944) and given his own house. He made it his business to seek out any Jewish servicemen in the locality and always enter-
tained them for Friday night (eve of Sabbath) *kiddush* (Jewish religious
supper) in his quarters; what Margaret proudly, rightly and movingly
describes as 'keeping the Jewish boys together in some way by inviting
them to his house'. In early December 1944, he developed a tropical ulcer
on his leg and had to spend the period 4 to 20 December in hospital in
Nairobi, returning to Mogadishu by air with a leg in plaster and using a

walking stick, just before Christmas. This meant he was unable to go on the next bush training patrol with his men, and his second in command went instead. This proved to have a fateful and tragic outcome.

Just after Christmas, on 28 December, a captain and sergeant of the British Military Police, stationed in the camp, came to ask Simmon if the men could have some of the old Italian signal rockets stored in a hut, for the New Year celebrations with the African troops. Simmon agreed and, taking the keys, hobbled along with the men to unlock the doors. As the two men and an African askari entered the hut, there was a huge explosion, which was heard clearly in central Mogadishu.[33] Without hesitation, Simmon plunged into the inferno and pulled out one man; then, his clothes now ablaze, he plunged in again to pull out a second man; attempting to enter a third time, other soldiers pulled him away, as he was so badly burnt. Throughout all this, he would have been unable to use his stick, dragging men out of the flames, and would have been much hindered by his leg plaster. The African soldier had died and the by now badly burnt three survivors were rushed to hospital;[34] the two MPs died that day and Simmon succumbed on 30 December.[35]

On 2 January 1945, Margaret received a telegram at her home in Hemel Hempstead,[36] saying Simmon was gravely ill in hospital with third degree burns; Margaret called a relative who was a nurse to ask for some explanation of this, and it was she who called Margaret's mother, who came over immediately to stay with her.[37] Two days later, the day before Anne's third birthday, the second, fatal telegram arrived announcing Simmon's death. He was 28 years old. Margaret was devastated; Simmon had never held his second daughter.

Margaret remembers much of these events as a blur; with no telephone at home, she went at around 2 p.m. that day to telephone her sister-in-law Blanche from a public call box, at work, and told her the terrible news. Blanche was then allowed home immediately to inform her parents in Camden that afternoon. Morris and Blanche then journeyed to see Margaret and about two days later Margaret went to see her parents-in-law at the house in Camden.

Simmon's effects were eventually sent home to Margaret; these included various personal items, but most important, his violin and viola. A treasured watch she had given him with his name inscribed on it, which in fact she had inherited from her grandmother, never arrived, however, and was probably stolen.

At Pearl's house the news came as a bombshell. Sheila and Rhoda remember their mother receiving constant phone calls that Simmon was very ill. Sheila could not quite believe what she was hearing and being about 10 years old then, got younger sister Rhoda to do something. The children had a game whereby when eating a fried egg – as they were that evening – they would break the yoke and make a wish. Sheila said that all the cousins should make a wish that Simmon gets better quickly; she then told young Rhoda to go and tell their mother what they had wished, for Sheila deep down knew that the worst had happened. Their mother, standing in the kitchen, sadly replied that Simmon would not get better, and that he had in fact died. Pearl was speechless for some time and that was how Sheila remembers that terrible day. How the news was broken to Simmon's parents she does not recall but she remembers that Freda especially was beside herself with grief at the cruel loss of her so talented and gentle son.

In April or May 1945, Sheila was sent by Pearl on a mission – to stay for ten days with her aunt Freda to try and cheer her up. Sheila remembers taking this very seriously and indeed she met with a partial success; they played games together and went shopping, Sheila trying desperately to distract Freda – and Morris – from their grief, alone in the house whilst Blanche, their daughter went to work.

At The National Archives in Kew, the author discovered the War Office (WO) Diary of 'HQ Troops East Africa Command, Mogadishu'.[38] In the monthly summary for January 1945 it states tantalisingly, on 10 January, 'court of inquiry (C. of I.) into an explosion at the Gendarmerie', in the minutes referring to December 1944. However, in the notes following there is no sign of any minutes of the meeting[39] where it was discussed, or any copy of the inquiry itself.

A Jewish neighbour in Hemel Hempstead, on hearing about Simmon's death, came to give her condolences, but also astonished Margaret by telling her that her nephew – a Jewish soldier in East Africa – had been a frequent Friday night guest at Simmon's house in the training school and had attended his funeral. One can only imagine Margaret's feelings at such an amazing coincidence. Sadly she does not remember the name of the serviceman.

Margaret drew great strength from her Jewish faith and learned to accept the terrible blow dealt to her, with courage and fortitude. She knew for Simmon's sake and that of her daughters, that she had to go on and make the best of her life. An officer's wife from the SLI, whom Margaret had got to know in Northern Ireland, wrote a particularly moving letter to her.

Many other letters of condolence arrived, but one in particular was informative. It came from a retired British regular army officer, Major Arthur McKinstry, who lived at Limuru in Kenya, growing coffee. He had lost his only son serving in the RAF and had adopted Simmon as a kind of surrogate. His letter raged because he knew that an order of 1942 had instructed that the Italian rockets be dumped as unstable. This order had never been carried out by the CO of the time. It was almost certain that the hobnail boots of the men, scraping on the concrete floor of the hut, had created a spark which caused the explosion.

Simmon's death was announced on page 6 of the *Daily Telegraph* on 16 January, and via the British Jewish Military Chaplains department, in the *Jewish Chronicle* on page 16, on 26 January 1945.

Many tributes came. Lieutenant Colonel Richard E. Thorne, deputy commandant of the Somalia Gendarmerie, wrote to Margaret on 2 January 1945,[40] expressing his deepest sympathy; he had looked upon Simmon as a personal friend and 'an extremely efficient and outstanding Officer in every way ... he was more than anyone responsible for the [Training School's] unqualified success. He was undoubtedly looked up to with respect and affection by all the men who passed through his hands, in the neighbourhood of two hundred, and by his permanent staff.' Simmon was still conscious, at that time, in the hospital, to where he and the others had been rushed. Thorne went on:

> He talked to me saying first 'I am terribly sorry about this, Sir' ... this was because we were together reorganising the School and he had just prior to this been in hospital with a bad ulcer on the ankle which would not heal and he felt that he was again incapacitated. He then asked me, 'What happened to the native – did he get away?' I tried to set his mind at rest over this – to save the shock – although I knew he had not been able to be got away. I feel you would like to know this as it again shows how his reactions even then, were consideration for others. Mercifully he suffered little if anything. We buried him on the morning of the 31st [December] with full Military Honours and a tribute to the affection and regard with which he was held was shown by the fact that no less than 50 Officers and 10 other ranks attended – a very large proportion of our strength here ... I feel very deeply myself the loss of a friend and a very gallant Officer and gentleman.[41]

On 22 January, Colonel P.R. Munday, the CO of the Gendarmerie, added his own tribute, writing to Margaret:

> of [his] sincere sympathy ... in the tragic loss of Captain Latutin, who died so gallant a death ... I was away ... when the fire occurred ... his undaunted courage and magnificent selflessness in his determination to effect a rescue ... are beyond praise. I have lost in him a most valued Officer, who was doing his work at the Training School for which he had been specially selected, exceedingly well and he was very popular amongst his men who all appreciated his ability to instruct and his firmness of character. As a friend also I mourn his loss, as he was a most charming person in private life. His

funeral was well attended by all the available officers who form the garrison and he was afforded full military ceremonial. Major Mckinstry who knew him was also present.[42]

Some time later a major of the Somalia Gendarmerie wrote to Margaret to say that he would be in England in due course and would like to meet her for lunch at the Overseas Club in St James's. Margaret agreed and dressed for the occasion. The officer eventually arrived late and somewhat the worse for drink, and he invited her to a restaurant in Jermyn Street. Here, he egotistically and tactlessly regaled her with how he had enjoyed a 'good' war in Somaliland but this was the first time he had home leave in five years. Margaret thought – but did not say – that her beloved Simmon would never have the home leave that this man was enjoying. As the luncheon wore on, Margaret was eventually able to bring herself to ask him if Simmon realised how badly burnt he was; he sharply replied that he had no idea. But he patronisingly reminded her of the Officers' Families Fund that could provide her with some assistance. Afterwards Margaret took him for a short meeting with Simmon's parents in Camden, although only Morris was strong enough to see him. Two weeks later Margaret received a grant from the Officers' Families Fund for her two daughters; although she regarded it somewhat as blood money – given the nature of Simmon's death – she accepted it for the childrens' sake.

One day in April 1945, then three-and-a-half-year-old daughter Anne was talking with Margaret, and she asked if it was true that her daddy was never really coming home. Margaret explained that this was true. Anne asked, then where will he go? Margaret explained that when a match is struck and then goes out, we know that there has been a flame but it is now gone; we do not know where it has gone but we do know that it once was bright and strong and has now gone – just like daddy. This apt and moving explanation seemed to satisfy Simmon's little girl.

The Award and Remembrance

On 2 February 1946, a letter was sent from Brigadier D.H. Wickham, chief British Army administrator in Somalia, to Civil Affairs Branch in Nairobi.[43] Nairobi had clearly requested witness statements of the incident at Mogadishu, and Wickham had to reply, 'both the persons carried out of the burning [explosives] store by Capt. Latutin died before they were able to make any statement. I enclose however, a report by No. 132 Sgt Aden Abdi of the Somalia Gendarmerie, who was an eye-witness of Capt. Latutin's action.'

The reader will understand why I now quote his statement in full:

I remember the day in December 1944, just after Christmas, when a fire broke out at the Somalia Gendarmerie Training School in Mogadishu. Between the hours of 1500 and 1530 I was in my barrack room when I heard shouts of 'Fire, Fire!' and simultaneously a number of explosions. I ran out of the barrack room and saw the scene of the fire. On my way I sounded the fire alarm. On arrival at the store, the first person I saw was Captain Latutin, whose clothing was aflame, dragging the Military Police Sergeant Major though the doorway of the store. The Sergeant Major was naked except for a pair of smouldering boots. Captain Latutin laid the Sergeant Major clear of the doorway, and then immediately dashed back into the store, to return in a very short time, dragging the Military Police Captain with him. The Military Police Captain was naked. Captain Latutin's clothing was by this time practically burnt off him, and his hair was alight. I rushed up to take off Captain Latutin's clothing, but he ordered me to attend to the other two which I did. Myself and some other Gendarmes put all three burnt men into a truck and took them to the De Martino Hospital.[44] The fire continued all the afternoon and it was most dangerous to approach the building on account of the continual explosions.

I was the first person to arrive at the scene of the fire, and I feel sure that Captain Latutin would not have died had he not gone into the blazing building to bring out the Military Police Captain, because when I saw Captain Latutin the first time, after he had dragged out the Sergeant Major, he was not badly burnt.

On 29 May 1946, Sir Robert Knox, DSO, received a letter from the War Office,[45] saying: 'Dear Robert, I submit the attached citation for the posthumous award of the George Cross to Captain Simmon Latutin, Somalia Gendarmerie. The recommendation has been forwarded by the G.O.C.-in-C. [General Officer Commander-in-Chief] East Africa Command.'

All of this was of course completely unknown to Margaret at the time. Some eighteen months after Simmon's death, Margaret, then living in Harrow[46] on just her widow's war pension, wrote to the War Office asking if some kind of recognition could be given to Simmon, perhaps a posthumous Mention in Despatches, so that she would be able to explain in some small way to her two children why their father had died in a non-combat zone. After some time, a reply was received to the effect that a George Cross was going to be awarded to Simmon in recognition of his supreme courage in the incident in trying to save the three men;[47] the medal is the highest award for gallantry that can be bestowed, given when not in the face of the enemy. And so it was announced in the press the following day, the *London Gazette* publishing it on 6 August 1946, promulgated on 10 September, and *The Times* and the *Daily Telegraph* on 11 September 1946.[48], The *Jewish Chronicle*[49] announced the award on its front page on 13 September 1946, quoting in full the GC Citation that was in *The Times*:[50]

> It was on December 29th 1944 that a fire occurred at the Training School Store, Somalia Gendarmerie, Mogadishu, while some Italian rockets and explosives were being taken out for another unit about to hold a New Year's entertainment. Captain Simmon Latutin, together with one officer, a Company Sergeant Major and a personal boy, were in the store selecting explosives, Captain Latutin standing in the main doorway. For some unexplained reason, a fire broke out and almost simultaneously, a great number of rockets began to explode and burn. There were some 70 cases in the store.[51] The force of the explosion and the fire turned the store into an inferno.
>
> Regardless of the detonating rockets, the intense heat of the fire and the choking clouds of smoke, Captain Latutin plunged into the storeroom and succeeded in dragging out the officer who was almost unconscious due to his burns.[52] By this time Captain Latutin's clothes and body were alight, but unhesitatingly he rushed again into the inferno and rescued the Company Sergeant Major, who by this time, owing to the fire, was quite naked. The body of the personal boy was recovered later, but was unrecognisable due to its charred condition.
>
> The heroism of Captain Latutin was outstanding as he fully realised the acute danger he was in as he twice entered the building ablaze with explosives and flames. His unquenchable determination to succour the injured is illustrated by his second entry into the store, even though his own clothes and body were alight. His action was illustrative of the finest degree of British courage and a magnificent example of undaunted selflessness.
>
> Captain Latutin died next day as a result of his injuries.

The original citation goes on: 'Despite the fact that only one   eyewitness is available, the evidence of the extremely gallant conduct and determined heroism of Captain Latutin is unassailable.'[53]

There were other tributes; on 11 September the *Daily Express* described the award to 'a sturdy young man who sat in mufti[54] playing the viola at wartime symphony concerts in London', quoting Margaret as saying:

> After he joined the Army in 1940, he continued to play with them when he was on leave. He was a quiet man ... whatever job Simmon

had to do he did it thoroughly. He was in charge so he went along ... he never knew his efforts had been in vain nor realised how badly he had been burnt. For that I can be thankful.

The *Daily Graphic* newspaper of the same day carried a similar, but shorter story[55] and the minutes of the board of the LSO noted on 16 September the award of the GC to Simmon.

The Jewish Year Book announced the award in the edition of 1947 on pages 312 and 320. However, his regiment did not officially know until November 1960 about the award, because he had been seconded to the Somalia Gendarmerie.[56]

Disappointingly, none of the three local Camden newspapers mentioned one word of the award in 1946 or in 1947,[57] even though they featured plenty of stories about locals being given MBEs, MCs and other decorations; one is left wondering at the motives for this.[58]

Within a few weeks, the major from the Somalia Gendarmerie wrote to congratulate Margaret on the award of the George Cross to Simmon, but suggested that they would have liked to have proposed the award themselves. Margaret politely but firmly replied that they had already had eighteen months to do this and that was surely long enough.

The posthumous investiture took place at Buckingham Palace on 2 December 1947 (announced in *The Times* on 3 December[59]), postponed slightly as the king was abroad on an official visit to South Africa in the weeks before. Margaret's mother's attitude had somewhat altered by now, as a George Cross award was something, of course, that she could be proud of. But Margaret alone was invited to attend with her children.[60] It was bitterly cold, and she and Blanche and the two children took a taxi to the Palace.

Margaret remembers the ceremony as quite low-key, with quiet string music being played in the background. Anne, Simmon and Margaret's daughter,[61] remembers that the seats were arranged in pairs, for the two people invited for each family, and pinned to the seats were raffle ticket style numbers. She said to Margaret that she had better sit on a specific chair which she chose of the two, so that Margaret would not get hurt by the pin. She also remembered being disappointed when told by Margaret that the king was the man in the uniform, as she was expecting someone with a huge crown and cloak.

One other George Cross was presented first to an elderly couple just before, and then Margaret and Anne were called forward. The king looked very ill, and sadly he stuttered when he spoke to Margaret and she was unable to understand what he said. She remembers clearly, though, that she replied to the king, 'I am very proud of him.' The king presented her with the medal in an open case as toddler Anne, in her light tweed coat, stared at him, finger in her mouth. Quite nervous, they both forgot to curtsy. Having been told mistakenly by her mother that only one child could attend, she had taken Anne, as the older child, to the ceremony. At one stage, overawed by the plush surroundings, Anne whispered to her mother, 'Do they have marble statues in their bedroom too?' Elisabeth, meanwhile, was taken for a walk to St James's Park by her aunt, Blanche Latutin, to feed the ducks. As a result, for many years the medal was given to Elisabeth to keep, but is now on permanent loan to the SLI regimental museum in Taunton.

After the investiture, all four went for a coffee and snack and returned home by bus to Simmon's parents. They were of course deeply grieved by his death, especially his mother, and they never really recovered from it. Anne and Margaret both remember vividly when they arrived in Camden that Freda wept ceaselessly, but Simmon's father silently took the medal in its case over to the window, to the sunlight, and gently turned it over to read the inscription. He then slowly, carefully and gently handed it back to Margaret.

On 27 April 1946, the LSO held a concert at the Albert Hall in memory of those members who had perished during the war. It was called 'A Tribute to the members of the LSO who gave their lives in the cause of freedom 1939–45'. Anne remembers attending the first half with family members, and that the programme had Simmon's name inscribed on it[62] along with six others.

Sadly, Simmon's mother died on 30 May 1953 and within seventeen days his father too had passed away, on 16 June; they were aged just 58 and 66.[63]

Simmon is remembered on the memorial to Commonwealth servicemen and women of the two world wars (GC and VC section) which is in Constitution Hill, near Hyde Park Corner; at the Royal Academy of Music War Memorial in the Marylebone main building[64] and in the RAM magazine, *Roll of Service*, published in September 1945;[65] on the Second World War memorial at Golders Green synagogue, Dunstan Rd, NW11;[66] on a large memorial on the grave of his parents at Willesden Cemetery;[67] on a Roll of Honour in the former Harrow synagogue, Vaughan Road;[68] and of course in both the Somerset Light Infantry (Taunton) and Jewish Military (Hendon) Museums.

The memorial at Golders Green synagogue was inaugurated in October 1954,[69] presided over by Reverend Isaac Levy, senior Jewish chaplain to HM Forces, attended by Reverends Newman, Livingstone and Tashlicky. Alderman Bernard Waley-Cohen – later Lord Mayor of London – unveiled it and two members of the Royal Horse Guards formed a Guard of Honour, with several Standards of the north-west London branches of AJEX on parade.

South Africa

After the war Margaret was financially insecure, earning only a poor living copying music manuscripts as a freelance. Then, through an old pre-war friend of Simmon's, Joe Sack,[70] she met a South African who told her she could get a much better paid job in an orchestra in South Africa; so off she went in March 1948 to Cape Town. Employing an African domestic and nurse for her girls, Margaret was soon playing in the Cape Town Broadcast Orchestra, and with various string quartets; she also got a music teaching post at the University of Cape Town and managed in addition to take a diploma in music teaching. Margaret spent five-and-a-half years in South Africa,[71] soon meeting a German Jewish refugee, Michael Liebert (born in Berlin, his family had sent him to family friends in South Africa in 1935; they remained and had died in Auschwitz). She and Michael married in December 1948 at the Cape Town City Hall. Michael had served in the South African Army in the Second World War. Whilst in South Africa, the past revisited her again on one occasion as she met a former RAF officer, who knew Simmon; but for an injury he had received at the time, he had meant to attend his funeral in Mogadishu the day after he died.

Michael was an ideal stepfather to the girls who, after all, did not remember or know Simmon – although Anne did remember the press attention the family got at the announcement of the GC and at the investiture in 1947. However, after much hardship, some unpleasant experiences with her new in-laws and the rise of the racist apartheid regime, Margaret and Michael decided to move back to the UK in August 1953 (Margaret had wisely rented out her Harrow house whilst abroad and so they had somewhere to live).

Simmon's grave was eventually moved to Nairobi Commonwealth War Graves Cemetery (grave 1.3), Ngong Road,[72] albeit without Margaret's knowledge. Later, she received an invitation from the War Office with a free (!) ticket to attend the official opening of the cemetery, and recommending an inexpensive hotel to stay in, if she could fly herself out; but Margaret had to politely refuse, saying she was working full time with two small children and anyway her late husband was buried in Mogadishu. She received a very curt reply saying the body had been moved. Margaret's second husband Michael, however, had a former refugee cousin in Nairobi, and she attended the ceremony on Margaret's behalf and took a photograph of the CWGC headstone, carved with the Star of David.[73] Inscribed on the foot of the white Portland stone grave is Margaret's own tribute: 'We can never forget your unselfish courage in true service to mankind.'

In Harrow, Margaret got a job as a music teacher in a local secondary school, and Michael became a successful salesman and manager. At the

age of 19, Anne became head girl at St Paul's Girls' School – the first
Jewish girl to hold the post in the school's history. But Margaret fell ill
with arthritis in her hands and spine, and had to retrain as a teacher of
English to foreign students. She later wrote a book on music teaching. In
1971, they moved to Walderton, near Chichester, West Sussex where
Margaret ran the local playgroup. In the 1980s, Michael sadly became a
sick man, and he died in December 2004. They had fifty-six years of
happy marriage.

Margaret had been close to Simmon's sister Blanche (who married in
1946) for many years, but eventually they drifted apart when Margaret
moved to West Sussex. Sadly, Margaret was never even told when Blanche
died quite young of cancer.

After

For many years Margaret was invited to and attended SLI annual reunion
dinners in London, until she moved to West Sussex, and she once
attended an SLI 'Beating Retreat' at Wells Cathedral with one of her
granddaughters; they were presented to Princess Alexandra, then Colonel
of the regiment, on that occasion.

In 1979, a letter appeared in the *Jewish Chronicle*[74] from Joe Sack, the
founder and then managing editor of the *Orchestra World* magazine. Previously music editor of the *Rand Daily Mail*, but living in London in 1979,
Joe had been a cello and composition student with Simmon at the RAM
in the 1930s and also knew Margaret, of course. Responding to a letter
about Jewish holders of the George Cross, Joe wrote movingly and with
emotion about how Simmon's family had made a lonely student from
South Africa so warmly welcome in their humble home. He said Simmon
was 'like so many true heroes, a quiet, modest, retiring young man, as big
in heart as he was in stature'. They had been in the London Symphony
Orchestra together, and he declared Simmon one of the best viola players in Britain at that time. When war came, they went their own ways,
promising to meet up again. In May 1943, Simmon wrote to Joe telling
him of his posting to East Africa – a letter Joe still had in 1979 – and they
did almost meet in Durban when Simmon was en route and Joe in the
South African Air Force; but they only managed a telephone chat and they
sadly never spoke or met again.

Simmon's daughter Anne has had a distinguished career as a university
academic in sociology. Elisabeth has had a long and varied career in
primary education and – perhaps not surprisingly – is a talented string
player (cello) like her illustrious Father.[75]

But the last word must rest with Simmon. He left a letter for Margaret in case of his death,[76] and in it he predicted that 'We Latutins will

make our mark.' So they have, living up to his ideals of service and devotion to duty.

Acknowledgements

Margaret Latutin was unstinting in her help, making many audio tapes, writing letters, reading drafts of the manuscript and speaking with the author on the telephone on numerous occasions, despite her 89 years. Without her enthusiasm and assistance this study would not have been possible. Sadly, Margaret died suddenly on 6 April 2009, but she did see the final version of this chapter.

I would also like to thank Jack Green (cousin of Margaret); Simmon Hill (son of Blanche Latutin); Simmon Latutin's cousins Sheila, Rhoda, Marlene and Maureen; Simmon and Margaret's daughters Anne and Elisabeth; Anna Charin of the *Jewish Chronicle* Library; the staff of the Tower Hamlets Local History Library; the staff of The National Archives – TNA – (formerly Public Record Office) at Kew; Bridget Palmer of the Royal Academy of Music Library and Archives; Mark Aston of the Camden Local History and Archives Centre; Karen Nathan of the United Synagogue Burial Society; Charles Tucker of the United Synagogue Archives; Peter Bowbeer of the London Metropolitan University; Naomi Hill of Golders Green Synagogue; the staff of the Bushey and Willesden United Synagogue Cemetery offices; Bob Thomson of the Harrow Local Studies Library; the curator of the Somerset Light Infantry Museum in Taunton, Lieutenant Colonel David Eliot; Mary Connor of the Commonwealth War Graves Commission; Marion Hebblethwaite of the GC Database; the staff of the Reading Room of the Imperial War Museum, Lambeth; Jack Cowdrey of the Royal Albert Hall Archives; Libby Rice of the LSO Archives; the Army Records Office, Glasgow; Peter Baron and Tony Kearney of the *Northern Echo* newspaper, Newcastle; Helen Charlton of the *South Shields Gazette*.

Notes

1. MoD leaflet definition.
2. Thanks to Mark Aston of the Camden Local Studies and Archives Centre for consulting the Electoral Registers for the 1930s. The family, though renting all the house, lived only in the lower half. It is still there today.
3. The information on Simmon Latutin's personal life for much of this paper comes from the author's taped interviews and telephone calls with Margaret Latutin-Liebert, Simmon's widow, between March and June 2006, from her home in Gloucestershire. She was in her ninetieth year and a great-grandmother.
4. Information confirmed by Margaret Latutin-Liebert.
5. Also spelt as Krafchig in Simmon's army records.
6. Taped interview with author at the house of Simmon Hill, May 2006; Sheila is sister to Rhoda.
7. It is now part of the extensive London Metropolitan University; the North London Polytechnic Day School for Boys moved about half a mile to the east in 1922, to Highbury Grove, to become the Highbury County School by the time Simmon was a pupil there – but was probably still

known to locals as the NLP School (thanks to Peter Bowbeer, operations manager at the LMU Library in Holloway Road, who extracted this information from the school's annual report of 1921–22).

8. Margaret says his name was on the honours board showing this in the student canteen at the RAM.

9. Thanks to nephew Simmon Hill for providing a copy of the scholarship certificate issued by the RAM.

10. Student Register viewed at the RAM, thanks to Bridget Palmer, assistant librarian and keeper of archives at the RAM.

11. This was at the Theatre Royal in Brighton, with the Brighton Repertory Company, with whom he stayed for two seasons (army records). His CV in his army records show that between 1932 and 1940, Simmon played with the Band of the Royal Marines, the London Philharmonic, the London Film Symphony Orchestra, the London Ballet Orchestra, the London Mozart Orchestra, the London Theatre Orchestra, the Queen's Hall Orchestra, the Royal Opera House Orchestra, the Isidore Schwiller Sextet, the Rael String Quartet and the Fortune Theatre Orchestra – as well as teaching!

12. Simmon was already leader of the viola section of the senior student orchestra at the RAM – information from Margaret.

13. Langham Place, London W1.

14. LSO Archives, Barbican, with thanks to archivist Libby Rice.

15. He was in the army shortly after this – see note 20 below.

16. LSO board minutes, LSO Archives.

17. Another address given on the Jewish Chaplain Cards was 68 Brondesbury Rd, London NW6.

18. She also had a small legacy from her parents.

19. 4 December 2006.

20. His AJEX Jewish Chaplain Card says he was entered on 18 July 1940 (there are 70,000 of these cards at the Jewish Military Museum in Hendon, which now can be consulted, by appointment, on a database and online. They were drawn up by the many Jewish military chaplains throughout the Second World War).

21. Professor Raphael Loewe, MC, comments:

At the outbreak of war, men adjudged unsuitable, because of defective eyesight, etc, for active combat were called up into the Pioneer Corps, some units of which consisted of refugees and others whom it would have been unacceptable to expose to risk of capture. But this did not mean that in the unit without refugees, at Clapton, to which Simmon and I were both directed, there was no weapon training. At first one would not, if one's eyesight was below standard, be considered for a Commission. The debacle at Dunkirk occurred just as examinations at the universities were taking place, after which there was a vast intake of new students, and new graduates into the armed services. I joined up on 15 August 1940, and young men just down from college were not slow in seeking each other out. I first met Simmon and Margaret in the bar of a hotel in Clacton. My father Herbert Loewe had just died in the October, and Margaret was sufficiently au fait with the Jewish community to have seen the obituaries and to identify me as his son; and the three of us rapidly became good friends. One feature of the realistic administration of Churchill's national government was that approximately from the turn of 1940–41, men whose sight with the aid of spectacles would be perfectly adequate would be commissioned as officers in the army and fairly early in the new year I proceeded to an OCTU in the Isle of Man, about a year before Simmon was similarly sent for training at Heysham. We never met again, although for a while we were in occasional correspondence. I myself was wounded in Italy in September 1944, and it was only early the following year, after repatriation in a hospital ship, that I learnt from my mother of Simmon's death, although not of its heroic nature. I much valued his friendship and admired the gentleness of his character and his gift for drawing out those who felt unsure of themselves. And I much regret that post-war circumstances meant that Margaret and I lost touch.

22. Army records.

23. Army records.

24. His Commission was gazetted on 11 and 17 September 1942 in the *London Gazette*, p.3956, as 242974, 2nd Lieutenant, Somerset Light Infantry from 21 August 1942 – see *LG* website.

25. Telephone conversation with Jack Green, May 2006.

26. Paul Beard, BBC Symphony Orchestra website.

27. Personal taped interview with the author at the house of Simmon Hill, May 2006.

28. His Jewish Chaplain Card states that whilst overseas in April 1943 he was sent a Bible and 'T. & B.', which could be a *Tallit* (Jewish prayer shawl worn by men when at prayer) and Bag, or

Tephillin (phylacteries) and Bag.

29. Elisabeth was born 7 September 1943 in Colchester, whilst Margaret was staying with friends at Grout's farm in Tolleshunt D'Arcy, ten miles east of Colchester. Rose, a family cook at Margaret's childhood home, had become a firm friend and it was her husband's farm where Margaret went to stay at this time, so they could look after Margaret and her children.

30. Margaret did not keep his letters from army days.

31. Rhoda thinks it was 'Mares eat oats and does eat oats and little lambs eat ivy … ' – written in 1943 by Drake, Hoffman and Kingston, and sung by Al Trace (see internet).

32. Simmon's Obituary in the *Harrow Observer and Gazette*, 12 September 1946 – thanks to Bob Thompson of Harrow Local Studies Library.

33. A Somali Gendarmerie officer to Margaret after the war.

34. According to the same officer, this was done within fifteen minutes – telephone call to Margaret, 1 November 2006.

35. These dates are from the *War Diary* of the HQ Troops Somalia (Mogadishu) TNA 69/18292 – see below. The author has been able to trace the names of the two men whom Simmon tried to save. A search of the CWGC website for Ngong Road, Nairobi, shows that only two other burials were dated the same day of the incident in Mogadishu – 164547 Captain James Long, Leicestershire Regiment, and 779283 Company Sergeant Major Thomas Carruthers, Corps of Military Police (from Durham). Mary Connor of the CWGC confirmed from the records that the remains of both these men were moved at the same time as Simmon's from Mogadishu, where they died. TNA WO169/18292 confirms and states clearly: '*28/12/44* explosion at Gendarmerie 1600; 1700 Long and Carruthers injured as a result of explosion; 2100 Long and Carruthers died. *29/12/44* 1600 Long and Carruthers buried with full military honours in Italian civil cemetery. *31/12/44* 1000 Captain Latutin buried with full honours Italian civil cemetery.' Efforts by the author to find the family of CSM Carruthers, via Durham newspapers, were successful, but they declined to take part.

36. At 30 Langley Avenue, a rented house. Margaret later had to leave this address with her two small girls, and stayed at various friends and relatives over a gruelling nine-month period. As a result, many condolence letters never reached her via the Latutin parental address in Camden Town (see note 40 below – correspondence between the author and Margaret in April 2006).

37. Interview with Margaret, June 2006.

38. WO 169/21761, The National Archives (TNA).

39. Further searches in the files of the WO, Foreign Office, Colonial Office, etc, revealed nothing further.

40. Margaret never knew of this or the following letter until April 2006 – sixty-one years later. For unknown reasons it appears the letters were never forwarded or shown to her.

41. Quoted from the original letter in the possession of Simmon Hill.

42. Ibid.

43. T 351/35 TNA.

44. Built during the First World War and named after the then Italian governor of Mogadishu; it was the city's general hospital.

45. T 351/35 TNA.

46. At 62 Walton Drive; the house was ultimately given to her by her mother *after* the kudos to the family of the GC award had been announced, but until then she had to pay her the equivalent of a mortgage, as her mother had otherwise disinherited her over her marriage to Simmon. Later, however, Margaret's brother gave a her a share of the profits when the family business was sold.

47. He also has the Defence and War Medals.

48. Thanks to the staff at Victoria Library, Westminster.

49. Thanks to Colindale Newspaper Library.

50. Taken from the *JC*; *We Will Remember Them*, by Henry Morris and Martin Sugarman (London: Vallentine Mitchell, London, forthcoming); and *The Times*.

51. The original citation from T351/35 at the TNA says 170 cases.

52. The *Daily Express* article – see note 55 below – mentions that Simmon's leg was in a plaster cast.

53. Readers will note the clear discrepancy; that in Abdi's account Simmon first brought out the sergeant; the official citation, however, says it was the officer. The author's view is that Abdi probably got it right and the citation may have been changed for reasons of protocol, perhaps reflecting the classist prejudices of the time. Simmon would hardly have had the time, ability – in a smoking inferno – or inclination to have done anything but grab the first man he could see.

54. Civilian dress.

55. Cuttings in the GC file for Simmon in the Imperial War Museum archives.

56. Regimental magazine of the SLI, *The Light Bob*, 1961, II, 1, p.51 – with thanks to the SLI Museum curator, Lieutenant Colonel David Eliot.

57. The *St Pancras Chronicle*, the *Hampstead and High Gazette* (*Ham and High*) and the *North London Press*.
58. Thanks to the staff at the Camden Local Studies Library in Theobald's Road.
59. 'Court Circular', *The Times online*, with thanks to Terry Hissey who confirmed this with The Chancellery of The Orders of Knighthood at St James's Palace. There were no names mentioned, however, in *The Times*'s announcement – only that posthumous awards to families of men killed were being made that day. The *Daily Telegraph* court circular also mentioned the award on page 4 on 3 December 1947.
60. Local reporters from the Harrow press came to the house to take photographs.
61. Taped interview with the author at the house of Simmon Hill in May 2006.
62. Conducted by Anthony Collins, the solo pianist was Benno Moiseiwitch; the concert consisted of Elgar's 'Cockayne'; Heming and Collins's 'Threnody for a soldier Killed in Action'; Rachmaninov's second piano concerto; and Brahms's Symphony Number Four (thanks to Jack Cowdrey of the Royal Albert Hall archives).
63. They are buried next to each other at Willesden Jewish Cemetery, Beaconsfield Lane, London (buried 1 and 18 June respectively) – graves LX24/104/105; they had been members of Golders Green synagogue in Dunstan Road.
64. The original memorial was unveiled by the Duchess of Gloucester on 20 March 1951 – see *RAM Magazine* issue, May 1951. Until 2006, this memorial did not mention Simmon's rank or award of the George Cross and this caused some dismay in the family and the wider Jewish community. But in March 2006, in response to a letter from the author, with permission from Margaret, the RAM happily agreed to install an additional plaque beneath the existing war memorial, describing Simmon's deed and the GC award. On 4 December 2006, the new plaque was unveiled by Margaret Latutin, in a ceremony organized by AJEX, the RAM and the VC and GC Association, with the SLI veterans. Four generations of the Latutin family attended, together with Jewish war veterans and civic dignitaries, including the deputy mayor of Camden, Councillor Dawn Somper; the secretary of the VC and GC Association, Mrs Didy Grahame; Lieutenant Colonel David Eliot, curator of the SLI Museum in Taunton; Harold Newman, national chair of AJEX; and over twenty-five Jewish war veterans, with twenty-five family and friends of the Latutin clan (photo and report in the *Jewish Chronicle*, 8 December, p.13, and the *Ham and High*, 14 December, p.10). A video of the event and copy of the proceedings (which included Jewish biblical readings, the Hebrew Kaddish prayer for the dead, and the carrying of the AJEX National and Westminster branch Standards) is in the AJEX Museum Archives. At a reception later in the RAM, the author related to the assembled guests, the background to the GC award and Margaret responded with a moving speech; she was presented with an AJEX eightieth anniversary plate as a memento of the day.
65. Nowhere in the RAM records is there any descripton of Simmon's GC; a disappointing oversight.
66. Close relatives of the family are still members there; Blanche's son Simmon Hill is named after his illustrious uncle; he and his wife Naomi are prominent members of the congregation today.
67. Sadly this is almost illegible but the author managed to decipher Simmon's name and GC.
68. This synagogue is now closed and the whereabouts of the black wooden board with its gold lettering is, sadly, now unknown; with thanks to Simmon Hill for this information.
69. *JC*, 8 October 1954, with photograph.
70. See note 74 below.
71. She kept in regular touch with both sides of the family.
72. Just south-west of the city, on 20 January 1946.
73. Margaret had refused to have the George Cross symbol on the headstone, which is the custom with this very highest of awards, and insisted the Star of David be inscribed, with the GC letters after his name, instead.
74. 12 December.
75. On 18 November 2007, Annabel Hill laid a Magen David poppy posy in memory of her great uncle Simmon during the formal wreath-laying at the AJEX Annual National Parade in Whitehall at the Cenotaph. In 2008 Camden Council sadly rejected a request to put a plaque on the wall of the house where Simmon was born and lived for many years.
76. She never kept it, as it was too heartbreaking.

Red Devils: Jews at the Battle of Arnhem

The incredible courage and searing self-sacrifice of the men who fought at Arnhem has passed into history as one of the classic, epic, awe-inspiring but tragic battles of the Second World War. Despite dreadful odds against them, of arms and troops, the men of the 1st Airborne and attached units fought ferociously, with relatively light weapons but unsurpassed bravery and endurance, against numerically superior and heavily armed German Panzer Units. Five VCs were won and numerous other awards were made. In addition, many RAF, USAAF and RCAF squadrons took part transporting both men and supplies in the most hazardous of conditions, and equally courageous and stoical were the brave Dutch citizens of Arnhem – many in the Resistance – who were so sadly caught up in the fighting, and who – to this day – feel such an intense loyalty to the Allied veterans and their descendants over sixty-five years later.

It is not my purpose here to describe the battle – this has already been done in numerous superb books. My aim is simply to list the parts played by Jewish servicemen in this battle, as another 'for the record' project, to help dispel the myth that Jews were 'not there'. What follows is what I discovered during many months of research between 1996 and 1999, using numerous written and oral sources.

Casualties

Unless stated, all are buried at Oosterbeek Airborne Cemetery, Arnhem. Initial information came from Henry Morris's books, *We Will Remember Them* (hereafter *WWRT*) (London: Brassey's, 1989) and *We Will Remember Them: An Addendum* (London: AJEX, 1994); his data came from veterans and their families as well as over 70,000 Jewish Chaplain Index Cards kept at the AJEX Museum, which although not complete were compiled by the British Jewish chaplains whenever they met or heard of Jewish Forces personnel. The cards were cross-checked to confirm all the list, where possible – killed or survived – as being Jewish. Various other printed sources were also used and are quoted where appropriate.

In addition, the Commonwealth War Graves Commission (CWGC)

Registers at the Imperial War Museum (IWM) were used as verification, as well as wartime issues of the *Jewish Chronicle* (*JC*).

Those Who Served

I am indebted to the research carried out by the late Jack Lennard of the Hull Association of Jewish Ex-Servicemen and Women, and Hull Wilberforce Society, for use of his unpublished book, *Jews in Wartime* (hereafter *JIW*), given by his daughter Phillipa Bahari. Jack had interviewed many Jewish Arnhem survivors, since deceased. Other sources are named. The *Jewish Chronicle* was consulted at the library of University College, London, and Tower Hamlets History Library, London. Numerous other books on Arnhem were read but gave little help and so are not listed here.

Some of the most helpful publications, however, included Leo Heaps, *The Grey Goose of Arnhem* (London: Weidenfeld and Nicolson, 1976); Martin Middlebrook, *Arnhem 1944* (London: Penguin, 1994); *Pegasus Journal*, 1946–97 (published by the Airborne Museum, Aldershot and kept at the IWM and British Library); M. Dank, *The Glider Gang* (Cassell, 1977); letters from the Secretary of the Polish Airborne Forces Association, Irena Hrynkiewicz; Adrian Groeneweg of the Hartenstein Airborne Museum, Arnhem; the staff of the Imperial War Museum Reading Room; and of Battersea Park Library in Battersea; and Philip Reinders of the Arnhem Battle Research Group, Holland. Corporal Lawrence Scott/Solomon, GM, was also of great assistance in guiding me to many of the 21st Independent Parachute Company (hereafter 21st Independent Paras), which contained many German and other European Jewish refugees determined to defeat Nazism and avenge their families and People.

I would also like to thank Patrick Gariepy of Oregon and AJEX Museum curator Henry Morris, as well as former AJEX chair, Gerald Bean, for their help and encouragement; and of course the countless veterans, Jewish and not Jewish, and their families and friends, and the Arnhem, RAF, Market Garden and Airborne Veterans Associations, as well as the AAC (Army Air Corps), USAAF veterans and Glider Pilot veterans who wrote to me with much information and kindness. Their names are mentioned in the list and its completion would not have been possible without their help. Texts that were sources of information are also named.

A thorough search of the AIR 27 files at The National Archives at Kew revealed many Jewish names of RAF and RCAF crew who were dropping and towing in men and supplies at Arnhem as members of the sixteen squadrons of 38 and 46 Group, but though the staff at RAF Innsworth Personnel department in Gloucester (and the Army Records Office, then in Hayes) tried hard to verify some names as being Jewish, lack of resources prevented a full search by them. Many more names could be added in this way, I know, but I fear this may never be possible. Furthermore, records at Innsworth and Hayes often stated that veterans were not Jewish even though the Jewish Chaplain Cards clearly say they were. This is explained by the fact that many Jewish servicemen preferred to hide their true religion in case of capture by the Germans and attested on enlistment to being of other religious denominations. I know that at least four graves at Oosterbeek – Privates Abraham Fenton, Francis Yapp, Frank Dobrozynski and Walter Lewy-Lingen, aka Landon/Langdon – have crosses on the headstones, but all the men were definitely proud Jews. The Commonwealth War Graves Commission, however, has declined to act on putting this right. Furthermore, Private Haikin's grave had no religious symbol on it at all, even though he was Jewish, but this has now been changed at his brother's request (letter from CWGC, October 1998, and telephone contact with his brother).

A Teletext announcement inserted by Sydney Goldberg of Kenton AJEX brought some moving and helpful responses from veterans and historians from all over Britain and overseas – from as far away as New Zealand, Canada, the USA and Israel. Responses also came from veterans via letters placed in the *Jewish Chronicle* and other Jewish newspapers abroad (including the English-language *Jerusalem Post* in Israel), the *Kindertransport Association Journal*, *Canadian Jewish News* and others; also the *AJEX Journal*, *Saga Magazine*, *Wartime News* magazine, the *War Widows Magazine*, the magazine of the Association of Jewish Refugees, the *USAAF Veterans Journal* and the *British Legion Journal*.

In addition, with regard to both lists of men, sources contained numerous names which could definitely have been Jewish, plus noms de guerre used by those who did not wish to be recognized as Jews in case of capture; in addition other men had one Jewish parent, and at least two have admitted this to me but did not at first wish to be included; they later changed their minds.

Twenty-eight Polish Jewish Airborne Soldiers (from the relatively small Polish Brigade) fought at Arnhem, of whom ten were officers – see Benjamin Meirtchak, *Jewish Military Casualties in the Polish Armies in WW2* (Tel-Aviv, Israel, 1995). Many more did not admit to being Jewish; it has been possible to trace the names of only about half of them here.

Mr A. Witko, formerly of the Polish Section of the British Army Records Office in Hayes was extremely helpful in providing further details of the Polish Jewish Airborne men. Some had enlisted as Catholic and atheist – and one even as C. of E., extremely unlikely for a Pole. This yet again is clear evidence of the fact that many Polish Jews lied about their religion (for fear of capture by the Germans as well as anti-Semitism in the Polish Forces) and obviously the real number of Polish Jews serving is greatly underestimated.

The 21st Independent Paras included at least twenty-six Austrian, German, Polish and Czech anti-Nazi Refugees, who volunteered from the Pioneer Corps (Middlebrook, *Arnhem*, p.33), using mostly Irish and Scottish noms de guerre – almost all of whom were Jewish. In the novel by Zeno (aka Lamarr) Allerton, *The Four Sergeants*, their courage is described as outstanding by the author, who fought with them. Survivors Solly Scott, Peter Block and many others attest to this, as does Major General R.E. Urquhart in his book, *Arnhem* (p.29).

As veterans pass away, fewer and fewer are able to bear witness that many of their comrades in the battle were Jews, for it is only by word of mouth that such names have emerged, particularly if such names had been anglicized and so gave no clue to the Jewish connection. Several examples of this are clear in the list. So many will never be known – the lesson being that this study should have been undertaken twenty years ago.

One of the most moving accounts, witnessed by several independent veterans (see below), Jewish and not Jewish, describes an incident on the eve of departure for Arnhem, at one of the airfields. Several Jewish Paras gathered under the wing of a glider to hold a short service to mark the Jewish New Year (Rosh Hashana), with a Jewish chaplain at the base. For despite the fears and sure knowledge that many would not return, the Jewish lads remembered their 4,000 year old heritage and met together to pray before what they knew would be a bloody battle against the evil forces of fascism and anti-Semitism, in which they were about to take part. It has not been possible to identify the chaplain but the airfield was probably Tarrant Rushton. This was indeed a most poignant moment for the author, when the story was related to him.

In the author's view, it is certain that the numbers of men in this study could probably be doubled if it were possible to verify religious denomination. The thirty-eight Jewish known killed in action (out of the total of 1,200) represent 3.2 per cent of total casualties, far in excess of the Jewish percentage in the general population (about half of 1 per cent). If we exclude one RAF, one RCAF and one USAAF casualty, the figure is 2.9 per cent – still way in excess. The 218 Jewish participants were 2.18 per cent of the total (10,000), again well in excess of the percentage in the general population. If we exclude the air force personnel, it is still 1.9 per cent. However, if we add back into the equation the fact that I do not have all the Polish Jewish names and the Jewish 21st Independent Paras' names, the figures increase again quite considerably.

16.1 Platoon Sgt Norman 'Sonny' Binnick, MM for gallantry at Arnhem and POW, 21st Independent
Paras.

16.2 Taken just before take-off to Arnhem, Doctor Capt. P. Louis standing far left, with the 133 Para
Field Ambulance. Capt. Louis was killed in action.

Those Who Died

1398796 Flight Sergeant/WO Mark Azouz. DFC, RAFVR, 196 Squadron. KIA Arnhem, aged 22. He made four supply flights over Arnhem in his Stirling III LK 557, taking off from Keevil on 17 September at 1055 hrs and returning at 1600 hrs; from Wethersfield on 18 September at 1150 hrs towing a Horsa, returning at 1725 hrs; on 19 September at 1310 hrs, returning at 1820 hrs having dropped twenty-four containers and four panniers but sustaining damage from light and heavy flak at the TRV and LZ; and on 21 September in LJ810, leaving at 1200 hrs, dropping a similar load at Arnhem and hit by flak – but he was attacked by three to five FW (Focke-Wulf) 109s and shot down at 1415 hrs (see PRO AIR 27 1167), and was killed. He kept the plane in the air whilst all but one of his crew (the rear gunner) escaped. It being Yom Kippur, he could have taken leave that day but refused, as men at Arnhem were waiting for supplies. According to his log (now at the AJEX Jewish Military Museum) an entry of 19 September states: 'Re-supply containers (Glider, Operation Market – Arnhem). Badly hit by flak – counted 27 holes' (see medals display and portrait at AJEX Museum). He was son of Ralph and Esta of 43 Park Rd, Chiswick, London. His portrait and medals are at the AJEX Museum, presented by his family in the late 1980s. He was buried Nijmegen, Jonkerbos Cemetery; his Jewish Chaplain Card at the AJEX Museum says he was originally buried at Nieuweweg alongside the house of Mr J. van Uum, B.31, Wijchen, Holland – a farmer – at map ref. 630592 1:25,000. Photo *WWRT*, p.183. His mother Esta died in Israel in 2009, over 100 years old.

283359 & 1922/59/I Private Anatol Bier. 1st Polish Independent Para Brigade. KIA Driel, 22 September 1944, aged 22. He was born in Krakow on 13 January 1922, son of Szymon and Adela, née Margulisz. He served Iran/Iraq/Palestine in 3rd Para Battalion and was awarded the Polish Field Para Badge with four British medals. He had been deported to the Soviet Union in 1940. His field burial was in the grounds of the Schuijling, near the Post Office at Driel, and his name is on the Roll of Honour at Nijmegen/Groesebeek War Museum, as well as the Polish memorial at Driel itself. There is no religious symbol on his grave at Oosterbeek. Photo in *WWRT: Addendum*, p.51.

14623928/13807288 Private Timothy Alexander/Adolf Bleichroder (Bleach). Jewish refugee born in Hamburg, 7 January 1922, into a banking family; came to UK in 1936; was interned 1940; deported to Australia on *Dunera*; joined 229 Coy Pioneer Corps in January 1942 at Ilfracombe, then Paratroops fighting in North Africa and Italy before Arnhem – 21st Independent Paras, AAC. He was KIA 25 September

1944, aged 22, during the retreat to the Rhine. Son of Bernard and Julie, brother of Beate Robertson and Irene Wright. Memorial, no known grave. Letter and photo from sister Irene. His medals were donated to AJEX Museum by his family in 1998. Letter also from German researcher Peter Leighton-Langer of Bensheim, Germany, July 1998. Veteran Harry Ford was with Bleach as they tried to cross the Rhine; Ford was badly wounded in the neck and passed out. Bleach had said he would try to escape into the marshes. When he came to, Ford was a POW and never saw Bleach again. Ford says the Germans had said they would kill all Pathfinders if captured.

1143320 Private Frank Percy Dobrozynski/Dobrozyski/Dobrovski. 1st Battalion Para Regiment, AAC, 'T' Coy, No. 9 Section, 11th MMG Platoon. KIA 19 September 1944, aged 26. Son of Isaac and Rose of Landseer Rd, Holloway, London; husband of Florence Rosa, née Whitehead, of Upper Holloway. Brother of John (POW), Albert (8th Army) and Vera. Cross on grave in error. Comrade Corporal Lionel Joe Gettleson saw him killed after their jeep with mounted Vickers MG received a direct hit near the Rhine Hotel. Andy Milbourne was seriously wounded with him. Comrade Doug Charlton (secretary and archivist, 1st Battalion OCA) says family were Polish Jews who had come to England in 1936; his family would give the men typical Polish Jewish cakes and buns to eat when on leave in London. He says that they persuaded Frank to say he was C. of E. to avoid ill-treatment if captured; also that he was excused Church Parade by Padre Captain Talbot Watkins. Obituary in *North London Press*, 20 October 1944 (Colindale).

1209750 LAC Roffer James Eden. RAFVR Radar Unit. KIA 20 September 1944, aged 31, by a shell at the Hartenstein HQ, Oosterbeek, whilst repairing a wireless to attempt contact with outside air support. Husband of Annie of Victoria, London. Photo *WWRT*, p.195.

6462382 Private George D.R. Alexander Emmanuel. 10th Battalion Para Regiment, AAC. Died of wounds, 20 September 1944, aged 28. Son of Montague Rousseau and Florence of 7 Radnor Rd, Paddington, London W2 (*JC*, 16 and 30 March 1945). He was a former TA soldier; although already wounded, he volunteered to go forward and silence a German six-pound gun. This was accomplished but he was wounded in the chest and died later.

P/237410 Lieutenant Rudolph Julian Falck. PC, then Para Regiment, AAC, 1st Airborne in 1943 – CO and Intelligence Officer No. 4 Section, Divisional Provost Coy, Corps of Military Police, att. Divisional HQ.

KIA 25/26 September 1944, aged 24. Son of George and Elizabeth; husband of Pauline Mary of Epsom. Memorial, no known grave. Falck was a German/Dutch refugee. He jumped with second lift into intense fire from the ground. His comrade, John Hamblett, in his book *The Pegasus Patrol* (1998) – photo in book and at AJEX Museum, and interviewed by the author at the Hartenstein Airborne Museum, Arnhem in September 1998 – describes how an eyewitness named Lance Corporal Stanley Reast gave testimony in 1993 that he buried both Falck and a Corporal Jack Newby in an orchard near where he found them dead, propped up against a lamp post, where they were killed during the defensive battle near the Hartenstein HQ. In 1945, Newby's body was found with his ID tags but Falck had removed his ID (in case of capture by the Germans); Reast, however, had seen his chequebook and knew that it was Falck; both bodies were buried – it is almost certain – in one grave with only Newby's name on (Hamblett, *Pegasus Patrol*, pp.133–4). Hamblett struggled to have Falck's name put on a proper headstone at Oosterbeek and removed from the Groesbeek memorial, but the CWGC declined as they are 'unable to prove identity'. Falck's daughter survives him.

0-744867 Navigator 1st Lieutenant Jacob Feldman. 314th US Troop Carrier, 61st Troop Carrier Squadron. Returning from Arnhem in aircraft number 42-92839, he was shot down by flak on 18 September 1944 and crashed west of railway bridge at Rhenen, Holland – based at Saltby. All the crew KIA: Warren S. Egbert, Jnr, Pilot; 2nd Lieutenant Horace M. Jerome, Co-Pilot; Crew Chief T/Sgt David L. Desantis; Radio Operator Sergeant Jacob J. Yapel. Feldman was buried after disinterment, in New York – see J. Hey, *Roll of Honour at Arnhem* (Arnhem: Airborne Museum) and letter from Admiral David E. Mondt, 62nd TCS OCA, Boone, Iowa, USA, 16 January 1999.

332693 Private A. (Abraham?) Fenton (probably Feinstein). KOSB, No. 2 Platoon/Airborne. KIA 21 September 1944, aged 26. From Glasgow, son of A. and Mary Jane Fenton. Buried with a cross on his headstone at Oosterbeek, but Sid Goldstein and Captain G. Gourlay (listed below) say he was Jewish and had changed his name on enlistment. Field burial at the White House on Van Dendenweg (Hartenstein Museum).

3458590 Staff Sergeant Cyril Fisher. Glider Pilot Regiment, 'D' Squadron, AAC. KIA 22 September 1944, aged 25. Son of Harry and Rose of Edgware, Middlesex. Memorial, no known grave. Photo *WWRT*, p.85.

1561122 Sergeant Ronald Franks. 1st Wing Glider Pilot Regiment, 'D' Squadron, AAC. Had already fought at Caen after D-Day. Of 27 East St, Barking; son of Mr and Mrs H. Franks. Died of wounds as a POW, 22 October 1944, aged 25 – *JC*, 27 October 1944 and 16 February 1945. Photo *WWRT*, p.87. Letter from niece Mrs A. Sarner and cousin Alan Cass.

Goldstein. Veteran Sergeant John/Jack Foyer 7018830 1st Paras was in a trench with Lonsdale Force and saw a Para's body with ID tag 'Goldstein'. There is no such name on the Roll or in the CWGC site or Jewish Chaplain Cards, so this man remains another Jewish mystery.

30053853 Corporal Moszek Gro(u)man. Polish Paras (Meirtchak, *Jewish Military Casualties*). Born 18 December 1912, Grojec, Warsaw, son of Zelek and Cyrla, née Liber. Fought in Poland 1939; served Iran/Iraq/Palestine, Polish 3rd Para Battalion Field Ambulance. Awarded Polish Field Para Badge, Wound Badge and four British medals. Had been deported to Soviet Union as POW, 17 September 1939 to 24 March 1942. Wounded/died of wounds at Arnhem. Lennard informant claims he survived and went to live in Israel post-war.

5837015 Private/Lance Corporal Bernard Haikin. Born May 1920, son of Katia, née Censor, and Yasha Haikin; divorced from Barbara. Enlisted 11 December 1941 in Suffolk Regiment /REME/RAOC, then 156 Battalion Para Regiment, AAC. KIA 25 September 1944, aged 24, near the Sonnenberg House (P. Reinders). Lived at 46 Milner Square, London NI – AJEX Index Cards and photo. Brother of Gloria Sachs of Milman Mews, London WC1 (*Pegasus Journal*, April 1970 and MoD records) and Jack (Israel), Harry and Norman. Mother and stepfather were Mr and Mrs Steiner of 64 Langdale Buildings, Wicker St, London E1. Letter from Edna Jordan, née Saunders (1 January 1999), who was a friend of Bernard when she was in the Land Army in 1944. She visited his observant family one Saturday for Sabbath lunch and his father 'wore a skullcap'. She has since met the family as a result of the author's research. A friend, Harry Miller Oberman, knew Bernard from the age of 4 and wrote (2 January 1999) that the family lived at 17 Harper Street, Theobalds Rd; father was a tailor who worked from home. Bernard and he attended St John's School, Fisher St, Southampton Row, London WC1, then Hugh Middleton Central School in Clerkenwell. They were both in 21st City of Westminster Jewish Scouts which met at Great Portland Street Synagogue. There was no religious symbol on Haikin's grave, but in 1998 his brother and sister requested a Star of David be inscribed and this has been done.

P/174343 Captain John Miles/Myles Henry. 10th Battalion Para Regiment, AAC, HQ Coy Intelligence Officer. KIA 19 September 1944, aged 23, whilst rescuing a comrade under fire – see R. Brammall, *The Tenth* (Eastgate, 1965), p.62. Son of Arthur and Margaret; husband of Pamela Evelyn, née Morris, who later lived in Sweden and remarried as Mrs Lamm in Ludvika, now in Auckland, New Zealand. Letter from comrade Fred Duncan 'Jacks' Jackson of Christchurch, New Zealand, who served with him at Arnhem, and sent a photo of John's headstone at Oosterbeek. Also a letter and photo from his widow, Pamela E. Henry-Lamm, in New Zealand. John's daughter and grandchildren live in Sweden; Pamela was pregnant with John's daughter when he was killed. Letter from comrade Frederic Jenkins (12 December 1999) describes how Miles gave him a drink from his flask when he had been knocked out on 19 September. Biography of Henry is in his wife Pamela's book, *I've Had My Dance*, published in New Zealand, in AJEX library.

6021874 Sergeant Maurice Kalikoff. 2nd Battalion Para Regiment, AAC, 'S' Coy Mortar Section. WIA Arnhem Bridge, 20 September 1944; i/c mortars on 'grassy' island at Eusebius Square, near bridge, with Colonel Frost; having run out of ammunition, he and two of his men retreated to a house which then received a direct hit, fatally wounding Kalikoff (telephone call from comrade Bill Bloys, from Essex). Died of wounds as a POW 27 October 1944, aged 28, buried Rheinberg Cemetery, Germany. Son of Phillip and Dora of 260 Upper St, Islington, London (*JC*, 1 December 1944 – photo). James Sims, author of *Arnhem Spearhead* (London: Imperial War Museum), fought with Maurice and described him: 'golden hair and moustache and blue eyes and soft spoken'. He had fled the Ukraine as a child in the 1920s with his parents and sister and was 'very popular with the men despite being a strict disciplinarian and trainer' (letter to author). He was about five foot ten inches tall. Sims relates the following:

> Just before Arnhem, Maurice had a bee in his bonnet about us achieving a quick exit and a tight stick, so he had us hobbling through a Nissen hut with a kit bag on our leg and with full equipment. As this was early September, it was very hot and uncomfortable and we moaned a bit, but Maurice was determined we would get it right. Came the 17th Sept. 1944 and I had just landed by parachute and was gathering myself together to make for 2 Para yellow flare rallying point, when I met Maurice obviously searching for something. It turned out that his kit bag had broken free and he could not find it. I found this very amusing but he didn't. That was

the last I saw of him although we were never more than about 50 yards from each other [at the bridge with Colonel Frost].

629281(6)7 Private Denzil (Denny) Meyer/Myer Keen. 'A' Coy, 10th Battalion Para Regiment, AAC. KIA 19 September 1944, aged 21. Son of John and Elizabeth of Scotch Fir Cottage, West Chiltington Common, near Pulborough, Sussex; letter from Albert Slesinger says parents owned a boarding house at 158 Sutherland Ave, Maida Vale, London W9. Groesebeek Memorial. Volunteered at age 17 in the Buffs. Letter from sister Helen Barnett, and *JC*, 6 April 1945. Photo at AJEX Museum. A close friend, Ron Pang, who served with Denzil in the Paras before Ron was posted to the Far East, has researched into the manner of Denzil's death in action and describes it in detail in a letter in the author's possession. Going into nearby woods towards Oosterbeek to destroy a German tank, Keen was badly wounded, losing a leg, and brought back to be evacuated to the RAP. He was laid across the front of the colonel's jeep but as it pulled away the jeep received a direct hit from an enemy tank and the occupants were all killed. This is from an eyewitness account given to Ron Pang by surviving participants in the event described above: Ernie Whadcote, Johnny Stillwell and Tom Harding. The informants further told Ron that just before take-off to Arnhem, all the Jewish men attended a service with the Jewish chaplain, and were told that as they had seen active service in North Africa, they were given the option of not going in with the first drop. They all said at once that they would go in with their comrades, and when this became common knowledge, the whole battalion were very impressed. Denny was described by this informant as a 'tall fellow, well built, got on well with everybody, a bloody good mate'.

Private Maurice Kingston, aka Cohen. *JIW.* No further information is available.

14623912/13803244 Private Walter 'Lew'/Lou Landon/Langdon (real name Lewy-Lingen). 21st Independent Paras, Para Regiment, AAC. KIA 20 September 1944, aged 24; posthumous Certificate of Gallantry for crawling out in full view of the enemy and silencing a German cannon with a PIAT, being then mortally wounded. Son of Richard (German High Court Judge) and Marie Gertrude – see N. Bentwich, *I Understand the Risks*, (Gollancz, 1950), and *JIW*, and numerous references by other survivors who speak of him as a giant of a man and very gentle. Sergeant Ron Kent, *First In: The Parachute Pathfinder Company* (Batsford, 1979), who was at Arnhem and knew Landon, describes his behaviour as 'one of the many gallant acts of the Company's large Jewish contingent' and says Landon was recommended for a VC (p.110). Photos at AJEX Museum. Buried with a cross on his grave, although his sister says the family converted in Germany in the 1930s. Field burial at Hotel Schoonord (Hartenstein Museum). Chemistry student at Balliol, Oxford, before joining 93 Pioneer Corps and later the Paras. Aunt in Oxford and sister Marianne in Sutton Coldfield. He also fought in North Africa and Italy.

1478958 Staff Sergeant John Oliver Levison. 2nd Wing Glider Pilot Regiment, 'E' Squadron, AAC. KIA 19 September 1944, aged 23 – see R. Seth, *Lion with Blue Wings* (Gollancz, 1955), p.238. Not in *WWRT*. Son of Arthur J.G. and Lydia Levison of Farnham, Surrey. Tbc/cross on grave.

112068 Captain Percy Louis. RAMC, 133 Para Field Ambulance, att. 1st Airborne Medical Staff HQ, MiD. KIA 25 September 1944 (Sunday night or Monday morning), aged 29. He volunteered to cross from the south side of the Rhine to the besieged troops in Oosterbeek by assault boat with his CO under a Red Cross flag. Was captured then eleased to return to south bank. That night he returned with 4th Dorsets in an attack to get more supplies through, to west of Arnhem – see Lieutenant Colonel Howard Cole, *On Wings of Healing* (Blackwood, 1963), p.129. Killed and lost during the night crossing back for more medical supplies. Son of Mr S. and Mrs R. Louis of 5 Ranelagh Close, Edgware, Middlesex. Memorial, no known grave.

7369132 Sergeant Micky/Gerry Myers. *JIW* – 16th Para Field Ambulance batman for the surgical team of the RAMC at St Elizabeth's Hospital and of Captain Dr Lipmann Kessel (listed below). Attempted escape with a nominal roll of the wounded treated by Kessel, and a letter to Kessel's girlfriend Peggy. May have survived as a POW: letter from Niall Cherry, author of *Red Berets and Red Crosses*, a history of the 1st Airborne Medics, and P. Reinders. Information also from QMS Eddy Pruden.

Pilot Officer T.I. Pervin. RCAF. KIA 22 September 1944, aged 30; buried at Groesebeek.

1094468 Sergeant Max Rams. 'D' Troop, 1st Air Landing AT Battery, RA. KIA 18 September 1944, aged 28; memorial section 28, panel 1; letter from Louise Robson of Neath, widow of Max's Welsh friend Sergeant Cyril Robson; also from John C. Howe, veteran friend; Jewish Chaplain Cards at AJEX Museum. Arnhem veteran Lieutenant Edward E. Shaw described Rams as 'tall, handsome, with a moustache, well educated and a very fine soldier in every way' (letter from Louise Robson) and 'large, flamboyant, strong and fit, he stood out and is remembered with affection by all' (Howe). Father of Allan and David Rams in Hamilton, Canada (personal call). Eyewitness 273321 Lieutenant Geoffrey Ryall (a 'D' Troop officer), spoke to the author and described how he joined Rams's gun team on landing zone L where he had parachuted in, and then all moved off towards the bridge with 3rd and 4th Battalions of the Paras. En route they were held up by German machine guns and snipers, so Max took a rifle and decided to go after them. He was wounded, however, and against advice he made his way to a CCS. This was overrun at the time or later by SS troops and the men there were POW. Witnesses say they never saw Max afterwards and a long investigation was carried out later; they believe he was murdered but there is no proof. His body was never found and it may be buried in one of the unknown graves at Oosterbeek. Howe's notes include a statement by Doug Stone, bombardier to Rams, who says the RAP where Max went was at Mariendaal, and as it was overrun by SS Germans, they shot all the wounded as the British counter-attacked. P. Reinders of the ABRG confirms that the RAP was near a house called De Vergarde, ref. 709782, where a mass grave was found after the war. An unknown bombardier was subsequently buried in grave 1C 18 at Oosterbeek and an unknown sergeant (Rams?) at 1C 19; all this is confirmed in an email from Canada, from Max Rams's son, David, to the author on 11 December 2003. The letter from John Howe describes how Max fought in Sicily at the capture of the Primasol bridge, landing by glider; the capture of Taranto naval base in Italy, landing from naval destroyers; the capture of Foggia; and fought up to Cassino. On the journey back to Europe, Max was remembered for the fun he created with 'housey-housey' games (bingo). In UK he was heavily involved in changing guns from six- to seventeen-pounders, for which the Hamilcar glider was designed, when stationed at Helpringham, Lincs. After seventeen operations were planned and cancelled, they were sent to Arnhem. Three of the four guns of 'D' Troop were all destroyed on landing and only Max's gun survived. Howe says that Max was remembered for his statement that he would never be taken alive, and he may have taken his own life – but there is *no* evidence for this.

14441856 Private Erwin/C. Max Rivers (Rothbart). 1st Battalion Suffolk Regiment att. Airborne. Economics student at Keynes College, Cambridge. Died of wounds 25 November 1944, aged 30, buried Overloon. Married to Myfanwy Christina from Bayswater (*JC*, 5 September 1997 and Bentwich, *I Understand the Risks*, p.148). Son of Otto and Cecilie; lectured at Cambridge University. Not listed as Arnhem death by Hey, *Roll of Honour, Battle of Arnhem*, published by the Airborne

Museum, Aldershot. Before the battle he wrote: 'Also I rage when I suddenly see waiting death behind the calming mechanism of Commandos, dispositions and planned movements. It helps me that I know what I am fighting for.' See Peter Leighton-Langer, *The King's Most Loyal Enemy Aliens*.

Corporal Rodney. No further details – see Bentwich, *I Understand the Risks*, p.97–8: possibly Rodley (see next entry).

14623901/13804684 Corporal Hans Rosenfeld, served as John Peter Rodley. 21st Independent Paras, Pathfinders, AAC. University mathematics student. KIA 23 September 1944, aged 29, by a ricochet in the neck defending his trench in the garden of the house at Stationweg 8 – another source says by a grenade after he refused to surrender. Buried Oosterbeek. Came to England from Dusseldorf in 1939; Paras 1942; also fought North Africa and Italy; injured whilst training as a glider pilot. Married Rachel Kay; their son, Nigel, was 3 years old at the time of Rosenfeld's death – *JC*, 19 December 1944 (now works for UN and is a university lecturer). His sister Ruth Ellern, formerly in Leeds, now in Tel-Aviv. Son of Richard and Minna Rosenfeld, murdered in the Holocaust. Photo Middlebrook, *Arnhem*, and *JC*, December 1944 and letter from sister. Photos also from Steve Nicholls of Sheffield.

14219614 Sergeant Theodore Albert 'Ruby' Rube(i)nstein. 2nd Wing Glider Pilot Regiment, 'E' Squadron, Down Ampney, AAC. KIA 22 September 1944, aged 21; formerly of RW Fusiliers. Son of Ernest and Annie of 23 Teilo Rd, Cardiff. Photo *WWRT* p.153. Killed by a flamethrower (letter from brother of a comrade, Captain L. Futter and *JC*, 2 November 1945). Ruby got his wings at North Luffenham. He was six foot two inches tall, and much liked by his friends (telephone call from comrades Mr Hands and Mr Renard).

13803084 Sergeant Ernest Simion/Simeon. 2nd Wing Glider Pilot Regiment, 'F' Squadron, AAC. KIA 20 September 1944, aged 24. German Jewish refugee born in Berlin, 8 August 1920, son of Eva/Erna Simion of Hampstead and Gunter Levy (divorced). Came to UK in 1939 and worked as a mechanic in Co. Down, Northern Ireland; then interned; joined Pioneer Corps, then REME. Joined the Glider Pilot Regiment at Fargo on Salisbury Plain (telephone call from comrade Mr Price, who served with him, and comrade Richard Long). Letter and photo from cousin Wolf in London. A letter in AJEX Archives from his co-pilot S/Sergeant Ron P. Gibson, written 23 November 1944 from the sergeants' mess at RAF Broadwell, Shilton, Oxon., says they took off from Tarrant Rushton:

I only knew 'Sim' for a very short time, but what I knew I liked. We had a smooth flight over Holland on Sept. 17th ... [with] a jeep, an anti-tank gun and two of the gun crew from the Border Reg. ... at Aldeburgh turned south-east over North Sea. As we passed over the dunes [on Dutch coast] we ran into some flak ... our tug pilot pulled us into some cloud to avoid [it] ... then below cloud over flooded Lower Holland ... As we approached the landing zone at Arnhem we could see some big fires blazing in the town and along the railway line on one edge of the ploughed field where we had to land. We released from ... 3,000 feet and had to weave our way through a host of gliders that all seemed to aim for the same point. We touched down in a ploughed field on the side of a pine wood ... unloaded the gun and jeep ... hacking the tail off .... few enemy in the woods at that time ... eerily quiet ... then drove off to our rendezvous at 1.30 [pm] ... in the evening we passed through ... Wolfheze, where people stood by their garden gates, waving and saluting and pushing apples and pears into our rucksacks [and] met our first opposition down the village streets ... snipers and an armoured car.

We took up positions in the gardens of the houses and ... just before dark moved into a little pinewood ... we dug ourselves foxholes along the edge of the wood ... for the soil was sandy. During the night we took turns on patrolling the edge of the wood ... on the following morning I was separated from Simion ... as he was sent forward. In the morning I joined up with Simion again and ... there was an enormous amount of firing all around us. In the evening we moved out to ... Oosterbeek Park ... beechwood ... and dug ourselves in [but] very thinly held. I was separated from Simion again. He was in a foxhole about 50 yards from mine ... all through the night we were mortared. On the early morning of Wednesday a party of Jerrys ... suddenly ... burst through the corner of the woods where Simion was and threw some grenades into the backs of the trenches [and] ... another party of SS troops dashed across the road under cover of Spandau fire and killed or wounded them with sub-machineguns and grenades ... I looked down to Simion's corner and saw it occupied by the SS who were hauling our wounded out of their trenches. I saw one man standing up being searched by an officer but couldn't recognise him as Simion. I made a dash and was able to join the rest of our squadron who had drawn back ... this is all the information I can give up to the moment Simion was missing.

Samuel Swarts. Royal Netherlands Resistance Section Leader. Born 26 July 1917; KIA with Paras at Arnhem, 20 September 1944. Buried at Oosterbeek among the Paras with whom he fought. Story recounted by Tom Van Soest, who is a retired Dutch Army colonel and as an 11-year-old boy was a guide to the Paras at Arnhem in Jack Watson's Recce jeep. He fled with them over the Rhine and did not see his family for eleven months.

6032180 Private Alec Louis Taylor. 'A' Coy, 3rd Platoon, 8 Section, 4th Battalion Dorsetshire Regiment. KIA 25/26 September 1944, aged 20. Son of Henry and Fanny of 76 Cazenove Rd, Stoke Newington, London N16, brother of Mrs A. Lever (letter) and Mrs H. Brandt (letter). Comrade Frank Porter, in a telephone conversation with the author, emotionally described how Alec had told him as they crossed the Rhine that night that he did not want to be captured under any circumstances because he was Jewish. Photo AJEX Museum.

14688322 Private Anthony William Verhoeff. 10th Battalion Para Regiment, AAC. KIA 18 September 1944, aged 19. Son of Anthony and Alida of Golders Green, London. Memorial, no known grave.

6846961 Sergeant Pilot Julius (Jules) Wisebad. Glider Pilot Regiment, AAC. KIA 18 September 1944, aged 25. Memorial, no known grave (*JC*, 6 October 1944). Jewish Chaplain Card – 5 Handley Rd, Hackney, London E9; married 2 June 1944.

148579 Captain Ernest Mariel 'Oscar' Wyss. 'D' Coy, 2nd Battalion, S. Staffs. KIA near Elizabeth Hospital, Utrechtway, by a tank shell whilst attacking it, 20 September 1944; landed by glider. A very popular officer. Letter from Sergeant H. Dalton who witnessed his death, describing Weiss as Jewish and 'the bravest man he ever knew' and saying that we 'should be proud of him ... I will never forget him.' He was left with Padre Buchanan to bury. No Jewish Chaplain Card – tbc. Cross on grave. His story is told in the book, *A Bridge Too Far*.

3597285 Private/Trooper Francis 'Buster' Yapp. 1st Battalion Border Regiment/Airborne Tank Squadron. KIA 18 September, aged 26; husband of Joyce of Sale, Cheshire – information from comrade Sergeant E.J. Peters, who was with him when he was killed and remembers him saying, 'I am a Jew and will be shot if captured', and Private Owen Delvoir. He was first buried at Sonnenberg House along the Hoofdlaan–Oosterbeek road; now at the Oosterbeek Cemetery. Jewish Chaplain Card. Cross on grave in error.

Harry Yentis. KIA – *WWRT.* No trace at CWGC: probably fought under another name (tbc).

6476988 Lance Corporal Harry Zimmerman. 7th Battalion Somerset Light Infantry/Royal Fusiliers/City of London Regiment, KIA 1 October 1944, aged 24. Son of Mr and Mrs J. Zimmerman of 18 Arran House, Stamford Hill, London N16. Photo *WWRT*, p.179.

'John Christie'. Just before Arnhem, an unknown Jewish Paratrooper of German origin was given – in order to protect him if captured – the ID discs of an actual British officer, John Christie. The Jewish Para was killed at Arnhem and in 1956 the real Christie visited Oosterbeek and saw his own name on the gravestone. To this day it has been impossible to identify the Jewish Para buried there. Inquiries to the *Daily Telegraph* when Christie died in September 1999, about the story told in his obituary, brought no response from the family. In any case Christie probably never knew to whom the ID discs had been given that fateful day. So there is an unknown Jewish Para buried at Oosterbeek, killed at the battle of Arnhem.

(A total of 38)

Known To Have Been Wounded and/or POW or Escaped

PO later S/L Reginald Otto Altmann. DFC. 271 Squadron. Flying Dakotas from Down Ampney, tugging Horsas; dropped supplies on 18 September at Arnhem; mentioned in *Jewish Year Book 1945–46* as gazetted with a DFC. PRO Records AIR 1594.

128694 F/O later S/L Stanley James Alexander Asher. 620 Squadron. Took off from Fairford 17 September in Stirling IV LJ930 at 1010 hrs to drop men and supplies, returning at 1440 hrs. Jewish Chaplain Cards and AIR 27 2134 at PRO.

1519228 Gunner Isidore/Jack/Jacob Askins. RA. Father of three, Welford Rd, Crumpsall, Manchester 8 – Jewish Chaplain Card. Letter from Hadassah Rockman, Israel, and friends in Manchester/Bradford. Not confirmed.

Lieutenant Charles Aspler. 23rd Field Coy, Royal Canadian Engineers. Took part in evacuating Airborne under fire across the Rhine night of 25/26 September – letter from son Joseph of Kirkland, Quebec.

PLF/1920 2nd Lieutenant (Infantry) Karol Maksymilian Aszkenazy.
Born 18 May 1920 in Vienna, son of Joachim and Klara, née Gutman.
HQ 1st Independent Polish Paras; awarded Field Para Badge and four
British medals.

13805440 Backwitz/Bachwitz, fought as Chris Blakely. Jewish refugee
(*JIW*). Veteran Harry Ford says he was with Bachwitz when he
volunteered to swim the Rhine and bring in Polish reinforcements. In
the UK, Bachwitz went to see Ford's mother to assure her that Harry
was alive as a POW. PC and 21st Independent Paras; also served North
Africa, Italy, Norway.

14429091 Private Philip Banks/Levy. 10th Para Battalion. Fought at
Oosterbeek crossroads; information from personal interview. Born 4
January 1925 at the Jewish Lying-In Hospital, Commercial Road,
London E1. Served Merchant Navy; torpedoed; volunteered army and
1st Airborne. Parachuted into Arnhem, WIA/POW Fallingbostel Stalag
11B, then *Arbeitscommando* in a lead mine in Hartz mountains. Escaped
and reached Dutch border; betrayed by Dutch Green Police; beaten and
given twenty-eight days in cooler and then returned to mine. Then
forced march to other camp but escaped to American lines in April 1945.
Now lives in Northampton; was a Regular till 1966. He confirms that
many of 21st Independent Paras – with whom he fought – were German
Jews but to this day will not admit their religion or talk to strangers about
their backgrounds (see below). Banks is mentioned in Bramall, *The Tenth*,
pp.63, 84, 111, as being at LZ 'L', firing a Bren in a bombed house in
Oosterbeek, and using some German he learned from his Jewish
grandmother to bring in wounded to the Apeldoorn Barracks hospital.
Photo AJEX Museum and *Sunday Express*, September 1994.

30029060 Private Roman Barman. Born 19 November 1924, Rokitno,
Saany, Wolyn, son of Mejer and Merka, née Olszanska. Served
Iran/Iraq/Palestine and 3rd Polish Paras; awarded Field Para Badge and
four British medals.

6472456 Gunner/Lance Corporal Alfred/Abraham Barnett. RA/R Fusiliers
att. 1st Airborne. Came in from Tarrant Rushton by Hamilcar glider
towed by a Stirling. As it was eve of Rosh Hashana (Jewish New Year),
he took part in a service held by the Jewish chaplain for Jewish personnel that evening. As the glider came down in the thick of the fighting,
the chains holding a seventeen-pounder cannon snapped and the
barrel swung round almost hitting him. WIA by shrapnel in legs;
escaped across Rhine with Canadian Engineers and remembers pouring
rain and it being the eve of Yom Kippur (Day of Atonement). Husband

of Mrs S. Barnett of 148 The Drive, Ilford. Personal interview AJEX, photo at AJEX Museum. Born 25 February 1915 in Brick Lane, Whitechapel, London; called up in June 1940; fought in North Africa and Italy before training as a para at Ringway with 1st Airborne.

13807673 Nicholas Berblinger/Barblinger, fought as Allington. Jewish refugee (*JIW*), possibly born in Russia; fought in Spanish Civil War, French Foreign Legion; interned at Oran; joined PC and then 21st Independent Paras; also fought North Africa and Italy.

Bernard Berman. Pilot 310th Squadron, 315th Troop Carrier Group USAAF. Letter from Irving Sternoff.

954033 Lance Corporal Cyril Bernstein/Benton. Radio Operator, 11th Battalion Paras, 4th Brigade. WIA in back, arms and legs, he tried to swim the Rhine but was captured; POW Stalag 12A Limburg/IVB Muhlburg, from where he tried to escape; finally liberated by Red Army – personal interview. Father from 103 Galleywall Rd, London SE16. Photo at AJEX Museum.

4752181 Platoon Sergeant Norman (Sonny) Binick. MM (*JC*, 10 November 1944). WIA/MIA/POW; Pathfinder Coy, 21st Independent Paras. From Glasgow – letter from comrade Lawrence/Solomon Scott, whose father was Jewish. Kin given as J. Rafael, 10 Noorcroft Rd, London NW2. One of the three first platoon sergeants of 21st Independent Paras from its inception in June 1942. Wounded by a mortar shell (Kent, *First In*, p.125). Photo at AJEX Museum.

Sergeant Block. 'B' Squadron, Glider Pilot. P. Reinders.

Private 'Mo' Bloom. 1st Border Regiment. Letter from comrade 2981724, Private A. Sandy Masterton.

J42319 P/O Max Blugrind. 573 or 437 Squadron. Took off 17 September 1944 in Dakota KG327 from Broadwell at 1002 hrs, returning 1517 hrs, dropping supplies and men at Arnhem (RAF Innsworth and PRO AIR 27 records).

6803522 Capt. Peter Isidore Brett aka Bretzfelder, R.F., son of Alfred and Raie, née Prince, of Stoke Newington, husband of Doris.

Lol Brand. RAMC att. 21st Independent Paras. Jewish refugee; letter from Solly Scott (tbc).

6465423 Sergeant Myer H. Bromnick. 1st Para, 'S' Coy, 6th Platoon, No. 6 Section, MiD twice. Born in Mile End, London, son of Mrs S. of 8 Grange Court Road, Stoke Newington, London N16. MIA/POW, seriously wounded – *JC*, 12 January 1945. Husband of Helene (letter from widow). Refused to change his Jewish ID in the Airborne. Photo at AJEX Museum. He noted many pro-Jewish slogans written on the sides of the gliders before take off – letter from widow in *JIW* notes.

1612604 WO David Butterworth. 271 Squadron, RAF. Son of Lewis and Leah Butterwasser, born 21 June 1922 at 2 Fenton St, London E1; took off Down Ampney in DC3 dropping Paras and towing glider with Paras on day one and then two more supply drops over Arnhem; almost shot down when he warned pilot of approaching fighters through the astrodome; recommended MiD but not awarded – interview 22 July 2000.

Major Cahn. *JIW.*

Maurice Canter. *JIW.*

WO B.N. Caplan. 233 Squadron. Flying from Blakehill Farm to Arnhem in Dakota KG 441 on 18 September 1944, dropping troops and equipment and towing glider; took off 1050 hrs and returned 1635 hrs. PRO Records AIR 1433.

Private Carr. Name given by AJEX veteran who could not remember any further details. Could be A., T. or T.S. Carr.

Private Sam Clamp. Information from Gerry Flamberg, MM. With the Mortar Platoon in 156 Battalion (P. Reinders, ABRG).

1553155 Private Jack Cohen. Ox. & Bucks. Light Infantry, att. Airborne, part of Divisional HQ Defence Platoon. See Longson and Taylor, *An Arnhem Odyssey*, p.86, photo. Of 122 Church St, Chesham, Bucks. – Jewish Chaplain Cards and photo at AJEX Museum. Army Records Office verified religion.

7016526/7106826 Private Harry Cooper. 1st Ulster Rifles, att. Para Regiment, att. Brigade HQ. Landed in glider, POW – personal interview. Son of Michael Cooper, 17 Balham Hill, London SW12.

T 14572938 Driver Joseph Gerald Cooper. RASC/RCOS/East Lancs Regiment. WIA three times: Middle East; D-Day, Caen, Ardennes; Reichswald Forest. Born 19 August 1923, Stepney, son of Mrs E. Cooper, 54 Mulberry St, London E1. Was at Driel with the Poles when they tried to get across to the Airborne at Arnhem, giving covering fire – Jewish Chaplain Card, photo and interview.

J16824 F/O George A. Coppel. 233 Squadron. Took off for Arnhem from Blakehill Farm on 18 September 1944 in Dakota KG400 at 1050 hrs returning at 1635 hrs. AIR 27 1438 at PRO; Innsworth records.

5884355 Sergeant Sam or C. Coster. 'K' Troop 1st Battalion Paras. From Ealing. POW at Fallingbostel – statement from comrade Doug Charlton, secretary/archivist of 1st Battalion OCA. Excused Church Parade. P. Reinders claims he escaped over the Rhine.

7896515 Private Lionel Cuckle. 11th Battalion Paras. POW with Cyril Bernstein and Sydney Goldstein, Stalag 4B (?), no. 025995; letter also from son, Howard. Born Hull, 2 March 1914. MIA – *JC*, 10 November 1944 and 1 December 1944 – photo. Wife lived at 164 Coltman St, Hull, and parents at 402 Anlaby St, Hull. He was friend of Jewish SOE agent Isidore Newman, MBE, murdered at Mauthausen death camp.

Flight Sergeant Edward Danziger. RAF, 298 Squadron in Halifax, ML MLP. From Tarrant Rushton to Arnhem on 17 September, from AIR 27 1654 at PRO and Innsworth.

Sergeant Glider Pilot George V. Joseph Peppi De Liss/DeLiss/Delitz. AAC, 'A' Squadron. Austrian Jewish refugee; friend of Louis Hagen, illustrated his book on Arnhem. Information from talk with L. Hagen.

Louie De Marco. 1st Battalion Paras. Son of a puppet-maker in Aldgate – telephone message from Bill Bloys of Essex.

Private 14623924/13814390 Descarr/Dossmar, fought as Bernard Kenneth Dawson. 21st Independent Paras. Jewish refugee from Vienna, born 1915; husband of Audrey (*JIW*) Letter from Solly Scott/21st Independent Paras archives.

Issac de Vries. Dutch Jew in hiding who left his safe-house to guide the remnants of Major Lonsdale's 11th Battalion Paras to the Rhine and then crossed with them (Middlebrook, *Arnhem*, p.435). Dutch King's Medal for Freedom and Dutch War Cross. Lives in Israel. Photo courtesy of Adrian Groneweg of the Arnhem Hartenstein Museum. Medals at Hartenstein Museum.

5729990 Private Lewis Diamand. 'D' Coy, HQ 1st Airborne and 6/7th Battalion Dorsets. Volunteered May 1940. Son of J. Diamand of 56 The Charter Rd, Woodford Green, London – information from Jewish Chaplain Cards and nephew David Van Loewe.

11260470 Private Bernard Dresser. AAC, Mortar Platoon. Of 12 Fieldland Terrace, Leeds, 7; husband or son of Jane. In Stalag 4B as POW no. 89570; escaped.

Rusty Ericson/Erickson, aka Isaacs, or Isaac Erickson. 'S' Coy, 1st Battalion Paras. From Stepney/Whitechapel. Escaped across Rhine via

Jonkerbosch convent school at Nijmegen with Doug Charlton (listed above) who testified that they persuaded Isaacs to change his name and religion on his ID in case of capture. WIA; returned to UK.

14456069 Sergeant Joseph Dan Faust (Fauschlager). 1st Airborne Recce Squadron. Personal interview. Lived at 302 Watford Lane, London NW4. Son of Mr and Mrs R. Fauschlager. Also in S.A.S.

13804402/14623920 Jurgen Fenner, aka Fenyce. AAC/RF. Son of Mrs L. Fenner of Vienna, Jewish refugee (*JIW*). Veteran Harry Ford was with him at Arnhem.

P14137 Lieutenant (Cavalry) Jerzy/George Zygmunt Bereda Fijalkowski. 1st Mounted Rifle Regiment in 1939 Polish campaign, 21st Lancers in France, 3rd Para Battalion. WIA, escaped; died of wounds 28 April 1945 (Meirtchak, *Jewish Military Casualties*); winner of Virtuti Militari (Polish VC) and Field Para Badge and four British medals. Born 19 December 1917/15 July 1920, Warsaw (Witko)/ Ostrow Mozowiecki, son of Zygmunt and Halina, née Barylska. Buried Donnington, England. Enlisted as RC.

1500732 Driver Joel Fiskin/Fisken. Nephew of Mrs G. Spoont of 128b South Portland St, Glasgow: information from Jewish Chaplain Cards; assumed to be the same RASC despatcher mentioned in *Journal of the RASC* (November 1944), p.54, as having baled out with his crew after being shot down dropping supplies over Arnhem and found by Polish troops. They were taken to British HQ and fêted by the General, who knew the base they had come from.

6856426 Private Gerald Flamberg, aka Lambert. MM, 156 Battalion Para Regiment. Of 12 Meynall Rd, Hackney, London. Wounded/MIA/POW – *JC*, December 1944 and 12 October 1945; stopped a German tank single-handed. Later founder of Jewish anti-Fascist 43 Group after war, against Mosely. Picture at AJEX Museum and *JC*. Letter to his parents from CO said:

> Your son displayed great courage, attempting to destroy an enemy armoured vehicle ... when his RSM was wounded, he stood up in the open and fired an anti-tank gun at it and throwing a bomb at it, continued to endeavour to destroy it. During this he was wounded but continued to fight. Truly a son to be proud of ... 'a great fighter in battle and in the ring'.

3317365 Lance Corporal Philip Fox. HQ Coy, Signals 1st Battalion HLI. Was at southern end of bridge during the evacuation of Paras, covering withdrawal across the Rhine – personal interview. Of 28 Sholebroke Terrace, Leeds 7.

13116161/13803486 Lance Bombardier Kurt/Kenneth D. Fraser, aka Fleischmann. RA/1st Airborne. WIA/POW, Stalag 12A, no. 13116161. Son of Mr S. and Mrs Fleischman, 10 West Heath Drive, London NW11; cousin of Henry Kissinger – *JC*, 4 May 1945.

Corporal A.E. Freeman. Served as Ward, 10th Paras – see Middlebrook, *Arnhem*, p.479 (tbc).

R171414 WO Max Frieman. RCAF. From Montreal. Took off in Stirling 4EZY from Harwell with 570 Squadron to Arnhem at 1145 hrs, returning at 1615 hrs. From records of Canadian Jewish Nominal Roll of the Canadian Jewish Congress, and AIR 27 at the PRO.

Corporal Walter Reginald Frimond. *JIW*. Jewish Chaplain Card shows him as 6093421, Queen's West Surreys, Westminster Rifles, 11th Battalion, KRRC; son of H. Frimond, 3 Anlany Rd, Bedford.

14672427 Signalman Bernard Fryman. No. 1 Coy HQ 1st Airborne Divisional Signals. His adjutant was Captain L.L. Golden – letter.

Captain Leonard Futter. Hampshires/Commandos/6th Airborne/1st Airborne. Born 16 May 1919. WIA/POW; friend of Sergeant T.A. Rubinstein – letter from brother. Emigrated to Canada in 1946 and never heard of since.

1874903 Flight Sergeant Walter Garretts. 196 Squadron, Stirling Mk. IV LJ502 – D for Dog. From Keevil, piloted by H. Hoysted, DFC; five drops over Arnhem, two towing gliders: 17 September, leaving at 1045 hrs and returning 1505 hrs with heavy flak damage after glider release at 2,500 ft over Arnhem; 18 September; 19, 21 and 23 September dropping supplies. Personal letters. Son of Nathan and Esther Garretts of The Castle, 44 Commercial Rd, London E1. Born 13 February 1925. Jewish Chaplain Card and photo. Also flew twenty-three other missions on D-Day, Rhine Crossing, and SOE and SAS drops all over Europe.

P/3273 Lieutenant (Medical Corps) Dr Ludwik George Gelber. Born 15 April 1917, Lvov, son of Jozef and Dordia, née Alper. Served in France 1940, 10th Ambulance Coy, 10th Armoured Cavalry Brigade, 4th Para Battalion Field Ambulance; awarded Field Para Badge and four British medals. Enlisted as C. of E.

1286389 F/S Philip Gold. 296 Squadron in Albermarle V1813 from Manston. AIR 22 1644 at PRO; RAF Innsworth; Jewish Chaplain Cards.

3326465 Private Frank Goldberg. POW no. 90546, Airborne/7th KOSB/HLI. From Glasgow: letter from Captain G. Gourlay. Married Mrs E. Goldberg; moved to 28 Estreham Rd, Streatham, London.

WO, D.J. Goldberg. RAF. In 196 Squadron with Azouz and Hartman; flew from Keevil on four missions to Arnhem: on 17 September at 1055 hrs returning at 1630 hrs, in Stirling LK 510; on 19 September from Wethersfield at 1300 hrs returning at 1815 hrs, having dropped twenty-four containers and four panniers; on 20 September at 1200 hrs returning at 1705 hrs, dropping a duplicate load but sustaining light flak damage; on 23 September in LJ 502, taking off at 1405 hrs and returning at 1920 hrs, having dropped another load. PRO AIR 27 1167.

229206 Major Lewis Lawrence Golden aka Goulden. OBE. Adjutant 1st Airborne Divisional Signals Author of Echoes of Arnhem (W. Kimber, 1984); Council of Westminster Synagogue post-war. Born 6 December 1922, Ealing, London. Only the second Officer of Signals appointed to Para Brigade. Escaped by swimming the Rhine; photo AJEX Museum and letter from CO Major General Anthony Deane-Drummond, then Second in Command, 1st Airborne Signals at Arnhem. Served also North Africa, Italy, Sicily, Normandy and India.

Henry Goldman. Pilot 309th Squadron, 315th Troop Carrier Group, USAAF. Letter from Pilot Irving Sternoff.

2364378 Private Phillip Goldsmid/Rubinstein. Para Regiment/RCOS. Escaped by swimming the Rhine; had been an army boxing champion. Moved to Israel aged 59, on a Kibbutz, died 1989. Letter from daughter Mrs Billie Josephs. Photo AJEX Museum. Uncle of Killarney House, Monument St, EC1.

5674773 Sergeant Ben Goldstein. 156th Battalion 1st Paras. Volunteered from 13th Foot SLI; platoon commander was Dennis Kayne. MIA/POW: *JC*,15 December 1944 – photo. Personal interview. Remembers taking off on Rosh Hashana and holding a short service with Lieutenant Kayne and Gerry Flamberg beneath a glider wing, just before. Born 22 March 1919, Brady St, London E1; parents from Tetworth, Oxford. Brady Jewish Boys' club. Married to Doris; of 54 Foburg Rd, Clapton, London E5.

Sergeant Len Goldstein. Glider Pilot. Refugee – *JC*, 13 October 1944.

1527851 Private Sidney Goldstein. 'D' Coy, 16 Platoon, 1st Independent Paras/7th KOSB. POW (personal interview AJEX) with Bernstein, Lee, Josephs, Cuckle. Batman to Lieutenant P.B. Mason, a Canadian Loan officer. Landed Ginkel Heath. Captain George Gourlay (letter) mentions him in a book, *Off at Last*, when Goldstein was asked to try Yiddish in communicating with local Dutch civilians. Photo AJEX Museum. Name found with Gourlay on glider list in AIR 27 records at PRO. In Stalag 4B, hut 26 – letter from comrade Bob Barrett.

Sergeant/Captain Benjamin Goodman. Airborne Divisional HQ, 2nd Paras. Information from 6th Airborne and AJEX member, Private Ivor Rimmon, and comrade at Arnhem, Sergeant Dalton. From Richmond, London.

5503715 Private A. G. (Jack) Gordon. Son of Reverend M.L. Gordon, minister of the Southampton Hebrew Congregation – *JC*, 13 October 1944. Of 47 Archers Rd, Southampton/Winchester.

Private Green/Grunen. 3rd Battalion Paras. Probably a Jewish refugee – telephone call from comrade John Reed.

14417002 Sergeant Frank Ashleigh Greenbaum. Glider Pilot, 'A' Squadron, AAC. Born Stepney, 23 December 1924. MIA/POW at Stalag 7 near Luchenwald. Of 480 Finchley Road, London: *JC*, October 1944. Took off from Harwell on 18 September. Telephone conversation. Photo AJEX Museum.

P/10952 2nd Lieutenant (Engineers) Mieczyslaw Grunbaum. Born 4 July 1921 Kalisz, Poznan, son of Marek and Paulina, née Krauze; served France 1939–40 and Para Engineers; awarded Field Para Badge, Virtuti Militari and four British medals; wounded at Arnhem, then KIA 14 April 1945.

13805451/13807110 Captain Tony (Anton) Guttmann, fought as Gordon. 21st Independent Paras. Jewish refugee (*JIW*) and mentioned also by Mrs Rita Stanleigh (see Stanleigh, her husband, listed below) and Peter Block. Later lived in Israel as port engineer at Ashdod or Ashkelon. Photo AJEX Museum. Also fought North Africa, Italy, Norway (ADC to GOC), India (Air Landing Division).

Sergeant Louis Hagen, served as Lewis Haig. Family name Levy. Glider Pilot, 'A' Squadron, AAC, MM for bravery at Arnhem and taking several POWs. See Middlebrook, *Arnhem*. WIA; escaped by swimming the Rhine; author of best-selling book *Arnhem Lift*. Photo at AJEX Museum and personal call. Born Potsdam, 30 May 1916. Also served REME/RAOC/RA and in India 1945. Son of Berlin bankers, came to UK in January 1936.

1921/171 Lance Corporal Nissan Hajtler. Born 4 January 1921, Warsaw, son of Abram and Sura, née Goldberg; served Iran/Iraq/Palestine, 1st Battalion 1st Independent Polish Paras/4th Warsaw Rifles/4th Polish Infantry Division, awarded Field Para Badge and four British medals.

14428984 Sergeant Glider Pilot Harold Halmer. Son of L. Halmer, 83 Mexborough Gdns, Leeds, 7 – Jewish Chaplain Card and letter from brother of friend, Bernard Spencer.

Henry Harding, aka Heindrick Getting. 10th Battalion Paras. Letter from comrade Norman Dickson in Isle of Man.

2337596 Sergeant Ephraim David Hardman. Royal Signals att. Airborne. Of 351 St Cheetham St, Salford – JIW.

Sergeant Harris. Jewish refugee – *JIW*.

1601174 WO Leo Hartman. 196 Squadron, RAF. Of 80 Hindle House, Arcola St, Hackney, London N16. Was in crew with Mark Azouz (KIA), B for Baker as Air-Bomber; baled out. Although his plane was badly damaged by ground fire, Azouz dropped the supplies and then made for home, being shot down by German fighters en route – *JIW* and letter from Walter Garretts, listed above.

Rachel Didi Ross (Hertz) born Rotterdam. Resistance, helped evaders, POW, escaped, lived in Israel, awarded Dutch Medal of Freedom and British Kings Commendation for Brave Conduct.

Captain Leo Jack Heaps. MC. Born 7 July 1922, son of a Winnipeg MP; was wounded in Normandy, where his brother also won the MC; Canadian Infantry Corps of Winnipeg att. 1st Airborne; captured 24 September; escaped then MIA, then turned up on south bank; returned to north bank and worked with Dutch Resistance, bringing 150 evaders home in Operation Pegasus, including Brigadier Lathbury and Major Tatham-Warter (see Hamblett, *Pegasus Patrol* pp.144–5 and *Canadian Jews at War*; photo at AJEX Museum). Author of two books on Arnhem; described by General Urquhart as 'having a charmed life!' It is likely Heaps was working on some secret SOE mission not known even to Urquhart. He seemed to appear at odd times in vehicles during the heat of the battle, solving problems as a mobile freelance (Urquhart, *Arnhem*, pp.54–5). He led the attempted breakthrough with three Bren carriers to the bridge to relieve Frost and bring supplies, but it failed (Urquhart, *Arnhem*, p.100).

183813 P/O Captain Jack Aubrey Herman. RAFVR, 644 Squadron Halifax V2PN LL218 at Tarrant Rushton to Arnhem. Of 72 Sandringham Gdns, London N12. Jewish Chaplain Cards and PRO Records AIR 2159.

30017723 Lance Corporal Israel Herszkowicz. Born 1921 Tarnow, Krakow, son of Izak and Sabina; served Iran/Iraq/Palestine, 3rd Para Battalion; awarded Field Para Badge and WIA Badge, 26 September 1944 at Arnhem, and four British medals.

Marcelle Herz. Dutch Resistance. Organized food supplies for the several hundred British evaders hidden in the Ede-Appledoorn area during months of waiting to escape.

Captain (later Colonel) Alfred John Hines. MC and bar, MiD twice; deputy to Commander, RE (CRE) Brigadier Wolf Myers at Arnhem. Parachuted at Ginkel Heath 18 September and responsible for coordinating evacuation on south bank of Neder Rhine with 43rd Wessex Division; awarded also Orange Nassau 1st class by Queen Wilhelmina. Served also Greece; Crete; North Africa (WIA); Sicily; Salerno (WIA); Normandy; Berlin Blockade; Suez, 1956 (Para).

30030453 Private/Lance Corporal Henryk Hirschfeld. Born 22 August 1918, Krakow, son of Zygmunt and Anna, née Lewicka. Served France 1940, 1st and 3rd Para Battalions; awarded Field Para Badge, Army Medal and four British medals. Enlisted as RC.

Sergeant 3533597 Harry Hoffman, or 'Big H'. 3rd Battalion Paras. Died 18 November 1997, aged 80 – obituary in *Pegasus Journal*, June 1998; buried Carleton Cemetery, Liverpool/Blackpool (?). POW Sicily, escaped; WIA, awarded American Purple Heart; escaped three times. Son of Mrs S. Hoffman, 10 Maud St, Manchester 8. Jewish Chaplain Card and photo.

174451 Lieutenant Gerald Maurice Infield/Infeld. 1st Battalion Paras, 1st Brigade. Born London, 1 June 1921. Fought at the bridge with Colonel Frost's men; MIA/POW at Oflag 79 near Brunswick – *JC*, 27 October 1944 and 24 November 1944. Son of Major H. Infield, MC, Flat 5, 217 Sussex Gdns, London W2. Telephone call. Photo at AJEX Museum. Personal interview.

105108/6967708 Captain Barry Barnett Ingram. OC Mortar Platoon, Glider Loading Officer, 1st wave, Air Landing Glider Regiment, 1st Battalion Border Regiment, 1st Airborne. POW after four days of evasion. Lived at 538 Finchley Rd, London NW11 – from records of Hartenstein Airborne Museum, Oosterbeek, Adrian Groeneweg and letters from wife Eileen and comrades Colonel Newport and Reverend Royall. Photo at AJEX Museum. MiD for his actions on 22 September 1944 (letter from comrade Pat Slote).

1078143 Gunner Israel Isaacs. RA attached 1st Airborne. WIA. Brother of Reverend S. Isaacs, British Jewish army chaplain. Lived at 45 Rostrevor Ave, London N15 – *JC*, 13 October 1944.

6149848 Staff Sergeant Samuel Gregory Isaacs, aka Murray. DFM Glider Pilot. Born 30 April 1920, Walworth Road area of London, son of Samuel and Rose. 10th Battalion East Surreys then glider pilot in North Africa, Sicily, Italy, D-Day, Arnhem (DFM), India. Saw much fighting and was an evader.

14429044 Sergeant Charles Izon. Royal Fusiliers/Ox. & Bucks./ KOYLI/Commandos, att. 1st Airborne. Born 5 October 1925 in Birmingham. Volunteered aged 17 in 1942, wounded at Caen, Normandy; severely WIA Arnhem; POW. Letter and interview with wife Sylvia. Photo at AJEX Museum.

1084603 Bombardier Abraham Solomon Jacobs. RA, 'B' Troop, No. 1 Air Landing Battery/1st Airborne. WIA aged 34 – *JC*, 17 November 1944. Lived at 49, Dixon Ave, Glasgow, son of Mrs Max Jacobs. Met another Jewish Airborne man and they greeted each other in the midst of the battle with '*Shema Yisroel*'. Photo at AJEX Museum.

14690953 Private D.H. Jacobs. 181 Air Landing Field Ambulance (Cherry's *Red Berets and Red Crosses*). Jewish Chaplain Card.

2nd Lieutenant Jerome Jacobs. USAAF fighter pilot ASN 0-819592, 364th Fighter Squadron, 357th Fighter Group. Shot down in his Mustang supporting Paras at Arnhem, 19 September 1944; POW. Son of Samuel and Sophie, 147th St, Flushings, NY – info from reader M. Moscow of USA.

6849171 Private 'Danny' Daniel Josephs. AAC/11th Battalion, KRRC. POW with Sidney Goldstein (personal interview with SG) and P. Reinders information. Stalag 12A. Jewish Chaplain Card. Married to H. Josephs, 52 Downs Court, Hackney, London E8, and 1 Dufours Place, London W1.

Pilot Harold Kaminski. 315th USAAF Troop Carrier. From Cleveland Ohio – letter from L. Zurakov.

249279 Lieutenant Dennis Benjamin Kayne. 156th Battalion, 4th Para Brigade. MIA/POW, Wednesday 20 September 1944; removed his Jewish ID before capture near Wolfheze (Middlebrook, *Arnhem*). Son of M.I. Kayne of 18 St George's Rd, Golders Green, London NW11; grandson of Rabbi J. Kyansky, minister of Newcastle-upon-Tyne Hebrew Congregation; husband of Monica. Described by his lieutenant colonel in North Africa as 'quite the best IO in the 8th Army'. Photo at AJEX Museum.

13804344 Private Bob Kendall, aka Kraus. 21st Independent Paras. *JIW.* German refugee from Sudetanland. Letter from wife of comrade, Mrs Rita Stanleigh (see Stanleigh listed below). Lived in Holland (married to a Norwegian woman named Siss, now in Colwyn Bay) where he died after war. Photo at AJEX Museum. Also served North Africa, Italy, Norway, Palestine.

30030285 Private/Corporal Kersch/Heszel Krugman. 4th Para Battalion, HQ Coy, Ist Independent Polish Paras. *JIW.* Born 18 September 1911, Bialystok, son of Tefio and Chaja, née Bryskja. Awarded Polish Army Medal and four British medals.

227647 Captain Surgeon Alexander William (Dan/Paul) Lipmann 'Lippy' Kessel. MBE, MC. RAMC att. 1st Airborne, 16th Para Field Ambulance. Aged 29. From Pretoria, South Africa; died 1986 after a successful career as a doctor in London; buried at Arnhem civil cemetery, opposite Oosterbeek Cemetery, with his comrades in accordance with his last wishes – see Middlebrook, *Arnhem.* Saved the life of the severely wounded Brig. John Hackett, CO 4th Para Brigade, who was disguised in the St Elizabeth Hospital at Arnhem as 'Corporal Hayter'. He helped smuggle arms out of the hospital for 'mock burials' in the grounds; these were later dug up by the Dutch Resistance. Escaped from Appledoorn Hospital with several other Airborne doctors after being given permission by the senior MO. At a safehouse he met the wounded evader Brigadier Hackett (wearing a Star of David badge – see Lipmann Kessel, *Surgeon at War*, p.173) again and operated on him for the second time on 15 February 1945. Photo at AJEX Museum and Hartenstein Museum. Jewish 6th Airborne veteran Ivor Rimmon described how General Hackett had himself organized Kessel's burial at Arnhem with an Orthodox rabbi at the local cemetery. Medals at Hartenstein Museum. Eddy Pruden recalls that Kessel once took on the regimental wrestler in a sporting event in North Africa.

30017776 Sergeant Albert Leon Kurzweil. Born 14 June 1916 in Lvov, son of Moric and Klara, née Gelles. Served 1939 Poland, France 1940, 2nd and 4th Para Battalions; awarded Field Para Badge and Army Medal and four British medals.

PLF/1890 2nd Lieutenant (Infantry) Gustav Jozef Tadeusz Lambert. Polish Paras. *JIW.* Born 23 July 1890 in Bihac Yugoslavia; served Polish regiment in Austro-Hungarian Army, 6 August 1914 to 28 November 1916; Engineers Lubiana, Slovenia and Zloczow, Poland, 10 January

1917 to 1 November 1918; POW, Polish Independence Organization, July 1917 to 11 November 1918. Served Polish Army 11 November 1918 to 25 January 1928. Deported to USSR 1940–41 where he enlisted 19 May 1942 into Polish Army in Iran. Enlisted as RC.

Sergeant John Latz. 3rd Battalion Paras. Right-hand man of Major John Audrey and of CO Colonel Lonsdale; telephone call from comrade Private John Reed, who described him as tall, smart with a dark moustache; mentioned in the book, *The Red Beret*.

Ira Lazarus. Pilot 309th Squadron, 315th Troop Carrier Group, USAAF. Letter from Irving Sternoff.

Philip Lebor. Managed to swim the Rhine to escape – *JIW*.

Fred Lee. 21st Independent Paras. Letter from Solly Scott. Was awarded a Dutch gallantry medal (tbc).

Private WO Harry Lee. 11th Battalion. POW with Bernstein and Goldstein.

Gerald Leigh. *JIW*.

WO Joseph Lemberg. USAAF, 34th Troop Carrier Squadron, 315th Group. Letter from Colonel William Brinson, Florida, USA.

1892611 F/S Aubrey Hyman Leon. 570 Squadron. Took off from Harwell to Arnhem on 17 September 1944 in Stirling IV V8D LJ616 at 1113 hrs and returned 1543 hrs. RAF Innsworth, Jewish Chaplain Cards.

6346510/73127 Lieutenant Robert Hugh Levien. CO 4th Platoon, 'B' Coy, 2nd Paras. Parachuted from Dakota 17 September 1944, POW after three days, ending at Oflag 79. Was on the bridge with Colonel Frost and knew Sergeant Kalikoff. Of Jewish origin through his parents and grandparents. Telephone call from him. Photo in John Frost's book and at AJEX Museum.

J23365 FO/Navigator Elliot Levitan. 196 Squadron, RAF. Took off from Keevil 23 September 1944 in Stirling EF272 at 1410 hrs, returning at 1010 hrs, dropped twenty-four containers and four panniers to Paras, his air bomber being injured in flak; RAF Innsworth confirm him as Jewish. Squadron records at PRO in AIR 27 1167.

Corporal Levy. RASC Dakota Despatcher at Arnhem. No. 2 to Lieutenant E.J. Younghusband. Wounded by ack-ack shrapnel whilst in doorway pushing out panniers to the Airborne at low altitude over Arnhem; reached hospital in England: from article by Lieutenant Colonel

Packe, 'The RASC at Arnhem', *Journal of the RASC*, November 1944, p.53 – AJEX Museum Archives.

7391545 Private Alfred Levy. RAMC att. Airborne 133 Field Ambulance. MIA/POW – *JC*, 3 November 1944, aged 24. Lived at 40 Scott Hall Rd, Leeds; mother from Middlesex. Personal letter. Forced landing in southern England en route, took off again next day. Landed Wolfheze and proceeded to Hartenstein Hotel and Oosterbeek. Left behind to care for wounded. POW Stalag 12A and 4B, Muhlberg and Leipzig, no. 77334. Photo AJEX Museum.

14492014 Private Gerald Levy. 3rd Battalion Paras. Landed Ginkel Heath, aged 17. Formerly 2nd Cadet Battalion Jewish Lads Brigade (Royal Fusiliers). His group held south-east corner of 'the Cauldron' and he was at Oosterbeek church, wounded, and part of Lonsdale Force – *AJEX Journal*, November 1994, and personal interview. Photos at AJEX Museum.

6849029 Private Harris Levy. 11th Para Regiment. WIA/MIA/POW – Stalag 9C, no. 52901 – *JC*, 3 November 1944 and 24 April 1945. Son of Mrs S. Levy, 82 Decking Road, Tonbridge, Kent. His CSM wrote: 'Your son's conduct and courage was of the highest order and I was proud and honoured to fight with him. He stuck to his guns until he was carried out (wounded in both legs) and even then asked to go back.' Photo at AJEX Museum.

Sergeant Harry Levy. *JIW*; photo in Hamblett, *Pegasus Patrol*, p.49, with HQ section of Provost Coy.

Sergeant Louis Levy. 'G' Squadron, Glider Pilot Regiment. Later served Palestine – information from P. Reinders and Eric Kemish (veteran).

1058297/187881 WO later PO Vivian Marcus Levy. 271 Squadron. From Down Ampney flying Dakotas tugging Horsas, took off on 17 September 1944 in Dakota III F2 601 at 0944 hrs and returned from Arnhem at 1525 hrs; again on 19 September in F2 615 at 1231 hrs, returning 1740 hrs. AIR 27 file 1574; RAF Innsworth; Jewish Chaplain Cards.

13805077/13804344(?) Staff Sergeant Martin David Lewin, fought as Lewis. Born Tempelburg, Germany, 22 January 1922. One of the first of 21st Independent Paras to land; served with Lewy-Lingen, aka Landon (KIA) – see *I Understand the Risks*, p.99. German refugee – *JIW*. Fought Africa, Italy (WIA by sniper behind German lines) and served in Norway (in the last drop to reinforce the Resistance in 1945) as well as at Arnhem. In Sachsenhausen concentration camp, aged 16, got to England February 1939, all his family perishing in the Holocaust; interned

Isle of Man; Pioneer Corps December 1940; recruited by Major Lander into Airborne, serving six years. Refused to serve in Palestine. Left for USA in August 1948 (letter to author). Photo AJEX Museum. Married Irene Ohnstein (born Berlin), father to three children.

6469132 Sergeant Michael Lewis. *JIW.* 1st Airborne photographer. See Middlebrook, *Arnhem*, p.111. Fought with 2nd Battalion Paras in North Africa (El Aounia) and Arnhem. Lived at 40 Mand St, Manchester. Photo in Longson and Taylor, *Arnhem Odyssey*, p.142 and at AJEX Museum, and IWM offices, Film and Sound Archives.

918417 Corporal Jack Alfred Linden. *JIW.* 1st Para Brigade Intelligence, 89 Paras, Field Security Section. MIA/POW – *The Times*, 11 October 1944. Son of Mr and Mrs R. Linden, 289 Bracknell Gdns, London NW3 (AJEX Index Cards and P. Reinders). Photo from Corporal Deeley of Intelligence Corps Museum; says some of the section spoke Yiddish, so there were probably other Jews in 89 FSS.

Private McManners. Jewish refugee – *JIW*; possibly McManus, below.

Sergeant Martin Maxwell, aka Max Meisels. Para Regiment/Glider Pilot, AAC. Austrian Jewish Refugee adopted by Webber family in London. Wounded/missing – *JC*, 20 October 1944. POW Stalag 11 Fallingbostel near Hanover (*JC* and personal interview). Photo AJEX Museum. Also landed on D-Day. Made video with Steven Spielberg Foundation, telling his story, where he gave his *Tephillin* (phylacteries) to a Christian chaplain, to care for, before take-off – and afterwards got them back.

14623408/354553/13805573 Private Heinz Mendelsohn, fought as Johnny Melford. 2nd Battalion Sussex Regiment then 21st Independent Paras. Refugee from Berlin, born 13 September 1922. Volunteered for Paras in early 1943 – *JIW* and letter from P. Block. Kent, *First In*, p.132, describes how Melford was wounded when a bullet passed through both cheeks as he yawned, giving him dimples for life. Served from March 1941 to August 1946, later commissioned into the Royal Sussex Regiment – letter to author and photo at AJEX Museum. Also fought North Africa, Italy, Yugoslavia.

1465052 RAF Corporal Samuel Mendoza. Husband of Mrs M.J. Mendoza, 17 Streathbourne Rd, London SW17. Electronics ground staff att. Paras – Jewish Chaplain Card, and photo of his RAF group after escape from Arnhem sent by niece Anne Mendoza/Ross.

13807470 Sergeant Mertz, fought as 14623944 John McManus. Refugee – *JIW*, P. Block and P. Reinders. Fought with 21st Independent Paras, also in North Africa, Italy, Norway and Palestine.

Lieutenant Colonel Mervin Mirsky. Staff Officer, Canadian Army HQ. Present at the drop and the bridge 'Block' – letter from him in Canada.

10584589 Private E.V.B. Mordecai. 1st Airborne Division Field Park, RAOC. At the bridge – Middlebrook, *Arnhem*, p.481 (tbc) POW no. 117843, Stalag 11B (P. Reinders).

Colonel (later Brigadier) Edmund Charles Wolf Myers. DSO (22 April 1943), CBE (6 January 1944), Bronze Lion of Netherlands (20 March 1947), MiD (10 October 1952), American Legion of Merit. Information from *WWRT: Addendum*. Son of Dr C.S. Myers, psychologist to BEF in France in First World War, and Edith Seligman. Born 12 October 1906, died 6 December 1997, aged 91. At Arnhem was Airborne Divisional Commander of the Royal Engineers and known as 'Tito' to his men – had fought with the partisans in Greece as member of SOE. Sent by Urquhart, at the height of the Oosterbeek fighting, across the Rhine to link up with XXX Corps and tell Horrocks and Browning to get a move on. Then led and accompanied the Polish Paras across the Rhine to support the British; returned (after discussion with Captain Heaps – see below) to accompany the Dorsets across in a DUKW to do the same, on night of the 24/25 September, with three important letters for Urquhart. Reached beleaguered Hartenstein HQ at 6.05 a.m. with order to withdraw all Paras south across the river. Myers in overall command of the evacuation on the last night, selecting routes and fixing ferrying; Urquhart (p.143) says: 'There was no need to underline just how vital were his technical experience and his qualities of character to the division's survival.' (Long article on his Yugoslav activities in *JC*, October 1944 and *JIW*. Author of a book on his SOE exploits in Greece, *Greek Entanglement*. Obituary, *The Times*, December 1997, and photo at Museum.) Also fought in Korea, where he was MiD.

2578967 (?) QMS R (Ronald/Raymond/Rudolf?) Nabarro. 1st Airborne Recce Squadron Photo in J. Fairley, *Remember Arnhem* (London: Imperial War Musuem, 1978).

14442780 Private/Sergeant David Nussbaum, fought as Neville Niven 9th Paras. Shot down and badly injured in glider en route to Arnhem drop. Born Gelsenkirchen, Bochum, Germany, 16 July 1925, and came with *Kindertransport* to Britain. Served TA and No. 3 ITC. Letter from wife Gertie in Bristol Road, Birmingham. Died 1990. Photo at Museum.

0-807301 2nd Lieutenant Navigator Sherman I. Phillips. 61st US TCS. Took off Saltby, on three flights over Arnhem. From Brooklyn, New York. Letter from Admiral Mondt – see Feldman, listed above.

Lieutenant H.M. Pollack/Pollak. Pioneer Corps to 21st Independent Paras, MC. Later served in Burma. Information from Leighton-Langer, *King's Most Loyal Enemy Aliens.*

13807478 or 87 Private George (Harry Pistol) Preger, fought as Bruce. 21st Independent Paras. Austrian refugee. *JIW* and talk with Schilling, but Block says was not at Arnhem.

Private Rosen, fought as Radwell. Refugee – *JIW*.

207030 Sgt. Ronald Rose. Glider Pilot.WIA and escaped across Rhine but maybe POW Stalag 11B, No. 118468 and P. Reinders ABRG – letter from widow in *JIW* notes.

4914584 Private/S/Sergeant Ronald or S. Rosenberg. Glider Pilot, 2nd Battalion S. Staffs. Regiment. From Brighton (*JIW*). POW Stalag 12a, no. 891879 (P. Reinders; Middlebrook, *Arnhem*, p.479).

4915089 Sergeant John Noel Rosenberg/burg. MM for gallantry and distinguished service in the field (P. Reinders), AAC. AJEX Jewish Chaplain Index Card. Gazetted 9 November 1944. 156th Paras, C Company, 10 Platoon.

Sergeant Rosenbloom. MM, 'T' Coy, 1st Battalion Paras. Sniper and sergeant instructor – information from Mr Tom Angus Craig of Burnley who served with both Rosenbloom and John Rosenberg after Arnhem, and P. Reinders. When 1st Battalion went to Palestine, the two sergeants did not serve. Telephone call as a result of Teletext advert.

13801214 Rosenthal, fought as Redferne. 21st Independent Paras. *JIW*.

1596358 St Sergeant Harvey Rossdale. MIA/WIA 27 October 1944. Lived at 124 Biddulph Mansions, Elgin Avenue, London W9. May not have been at Arnhem (tbc).

7403928 Private L.S. Rubin. 181 Para Field Ambulance (Cherry, *Red Berets and Red Crosses*). No Jewish Chaplain Card found.

3326640 Private Sidney Rubinstein. 'A' Coy, 1st Platoon 7th KOSB/HLI/Airborne. POW. From Glasgow – letter G. Gourlay and *JC*, 25 May 1945. Jewish Chaplain Card – son of Mrs J. Rubinstein, 166 Gorbals St, Glasgow 5. Served a sentence for insubordination in Glasgow barracks.

30100326 Sergeant David Salik. Polish Paras. Born 20 February 1914, Sande/Sanok, near Lvov, son of Salim and Rozalia, née Tyn. POW Russia 18 September 1939 to 9 February 1942, escaped (*JC*, Spring 1997). Served in Poland 1939; Iran/Iraq/Palestine 1942; Para Field Ambulance, 3rd Para Battalion; awarded Field Para Badge, Army Medal, Bronze Cross of Merit with Swords, and four British medals. Photo AJEX Museum and personal interview.

14213424 Private Jack Saltman. 'A' Coy, 1st Platoon KOSB/1st Airborne, Medical Orderly. Son of Louis Saltman of 3 Marchmont Cres., Edinburgh 9. POW – *JC*, 1 December 1944 and letter from Captain G. Gourlay – Jewish Chaplain Card.

Private Gustav 'Gus' Sander. RAMC Field Ambulance and Intelligence MID, POW, escaped 7 times. German refugee. Later lieutenant in Middlesex Regiment, commanding 6th platoon, 'B' Company; KIA in Korea, 30 October 1950, during attack on village of Tae-Dong near Chongju; commemorated on plaque at Pusan CWGC Cemetery. Letter from comrade Peter Davis, TD, and Mr Barrett, Korean War archivist of Middlesex Regiment. Also letter from nephew Mark Sander. Photo and archive at AJEX Museum.

13805947/14623980 Sergeant Schilling. Fought as Harold Bruce, 21st Independent Paras. German refugee from Berlin – *JIW* and personal call. Gordonstoun School. Also fought North Africa, Italy, Norway.

13807724 Schivern. 21st Independent Paras. Refugee – *JIW*.

Robert Schlesinger (?), aka Bobby Shaw. All information from comrade QMS and WO Eddy Pruden, 7348767, 16th Para Field Ambulance. Schlesinger wore a Methodist dog-tag and was a Viennese Jew. He lived in a children's home near Bolton and then was interned; later went to the PC and then Intelligence Corps, as he spoke German. He then volunteered for the Paras in the 1st Para Brigade at Arnhem, where he was POW; he met Pruden in Stalag 2A near Brandenburg. He told Pruden that he had captured an old German schoolfriend at Arnhem, who then captured him later! His brother had a pub in Dalston, London, after the war and Bobby was in the rag trade.

Eric Schubert-Stevens. 21st Independent Paras. Austrian origin, according to comrades. Originally Dorset Regiment. No Jewish Chaplain Card and probably enlisted as C. of E.

23(5)97136 Signalman Ellis 'Dutch' Schultz, aka Schulberg. RCOS. Interview with B. Fryman, 1st Airborne Division Signals, 'E' Section, C.O. Captain L. Golden (listed above). Lived Harrogate after war –

call from comrade John Harris. Evader – letter from comrade Sig. George Ball. Son of Bernard of 178 Mayfield Rd, Edinburgh – AJEX Chaplain Cards and P. Reinders.

160552 2nd Lieutenant Ralph Harding Schwartz. Assistant Adjutant, S. Staffs. Regiment. Jewish Chaplain Cards and information from P. Reinders.

5731130 Corporal Laurence Scott/Solomon/Solly Scott. 21st Independent Paras. Father Jewish and fought in First World War. Born London, 13 March 1920. Sergeant in Metropolitan Police 1946–76, winning the GM in 1967. Escaped across the Rhine with Canadian and Royal Engineers, paddling when motor failed. Details from himself by letter and telephone calls. Photo at AJEX Museum.

14564670 Sergeant Horsa Glider Pilot Raphael Shovel. 'F' Squadron. WIA, aged 21; escaped during evacuation – letter and Jewish Chaplain Card. Served also D-Day and assisted in UK in preparation of Israel's War of Independence.

J23634 FO Ernest Frederick Siegel. RCAF. 570 Squadron took off from Harwell in Stirling 4-E7Y EF 306, Air Bomber, on 17 September 1944 at 1145 hrs, returning at 1615 hrs. AIR 27 records at PRO.

Sergeant Glider Pilot Simon. AAC. German Jewish refugee; friend of Hagen – information from Hagen. Could be E. Simeom, KIA.

Sq. Ldr. Philip "Smuggler" Smulian, dropped supplier on Arnhem. From South Africa RAF 512 Sqdn. – awarded A.F.C.

13804270 Sobotka. 21st Independent Paras. Refugee – *JIW* and P. Block letter.

5043849 Lance Corporal Bernard Soley. Medical Orderly 4th Dorsets. Helped evacuate Airborne wounded from Arnhem across the Rhine downstream, 300 yards from the bridge; WIA. Photo and letter at AJEX Museum.

14646399 Private Max Sorkin. 8th Battalion, Middlesex, Wessex Division. Mortar and heavy machine-gun support to Airborne near the bridge at Arnhem – letter and personal interview. Was 18 years old in 1944; now lives in Aylesbury.

Private Mane Spiegelglass. DCM, 156 Para Battalion, Para Regiment. German refugee, aged 21. *JC*, 8 and 22 December 1944, and P. Reinders. May have used another name

14623976 or 47/13801629 St/Sergeant John Hubert Stanleigh (nom de guerre)/Hans Schwarz. 21st Independent Para Coy and bomb disposal.

Born 5 July 1919 in Poznan, Poland. Personal interview with comrade, Laurence Scott. Stanleigh was sent on a secret mission to France after D-Day to contact French Resistance, before Arnhem operation. Recommended MM but ineligible due to nationality. Was a founder of Ex-Services CND after the war. Photo at AJEX Museum and letter from wife Rita in Bristol. Also MoD records. Also fought North Africa, Italy, France and Norway.

0-701063 Flight Lieutenant Pilot Irving J. Sternoff. 309th Squadron, 315th Troop Carrier. Dropped Paras into Arnhem – letter to author, December 2000. Lives Kirkland, Washington, USA. Fifty-five holes in Dakota on return from one drop carrying British Paras. Also dropped troops in Normandy, Battle of the Bulge and many other missions.

Subkovitch. Paras. Information from G. Levy (listed above). No further details known, but there was a Sergeant Alfred Supkovitch, no. 1893423, RAF, 207 Squadron, MIA/KIA, of 141 Fieldgate Mansions, Romford St, London E1, KIA 19 September 1944 – *JC*, 26 January 1945.

6091548 Sergeant Malcolm Sumeray. 11th Battalion Paras. MIA/WIA/POW – letter from brother. Born 6 June 1919 in East End of London. Queen's Royal West Surreys. Son of Isadore and Cissy of 16 Gloucester Gdns, London NW11; former JLB member, *JC*, 9 March 1945. Malcolm was severely wounded in the head, arms and legs by tank and mortar fire and left for dead. Weeks later, a German broadcast announced him as POW, but Whitehall said German broadcasts were not official and he was still presumed killed. Months of anxiety passed until a letter from him reached his home in February 1945 (cutting from late 1940s *Golders Green Gazette* from friend Danny Miller and wife Jose).

3658220 Private A Sunderland. 13th Battalion Paras. MIA/POW, Stalag 12A, no. 26067, Dorset Regiment. Son of Mr and Mrs H. Sunderland, 22 Salisbury Drive, Prestwich, Manchester – *JC*, 15 December 1944.

30068370 Lance Corporal Jozef Szreiber. Polish Paras. Born 11 February 1922, Warsaw, son of Jakub and Adela, née Gingold. 2nd Para Battalion, awarded Field Para Badge and four British medals.

Lieutenant Albert Louis 'Tan' Tannenbaum. 2nd Battalion, Paras HQ Coy. WIA/POW. Son of Mr and Mrs J. Tannenbaum, 46 Basing Hill, Wembley Park, London. East Surreys, commissioned in the field North Africa; 1st Airborne evader; wounded attempting escape – *JC*, 5 January 1945, and photo. Also photo in General John Frost, *A Drop too Many*, at AJEX Museum, and letter from CO Lieutenant Colonel D.E.C. Russell.

P/1364 2nd Lieutenant (Medical Corps) Dr Henryk Urich. Polish Paras. Later Professor of Neuropathology at the London Hospital, Whitechapel. Born 15 August 1916, Vienna, son of Joachim and Maria, née Rosenstock. Served France 1940, Ambulance Coy, 4th Cadre Rifle Brigade, and 3rd and 1st Polish Paras; awarded Field Para Badge, Cross of Valour and four British medals.

Unknown. Dutch Jewish woman in hiding in Oosterbeek who donned a British helmet and ran out under fire to bring back parachuted food containers for British troops (Middlebrook, *Arnhem*, p.400).

Captain Maurice Victor. Royal Canadian AMC, Knight Officer of the Order of Orange Nassau with Swords (*Canadian Jews at War*, Canadian Jewish Congress, 1948), att. 1st Airborne. Born Camora, Saskatchewan. Escaped.

T/S P.D. Waterman. USAAF WO serving with RAF. Took off from Harwell 295 Squadron. AIR 22/1644 at PRO. Verification of religion required.

Sergeant Weiner. Leader Section 4, 8th Platoon, 'B' Coy, 1st or 4th Para Brigade. May be a pseudonym: see Tom Angus, *Men in Arnhem* (London: Leo Cooper) p.77.

P/13677 Private/Lieutenant (Witko) Paul/Pawel Weitzen. (Medical Corps) Polish Paras. *JIW*. Born 18 November 1908, Stanislawow, son of Izak and Genia, née Zukier. Served France 1939–40, 10th Ambulance Coy, 10th Armoured Cavalry Brigade, and 2nd and 3rd Para Battalions; awarded Army Medal and four British medals.

289605 Sergeant Hyman Woltag. Glider Pilot, 'C' Squadron, former JLB. WIA; husband of Mrs B. Woltag, 101 Edgware Court, Edgware, Middlesex – *JC*, 6 October 1944. Flew from Tarrant Rushton; wounded in back by shrapnel but managed to escape across the Rhine with friend John McGeough on night of 25 September – letter from John McGeough of Cheadle in Cheshire.

Hyman Yallow/Yellow. From Hendon; article in *Ham and High Gazette* November–September 1945/46,seen at Holborn Local History Library.

J38588 F/O William Zelicovitz. RCAF 437 att. RAF as Acting Squadron Leader. Squadron took off 23 September to Arnhem from Blakehill Farm in Dakota F2639 – PRO Records AIR 1876 and Jewish Chaplain Index Cards at AJEX Museum. Zelicowitz described sorties over Arnhem as 'us having the sh— kicked out of us but going back for more!!'

Aircraft were lost and damaged on each flight. Died June 1997 – letter from son Martin in Toronto and photo at AJEX Museum.

4804144 Corporal Ernest Abbott Zitman. 89th Field Security (Intelligence). POW no. 118794 Stalag 11B (tbc) – P. Reinders. Photo at AJEX. Fluent Icelandic speaker, joined 89 FS section from 319 in Faeroe Islands. Jumped with 4th Paras 18 September 1944, WIA 22 September, POW 25 September. From 'G' Intelligence supplied by Graeme Deeley, of Airborne Regiment Research; report states: 'Cpl Zitman distinguished himself, putting out fires under trying circumstances, bagging a sniper on 21st, carrying wounded and keeping up morale, until he himself was wounded and evacuated.'

2087757 Corporal Desire David Charles Zucker. RA then 89th Field Security. Photo at Hartenstein museum with Zitman and AJEX. At Arnhem, according to Intelligence Corps Veterans records. Jewish Chaplain Card – wife at 26 Carlton Mansions, Holmleigh Rd, London N16.

Len Zurakov. Radio man to Lazarus USAAF (listed above), 309th Squadron, 315th Troop Carrier. Tape from Sternoff and letter from Len – now lives in Israel. He wrote: 'We dropped British Paras at Arnhem and the sight of them being shot down as they landed was terrible.'

Fin? 1st Forward Observer Unit, RA, formerly RWK Regiment. Other name not known – letter from Mr Brearton, Arnhem Veterans Association; could be Gordon Finglass, WIA/POW, 6346424 21st Independent Paras, died 1997 – archives at Airborne Museum, Aldershot.

(A total of 179)

Awards

DFC	2
DFM	1
Certificate of Gallantry	1
MM	5
MiD	4
OBE	1
MC	5
CBE	1
DCM	1
Polish Virtuti Militari	2
Polish MM	5
Polish Bronze Cross of Merit	1
Polish Cross of Valour	1
Bronze Lion of Netherlands	1
Dutch War Cross	1
Dutch Knight Officer of the Order of Orange Nassau	2
Dutch Medal of Freedom	1
Kings Commendation for Brave Conduct	1

Lionel Pekarsky, aka Pack, led the team which designed the heavy gliders for carrying vehicles used at Arnhem, for Fairey/De Haviland. Born 1913, died 2003 – obituary, *The Times*, undated.

This study has been published by the *Military History Society Journal* and on the internet, and also placed with the British Airborne Museum, Aldershot; the Arnhem Airborne Museum, Oosterbeek, Holland; the Imperial War Museum, The National Archives and British Libraries; the RAF Museum, Hendon; the Arnhem Battle Research Group, Holland; the Arnhem Battle Veterans Associations; and many individuals around the world who helped the author complete this work.

Three further possible Jewish Paras at Arnhem, taken from Special Forces Arnhem website are – Lt. Bruno Henry Haeffner, Gilder Pilot; Lt. Martin Kauffmam, KOSB, WIA, POW; Lt. Eric H. Steele-Baume, born 1-1-1910, lived in Brighton, Cameronians 1932–1958.

Lieutenant Marcus Bloom ('Urbain'/'Bishop'), MiD: A Jewish Hero of the SOE[1]

Early Life

Marcus Reginald Bloom was born in Tottenham, north London, on 24 September 1907, into an orthodox Jewish home,[2] the second of four brothers (Alex, Marcus, Bernard and Jenice)[3]. He was the son of Harry Pizer (Percy) Bloom – born in East London in 1882, to poor Polish Jewish immigrants – and Anna Sadie Davidoff, born in Russia around 1882 and brought to England the same year. Anna's family were small shop-keepers, also in the East End. Anna and Harry were married in the early 1900s and the newly-weds moved from a Brick Lane 'over the shop' address and rented a house in Tottenham, where Alex and then Marcus were born. From a very young age, Harry (who died in 1949; Anna died in 1946) had been a successful small businessman so when the Zeppelin raids hit the East End during the First World War, Harry had by then earned enough to move his family away to the safety of Hove in Sussex, where the family lived at 13 Medina Villas[4] until 1929. As a young man, and after attending Cranford College in Maidenhead and later Hove High School, Marcus often helped out, working at his father's cinema in Wandsworth[5] south London, or in their mail order textile firm, or at their restaurant business in Hove. Just before the Second World War, when his parents separated, and the family – now quite well-off – were living in various hotels around London, Marcus moved to Paris.

Bernard Bloom describes his brother Marcus as having a great sense of humour and a love of good food and the cinema. He was by far the most adventurous of the brothers and thus it was he whom their father sent to Paris in the 1930s to run the mail order business, Sterling Textiles. He took an office in the Boulevard Haussman and learnt French. He employed Baron Michel de Tavenau as his manager and it was he who taught Marcus how to ride, play polo and shoot. As the business prospered, Marcus took an expensively-furnished apartment in Clichy. His life changed and he mixed with the wealthy French minor aristocracy. He owned a white Arab pony called Rajah, a Great Dane dog called Sphinx and a pale blue convertible Delage car which he drove wearing a white flying helmet. With his girlfriend Germaine Fevrier (who was from Village du Tot, Barneville-sur-Mer in La Manche, Normandy), he and the baron were often seen at race meetings. He was generous to his friends in France and England and adored his mother, for whom he always bought expensive gifts. After five years, however, the firm closed, following a court case in England when the *News of the World* newspaper questioned the morality of mail order as a means of selling to the public.

Marcus returned to London and married Germaine in March 1938 at St Marylebone Registry Office, and they took a flat in north-west London. Germaine was unhappy in England and went back and forth to France, where she happened to be – and was trapped – when the Maginot Line collapsed before the German Blitzkrieg in 1940.

SOE

Marcus had originally volunteered within forty-eight hours of the outbreak of war on 3 September 1939, and he was interviewed at Clapham Junction recruiting office by a staff sergeant. Marcus told him he spoke fluent French and wished to use it in the service of his country. Three weeks later he was summoned to the War Office with Bernard accompanying him. He was interviewed by a major, but turned down. They had not tested his French or knowledge of France and asked only about his religion, job and the birthplace of his parents. They said that as his mother had not been born in England, he could not be recruited for the use of his French, hence the rejection. Angry but undeterred, in mid-1941 Marcus enlisted as a private in the Royal Artillery and by December 1941 was an officer.[6] He was soon summoned to SOE offices at Norgeby House in Baker Street. Met by Vera Atkins (the formidable PA to Colonel Maurice Buckmaster, the leader of the French Section of SOE[7]), he was brought before the colonel who – to Marcus's surprise – was wearing a casual sports jacket and trousers.

Marcus's file was lying unopened on Buckmaster's desk (he had given shooting and riding as his hobbies); he stared for a few moments at Marcus and then said, 'Tell me fully what you were doing in France for five years.'[8] Marcus explained in detail and the interview continued half in French, half in English; Marcus said he knew Paris and La Manche well and had travelled on business all over Europe, and that he was 'willing to undertake special duties'. Finally Buckmaster said, 'I must tell you that the people who work for us are taking on a dangerous job … and it is not for the faint-hearted. You should now return to your unit and in the meantime I will consider whether we can use you. If you have second thoughts about it please advise your Commanding Officer.'

Three weeks later Marcus was summoned again to see Buckmaster,

17.1 Lt Marcus Bloom, MiD, SOE, murdered at Mauthausen Death Camp.

17.2 Bernard (left) and Jenice Bloom, brothers of Marcus, at a Mauthausen Camp commemoration, representing the British inmates, in May 1970.

who was this time in uniform. 'Since I have not heard from your CO, I must assume you still wish to join our organisation.' Marcus said he did. 'I have decided that you are suitable material ... you must not discuss your activities with anyone. All your work will be top secret.' The colonel stood up and, in a complete change of tone, put out his hand to Marcus and said, 'Welcome to the Firm. I wish you every success in your training.'[9]

Marcus was formally accepted into SOE 'F' (French) Section on 24 February 1942[10] and was sent to Scotland for his initial assault-course training, which must have been particularly hard for a man of his age (he was then 35 years old). With balding red hair and moustache, hazel eyes, and standing five foot eight inches tall, an excerpt from his paramilitary training report at Arisaig (see Appendix 1) by his instructor says: 'Hardly the build for hard work on the hills, but always gets there with a smile on his face although completely done in. He has plenty of "guts" and is an extremely able man. He has a very sound knowledge on all branches of the training, and has done exceptionally well.'[11] The commandant's report (dated 15 and 17 May 1942) went on to say:

> MICHEL[12] has done very well indeed. His willingness to try anything has been an excellent example to the others. Possessed of a keen sense of humour, he has been the life and soul of the party. He is a very nice fellow who has plenty of intelligence and 'guts'. Company seems to stimulate him to greater efforts, so he should work very well with others. Seems very English.[13]

Opposed to this is a nasty quote in the book by Sarah Helm,[14] where Roger de Wesselow (major, Coldstream Guards[15]), head of an 'F' Section Training School at Wanborough Manor in Surrey, in an official training report, makes the anti-Semitic remark that 'physical effort seems to come hard to this pink yid',[16] adding that Bloom 'keeps under his shell the usual racial nimbleness'. In the same report, Lieutenant R.F. Turner describes Marcus as 'slightly Jewish in his outlook and appearance'. What this can mean, readers can only judge for themselves. Thus was the racism of the officer class at that time.

Marcus then continued at Wanborough Manor to train as a wireless operator (WO) in Morse code, decoding and repairs of equipment. After this he was sent to Ringway near Manchester for parachute training and was then recalled by Buckmaster, who told him he was needed in the field urgently. What he did not say was that SOE were losing WOs at an alarming rate.

'Urbain'

Marcus was given a short leave; his mother was no fool and realized there was some French connection and that this meant dangerous work somewhere behind enemy lines. He consoled her with the fact that there were plenty of escape routes if things went wrong.[17] Back at Baker Street he was given the code name 'Urbain'[18] and, like all agents, a fictitious new background. Dressed in authentic all-French clothes and personal items, with his false papers in the name of Michel Boileau or Blount,[19] money and briefcase wireless set, he was embarked on a troop ship – much to his surprise – to Gibraltar in August 1942. There he was joined by another SOE agent. From here he sent a telegram to his brother Bernard, who was in a military hospital in Ranchi, India, saying, 'Many Happy Returns of the day, get well soon, I salute you. Marcus.' This in fact was the last time Bernard Bloom ever heard from his brother.

According to Bernard Bloom's research, one morning some weeks later (probably about 18/19 October), Marcus was warned to prepare himself, and that night was put aboard a naval motor torpedo boat with his colleague, and taken in darkness to a submarine lying offshore, which they boarded. Travelling all night, the submarine surfaced in the early dark morning and Marcus and his colleague, with the captain and two sailors, went onto the conning tower. Then they launched a small rubber dinghy tied to the submarine and peered out to the nearby dim coastline. Suddenly, from slightly inland, a light flashed the code letter 'Q', the arranged signal, and the two agents and two sailors embarked on the dinghy and rowed towards the shore.

There is, however, a different official version of this. Richards[20] says that Marcus was inserted after an eight-day journey by the Polish SOE felucca *Seadog*, commanded by Captain Buchowski in Operation Watchman III, Overgrow and Dubonnet[21] on the night of 3/4 November 1942 at Port Miou near Cassis in southern France.[22] With him were SOE agents Lieutenant Colonel George Starr, DSO, MC; Mary Herbert; Mme M.T. Le Chene; and the famous Odette Sansom, GC.

Into France

Whatever the truth, on reaching the beach near Cassis, two men appeared from behind a hut and told the SOE agents to follow them. According to Tickell[23] the reception party was headed by Resistance leader Marsac, of the nearby Marseilles Group. After a night in a safe-house nearby, they continued their journey next day by train to Toulouse, where the other agents left Marcus for different assignments. Marcus was to work with the Resistance circuit named 'Pimento'.

M.R.D. Foot (SOE's official historian) describes Marcus's arrival less flatteringly.[24] He alleges that Marcus arrived at Toulouse railway station wearing a conspicuous, loud check coat and smoking a pipe. He made contact correctly in a warehouse – as arranged – with his control, Tony

Brooks.[25] When they met, Marcus held out his hand and with a broad grin and in his cockney voice allegedly said, 'Ow are yer, mate?' Brooks thought this a breach of security – using English in a place where informers may be listening. In addition, Marcus had already spent twenty-four hours in Toulouse chatting in the flat of Maurice Pertschuk (he and Pertschuck – another Jewish agent – had trained together in England[26]) and in fact had allegedly – against all security rules – made this rendezvous arrangement in England before they left for France. As a result, Brooks passed Marcus on to Pertschuck, whose WO and second in command of the circuit he then became. However, Foot gives his source (in a note) for this information as 'private' and there is, therefore, no way this can ever now be confirmed or denied – especially as Marcus and Pertschuck did not survive to respond to the truth or otherwise of this anecdote.

Opposed to this view is that of French SOE agent Robert Martin, in his debrief in London, who described Marcus as 'willing and courageous if temperamental, and anxious to do more important work than being a W.O'.[27]

Be that as it may, in the following months, beginning 8 January 1943,[28] Marcus worked very successfully and sent and received many messages to and from London (estimated at over fifty), having to keep constantly on the move to avoid the German radio detection vans. Marcus also assisted in sending and receiving messages for Starr in circuit 'Wheelwright'.[29]

One of his favourite ploys was to sit on a river bank pretending to fish whilst using the rod as an aerial. Another fellow agent described how Marcus also transmitted in open country using a long forked pole to tap the current from overhead cables. Although cars were often stopped by the Germans and Vichy French, and searched for black-market goods, Marcus persisted bravely in using his *permis de circular* in the service of the Resistance group in which he worked.[30] He also organized receipt of four drops of stores for his circuit,[31] which included much arms and explosives for the Resistance,[32] as well as assisting RAF evaders to get to Spain on at least one occasion.[33] Marcus also assisted in carrying out repeated acts of sabotage on telecommunications and railways.[34] In late spring, Pertschuck had to visit Marcus to repair his radio for him. Occasionally, Germaine would also visit Marcus from Normandy.

Marcus, now working comfortably in circuit 'Prunus' with Pertschuk,[35] received instruction from London to plan to destroy the Toulouse powder (explosives) factory that Pertschuk had been investigating. For this work, Marcus was Mentioned in Despatches.

Betrayal

Marcus was hiding out at the Château d'Équerre at Fonsorbs with the Vicomte d'Aligny, when at dawn one day in April 1943 (certainly before

15 April[36]), the villa hideout of Marcus and his comrades[37] was betrayed and surrounded by SS troops. Although escape was attempted, they were all captured. Marcus and a Spanish member of his group, Robert, ran into the surrounding wood, handcuffed together, firing pistols at the pursuing Germans, and made it an astonishing fourteen kilometres away to a local gendarmerie,[38] having crossed a river seven times to throw the Germans off their trail; but Robert became exhausted and suggested going to the French police at Murray (near Toulouse) where the *capitaine* was a known Gaullist. Arriving at 5 a.m., however, a different officer (a brigadier) said he would fetch the *capitaine*. But he disappeared and instead the Gestapo arrived. One story is that the French police gave them away at their hideout, another that it was a local SOE double agent; nobody really knows to this day. According to Foot it may have been the Franco-German double agent Roger Bardet, known as 'Le Boiteau'.

On 17 July 1945, after the war, British Intelligence Captain Hazeldene interviewed M. Colle at 27 Rue Lepic in Paris. Colle had shared a cell with Marcus at Fresnes, between 23 March and 25 May 1944, and told the story that Marcus related to him. In fact, Marcus had been arrested at the château at 10 p.m. on the night of 13 April 1943 by the Gestapo; he substantiated the rest of the story of Marcus's capture.

Later that day Marcus was seen, his face covered in blood, being escorted to the military prison in Toulouse.[39]

Foot argues that, again defying security training, Marcus and Pertschuck had previously held a meeting at a black-market restaurant where all seven leaders of 'Prunus' were sitting at a single table, chattering in English over dinner.

Foot's assertion, that security among 'Prunus' agents was lax, was challenged after the war (according to Bernard Bloom) and some SOE agents successfully sued Foot for giving a misleading picture in his book; Marcus, of course, was dead and so could not speak out.

The SD (Sicherheitsdienst – Nazi Party Security Service) had arrested Marcus and found among his belongings a photo of Pertschuck in British uniform; somehow this had escaped security detection in England before he was inserted into France. This was disastrous as it not only blew Pertschuck's cover but the Germans could use it against other captured agents who knew Pertschuck. It could even be used to suggest that the Germans had a spy in Baker Street – also useful to get captured agents to confess.

Josef Goetz, the SD Section IV Paris wireless expert, was sent imme-diately to Toulouse to try to 'play' Bloom's captured wireless and codes to the British (pretending he was Bloom). But Bloom behaved impeccably and gave no information to his torturers. The British thus knew at once from Goetz's faulty messages that Marcus had been captured. Goetz did not know Marcus's security check and Baker Street sent one particular set of messages asking Marcus to meet them at 'the Green pub' that only Marcus would know about (in fact it was the Manchester Arms in Baker Street, frequented by SOE personnel when at HQ). Goetz's puzzled replies to this request showed clearly that he was controlling the wireless[40] and not Marcus.[41]

Taken to Paris, Marcus was imprisoned at the notorious Fresnes prison in the suburbs of the French capital, a building that was host to many SOE agents during the 'silent war'. In his cell were two French Resistance workers, one Spanish *passeur* and a third Frenchman who was railway controller at Montparnasse, named Leopold Turcan; he was accused of passing information on railway movement to the Allies.[42] All of them were demoralized and unkempt but Marcus struck up a friendship with Turcan who, like Marcus, knew Paris well.

Interrogation

Next day Marcus was taken in manacles to that other notorious location in Occupied France, the Gestapo HQ in Avenue Foch in the centre of Paris, where he was questioned about his Resistance circuit, codes and comrades as well his superiors in London. He refused to say anything but his name, rank and number. He was then marched down a corridor to another room and shoved violently inside. He was pushed into a chair in the middle of the room by two men in suits. One man stood in front of him and again Marcus refused to answer questions, upon which he was struck fiercely in the face by the back of the Gestapo man's hand. Again he refused to answer questions and so the second man came from behind and pointed a revolver at Marcus's temple. Yet again he refused to answer and he was struck on the head by the butt of the gun. He fell to the floor, blood running down his face, as one of the men kicked him. The interrogators left the room and another guard helped Marcus up and he was driven back to Fresnes.

At one point it was rumoured by a sympathetic member of the French Sûreté that Marcus had been executed in Fresnes in July 1943, a rumour which proved untrue.[43]

In the cell, Turcan bathed Marcus's wounds with water and he slowly recovered, helped by his anger at those who had beaten him but got nothing out of him. To keep up morale, Marcus persuaded the others to keep clean, exercise, wash their clothes, shave and have daily discussions. Through his strength of character, he welded their resolve to resist.

Marcus's brother Bernard met Turcan many times after the war, and Turcan testified to the way in which Marcus had helped him stay alive. He too was taken and beaten at Avenue Foch, and in return Marcus nursed him back to health. When Germaine heard he had been caught and was in Fresnes, she moved to Paris and had food parcels smuggled into him – at great risk to herself – which he always shared with his cellmates.

On a second occasion, Marcus was taken to Avenue Foch and severely beaten about his body; again he said nothing. Much of the time at Fresnes he spent talking to Turcan about his work before he was captured. He also resolved to escape by trying to convince the Germans that if they moved him to a camp, he would be more cooperative; his idea was that whilst in transit he would find it easier to make his getaway than from a high security prison like Fresnes. Turcan advised against this but eventually Marcus succeeded and bid farewell to his fellow prisoners.[44]

Mauthausen

Bernard Bloom has been unable to find any information about the next fifteen months of Marcus's imprisonment in Germany. However, the author discovered the personal archive, at the Imperial War Museum, of the late Vera Atkins.[45] It reveals that her immediate post-war research and interviews with German war criminals and eyewitnesses in many camps and prisons, over a long period of time,[46] showed that Marcus had arrived at Mauthausen from a fortress-style camp called Ravitch (Ravitsch) on the Polish/Silesia border, north-east of Breslau (now Wroclaw), some time in August 1944. This was owing to the rapid Soviet advances, and they were marched west by the Germans towards Dresden, then taken to Gusen,[47] a satellite camp of Mauthausen, near Linz in Austria.[48] Marcus either met other Dutch and British SOE agents and even one American at Gusen, or they all had come from Ravitsch together. In any case they formed a cohesive group and always kept themselves separate and well fed as far as they could. They were much admired by the other prisoners.

Another letter in the Vera Atkins archive, dated 14 September 1945, is written by Captain Rousset (French agent 'Leopold'), who was also a prisoner of war. He had been at Fresnes for three months with Marcus. He says he had been at Ravitsch from 18 April 1944 and that he saw the Allied SOE prisoners dressed in blue prison uniform, with a white triangle marked with 'I' on the back, and that they were all kept together in the same wing of the camp. It appears Marcus arrived there in May 1944.[49]

On July 30 1944, following the aborted attempt on Hitler's life, orders reached various Nazi camp commanders from General Keitel on 18 August, that 'terrorists' and saboteurs should be severely dealt with. Marcus and his comrades realized that this was a death sentence for them.

On 2 September 1944, the group was taken by lorry from Gusen, through the village of Mauthausen and up hill to a dark, granite fortress which was the notorious Death and Labour Camp. In front of two high double gates, a guard telephoned and then the gates slowly opened as they drove into a large cobbled courtyard. To the left stood the main prison wall, to the right were arches, each with green double doors. Ahead was a house with a long stone balcony and in front stood the SS commandant of the camp, looking at them. Some archway doors were opened and the men were shoved through these. In the camp records it is recorded in section 16: 'arrivals Sept. 2nd … 47 Allied soldiers; 39 Dutch; 7 Britons; 1 USA'.

The archway cavern in which these forty-seven SOE men were placed was usually a transport depot, cold and dank. There was no food that night and only thin gruel and black bread the next day. On the third afternoon, each man was ordered to open his shirt and numbers from one to forty seven were painted on their chests. This was the order in which they were to be shot.

The End

On 6 September the weather was warm and sunny. The doors were thrown open and the men were ordered outside to form up in twos facing the commandant's house in the courtyard. Witnesses believe Marcus was number three, although a list in the Atkins archive shows him as number twenty-nine, with prison number 96529.

From the courtyard it appears that the men were taken to the right up some steps, but instead of going into the main camp they were turned, heavily guarded, down a narrow path (away from the prison) that was partly earth and partly covered in irregularly-laid stone slabs. Eventually they came to a vast, deep granite quarry, with a sheer drop from the path on which they were walking. A bluff jutted out into a platform feature overlooking the quarry which the Germans called 'the Jew Jump'. Here many Jews were pushed to their deaths. The prisoners were marched to the notorious 180-step staircase, built of uneven granite slabs and diffi-cult to negotiate, leading down into the quarry. Looking down they could see that the rest of the emaciated camp inmates had been assembled below and were peering up at them. The SOE men scrambled down the steps; they were in better condition than the other prisoners. They were then lined up with their backs to the quarry wall. Armed SS and a mounted machine gun faced them.

Then an SS officer moved forward and screamed at the first man (a Dutchman) in English: 'You will go over there and pick up a big stone and put it on your shoulder. You then run up the stairs.' The Dutchman started to move, pushed by a guard. He put a heavy rock on his shoulder as the officer yelled '*Schnell! Schnell*. The Dutchman started to climb the stairs, the armed guard behind him. After about fourteen steps, the officer shouted '*Feuer!*' The guard shot and the Dutchman fell dead. This horrific charade was meant to comply with Keitel's order that the SOE men were to be shot trying to escape.

The second man was murdered in the same way and then Marcus came forward. He ran up the steps with a rock but suddenly turned and threw his rock at the guard, striking him fully in the chest; he fell tumbling to the bottom of the steps. Marcus then made a defiant run for it up the stairway of death, but the machine gun cut him down.[50]

It took two days to shoot the whole group. It was witnessed by hundreds of prisoners. They never forgot the courage of Marcus Bloom and his comrades.

The Atkins archive contains a letter, until now unknown, from Professor Karel Neuwirt of 11 Zborovska Mor, Otsrava, Czechoslovakia, to Mr Vaclav Pistora of Prague 1, c. 194, dated 19 December 1945. It gives a slightly different version of events and says he witnessed the Allied soldiers being dragged into the camp by SS Obersturmführer Schulz (Kommandant Ziereis was in overall command). They were still wearing their army uniforms (contradicting Rousset) and they then had their heads crudely shaved with blunt razors. Then a particularly brutal *Blockführer* called Farkas (a German Slovak from Bratislava) was called to march the men away towards the infamous quarry. It was then allegedly SS Hauptscharführer Spatzenger and Kapo Paul Beck who murdered the first group of prisoners, on that afternoon of 6 September. The rest were taken the next morning. Neuwirt also named SS Oberscharführers Karl Schulz, Werner Fassel and Prellberg, and SS men Diehl, Klerner and Roth, as well as Hauptscharführer Wilhelm Muller (chief of the crematorium) as particular participants in the war crime. Neuwirt went on to name another surviving witness as Casimir Clement of 11 Ave Marceau, Solidarite Catalene, 16e, Paris.

Another letter[51] dated 12 December 1945 is addressed to Lieutenant Commander Pat O'Leary at 4 Rue de Valois Paris, 1er – a very famous and highly decorated member of SOE who was also at Mauthausen. This was sent from Victor Pistora (almost certainly the Vaclav Pistora mentioned above), another eyewitness to the executions. His testimony adds that the SOE men arrived at 1 p.m. that fateful day, but that they were also given a shower and then made to change into prison garb, and had a number inscribed on their chests in indelible pencil. They were registered by a prisoner clerk, a Czech friend of Pistora, Mr P. Dobias. The first twenty-one were murdered that afternoon. At about 5 p.m. the remaining twenty-seven were returned under heavy SS armed guard, carrying the bodies of their comrades on carts and into the main camp where the others spent the night. The following day the surviving group were marched to the quarry and were all machine gunned at about 7.30 a.m. He ends his letter by stating that Professor Neuwirt was his good friend and as a clerk knew all the men and their home addresses.

There are also two more documents in the VA files dated 6 June 1945, from AMX (American Intelligence) to Vera Atkins at Field Intelligence in the British Occupation Zone of Germany. One lists the forty-seven names of the men 'shot whilst trying to escape' and was obtained from a captured German corporal who witnessed the killings and was in US custody. Remarkably it contains the name of Captain Isidore Newman, MBE (mistakenly named as Mattheo or Matthieu Newman and corrected in her own hand by Vera Atkins), code-name 'Julian', another famous Jewish SOE agent; it is moving for the author to know that this study reveals for the first time that they both died together at Mauthausen.[52]

The second document is a follow-up to the first and states that 'Josef Pelzer, a German Kapo of the Strafkompanie at Mauthausen, witnessed the executions and named specifically SS man Gockel (a German) and Kisch (a Yugoslav) as the murderers.' Strangely, in his deathbed confession on 24 May 1945, after being fatally wounded in a fire-fight with American troops, Kommandant Zereis never mentioned the murders of the Allied SOE men in his camp, even though he detailed many other atrocities of which he was guilty.

Afterwards

The parents and wife of Marcus were notified of his death soon after the war.[53] A Colonel Ravensdale had written to Germaine that the only effects left in the care of the War Office were Marcus's wedding ring, which he sent to her together with his MiD Oak Leaf and Citation. Marcus's estate had come to £521-8s-10d (£521-45p) which was to be shared between her and his brothers. But Germaine was destitute and she explained to the War Office that she had borrowed 40,000 francs from friends to supply Marcus with food and clothes when he was in prison at Fresnes and spent a further 10,000 francs of her own. The British Government soon agreed to pay this back to her. In a letter of 3 September 1946, she also complained to Colonel Ravensdale at the War Office that two expensive shooting guns owned by her and Marcus had been left in the care of Marcus's regiment and she wanted them returned to her; and that her parents-in-law were not being very helpful in giving her some of Marcus's possessions to keep. She especially asked about the guns as a reminder 'of the many happy hours spent with my husband'. But they had disappeared.

Remembered

So ended the life of a brave man.

Marcus is remembered at the Brookwood memorial, in Surrey, to SOE agents with no known grave, panel 21, column 3; at the SOE French Section memorial at Valency near Paris; on a plaque on his mother's grave at Edmonton Federation Synagogue Cemetery, Montague Road (London) in block X, row 10, grave 33;[54] on the war memorial of the St John's Wood Synagogue in Grove End Road (formerly in Abbey Road); and of course on a memorial at Mauthausen Camp itself,[55] together with Isidore Newman. Marcus's family also erected a private obelisk memorial at Mauthausen, inscribed with his name, soon after the war.

An 'F' Section Summary (PRO HS9/166/7) says: ' The risk of sending to the Field this officer with his imperfect French and his Anglo-Saxon Jewish appearance, was only justified by an extreme penury of WT operators. He was very courageous and fought to the finish ... it is clear he did a good job for many months.'

Describing Marcus's SOE career, Buckmaster's citation for the MiD included: 'For his courage and devotion to duty during his clandestine mission to France, it is recommended that Lt Bloom be Mentioned in Despatches.'[56]

But perhaps the most moving tribute to him was written in an unsigned testimonial report in French from his comrades in circuit 'Prunus', written on 1 May 1945:[57]

> Designated as a radio controller for the Pimento Circuit, and to train circuit members in the use of the 'S' phone, Marcus was sent on to work for Prunus. Due to technical difficulties, he was unable to transmit for some five months, but he passed his time usefully helping with the accumulation of important stocks of munitions, and in several acts of sabotage, notably the destruction of an enemy train around January 1943. He made important contacts with local postal workers which later allowed us to carry out important jobs. He began transmitting in March 1943 and sent and received many important messages until his arrest in April 1943. He was probably denounced by one of his contacts and sent to Fresnes, where he was kept until March 1944. In spite of his accent and British appearance, he never hesitated to accept dangerous missions. When he was ordered to do the demanding job of radio controller, he accepted this despite the fact he knew full well that he was not particularly well qualified for it. His great courage and composure always hugely inspired all those who knew him. We mourn the loss of this congenial and courageous officer. He fought a gun battle with the Gestapo, although heavily outnumbered, until running out

of ammunition, killing several of them. He is remembered here by us all with enormous respect.[58]

Acknowledgements

I would like to sincerely thank Bernard Bloom, brother of 'Urbain', without whose wholehearted support this article could not have been written. It was Gerry Bean of AJEX whose superb survey of Jewish service in the Second World War first put me in contact with Bernard, whose own very distinguished war service in North Africa, Burma, the Middle East and Italy is in itself an amazing story too, albeit of survival.

The staff of the Imperial War Museum Reading Room were, as usual, extremely helpful, as was Mark Seaman – an SOE expert – of the Cabinet Office. The readers' advisers and librarians at The National Archives were of great assistance. I would also like to thank Gill Bennett, chief historian of the Records and Historical Department at the Foreign and Commonwealth Office, Whitehall; Louise Pilley of Brighton and Hove Sixth Form College; Hadira Elkadi for her French translation skills; Philip Bye of the East Sussex Records Office; and Captain Ms Decia Stephenson of the FANY Records Office, Chelsea Barracks.

Appendix 1

Marcus's paramilitary report from Majors Watt and Bush at Arisaig, Scotland, on 15 May 1942, stated that his physical training had improved greatly despite his size, but that rope, fieldcraft and close combat work were not too good ('Cannot imagine him really getting tough with anyone'). However, with weapons, explosives and signalling, he was very good, as he was with report-writing, mapwork, tactics, boatwork and navigation.

On a two-day course at Loughborough (21–22 August 1942), Training Sergeants Stebbing-Allen and Fox reported to Captains Angelo and Hilton and Major Lee that Marcus had done remarkable work with complete mastery: painstaking and intelligent. He had passed all the tests in Making Initial Contacts ('natural manner, remembering the password in a crowded cafe'), Following Suspects ('did not lose his man, good use of cover'), Boites Aux Lettres ('finding and retrieving messages, hiding messages'), Message Passing ('did not arouse suspicion in a crowded café'), Verbal Messages ('passed perfectly despite distracting deliberate interruptions'), Cover Conversations ('perfectly arranged before questioning with another student'), Interrogation ('had a false life history and documents all convincingly carried out'), Security ('discreet, always hiding his wireless and papers and keeping door locked').

Appendix 2

On 6 November 2006, the author met Dr Premysl (Prem) Dobias, the clerk mentioned above at Mauthausen Camp, when viewing the Rex Bloomstein documentary *KZ* at the UK Jewish Film Festival. Prem, aged 94, living in London, had been a non-Jewish Czech political prisoner at Mauthausen (a former doctor of law from Charles University in Prague) and spoke briefly to the audience after the film. The author later contacted him about Marcus Bloom. He said he remembered Bloom very well. Bloom had been brought to Prem's desk that day in September 1944, to be registered as an inmate on arrival, on a small transport, which meant they were prisoners deemed to be 'dangerous to the Reich'. Marcus was 'dressed in civilian clothes, looking haggard but still confident'. Prem related how his whole demeanour was that of an 'honourable British officer who clearly had open and courageous contempt for the SS', who were standing around and bullying everyone into speeding up the clerical procedures. As a prisoner himself, Prem was not permitted to talk to the other prisoners but managed 'a few whispered words under his breath as he typed out' Marcus's details. He described Marcus as a true '*mensch*', using the Yiddish meaning of the word – a true man – and developed an immediate and enormous respect for him in just those few minutes that they met. He never saw him again.

Notes

1. E. Cookridge claims Marcus also had the code-name 'Jack'. See *Inside SOE* (London: A. Barker, 1966), p.632.
2. Telephone interview with brother Bernard Bloom in June 2002.
3. Much of the material on Marcus's early life is taken from his brother's autobiography: Bernard Bloom, *Soon or Late* (published privately, 1994 and donated to the AJEX Jewish Military Museum).
4. Sussex Directory 1899–1938; thanks to Philip Bye, senior archivist, East Sussex Records Office, Lewes.
5. Super Shows Ltd., 32 York Road, Battersea.
6. Marcus's Jewish Chaplain Card (there are 70,000 of them from the Second World War, stored at the AJEX Museum) states that his number was 1113627 and he attended the 124 OCTU at Llandrindod Wells. He was commissioned 2nd lieutenant 26/5/42 and 1st lieutenant 6 October 1942 – PRO HS9/166/7.
7. See Chapter 14 in this book, 'Daughters of Yael: Two Jewish Heroines of the SOE'; also in *Bulletin of the Military History Society* (February 2000), pp.127–45; also in *Jewish Historical Studies*, 35 (1996–98) pp.309–28; also *The Military Advisor* (California: J. Bender Publishing, 2002). This article gives fuller details of SOE training, etc.
8. Bloom, *Soon or Late*. pp.235ff.
9. The Commonwealth War Graves Commission entry for Marcus lists him as Lt, no. 236314.
10. Bloom's personal SOE file at the Foreign and Commonwealth Office (FCO), now at The National Archives (TNA), Kew.
11. FCO, now at TNA.
12. His training name.
13. FCO, now at TNA.
14. *A Life in Secrets: The Story of Vera Atkins* (London: Little, Brown, 2005), p.286.
15. Marcus Binney, *Secret War Heroes of the SOE* (London: Hodder & Stoughton, 2005), p.242.
16. PRO HS9/166/7.
17. PRO HS6/472 – a document shows he was given the address of the British Consul at 35 Passeo de Gracia, Barcelona, if ever he had to escape to Spain.

18. There is some confusion over this name, as M.R.D Foot, *SOE in France* (London: HMSO, 1966), p.219, also uses another code-name, 'Bishop' – but it is not clear whether this is the name of a local Resistance circuit, or agent code-name, or his transmitter code-name (see also PRO HS6/422).
19. PRO HS6/423 and HS9/166/7 – he also used the agent name Henri Duval.
20. B. Richards, *Secret Flotillas* (London: HMSO 1996), p.570.
21. Ibid., p.677.
22. The FCO file says 8 November.
23. J. Tickell, *Odette* (London: Chapman & Hall, 1949), p.154.
24. Foot, *SOE in France*, pp.274–5.
25. Major Anthony M. Brooks, MC, aka 'Alphonse'.
26. Foot, *SOE in France*, p.219.
27. PRO HS6/423.
28. His original wireless set did not work and hence the delay until it was repaired (PRO HS6/422).
29. Records of the FANY at Chelsea Barracks, London; thanks to Captain Ms Decia Stephenson.
30. PRO HS6/423.
31. Foot, *SOE in France*, p.274.
32. PRO HS6/422.
33. Ibid.
34. FANY Records.
35. Lieutenant Maurice Pertschuk, MBE (code-names Martin Perkins, Gerard, Martial and Eugene), worked with Odette Churchill, GC, and Peter Churchill, famous SOE agents. Pertschuk was betrayed and sent to Buchenwald where he was hanged on 29 March 1945, hours before the American liberation of the camp. Born in France, Maurice was brought up in England. A younger brother of his was also in the SOE.
36. The exact date is thought to be 12 April, which was the date of his last message to London (PRO HS6/422).
37. PRO HS6/423.
38. Evidence from Agent Portier, 28 November 1943, HS9/166/7.
39. PRO HS6/423.
40. PRO HS6/422. There is a long correspondence about this matter in the file, before Baker Street decided Marcus must have been captured.
41. In one report (PRO HS6/422), one SOE officer at HQ criticizes the fact that Marcus had been sent into the field without a 'slip in' phrase – that is to indicate that he was compromised; one example is 'Tell the parents I am OK', which in fact would mean 'I am not OK.'
42. Turcan is mentioned in G. Martelli, *Agent Extraordinary* (London: Collins, 1960), pp.78 and 191.
43. PRO HS9/166/7.
44. It was from personal testimony from Turcan that Bernard Bloom learnt of Marcus's experiences in SOE before he was captured, and of course his witness testimony to events at Fresnes.
45. VA files, Imperial War Museum, Department of Documents, box 1, Mauthausen folder.
46. Helm, *A Life in Secrets*.
47. For detail on this camp see PRO HS6/630.
48. There were three camps at Gusen, and these were but three of forty-eight sub-camps. (Mauthausen Museum booklet, 1970, p.5).
49. WO 311/607 at PRO.
50. The eyewitness accounts of Marcus's time at Mauthausen and the manner of his death were given as personal testimony to Bernard Bloom by Yugoslav prisoners who survived and who met Bernard at two camp post-war commemoration events at Mauthausen.
51. VA files.
52. Newman was a graduate in French at Newcastle University, and after joining the Royal Signals was recruited by SOE. He was also WO to the famous Odette and Captain Peter Churchill. He was betrayed in Normandy just before D-Day on his second drop into France. See chapter 18.
53. The address had been at 9 Brownlow Court, Lyttleton/Littleton Rd, East Finchley, London N2.
54. As SOE 'did not officially exist' and was not widely known of until the 1950s, the 1946 inscription says Marcus was in British Intelligence.
55. Photograph in Henry Morris, *We Will Remember Them* (London: Brassey's, 1989), p.24. At the PRO, document FO 120/1185 contains a letter showing that Alexander, Bernard and Jenice Bloom were co-chairs of the British Mauthausen Memorial committee.
56. HS9/166/7.
57. Ibid.
58. FCO file, now at TNA, Kew.

The Teacher from Hull:
Capitain Isidore Newman, SOE, MBE

Isidore ('Izzy') Newman was born in Leeds on 26 January 1916, son of Joseph and Mrs Tilly Newman, née Cohen, pious and very poor Jews who had come as immigrants to Britain from Lithuania in 1909. Joseph's original family name had been Naviprutsky, but they had changed it when they immigrated.[1] He came from a large family of thirteen brothers and sisters, most of whom stayed in Europe and, sadly, perished in the Holocaust. Two younger brothers, however, escaped with the Polish Army in 1939 and eventually got to Israel, where their families live to this day.[2]

The Newmans had married at New Briggate Synagogue on 11 June 1912, Joseph then living at 8 Gledhow Terrace and Tilly at 22 Whitelok Street.[3] They were both tailors and pressers. The family lived at 11 Kepler Street (or Grove),[4] Leeds, at the time of Isidore's birth.[5]

Isidore was the middle one of three brothers. The older was Benny, aka Bernard, born in 1914.[6] Although extremely clever, Bernard developed acute mental illness as a young man and was in and out of institutions for much of his life.[7] He died in Hull some time in the 1970s or 1980s. The other brother, Harry, seventeen months younger than Isidore, was slightly physically disabled. He became a medical technician in the Royal Victoria Infirmary in Newcastle, married a non-Jewish girl and appears to have lost touch with the family after Joseph and Tilly died.

In 1922 when Isidore was 6 years old, he and his family moved to Durham. An old family and school friend, now Dr Nat Cannon,[8] remembers clearly that the family lived at 6 Cross Street and that Isidore's uncle Isaac Cohen (Tilly's brother) lived at 9 Cross Street in Durham City.[9] Both Isidore and Nat attended the St Margaret's Elementary (primary) School[10] and later the Johnston Grammar School. Isidore attended the local synagogue of the very small Durham Community, where his father was a cantor, located then at 107 Laburnum Avenue.[11]

Isidore was a keen athlete,[12] enjoying cricket, football, swimming and cycling, but he was especially interested in learning French. He successfully completed his matriculation (aged 16) and Higher School Certificate (aged 18), and in 1934 went up to Armstrong College, Newcastle – then part of Durham University – to read French, English and Latin. Here, he and Nat Cannon (studying medicine), both with slight Geordie accents, met on occasion, although Nat was four years older than him. As Isidore wrote in his SOE file on 18 August 1941:

> The exciting life of a young student began for me; I studied, I played games, I was interested in everything ... French language, literature and customs was my special study.[13] In June 1936, at the beginning of the holidays, I decided to go to Belgium with a friend (I corresponded with a young Belgian student at that time). We left Dover for Ostend, then for Brussels. As it was necessary for us to write a thesis for our B.A. degree, we installed ourselves at the University there – in the 'Cite estudiantine' in order to use the books in the library. When the thesis was finished, we went to Bruges and to Blankenberghe, then to the French coast for a few days; finally from Antwerp, we returned to England. In 1937 I obtained my B.A. degree (2nd class honours) and in 1938, after a year of study, I obtained the D.Th.P.T. (Diploma in the Theory and Practice of Teaching[14]) from King's College, Newcastle. I left the University and settled in Hull as a teacher in a primary school.

Isidore's father, Joseph, later became a successful cloth merchant, but by 1938, he became bankrupt and moved with his family to Hull, where Joseph was able to find only a more poorly paid job. This was as *shomer* to the local Jewish Community[15] as well as *Shammes/Baal Tephilah*[16] to the now disbanded Hull Central Synagogue (this was in Cogan Street but was bombed during the war and later moved to Park Street[17]). The family lived at 62 Etherington Drive and later at 137 Clumber Street, Princes Avenue,[18] in Hull.

It was whilst in Hull that Isidore became engaged,[19] but it has been impossible to discover the name of the lady. A contemporary of Isidore[20] remembers, as a teenager, one of the women of the local Hull Community saying that Isidore's mother felt that he – with his good looks and education – was a good catch for any local Jewish girl. Rita Charnah, who knew Isidore in Hull, related to the author how her brother Aubrey Gordon had been a fellow teacher with Isidore at Middleton Street Primary School[21] and they often played cricket and football together for the Judeans, the local Jewish athletic club.[22] Rita also knew that Isidore was a boyfriend of her cousin Dorothy 'Dolly' Marks, also a primary school teacher in Hull, and she may have been the mysterious fiancée. Other sources suggest the fiancée may have been Rita Cuckle,[23] and according to her husband, Lesley Simmons,[24] Rita described Isidore as a very handsome young man, with a widow's peak hairline, who spoke perfect French, and whom she dated on several occasions.

Judah Rose[25] and his wife Rhoda became good friends with Isidore –

18.1 Capt. Isidore Newman, MBE 'for gallantry', SOE agent murdered at Mauthausen Death Camp. The once 'Lost Portrait' donated by the family to the AJEX Museum in 2008.

18.2 Isidore Newman on leave in Hull with, left to right, Dolly Marks (his girlfriend) and friend's wife Rhoda Rose. Photo courtesy of Judah Rose.

whom they nicknamed 'Winkie' – when he lived in Hull because Dolly lived nearby and she often brought him to Judah and Rhoda's house on Sundays, to play music and have tea. Isidore was full of good humour, and often all four would go cycling in the countryside around Hull. Judah remembers Isidore was a smoker and once accidentally burnt a hole in the arm of their settee. The settee – with the hole – remained in Judah's house until quite recently, as a sad reminder of those days of friendship with the scholarly young man who became all too soon a brave SOE agent.

It was from Hull that Isidore joined the army (as no. 2350538) on 29 August 1940 and trained as a radio telegraphist with the Royal Corps of Signals (RCOS) at Catterick for six months. Here he was seen by a Jewish Army chaplain, Reverend P. Cohen, on 22 September, and given the standard military Jewish prayer book and the former Chief Rabbi's *Book of Jewish Thoughts*. Cohen saw him again on 1 December.

After being posted to Scarborough, Isidore was sent to Kent for four months as a signalman. He was then commissioned as 1st lieutenant (no. 216306) and finished OTC (Officer Training Course) on 9 July 1941, from where he went to Sheffield with 12th Light AA (Anti-Aircraft).

At some stage soon after OTC, Isidore appears to have been stationed with a Royal Artillery battery in Hull. Malcolm Shields (then Schultz) remembers as a young teenager that Isidore frequently used to come for Friday evening (eve of Sabbath/*erev Shabbat*) meals at his house because his mother and Isidore's mother had been childhood friends.[26]

Malcolm, then in the army cadets at the local Hymers School, asked Isidore if he could organize it so that the cadets could come and visit the AA battery on Costello playing fields in west Hull, where they were stationed for the defence of the city. Isidore promised to see what he could do and a few days later rang to say he had organized a visit for the cadets. Malcolm remembers with great glee how almost a hundred boys were taken to the battery and how Isidore had set up a full, dry-run demonstration of how the guns worked, lasting the whole afternoon. Malcolm, when asked by the author, described Isidore as a handsome and athletic man whom the boys really looked up to on that day.

On 1 August 1941, Isidore was sent for wireless officer training with SOE, in Colonel Buckmaster's 'F' (French) Section.

Training

Isidore was a good SOE student. A report of 7 August 1941[27] by one of his trainers, Lance Corporal MacAlister, stated that 'he was in good physical condition ... standing 1.8 metres tall, dark, with black hair, brown eyes and good looking; above average intelligence ... and after only two weeks had a good knowledge of French and French customs; he enjoys the training but has written some indiscreet letters.'[28] On 14 August: 'he is self assured and thinks with precision'; and on 28 August: 'sometimes seems depressed … he went for a long walk yesterday saying he was suffering from nostalgia (?). His French vocabulary is improving and he does excellent work instructing other students in Morse code. Colloquial French not good but he is a patient and excellent teacher of wireless and Morse.'

At some stage he met the delightful Leo Marks, MBE, who was the Jewish chef de codage at SOE and taught all the agents the required skills in coding and decoding messages.[29] In his book (see note 29), on page 80, he describes Isidore as 'one of Buckmaster's best operators'.

In a second report by a Corporal Edgar on 23 October 1941, Isidore is described as 'good at PT; knows a lot and so this makes him a little unpopular with others in the group'. By 27 October, a cryptic message from SOE said it has 'been decided that the progress he [Newman] has made justifies his selection for work of a very responsible nature abroad … kindly take the necessary action and get posted to us from 1.11.41'.[30] On 1 November he was promoted to 2nd lieutenant and given the training name 'Athlete'. On 16 December he received a postcard from the Jewish chaplain, congratulating him on his promotion. Later he had a spell in hospital, having broken his leg whilst training in Scotland[31] (the family story was that it occurred whilst parachute training, though this usually took place at Ringway, near Manchester, for SOE agents). He was certainly visited in a hospital by Reverend Chait of the Army Jewish Chaplaincy on 4 and 25 February 1942.[32] Rita Cuckle remembers him coming home on leave with a limp, probably in late 1941, which he said was acquired during a training or car accident.[33]

First Mission into France

Code-named 'Julien' (code Georges 49 WO)[34] and Mathieu Elliot, with a further false name of Joseph Nemorin, Isidore was sent into the field on 31 March 1942, to southern France. He was to work with agent 'Olive', aka Lieutenant Francis Basin, in Operation Dividend, with circuit 'Donkey-man'. Fortunately the famous SOE agent Peter Churchill (aka Raoul/Michel, later married to the agent Odette Sansom, GC) was to accompany Isidore, with agent Edward Zeff and two others, and he has left a vivid account of this episode in his book,[35] which I paraphrase here, for it gives a detailed and exciting picture of a typical clandestine operation.

Churchill first met Isidore at the London HQ of SOE, describing him as 'tall, dark and in his early 20s'; with him was Edward Zeff, another Jewish WO, short and middle-aged', also to be inserted into France.[36] They both spoke 'faultless, rapid French and their appearances [Churchill was pleased to note] were such that they would pass unnoticed in any French crowd, train or restaurant'. With their French clothes and accessories in their suitcases, Isidore and Zeff were each given a money belt with 100,000 francs and smaller notes for their wallets; they also carried false ID cards, various passes, photographs, old newspaper clippings and local tram tickets – all as evidence of their cover stories which they had committed to memory.

On 26 February all three took the train to Bristol, and then flew on a Curtis CW20 aircraft to Gibraltar. Here they were met by Captain Benson of Military Intelligence, who took them to the Rock Hotel. Due to the Malta crisis, their submarine transport was going to be delayed, so they used their time practising landing with the folboat (folding commando boat) canoes, in the sea beside the airfield, and also learnt how to climb down at night from a submarine into a floating boat, in the centre of Gibraltar harbour.

Finally, at the end of March, they departed by submarine P42 (HMS *Unbroken*), commanded by Lieutenant Alistair Mars, to the Riviera region at Antibes in France.

The craft was very small but the officers and petty officers were very kind in giving up their bunks on the ten-day voyage, for in addition there were two other agents with them to be dropped at another location by Churchill, making five extra passengers in all for the gallant Captain Mars to cope with. All five agents were given naval overalls for the voyage, to cover their French suits. Despite frequent excursions to the bridge each night for fresh air, Zeff suffered a little from claustrophobia on board, but Isidore seemed to enjoy the trip and the camaraderie with the crew; this was very strong, each admiring the courage of the others' work.

After nine days, they finally reached the Riviera coast and patrolled back and forth at night on the surface, allowing Churchill to carefully reconnoitre exactly where they were to land and pinpoint the bay and buildings he knew from a previous mission weeks before. Next dawn they dived and then used the periscope until Churchill exactly located his landing site at Antibes. That night by a half moon, they surfaced four miles offshore.

Suddenly, Mars spotted a fishing boat coming in their direction; it later transpired that it was an SOE felucca trying to land other agents in an uncoordinated operation. So Churchill had to abort his landing for that night, causing much consternation among the agents.

The following day, submerged, the submarine again cruised back and forth looking for the right landing place; to pass the time, Churchill drew a plan of the site showing the concrete steps leading up from the rocky beach to circular gardens above and the view along Avenue Marechal Foch, up to house number 31. This was the rendezvous, the home of the Jewish Resistance leader, Dr Louis Levy ('Louis of Antibes')[37] whom Churchill knew well.

Darkness fell, the town lights went on and the inhabitants slept; at midnight the submarine surfaced slowly. From two miles out they spotted some unidentified, moving, powerful lights inshore (these later turned out to be highly-illuminated French fishing boats). Nevertheless, Captain Mars ordered the folboats to the forward hatch and told Churchill he should go ahead and disembark; he would watch for his pencil torch light on his way back.

The Landing

This took place on the night of 21 April as Operation Delay II.[38] Churchill slid down a rope into the folboat with one radio and suitcase already placed in the back seat. Now, 1,500 yards from shore, a French-speaking agent was stood to on the bridge to deal with any inquisitive French fishermen, who would be told they were a French submarine from Toulon, laying mines, and they had better get away. The machine guns and three-inch gun were also manned, in case.

Churchill intended to land, unload and hide the case and radio in the gardens, and then return for the second boat with Isidore and Zeff and the second radio and case. He was interrupted, however, by one of the brightly-lit fishing boats and immediately paddled hurriedly back to the submarine. Here he breathlessly recited to Mars what had happened, but Mars, calmly amused, told him a fishing boat had come to the submarine too and said they were about to make for home – it was safe to return to shore. Also, Isidore and Zeff were already in their boat and waiting for him 200 yards to starboard. So Churchill paddled to them and they all set off towards the dark bay shore. Churchill, however, went too fast and, turning, realized he had lost the other boat in the dark. He again turned and after 100 yards found them; he told them sharply to speed up, but Isidore told Churchill that his speed was leaving a very visible phosphorescent wake and he needed to slow down. So they agreed to approach at only two knots.

Almost running aground on the treacherous rocks, they finally found the concrete steps. Churchill unloaded his canoe, changed from gum boots into plimsolls and turned his boat around ready for a rapid departure. He then held Isidore's canoe whilst they disembarked. After tying the empty canoe to his stern, he then carried the case and radio, separately up the steps – leaving Isidore and Zeff below – keeping one hand free to hold his Colt revolver in case of meeting any uninvited guests. He returned to bring Isidore and Zeff up to the gardens and left them hiding in the bushes whilst he went to check the location of the Levy house. He said they would know when he came back as he would whistle the tune of 'Le Madelon'. Suddenly, two French policemen on bikes approached, with headlights on, and they all ducked as the policemen passed by, oblivious of the hidden men.

In the dark, Churchill had difficulty finding the correct road that he thought he knew so well. He searched west and east and forwards, not able to find it, careful to whistle the tune as he passed Isidore and Zeff each time. It was 3 a.m. and light was approaching. Suddenly he found the avenue and went straight to number 31, where Dr Levy's name plaque was clearly fixed to the wall. Relieved, he returned to his comrades and explained they had to go three turnings up on the right and return before dawn for the other radio and case that he would now fetch and hide. They all shook hands; nothing was said but Churchill wrote that 'there was a world of feeling in our handclasps'.

Churchill returned to the submarine for the second radio and case but the current had forced the vessel nearer to shore and sideways; using his flash light, however, he soon found them. Second in Command Lieutenant Haddow[39] helped him load the radio and case into the folboat, and told him to hurry back as dawn was fast arriving. But as Churchill again approached the steps, he noticed several shadowy figures moving around. He drew his revolver and placed it on the bow with lanyard attached, then turned the boat in case he had to make a quick retreat. Then he spotted a bald head which could only be his old friend, Dr Levy.[40]

Warmly shaking hands and without taking breath, Levy, with good humour, demanded to know from Churchill, where were the false baptismal certificates he had ordered for his daughters?[41] Churchill replied, with equal humour, that he had brought agents and radios, so why worry about paperwork? Peering around, he demanded to know who these other men were with Isidore and Zeff. 'Some of the gang to watch the fun', said Levy. Churchill agreed, with Dr Levy, to take agent Bernard[42] back with him in the folboats; they all shook hands and Churchill disappeared into the night, back to P42.

Others in the welcoming committee had included Henry Frager (aka 'Paul', a French architect and agent, later betrayed and executed by the Nazis; he was a former First World War and Second World War artillery officer) and Guillain de Benouville. In their slightly different account, they remembered:

> from our little boat I watched the submarine surface slowly, with tears in my eyes ... from England they had come to fight on our side ... for France ... the sailors threw a rope to us and pulled our boat alongside . The three agents jumped down shook hands and stuffed packets of cigarettes into our pockets. We embraced them, patted their shoulders, their faces ... you must remember that for us this was the first sign of action against the German conquerors of Europe

by our friends, the free Anglo-Saxons. 'What a joy', cried Henry Frager and we all repeated his words.[43]

The Mission

In a report written by himself on his return from France, Isidore described this mission. The first two weeks had been quiet whilst he found a suitable safe-house for his radio transmissions, one not too surrounded by other buildings. However, after a short time his French agent Olive (Lieutenant Francis Basin) was arrested, and was replaced by Baptiste who took up residence in the house opposite. This agent was too careless with security matters, and Isidore shared this unease with his colleagues, agents Hilaire and Arnaud.[44] On one occasion, Baptiste had openly called on Isidore at 9.30 one evening, behaving in a very suspicious manner in the street and unnecessarily arousing the curiosity of an Italian woman living nearby. A second agent, Carte,[45] came as a replacement, but he too proved difficult, insisting Isidore send messages only as he (Carte)submitted them, leaving no room for Isidore's own training and initiative in abbreviating them.

One evening, the police arrived at Isidore's house and Carte warned him to go to a known safe-house, of a Dr Picot in Cannes; but Picot's wife refused to take the risk and Isidore was forced to move on to yet another unsuitable house – being watched by the police – belonging to agent Baron. Ultimately, by the night's end, he was forced to find his own residence.

Isidore sought assistance from agents Romano and Audouard, of Resistance group Croupier which had given him excellent help in the past. But Carte had fallen out with this group for some reason. As Isidore had been looked after for months in Audouard's house, he ignored Carte's objections, who then threatened never again to help him.

At this point, agent Raoul, who until then had been friendly and helpful, became very authoritarian, accusing Isidore of taking too long to decipher messages, among other things. He ordered him to transmit only in the very early morning hours, even though he knew this to be the most unsatisfactory time of the day to do so.

The police surveillance increased and Isidore suggested he take a two-week break, allowing Arnaud to fill in for him, but Raoul refused, blaming Isidore for arguing with Carte, despite Isidore's protests about Carte's unreasonable behaviour towards him.

Raoul then ordered Isidore back to London by the next felucca, for breaking with Carte, accusing Isidore of being dangerous to the discipline of the group – which was clearly absurd. Isidore asked to simply be moved elsewhere to another group, but Raoul refused and said, 'No, you will take the boat. If you don't take it, I will.' He ordered Isidore to pass his set, codes and crystals to Arnaud; this was a major dilemma, as orders from London were always that the wireless operator is master of his own set. Isidore contemplated leaving the area and contacting London himself and asking HQ for instructions, but eventually gave in. Raoul ordered him to speak to nobody and leave for group Antibes at Marseille to await the felucca. As the boat did not arrive, Isidore went to Arles to agent Ulysse, to try to contact London. When they found out, Carte and Raoul were furious, even though the Arles group wanted to keep Isidore as their WO, swapping him for Ulysse. This was turned down and, very unhappy, Isidore returned to London, reaching Britain on 23 November 1942.

Isidore's extraction was carried out as Operation Watchman 3/Overgrow/Dubonnet on the night of 3/4 November at Port Miou. With him were John A.R. Starr, younger brother of agent George Starr; agent 'Richard' and his son; and agent 'Quintet' Jaboume, whilst being inserted were George Starr, Marcus Bloom,[46] Mary Herbert, Mme M.T. Le Chene and Odette Sansom (later GC) – quite a famous group of people.[47]

In his debrief report, Isidore wrote that he had been witness to how badly Carte had treated agent Hilaire – who had a broken leg following his parachute jump into France – leaving him to recover in an unoccupied house with insufficient food, as a result of which his morale suffered badly. Hilaire later refused to have anymore to do with Carte, finding his own house and refusing to divulge the address to Carte. Isidore noted that agent Romano had also been badly treated by Carte, refusing help from Romano's enthusiastic Croupier group who had found many safe-houses for agents in southern France and were devoted to helping the Allies. He failed to recognize their huge potential.

Isidore ended his report by saying he had received only 10,000 francs from agent Olive at the beginning of his mission, and nothing in the Field, despite the initial agreement from Major Bodington in London. He also asked that a BBC radio message be sent to his friends in the Resistance to let them know he was safely back in England, to read, 'Vous serez toujours dans mon coeur. Mille baisers d'Andre', to be transmitted on 25 November 1942.

Churchill's Version

Peter Churchill's own account bears out what Newman said. Foot neatly summed it up:[48]

> Newman quarrelled with Girard, who had no appreciation of the dangers Newman ran, and insisted – to Churchill's as well as Newman's horror – on having his verbose messages transmitted exactly as written. This was more than Newman's professional integrity could stand.

Churchill thought it of overriding importance to keep on good terms with Gerard, so he reluctantly sent Newman home on the November felucca. Newman expressed himself forcibly, on reaching London, at Churchill's treatment of him, but appears later to have relented.

Churchill's own account in *Duel of Wits* (pp.97–133, passim) is more detailed. He had been asked to return to Antibes in late August 1942, dropping by parachute near Montpelier and making his way to Cannes. He and Isidore met up at Villa Isabel at 6 p.m. on the day he arrived and had a joyful reunion dinner. Isidore was looking forward to working for Churchill but told him the local set-up was not a happy one as Carte was too demanding concerning radio transmissions by Isidore, which were always from the one safe-house, a very dangerous practice as it would ease the finding of the radio by German detector vans. Cannes was also a major attraction for the Resistance as Isidore's radio was the only working one in the region, and a radio meant contact with the outside world – and this meant huge pressure on Isidore.

After dinner, Isidore handed Churchill a message from London and then went to bed.

Next day they met again after lunch at the prearranged rendezvous in the Jardins Fleuries, beside the Majestic Hotel, in the shop of Roger and Germaine Renaudi; this fancy-goods and buttons shop had an entrance into the gardens and another to the street behind, with views both ways through a curtain in case of uninvited guests; it was the Carte group meeting place. Isidore handed Churchill the day's decoded messages, written in neat block letters on a small piece of paper:

NUMBER 57
FOR MICHEL [Churchill]
REPEAT STAND BY TONIGHT WATCHMAN [a Felucca insertion] BRINGING SIX AGENTS INDEPENDENT STOP ONE TON MATERIALS TO BE SUNK WITH LINE TO BUOY POINTE DE LESQUILLON COLLECT ONE TON TINNNED FOOD STOP MAXIMUM PASSENGERS RETURN PIERROT AND TWO OTHERS TO LEAVE SPACE RAF MEN EMBARKING ELSEWHERE STOP SIGNAL BOAT TO SHORE RED M FOR MOTHER SHORE TO BOAT WHITE O FOR OSCAR ENDS.

NUMBER 58
FOR MICHEL
WELL DONE HALIFAX REAR GUNNER SAW YOU SPINNING. KEEP W/T MESSAGES YOUR LENGTH GOOD LUCK LOVE AND KISSES ENDS.

Churchill asked why the soppy stuff at the end and Isidore explained that it helped to confuse decoders. Churchill wrote down and told Isidore to send:

YOUR 57/8 OK STOP NUTS ENDS

Incredulous, Isidore asked if he was sure he wanted that message sent. Churchill confirmed and added, 'Perhaps they will sack me and give me a job in the Cabinet!'

Noticing lots of comings and goings in the shop, consisting mostly of people not actually buying anything, Churchill commented that security was lax. Isidore explained that the naturalness of the people does the job instead; there is no-cloak-and-dagger whispering that would give the game away, even though that is what they were taught to use in training. Churchill replied that as a result, any one person caught would know too much about everything, but Isidore said it was unavoidable. Churchill decided he was going to take matters in hand. Isidore concluded by giving Churchill a rundown on what the different individual group members did, and then they parted company. But Churchill was very nervous about Isidore being mixed up with such lax methods which endangered him.

At a meeting in the house later that day, Carte complained to Churchill that Isidore was undisciplined because he complained openly about the length of messages Carte asked to be sent. Churchill tried tactfully to explain that their training was to send only messages that were urgent and short. Carte replied that all his messages were urgent and if Isidore did not comply, he wanted a new WO. Churchill said he would consider this, and could see that a problem was brewing between these two dedicated and determined men.

The following day Isidore took Churchill to meet the Jewish second in command of the group, Porthos. The Gestapo in Paris had a one million francs price (about £5,500 at that time – 177fr. to £1) on his head.[49] Churchill's thoughts were that if he was as clever and resourceful as all the other Jewish agents, all would be well.

In Report 1 to London, made on 10 September 1942, Churchill mentions that Isidore is extremely overworked and has a fever; he often refuses food as he is too busy – a great sap on his long-term health and energy.[50] So agent Ulysse was helping Isidore with decoding tasks. In Report 3 (18 September) he describes Isidore as 'working like a Trojan' and says he will be pleased to 'recommend him for great devotion to duty'.[51] In Report 4 (24 September) he describes how Isidore had to leave town on several occasions as it appears copies of his messages have been found left carelessly lying about in the houses of group members.

In Report 7 (8 October) Churchill describes a very tense meeting with Carte where he defended Isidore – and Britain – against slanderous allegations of poor support. Churchill made it very clear to Carte that Isidore had been a WO for six months and working exceedingly long hours under constant stress and fear of betrayal or discovery; if he sometimes lost his temper and used bad language, it was perfectly understandable. Excellent WOs were very rare and he, Churchill, never had any problems with him. It was also clear (though Churchill kept this to himself) that use of the much slower courier system to send and receive messages via Spain was due to Carte's behaviour towards Isidore and making his life so difficult; this was causing huge problems for the Resistance groups and their work.[52] However, owing to the danger such a rift posed, Churchill reluctantly said Isidore would have to be sent home.

The news was broken gently by Churchill, who confessed to liking Isidore very much at all levels. Isidore was much hurt but Churchill insisted he needed a break anyway, and that he should put all the problems with Carte in his debrief report when he returned to London. Meanwhile he was to 'behave' with Carte – though it turns out he did not.

Isidore had done well, transmitting over 200 messages to London over a period of eight months; many were sent from Villa Isabel, Route de Frejus, Cannes – owned by Baron de Malval (aka agent 'Antoine'); Adam Rabinovitz ('Arnaud') also often worked from this location.[53] An unsigned report in HS9/1096/2 says Isidore was:

> an extremely capable radio operator – technically the best we have ever had – but his temper was uncertain and he was not a diplomat ... he maintained almost daily W/T communication and ... in spite of the strain of operating in occupied territory and the constant efforts made [by the enemy] to detect his set, he seldom missed a schedule [pre-arranged transmission], and his messages were always clear and accurate.

Lieutenant Basin, who survived the war, described Isidore thus: 'Poor Julien, he was an excellent radio operator, cheerful, hardworking and courageous.'[54]

Isidore had been promoted to captain whilst in France, on 21 September 1942, and on his return SOE wanted him to return to the field with the December moon, to a new area; he readily agreed. First he was to report to Training School S2 for one to two weeks, in order to learn the latest radio techniques. Unable to return by the December moon, however, he started the course instead on 31 December 1942.

In March 1943, Peter Churchill bumped into Isidore at SOE HQ, who was wearing his General Service uniform and three captain's pips, and on his left breast was the ribbon of the MBE. Churchill wrote,[55] 'He paid me the great compliment of asking if he might be my radio operator again'; sadly, this was not to be.

Sometime in early 1943, Isidore by chance met his cousin William Wolfe Newman, a doctor and captain in the RAMC, at a station in London; William was a brother of his cousin Eric (see Acknowledgements). In a telephone interview with Eric in November 2005, he said that the one abiding memory he has of Isidore is through the story told to him by William. Isidore and William shook hands and chatted, but as they parted on that platform in a London railway station, Isidore said that he was going into France and that he would probably never see him again. This transpired to be sadly true and so William was the last family member to see Isidore alive. Rita Cuckle also related how Isidore was due to come to tea with her on a forty-eight-hour leave at one time, but called to say he could not make it 'as there was a flap on'; she never saw or heard from him again.

Again into France

On the night of 19/20 July 1943, Isidore left by Lysander aircraft for his second mission. He was piloted by Flying Officer 'Mac' McCairns in Operation Athlete after a two-day wait due to bad weather; in fact McCairns wrote that the weather during the flight was very bad over the Channel and he had fifty minutes of very strenuous flying to endure.[56] With the additional code-name of 'Pepe', and false name of Pierre Jacques Nerrault, Isidore was to work in the Rouen area with agent 'Clement' (aka Major Staunton, aka Phillipe Liewer) for the Salesman circuit. He landed just east of Tours on a landing area code-named 'Grippe,'[57] with agent 'Anthelme'.[58]

Much of what is known about this mission comes from a report by Staff Sergeant J.M. Clark of 327 Field Security/Intelligence, British Liberation Army (BLA), written on 15 March 1945, for his superior officer.

Clark arrived in Rouen in October 1945 and was introduced to a woman, Mme Denise Desvaux (of 2 Rue de Fontenelle, previously of Rue Jeanne d'Arc). A well-known couturière, she told Clark how her friend introduced her to Captain Charles Clement of the Normandy Resistance, and she agreed to have Isidore billeted with her, posing as her nephew, for eight months from some time in August 1943.

Desvaux knew exactly what Isidore's job was and described how he was sending radio messages daily, sometimes from her house and some-times from other safe locations in Rouen. She also met French comrades of Isidore – naming Serge and Lieutenant Henri Pacquot (later evacu-ated to England after being wounded in a firefight with a German patrol).

Isidore was described by other members of his group as very security-minded, never transmitting from the same place twice and often cycling 1,000 miles per month to achieve this by leaving Rouen for distances up to forty miles before sending messages. In an area thick with enemy troops and Gestapo, Isidore worked untiringly, making possible the delivery of arms to his circuit on a large scale.[59]

Isidore remained in Desvaux's home until March 1944, when Serge was arrested by the Rouen Gestapo (whilst Clement was in England) and under torture appears to have named others in the Resistance. As a result, the Gestapo, accompanied by French Inspector Ali, raided Desvaux's home on 9 or 10 March, arresting Isidore and Desvaux.[60] They were taken for interrogation to the Palais de Justice in Rouen, and London heard on 11 March. Over eighty other agents had also been arrested.

But after a week, Desvaux was released, explaining that she and Isidore had a pre-arranged story to exonerate Desvaux from any knowledge of Isidore's activities. They took all Isidore's possessions, including 50,000 francs for use in the Resistance, but not the radio as this was not there. Desvaux was able to visit Isidore in jail and take him food and other comforts; he gave her his mother's address in Hull, and she says that she was told by the Germans that as a British officer, Isidore would be treated as a POW and might even be exchanged.

Sometime in April, part of the Palais de Justice was destroyed in an air raid and Isidore and Serge were taken to Paris, to 3 Rue des États Unis, a private house that had been turned into a Gestapo prison. This was reported to London on 27 June. Agent George Starr[61] said he saw Isidore at the Gestapo interrogation centre in Paris, at the notorious 84 Avenue Foch, for two or three days, where he was actually put in Starr's cell whilst Starr himself was kept in the guard room; Isidore had apparently recognized a tie Starr was wearing that he himself had bought in Selfridge's in London. Starr says that Isidore then disappeared, perhaps back to Rue des États Unis. Another report says Isidore was at some time in the German transit prison at Compiègne, which would have been the usual route on which captured agents were taken. It appears that he was then taken to Dara in Silesia, then to Ravitsch, together with agent Rousset ('Leopold'). He had sent fifty-four messages to London on this mission.

Another document in Isidore's SOE file, however, claims, that he had worked almost alone with the commander of the Rouen Resistance, codenamed Lieutenant 'Cicero', and it may have been he who gave Isidore away, as that evening they had arranged to meet for dinner.[62]

Denise Desvaux herself wrote to Isidore's mother after the war. She described him as a sweet and charming man and said that she had been a second mother to him, enjoying their trips to Paris and also listening to his plans for his post-war life. He had apparently sent at least one letter to his mother in Hull, via another agent who was extracted to England. She went on to say that Isidore felt happy and secure in her home, always looking forward to returning there after his long journeys to carry out his transmissions. She ended by saying she hoped to come and visit her in Hull, but there is no indication that this happened.

But Isidore's parents were sceptical; in a letter to the War Office of 20 November 1945, in response to Desvaux's letter, Joseph Newman asked how was it that the Gestapo released her so quickly? And how did they know Isidore was a British officer? Did she in fact betray him? We will probably never know.

Mauthausen and the End

It is clear from the records that Isidore's end was similarly tragic to that of Marcus Bloom, another courageous British Jewish SOE officer.[63] From the fortress camp of Ravitsch on the Polish/Silesia border near Breslau, Isidore was taken to Gusen, one of the many satellite camps of Mauthausen, probably sometime in August 1944, and then to Mauthausen itself at the beginning of September.

A French POW, Captain Rousset – already an inmate at Ravitsch – testified to seeing forty-seven Allied agents arrive together, Bloom and Newman among them. He said that they were wearing blue prison uniform, with a white triangle marked 'I' on the back and that they arrived sometime in April 1944, and were kept together in the same wing. In August they were marched west as the Russians advanced, and taken to Gusen near Linz, Austria. The agents remained a tight-knit group and were much admired by the other prisoners for the dignified and disciplined way in which they all behaved.

Following the failed attempt on Hitler's life on 30 July 1944, Keitel issued orders to Nazi camp Commandants on 18 August, to deal severely with 'terrorists and saboteurs'. So on 2 September the agents were taken from Gusen to the dark, granite fortress of Mauthausen death and labour camp itself. On that date, Section 16 of the camp record states: ' arrivals ... 47 allied soldiers; 39 Dutch, 7 Britons; 1 USA'. On the third afternoon, all the agents were ordered to open their shirts, and numbers from one to forty-seven were painted on their chests.

Isidore was listed as prisoner no. 96535 in documents found after the war.[64] On the morning of 6 September, he and his comrades were formed up outside their cavernous cell under heavy guard and marched towards the notorious camp quarry, down the 180 stepped staircase into its bowels, where the other emaciated camp inmates stood in silent witness. An SS officer moved forward and screamed at the first man (a Dutchman) in English, 'You will go over there and pick up a big stone and put it on your shoulder. You then run up the stairs.' As the Dutchman climbed, the officer shouted '*Feuer*' and the prisoner fell dead. This horrific charade was meant to comply with Keitel's order that the men were to be shot 'whilst trying to escape'. And so Marcus and Isidore were murdered at Mauthausen death camp on 6 September 1944, together with the forty-five others, mostly Dutch agents; they have no known grave.[65]

In a post-war debrief, agent Rousset said[66] that after his own interrogations on 18 April 1944, he had been taken from 3 Rue des États Unis to a bus in which other captured agents including 'Pepe'/Newman and his organizer Claude Malraux (brother of the famous Andre) were already seated. With nineteen others they were driven to Fresnes prison outside Paris and then to a railway station at Vaire-sur-Marne; from here they were taken to Germany via Maastricht, Dusseldorf, Leipzig and Dresden, to Breslau and Ravitsch. Here they had been put in chains but were allowed to speak to each other. They managed to persuade a Georgian SS guard to take and post a list of prisoners to Clement via an agent called Charles at Rue St Ferdinand in Paris, pretending it was a letter to a relative. It did reach London. They were badly treated, in solitary confinement with bad food, and handcuffed at night, wearing convict clothing; they were put to rope-making during the day and had only half-an-hour's exercise. On 19 May Rousset was sent back to France and never saw Isidore again until that day in Mauthausen.

Tributes and Aftermath

General Gubbins' citation for Isidore's MBE[67] reads at the end: 'For his courage and devotion to duty during his two clandestine missions in Occupied France, it is recommended that Captain Newman be appointed a Member of The Order of the British Empire (Military Division).' This was gazetted on 31 January 1946 and sent to the *Jewish Chronicle* on 2 February. He was also given a posthumous Mention in Despatches. The family also received several letters from members of Isidore's French Resistance colleagues, praising his work,[68] and an official War Office letter to the family said:

> I have known your son since he joined this department in the summer of 1941 and have taken pride in his work and career. He was one of the keenest and ablest of men and has done an important job ... him and others like him ... made a very important contribution towards the liberation of Europe, with the minimum loss of lives to our Allied Armies and the civilian population of France.[69]

Squadron Officer Vera Atkins (née Rosenberg), the formidable Jewish administration officer of 'F' Section, SOE,[70] wrote on 6 June 1945 to Mr Wolff of 13 Bowlalley Lane, Hull (solicitors of the Newman family) expressing 'the deep regret of herself and Colonel Buckmaster [commanding officer of 'F' Section] on the death of this gallant officer we knew so well'. It was Vera who had seen an American Intelligence report naming the murdered agents at Mauthausen and noticed that Newman had been recorded on the list as Matthieu, one of his code-names; she corrected it in her own hand.[71] The *Jewish Chronicle* announced his death on 13 July 1945 (p.5).

Marcel Ruby, a very young and decorated French Resistance worker at the time, describes Isidore as 'a particularly able man, hard working and very brave'.[72]

Colonel Maurice Buckmaster had in fact written a more detailed appreciation of Isidore, quoted in the *Hull Daily Mail* of 13 September 2004, from the edition of November 1946, detailed in an article on the sixtieth anniversary of Isidore's death:

> At great personal risk he continued for many months to transmit and receive Morse messages to and from Supreme Allied HQ ... essential to the successful execution of our part of the war effort. This consisted of supplying liaison officers, arms and ammunition and explosives to French patriots who would thus be able to co-ordinate their efforts to liberate their country. Having successfully completed his first mission in the south east of France, he returned to London and volunteered to return again to another part of France ... After carrying out invaluable work in reconstituting a previously decimated resistance group in Normandy, he was arrested by the German forces and executed. Never did he betray any secret information despite intense pressure on him to do so. His colleagues have spoken in glowing terms of his readiness to help at all times and of his imperturbable sangfroid. I am happy to record this tribute to a very brave man of whom the French Resistance chiefs, as well as his British compatriots, are and always will be proud.

Before he died in 1992, Buckmaster gave a copy of a book in French, about the French Resistance, to Ronald Oliver, a school friend of the Newmans; in it is quoted 'La mort de Izzy Newman, l'excellent radio 'Julien' dans la Résistance'.[73]

In a letter to Arnhem Jewish veteran Lionel Cuckle, of Hull AJEX, Peter Churchill wrote: 'you will see in my book *Duel of Wits* that Newman was not the only Jew to cover himself in glory – they were legion' (quoted in the *Hull Daily Mail* of November 1946).

Newman's group had had many successes during his time as WO,[74] including sinking a 900-ton German minesweeper at Rouen, in September 1943; destroying an aluminium alloy factory at Deville, which produced material for the Luftwaffe, in October 1943; destroying electricity supplies at Yainville and Dieppedelle; derailing a German troop train, causing many deaths and casualties, also in October 1943; and sending much intelligence on the German naval dispositions at Le Havre, back to London.

Hull Community member Warren Winetroube, who was articled as a young solicitor at the time, told the author how from the time Isidore was declared missing, Joseph Newman haunted the offices of his law firm, Myer Wolff. Joseph pleaded with them for over two years to write on his behalf to the War Office, concerning the whereabouts of his son, and of course they helped as much as they could. Rita Cuckle too often visited the Newman family after the war to console and support them.

Heartbroken, Joseph and Tilly Newman made their first trip to London on 2 December 1947,[75] to receive their son's MBE from the King, who expressed his pleasure at being able to acknowledge Isidore Newman's gallantry in this way. Local members of the Jewish community remember how Isidore's parents had idolized him;[76] he had been a handsome and scholarly man with a bright future, who had broken from relative poverty into the teaching profession in the 1930s – no mean feat for a working-class Jewish boy. Joseph and Tilly never really recovered from his death.

For many years after the war, virtually up until he died, Joseph Newman could be seen with the Hull Jewish Ex-Servicemen and Women contingent in Hull, marching proudly on Remembrance Day with his son's medals pinned on his right breast.[77]

Isidore Newman is remembered on the Memorial to the Missing, panel 21, column 3 at Brookwood Commonwealth War Graves Commission Cemetery,[78] at the SOE French Section memorial at Valencay near Paris, and on the Roll Of Honour of the Pryme Street Synagogue in Hull (erected by the Hull branch of AJEX in November 1994 on the approximate fiftieth anniversary of his death). He is also remembered on a Dutch war memorial with many Dutch SOE agents, including Lieutenant Marcus Bloom, at a location the author has not been able to determine, possibly at Mauthausen camp itself. At his old secondary school in Durham, then Johnston's Grammar and now on a new site as a comprehensive at Crossgate Moor, Isidore's name is inscribed on a war memorial in the main school hall.[79] The two Second World War panels were added in June 1948 alongside the First World War memorial, following a service of remembrance.[80] After the war, Isidore's uncle Isaac also endowed a prize for French at the school, in his memory,[81] and although it had fallen into disuse, the current head of languages, Bernard Clark, has revived it as a result of this author's research. It was awarded at the Gala Theatre in Durham, in September 2006, for the leading sixth form linguist, in Isidore Newman's name, for the first time in decades.[82] Curiously, however, Isidore is nowhere recorded on a Durham or Newcastle or Hull City war memorial, so far as the author can discover.

On the memorial stone at the Ella Street Jewish Cemetery in Hull, on his parents' grave, the inscription reads in Hebrew: 'In memory of the soul of our soldier, Isidore son of Joseph – Isidor bar Yosef – who was taken in war on the 8th day of the month of Ellul 5705', and in English: 'Captain Isidore Newman, MBE, beloved son of Joseph and Tilly Newman, died 6th Sept 1944 aged 28 years, whose high courage and magnificent leadership were an inspiration to all those with whom he served and whose memory they will forever honour. He died as he lived – bravely.'

Sadly, at time of writing, the stone is now cracked in two.

Acknowledgements

I would like to thank the staff of The National Archives (PRO) in Kew, and of the British Library in Euston; the staff of the Imperial War Museum Reading Room and Department of Documents in Lambeth; Mr Perris and Mr Aubrey Coupland of Hull AJEX; David Lewis of Hull Jewish Community Archives; Geoffrey Rossman of Newcastle-Upon-Tyne AJEX; Hull *Daily Mail* Archives; Mark Seaman of the Cabinet Office (formerly of the Imperial War Museum and SOE specialist) for his guidance; Dr M. Stansfield of the University of Durham Archives; Susan Oldsburgh of Newcastle Jewish Community; Murray Freedman of Leeds Jewish Historical Society of England; Dr Nat Cannon of Vancouver (formerly a Durham City resident); Vivien Cartwright of Leeds Local Studies Library; Judge Israel Finestein (formerly of Hull); Rita Charnah and Judah Rose of Hull who knew Isidore; Warren Winetroube of Hull who knew the family; Eric and Graham Newman of Leeds and London, first and second cousins of Isidore; Lesley Simmons, Howard Cuckle and Fran Harris of Hull; Paul Leaver of Hull City Archives; Jacqui Rodgerson of Durham Local Studies Clayport Library; Carol (surname unknown) of the Hull Local Studies Library; Keith Feldman (Jewish Chronicle Librarian); Mr B.T. Clark and Denise Scrivens of Johnston's School; Mrs D. Mowbray-Pape of St Margaret's School; Mike Robson (Johnston's School historian and former pupil); John Dickson of the North East War Memorials Association.

Notes

1. Thanks to Graham Newman of London, Isidore's second cousin – correspondence November 2005.
2. Thanks to Eric Newman of Leeds, Isidore's first cousin and contemporary, and father of Graham – correspondence, November 2005. Eric spent many childhood days with Isidore in Durham.
3. Thanks to Murray Freedman of the Leeds JHSE for this information from the Newmans' marriage certificate.
4. Thanks to Vivien Cartwright of Leeds Local Studies Library.
5. From Isidore's birth certificate, courtesy of David Lewis, archivist of the Hull Synagogue and Jewish Community.
6. Yorkshire 'births, marriages, deaths' website.
7. Benny had to leave Johnston school in the sixth form, having shown great promise for the future

(personal letter from the late Ronald Oliver, who knew the brothers Newman, to school historian Mike Robson – copy with author).

8. Of Vancouver, Canada – aged 94 at time of writing.

9. Correspondence with Dr Cannon, October 2005, with thanks to Susan Oldsburgh of Newcastle Jewish Community. The *Durham City Directory 1931* lists Joseph and Isaac as 'general dealers' (p.15) – thanks to Jacqui Rodgers of Durham Clayport Library.

10. On the Honours board at the school are listed the pupils who went on to grammar school, and in 1927, Isidore's name was added; the board is still in the old school building, which is now an arts centre – thanks to the head teacher, Mrs D. Mowbray-Pape (page 25 of a booklet published by the school, celebrating their hundredth anniversary in 1961 – thanks to Jacqui Rodgerson of the Durham Clayport Library).

11. L. Olsover, *The Jewish Communities of North East England* (Newcastle: Ashley Mark, 1981), p.296.

12. PRO/TNA HS9/1096/2 (hereafter HS9/1096) – Isidore's personal SOE file.

13. Ibid.

14. Thanks to Dr M. Stansfield of the Durham University Archives.

15. A *shomer* ('guard' or 'keeper' in Hebrew) is someone who ensures all food consumed in the community, sold in its shops and prepared at weddings, barmitzvahs and other events, is strictly kosher according to Jewish religious belief. Thanks to Mr Perris Coupland of Hull AJEX who remembers Joseph and Isidore Newman well.

16. The *Baal Tephilah* (Master of Prayers) oversees the order of prayers and general ritual in the synagogue and like the *shomer* is regarded as a senior dignitary of the congregation. However, although much respected, those holding such posts were often quite poorly paid. Thanks to David Lewis of Hull Jewish Community Archives for this information from the Community's records.

17. The Annual Report of the Hull Central Hebrew Congregation of 1958–59 shows Joseph as 'Beadle and Collector' – thanks to David Lewis. Joseph died 10 April 1966, aged 86, and Tilly on 28 March 1956, aged 67; both are buried in Ella Street Jewish Cemetery.

18. AJEX Jewish Chaplain Card for Isidore Newman, at the AJEX Jewish Military Museum in London.

19. HS9/1096.

20. Telephone call from Fay Wolfson in answer to author's request for information in the *Jewish Chronicle* letters page.

21. Isidore taught at the boys' primary school, but no school records from that period survive. Minutes of the Hull City Education Authority staffing sub-committee, however, show that he began teaching there in September 1938, aged 22. Sadly, the school closed in 1941 and the building was demolished in 1994. My thanks to Paul Leaver of Hull City Archives.

22. Telephone conversation with Rita Charnah, November 2005.

23. Thanks to Aubrey Coupland of Hull – telephone call to author, November 2005.

24. Lesley Simmons telephone call with author, January 2006 – with thanks to nephew Howard Cuckle of Leeds/Hull.

25. Telephone call with author, November 2005 – thanks to Judge Israel Finestein.

26. Telephone calls with Malcolm Shields, January 2006; he lived then at 218 Kingston Road, Hull.

27. HS9/1096.

28. Perhaps to his fiancée or parents?

29. For his story see Leo Marks, *Between Silk and Cyanide* (London: HarperCollins, 1998).

30. HS9/1096.

31. Thanks to Hillel Bender, aged 83, now of Cheltenham, then of Newcastle – telephone conversation November 2005; he was married to Sheila Cohen, Isidore's first cousin, who told Hillel about the broken-leg incident after they were married.

32. Jewish Chaplain Card at AJEX Jewish Military Museum.

33. See note 24 concerning Lesley Simmons and Hull DM, November 1946.

34. E.G. Boxshall and M.R.D. Foot, 'Chronology of SOE Operations with the Resistance in France in WW2', 1960, sections 17 and 22; manuscript at IWM Reading Room.

35. Peter Churchill, *Duel of Wits* (London: Hodder and Stoughton, 1957), pp.15–3.

36. Zeff was captured but survived the war in a Nazi camp.

37. E.H. Cookridge, *Inside SOE* (London: Arthur Barker, 1966), pp.151–9, passim.

38. Richard Brooks, *Secret Flotillas, Vol. 2* (London: Frank Cass, 2004), p.365; Peter Churchill calls it 'Operation A' in *Duel of Wits*, p.20.

39. Tragically, later killed in the war.

40. Sadly, Dr Levy was betrayed three years later and died on a forced march between two Nazi death camps.

41. Levy had bought a house in his daughters' names and so needed the certificates in case the Germans should try to confiscate his house from him, as a Jew. These were later dropped by parachute and had the desired effect.
42. Emmanuel d'Astier, a French naval officer.
43. Cookridge, *Inside SOE*, pp.151–9.
44. Arnaud was radio operator Adam/Adolphe Rabinovitz, another famous Jewish SOE agent, who worked for Churchill after Isidore left for England. He was later murdered by the Gestapo.
45. Carte was a well-known French artist, Andre Girard; owing to his behaviour with Newman and others, he was not used by SOE again (HS6/382).
46. See article/chapter on Marcus Bloom by Martin Sugarman; Ch. 17 in this book.
47. Brooks, *Secret Flotillas*, p.215.
48. M. Foot, *SOE In France* (London: Frank Cass, 2004), p187.
49. Sadly, he was betrayed and executed by the Nazis later in the war – see Churchill, *Duel of Wits*, p.319 – but is known to have been exceptionally bad on security.
50. Ibid., p.115.
51. Ibid., p.119.
52. Ibid., p.131.
53. Brooks, *Secret Flotillas*.
54. Cookridge, *Inside SOE*.
55. Churchill, *Duel of Wits*, p.126.
56. Hugh Verity, *We Landed by Moonlight* (Manchester: Crecy Books, 1995), p.198.
57. Ibid.
58. Foot, *SOE in France*, p.361.
59. Taken from his citation for his MBE, written by Major General Gubbins, commander of SOE, 21 November 1945.
60. There is no evidence that Isidore's radio had been detected by a German detector van, as some sources suggest.
61. In a debrief report of May 1945 – the Vera Atkins archive at the Imperial War Museum, London, Department of Documents (hereafter IWM DofD, box 1, file 2/1/9-10).
62. HS9/1096.
63. For the dreadful details of the shootings and eyewitness survivor accounts, see Martin Sugarman, 'Lt Marcus Bloom', *Jewish Historical Studies*, 39 (2004), pp.183–96, especially pp.191 ff; also website Marcus Bloom, using a search engine; in Ch. 17 in this book.
64. Vera Atkins archive, IWM DofD, box 1, Mauthausen file.
65. For further eyewitness accounts see article/chapter on Marcus Bloom by Martin Sugarman.
66. HS6/578.
67. Announced in the *Jewish Chronicle*, 12 April 1946, p.14.
68. *Hull Daily Mail*, 16 June 1945.
69. Ibid. See also *The Times*, (p.7), and *Daily Mail*, front page, 13 May 1945.
70. For detail on the amazing administration officer of 'F' Section, the Jewish Vera Atkins-Rosenberg, and her connection with all the agents, see Sarah Helm, *A Life in Secrets: The Story of Vera Atkins and the Lost Agents of SOE* (London: Little, Brown, 2005) and Martin Sugarman, 'Daughters of Yael: Two Jewish Heroines of the SOE', *Jewish Historical Studies*, 35 (1996–98), pp.309–28; also *Bulletin of the Military History Society*, February 2000, pp127-45; also *The Military Advisor Journal* (R. Bender, California, USA) 2002; also Chapter 14 in this book; and by title on the internet using a search engine.
71. Vera Atkins archive, IWM DofD.
72. Marcel Ruby, *F Section SOE* (London: Leo Cooper, 1985), p.120.
73. Copy of letter to Mike Robson from R. Oliver.
74. HS6/469.
75. *Hull Daily Mail*, 18 October 1947 and 6 December 1947; it was announced in the *Jewish Year Book* in 1947, p.313. Also a commemoration article in the *Hull Daily Mail*, 13 September 2004, p.53.
76. Testimony from Rita Charnah of Hull, who knew Isidore and his family.
77. Letter from Mr Perris Coupland of Hull AJEX.
78. See the CWGC website.
79. Thanks to Denise Scrivens of Johnston School staff.
80. Michael Robson, *History of Durham Johnston School* (published privately, 1998), p.109.
81. Ibid., p.108.
82. Telephone conversation and emails with Mr B. Clark of Johnston School.

Major Richard 'Ruby' Rubinstein: with the SOE in France and Burma

Richard Arthur Rubinstein was born in Baker Street, London, on 29 August 1921, son of Arthur Bernard (born in Birmingham) and Floris Rubinstein (née Newport, born in London). They had married in 1920 after Floris converted to Judaism; they belonged to Marlborough Place (formerly St John's Wood) synagogue, where Richard learnt his Hebrew and was barmitzvah. Arthur was an importer of millinery and associated goods for the clothing trade, and his father had come as a Jewish immigrant to Britain from Latvia in the early nineteenth century. Richard's grandfather, Bernard, had been a junior officer in the Tower Hamlets Rifles Volunteers, a mostly Jewish unit. He married the sister of his company commander, Julia Lazarus, scion of the old Exeter Jewish family. Bernard's father, Joseph, was president of the synagogue in Mitau, Latvia and allocated stall-holder areas for pedlars in the ghetto market. Only pedlars among the Jews were permitted to travel, and through them Joseph established an underground escape network to save young Jewish boys from the tortuous experience of compulsory service in the Czarist Army, where they were put in high-risk battalions in the hope that they would be killed or simply forget their Jewish roots. Perhaps in some way Richard's wartime secret work in SOE could thus be seen as the continuation of a family tradition in clandestine operations.

Richard went to University College School between 1929 and 1939 and then won a place at Imperial College, London, to read aeronautical engineering. Meanwhile, as the 1930s' war clouds gathered, asked by his mother not to join the OTC (Officer Training Corp) at school in 1934, he instead joined the Territorial Army at the Duke of York's Barracks, Chelsea, on 23 March 1938; he was only 16 but, with the connivance of the recruiting officer, he lied about his age to get in. He attested as C. of E. and was now a member of the Royal Engineers, as Sapper no. 2051152 (321 Company, 26 Anti-Aircraft Battalion); this later became 26th Searchlight Regiment, Royal Artillery, in August 1940. Mobilized at the Munich crisis whilst still at school, and then temporarily demobbed, he was at a Territorial Army camp in August 1939 when war was declared and so never was able to take up his place at Imperial College. He went straight into the Forces.

In charge of a sound locator during the London Blitz, he sometimes faced anti-Semitism in the barrack room but was always able 'to look after myself'.[1] Aged 19 in February 1941, he successfully tried for a Commission, passing out in June as 2nd lieutenant no. 193114 from 133 OCT Unit. He became a Searchlight troop commander (69 Searchlight Regiment, RA, Royal Fusiliers) in Norfolk, commanding six searchlight sites and over eighty men, using a motorbike to keep control over a fifty-mile circuit. By 1943 he was a Searchlight battery training captain in charge of over twenty-four searchlights in Wiltshire, sometimes flying with the RAF night-fighters, to check on the performance of his lights to form a neat cone to indicate a target to the fighters, and also flying with new bomber crews to help them interpret the night sky and avoid the searchlights that they would meet over enemy territory.

By 1943 he wanted to take a more active role in the war, but was rejected by the RAF and Commandos. He married his sweetheart, Gay Emily, née Garnsley, in April 1943 and then saw a notice at his HQ asking for volunteers to work in occupied Europe, language skills not essential. He applied and was sent on a three-day selection course in August 1943, at a large country house near Petersfield in Hampshire. Promoted to captain, he was accepted with the comment, 'he appears well motivated but is he tough enough?' After six weeks he was ordered to report to a London address near Trafalgar Square, from where, on 17 November 1943, he was sent to another country house – Hatherup Castle near Swindon.

Richard was to be trained for an SOE Jedburgh team to be inserted into north-west Europe. Most teams were intended for France. They comprised one British or American officer, an officer of the country of insertion and a sergeant wireless operator (WO) of the same nationality as one of the officers. Jedburghs were unique in being the first military group that was truly international and were under joint SHAEF[2]/SOE command. Their aim was to parachute in after D-Day – ahead of the advancing Allies – with arms and other supplies, wearing full British or Allied uniform, and to work with the SAS and French Resistance to harass the enemy, en route to Normandy from various parts of France, who were attempting to stop the Allied invasion. They were to aid the advancing Allies in whatever way they could, depending on the local situation. At Hatherup (SOE Special Training School – STS – No. 45), the British and Americans trained together up to January 1944 and then they were all moved to Milton Hall (two miles from Peterborough) where the French members joined them in a cohort of 300 men to make up 100 Jedburgh teams.[3] Milton Hall was part of the Fitzwilliam estate and was the permanent home of the European Jedburgh teams, commanded first by Lieutenant Colonel Frank Spooner and later by Lieutenant Colonel Musgrave.

In Richard's first training report,[4] dated 4 December 1943, it was questioned whether 'his temperament would stand the strain of action', although he 'was very keen and confident'. His seventh report, on 4 March 1944, described him as 'a leader who obeys orders ... mixes well with the French to practise the language ... keen, aggressive and popular'. By his eighth report, 13 March 1944,[5] he 'spoke French fairly well' and was 'practising continually to improve ... was very fit with lots of endurance ... was a forthright type that people would have faith in, with above average organising powers ... keen, quick, estimates situations well, has leadership ability, is intelligent and contented with his work'. His Company commander, Major B.W. Gilmour, wrote: 'he is the type who can do all three duties equally well (liaison, organisation, leadership) ... his French is easily understood, he has plenty of tact and drive and personality ... can be trusted to do any job well ... a first-class officer in every way and is very popular with all nationalities'.

Further intense training included parachute jumps at Ringway; the study of German army weapons and tactics; explosives and sabotage; unarmed combat; ambush and guerrilla techniques; and radio operation. Richard was given the code-name 'Augure' and also false French identity papers[6] (in the name of Robert Andre Richard, which maintained his own initials, so it could easily be remembered) as an industrial designer, in case he ever had to make an escape in civilian guise. The risk, however, was very great, as the records show that few SOE/SAS captives – in uniform or not – escaped execution. They were given wireless skeds (schedules) for reporting in.[7]

Into France

On the night of 5 August 1944 at 2200 hrs, Richard's team – known as Douglas 1 and consisting of a British Tank Corps WO, Sergeant John D. Raven, code-name 'Halfcrown',[8] and French officer Jean Roblot, cover-name Jean Ronglou, code-name 'Anachorere'[9] – was joined by 2nd Lieutenant J. Poignot from the local FFI (Forces Français de L'Intérieur) group, and took off from Fairford in an RAF Stirling.[10] Richard was dressed in full British paratroop uniform with a captain's rank and gear, armed with a .45 Colt revolver and M1 carbine with folding stock, a commando knife, and five million francs for local purchases and wages for the French Resistance. However, they could not find the DZ (drop zone)[11] and so returned to Fairford until next day. This was fortuitous as their supplies had not arrived at Fairford to accompany them and were to be dropped for them later. The following day, 6 August, they went to Keevil and took off at 2315 hrs with two Stirlings. They were dropped successfully this time with all their nine 'supply packages' into Brittany, just north-east of Vannes,[12] at an SAS base named Dingson,[13] with seventeen French Breton

SAS reinforcements, to work with the local Resistance to help cut off the German naval bases garrisons from Normandy, especially around the port of L'Orient. They were met by 150 local people of all ages and then marched to a prepared camp site.

To get to the local Resistance HQ it was necessary to travel by lorry and boat from Nostano, but there was room for only six packages, and two were hidden at the DZ – one having been lost. Security was not good, and the day following the drop, one of the women Resistance workers was arrested by the Germans. Hiding in woods, Richard's team then went to pick up the packages at Nostano and arrived ten minutes after a German search party had left – fortunately finding nothing. From the woods and away from prying civilian eyes, they made their first contact with London at 7.15 a.m. on 7 August. That night they were moved to the safety of local FFI HQ.[14] This was the house of M. Tristan, Deputy for Morhiban, and the 5,000,000 francs were handed over. They were then hidden on 8 August at a small oyster farm where they stayed for a week, sending many messages to London but making only poor contact with Mission Aloes, a French Resistance Group. On 16 August they moved to FFI HQ at Vannes and made contact with the US Army.

In his report, Richard complained of poor responses from London for supplies to the SAS and FFI, which lowered his standing with the locals.

Most of the Brittany countryside was empty of the enemy by now, but they were still strong in the port areas and it was here that the Germans had to be harassed and contained. Richard's team also assisted the SAS with the landing of several gliders carrying arms for 3,000 men and, later, Dakotas with further supplies.[15] By late August their job was done. Richard thought that they had really arrived too late to be of real use to the FFI,[16] as much of the information on local German strength was already known to the Americans, and so they were extracted by Dakota to Normandy and thence by plane (which was also carrying wounded troops), to Hendon aerodrome on 24 August. Here Richard faced the irony of Customs charging him duty on a silk dress-length he had bought in France for his wife Gay – a red flowered pattern, she remembers.

He and Gay then enjoyed some leave on a friend's boat, sailing the Thames, but with orders to ring in every day to HQ at Milton Hall. After four days he was recalled and told that his team would soon be dropped again, this time as Douglas 2, into eastern France. During the week preceding the drop they underwent some further training, and then the day before, Richard's WO, John D. Raven, was injured by a misfiring pistol and was replaced by a young and not too experienced American, John T. Van Hart.[17]

Following a poor briefing, they flew from Harrington aerodrome (near Skegness) on the night of 15 September in an American OSS Liberator and dropped in Jura, twenty-eight kilometres south-east of Besançon, on a plateau near the village of Reugney,[18] with several packages, some of which were lost when parachutes failed to open.

Their job was to assist the active local Maquis in working together and harassing the German lines as the American and French forces were advancing north from the Rhône Valley region after the Allied invasion of southern France. However, the area was already mostly liberated, but after a few days, the Arnhem airdrop had occurred in Holland and Richard's team were ordered to march north with the Resistance along the west bank of the Rhine, in the valley of the River Doubs, and generally help create havoc among the Germans, to prepare for an Allied Rhine crossing. But with failure at Arnhem, an autumn Rhine crossing could not take place, and so the team were told to report on German troop movements. Here, near Montbeliard, they did important work gathering information for the advancing Free French Forces for the capture of Belfort. But again the response from London was poor and eventually Douglas 2 was ordered home.

They split up for safety reasons, and Jean took the American WO and went in one direction and Richard found a German motorbike and went in another. About twenty-five miles east of Besançon, Richard met the French Army, who were quite suspicious of him, as he was riding a German vehicle whilst wearing British uniform, and he was arrested and tied to a tree. He suggested that they call his HQ to verify his SOE story and to use the coded message, 'I have lived at number 77 since 1927' (his address in West Hampstead at 77 Broadhurst Gardens).[19] This proved his identity and he was released, just as his comrade Jean turned up to find that the French were from his old regiment that he had left in 1943 (when joining SOE) in North Africa. He told Richard and the WO to go on alone as he was staying to fight with the French. Richard told him that this was fine, as their work was finished, but suggested that he should go to visit his parents first. He never did, and soon afterwards was tragically killed in heavy fighting against the Germans, in the Rhine Valley forest area in November 1944, leading a company infantry attack.

Richard made his way to Paris SOE HQ, using his letter of authority (which all Jedburgh team members carried, ordering whoever it may concern to assist the holder in any way possible) to obtain petrol. After a short leave he was returned to the UK by Dakota on 4 October 1944 and given some more time to spend with Gay, whose aunt lent them a car to use on a holiday.

For his work in France, Richard was Mentioned in Despatches (*London Gazette*, 30 August 1945) and awarded the Croix de Guerre avec Étoile Vermeil (Bronze Star). His citation reads:

Capt. Rubinstein volunteered for missions in occupied France and was dropped with an Allied team for the first time in Morbihan on Aug 6th 1944 and the second time in Jura on 15th Sept. 1944. Although these two areas were particularly heavily controlled by the enemy, he was able to organize an important information system, which proved to be most useful for the Allied advance. This officer displayed the greatest bravery under all circumstances as well as complete devotion to his mission and to the common cause. Signed by De Gaulle, 16th Jan. 1946.[20]

Burma

Recalled to SOE in London, Richard was given the three options: of returning to the army, of dropping into Germany with the SAS to release Allied POWs,[21] or of going to Burma. He chose to go to Burma. Higher authority also agreed that those who had the experience of fighting with the Maquis in France would be the first and best available to be switched to Burma after VE-Day.[22]

American Jedburgh members were off to help Chiang Kaishek's Nationalist Chinese, the French to fight in Indo-China and the British to Burma. At one point, in one of those strange ironies of war, Jedburghs were fighting on opposite sides as the Chinese advanced into French territory.

Richard left London on 3 November 1944, arriving in Bombay via Liverpool and the Mediterranean on the SS *Otranto*, in December 1944, having had all the appropriate inoculations. Richard was attached to the famous Force 136 of SOE, based on a small, idyllic beach coconut plantation near Colombo in Ceylon (Sri Lanka), called Horuna. At that time Slim's 14th Army was fighting its way south from North Burma with the Chinese, towards Rangoon, which he wanted to reach before the monsoon broke in June, and he welcomed any help SOE could give him in organizing friendly Burmese to help harass and destroy the Japanese behind their lines as they made their fighting retreat. The Burmese leaders had been as anti-British as they were anti-Japanese, but they soon realized, when the Japanese occupied them, that the British were by far the lesser of two evils, and offered to help SOE.

The evening before insertion, extra pockets were sewn on tunics, seams strengthened, rifles zeroed and rucksacks repacked. The limit was forty-five pounds (about eighteen kilos) but with emergency rations, medical kit, wireless parts and ammunition, it was quickly exceeded. After the usual hectic briefing (they had not been warned for the mission until 2000 hrs on 23 January; there were no written orders and only a brief verbal background – none of which exactly inspired confidence.[23]), interviews,

19.1 Major Dick Rubinstein, SOE in Burma jungle with a captured Japanese officer's Samurai sword (foreground).

19.2 Dick Rubinstein, SOE, MC and Cr de Guerre, with Kachin guerrillas in Burma, preparing for an ambush mission (standing left).

preparation of codes, and maps and reports to digest, on 25 January 1945, Richard took off at 1800 hrs for Operation Dilwyn/Monkey[24] in an RAF Liberator from Jessore, about fifty miles north-east of the SOE operational HQ in Calcutta. He was parachuted by night with two comrades, Major Hugo E. Hood (Somerset Light Infantry) and WO Ken Brown (Royal Tank Regiment), landing at 2130 hrs. They were to assist an SOE intelligence group led by William 'Bill' A. Howe, MC (a former rice-buyer who had lived in Burma for some years, alive today and over 90 years old, who was the senior British officer on the ground); Howe's Burmese second in command was Captain Kum Ge Tawng Wa, and his Resistance group of about 200 men. They dropped, guided by fires, with their radios and a load of arms and other supplies onto a small plateau. Approaching the drop zone, the exit hatch in the aircraft was opened by the dispatcher and all Richard could see was a beautiful tropical moon and thick forest; he was very frightened, and to calm his nerves during the long flight, chewed gum with such ferocity that it ended up all over his lips and chin. Suddenly he was pushed out into the silent, dark world below. He fully admits that he was always more afraid of the jump than of what awaited him on the ground.

This was Kachin country, a cheerful hill people, fiercely loyal to Britain – indeed, many had been soldiers in the British-led Burma Rifles and so formed the core of the Resistance groups. They were met with hot coffee and then conducted to a comfortable hut with bamboo mats and blankets to sleep in. One subadar major with twenty years' service told Richard in excellent English that he had been to Britain for King George VI's Coronation in 1936, as ADC to the representative of the Burma Army, and had stayed at Wellington barracks in the Mall.

The arms were distributed and immediately the British Army training and discipline of the Kachins took over as they formed up and started drilling and marching. Richard remembers being most moved and impressed by this experience. Many still wore bits of old British Army uniform – belts, puttees, hats – which they had kept since the 1942 retreat and now proudly wore. As time went by more and more former British Army veterans joined up and were given ID discs and by the end of January they numbered about 350.

The Jedburghs had some army rations but generally depended entirely on the Burmans, who accepted them completely. They ate local food such as fruit, rice with chillies, and stewed meat and vegetables; Richard and the Jedburghs would sometimes supplement this with bartered eggs, buffalo milk and the occasional chicken. On special occasions a larger animal would be killed for a communal feed-up. They lived in the field with the Burmese, sleeping in thatched huts or in the open with mosquito nets.

In the area of Kutkai/Kutkhia, cool at about 4,000 feet altitude and twenty miles square, the country is very wild and, at that time, was largely unexplored – in appearance rather like parts of Scotland, with forested and grassy hills, heavily forested valleys, and few roads. Within five days, the group was ready, after some basic training, to go on the offensive. Richard organized and supervised many ambushes of Japanese military targets, mining and shooting up convoys on roads, in camps and along paths, inflicting many casualties, the Burmese often going in close with their *dahs* (short swords). Intelligence on the whereabouts of the Japanese and their movements would arrive from many local Kachin sources. It was also necessary to provide a small detachment to prevent the ravages of Chinese deserters and local bandits from attacking the villages of the Kachin whilst the men were away fighting the Japanese.

Some amenity drops organized by Richard, to assist the well-being of Kachin communities, resulted in replies from HQ BCS (Burma Country Section) that they could not keep acting as 'fairy Godmother', due to scarce resources. The teams on the ground rather resented this attitude, but nevertheless such drops were periodically made.

Generally, the Burmese preferred to be told how to deploy and to be given firm and clear instructions, and then wished to get on with the job without any interference from the Jedburghs. They were extremely tough, fierce and courageous and wanted to keep their leaders (the British SOE, who after all supplied them with their means to resist) safe and sound at jungle HQs, whilst they, by and large, did the face to face fighting. They rightly protested that the British, wearing trousers, with lighter skins and especially being much taller than the Burmese, were simply far too conspicuous in the bush.

By 7 February, six actions had been fought (on 1, 2, 3, 4, 6 and 7 February), in which 109 Japanese had been killed, thirty-one wounded and forty-two taken POW – later evacuated (Operation Cheetah report).

By the end of February, Richard's men had despatched even more Japanese and wounded dozens of others. Groups of ten to twenty guerrillas would occupy concealed camps or outposts and, after reconnoitring for enemy bivouacs, would attack at night. Japanese stragglers would also be constantly picked off, day and night. Burmese casualties were very few. To support these fighting patrols, there were two mini-HQs, where fresh supply drops could be made, and from which the outposts were reinforced and supplied. They also formed a camp for local refugees and arranged drops for them of food, salt, blankets, clothing and medical supplies. On one occasion, forty-five Indian escaped POWs arrived and their evacuation was arranged with SOE. They even recovered material looted from the Kachins by Chinese deserter bands.

Among the Burmese fighters with Richard was Duwa (Chieftain) 'Rusty' Shan Lone, who already had an MC and OBE from 1942. He worked with another Resistance group some miles from Richard's and they soon amalgamated to form a 400-strong anti-Japanese unit.[25]

As Chiang Kaishek arrived in March from the north, Richard and his team were ordered out (in Dakotas, which brought more arms for the Resistance; they used a captured Japanese landing strip at Kutkai) after almost two months behind enemy lines. With them went thirteen young Kachins to join the Jedburghs as armed SAS-style soldiers for Force 136 (Special Forces), in more hostile Central Burma.

Richard was meant to collect arms and pay the guerrillas at army rates; in fact, many weapons were deliberately left behind so that the Kachin could protect themselves later from local outlaws and Chinese deserters. A last supply drop of cloth and salt was arranged and Richard gave away several thousand pounds in silver rupees, whose sparkle the Kachin delighted to see; they mistrusted paper money. At Kongsa they even reopened the local church and market (the bazaar) and a small hospital. A peace party (*manaus*) was held, with speeches and religious thanksgiving ceremonies to Richard and his team; there was dancing in full silk and feathered headdresses and swords, and some amusement when Richard was asked to demonstrate English dancing. There was of course a huge feast and the killing of a buffalo. Touching gifts were exchanged – native crafts for tobacco and sweets – and many goodbyes. It was particularly moving when everyone stood and sang 'God save the King' in English and Burmese.

Richard's debriefing report did make some criticisms of HQ – namely, lack of information of exactly where Allied troops were, to save them sending raiding parties into areas that the enemy had already left; too few supply drops for local people who were sacrificing so much to help the Allies; lack of interpreters with the Jedburgh teams; poor radio procedure by HQ; too few medical supplies; and they wanted British blankets and groundsheets replaced by USA hammocks and sleeping bags.

Pyinmana

Arriving in Calcutta, Richard's team went to their rest-house in a block of flats run by SOE, re-entering the unreal world of peacetime India; here the team let off steam and scrubbed away the stench of their unwashed sojourn in the wildest of jungles, wrote their reports, were debriefed and then were returned to Ceylon. Their hut at Horuna was now adorned with trophies – mostly Japanese swords and flags – and they had adopted a green parrot.[26]

Newly-arrived teams from Europe were sent on acclimatization training in the thick Ceylon jungle, but Richard's men were spared that and disappeared on leave into Colombo until needed.

After a week, they were informed that as veterans of the Burma guerrilla campaign, they were very highly valued. Richard (now a major) was made a team leader and, with Dick 'Doc' Livingston, a Rhodesian, who had just been with SOE in Greece, and Ken Brown again as WO, was to be dropped now into Central Burma as Operation Chimp;[27] they would be one of a number of Jedburgh teams to be dropped near Rangoon. On reaching Calcutta, however, Richard developed an infection from some scratches he obtained on the beach in Ceylon and was hospitalized for three days. By this time his mission was switched to the Mandalay area and was now urgent, as Slim's forces were approaching the town and needed immediate support from the SOE agents. After sleeping all night at the airport, within eight hours of leaving his sickbed, Richard was with his team in a Liberator, at 0700 hrs over Burman jungles again, this time dropping by day at 10.15 a.m. on 9 April 1945. They parachuted in, twenty miles north of Pyinmana, landing in a dry river valley about fifty yards wide, surrounded by forest, at map reference IQ434460 – in full view of the Japanese. Richard noted that only one smoke fire guided them in and there was no recognition signal.

There were five in his team, as he had two Burman Army men with him as interpreters. Two of the team fell in trees, but without injury, and two containers collided and crashed to earth spilling their contents – but by the time the Japanese arrived, all had disappeared. This time Richard's men[28] were welcomed by communist fighters of the AFO (Anti-Fascist Organization), and taken by bullock cart for about twelve hours into the Sittang valley, along which ran the main roads and railway, to the village of Kyatahaung, where they arrived around 2 a.m. on 10 April. With them came about ten containers of rifles, Brens, grenades and so on, for the guerrillas. With the help of two ex-Burma Rifle havildars, the men were quickly trained and sent off in small groups by Dick to scout for Japanese, now retreating in large numbers from Slim's advance down the valley, as they fled into the surrounding jungle in order to avoid the ambushes and the air attacks. Tracks were easy to follow as the Japanese split-toe shoe prints were easy to spot.

The objective of Richard's team was to report on all Japanese troop movements in order to call in air strikes; contact and arm the local Burman Defence Army Resistance; and prepare a local drop zone for arms. On 10 April they called in the first bombing raid on Japanese targets at Kayanzatkan; on 11 April, six Japanese were killed in three encounters and the HQ moved to Gwegyi. On 13 April at 1700 hrs, the first drop of arms was successfully completed and the drop zone cleared within twelve minutes. On 14 April a group of twenty-five fighters ambushed and killed thirteen Japanese, and captured arms and documents on the road to Myola-Gwegyi (parallel to the Rangoon–Mandalay road) down which the Japanese were retreating in quite large numbers. On 15 April, five more Japanese were killed at Kyatchaung; within ten days Richard's men had ambushed, captured and killed as many as forty-eight Japanese, including, at Kyatchaung on 10 April, a major-general and his staff[29] of six senior officers (four captains and two lieutenants) and eleven others (mostly NCOs); a large amount of documents were also captured and sent rapidly by runner to Slim's forces to the north, and handed to Major Boyt who was the 5th Indian Division's liaison with SOE. The report on this coup got back to London and had a profound effect on policy towards increasing support for Force 136 and SOE and the Burmese Resistance in general.

When the Japanese were in small groups, they ambushed them directly; when they came across larger concentrations and targets such as stores and buildings, they simply radioed for air strikes. It was rarely possible to take prisoners and in any case this was not the wish of the Burmese who were doing the fighting; any Japanese left alive after the first bursts of fire often blew themselves up with grenades.

On 16 April, more Japanese were killed and on 17 April, two POWs were taken but shot trying to escape. Several other successful ambushes were made and, in all, around Pyinmana and later further south in Toungoo, they inflicted over 400 casualties on the enemy.

On 17 April, Richard went to make contact with the Burmese Defence Force (or Burmese National Army), leaving the local guerrillas to fight on. With twenty men, and two elephants to carry their kit, they covered only thirty miles in three days, due to the need to lie-up to avoid the Japanese en route. Even then they made contact, and on the night of the 17/18 April killed ten Japanese at Kyatchaung. On arrival on 20 April, at the BDF HQ at Thindwindaung, they were put in comfortable huts and able to wash each day from well water, wearing cotton sarongs – the climate being considerably hotter here. Richard was able to perfect the skill of bucket filling from a well and also enjoyed the local green tea, taken without milk whilst sucking a stick of brown sugar. On the first night the Japanese attacked the HQ but were beaten off. Richard's team were given the assistance of a 14-year-old boy who had been a cadet officer with the BDF; when they had gone over to the Allies, they killed their Japanese instructors and reported to the guerrillas. On 21 April Richard was called to meet with Major Boyt on the road[30] and, wearing a sarong, disguised as a Burmese, he was taken by a guide for a meeting – much to the amusement and wolf-whistles of the Tommies who saw him. He was then ordered back to continue his campaign, taking a large tin of jam for his team as a gift from the local quartermaster. He got back to his guerrillas on 24 April, having again to lie-up on occasion to avoid Japanese patrols.

For three weeks they worked together with the BDF although there was some tension with a few of the Japanese trained officers. At

Thindwindaung, they were attacked on 23/24 April by the Japanese with little result, but on 25 April a Japanese officer was killed. Other groups in the area reporting to Richard killed fifteen more of the enemy on 25 and 26 April, also taking one POW. On 4 May Richard visited Gwegyi to coordinate further operations and collect two POWs caught on 2 May – one of whom was wounded – and to bring them back for evacuation. On 5 May, ten more Japanese were killed and on 8 May seven more. It was then decided that the area was free of the enemy and orders came to Richard to withdraw.

At this point Richard had to conduct delicate political negotiations with the various Burmese Resistance factions to achieve peaceful disarmament. By 12 May he had moved his HQ back to Pyinmana and on 14 May to Gwegyi again. On 18 May he organized another supply drop. On 21 May Ken Brown was taken ill and Richard acted as WO till his return on 23 May.

After the usual goodbyes (but decidedly no pay, as the BDF was determined to be independent of the British) and thanksgiving, Richard rejoined his guerrilla group and on 30 May his team were ordered seventy miles south to the river crossing near Toungoo, where it was expected the Japanese would try to break across and flee further into Thailand. Here they were to meet another team, code-name 'Reindeer', and put themselves at their disposal. Trucks from the army first arrived and, as agreed beforehand, took back the British arms from the Burmese, but Richard turned a blind eye and allowed them to keep the Japanese weapons they had captured.

On arrival at Taungoo on 3 June, Richard discovered within minutes from a runner that Reindeer's commander, Major Dave Britton[31] – also from Milton Hall – had ventured out with his fighters on that very day against their advice and, being tall, had been killed by a sniper whilst scouting along the Sittang river bank. Richard thus stayed with Reindeer (together with radio man Sergeant R. Brierley) in place of Dave Britton, on the west side of the Sittang river, and Dick Livingston re-formed Chimp with Ken Brown to operate on the eastern river bank, and allied the team with Reindeer's.

Richard's job now was to report to the army all Intelligence on the Japanese attempts to cross the Sittang, in order to set up attacks on them by air and artillery, and wherever possible actually engage with them if they tried to retreat across the river.

During a period of two months, Richard's force reported on all Japanese forces – two Divisions – as they concentrated for the breakout across the Sittang. They also were expertly ambushing and killing dozens of Japanese, at one time capturing the order of battle for the breakout.[32] So successful were they that Richard began to question the kills reported by his Burmese force, but on inspection found them all to be true. The proof came in the form of a delivery of a lot of small green-leaf packages which, when opened, were found to contain dozens of Japanese amputated right ears.

Another ruse was to give the Burmese villagers a device which shot coloured flares. Whenever the Japanese broke into a village looking for food, this would be activated and then British artillery could be directed onto the village, even though the Burmese knew it might cause their own people casualties if they had not got away in time. Such was their hatred, by then, of the Japanese.

In addition to all this Richard's force guarded villages from foraging Japanese stragglers, stored rice in safe caches for local Burmese and supplied them with food and medical supplies. They patrolled constantly, allowing British troops to rest after their exhausting advance south, and received cheerful recognition from Tommies whenever they returned with the Japanese prisoners whom it was now possible to take.

By June, the British had a trap prepared along a twenty-mile front of the river and road, waiting for the 10,000–15,000-strong Japanese force to make their move to cross. Meanwhile, Richard's two teams had removed all boats from the river to deny any ferry transport to the enemy. When the battle came, it lasted for a week and the Japanese were annihilated; bodies littered the river and its banks and the stench of death was every-where. In one instance, a large country boat was left deliberately at a mooring and as the Japanese got in they were ambushed at point-blank range. The boat was then re-moored to await the next group. Richard's estimate in his report was that up to 2,500 Japanese were killed by his group of 1,000 fighters alone, and over 200 prisoners were taken. Eventually the Japanese surrendered.

Skirmishing continued until August/September 1945 and the dropping of the atomic bombs; Richard's men were then leaving leaflets in the jungle for scattered Japanese telling them to surrender. Until early October 1945, Richard was collecting up arms from the Burmese and was back and forth to Rangoon in Stimson light aircraft to give reports to forward HQ of SOE.

Finally he was back in Horuna, Ceylon, where he and Dick Livingston parted, but they were to remain friends for many years. Richard then volunteered to be parachuted into POW camps with doctors to relieve the misery among the British and Allied prisoners. But he was told he had done more than his share of dangerous work and was sent instead to Cal-cutta to organize the reception and care of agents coming out of the field for rest and recovery. Many had to be extracted from deep inside Malaya, Indo-China and Indonesia, for example, and this would take months. Danger still abounded and British troops, encouraging Japanese surrender, were still being killed. Richard prided himself on meeting every SOE group that came out of the field and taking care of them in a safe-house with the cover name of 'The School of Eastern Interpreters'. He encouraged the local detachments of FANY[33] to spend time with these men and accompany them at barbecues, bonfire parties and generally help them have fun and readapt to normal life – all strictly above board. Indeed, some agents had already got to know some FANYs at a distance when they occasionally – and against orders – inserted frivolous messages at the end of wireless transmissions from behind the lines. The result of this socializing in the house was sometimes even marriage between the participants. Even General Gubbins (SOE commander) attended some of the parties and thoroughly enjoyed himself.

For his work in Burma Richard was awarded the Military Cross. The citation read:

> Major Rubinstein was landed by parachute behind the enemy lines in January 1945 and by his initiative, determination and efficiency, contributed materially to the effectiveness of the guerrilla forces then operating in the Kutkai area (of Burma). On returning in March 1945, he immediately volunteered for further operations, and early in April 1945 was dropped by parachute near Pyinmana. Here, in an area through which large numbers of Japanese troops were passing daily, he quickly organised the local Burmese resistance forces with such success that ten days after landing, he and his forces ambushed a party of the enemy, killing one Major General, six officers and seventeen other ranks, the majority of whom were NCOs. From the period 8th April to 8th June Major Rubinstein's party of guerrillas, operating firstly in the Pyinmana area and later south of Toungoo, inflicted over 400 casualties on the enemy.
>
> The success of the operation was entirely due to Major Rubinstein's initiative, determination and personal courage.[34]
>
> [*London Gazette*, 7 November 1946; his award is also recorded in the *Jewish Chronicle* of 29 November 1946, p.11, and in the *Hampstead and Highgate Gazette*.]

Despite all the danger, Richard says he always felt safe because his Burmese comrades were constantly with him day and night, guarding and patrolling their camps and trails; he pays great tribute to their simple courage and excellent behaviour.

Afterwards

SOE sent Richard home in January 1946 and he arrived in London on 9 February.[35] His parents' home had been destroyed by bombing but, in a small wardrobe, his school blazer and grey flannel trousers had survived. He was sent to take charge of 404 POW camp in Devon, from April to August, till his demob. Sergeant Major Rice (a former POW himself of the Japanese) happily agreed to take full responsibility for the running of the camp, as long as Richard attended various parades, leaving Richard free to study his textbooks in order to prepare for university. With the constant support and encouragement of his wife Gay, he gained entry to Imperial College in October, for two years, winning the student of the year medal. He also rejoined the Territorial Army Anti-Aircraft Regiment (604) in May 1947. On graduating, however, it was very difficult to find work in the aeronautical industry, and so he joined ICI on Merseyside as a senior workshop manager. In April 1949 he was appointed to command a company of the 13th Battalion Lancashire Parachute Regiment (TA), using his parachute skills gained with SOE, and he held various TA Staff appointments until 1956. Later, with their two sons, he and Gay moved, as Richard took a job which was more engineering-based, with De Havilland/Hawker Siddeley in Hatfield, with whom he stayed until retirement. He retired from the TA in 1971.

Richard attended special Jedburgh team reunions (which have been in London, Washington and Paris over the years) and also with the French Resistance and American OSS[36] veterans; he was a senior and active member of the Special Forces Club after the war and on its Benevolent Fund Committee. The last large formal Jedburgh reunion was in St Malo in France for the fiftieth anniversary of D-Day in 1994. He would have loved also to visit comrades in Burma but political problems there made this impossible.

In one article, Richard wrote on the fortieth anniversary reunion in Paris: 'the tears flowed and we remembered ... I am proud to have been of that number then and I was proud to be of them again in Paris 40 years on.'[37]

In May 1996, a memorial to all the Jedburghs killed in action was unveiled in Peterborough Cathedral, and Richard had a large part to play in organizing this.[38]

Richard's Decorations are the MC, 1939–45, France and Germany and Burma Stars, Defence and War Medals, Mention in Despatches, Territorial Decoration (*London Gazette*, 19 March 1952) and Croix de Guerre.[39]

Though not practising in any way, Richard is very proud of his Jewish name and roots, as are his sons who have not changed their surname. Even Gay – who comes from Wellington in Somerset – has a Lazarus in her family tree and this could conceivably be from the same family as Richard's Exeter grandmother.

Like all brave men, Richard is extremely modest and if truth be told did not even want this article to be written. But it is for me a great honour, and the duty of those who come after such people and so enjoy the liberties that they fought to preserve from the evils of fascism, to ensure that what they did is carefully and accurately reported and preserved. They were ordinary people who did extraordinary things in extraordinary times – thank goodness. The Jewish and wider community can be justly proud of Major Richard Rubinstein.

Acknowledgements

I could not have completed this article without the untiring help of Richard and Gay Rubinstein, on whose time I imposed. The staff of the Imperial War Museum Reading Room were of inestimable help, and my thanks as well to the AJEX HQ staff who first put me in contact with Dick Rubinstein when they met him at a Duxford reunion in 2002. Howard Davies of the Acquisitions Section of the PRO was also very kind in arranging for me to have unique access to Richard's file, once permission was granted.

Notes

1. Some of the section of this paper set in France is drawn from a long interview with Richard, conducted by the author, at his home in Hendon in October 2002. Much of the Burma section is drawn from the R. Rubinstein/Jedburgh file at the Imperial War Museum Department of Documents (hereafter IWM DofD) as well as from the interview.
2. Supreme Headquarters Allied Expeditionary Force.
3. Jedburgh team website.
4. PRO HS9/1289/2 – Richard's personal SOE file (hereafter HS9). He was in Section C, Company 1, under Lt Bank.
5. HS9.
6. Now in the Imperial War Museum.
7. Odd days – 08.30, 15.00; even days – 10.00, 17.00; nights – 22.00, 02.00.
8. The Special Operations Squadrons which inserted agents were called 'Carpetbaggers' – Jedburgh teams website.
9. Jean was a patriotic regular infantry officer who had been wounded fighting the Germans in 1940 and saw participation in SOE as the only way to help liberate France.
10. Douglas 1 was part of Mission Aloes under the French Colonel Eono and it was to get the French Resistance to work with the SAS under Brigadier McLeod, to assist the US 3rd Army advance. The BBC announced their impending arrival on 2 August with one of the now famous radio messages from London to occupied France – in this case, 'Le châpeau de Napoleon est-il toujours à perros gyer?' (PRO HS7/18.) It was estimated that the work of Douglas 1 and three other Jedburghs in the area saved the use of one whole Allied Division in Brittany.
11. PRO HS6/502.
12. The DZ map reference was incorrect and they had to search for fifty minutes, during which they were fired upon and hit by German anti-aircraft fire whilst the pilot took drastic evasive action which caused chaos in the aircraft. Confusion was not uncommon; in one report on Aloes, Richard is described as a French officer (HS6/363).
13. PRO HS7/19.
14. PRO HS6/502.
15. IWM DofD file on R. Rubinstein contains two manifests dated 24 August 1944 for aircraft KG592 (PO McLoughlan and four crew) dropping at Vannes 90,000 9mm parabellum (Sten gun ammunition), 600 grenades, fifty 2" mortar bombs HE (High Explosive) and four packages of medical supplies for the SAS; another aircraft, KG367 (PO Wood and four crew) dropping fifty-four packages of .303 bullets and one 1" illuminator (Verey pistol and cartridges).
16. PRO HS7/19.

17. Letter from Richard Rubinstein; a report in PRO HS6/502 shows that this wound may have been self-inflicted on 7 September at 07.30 and was the subject of an enquiry.
18. Letter from Richard Rubinstein.
19. Richard's AJEX Jewish Chaplain Card – one of 70,000 kept at the museum.
20. Original with Major Rubinstein; copy at AJEX Jewish Military Museum, London.
21. This scheme came about because the Allies believed that the Germans were preparing to liquidate POWs. The idea was that an SOE/SAS team of about a dozen heavily-armed men would go to each camp with information about the commandant, his staff and conditions in the camp, and warn them that if any POWs were harmed as the Allied armies closed in, the Germans would face war crimes trials. Eventually, the plan was more or less abandoned.
22. R. Rubinstein, 'Burmese Experience' – report of January 1949 at IWM DofD.
23. Report on Operation Cheetah, IWM DofD.
24. This was the overall name of the insertion of Jedburghs in Burma at this time; the code-name of Richard's specific mission was Operation Cheetah II (telephone interview with Richard, November 2002).
25. R. Rubinstein, 'Lone Survivor', *Special Forces Club Newsletter*, Autumn 1996, p.8. Shan Lone was born in 1910, became a Baptist and went to university, later serving in the Burmese Civil Service. At the outbreak of war he was the first Kachin to be commissioned, won an MC in 1942 fighting the Japanese, and then fought with the Chindits and SOE Force 136, winning, as a major, an OBE and MiD. He retired in 1974 and later went to live in the USA; Richard stayed in touch with him till he died.
26. Letter from Richard to Gay, at IWM DofD.
27. Chimp and Reindeer were part of Operation Nation (telephone interview with Richard, November 2002).
28. Major R.A. Rubinstein, RA (RE); Captain C.R. Livingston, RE; Sergeant K.J.W Brown, RTC; Ko Thein Aung; Ko Sein Maung. From Secret Report of Operation Chimp 195/375, IWM DofD.
29. This general's sword hangs proudly today in Richard's house; the author can testify that it is still razor sharp. The general's red and gold collar tabs were given to the Imperial War Museum.
30. The Burman runner bringing the message had been stopped and questioned twice by the Japanese en route but managed to bluff his way through, and that night two HQ guards had been killed by Japanese infiltrators.
31. Major D.J.C. Britton (Operation Reindeer Secret Report 205/375/40, 5 September 1945 – IWM DofD).
32. R. Rubinstein papers at IWM contain a translation from the Japanese of this fascinating document.
33. The Field Auxiliary Nursing Yeomanry, a women's corps that did most of SOE's clerical and coding work in various theatres of war, though some were also SOE agents.
34. Original with Major Rubinstein, copy in the AJEX Jewish Military Museum, London.
35. Some of Richard's exploits are mentioned in a standard work on SOE in Burma: Charles Cruikshank, *SOE in the Far East* (Oxford: Oxford University Press, 1983), pp.35, 184, 186.
36. Office of Strategic Service, similar to the SOE but later to become the CIA.
37. *Hawker Siddeley News*, 1985, undated.
38. *Special Forces Club Newsletter*, Autumn 1996, pp.4–5.
39. MoD Records document, April 1993.

British and Commonwealth
Jews in the Korean War

For help in compiling this list of almost 100 names I would like to thank Sidney Goldberg, former Vice-Chair of AJEX, and Henry Morris, AJEX Museum Curator, for all their encouragement. I would also like to especially thank the many veterans and their families, Jewish and non-Jewish, who wrote to me from all over the world – including Canada, the USA and Israel – with information. Without their assistance the work could never have been started.

As with all such studies this list will always be incomplete. Information can come only from surviving veterans who make themselves known through appeals in Korean War veterans' journals, and other magazines and journals. I placed appeals in the *AJEX Journal*, the *Jewish Chronicle*, Korean War veterans' groups' journals, the *British Legion Journal* and other related publications.

Major Isaacs (see below) testified to the author that there were many Jewish servicemen serving with him among the Royal Fusiliers in Korea, and several killed whom he helped to bury. We both concluded that they must have attested to being C. of E. and/or changed their names on being called up for National Service, as records of burials and other rolls or casualty lists reveal very few Jewish names. We will thus never really know the full extent of the Jewish community's contribution. However, by scanning the War Diaries of the Royal Fusiliers at the Public Records Office, I discovered many names, cross-referenced with the AJEX Jewish Chaplain Cards, of Jewish lads who served (indicated as PRO-RF in the text). We know that not all the cards are complete, and hence it is always the case that some veterans' cards cannot be found.

The *JC* of 31 July 1953 stated that there were 4,000 Jewish servicemen and women serving in the Allied Forces in Korea, mostly American.

Served

Walter Alt. Royal Canadian Corps of Signals, formerly British Army, Second World War; born in Austria; billeted Merryhill barracks, Glasgow; emigrated to Canada after Second World War to serve in Canadian Army in Korea. (He is possibly 13120004 Abraham Alt as per Jewish Chaplains Cards – Pioneer Corps, sister Linda Libenson of Ramat Gan, Israel.) Information from Mr Guest of Bristol who served with him; he says Alt was a judo expert and had War, Defence, Korea and UN medals. To be clarified, but a Private Allt is mentioned on pages 125–7 in Jefferson, *Assault on the Guns of Merville* (London: John Murray, 1987), as member of the Paras on D-Day. This could be the same man.

Abingold, from Liverpool, named as serving in Korea in *JC*, 8th May 1953, p.18.

421996 Captain Isidore Apter. RADC, son of Mr P. Apter, 25a Thompson St, Barry, Glamorgan – AJEX card.

22168031 Private Anthony Babot, Middlesex Regiment. Son of Mrs F. Babot, 174 Chamberlayne Road, London NW10. *JC*, 23 May 1952, p.32.

22759423 Sapper David Back. RE, son of Mrs Back of 274 Camden Rd, London NW1 – AJEX card.

349943 Major Michael Arnold Balcon. RA/1st Battalion Royal Warwicks; 41a Maresfield Gdns, Hampstead – AJEX card.

116515 Squadron Leader Cyril Stanley Bamberger. DFC and bar, RAF (Second World War), Battle of Britain ace: see K. Wynn, *Men of the Battle of Britain* (London, 1999); RAF Intelligence, Korea – AJEX

card; of Jewish origin.

2430125 Bernard Bellman. RAF, AT Control, also Berlin Airlift. From Edgware.

2328455 Harold Gershon Benjamin (now Bennett). RCOS – AJEX card and interview; Second World War veteran of Lofoten Islands Commando raid, Iceland, North Africa. Son of H. Benjamin of 42 Banstead Grove, Leeds 8, later of Lincoln.

22943686 Corporal (later Dr) H. Bentley. RAMC, Stanmore; later IDF in Six-Day War.

22985360 Private Aubrey Bernstein. RASC; 128 Hindle House, Arcola St, Hackney, London E8 – AJEX card.

Geoffrey Brice. FAA; HMS *Glory*.

22611667 Private Frank Frederick Carson. RAPC; 47 Parkholme Rd, Dalston, London E8 – AJEX card shows he was in the BAOR and posted to Korea in 1951 (PRO-RF).

Lieutenant Brian Charig. died December 2006 – obituary, *JC*.

22992559 Private Victor Cohen. RAOC – 1st Comm. Division; 28 Lime Grove, Hoole, Chester – AJEX card.

14452236 Sergeant Julius Cohen. KSLI; 3 Ribstone House, Morning Lane, Hackney, London E9 – AJEX card.

David Cohen. Information from L. Keene; no more known.

22493698 Fusilier H. Cohen. 1st Battalion, Royal Fusiliers (PRO-RF) – no card identified.

Major Elliot L. Cohen. OBE, CO 'B' Coy, 1st Battalion Royal Canadian Regiment

at Hill 355 (Little Gibraltar) in October 1952, heroically defended against heavy Chinese tank and infantry attack – Korean War Official History at Imperial War Museum Library/*JC*, 31 October 1952, p.24.

22650106 Private Gerald Cohen. 1st Battalion Royal Fusiliers, from London – information from Feinstein and AJEX card.

7893184 Trooper Frank Cornell. RAC, husband of Mrs T. Cornell, 9 Primrose Hill Court, London NW3 – AJEX card.

22937819 Sapper Malcolm Collins. RE, of 62 Easterley Rd, Leeds 8 – AJEX card says he was posted to Pusan.

S/22637658 Lance Corporal Conrad Percy Drogie. 38/39th Platoon, RASC; 19 Wensley Rd, Kersal, Salford, son of Henry – *JC*, 24 April 1953/Jewish Chaplain Cards. Was involved in assisting with bringing of the dead and wounded back from the front.

Tom Driberg. MP, war correspondent.

427856 Captain K. Dickinson. RAMC, possible MC; 54 Portland Rd, Edgbaston, Birmingham 16 – information from AJEX cards and Colin Ross (below).

RM7021 John Dickson. 45 RM Commando; 35, Kensington Drive, Woodford Green.

Joseph Dickson. RN, brother of John Dickson, above.

ZD10253 Captain Graham Gershon Dixon. Canadian Royal 22nd Regiment, Infantry; born 29 January 1931, Montreal; regular soldier for sixteen years, enlisted as a private in 1948 – personal letter.

20.1 Fusilier Teddy Greenbaum, 1st Bat. Royal Fusiliers, on the front line in Korea.

20.2 Bren Gunner Jack Feinstein, 1st Bat. Royal Fusiliers, on the front line in Korea.

22933997 Sergeant Vivian Dubow. 'E' Troop RCOS of 19th Field Regiment, RA – AJEX card; 30 Winchester Ave, Penylan, Cardiff.

Acting Sergeant 23093366 Howard Peter Ellerman. 'C' Coy, RAMC, December 1954 –December 1956, Japan and Korea – personal interview and AJEX cards. 1 Empire Mansions, Mare St, Hackney, London E8.

22860834 Private Alfred Ellis. Royal Irish Fusiliers, to 1st Battalion Commonwealth Division; son of D.J. Ellis, 7 Morval Rd, Brixton, London SW2 – AJEX cards.

433532 Captain Henry Engelsman. RADC; 22 Ballogie Ave, London NW10 – AJEX card.

22650111 Fusilier Jack Feinstein. Bren gunner, 1st Battalion, 'D' Coy, 12 Platoon, 3 Section, Royal Fusiliers; served at battles of Inchon, The Hook (with Duke of Wellington's Regiment), Hill 355 (with US Forces); from Amhurst Rd, Hackney, London – AJEX card. After a night patrol and ambush of enemy troops, his platoon returned for hot soup served by cook Fusilier Harold Weinberg.

2239370 Private Samuel Fineberg. AJEX card; 29th Field Ambulance, RAMC; son of Mrs S. Fineberg of 10 Bellot St, Cheetham, Manchester.

Sergeant Alec 'Moishe' Freedman. born 20 November 1928, Stepney; Middlesex/'B' Coy, 1st Battalion Leicestershires; Battle of Italy Hill (Hill 317); resident at Royal Hospital Chelsea. The Leicesters attacked 317 on the night of 6 November 1951 but were not successful, taking heavy casualties. Personal interview and photo, AJEX Museum.

23022452 Private Bertram Gabriel. RAOC – AJEX card; 41 Rutherglen Rd, Glasgow 5; 1954 Korea and Japan.

Fusilier 22594482 A. Goldstein. PRO-RF, no AJEX card found.

22650113 Fusilier E. Teddy Greenbaum. 1st Battalion Royal Fusiliers; London – information from Feinstein and AJEX card.

Gilmour/Gilmore aka Ginsburg/Ginsberg. RADC – information from L. Keene.

T22911049 Driver Sidney Hearne. RASC – information from Kosmin, listed below; 73 Brune Hse, Toynbee St, London E1 – AJEX card.

22868160 Private Dennis Herman. RAOC; of 21 Leadale Rd, Clapton, London N15 – AJEX card.

22457395 Trooper H. Hyams. 5th Dragoon Guards.

22361530/414377 Major Bernard Arthur Isaacs, aka Irvine. MC, MiD twice, US Citation; KRRC/1st Battalion KSLI/1st Battalion Royal Fusiliers – personal call: said 15 per cent of City of London RF were Jews and he was present at the burial of many. Volunteered 1948, aged 17, for twenty-one years' service; Sandhurst; RF att. Middlesex and Gloucestershire Regiments, then US 5th Cavalry liaison officer. WIA and POW, reported believed KIA. Escaped with ten others; only three survived; rescued General McArthur's son – the general gave him a gold Rolex watch as a reward. Recommended for a VC in the same action with Speakman, VC, but given MC instead. On return to UK, not expected to live, due to malaria, but grand-father doctor (paediatrician to the royal family) admitted him

to Hospital for Tropical Diseases, and he survived; later gave a talk to the Liberal Jewish Synagogue, where he met his wife. AJEX card says father was G.H. Isaacs of 49 The Ridgeway, Golders Green, London.

Major Jaffey. OBE, Canadian Forces.

S/22451246 Corporal Barry Karsberg. RASC/Royal West Kent Regiment; 402 London Rd, North Cheam, Surrey; son of E. Karsberg; sailed on HMT *Empire Pride* to Japan and Korea – *Jewish Chronicle*, 17 October 1952, p.13, and Jewish Chaplain Cards.

Colonel Alfred G. Katzin. of South Africa, personal representative of UN Secretary General Trygvie Lee – *JC*, 21 July 1950.

23171332 Private Leon Keene. 1st Battalion Royal Sussex Regiment and ACC of 15 Manor Hall Ave, Hendon, London NW4 – AJEX card and personal call. Knew the USA Jewish Chaplain Chaim Potok, later a famous writer.

413358/2234477 Lieutenant Michael S. Kisch. 2nd Field RE; son of the late Brigadier Kisch, KIA in WW2 and Mrs R. Kisch, 2 Kensington Court, First Ave, Hove, Sussex – AJEX card.

22943980 Private Gerald Emmanuel Kosmin. Royal Signals radio mechanic; 68 Holders Hill Drive, London NW4 – AJEX card.

22493234 Corporal Lionel Krimholtz (now Kaye). RAOC; Base Ammunition Depot, Zong Zang, near Pusan; 149 Grundy St, Poplar, London – AJEX card.

Private, formerly S/Sergeant Second World War, 6631255 Godfrey Langdon. RCOS; Perrin Rd, London W3; fought with RA at Imijin

River supporting the Gloucesters. Recommended for MiD. Telephone call and correspondence from nephew Julian Lewis. Langdon was one of four brothers who were in the TA and fought throughout Second World War (including France and North Africa), and father in First World War; photos at AJEX Museum, and AJEX cards.

S/227443822 Private Leon Lehrer. RASC – AJEX card; 30d Greencroft Gdns, London NW6.

Lieutenant A. Levy, from Istanbul; ADC to Commanding Officer of Turkish Brigade (from *Jewish Chaplain Bulletin of the USAC*, July 1953).

1485439 Acting Sergeant H. Levy. RWK att. RF, WIA 27 June 1953 – see *Casualties Sustained by the British Army in the Korean War* (CSBAKW – privately published pamphlet from Korean War Veterans Association), p.18. Unable to locate AJEX card – on PRO-RF roll.

Lieutenant Meyer Michael George Levy. Princess Patricia's Canadian Light Infantry, 'D' Coy, 10th Platoon – see H.F. Wood, *Strange Battleground: Official History of Canadians in Korea* (Canadian Ministry of Defence, 1966), p.77. Formerly SOE 136 Force Malaya 1944–45; died Vancouver, October 2007; MiD.

Barry Lobell (not real name). POW of the Chinese – mentioned in Finchley Synagogue magazine, August 2001; refused to divulge any further information.

22318551 Sapper Jonathan Ellis Manasseh. RE; son of E.S. Manasseh, 57 Camden Hill Rd, London W8 – AJEX card.

21127179 Private D. Marks. MIA/POW 26 April 1951; Gloucestershire Regiment – see P. Gaston, *POWs of the British Army in Korea 1950–53*, p.16; AJEX card not found.

Private D.H. Marks. Duke of Wellington's (West Riding) Regiment, WIA 6 June 1953 (CSBAKW, p.50); AJEX card not located.

Lieutenant Colonel R.L. Marks. 26th Field Ambulance, RAMC; no AJEX card located.

22307199 Private Maurice Martin Mazin. RAOC, 1st Comm. Division; son of Mrs E. Mazin; 122 Clapton Common, London E5 – AJEX card.

22559891 Lance Corporal H. Miller. BAOR posted to Korea on PRO-RF roll – AJEX card.

Colonel E.C. Wolf Myers. Engineers; MiD for gallantry, January to June 1952 – *Jewish Chronicle*, 17 October 1952, p.13; a highly decorated regular officer who served at Arnhem and in SOE in Yugoslavia in Second World War. See Arnhem archive at AJEX Museum. Died in 1997.

2201375 Lou Myers. Born 26 October 1927, Shoreditch; Second World War Royal Marines in North Africa, Combined Operations/SAS; Israel Machal 1948–50; Korea 1950–52 – personal interview.

22541117 Corporal Solly Myerthall. RASC; son of Mrs J. Myerthall, 5 Prestonfield Gdns, Edinburgh 9 – AJEX card.

22859663 Sergeant Eric Jack Orbaum. RASC; son of F. Orbaum, 2 Norfolk Rd., Leeds 7 – AJEX card.

22576845 Private Morris Ottolangui. ACC att. RF, 'D' Coy, 1st Battalion; son of Julia Ottolangui of Wistaria House, 42 Huntingdon St, St Neots, Huntingdonshire – PRO-RF roll and AJEX card.

Private Peter Phillips. Royal Fusiliers – information from Alan Shaffer.

22929428 Lance Corporal Sam Phillips. RAMC, 26th Field Ambulance; born 7 August 1934 in East End of London; evacuated to 13 Abbotts Way, Northampton; served in Japan and nine months in Korea, British and Commonwealth Communications Zone Medical Unit; UN Korea Medal – personal call/AJEX cards.

Private Joe Rairu. Royal Fusiliers – information from Alan Shaffer.

22616095 Craftsman Louis Rapaport. REME and 1st Battalion DLI; 586 Wilmslow Rd, Manchester 20 – AJEX card.

FX584695 Petty Officer John 'Jack' Renack. Fleet Air Arm, from Cable Street (51 Cannon St Rd); Second World War comrade of Emmanuel Penner, with whom he served – personal interview – AJEX card.

22943905 Acting Sergeant Issy Rondell, aka Reynolds. 29th Brigade, RA; met with the author on AJEX Parade, November 2001; born 11 August 1935 in Kalisch, Poland, and survived Nazi death camps. Lived at 121 Old Montague St, London E1. In UK he joined the army and was posted to Korea in RA and then a special airborne unit, owing to his language abilities which included Polish and Russian – AJEX card.

22895132 Sergeant Harold Colin Ross. 26th Field Ambulance, 1st Commonwealth Division, section commander Battle of The

Hook, and Stand of the Gloucesters, many of whose casualties, as well as North Koreans, came through his RAP. Remembers the American Jewish chaplain clearly. Letter and call to author. Born Sunderland 11 July 1931, 25 Whitburn Bents Rd, Seaburn – Jewish Chaplain Card/photo.

23179534 Private Arnold M Schwartzman. 1st Battalion Royal Sussex Regiment and RAEC; parents of the Hotel Majestic, Lewis Cres., Cliftonville – AJEX card and call from Keene (listed above). Now lives in Los Angeles.

22508074 Fusilier A. Shaffer. 1st Battalion Royal Fusiliers, BAOR, posted to Korea – PRO-RF roll and AJEX card.

22928876 Stanley Share. 15th Coy, RASC; 13 Hazon Way, Epsom, Surrey – AJEX card.

14472846 Intelligence Sergeant (later Major) David Sharp. BEM, born Hackney 12 January 1928, barmitzvah at Singers Hills Synagogue, Birmingham. Formerly 22 SAS Malaya, then HQ 29th Independent Infantry Brigade Group att. 1st Battalion Royal Northumberland Fusiliers; at time of capture in Korea was with UN Partisan Forces behind the lines; last and 946th POW to be released in September 1953, aged 25; son of Mr and Mrs Harry Sharp – AJEX cards, AJEX Museum. Volunteered September 1946 as a regular in Malaya. Captured at Imjin River, 25 April 1951, three times wounded. From 1 Moorcroft Rd, Moseley, Birmingham. In *Jewish Chronicle*, 13 April 1953 and November 1953; *Daily Express*, 7 September 1953. Awarded BEM (Military) for 'gallant and distinguished services whilst a POW in Korea' and US Gallantry Award. Made sev-

eral attempts to escape and was in fact engaged on an escape near the end of his captivity. Was incarcerated in the notorious 'wooden boxes' and gave up the chance of a GC award because, as senior NCO, he recommended a comrade, Fusilier Derek Kinne, in his stead. Arrived home on troopship *Dilwara* at Southampton. WIA/MIA and beaten badly by guards; charged as a war criminal because he refused to give information. Now a major (retired), he was CO of the 16th Independent Paras, and is today a trainer of Special Forces and Government Agencies, especially in Africa. Personal letter and interview. Never married.

22387810 Gunner Neville Silver. RA; 762 Mansfield Rd, Nottingham; Hong Kong and Korea – AJEX card and letter. Served December 1951 to April 1952, 14/24th Battery 61st Light Regiment of RA sound ranging (i.e. locating position of enemy guns) – Jewish Chaplain Cards and photo.

22700971 Private Phillip M. Silver. RASC; son of M. Silver, 19 Terrace Rd, Liverpool, 16 – AJEX card.

2258037 Fusilier Maurice Solomon. 105 Lewis Flats, Dalston, Hackney, London E8; BAOR, posted to Korea – PRO-RF and AJEX card.

23271186 Private Eddie Sonsky. 1st Battalion Royal Sussex Regiment; 92 Eric St, Mile End, London E3. AJEX card and call from Keene (listed above).

22409862 Fusilier Ivan Steinberg. Royal Ulster Rifles/ Royal Irish Fusiliers; son of M. Steinberg, 398 Bancroft Rd, London E1 – AJEX card.

Lady Sybil Summers. of Biggin, ATS/Army 61, Boydell Ct., St John's Wood.

23136318 Private Joel Sylvester. RASC; 22 Meadway, Welwyn Garden City – AJEX card.

22521609 Sapper R.L. Szapira. RE, 55 Field Squadron – AJEX card.

22622159 Fusilier Michael Micky Taylor. Information from Feinstein; 'B' Coy 1st Battalion, RF – AJEX card; son of A. Taylor of 44 Hadford Rd, London NW11.

Lieutenant Commander Alan Tyler. RN, born 1924, London, served Second world War and worldwide postwar, including Malaya; in Korea at time of fighting and armistice, with HMS *Birmingham*. See autobiography, *Cheerful and Contented* (Book Guild, 2000) – AJEX card and interview.

22244052 Sergeant R. Wainstein. APTC att. RF – PRO-RF but AJEX card not located.

22622146 Fusilier Harold Weinberg. 1st Battalion, RF – see Feinstein above; 7 Cookham Bldgs, Old Nichol St, Bethnal Green, London E2 – AJEX card.

22486122/421197 Lieutenant Michael Wolff. Platoon 2, 'C' Coy, 1st Battalion, RF – PRO-RF roll and AJEX card.

23081754 Lance Corporal Norman Zetter. RAOC att. S. Staffs. Regiment; son of Mark Zetter, 10 Headleigh Rd, Westcliffe-on-Sea, Essex – AJEX card and interview.

Unidentified. Jewish member of KOSB, 1st Battalion, 'A' Coy, from London; was Coy Clerk, KIA in Korea; had previously served in Palestine and Hong Kong – information from comrade Leonard Jones.

Killed in Action

414788 Lieutenant Andrew J. Albrecht, RIDG (Dragoons), KIA 20 June 1952, buried Pusan, grave 22-4-1450.

Lieutenant Joseph Yehudi Levison. Princess Patricia's Canadian Light Infantry, KIA 20 May 1951 at Munsan, seven miles south of Panmanjon – Canadian Book of Remembrance, Korean War, and photo of grave donated by Group Captain Simon Coy, military attaché British Embassy in Seoul.

2277176 Cpl. Barnett Lipschild, R.E., born Nkana, Northern Rhodesia, 23-4-31 killed 13-5-53, buried Pusan Grave 39-83-399.

22290920 Corporal Montague Ritterband. 'B' Coy, 1st Battalion KSLI/formerly 14422233 2nd Battalion, Rifle Brigade/att. Army Air Corps, in Second World War; son of Marcuse/Martin R. Ritterband of Northampton (owned philatelist shop at 226 Wellingborough Road), brother of Daniel Ritterband of 30 Fairways, Brighton 5. Re-enlisted 29 December 1949; arrived Korea 4 September 1951; notified in *Jewish Chronicle*, 7 December 1951, that he was KIA 17 November 1951, aged 26; Jewish Chaplain Cards.

Army casualty office confirms burial at UN Memorial Cemetery, Pusan, South Korea, plot 23, row 6, grave 1616. Name inscribed on War Memorial in Abington Square, Northampton, 1998. Montague joined Home Guard, aged 15, during Second World War, then Belgian and Norwegian Merchant Navies; joined army at age 17; eventually joined Paras, serving in Belgium, Holland, Germany, Sumatra, Thailand and Malaysia, making at least eight operational jumps during Second World War. Demobbed in 1946, fought in Israeli War of Independence, then rejoined army; KIA in Korea, just when due for leave. Letter from brother and sister-in-law Betty. Decorations include 1939–45, France and Germany Medals, War Medal, General Service SE Asia 1945–46, General Service Palestine 1945–48, Korean Medal, UN Korean Medal, on permanent loan to AJEX Museum. Photo at AJEX Museum.

370959 Lieutenant Gustav 'Gus' Sander. Commander 6th Platoon, 'B' Company, Middlesex Regiment; MiD; KIA 30 October 1950, during an attack on Tae-Dong village, near Chongju. Padre 'Guz' Jones conducted the burial service in a small glade of trees with members of his platoon and other officers. His body was never repatriated and his name is commemorated on the memorial to those with no known graves at Pusan WG Cemetery. However, a body repatriated from North Korea in 1997 *may* be his; identification is awaited. He served at Arnhem in 1944 in Intelligence/RAMC(?), a Jewish German refugee. Letter from Middlesex OCA historian, Dan Barrett, and AJEX member Peter Davis, TD, who served with him in OCTU after the Second World War. Also letter from nephew Mark Sander who also donated Gustav's archive and medals. Photo at Museum, and of his memorial donated by Group Captain Simon Coy, Military attaché at British Embassy in Seoul.

Two un-named Hungarian Jews serving as medical orderlies with the Allies, KIA – *Jewish Chronicle*, 7 December 1951. Several Hungarian Jewish doctors and orderlies were serving in Korea as an option to internment in labour camps in Hungary to which Jews were being sent as part of a general anti-Semitic policy in that country.

Suggested Reading

This is a suggested reading list of books, chapters within books, and articles on Jews in the Armed Forces in the Second World War, by Jewish authors, or about Jewish Servicemen and Women by other authors. The list is not definitive and is periodically updated at the AJEX Museum; it also includes privately published manuscripts.

(For the First World War, see Harold Pollins's reading list in the AJEX files.)

Aaron, W., *Wheels in the Storm* (London: Roebuck, 1974).

AJEX, *70,000 Jewish Chaplain Cards* (London: AJEX Museum WW2 Index/online database).

AJEX Archives, *DSM* [Distinguished Service Medal] *Directory* – contains names of Jewish recipients of both world wars.

Alexander, J., *A Measure of Time* (UK: privately published, 2000).

Almog, Y., *Palestinian Jews in POW Camps in WW2* (Israel: 1992)(Hebrew).

Arton, M., *One Day in York* (London: Hazelwood, 1985).

Ashe-Lincoln, Lieutenant Commander F., *A Sailor's Odyssey* (UK: Minerva, 1995).

Atkins/aka Rosenberg, R., *Fair Shares and Romanian Oil* (London: Book Guild, 2005) – written by the brother of Vera Atkins.

Baker, K., *Paul Cullen (aka Cohen): Citizen Soldier* (Australia: Rosenberg, 2005).

Bard, M,. *Forgotten Victims: Abandonment of Americans in Hitler's Camps* (Boulder, CO: Westview Press, 1994).

Beckman, M., *Atlantic Roulette* (London: Tom Donovan, 1996).

Beckman, M., *The Jewish Brigade* (London: Spelmount, 1998).

Bellamy, B., *Troop Leader: A Tank Commander's Story* (London: Sutton, 2005).

Bentwich, N., *I Understand the Risks* (London: Gollancz, 1950).

Bentwich, N. and Kisch, M., *Brigadier F. Kisch* (London: Vallentine Mitchell, 1966).

Bercuson, D. J., *The Secret Army* (Toronto: Lester & Orpen Dennys, 1983).

Behrendt, G., *Long Road Home* (Israel: privately published, 2005).

Bierman, J. and Smith, C., *Alamein* (London: Penguin, 2000).

Bierman, J. and Smith, C., *Fire in the Night: Wingate of Zion, Ethiopia and*

Burma (London: Random House, 2000).

Bloom, F., *Dear Philip* (London: Bodley Head, 1980).

Blum, H., *The Brigade* (London: HarperCollins, 2002).

Bondy, R., *The Emissary: Enzo Sereni* (London: Robson, 1978).

Booker, M., *Collecting Colditz* (London: Grub Street, 2005).

Bower, T., *Maxwell* (London: Mandarin, 1988).

Bowyer, C., *Guns in the Sky* (London: Corgi, 1979).

Brown, G., *Commando Gallantry Awards WW2* (Canada: Western Canadian Distributors, 1991).

Brown, G., *For Distinguished Conduct in the Field: The DCM 1939–92* (Canada: Western Canadian Distributors, 1993).

Brickhill, P., *The Dambusters* (London: Pan Books, 1956).

Brickhill, P., *Escape or Die* (London: Evans Books, 1952).

Cailingold, A., *An Unlikely Hero* (London: Vallentine Mitchell, 2000).

CAJEX, *Cardiff Jewry Book of Honour* (Cardiff: CAJEX, 1951).

Casper, B., *The Jewish Brigade* (London: Goldston Books, 1947).

Centre de Documentation Juif Contemporarie, *Le Monde Juif*, 152 (Paris, 1994).

Chinnery, P.D., *March or Die* (London: Airlife, 1997).

Churchill, P., *Duel of Wits* (London: Hodder & Stoughton, 1953).

Canadian Jewish Congress, *Canadian Jews in Wartime* (Book of Honour) (Montreal: CJC, 1947/8 and online).

Cohen, R., *The Avengers* (USA: Phoenix Books, 2000).

Cohn, M. *Hannah Senesh: Her Life and Diaries* (London: Sphere, 1971).

Cole, H., *On Wings of Healing* (London: Blackwood, 1963).

Colville, J., *Lions of Judah* (London: publisher and date unknown).

Commonwealth War Graves Commission, *Register for Ravenna* – most of the Jewish brigade burials. Also Palestine Jewish POW graves in *Cracow Cemetery Register* (London: CWGC).

Cowles, V., *The Phantom Major* (London: Capital Books, 1958).

Creighton, C., *OpJB* (London: Simon and Schuster, 1996).

Dale, S., *Spanglet Or By Any Other Name* (London: pub. privately, 1993).

Daniel, R. and Johnson, B., *Ruby of Cochin* (Philadelphia, NJ: Jewish Publication Society, 1995).

David, S., *Mutiny at Salerno* (London: Brassey's, 1995).

Davies, J.A., *A Leap in the Dark* (London: Leo Cooper, 1994).

Dear, I., *Ten Commando* (London: Grafton, 1987).

Dominy, J., *The Sergeant Escapers* (London: Allan, 1974).

Drage, C., *General Two Gun Cohen* (London: Panther, 1954).

Dunkelman, DSO, Col./General B., *Dual Allegiance* (Canada: Formac, 1984).

Eberstadt, W., *Whence We Came: Whence We Went* (London: WAE Books, 2002).

Elkins, M., *Forged In Fury* (London: Piatkus, 1971) .

Falk, L. and Fredman, G., *Jews in American Wars* (USA: JWV of the USA, 1954/63).

Flederman, Lieutenant Alan, *And Direction Was Given* (London: Athena, 2008).

Forman, D., *To Reason Why: The Story of Lionel Wigram* (London: Abacus, 1993).

Forrester, L., *Fly For Your Life* (London: Panther, 1971).

Friedlander, G. and Turner, K., *Rudi's Story* (London: Jedburgh Books, 2006).

Freud, Major A.W., *Before the Anti-Climax* (London: published privately).

Fry, C., *Ken Adam* (London: Faber and Faber, 2005).

Fry, H., *Jews in North Devon* (London: Halsgrove, 2005).

Fry, H., *The King's Most Loyal Enemy Aliens* (London: Sutton, 2007).

Fry, H., *Freud's War* (London: History Press, 2009).

Gelber, Y., 'Palestinian Jewish POWs in German Captivity', *Yad Vashem Studies* (London) 14 (1981).

Gijbels, P. and Truesdale, D., *Leading the Way to Arnhem*: *The 21st Independent Parachute Company* (UK: Sigmond, 2008).

Golden, OBE, Major L., *Echoes of Arnhem* (London: W. Kimber, 1984).

Green, G., *Royal Naval Jewish Casualties in WW1 and WW2* (London: JHSE, 2007) and amendment to it in 2009 issue by Sugarman, M.

Green, M., *From Colditz in Code* (Glanville, Leeds: Jack Lennard, 1990).

Green, General M., *Dual Allegiance* (London: Parapress 1994).

Hagen, L., *Arnhem Lift* (London: Leo Cooper, 1993).

Hampshire, C., *Beachead Commandos* (London: W. Kimber, 1983).

Hardman, Reverend L., *The Survivors* (London: Vallentine Mitchell, 1958).

Haronvi, E. and Shiloach, R., 'Covert Operations with British Intelligence in WW2', from the book, *British Intelligence*, in English (publisher and date unknown).

Hay, P., *Ordinary Heroes* (London: Putnams, 1986).

Heaps, L., *Grey Goose of Arnhem* (London: Weidenfeld & Nicolson, 1976).

Heaps, L., *The Evaders* (London: Naval Institute Press, 2004).

Heilig, G., *Cry of The Nightjar* (100 Bomber Group Museum Association/City of Norwich Aviation, 1997).

Helm, S., *A Life in Secrets: Vera Atkins/aka Rosenberg, SOE* (London: Doubleday, 2004).

Herzog, C., *Living History* (USA: Phoenix Books,1998).

Hobsbawm, E., *Interesting Times* (London: Allen Lane, 2002).

Instone, G., *Freedom the Spur* (London: Pan, 1956).

Jackson, L., *Pawn on a Chessboard* (London: Book Guild, 2001).

Jefferson, A., *Attack on the Merville Guns* (London: J. Murray, 1987).

Jeffrey, B. *White Coolies* (Tonbridge: Angus and Robertson, 1954).

Jenkinson, J., *UXB: Unsung Exploits of RAF Bomb Disposal* (London: Woodfield, 1999).

Jewish Agency, *Jewish Palestine Fights Back* (London: 1945).

JNF, *Jewish RASC Companies* (Israel: 1986), in Hebrew.

Jones, L., *A Quiet Courage* (London: Corgi, 1990).

Jones, R.V., *Most Secret War* (London: Hamish Hamilton, 1978).

Jordan, DCM, F., *Escape* (New York, Cranbury, NJ: 1970).

Jordan, DCM, F., *Oflag* (New York: Durham Books, 1995).

JWB (Jewish Welfare Board), *American Jews in WW2*, two vols (New York: Dial Press, 1947).

Kagan, J. and Cohen, D., *Surviving the Holocaust with the Jewish Partisans* (London: Vallentine Mitchell, 1998).

Kaplan, J. *From Gorbals to Jungle* (Canterbury: published privately, 1988).

Kaplansky, E., *The First Fliers: Aircrew Israel War of Independence* (Israel: Israel Air Force Publication, 1993).

Katzew, H., *South Africa's 800 Volunteers for Machal* (Tel-Aviv, Israel: Telfed, 1997).

Kaye, Captain A./aka Alexander, K., *The Forgotten Army* (London: Regular Publications, 1950, 1996).

Kemp, A., *SAS at War* (London: John Murray, 1991).

Kemp, A., *Secret Hunters* (London: O'Mara Books, 1986).

Keneally, J., *Keneally VC* (London: Kenwood, 1991).

Kent, R., *First In: The Pathfinders* (London: Batsford, 1979).

Kessel, MC, Captain L., *Surgeon at Arms* (London: Leo Cooper, 1976).

Klugerscheid, A., *HM Loyal Enemy Aliens: German immigrants in UK Army 1939–47*, translated by E. Bohm (MA thesis, London, 2000); other theses on aliens in AJEX archives.

Kramer, R., *Flames in the Field* (London: M. Joseph, 1995).

Kurzman, D., *Genesis 48* (New York: De Capo Press, 1980).

Langley, M., *Anders Lassen* (UK: New English Library, 1999).

Latour, A., *Jewish Resistance in France* (New York: Holocaust Library, 1970).

Leasor, J., *Green Beach* (London: Heinemann, 1975).

Leasor, J., *The Unknown Warrior* (London: Heinemann, 1980).

Leighton-Langer, P., *The King's Own Loyal Enemy Aliens: German and Austrian Jews in WW2 British Forces* (London: Vallentine Mitchell, 2006).

Lennard, J., *Jews in Wartime* (Hull: unpublished manuscript, 1990s) – AJEX Archives.

Levett, G., *Flying Under Two Flags* (London: Frank Cass, 1993).

Levy, D.S., *Two-Gun Cohen* (London: St Martins Press, 1997).

Levy, H., *Dark Side of the Sky* (London: Leo Cooper, 1996).

Levy, Reverend I., *Now I Can Tell* (London: published privately, 1978).

Levy, Reverend I., *Witness to Evil* (London: Peter Halbag, 1995).

Macintyre, B., *Agent Zig-Zag: Eddie Chapman* (London: Bloomsbury, 2007).

Marks, L., *Between Silk and Cyanide* (London: HarperCollins, 1999).

Masters, P., *Striking Back* (London: Presidio Press, 1997).

Meirtchak, B., *Jewish Casualties in the Polish Armies WW2*, five vols (Tel Aviv: published privately, 1995).

Messenger, C., *Middle East Commando* (London: W. Kimber, 1988).

Messer, H.J., *Able Seaman: RNVR* (Devon: Merlin Books, 1991).

Millar, G., *The Bruneval Raid* (London: Bodley Head, 2002).

Montrose, A., *Soldier in WW2* (London, published privately, 1997).

Morris, E., *Guerrillas in Uniform* (London: Hutchinson, 1989).

Morris, H., *History of AJEX* (London: AJEX, 2000).

Morris, H., *We Will Remember Them: A Record of the Jews who Died in the Armed Forces of the Crown 1939–1945* (London: Brassey's, 1989).

Morris, H., *We Will Remember Them: An Addendum* (London: AJEX, 1994). Roll of Honour of Jewish UK KIA and Awards (updated joint version to be published with Sugarman, M., 2010).

Morris, P., *I've Had My Dance* (New Zealand: David Ling, 2005).

Mosseson, G., *Jewish War Veterans of the USA* (Washington, DC: JWV, 1971).

Museum of Diaspora, *Living Bridge* (Tel-Aviv: 1983).

Myers, Brigadier W., *Greek Entanglement* (London: Hart-Davies, 1955).

Naor, M., *Laskov* (Israel: Keter, 1989) – in Hebrew.

Nardel, Sydney, *Jungle Medicine and Surgery* (Sussex: Book Guild, 1999).

Nicholson, D., *Aristide* (London: Leo Cooper, 1994).

Nissenthal, J. and Cockerill, A.W., *The Radar War* (London: Robert Hale, 1989).

Nomis, L., *The Desert Hawks* (London: Grub Street, 1998).

Nussbaum, Rabbi C., *Chaplain on the Kwai* (London: Ulverscroft, 1987).

Owen, B., *With Popski's Private Army* (London: Astrolabe Books, 1996).

Oxford & St George Jewish Youth Club, *Fratres* – wartime magazine issues (London: AJEX Jewish Military Museum archives).

Pelican, F., *From Dachau to Dunkirk* (London: Vallentine Mitchell, 1993).

Peniakoff, DSO, V., *Popski's Private Army* (London: Reprint Society, 1950).

Perry, P., *An Extraordinary Commission* (UK: published privately, 1997).

Pertschuk, MBE, SOE, M. *Leaves of Buchenwald: Poems* (London: published privately) – presented by Odette Churchill, GC, to AJEX Museum.

Pollins, H., *Civilian Jewish Casualties in WW2 in Stepney and Outside Stepney* – two lists on Jewishgen website.

Pynt, G., *Australian Jewry Book of Honour WW2* (Sydney: Australian AJEX, 1973).

Rabin, L., *Rabin: His Life, Our Legacy* (London: Putnam 1997).

Rabinowitz, Rabbi L., *Soldiers from Judea* (London: Gollancz, 1944).

Reilly, J., *The Liberation of Belsen* (London: Routledge, 1998).

Richardson, A., *The Crowded Hours* (London: Max Parrish, 1952).

Rofe/aka Rolfe, MM, C., *Against the Wind* (London: Hodder & Stoughton, 1956).

Rogers, G., *Interesting Times* (London: published privately, 1998).

Rome, M., *Lest I Forget: With the Chindits* (London: published privately – AJEX Museum).

Rosmarin, I., *Inside Story* (Cape Town: published privately, 1990).

Rossney, H., *Grey Dawn: Normandy: Personal Recollections* (London: three works published privately, 2003–4).

Rubin, E., *140 Jewish Generals, Marshalls and Admirals* (London: Jason Books, 1952).

Rubinstein, N., *The Invisibly Wounded* (Hull: Jack Lennard, 1989).

Russia, *Memorial Book of Jewish Soldiers of the Russian Army 1941–45* (Moscow: 1945 – in Russian).

Sampson, A., *Bless 'em All* (London: ISO, 1990).

Sanders, E., *Irony of Luck* (London: published privately, 1995).

Sannitt, L., *On Parade* (London: Spa Books, 1990).

Schrire, T., *Stalag Doctor* (London: Wingate Books, 1958).

Seligman, A., *War in the Islands* (London: Alan Sutton, 1996).

Shepherd, B., *After Daybreak* (London: J. Cape, 2005).

Sides, H., *Ghost Soldier* (USA: Knopf, 2002).

Silver, L., *Sandakan: Conspiracy of Silence* (Australia: Milner, 1998).

Sington, D., *Belsen Uncovered* (London: Duckworth, 1946).

Sjajkowski, Z., *Jews in the Foreign Legion* (Ktav, Israel: 1975).

Slater, I., *Jacob's Ladder* (London: published privately, 1993).

Slater, R., *The Life of Moshe Dayan* (London: Robson, 1992).

South African Jewry Book of Honour (Johannesburg: SAJEX, 1950).

Spencer, R., *Looking Back Without Anger: A Jewish Refugee in the RAMC* (London: published privately, 1992).

Sugarman, M., *Jews in the Spanish Civil War* (see Virtual Jewish Library website for full article, also kept at AJEX Museum, London).

Sugarman, M., *Jewish Military Research for Beginners* (London: Shemot Magazine/JGSGB, March 2008), p.23.

Sugarman, M. and Maltman, S., *Jewish Firemen and Women in WW2* (London: AJEX, manuscript in progress).

Suhl, Y., *They Fought Back: Jewish Resistance in Nazi Europe* (New York: Schoken, 1975).

Suhl, Y., *Uncle Misha's Partisans* (London: Hamish Hamilton, 1973).

Sverdloff, F., *Jewish Generals of the USSR* (Moscow: 1993).

Syrkin, M., *Blessed is the Match: Jewish Partisans in Eastern and Western Europe* (Philadelphia: JBSA, 1947/1976).

Tenney/aka Tenenberg, L., *My Hitch in Hell: Bataan Death March* (USA: Potomac, 1995).

This England Books, *Registers of the George Cross and Victoria Cross* (London: 1985).

Tiefenbrunner/Tiffen, M., *Long Journey Home* (Israel: published privately, 1999).

Trepper, L., *The Great Game* (London: Sphere, 1977).

Tropp, A., *Jews in the Professions* (London: Maccabeans, 1991).

Tute, W., *Escape Route Green* (London: Dent, 1971).

Tyler, Lieutenant Commander A., *Cheerful and Contented* (Sussex: Book Guild, 2000).

Urquart, C. and Brent, P., *Enzo Sereni* (London: Robert Hale, 1967).

Van der Bijl, N., *Commandos in Exile* (London: Pen and Sword, 2008).

Victoria AJEX *The Role of the Jews in the Defeat of the Nazis* (Australia: 1991).

Ward/aka Wurtsburger, K., *And Then The Music Stopped Playing* (London: Aldous Books, 2006).

Warner, F., *Don't You Know There Is A War On* (London: published privately, 1985).

Weiner, H.P., *They Lost Their Freedom Fighting For Yours* (Israel: publisher and date unknown).

Weinrok, J. 'Cobber', *The Vaulted Sky* (Cape Town: published privately).

Weizmann, E., *On Eagle's Wings* (Israel: Steimatsky, 1979).

Willett, J., *Popski* (London: MacGibbon and Kee, 1954) – the definitive book.****

Willis, Lord T., *Lions of Judah* (London: Macmillan, 1979).

Wright, I., *Looking Back: The Story of Irene Bleichroder* (London: published privately).

Zeno, aka Lamar, aka Allerton, *Four Sergeants* (London: Atheneum, 1977).

Ziv, H. and Gelber, Y., in *B'nei Keshet* (*Bearers of the Bow*) (Israel: IDF, 1992) (Hebrew).

The First World War and the Second World War

Allon, Y., *Shield of David* (London: Weidenfeld, 1970).

Gumpertz, S., *Jewish Legion of Valour* (New York: CMH, 1946).

Hurwich, B., *We Are All On The Front Line: Military Medicine in Israel 1911–47* (Israel: Ministry of Defence, 2000).

JWV, *Jewish Veterans of the USA: 100 Years of Service* (USA: Turner Books, 1996).

Samuel, E., *A Lifetime in Jerusalem* (London: Vallentine Mitchell, 1970).

Note

J. Wiseman, MC, SAS Officer, appears in the following books:

Bradford, R. and Dillon, M., *Rogue Warrior: Paddy Mayne* (London: J. Murray, 1987).

Cooper, J., *One of the Originals* (London: Pan, 1991).

Kemp, A., *SAS at War 1939–45* (London: Signet, 1993).

McCluskey, J.F., *Parachute Padre* (London: SCM Press 1951).

Wellstead, I., *SAS with the Maquis* (London: Greenhill Books [date unknown]).

Index

Page references to endnotes will be followed by the letter 'n'. Page references to photographs will be in *italic* print